*TENTH EDITION*

# THE AMERICAN LEGISLATIVE PROCESS

## CONGRESS AND THE STATES

**William J. Keefe**
**Morris S. Ogul**
*University of Pittsburgh*

Prentice
Hall

UPPER SADDLE RIVER, NEW JERSEY 07458

**Library of Congress Cataloging-in-Publication Data**

Keefe, William J.
    The American legislative process : Congress and the states / William J. Keefe, Morris
S. Ogul.—10th ed.
       p. cm.
    Includes bibliographical references and index.
    ISBN 0-13-087703-4
       1. Legislation—United States. 2. Legislation—United States—States. 3. United States.
Congress. 4. Legislative bodies—United States—States. I. Ogul, Morris S., 1931- II.
Title.

KF4945 .K44 2001
328.73—dc21

00-027214

# To Martha and Eleanor

VP, Editorial Director: Laura Pearson
Executive Editor: Beth Gillett Mejia
Marketing Manager: Kara Brescia
Editorial Assistant: Beth Murtha
Interior Design and Project Manager: Serena Hoffman
Prepress and Manufacturing Buyer: Benjamin Smith
Illustrations: ElectraGraphics, Inc.
Cover Art Director and Designer: Jayne Conte

This book was set in 10/12 Adobe Palatino
by ElectraGraphics, Inc., and was
printed and bound by Courier Companies, Inc.
The cover was printed by Phoenix Color Corp.

© 2001 by Prentice-Hall, Inc.
A Division of Pearson Education
Upper Saddle River, New Jersey 07458

Printed in the United States of America

10 9 8 7 6 5 4 3 2

ISBN 0-13-087703-4

Prentice-Hall International (UK) Limited, *London*
Prentice-Hall of Australia Pty. Limited, *Sydney*
Prentice-Hall Canada Inc., *Toronto*
Prentice-Hall Hispanoamericana, S.A., *Mexico*
Prentice-Hall of India Private Limited, *New Delhi*
Prentice-Hall of Japan, Inc., *Tokyo*
Pearson Education Asia Pte. Ltd., *Singapore*
Editora Prentice-Hall do Brasil, Ltda., *Rio de Janeiro*

# CONTENTS

Preface                                                                    vii

Using the Internet to Study the Legislative Process    xi

## PART I
## LEGISLATURES AND LEGISLATORS
## IN THE POLITICAL SYSTEM

**1    The Legislative Task**                                              1

Discontent over the Legislature    3
The Functions of the Legislature    21
A Bill Becomes a Law    45
Notes    47

**2    Legislative Structures and Powers**                               53

The Constitutional Status of the American Legislature    54
Organizing the Legislature    61
Presiding Officers    63
Rules of Procedure    65
The Legislative Body: Size, Terms of Members, and Sessions    66
Bicameralism    72
Structure, Powers, and Policy    73
Notes    73

**3    Representation and Apportionment**                                 76

Representatives and Represented    77
The Representative System    84
The Malapportionment Issue    88

The Struggle for Equitable Apportionment  92
Notes  105

## 4 Legislators and the Electoral Process 110

Recruitment of Legislators  110
The Nominating Process  114
Congressional and Legislative Elections  117
Financing Congressional Campaigns  134
Elections and the Legislature  143
Notes  144

## 5 The Legislators 155

Social and Occupational Backgrounds of American
    Legislators  155
Legislative Experience: Tenure and Turnover  163
Pay and Perquisites  167
Privileges and Immunities  170
Legislators' Adaptation to the Legislature  170
Legislators and Legislative Norms  175
Legislator and Legislature  182
Notes  183

## PART II
## THE LEGISLATIVE STRUCTURE FOR DECISION MAKING

## 6 The Committee System 190

The Role of Committees  191
The Representativeness of Committees  195
Kinds of Committees  197
Committee Jurisdiction  206
Committee Members and Committee Chairs  208
Committee Staffs  218
Notes  222

## 7 Committees at Work 229

Committee Hearings  230
Investigating Committees  239

Committee Sessions    245
Committee Decisions    246
Committee Power    250
Notes    254

## 8    Debate and Decision Making on the Floor    257

From Committee to Floor    257
The Rules Committee of the House of Representatives    258
The Amending Process    268
Debate    271
Casting the Vote    283
The Multiple Points of Decision Making    286
Notes    287

*PART III*
*LEGISLATURES, PARTIES, AND INTERESTS*

## 9    Political Parties and the Legislative Process    291

Legislative Party Organization    291
Party Influence on Legislation    311
Party Responsibility in Congress    331
Notes    334

## 10    Interest Groups and the Legislative Process    344

Interest-Group Politics in America    345
The Lobbyists    347
Major Access Points in the Legislative Process    350
Special Techniques Used by Lobbies    352
Grass-Roots Lobbying    363
Pressures on the Parties    365
The Effectiveness of Interest-Group Tactics    366
Factors in the Effectiveness of Interest Groups    367
Legislator-Lobbyist Relations    370
Regulation of Lobbying    373
Interest Groups and Democratic Government    377
Notes    382

## PART IV
## INTERACTION WITH THE EXECUTIVE AND THE COURTS

### 11 The Chief Executive as Legislator                                    388

Societal Conditions and Executive Influence    389
The Legal Base for Executive Influence    390
Partisan Politics and Executive Influence    406
The Personal Dimension of Executive Leadership    408
The Effectiveness of Executive Influence: Overview    412
The Effectiveness of Executive Influence:
   The Problem of Measurement    412
Conclusions and Tendencies    415
Notes    417

### 12 Legislative Oversight of Bureaucracy                                425

Politics, Policy, and Administration    425
What Do Legislators Oversee, and How?    427
Legislative Oversight: Goals and Effectiveness    442
Notes    451

### 13 Legislative-Judicial Relations                                      457

Courts and Legislatures: Comparison and Contrast    457
The Courts: Personnel, Structure, Procedures    459
Legislatures, Courts, and the Separation of Powers    464
Legislatures, Courts, and Public Policy    466
Legislative Reaction to Court Decisions    472
Legislatures, Courts, and the Political Process    479
Notes    480

## PART V
## CONCLUSION

### 14 The Legislative Process: Problems and Perspectives                  487

Efforts to Reform the Legislature    487
The Continuing Problems    498
Conclusion    514
Notes    518

### Index                                                                  522

# PREFACE

The American legislature is the first branch of government. It is the legislature that decides which policy proposals will be considered, shaped, and turned into public law. New policy ventures require legislative approval; earlier political settlements rest on legislative forbearance. The ultimate responsibility for the direction and scope of public programs thus rests with the legislature. But the legislature is a remarkably open and accessible institution, and hence its decisions are often influenced by the preferences of outside interests and actors, including the chief executive.

The centrality of legislatures in the American system of government is a function of their prominent constitutional position, especially in the case of Congress. Legislatures, of course, are much more than the sum of their constitutional powers. They are places where individual political careers develop and expand and where political maneuvering is a way of life. Supported by their staffs and others, members invest unusual amounts of time and energy in protecting and enhancing their careers, and the legislature is singularly hospitable to their needs—for advertising their wares, gaining recognition and position, and heightening their advantages in the electoral process. The truth of the matter is that, for the typical member, nothing looms more important than his or her career. Failure to protect it, using the resources of the legislature, is more likely to stem from a lack of imagination than from a lack of opportunity.

More than any other institution of government, the legislature reflects the range and reality of American politics—in the behavior of the politicians who do business there, in the conflicts that are resolved there, and in the struggles that occur there to gain the benefits that government can confer or to avoid the penalties that it can impose. The legislature is a microcosm of all democratic politics. Inevitably, it holds a fascination for attentive observers and other democrats.

American legislatures warrant careful examination for a reason that goes well beyond the fascination of observers. They are changing institutions: their popularity fluctuates; media attention to them vacillates; events help to shape them; election outcomes influence them; strong leaders bend them; new members may alter their character. Legislatures also change by themselves—sometimes self-consciously and independently, sometimes in response to pressures from the outside, sometimes simply to serve symbolic purposes.

The American legislatures of the 2000s are by no means the same as those of earlier decades. Nor is what we know about them quite the same. The need to examine the evolving legislatures and to take account of the new literature on the legislative process provides the main justification for the preparation of this tenth edition.

At this point, scholars have developed no encompassing scheme for analyzing the legislative process useful enough to justify its exclusive adoption. In this respect, political scientists who engage in research in this field work under the same burdens shared by political scientists in all fields. Within this limitation, this book proposes to describe and analyze the American legislative process. We have sought to wring the most that we can from a variety of approaches and have drawn upon a wide-ranging assortment of studies—of legal, behavioral, normative, and historical dimensions. The only test invoked has been of their apparent appropriateness to a better understanding of the behavior of legislators and the functioning of legislatures.

The three major assumptions made in this work are central to effective analysis. First, we believe that legislative institutions should be viewed in relationship to larger environments and inclusive political systems. Accordingly, we have given the role of "outsiders"—political parties, interest groups, chief executives, and courts—at least as much attention as the legislative institution itself. Second, we believe that a comprehensive study of the legislative process requires careful examination of state legislatures as well as Congress. In each chapter, analysis moves between state and nation, depending on the nature of the inquiry and the availability of data or interpretation. Third, we believe that legislative institutions and processes can be illuminated by stressing such aspects of legislative life as the roles, norms, and perceptions held by the legislators.

Some account of the authors' perspectives may be of interest. Most important, we have tried to keep this volume from becoming disabled as a result of carrying a heavy load of our personal preferences and the incantations that they would tend to produce. Here and there a determined reader may encounter clues that suggest that the authors: (1) hold a bias in favor of legislative institutions that are responsive to majority opinions and impulses in the institution and the electorate; (2) believe that American legislatures today are to be neither extolled nor disparaged in the abstract and that specific analysis should precede assessment; and (3) conclude that there is nothing inevitable about the present ordering of American legislatures, even though major change probably will be associated with major alterations in the broader political system. Given this primary assumption, our analysis inevitably moves toward ascertaining the relevance of contemporary trends in American society for the legislative process.

American legislatures are not static institutions. Many changes have taken place in recent years, and this tenth edition examines these changes carefully. Among the topics that receive new or expanded analysis are the following: financing of congressional elections, popular evaluations of Congress, impeachment, initiative and referendum, term limits, gerrymandering, redistricting and the courts, recruitment of legislative candidates, PACs, representation, committee politics, committee-floor relations, rules, legislative strategy, party caucuses, party voting, divided government, independent counsels, and presidential leadership in Congress.

Humor is an important feature of legislative life. In legislatures, as elsewhere, humor diminishes tedium and tension. We have let it slide into our pages here and there—in accounts, for example, involving crab racing, Shamu, the Apache Belles, the cat versus bird controversy in Illinois, the albino deer of Pennsylvania, the real estate business of U.S. Steel, the front porch ruminations of Ethel and Homer concerning discharge resolutions in West Virginia, and legislative oversight in Kentucky. ("If you grab them by their budgets, their hearts and minds will follow.") The justification for tapping into the amusing world of legislators is, of course, to extract elements for the development of middle-range theories of the legislative process.

A number of colleagues, friends, and students assisted us in the preparation of earlier editions: Stan Berard, Lisa Campoli, Holbert N. Carroll, Edward F. Cooke, Joseph Cooper, Martha Ellis Crone, David Fitz, Ayeola Fortune, Paul Goren, Brooke Harlowe, Charles S. Hyneman, Charles O. Jones, Kathryn Keefe, David C. Kozak, Karl T. Kurtz, Thomas Mann, Albert J. Ossman, Albert Papa, Lynette Perkins, Philip Powlick, James A. Robinson, Fiona Ross, Myron Rubinoff, Deborah L. Solomon, and Sidney Wise. In the preparation of this edition, we received valuable assistance from Holbert N. Carroll, William Lies, James Tinnick, Janie Pegher Ondo, and from reviewers Paul Goren, Southern Illinois University; Jack Riley, Coastal Carolina University; and David Nice, Washington State University. Martha Keefe typed much of this edition; our daughter Jodi proofread most of the chapters. We want to thank Beth Gillett and Serena Hoffman of Prentice Hall for their assistance in the preparation of this volume.

Finally, a word is appropriate about the division of labor in writing this book. Chapters 1 through 10 and Chapter 14 were written by Keefe, and Chapters 11 through 13 were written by Ogul. Each author made numerous contributions to the other's work to develop an integrated book—consistent in approach, content, and style.

William J. Keefe
Morris S. Ogul

# USING THE INTERNET TO STUDY THE LEGISLATIVE PROCESS

Several widely used general search engines can provide information on specific topics such as impeachment of the president, social security, and health care. Among these are AltaVista (*www.Altavista.net*); Excite (*www.excite.com*); Infoseek (*www.infoseek.com*); Lycos (*www.lycos.com*); and Yahoo (*www.yahoo.com*). Metacrawler (*www.metacrawler.com*) is a site that searches several engines at once.

An excellent source of current and recent documents about Congress is Thomas (*http://thomas.loc.gov/#record*), named after Thomas Jefferson. Thomas enables one to reach the *Congressional Record,* a chronicle of the proceedings of Congress, its index and résumé of activity; the text of bills; an update on the status of bills; congressional hearings; and roll-call votes. Thomas also provides links to the executive and judicial branches, as well as to state and local governments.

CongressionalMegaSites (*httl://lcweb.loc.gov/global/legislative/mega.html*) lists and describes more relevant Web sites than most people, even serious researchers, could possibly use. For example, it provides links to Thomas, the House and Senate Web sites, "GPO Access" for the texts of congressional documents, "Capweb," "The Internet Guide to the U.S. Congress" (*www.capweb.net*), and GovBot (*http://ciir2.cs.umass.edu/GOVBOT*), which searches all government sites.

Much information concerning Congress and its activities can be obtained from two newspapers on Capitol Hill: "The Hill" (*www.hillnews.com*) and "Roll Call" (*www.Rollcall.com*). Both are widely read in Washington. The results of public opinion polls about public policy issues and governmental institutions can be found at the Web site for the Gallup Poll (*www.gallup.com*) or at Polling Report (*www.PollingReport.com*), which compiles and reports polling results from organizations such as Gallup, Harris, and Yankelovich. Congressional Quarterly, Inc., the publisher of *CQ Weekly,* offers several online sites, such as American Voter (*http://voter.cq.com/hot.htm*), a compilation of information and carefully screened political Web sites. The Dirksen Congressional Center (*www.pekin.net/dirksen*) provides online information about Congress and, perhaps more important, through its Congress Link (*www.congresslink.com*) offers an excellent list of Web sites with information on Congress.

Reams of valuable data and other information concerning campaign finances can be found at the Federal Election Commission Web site (*www.fec.gov*).

Online sources dealing with state legislatures are more difficult to find. The Library of Congress provides a listing of Internet resources dealing with state and local government (*http://lcweb.loc.gov/global/state/stategov.html*). Included is a listing of meta-indexes for state and local government information. Links are provided to the Web sites for the Council of State Governments, the National Center for State Courts, and the National Conference of State Legislatures, as well as to individual states. To reach the Council of State Governments directly, use *www.csg.org*; reach the National Conference of State Legislatures at *www.ncsl.org*. This site has materials on state legislatures, on policy issues in the states, and on links to other Internet sites, including those for each state legislature. Each state has a Web site, but as one could guess, they are uneven in quality.

FindLaw (*www.findlaw.com/11stategov/index.html*) provides links to state constitutions and laws, directories of state officials, and court cases.

An excellent guide to articles concerning the social sciences in scholarly journals is PAIS. Many colleges and universities provide online access to PAIS. A listing of politically relevant Web sites is *www.politicalresources.com/webnotes/issue_2-2.htm*.

This guide was prepared with the assistance of Mary Elizabeth Miller and Wendy Mann-Eliot of the Hillman Library, University of Pittsburgh.

# 1

# The Legislative Task

Complex social systems require institutions that will establish and maintain the legal order, receive and settle conflicts, set priorities, make and legitimize policies, and adapt existing rules of society to new conditions. These tasks are familiar to all democratic legislatures, though they are not assigned exclusively to them. The legislature is only one part of the apparatus for making authoritative social decisions. Constitutions, laws, and customs require it to share power and responsibility with the chief executive, the courts, the bureaucracy, the political parties, and in some cases, the public. Time, place, and leaders help shape the relations between the legislature and these other institutions. The legislature may choose to follow their lead, to join with them, to ignore them, to try to pit one against the other, or to struggle against them. In a word, the legislature is tightly linked in a web of complex and ever-changing relationships with other branches and political institutions.

Analysis of the legislature that focuses on the institution as a separate legal entity may contribute to forming valid and useful distinctions, but it will fall short of explaining the nature of the legislative process. The legislature is unable to maintain an independent group life. Rather, it is involved in an elaborate network of external relations, some that it has developed for its own purposes and others that have been thrust upon it. Legislative oversight of the administration, for example, emerged as a means of strengthening the institution's position and helping it to secure from the bureaucracy certain behavior termed "responsible administration." In contrast, executive initiative in the legislative process, an intrusion certain to be opposed by some members, often functions to stimulate the legislature to action, contributing to the development of new programs or to the abandonment or revision of old ones. No legislature is sufficiently insulated from outside pressure to control its own agenda, though it may well be able to control the pace at which it considers items on it. About the same thing can be said for those institutions dependent in some way on the legislature or susceptible to its influence. The course of their affairs as well as their effectiveness may in large measure be attributable to steady legislative interest and backstopping.

The legislature functions within a larger political system. It is linked with other institutions in various ways, and its decisions often reflect these interrelationships. Interest groups make claims upon it. Executive officials help shape its agenda and interpret and implement its legislation. The judiciary may be called on to explicate the meaning of its statutes or to examine their constitutionality. In its relationship with the executive branch and the courts, the legislature may have neither the first word, as represented in the origination of ideas for legislation, nor the last word, as represented in the determination of the constitutionality of its legislation. Within the legislature itself the process of reconciling the demands of competing groups and of choosing among alternatives may be influenced as much by outsiders as by legislators.

Linkages between the legislature and the general political-constitutional system may have major bearing on the behavior of legislators. The traditions, processes, and political cultures associated with elections and representation affect the kinds of people who are recruited as legislators, the conditions under which they hold office, the roles they select to play as members of the legislature, and the clienteles (organized private interests, the chief executive, the party, and others) to which they turn for information, cues, instructions, or support. Constituency interests may dominate the attention of some legislators or represent only one force among many for others. Members may be more responsive to constituents on some issues than on others, and be more receptive to the initiatives of the chief executive on some issues than on others. Members elected in districts or states of intense party competition may behave differently from members elected in districts or states of limited party competition. Legislators from one region may vote in a distinctive way regardless of their party affiliations. The overall political-constitutional system may be designed to make it difficult for public sentiment to find its way intact to the legislature; it may be relatively uncommon, for example, for one party to capture both houses of the legislature and the executive at the same time. If arrangements rule out party control, party management of the legislature and party responsibility for a policy program are similarly ruled out.

The legislature is not an isolated institution. The struggle to gain the advantages it can allocate (or to avoid the penalties it can levy) takes place both inside and outside its walls. Eventually, conflicts are likely to be brought to the legislature because arrangements made outside are inconclusive, precarious, or unsatisfactory, or because the legislature is in a position to contribute formulas for settlement and legitimacy to the provisions of settlement. The major decisions of the legislature ordinarily represent a temporary accommodation between private and public groups holding different objectives. As circumstances change and as elections upset old alliances and help to create new ones, consensus is impaired. A change in power relations gives rise to multiple demands that the legislature produce new settlements;

"business as usual," whether in the way the legislature is organized or in the character of the policy output, may be entirely unsatisfactory to those newly come to power.

The legislative process is much more than a legal system for taking inchoate ideas and turning them into firm statutes. In its most fundamental aspect, the legislative process is the center of critical struggles for political, economic, and social advantages.[1] The process is routine only when the questions are routine. To bring the process into focus requires the observer to understand the legislature's relationships with other major institutions and environmental forces, including political parties, interest groups, constituencies, the executive, the bureaucracy, the judiciary, and the electoral-representative system. These elements receive much more emphasis in this book than those that might be described as uniquely legislative.

## DISCONTENT OVER THE LEGISLATURE

Legislative assemblies have long been experiencing difficult days. Where totalitarian movements have been successful in gaining power, the independence and autonomy of legislatures have been diminished or lost altogether. Elsewhere, under democratic conditions, legislatures have declined in popular esteem, at times to the point of disrepute. American legislatures without exception no longer enjoy as great a measure of public confidence as was theirs in the early days of the republic. How great their fall from virtue has been is surely disputable, but there is no doubt that it has taken place.

The reasons for the decline of the legislature's prestige are more easily detected than weighed for significance. Discontent over the performance of the legislature appears to stem from a number of interrelated complaints. Briefly treated here and at length in later chapters, they are as follows.

*The legislature is not sufficiently responsive to majority preferences either in the electorate or within the institution itself.* Of all the charges laid against the legislature this one has been pressed most often and insistently. In years past the malapportionment of legislative districts was typically cited as the leading obstacle to majority rule in American legislatures. Majority sentiments in the electorate, according to this argument, could not find expression in the legislature because of a faulty system of representation in which rural and sparsely populated areas held a disproportionate number of seats at the expense of populous urbanized areas. Allegedly this imbalance resulted in the formation of public policy inimical to the interests represented by urban legislators. Today the malapportionment issue is of slight significance. A series of Supreme Court and state court decisions during the 1960s and 1970s firmly established the doctrine that legislative districts must be fairly apportioned, consistent with the principle of "one man–one vote," and in 1986 gerrymanders came under the review of the Court. In *Davis* v. *Bandemer*, the Court warned that redistricting plans will be invalidated "when the electoral system is arranged in a manner that will consistently degrade a voter's or a group of voters' influence on the political process as a whole."[2]

The lament that legislatures are not responsive to their own majorities, however, continues to be heard. At times criticism focuses on the fragmentation of legislative power that results from the weaknesses of the parties as instruments for building reliable majorities. Coalition politics may come to the fore when the parties are splintered. In the 105th Congress (second session), for example, the "conservative coalition" (a voting alliance of Republicans and southern Democrats aligned against northern Democrats) won 96 percent of the roll-call votes on which it appeared.[3]

The committee system is also a point of controversy. It is easy to find examples of committees whose composition and policy orientations are unrepresentative of the chamber as a whole and to identify committee and subcommittee leaders who are out of step with the main elements of their party. (See Chapter 6.) Intensely individualistic members and the growing power of lobbies also take a toll on the legislature's cohesiveness and its capacity to serve broad public purposes. Finally, there are the frustrations that accompany divided control of government, with one party in control of the executive branch and the other party in control of one or both houses of the legislature. Under such circumstances, it is all but impossible for even the most attentive observers to estimate the responsibility for policies adopted, problems ignored, and things left undone. In recent decades divided control of government has become a chronic condition of both national and state politics. At any one time about half of all state governments will be operating under conditions of divided party control. At the national level, every Republican president since the 1950s (Eisenhower, Nixon, Ford, Reagan, and Bush) has faced Democratic majorities in one or both houses of Congress. Democratic presidents encounter opposition majorities occasionally, as in the 104th Congress (1995–96) and the 105th Congress (1997–98).[4]

*Legislative politics and public policy formation are dominated by organized special-interest groups.* This assessment will be recognized as a variant of the first. It holds that the "public interest" is not often uppermost in the minds of legislators bent on favoring (or placating) a multitude of pressure groups. When agricultural policy is under consideration, farmers' organizations arrive with drawn specifications; when labor-management legislation is at stake, labor and business organizations lock horns; when trade legislation is under review, "protectionist" and "free trade" interests stumble over one another in their zeal to defend their positions; when campaign finance legislation makes its way to the agenda, each party moves quickly to its conventional interest-group position—for Democrats, support for limits on spending coupled with public funding, and for Republicans, support for curbs to rein in political spending by organized labor and to increase both contribution limits for individuals and spending limits for political parties; when corporate subsidy ("corporate welfare") programs (e.g., protecting companies' overseas investments against losses from political upheavals, research on clean coal technology, timber road construction in national forests, research on alternative energy sources) come under review, every affected interest shows up on Congress's doorstep; when the question of appropriating money for the International Monetary Fund (IMF) makes its way onto the agenda, intense conflict breaks out among conservative interests, with major business organizations favoring unhampered IMF funding as a way of protecting American exports, and antiabortion activists insisting on a requirement to restrict overseas family planning funds; when legislation to protect the environment is introduced, producer interests arrive, ready to do battle with conservationists.

To many observers, it appears that legislators fail to distinguish between private interests and the public good. All too frequently, some critics say, public policy overrepresents the interests of the most organized elements of the population. E. E. Schattschneider described the problem in this way:

> American government has grown great by meeting the demands made upon it. The catholicity and versatility of the governmental response to the demands made upon it seem at times to have been based on the assumption that all claims ought to be met regardless of their merits. . . . [Yet] sooner or later it becomes necessary . . . in any political system to *discriminate* among the demands. This involves the establishment of a public policy. No public policy could ever be the mere sum of the demands of the organized special interests. For one thing, the sum of the special interests, especially the organized special interests, is not equal to the total of all interests in the community, for there are vital common interests that cannot be organized by pressure groups. Government by organized special interests, without some kind of higher integration, must break down of its own weight.[5]

An appraisal of the Texas legislature in 1975 illuminates the problem of securing legislation to assist the disadvantaged and poorly organized elements of society:

> The legislature's [priorities] are most clearly seen in its biannual appropriations bill. Compare $400,000 for a moss-cutter on Lake Caddo with nothing for bilingual education. A healthy chunk of money for an old folks' home in the district of the chairman of the House Appropriations Committee, but nothing for the state's only black law school. Money to air-condition a National Guard armory, but no money to air-condition the state school for the mentally retarded. When it's a question of malnutrition, hookworm, or illiteracy against new equipment for the Texas Rangers, the Rangers always get what they need. In a state with

no corporate income tax, no corporate profits tax, no natural resources severance tax, wellhead taxes on natural gas and oil that fall below the national average, and a light corporate franchise tax, where does the largest chunk of Texas' money come from? From a regressive 4 percent state sales tax.[6]

Legislatures are frequently tarnished by accusations that special interests dominate policy outcomes. When the 98th Congress (1983–84) blocked the imposition of a withholding tax on interest and dividend income, it was accused of caving in to the banking industry, which had orchestrated a massive campaign for repeal of the law. "The conduct of some members of the American Bankers Association," said one House member, "is absolutely outrageous—frightening the elderly and poor into intimidating Congress." The House's action, observed another member, "will send a signal that the Congress of the United States is a patsy for a very well organized lobby."[7]

The influence of interest groups, conventional wisdom asserts, is linked to the strength of the legislative parties. Former Senator David F. Durenberger (R., MN) offered this observation: "Party discipline doesn't matter because parties don't matter. There's no discipline, just 30,000 special interests that we're all serving in one way or another."[8]

The belief that special interests exert inappropriate influence on legislatures has intensified as a result of the growing involvement of organized groups in financing congressional election campaigns. In the 1997–98 election cycle, the political action committees (PACs) of interest groups contributed $200 million to all Democratic and Republican candidates for Congress, with some candidates receiving more than half of their funds from this source. In comparison, in the 1978 election, PAC gifts to congressional candidates were only $34 million. Contributions by PACs to House candidates in 1998 totaled 37 percent of their campaign receipts. For Senate candidates the figure was 19 percent. Republican congressional candidates received 52 percent of all PAC funds, Democrats 48 percent.[9]

A striking fact in election after election is that congressional incumbents receive, on average, six or seven times as much money from PACs as their challengers. In the 1998 election, House and Senate incumbents garnered a whopping 87 percent of all PAC money.[10] (See data on the PAC–incumbent nexus in Table 1.1.)

Many observers wonder whether members' dependence on PACs to finance their campaigns compromises their role as representatives of the general public. Members also worry about the PAC problem. To quote former Congressman Richard L. Ottinger (D., NY):

> It is fundamentally corrupting. At best, people say they are sympathetic to the people they are getting money from before they get it; at worst, they are selling votes. But you cannot prove the cause and effect. I take the money from labor, and I have to think twice in voting against their interests. I shouldn't have to do that.[11]

TABLE 1.1    PACs, big money, and incumbents: House incumbents who received more than $500,000 from PACs and Senate incumbents who received more than $1 million from PACs, 1998 off-year elections

|  | No. of Incumbents | Percent of All Incumbents Seeking Reelection |
|---|---|---|
| House of Representatives | 64 | 16 |
| Senate | 20 | 69 |

NOTE:  Three open-seat House candidates also received more than $500,000 in PAC money. The average Democratic House challenger received $49,000 in PAC funds, the average Republican House challenger $45,000. On the Senate side, the average Democratic challenger received $96,000 in PAC funds, the average Republican challenger $281,000.

SOURCE:  Adapted from data in press release, Federal Election Commission, December 29, 1998.

*The legislature is seldom a force for innovation.*  This criticism rests on the belief that few if any significant changes are likely to result from a new session of the legislature. The caution and conservatism of the legislature, its unwillingness to experiment, and its inability to cast free from conventional ties very probably have served to stunt the interest of the public (or at least some sectors of it) in the institution and its policy processes. At times, change comes so haltingly as to be imperceptible. Temporization appears as policy. Duane Lockard has put the case this way:

> [Power in Congress is not] distributed in a neutral way; it favors the status quo. Congress is like the rest of American government: it is geared to grind slowly. Congress, through its formal rules and its informal practices, is an institution devoted inordinately to the prevention of action. Indeed it is so well equipped to stop legislation that even conservative interests at times have difficulty when they seek changes in the law. Usually conservatives need only to stop action to achieve at least their more limited goals, but liberal legislators, because they seek innovation more frequently, encounter obstruction from well-entrenched conservative opponents in addition to the usual difficulties in putting together majorities for their proposals.[12]

Writing in the early 1990s, Paul J. Quirk offered these observations:

> [The postreform Congress] has great difficulty deliberating responsibly or resolving conflict constructively on issues that elicit strong feelings from mass constituencies. . . . Accordingly, when Congress is forced to deal with issues like whether to cut Social Security payments, tolerate moderate levels of environmental pollution, ration high-technology health care, or especially, raise taxes, it is under exceedingly heavy pressure to act in conformity to the public's sentiments and prejudices about these subjects. When it is called on to resolve

conflicts among such sentiments—for example, to adopt a balanced program of benefit cuts and tax increases—this pressure leads to prolonged or permanent stalemate. Ultimately, the weaknesses of the postreform Congress in deliberating and resolving conflict on salient issues may outweigh its enhanced capacity for representation.[13]

Electoral upheavals, of course, can upset congressional stability. Following the Republican party's capture of the House of Representatives in 1994, for the first time since 1952, significant institutional changes were adopted and an activist policy agenda was put in place. Numerous rule changes were adopted at the opening of the 104th Congress (1995–96), leading to the elimination of certain committees, sharp cuts in committee staffing, tighter limits on committee and subcommittee assignments, a ban on proxy voting in committee, and term limits for leadership positions (six years for committee chairs, eight years for Speaker), among other things. Of greater importance, arguably, House Republicans lived up to their campaign promise to vote on each item in their "Contract with America" (including a balanced budget amendment, line-item veto, middle-class tax cut, capital gains tax cut, welfare reform, congressional term limits, and the like) during the first 100 days of the session. Supported by a remarkably cohesive party, the Speaker became the dominant player in Congress, at least for a time. But it did not take long for this burst of leader-dominated party activity to run its course. The most celebrated "planks" in the "Contract with America"—constitutional amendments to provide for a balanced budget and congressional term limits—were defeated, the former in the Senate and the latter in the House itself. Under the speakership of Newt Gingrich, partisan division occurred more frequently, culminating in the acrid impeachment proceedings in 1998. Following the 1998 elections, in which Republicans lost five House seats, disgruntled rank-and-file Republicans forced Gingrich to step down. A more affable and pragmatic lawmaker, J. Dennis Hastert of Illinois, was chosen to replace him.

*Institutional arrangements in the legislature obscure the public's view of the decision-making process and, moreover, make it difficult to fix responsibility for actions taken by government.* The legislature functions according to well-ordered routines, but even the most assiduous observer finds it baffling to follow the course of a bill through the legislative labyrinths. The haze that hangs over the lawmaking process is due chiefly to the complexity of rules of procedure, which opens up vast opportunities for maneuvering; the structure and design of legislative organization, which make the institution vulnerable to minority domination; and the weakness of the party, which diminishes the possibility of holding an organized and highly visible group accountable for decisions.

Lawmaking is unpredictable. Proposals must surmount numerous obstacles. A bill may be referred to a hostile committee and quietly pigeonholed, for example, or it may never win a place on the committee agenda because of the chair's opposition. It may die in subcommittee. Or having passed through a standing committee, a bill may fail to win clearance from the rules committee and thereby be lost. A rule to bring a bill to the floor may be defeated, in effect killing the bill without actually voting on it. A bill on the calendar may not be called up for consideration. A bill may be lost by recommitting it to committee "for further study" or emasculated by adopting an amendment that alters its purposes. In a word, why and how legislative decisions are taken are not easily discovered by outsiders. To the general public preoccupied with daily living, the design of the legislature appears to consist mainly of dark corners.

In the typical Congress, the legislative parties have only modest success in fostering responsibility in government. Their inability to close ranks and maintain cohesion on major legislation is well established:

> [The] parties, like the offices and committees, are tailored to suit members' electoral needs. They are more useful for what they are not than for what they are. . . . It should be obvious that if they wanted to, American congressmen could immediately and permanently array themselves in disciplined legions for the purpose of programmatic combat. They do not. Every now and then a member does emit a Wilsonian call for program and cohesion, but these exhortations fail to arouse much member interest. The fact is that the enactment of party programs is electorally not very important to members (although some may find it important to take positions on programs). What is important to each congressman, and vitally so, is that he be free to take positions that serve his advantage.[14]

So ambiguous is the concept of "responsibility" that almost anyone can be blamed or praised for a particular decision. On any given vote the press and commentators may supply an explanation along these lines: "The president failed to exert effective leadership"; "the defection of eastern Republicans cost the president a major victory in the Senate"; "the House leadership erred in its calculations"; "the opposition of conservative southern Democrats doomed the Speaker's plan"; "the vote was an overwhelming victory for the banking industry"; "the decision turned on the vote of the senator from West Virginia, who was in the debt of the senator from Oklahoma"; "the loss has been attributed to the defection of several key Democrats"; "the new members ignored the leadership's plea for party unity"; "a biparty coalition won a narrow victory"; "the bill that emerged from the conference committee was accepted reluctantly by a House leadership anxious to adjourn"; and so on. In the absence of responsible parties the public lacks the means by which to hold the legislature as a whole accountable for its decisions.

Put another way, responsibility in the American "separated" system is diffused. Charles O. Jones writes,

The tracking of policy from inception to implementation discourages the most devoted advocate of responsibility theories. In a system of diffused responsibility, credit will be taken and blame will be avoided by both institutions [president and Congress] and both parties. . . . In preventing the tyranny of the majority, the founders made it difficult to specify accountability.[15]

*The legislature is populated by insecure and timorous individuals whose principal aim is to stay in office.* This judgment has a wide currency and appears to be shared by all manner of critics, even two as unlike as C. Wright Mills and Walter Lippmann. Mills wrote,

> Most professional politicians represent an astutely balanced variety of local interests, and such rather small freedom to act in political decisions as they have derives from precisely that fact: if they are fortunate they can juggle and play off their varied local interests against one another, but perhaps more frequently they come to straddle the issues in order to avoid decision. Protecting the interest of his electoral domain, the Congressman remains attentively loyal to his sovereign locality.[16]

And Lippmann observed,

> In government offices which are sensitive to the vehemence and passion of mass sentiment public men have no sure tenure. They are in effect perpetual office seekers, always on trial for their political lives, always required to court their restless constituents. They are deprived of their independence. Democratic politicians rarely feel they can afford the luxury of telling the whole truth to the people. . . . With exceptions so rare that they are regarded as miracles and freaks of nature, successful democratic politicians are insecure and intimidated men. They advance politically only as they placate, appease, bribe, seduce, bamboozle, or otherwise manage to manipulate the demanding and threatening elements in their constituencies. The decisive consideration is not whether the proposition is good but whether it is popular—not whether it will work well and prove itself but whether the active talking constituents like it immediately. Politicians rationalize this servitude by saying that in a democracy public men are the servants of the people.[17]

The pessimistic views of Lippmann and Mills were of course set forth many years ago. But it is not hard to find contemporary observers who see legislators in about the same light:

> By shirking the hard work of lawmaking [in the New York state legislature] and turning it over to the leaders, legislators can devote themselves to the easier, more rewarding tasks of public office: meeting with constituents, interceding with the state bureaucracy, attending political events, and speaking out on issues. Such activities make legislators popular—many are minor celebrities in their districts—and they amount to the lightest of workloads: little wonder that so many lawmakers keep coming back to Albany decade after decade. The capital's political culture even supplies legislators with a ready excuse for the occasional vote that offends constituents: "The leaders insisted." (Eric Lane, former counsel to the New York Senate minority leader)[18]

The conventional wisdom you'll hear is that a few thoughtful letters have more impact than 100 names on a petition. That's generally true. But a lot of these new members are like cats on a hot tin roof. You turn up the heat and they start dancing all over. They can't take any pressure at all—including contrived pressure. (Staff Director of the Democratic Study Group of the U.S. House of Representatives)[19]

The reason the [Democratic] tax bill lost is that over 50 percent of Congress never served in a legislature before, never came up the route of having had party discipline. They've never been subjected to pressure before. And all of a sudden, it's pressure hitting them. There's a lot of talent in this Congress. But there's a hell of a lot of lack of courage out there, too, and I have to pay the bill for that. (former Speaker Thomas P. "Tip" O'Neill, D., MA)[20]

The Senate is on a hair-trigger. There's an absence of a long view. People are running for reelection the day they arrive. It's unbelievable. (former Senator John C. Danforth, R., MO)[21]

The Founding Fathers gave senators six-year terms so they could be statesmen for at least four years and not respond to every whim and caprice. Now a senator in his first year knows any vote could beat him five years later. So senators behave like House members. They are running constantly. (Senator Dale Bumpers, D., AR)[22]

[In 1999] the House, with an incoherence produced by the timidity of careerists, voted against declaring war [against Yugoslavia], against supporting the air war, against withdrawal of U.S. forces, against use of ground troops without congressional approval and against stopping what they will not support. (George F. Will)[23]

Members of Congress win election through the ceaseless monitoring and cultivation of voter desire. They keep that process up once they are sworn in. It is no accident that the overwhelming majority of staff people in any congressional office work on constituent service, not legislative research. . . . *Congress fails for an excess of responsiveness*. At no point in recent times has there been so wide a gap between what members are willing to propose in private . . . and what they are willing to endorse in public. . . . [They are] desperate to stay in office, and timid about saying or doing anything that might turn a fickle electorate against them. This—not the prevalence of PAC money—is what has rendered Congress so weak in dealing with hard national problems. (Alan Ehrenhalt, political editor of *Congressional Quarterly Weekly Report*)[24]

Now and then Congress's own doubts about its capacity to deal with difficult problems are laid bare. In 1985, for example, it passed the Gramm-Rudman-Hollings deficit-reduction bill, establishing yearly deficit-reduction targets in order to bring the budget into balance by 1991. The key feature of the law provided for automatic spending cuts to be made when the president and Congress were unable to agree on a budget that conformed to the target for any year. No mystery surrounded the rationale for this provision. By opting for automatic, across-the-board cuts, thus relinquishing its budgetary authority, Congress sought to protect its members from having to go on the record by voting for painful spending cuts that were sure to be felt in the constituencies. "Budget balancing by anonymous consent," one member called Gramm-Rudman, and another saw it as "a legislative substitute for the guts that we don't have to do what needs to be done."[25] The section of the law that provided for automatic spending cuts was declared unconstitutional in 1986,[26] leaving Congress to deal with deficit-reduction targets through the conventional workings of the legislative process. Unable to make any progress toward reducing the deficit, Congress in late 1987 passed a second version of Gramm-Rudman with a different mechanism for enforcing automatic cuts.[27] In the late 1990s, balanced budgets, unprecedented in recent years, could be traced more to a thriving economy and hence a growing tax base than to any newly discovered ability of Congress to grapple successfully with budgetary problems.

*The legislature is not sufficiently attentive to the need for developing and maintaining high standards of rectitude for its members.*   In the judgment of a host of critics, there is a dinginess about American legislatures that results from their tendency to overlook wrongdoings by members and their reluctance to adopt rigorous, enforceable codes of ethics. In response to several spectacular cases of wrongdoing in the 1960s—involving conspiracy, tax evasion, and misuse of public and campaign funds—the U.S. House of Representatives created a Committee on Standards of Official Conduct and the Senate formed a Select Committee on Standards and Conduct. These "ethics" committees are expected not only to investigate allegations of improper behavior on the part of members but also to establish and maintain standards of ethical legislative behavior. The creation of these watchdog committees undoubtedly has sensitized members of Congress to a variety of ethical questions, but such committees have not by any means put an end to unseemly or abusive uses of office and power.

Both houses of Congress now operate under relatively comprehensive codes of ethics. Adopted in 1977, the ethics rules were given an extensive overhaul in 1989 in legislation that also provided for significant pay raises for members. Provisions in the revised codes govern such matters as financial disclosure statements, the receipt of gifts, office accounts, franked mail, mass mailings, honoraria, other outside earned income, lobbying by former members, conversion of campaign funds to personal use, acceptance of travel expenses from private sources, and the practice of a profession (such as law) while serving in Congress. Included in the codes are these provisions: (1) Each member of Congress must file an annual financial statement showing income earned during the year, other income, gifts, financial holdings, liabilities, real estate holdings, and securities and commodities transactions. (2) The practice of making speeches for honoraria is banned. The House voted to ban honoraria in late 1989, at the same time raising its salary to make up for the loss. In mid-1991, the Senate eliminated honoraria and raised its salary to the House's level. Members can continue to charge a speaker's fee but the money must be directed to a charity.[28] (3) Members cannot be paid for professional services, such as working for a law firm or serving on a board of directors. (4) Members are prohibited from maintaining an unofficial office account ("slush fund") to pay for office expenses and also from converting campaign contributions to personal use. (5) To reduce the advantage of incumbency, members seeking reelection are prohibited from sending franked mass mailings less than sixty days before a primary or general election. Annual mass mailings are limited to three per year. Any House member who is a candidate for statewide office is prohibited from sending franked mass mailings to residents outside the district. (6) Former members and top staff are banned from lobbying the legislative branch for one year after leaving office. (7) And, of considerable importance, both houses changed their rules in 1995 to restrict the gifts that members can accept. Senate rules now provide that members cannot accept any gift or meal valued at more than $50, or more than a total of $100 in gifts and meals from any person in a year. Going one step further, the House voted to prohibit members from accepting any gifts or meals. (Members are allowed to accept gifts from family members and friends.) At the opening of the 106th Congress (1999–2000), the House eased its rule on the acceptance of gifts to match the Senate's restrictions.[29] Both houses ban their members from accepting free travel to charity outings and events, such as golf and tennis tournaments. Designed to limit the influence of lobbyists and special-interest groups, these rules prevent lawmakers from accepting almost anything of value. But they are still permitted to accept expense-paid travel from groups that invite them to give speeches at their conventions.

In addition, the 104th Congress (1995–96) passed the so-called Congressional Accountability Act, which ended Congress's exemption from major workplace and antidiscrimination laws. Affecting some 34,000 employees, the act was designed to prevent employee discrimination, provide for worker safety, and guarantee medical and family leave for congressional employees. The legislation also permits employees to sue Congress in federal court for violation of these provisions.[30]

The concern to improve the ethical climate of Congress was a response to a variety of scandals involving members during the 1970s. Included were charges, indictments, and convictions for income tax evasion, false reimbursement claims involving official expenses, acceptance of illegal corporate political contributions, extortion, kickbacks from staff, solicitation and acceptance of bribes, mail fraud, conspiracy to defraud the government, perjury, acceptance of legal fees for assisting private institutions to obtain federal grants, diversion of campaign funds for personal use, election fraud, and morals charges. The adoption of strict ethical codes was seen by many members as the best means for restoring public confidence in Congress. But there is no evidence that the codes had this effect.

Codes of conduct can help to illuminate misconduct and provide guidelines for behavior, but they cannot prevent the occurrence of ethical transgressions. During the 1980s, members of Congress were charged with a wide variety of ethical breaches, including, for example, charges involving bribery, false claims in records of official expenses, acceptance of gifts, illegal use of campaign funds, failure to file accurate financial disclosure reports, questionable payments to staff aides, and a miscellany of abuses of office for private gain. As a result of a Federal Bureau of Investigation (FBI) sting operation (Abscam), one member was expelled in 1980 for accepting a bribe—the first House member since the Civil War to be expelled—and two others resigned before disciplinary votes were taken. Several other House members implicated in the Abscam investigation were defeated for reelection. In 1989 the Speaker of the House (Jim Wright, D., TX) resigned from Congress following the ethics committee's decision to press charges against him for accepting substantial gifts from a Texas developer and for evading House rules on outside income and speaking fees. About the same time the House majority whip (Tony Coelho, D., CA) abruptly resigned rather than face an investigation of his personal finances.

Further damage to Congress's reputation resulted from the savings and loan crisis in the late 1980s and early 1990s. Several senators were charged with mixing official activities with fund-raising—aggressively intervening with federal banking regulators on behalf of a savings and loan association while soliciting and accepting $1.5 million in campaign contributions from it. Weeks of televised hearings of the "Keating Five" investigation doubtlessly heightened the public's perception that campaign funding practices are closely linked to political favoritism—in particular, inducing members to convey improper preferments to their benefactors.

Next came the embarrassment of the House check-kiting scandal, with disclosures that numerous members routinely had been overdrawing their accounts in the House bank (essentially a salary disbursing office with checking services). Talk-show hosts everywhere gamely risked apoplexy as they harangued listeners daily on the members' bad checks and "interest-free loans." The leadership soon abolished the bank, but the damage was done.

Congress's reputation suffered other setbacks when the chair of the House Ways and Means Committee was indicted on multiple counts of conspiracy, embezzlement, and obstruction of justice; when a Minnesota senator was indicted for misuse of funds involving billing the Senate for the use of his own condominium; and when a Pennsylvania congressman was indicted for accepting money from government contractors in return for favors. Still another nagging case during this period involved a prolonged Senate investigation of a member's alleged sexual harassment of many aides and other women.

The most recent troubles to visit Congress have involved the sexual misadventures of members. In late 1998, during the impeachment proceedings of

President Bill Clinton, several House Republicans, including the Speaker-to-be (Robert L. Livingston of Louisiana) and the chairman of the Judiciary Committee (Henry J. Hyde of Illinois) were embarrassed by the disclosure of past extramarital affairs; the Speaker-designate soon announced that he would not run for Speaker and would, in fact, resign from the House. The hard truth is that "sexual McCarthyism" has taken a noticeable toll on both Congress and the presidency, diminishing them in the eyes of the public and eroding institutional morale.

Abuse of power and misuse of funds have been major themes in congressional scandals in recent years, but with the exception of the relatively minor House bank controversy, only a small number of members have been involved in them. *Congressional Quarterly* estimated that some two dozen members have pleaded guilty or been convicted of crimes in the two decades between the mid-1970s and the mid-1990s.[31]

Such evidence as is available suggests that state legislatures are less likely than Congress to require members to adhere to stern codes of ethics. An extraordinary number of accounts have been published that suggest that state legislators are under the thumb of private interests, that they are careless in segregating their personal interests from their public responsibilities, and that they are indifferent to corruption in their midst. Consider the following reports of a party given by Harrah's Lake Tahoe gambling casino to welcome the Nevada legislature into session, of "payoffs" in the Illinois legislature, and of generalized corruption in the Maryland and Pennsylvania legislatures:

> [Legislators, their wives, secretaries, and secretaries' boyfriends] were treated to an all-expense-paid evening on the house, complete with dinner, champagne and entertainment by Robert Goulet. Nobody seemed to question the extending of such hospitality by a regulated industry to its regulators. Indeed, another such affair was scheduled for the following evening at the Nugget in Carson City.[32] [Nevada]

> Most of these [payoffs] are recorded as legal fees, public-relations services, or "campaign contributions," though a campaign may be months away. If questioned, the recipient simply denies that the payment had anything to do with legislative activity. This makes it technically legal. A somewhat smaller number of payoffs are not veiled at all; cold cash passes directly from one hand to the other. . . . A few legislators go so far as to introduce some bills that are deliberately designed to shake down groups which oppose them and which pay to have them withdrawn. These bills are called "fetchers," and once their sponsors develop a lucrative field, they guard it jealously.[33] [Illinois]

> Corruption is a familiar feature of Maryland politics, as jobbers, brokers, horse-racing fanciers and bank-charter addicts work their way through the legislative hall. . . . The Maryland legislature is, to be kind about it, the shoddiest of any of five state legislatures that I've had association with. . . . Maryland is a one-party (Democratic) state run out of the backroom gatherings of Eastern Shore and Baltimore area and Prince George's County legislators and gubernatorial

agents. Seldom are legislators in other states watched, cajoled and bullied by the governor's men as are those in the Maryland legislature. The legislature meets at night once a week, on Mondays. More Marylanders should go down to Annapolis on a Monday evening and watch the obvious shady goings-on— including call-girls from Baltimore waving from the public galleries to their "friends" on the floor of the legislative chambers below. Committees seldom escape the governor's hand. This year, one committee adjourned after defeating by a tie vote a bill he very much wanted. But half-an-hour later, committee members found themselves reassembled, after a talking to by the governor's agents. The bill was then approved with only two dissents.[34]

You can tell a lot about an institution by the individuals it reveres. Visitors to the Pennsylvania Capitol in Harrisburg are greeted by a statue of Boies Penrose—the 19th century state legislator, glutton, vulgarian, and leader of one of the most corrupt political machines in American history. . . . If Penrose were alive today, he would feel right at home in Harrisburg. An eight-month investigation by the [Philadelphia] Inquirer has found that the Pennsylvania General Assembly is dominated by a system Boies Penrose would be proud of. It is a system that allows an elite handful of legislators, operating in virtual secrecy, to spend millions of tax dollars enriching themselves and shoring up their political allies and organizations. It is a system that thrives on the politics of padded payrolls, secret slush funds, kickbacks, expense-account banditry and conflicts of interest. It is a system undisturbed by the wave of reform that swept across much of the nation after the Watergate scandal. And it is a system that has even survived the jailing of two of its leaders and five of its other members over the last three years.[35]

Bribery incidents do the most damage. When certain Arizona and South Carolina state legislators pleaded guilty to accepting bribes to support bills to legalize betting on horse and dog races and casino gambling (uncovered in 1991 sting operations), their legislatures as a whole doubtlessly suffered. Indeed, the public everywhere probably became somewhat more skeptical of their state legislative institutions.

The investigation of members for alleged ethics violations, and their occasional conviction and expulsion, also draw substantial attention to the legislature. In 1998, for the first time in 200 years, the Maryland Senate voted to expel a member for using his office to solicit gifts, including a Lincoln town car from a company doing business with the state. About the same time, with expulsion looming, a Michigan state senator resigned after it was discovered that he had been using a member of his legislative staff to work in his Detroit art gallery.[36] Media and public toleration of legislators' financial improprieties is, arguably, at an all-time low. The conventional wisdom is that legislators who violate the public trust, and are exposed, do irreparable harm to the institution.

Criticism of the legislature is always in style, and critics are not always reasonable in the distinctions they draw or fair in the illustrations they select. Accounts of the weaknesses, waywardness, or corruption of a few legislators, for example, will not support a case that the institution itself is corrupt.

Yet whether the indictments are convincing and square easily with the facts may be less important than that many estimable observers believe they are true. A little evidence goes a long way.

Some of the damage done to the public standing of the legislature is done, either thoughtlessly or deliberately, by legislators themselves. In his innovative study of House members in their districts, Richard F. Fenno, Jr., writes,

> [The] willingness of House members to stand and defend their own votes or voting record contrasts sharply with their disposition to run and hide when a defense of Congress might be called for. Members of Congress run *for* Congress by running *against* Congress. The strategy is ubiquitous, addictive, cost-free and foolproof. . . . In the short run, everybody plays and nearly everybody wins. Yet the institution bleeds from 435 separate cuts. In the long run, therefore, somebody may lose.[37]

Or, as former Speaker Thomas S. Foley (D., WA) put the matter, "Every day we are in session there are members of both parties that are openly critical of the institution. We pay a certain penalty for that."[38]

Perhaps what plagues the legislature most is its failure to hold the confidence of the public. It is extremely rare for as many as half of the people to express confidence in Congress, and often the proportion falls well short of that. In twenty Gallup surveys between 1973 and 1998, in fact, the confidence level averaged only 29 percent. (See Figure 1.1.) From 1992 to 1994, it averaged only 18 percent. Despite the unprecedented media attention given to Congress and its new Republican majority in 1995, popular confidence in the institution reached only 21 percent. Congress's highest ranking in the last several decades occurred in 1974, when it held televised hearings in the impeachment proceedings of President Richard Nixon. Even then, only 42 percent of the public viewed Congress favorably. The rancorous partisanship that characterized the impeachment proceedings of President Bill Clinton in late 1998 and early 1999 clearly took a toll on Congress's (and the Republican party's) standing with the public.

The results of a 1994 *Washington Post*–ABC News opinion study say something about the depths of popular suspicion of Congress. Eight out of ten voters in this national survey contend that members "care more about keeping power than . . . about the best interests of the nation," "care more about special interests" than they do about the average person, and quickly "lose touch with the people." Three out of four voters say that candidates for Congress "make campaign promises they have no intention of fulfilling," and less than one out of three believe most members "have a high personal moral code." The appraisals could scarcely be worse. Why has Congress not performed better? More than half of the respondents charge it up to partisanship—the inability of the parties to work together. This survey, like all

**FIGURE 1.1   Confidence in Congress, 1973–98**

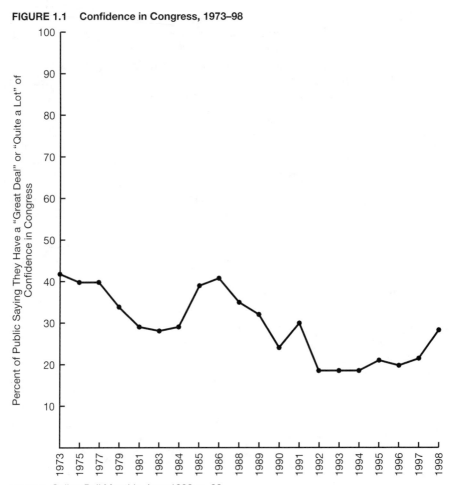

SOURCE: *Gallup Poll Monthly,* June 1998, p. 23.

others, captures the public disdain for Congress. But what it also shows is that a surprisingly large number of voters have only the vaguest idea of what Congress is doing. Less than one-third of the persons in this sample were aware that Congress had just passed a landmark deficit-reduction bill or raised taxes on the very rich and cut them for the working poor—two of the major initiatives of the Clinton administration's first two years. Criticism of Congress, in other words, is not necessarily well founded. Nevertheless, it is troubling that the best-informed voters in this survey emerge as the institution's harshest critics.[39]

Congress's performance is seldom evaluated as favorably as the president's. Indeed, the public's assessment of the two appears to be related. When the president's popularity increases, Congress often benefits; when the president's popularity declines, Congress's standing usually dips as well. The temptation is strong to argue that Congress does not have much control over its own destiny. The same could be said, of course, for state legislatures.

It is a curious fact that Americans tend to approve of their legislators but disapprove of their legislatures. We "love our congressmen," Fenno observes, but "not . . . our Congress."[40] The chief reason for this anomaly is that the people apply different criteria in their evaluations of Congress and of individual legislators. In assessing the institution, as Table 1.2 shows, nearly one-third (30.8 percent) of the people invoke policy standards of one kind or another: How well has Congress dealt with the energy problem? Inflation? Unemployment? When the public is disappointed with the results, which is often the case, the reputation of the institution suffers. The state of legislative-executive relations also is likely to leave many voters disenchanted with Congress. Furthermore, a great many people are critical of the congressional environment, finding deficiencies in the institution's style and pace (inefficient, too slow, given to bickering and haggling), ethical standards, and "self-seeking" activities.[41]

In evaluating members of Congress, the public employs different and less rigorous standards. Voters seldom judge their representatives in a policy context—few members either receive praise or blame for the votes they have cast. Indeed, not many votes are even visible to constituents. The truth is that most voters evaluate their legislators in terms of their records of constituency service and their personal attributes.[42] The public's preferences are not lost on the member. He or she stays in office by taking care of political business at home, paying close attention to constituency matters, creating opportunities for claiming credit, winning public trust, and developing a personal style that fits the voters' expectations. No uncommon imagination is required to do these things. Thus, even while Congress as an institution is steadily disparaged, incumbents continue to win reelection, usually by comfortable margins. Of those seeking another term in 1998, for example, 98 percent of all House incumbents and 90 percent of all Senate incumbents were successful.

The public's evaluation of Congress, David Kimball and Samuel C. Patterson argue, turns on the discrepancy between expectation and perception—that is, the gap between what people think Congress should be like and what they believe it is like. Citizens want lawmakers who are honest, community-minded, and unconcerned with personal gain. But they have a sense that their representatives are too partisan and career-oriented and that the institution is "scandal-ridden, that it is ineffective and laggard, and that it is unresponsive and has lost touch with the public." Media coverage doubtlessly contributes to the public's negative image.[43]

**TABLE 1.2   Bases of public's evaluations of Congress and of members of Congress (in percentages)**

| Bases of Evaluation | Percent of All Responses | Favorable | Unfavorable |
|---|---|---|---|
| **Congress*** | | | |
| Policy | 30.8 | | |
|   Domestic | 30.1 | 7 | 93 |
|   Foreign-Defense | 0.7 | 100 | — |
| Legislative-Executive Relations | 19.6 | | |
|   Presidential Support | — | — | — |
|   Presidential Opposition | 19.6 | 25 | 75 |
| Congressional Environment | 37.1 | | |
|   Congressional Style and Pace | 23.1 | 30 | 70 |
|   Congressional Ethics | 4.9 | — | 100 |
|   Congressional Self-Seeking | 9.1 | — | 100 |
| Group Treatment | 1.4 | 50 | 50 |
| Other | 8.4 | 33 | 67 |
| Don't Know—Not Ascertained | 2.8 | | |
| Total | 100.1 | | |
| **Members of Congress†** | | | |
| Policy | 3.0 | | |
|   Vague Reference | 1.5 | — | 100 |
|   Specific Reference | 1.5 | — | 100 |
| Constituency Service | 37.7 | | |
|   District Service | 13.3 | 100 | — |
|   Constituent Assistance | 12.6 | 100 | — |
|   District Conditions | 3.7 | 100 | — |
|   Informs Constituents | 8.1 | 82 | 18 |
| Personal Attributes | 35.6 | | |
|   Personal Characteristics | 6.7 | 100 | — |
|   Reputation | 28.9 | 67 | 33 |
| Group Treatment | 3.7 | 100 | — |
| Other | 10.4 | 57 | 43 |
| Don't Know—Not Ascertained | 9.7 | | |
| Total | 100.1 | | |

*Question: "Overall, how would you rate the job Congress as a whole—that is the House of Representatives—has done during the past two or three years—would you say Congress has done an excellent job, a pretty good job, only a fair job, or a poor job? Why do you feel this way? Any other reasons?"

†Question: "Overall, how would you rate the job the member of Congress who has been representing this area during the past two or three years has done—would you say he or she has done an excellent job, a pretty good job, only a fair job, or a poor job? Why do you feel this way? Any other reasons?"

SOURCE:  Adapted from tables in an article by Glenn R. Parker and Roger H. Davidson, "Why Do Americans Love Their Congressmen So Much More Than Their Congress?" *Legislative Studies Quarterly,* IV (February 1979), 55, 57. This national survey was conducted in 1977 for the Commission on Administrative Review of the U.S. House of Representatives.

## THE FUNCTIONS OF THE LEGISLATURE

To begin the study of the legislature, we need to look at what it does. The functions of the legislature resemble the listings of a catalogue. No single, urgent theme ties them all together or dominates the rest; some represent a heavier investment than others; some appear as basic requirements, whereas others are simply the accretions that attach to a going institution. The hallmark of the legislature is of course its lawmaking function, and many pages of this book are concerned with how it carries out this role. Yet lawmaking takes up only a portion of the legislature's time. The legislature is also engaged in three other *central* functions—checking the administration, providing political education for the public, and providing representation for several kinds of clientage—and two *minor* functions—described as the judicial function and the function of leadership selection. What the functions of the legislature depict, in short, is the contribution of the American representative assembly to the governing process.[44]

### Making Law

The principal legal task of the American legislature is to make law. The expansion of government services and functions, especially in recent decades, has contributed to an endless procession of ideas for laws. Legislation covers an immense ground: virtually any stray idea can gain some kind of hearing among legislators; virtually any proposal stands something of a chance of finding legislative expression. The instability of legislation differs only in degree from the instability of fashion and public taste. No statute is likely to settle a matter for all time; at best it can only temporarily conclude a problem. In all probability, subsequent legislatures will undo the statute, rework it, perhaps remove it altogether. "Once begin the dance of legislation," wrote Woodrow Wilson, "and you must struggle through its mazes as best you can to its breathless end—if any end there be."[45]

The widening of knowledge in science and social relations seems inevitably to foreshadow a greater burden for the legislature. It is obvious that tomorrow's legislature will run no risk of atrophy for lack of legislation to consider; rather it will be put to the test of coping with a body of requests and problems both more numerous and more complex than government has ever had to consider in the past. The increasingly heavy and the highly visible investment in lawmaking is not, of course, evidence that the legislature occupies a superior position among the branches of government. What it does signify is the close relationship between the growth in complexity of society and the resulting requirements for standard means of adjusting conflict and for new forms of social control. (See Table 1.3 for a variety of evidence on the importance of the lawmaking function in Congress.)

A literal reading of the constitutional grants of power to the legislature

**TABLE 1.3 Legislative activity, House and Senate, various Congresses, 1953–96**

| | | | | | | |
|---|---|---|---|---|---|---|
| | | | *House* | | | |
| *Congress* | *Bills Introduced* | *Bills Passed* | *Recorded Votes* | *Time in Days* | *Time in Session Hours* | *Committee Subcommittee Meetings* |
| 83rd | 10,875 | 2,129 | 147 | 240 | 1,033 | n.a. |
| 93rd | 18,872 | 923 | 1,078 | 318 | 1,487 | 5,888 |
| 95th | 15,587 | 1,027 | 1,540 | 323 | 1,898 | 7,896 |
| 97th | 8,094 | 704 | 812 | 303 | 1,420 | 6,078 |
| 99th | 6,499 | 973 | 890 | 281 | 1,794 | 5,272 |
| 100th | 6,263 | 1,061 | 939 | 298 | 1,659 | 5,388 |
| 102nd | 7,771 | 932 | 932 | 277 | 1,794 | 5,152 |
| 104th | 4,542 | 611 | 1,340 | 289 | 2,444 | 3,796 |
| | | | *Senate* | | | |
| 83rd | 4,077 | 2,231 | 270 | 294 | 1,962 | n.a. |
| 93rd | 4,524 | 1,115 | 1,138 | 334 | 2,028 | 4,067 |
| 95th | 3,800 | 1,070 | 1,151 | 337 | 2,510 | 3,960 |
| 97th | 3,396 | 803 | 952 | 312 | 2,158 | 3,236 |
| 99th | 3,386 | 940 | 740 | 313 | 2,531 | 2,373 |
| 100th | 3,325 | 1,002 | 799 | 307 | 2,342 | 2,493 |
| 102nd | 4,245 | 947 | 550 | 287 | 2,291 | 2,039 |
| 104th | 2,266 | 518 | 919 | 343 | 2,876 | 1,601 |

SOURCE: Adapted from data in Norman J. Ornstein, Thomas E. Mann, and Michael J. Malbin, *Vital Statistics on Congress 1997–1998* (Washington, DC: Congressional Quarterly, 1998), pp. 160–63.

discloses a minimum amount about the lawmaking process. The fact that the legislature is empowered to make laws does not mean that it initiates the ideas for legislation. Indeed, for the infusion of ideas and the origination of most legislation, the legislature is dependent on familiar "outsiders"—the chief executive, administrative agencies, political interest groups, and various party agencies and party spokespersons. Most important among these "outside" interests is the chief executive, whose ideas for legislation and the ideas of the advisers, set forth in "administration bills," regularly provide the major items on the legislature's agenda. By and large, what the legislature brings to lawmaking is the power to represent the people and the authority to make social decisions; what it can leave is its distinctive imprint on the policies recommended by others. Neither in what it brings to the process of making law nor in what it leaves in public policy is its power trifling.

In its broadest sense, American lawmaking consists of finding major and marginal compromises to ideas advanced for legislation. The sifting and sorting of proposals accompanies the search for compromise—in caucus, in committee, on the floor, in negotiations with the executive, and in confrontation with interest groups. The details of bills are filled in at many stages in the legislative process, though especially in committees. One can say that any proposal of consequence serves something of a probationary period; its ultimate fate depends on how well its advocates succeed in bringing additional supporters to its side. The task is not simply to beat the drums to excite one's followers but to neutralize outward and probable opponents and to convince the uncertain. The decisive support may come from one or more interest groups newly won over to the cause, perhaps from a newly invested and sympathetic committee chair, perhaps from the chief executive who would incorporate the bill in "his" or "her" program.

The process of gaining converts to an idea, of strengthening a latent party position, or of putting together a winning coalition may and often does require more than a single session of the legislature. Today's opponents, under different circumstances (for example, a new administration, the aftermath of a sweeping electoral decision), may be tomorrow's proponents or at least reluctant supporters. A considerable number of the major bills adopted at any session of any legislature have failed of passage in an earlier assembly. Ordinarily, where major change is involved, support is won gradually, perhaps accumulated over a number of sessions. Many proposals are given trial runs in the full knowledge that they have no chance of passage. But another day may bring another verdict. In the American political landscape, what is currently unconventional may yet become orthodox with the passage of time: In the formation of public policy the principal testing ground for orthodoxy is the legislature.

In moving proposals through the legislature, advocates strive to attract and consolidate the necessary support—a majority at each stage of the process—without making major concessions to opponents.[46] The process of gaining support may call for tapering provisions from the optimal down to the acceptable—ranging from what is most desirable to what, if necessary, will do—and it may begin as early as the drafting of the bill and continue through to the penultimate decisions of a conference committee between the houses. A form of logrolling is likely to be an important element in the construction of legislation—that is, the preferences of other members are incorporated into a bill to increase its prospects for passage. And since lawmaking is not a zero-sum game, the participants are usually accustomed to outcomes best described as "partial wins."[47]

The steady working of compromise and accommodation may lead to a curious assortment of provisions, many of which entered the bill as concessions to potential supporters. The end product may be a bill that under the circumstances is the best possible, a bill that no one is particularly happy about, or a bill that has little chance of adoption. Getting a bill through the legislature requires ingenuity and leeway, and rare is the major proposal that ends up in law in the same form in which it was introduced.[48]

What you see in either legislation or roll-call voting is not necessarily what you get. The palpable merits of legislation may have less to do with voting calculations than the understandings and commitments that underlie it. Members help one another out by trading votes—logrolling from one perspective, reciprocity from another. And they are surprised when comity falls short. Thus, when a Colorado member from a sugar-beet district offered an amendment to bar tobacco sales from the Food for Peace program, a Kentucky congressman had these observations to make:

> I recall distinctly that last week, when sugar was in trouble . . . about 20 states which produce tobacco marched right down the road with that gentleman. They do not produce any sugar beets . . . or sugar cane in Kentucky. But when sugar is in trouble, sugar beets and sugar cane, the people in Kentucky are concerned about it.[49]

The norm of reciprocity can be threatened by fiscal constraints and budget caps. Reciprocity usually requires spending. When President Clinton requested a multi-billion-dollar supplementary spending bill in 1993 to aid the victims of the "Great Flood" in the Midwest, House conservatives were able to stall the proposal for a time (even defeating a rule to bring it to the floor) by insisting that this new spending be accompanied by reductions in other spending programs—"pay as you go," in other words. Early in the debate an Illinois congressman whose district had been particularly hard hit by the flood had this to say about the reality of congressional practice:

> When this gentleman was asked to come to the aid of California in their disaster [earthquake], for the disaster in Florida [hurricane], and the disaster in Texas [hurricane], I marched up that hill to help American people in need. Today what we get are theories about how to pay for it.[50]

Eventually, after members had properly positioned themselves on the deficit dilemma, the flood-disaster package was overwhelmingly approved, and without offsetting cuts.

Legislative policies, few of which are ever totally new, derive from a vast array of factors. In the most general sense, a policy represents a response to some kind of problem, one acute enough to intrude on the well-being of a significant number of people and their organizations or on the well-being of the government itself, one conspicuous enough to draw the attention of at least some legislators. In a more specific sense, legislation is generated by apprehension, unrest, conflict, innovation, and events. Rarely, if ever, do policies spring full-blown from a theory of society.

Not all legislation is the product of a slow, drawn-out process, marked by twists and turns, advances and backfilling. Legislation sometimes comes in spurts, typically in response to the media's cultivation of the public. Former Representative Leon E. Panetta (D., CA) observes how Congress responded to the drug issue in the 99th Congress (1985–86):

While this bill deserves our approval, it disturbs me that we are treating the drug issue as we do so many issues: An event triggers nationwide concern about a problem, three weeks of media coverage and magazine covers follow, quick drafting of legislation occurs followed by passage by the Congress and signature by the president—and then we forget the issue as we move on to another crisis. . . . The attention span of the American people and Congress for national problems is growing shorter and shorter.[51]

Neither the wide perception of a problem by legislators nor their recognition of a group's particular claims for government action necessarily leads to legislation. The prospects for legislative action increase when (1) the media concentrate on an issue, (2) the chief executive incorporates a proposal into his or her program, (3) influential interest groups mobilize their members, (4) the unorganized public becomes intensely concerned over the issue, (5) the parties and their leaders take up the cudgels, and (6) the formation of strong counterpressures fails to develop. On occasion major interest groups, the chief executive, the unorganized public, and legislative leaders act in concert to advance legislation. But more often than not, public opinion is inert and the other participants are divided. Change thus comes slowly, in bits and pieces, or perhaps not at all.

In the appraisal of David E. Price, congressional initiative in lawmaking turns on the type of issue involved and on the stage of the policymaking process. Concerning issues, he writes, "Congress acts more readily and easily on distributive issues that are responsive to discrete constituencies than it does on broader and more conflictual problems." And as for the stage of the policymaking process,

> One's estimate of Congress's capabilities is likely to be more favorable . . . if one is looking at the *early* stages of policy formation—the generating of issues, the gathering of information, the floating of new ideas, the development of the policy agenda. . . . On high-conflict issues, Congress often needs a strong push from the executive or a swelling of popular opinion if its scattered initiatives are to bear fruit.[52]

There are two special categories of lawmaking of constitutional origin. The first, involving the approval of treaties, is specified by the U.S. Constitution and technically brings only the upper house of Congress into the process. The second special category, the power to adopt constitutional amendments and thereby to alter the fundamental law, is a lawmaking function of both national and state legislatures.

The initiative in making foreign policy rests with the president. But the bare words of the Constitution afford only slight indication of Congress's prerogatives and opportunities for influencing presidential decisions and the broad thrust of foreign policy. In recent years the significant increase in the number of international agreements and in the requirements for enabling legislation to carry broad policies into effect have greatly augmented the responsibilities of Congress in the field of foreign policy. "Foreign" and "domestic" policies, more or less distinct in an earlier period, have now become tightly joined in much of the major legislation of any Congress. Moreover, the House, though it has no constitutional role of advising and consenting to the ratification of treaties, is virtually as instrumental as the Senate in shaping foreign policy through the exercise of its ordinary lawmaking powers and especially through its influence on appropriations. By the same token, the treaty-making power of the Senate does not reveal much about the chamber's overall responsibilities in foreign policy; treaty making, in fact, takes up only a small fraction of the time devoted to foreign policy questions. To quote Louis Henkin,

> Emphasis on the President's power to formulate foreign policy, with its roots in his control of foreign relations, should not depreciate the part which Congress continues to have in the formulation of foreign policy. Congress formulates major foreign policy by legislation regulating commerce with foreign nations or authorizing international trade agreements. The Foreign Commerce Power has grown enormously on the wings of the Interstate Commerce Power so that Congress now has nearly-unlimited power to regulate anything that is, is in, or affects, either interstate or foreign commerce. Congress, and Congress alone, also has the power to make the national policy to go to war or to stay at peace; it has determined United States neutrality in the wars of others. The War Powers of Congress include the power to legislate and spend as necessary to wage war successfully; to prepare for, deter, or defend against war; and to deal with the consequences of war. Under the "general welfare" clause, Congress can decide where, for what, how much, and on what conditions to spend, as in foreign aid. There are implications for foreign policy when Congress establishes and regulates the Foreign Service and the bureaucracies of various departments and agencies dealing with foreign affairs. The innumerable uses of the "necessary and proper" clause include many that "formulate foreign policy." Since foreign policy and foreign relations require money, which only Congress can appropriate, Congress has some voice in all foreign policy through the appropriations process. . . . Congress' unenumerated power to legislate on all matters relating to "nationhood" and foreign affairs may reach far beyond regulation of immigration, nationality, and diplomacy. . . . The Senate, in its executive capacity, is indispensable to the formulation of foreign policy by treaty. . . . If the Senate does not often formally refuse consent to treaties, it sometimes achieves that result simply by failing to act on them. Sometimes, too, it gives consent only with important reservations. When the Senate does consent to an important treaty, it is often because its views were anticipated, or informally determined, and taken into account. Occasionally it contributes to national policy by its actions and expressed attitudes on appointments of foreign service officers, cabinet members, and other important officials in the "foreign affairs establishment."[53]

The other special lawmaking function entails the formulation and adoption of constitutional amendments. The process by which constitutions are amended includes two main stages: proposal and ratification.

Amendments to the U.S. Constitution may be proposed by a two-thirds vote of both houses of Congress on a joint resolution or by a national constitutional convention summoned by Congress in response to a petition adopted by two-thirds of the state legislatures. Amendment ratification may be secured in either of two ways: by adoption of the resolution by legislatures in three-fourths of the states or by constitutional conventions in three-fourths of the states. Only the first-mentioned method of proposing constitutional amendments, joint action by both houses, has been used. Only one amendment, the Twenty-First, has been assented to by conventions held in the states; all the others have been ratified through the actions of state legislatures. Congress alone determines the method for ratification, and the president has no veto power over amendments.

The methods by which state constitutions are amended resemble those used at the national level. All states empower the legislature to propose amendments. Most commonly, a two-thirds vote of the elected members of each house is required to propose an amendment. Almost as many states require only a majority of members, and a few require a three-fifths vote. About a dozen states stipulate that a constitutional amendment must be passed in two sessions of the legislature before being submitted to the voters. In New Jersey, proposals are submitted to the voters if approved by three-fifths of all members of each house at one session or by a majority of all members of each house for two successive sessions. In Massachusetts, a proposed amendment must receive a majority of the vote of the members of both houses sitting in joint session.

Except in Delaware, which empowers the legislature acting alone to amend the constitution, all amendments proposed by the legislature must be ratified by the electorate, usually by a majority voting on the amendment. Three states—Minnesota, Tennessee, and Wyoming—require a majority of those voting in the election to approve the amendment. Nebraska requires that the majority vote on an amendment be at least 50 percent of the total vote cast at the election. In Illinois, the approval of a constitutional amendment requires a majority of all those voting in the election or three-fifths of those voting on the amendment.[54]

The most important difference between national and state practice in regard to the amending process is that the voters are directly involved in the ratification of state constitutional amendments but are bypassed in the ratification of national amendments. Since amendments to the national Constitution ordinarily are considered only by the state legislature, there is no opportunity for voters to vote directly on constitutional proposals. Few if any legislators will have been elected on the basis of how they stand on proposed amendments.

## Checking the Administration

The need to secure responsibility in government and to provide for the representation of the citizenry led to the creation of representative assemblies. An important point to remember, however, is that the legislature was not created to govern; this has been, rather, the responsibility of the executive power. It remains true, of course, that the legislature has a long-established concern with inquiring into administrative conduct and the exercise of administrative discretion under the acts of the legislature, as well as with ascertaining administrative compliance with legislative intent. In the usual phrasing, the legislature's supervisory role consists of questioning, reviewing and assessing, modifying, and rejecting policies of the administration.

The lawmaking prerogative of the legislature has always had the careful attention of legislators themselves—with good reason, of course, since this is the source of the institution's most important powers. In purely constitutional terms, the legislature's lawmaking power is as important today as ever in the past. Current experience shows, however, that much of the initiative and vigor in lawmaking is supplied by the chief executive. If the new balance in legislative-executive relations has been discouraging to legislators, it has also been instructive. Change invites reassessment. Executive leadership now tends to be accepted as inevitable in an increasingly complex and technical world. Moreover, scarce resources, including time and power, require prudent handling. Hence many legislators, as well as many scholars, have come to see legislative surveillance of the administration as a means of increasing the legislature's effectiveness. Legislative oversight, as it is now called, serves as an instrument whereby the legislature can resist executive domination and strengthen its overall position in the constitutional system.[55]

The following justification for legislative oversight may not embellish legislative theory, but it does make an argument worth noting: "People look at the Executive and say we don't trust those bastards. They look at the politicians in Congress and say we don't trust these bastards. The only question is can we trust *these* bastards to keep *those* bastards honest."[56]

The legislature has several devices available for reviewing, influencing, and directing the administration. Legislation itself is an obvious technique of supervision: New laws can be put on the books and old laws revised with a view to changing administrative behavior. Probably the most formidable of its devices, however, is its power to appropriate funds for the conduct of government. The appropriations process is a continuing source of anxiety for administrators, for it is here that agencies can be disrupted and programs undone, chipped away, or discarded. In the final analysis, the direction and scope of government are determined by the amount of money made available for programs.

Constitutional requirements for legislative participation in the appointment process open up additional opportunities for checking and influencing the administration. At the national level, a great many appointments are made by the president alone, under authority given by Congress, and still other lesser appointments are made by department heads. But major appointments, such as those of ambassadors, consuls, and judges, require

Senate confirmation. The custom of "senatorial courtesy" prevails in the submission of names to the Senate for *certain* offices, such as those of district court judges and U.S. marshals. This custom dictates that prior to nominating a person for a position in a state, the president will consult with the senators of that state, if members of his party, about their choice for the position. Should the president ignore their wishes and submit a name objectionable to them or simply fail to consult them, "senatorial courtesy" may come into play, with the senators from that state contesting the nomination. Courteous to a fault, the rest of the Senate ordinarily joins them in opposition.

The state legislature may participate in the formal appointment process in two ways. First, some state constitutions or statutes provide for election of certain administrative officials by the legislature. In over half of the states the auditor is selected by the legislature or one of its organs. A few state legislatures are empowered to elect the state treasurer. In addition to electing these officials, the Maine legislature also chooses the secretary of state and the attorney general. Second, as in the case of national practice, state senates (occasionally councils or both houses) must approve executive nominations for high-level positions.

In general, the governor's power of appointment is more hemmed in than the president's. In a great many states governors have to live with the fact that certain major administrative officers, such as the treasurer and the secretary of state, are popularly elected, and their independent status gives them control over appointments in their departments. And both in appointments that the governor makes alone as well as those that require senate confirmation, his or her power and options are circumscribed by political factors. There are state and local party leaders whose interests in jobs demand consideration, legislative leaders and factions to be mollified by patronage, and key supporters of the governor's own campaign to be rewarded. In the politics of appointment, the governor's view is not unlike the president's.

The appointive power presents both opportunities and problems to the governor. The appointment that wins some friends loses others; rarely are there as many jobs as there are claimants, and never are there enough good ones. Rejected job-seekers and their sponsors, unfortunately, have long memories. Yet in many states, despite its unhappy side effects, the governors' appointive power (coupled with other forms of patronage at their disposal) is the key to securing enactment of their legislative program. In varying degrees and in sundry styles, patronage is used by all governors to win over legislators to their proposals, but it appears to be most important to governors in one-party states. In the absence of meaningful party programs and commitments, the governor and the legislature may have little in common, and "when the going gets rough, he cannot rely on party loyalty but must turn to patronage." Used promiscuously, patronage in a predominantly one-party state may corrupt the minority party. "The more patronage [minority party members] can get, the less incentive they have to gain majority status; the more often they support the governor, the fewer issues their party has for the next campaign."[57]

As a rule few nominations are rejected by the legislature. Legislators generally want to avoid the imputation of obstructionism; hence any warfare over nominations that may occur tends to be guerrilla rather than open in character. Where a two-thirds vote is required for confirmation, there is ample opportunity for the "out" party, if it holds a sufficient number of seats, to exact concessions from the governor. The price of confirming an administration nominee to the public utility commission may be the appointment of an "out" party member to the same or some other commission; to be sure that bargains are carried out, the nominations may be confirmed in tandem. It is not unusual in some states for the minority party in the senate to withhold the necessary votes for confirmation until agreements on certain legislation or appointments have been worked out. When confronted by a hostile senate, governors are likely to make good use of "recess" appointments— temporary appointments for the interim between sessions.

Other legislative-executive encounters take place in committee hearings and investigations; these are treated elsewhere at length. Here it is sufficient to emphasize two things. First, these devices, especially investigations, are sometimes characterized by a doubtful blend of legitimate surveillance and the publicity aspirations of the investigator, notably the committee chair. As such, inquiries sometimes lead to embarrassing treatment of bureaucrats—a prospect unlikely to repel the typical legislator. Second, hearings and investigations need to be seen as instruments in the struggle between the executive and legislative branches—as powerful deterrents to administrative waywardness and carelessness.

## Educating the Public

A function of the legislature easily overlooked, though an exposition of it goes back at least as far as Walter Bagehot's classic analysis of the British House of Commons,[58] is the function of informing and instructing the public. "[Even] more important than legislation," wrote Woodrow Wilson in his volume on Congress, "is the instruction and guidance in political affairs which the people might receive from a body which kept all national concerns suffused in a broad daylight of discussion."[59] Wilson thought that Congress had failed to meet this obligation, preferring instead to engross itself in matters of legislation—in adopting, amending, and revising laws. Few if any current writers argue that today's Congress provides significantly better or more extensive instruction for the public.

The opportunities for the legislature to teach the public things it needs to know are more circumscribed than might appear at first glance. In the first place, the structure of the American legislature inhibits the teaching function. By any reckoning, a large share of the crucial decisions of any session of any legislature are made in committee, yet neither committee discussions nor decisions are as well reported or appear as important (or are viewed as openly) as the affairs of the chamber itself—even though the chamber's role frequently consists simply of ratifying the actions (or acquiescing in the inactions) of sovereign committees. At the state level, reporting of committee activities in depth is virtually unknown; committee jurisdiction and power are both uncertain and unpredictable, committee votes are not readily available and sometimes not available at all, and committee records are often unsatisfactory. The power of committees must be put down as a principal explanation for the failure of the legislature to highlight important matters of policy, to set forth alternatives in such a way as to make them intelligible to the public. If the public is an inattentive audience for legislative politics and, as a consequence, is unable to perceive the significance of decisions to be made, that is hardly surprising.

Another reason the legislature has been unable to master the teaching function lies in the volume and complexity of legislation itself. A sustained political exchange with and for the public over the purposes and meanings of policy, in the fashion of Wilson's dictum, is inordinately difficult under the press of hundreds and thousands of bills introduced each session. Informing the public of the choices available and making clear the stakes involved are tall requirements for a heavily burdened legislature. Indeed, legislators face a formidable task in instructing themselves on legislation.

To these obstacles to communication between governors and governed must be added the demands of errand running, the restless search for political security with constituents, the compulsion to campaign steadily for reelection—each urgency helping to shift legislative attention from the broad objective of educating the public to the more immediate and narrow objectives of getting the job done and retaining popular favor. It is no exaggeration to say that in the course of tending to the political shop, elaborate argument yields to expedient settlement, policy alternatives turn into slogans and issues, and conventional responses substitute for the effort to fathom and to explain the nagging problem or the new venture. Out of such an uncertain mélange a program of public instruction is not easily fashioned.

There is some irony in the fact that two of the activities of Congress that are most demeaned—unlimited debate in the Senate and committee investigations—have as a leading purpose the instruction of the public. Though the argument may be regarded as simply a veneer, the typical group of filibusterers justifies its action in terms of the need to alert and instruct the public:

> Mr. President, I think it is important for the Senate to be a deliberative body. There are many matters affecting the states, the nation, and the world which require extended debate. There are many matters about which the people of the country, who are busy making their livings, working at their jobs, and who do not have the time for deliberation or debate, as we do, will not be informed without extended debate to focus attention on an issue.[60]

Filibustering ("prolonged debate," in the argot of sympathetic legislators) has a goal beyond the education of the public. For success it may require the collaboration of the public and its organized elements. The fact is that major legislation frequently makes no great stir. By delaying the vote on a proposal, opponents seek to win time and to gain new support for their cause. With time, friendly interest groups still on the fence may be induced to enter the fray, and there is always the hope that the publicity generated will rouse the wider public to write, wire, telephone, or visit their representatives. Whatever the disruptive effects of a filibuster, the issue over which it arises gains publicity far out of the ordinary, and the public presumably acquires better insight and an improved opportunity to register a claim in the matter.

The same service is performed by committee investigations. These inquiries serve a variety of purposes, including the important one of exposing the presence of problems and abuses in private groups and public agencies. "No aspect of congressional activity other than investigations is as capable of attracting the attention of the public and of the communications facilities that both direct and reflect public interest."[61] Regardless of the motivations that underlie investigations, and they are doubtless diverse, members of Congress recognize the extraordinary opportunities they offer for influencing public opinion. The standard justification for an investigation is the presumed need for new or remedial legislation; nevertheless, the informing function actuates many inquiries and at times is controlling. Moreover, publicity by itself may lead to the correcting of abuses, thereby allaying the need for legislation.

Teaching is a reciprocal act. It requires a public that is attentive to what is being taught and a legislature intent on making its instruction clear and effective. By and large, neither public nor legislature satisfies these requirements; typically, the public is passive and absorbed in daily living, whereas the legislature is immersed in the negotiations and details of lawmaking.

There are additional opportunities for "educating the constituents" when the members are at home. In fact, however, relatively little instruction takes place. Members talk less about Congress as an institution and more about their individual power. When they do discuss the institution, it is usually to demean it. They "polish" their reputations, writes Richard F. Fenno, Jr., "at the expense of the institutional reputation of Congress."[62]

Even though the legislature's teaching function appears to be of limited effectiveness, changes in recent years do permit voters to learn more about legislative activities. Both Congress and the state legislatures, for example, have adopted *sunshine* (or antisecrecy) rules that open up most committee meetings to the public. In addition, there is a trend toward open sessions for party caucuses. Similarly, regular television coverage of Congress and many state legislatures gives attentive constituents a view of the legislative process and a chance to increase their understanding of policy issues. The effects of the new openness, however, are hard to measure.

There is a final point to be made. Emphasis on the teaching or informing function may lead to overlooking the nature of the legislative *process*, at least insofar as the American legislature is concerned. "Legislation is not merely a matter of persuasion through eloquent speeches or of taking votes backed by a party majority. It is essentially a matter of making adjustments and regulating action so that anticipated desires may be met."[63]

### Representing Constituents, Localities, and "Interests"

"I learned soon after coming to Washington," a Missouri congressman reported, "that it was just as important to get a certain document for somebody back home as for some European diplomat—hell, *more* important, because that little guy back home votes."[64] Members of Congress and state legislators alike spend much of their time running errands for constituents, answering their letters and telephone calls, interceding with administrative agencies on their behalf, and providing entertainment for them when they visit the capital. Probably no function of legislators exacts a greater toll on their time and energy than the purely service activity they are expected to perform. One study has shown that senators average 302 cases a week and representatives average 115.[65] Handling constituent problems may be especially important to House members, since they must face the voters every two years.[66]

What is more, constituents expect their representatives to pay close attention to them and to their districts. Table 1.4 shows the results of a national survey in which people were asked to define the most important tasks of members of Congress. The public's preferences are clear. Voters want their legislators to concentrate their attention on representing them and their districts. The four leading jobs (duties or functions) of the representative, as seen by the public, are closely related to constituency service, errand running, and constituency interests. In contrast, the public cares much less about the more general lawmaking responsibilities that make up the job of the legislator.[67] Purely and simply, for a great many citizens, representation begins and ends with the locality.

The fly in the ointment of errand running is obvious: Legislative matters too frequently are neglected because the member's time is preempted by constituents' requests. For some legislators errand running is a pretext for doing nothing with big problems. "There are congressmen elected year after year who never think of dissipating their energy on public affairs. They prefer to do a little service for a lot of people on a lot of little subjects, rather than try to engage in trying to do a big service out there in the void."[68] Or in the words of a congressional staffer:

**TABLE 1.4   The most important jobs of members of Congress in the view of the public**

| Job, Duty, or Function | Percent Mentioning |
|---|---|
| Work to solve problems in his district, help the people, respond to issues, needs, of our area | 37% |
| To represent the people, district, vote according to the wish of his constituents, the majority | 35 |
| Keep in touch, contact with the people, visit his district, have meetings, know his constituents | 17 |
| Find out what the people need, want, think, send out polls, questionnaires | 12 |
| He should attend all, as many sessions as possible, be there to vote on bills, legislation | 10 |
| Be honest, fair, as truthful as possible, keep his promises, should be a man of good character | 10 |
| Working on improving the economy, lower prices, stop inflation, create more jobs, reduce unemployment | 10 |
| Be knowledgeable, well informed about the issues, study legislation, pending bills before he votes | 9 |
| I expect him to pass fair, good bills, have a good voting record, make sure the right laws are passed | 8 |
| His positions on the issues, e.g., welfare, crime, etc. | 8 |
| Use media, newsletters to keep people informed of what he's doing, explain issues, bills pending, what's going on in Washington | 7 |

SOURCE: *Final Report of the Commission on Administrative Review,* U.S. House of Representatives, 95th Cong., 1st sess., 1977, pp. 822–23 (as modified). The total exceeds 100 percent because of multiple answers.

> Mr. _____ is a pothole congressman. We do constituency services. The constituents do not try to decide whether a matter is local, state, or federal; it all comes to us. It's like continually filling in the potholes in a street. The phrase means constituency service. We are known for our constituency services.[69]

Requests put to the legislator by constituents cover a wide sweep and have never excluded minor or awkward problems. The rule is that any request deserves a prompt response. Consider these observations by members of the Pennsylvania General Assembly:

> You know there are only four or five leadership positions on each side of the aisle and the legislators' . . . first reaction is survival. And the way he survives is not necessarily participating to any degree down here but keeping those people back in his legislative district happy. This can be done in many ways, but one way that is, I think, far more effective than how you voted on a particular bill, because 90 percent of the people don't know what goes on down here anyway, is getting their licenses, getting them out of trouble with the various administrative agencies or solving their problem. I know when I'd go home nobody would ask me how I voted unless there was somebody with an axe to grind, but if I didn't have the guy's license or if I hadn't taken care of these errands, not only was he provoked with me, but so was his family and pretty

soon I was a bad legislator, even though I may have been doing a very good job with the group down here. And they wouldn't vote for me at the election.

Christmas Eve, two years ago, I received a panicky call from a woman in my district who had just been called by the Department of Defense that her son had been killed in a crash in Alaska. She said she had reason to believe that her son was not on that plane. I spent several hours on the phone until I finally got someone at the Pentagon to check it out and sure enough her son had been scratched from that flight and was alive. I called that woman sometime after midnight with the good news. Of course, the easy way out would have been to tell her that I was a state representative and she had a federal problem.[70]

The volume of interactions between Congress and the executive branch is truly staggering. Some agencies receive several hundred thousand written communications and telephone calls from members and their staffs each year. Members want the bureaucracy to handle the problems that are troubling their constituents. As for the agencies, they cannot take Congress for granted. If they fail to respond in a timely and satisfactory fashion to congressional requests and inquiries, their relations with Congress are likely to deteriorate.

Catering to constituents is only part of legislators' functions in representation. They are also expected to be a guardian of district or state interests,[71] a bidding that is demonstrated by the following colloquy in the U.S. House of Representatives over the relocation of certain government facilities:

MR. GREEN (D., PA): [Would] the gentleman be willing to accept an amendment which would read like this: No funds appropriated in this Act may be used to close or facilitate the closing of the Frankford Arsenal in Philadelphia?

MR. MAHON (D., TX): . . . I am not aware of the status of the plans with respect to the Frankford Arsenal itself, so I would not accept the amendment.

MR. GREEN: . . . I would like to give my friends from Maryland an opportunity to stand up and say that they do not want any of the jobs that are now being held in Philadelphia to go to Maryland, where some of these jobs are currently scheduled to go. I did not want this debate to end before there was an opportunity for the Members from Maryland here to make it perfectly clear that they certainly would not want any jobs to leave the city of Philadelphia, considering its desperate unemployment situation. . . .

MR. BAUMAN (R., MD): . . . I would just like to say to my distinguished colleague from Philadelphia, the gentleman from Pennsylvania [Mr. Green], that there are no plans to transfer any jobs from Pennsylvania to Maryland at this point. . . . They may be considered at some point in the future, but nothing of that sort is proposed at this particular point.

MR. GREEN: And the gentleman from Maryland would make no special effort in that direction?

MR. BAUMAN: Mr. Chairman, the gentleman from Maryland would have to consider the situation at the time if such an event would occur.

MR. GREEN: Mr. Chairman, I would like to give the sponsor of this amendment . . . an opportunity to stand up and say that none of the jobs existing at the Frankford Arsenal would wind up in Maryland or Illinois or any place else.[72]

Every member, doubtlessly, wants his or her constituency to fare as well as any other member's in securing federal benefits. But their concern is not often voiced as bluntly as in these remarks by Representative Jay C. Kim (R., CA) in debate over the crime bill in the 103rd Congress (1993–94):

> We have a perception that our district will not get anything out of this thing. . . . We are tired of subsidizing someone else all the time. . . . We do not have any midnight basketball programs in my district. . . . Simply give us money, we will spend with the best of them. . . . California will lose $250 million in taxpayers' money . . . but Arkansas will gain a $44 million windfall. I do not see why California has to subsidize other states such as Arkansas. . . . Just give us money without any conditions attached. We know how to spend it.[73]

It would be difficult to exaggerate the attention that many legislators devote to securing federal projects for their states and localities. Some state delegations, for example, have had an extraordinary capacity to influence the location of defense facilities—with all the attendant benefits that derive from such expenditures. Consider the observations of President Johnson when, late in his administration, he visited a Lockheed plant in Marietta, Georgia, for a ceremony unveiling a new cargo plane: "I would like to have you good folks of Georgia know that there are a lot of Marietta, Georgias scattered throughout our fifty states. All of them would like to have the pride that comes from this production. But all of them don't have the Georgia delegation."[74]

Are legislators who "bring home the bacon" (grant money for projects in their districts) rewarded by the voters on election day? The answer is elusive, but on the whole, research has not uncovered a significant relationship between the distribution of particularized benefits and electoral support. A study by Robert M. Stein and Kenneth N. Bickers, for example, finds that, first, only the most vulnerable incumbents are disposed to seek increases in new awards and that, second, these awards have little or no impact on their electoral margins. Although certain politically attentive constituents are aware of the incumbent's successes in obtaining new federal money for projects, and regard their actions favorably, most voters are simply indifferent to the matter.[75] Examining pork from another perspective, the authors find that vulnerable incumbents who are successful in garnering new federal awards early in the congressional term are less likely to face quality challengers (those with experience in elective office) in the subsequent primary or general election. Bringing federal money to the district, in other words, helps some incumbents fend off the challenge of serious candidates.[76]

R. Michael Alvarez and Jason L. Saving offer interesting evidence on the connection between pork barreling and reelection. Analyzing the total flow of newly authorized federal spending at the congressional district level in the 1980s, they found that Democratic incumbents significantly benefited from pork sent into their districts. The more they secured in distributive benefits for their districts, the larger their vote share in the next election. Republican incumbents were largely unaffected by pork barreling. As the majority party at that time, Democrats disproportionately favored their own districts in distributions, and it worked to their advantage.[77]

Whether bringing more federal resources to their districts boosts incumbents' electoral margins may depend on their fiscal consistency—that is, whether their votes on spending are consistent with their credit claiming concerning pork for their districts. Patrick J. Sellers finds that in high-pork districts, fiscal liberals (who regularly support federal spending) do better electorally than fiscal conservatives. In low-pork districts, fiscal conservatives (who regularly oppose federal spending) have similar electoral success. In sum, as study after study has shown, not all incumbents profit equally from the distribution of pork. Consistency between the member's credit claiming on pork and his or her voting record is obviously important for some voters.[78]

Taking care of constituency problems is an important feature of committee politics. The appropriations committees, for example, often lace their bills with funding for local projects, and in the process build support for their measures. Logrolling comes to the fore, and not many members think twice about voting for a bill that carries direct benefits for their district. Shortly after he was elected chair of the House Appropriations Committee in 1994, David R. Obey (D., WI) commented, "I don't think it is a sin to help your district. You just have to make sure it's a legitimate request for help and that it fits the times."[79] Committee leaders also use distributive benefits to gain support for legislation that has a broad national impact. They do this "by tacking a set of targeted district benefits onto such legislation, using them as currency to purchase the votes of additional legislators for the leaders' policy preferences, much as political action committees make campaign contributions hoping to sway members' votes."[80]

The practice of earmarking appropriations for specific projects in districts is both routine and pervasive. When the budget of the Department of Defense is drawn up, for example, battles erupt between those members who want the Pentagon's university research funds awarded solely on the basis of merit review, which favors the leading research universities (and a small number of districts), and those members who want to spread the money around, using it for miscellaneous projects at smaller colleges and universities. Although the major universities wind up with the biggest share of the money, smaller schools also do well through earmarking (e.g., in the Defense Department's 1994 budget, a center on world languages and culture at Pfeiffer College, $250,000; the conversion of former military buildings to classrooms and dormitories at a new Monterey Bay campus in the California

State University system, $15 million; an institute to recruit female and minority students for aeroscience training at Hampton University, $3.75 million). Critics see earmarking in university research grants as "scientific pork," while defenders view it as a proper prerogative of lawmakers. Representative John P. Murtha (D., PA), former chair of the House Appropriations Subcommittee on Defense and champion of "academe's have-nots," offers this justification for earmarking: "A member knows better than anyone else what would go well in his district. It's a very important part of our process that if a member makes a request and it's related to defense, we try to do our best to fund it."[81]

The concern of members to safeguard their constituents' interests often collides with their other objectives, including budget cutting. Republican "deficit hawks," for example, can find their lives complicated (and their ideology compromised) when attempts are made to eliminate federal projects in *their* districts. Thus in 1993, a Republican member from Indiana with a reputation for sniffing out "pork" sought to eliminate a half-million-dollar grant for the National Center for Agricultural Law Research and Information at the University of Arkansas Law School in Fayetteville. The response of the conservative, first-term Republican who represented that district was not unexpected: "I normally about 99 percent of the time agree with the efforts the gentleman makes to cut federal spending. However, this agricultural law research center is in my district, and I do know it is doing an outstanding job. . . . It would be wrong to [deny it funds]." Democrats, of course, behave similarly—as in the case of those members who seek to cut the Pentagon's budget while at the same time working to protect defense contractors and military bases in their districts.[82] In legislative lexicon, "pork" is federal largesse destined for other members' districts.

Pork is omnipresent in public works legislation. In 1998, Congress passed the largest highway and mass transit bill in the nation's history. Packed with some 1,500 special projects, such as research grants for universities and the construction of bicycle paths, in addition to ordinary transportation items, the bill provided for spending $200 billion over six years. Virtually every congressional district became a beneficiary of federal money. Despite the opposition of fiscal conservatives, the bill was irresistible. Representative James A. Traficant, Jr. (D., OH), made this observation: "I was called the king of pork because I got five bridges funded. I don't apologize for any damn thing. You could call me anything you want on this House floor. But if you don't take care of your district, no one's going to take care of your district."[83]

Protecting the interests of their states and localities typically leads to trade-offs among the members. To broaden support for a public works bill to combat unemployment in the Northeast, for example, may require northeastern members to support legislation of peculiar importance to the Southwest, such as water projects. To pass a farm bill requires the votes of urban legislators, who in return expect the support of farm-belt members for programs to benefit the cities and their residents. Localism, in truth, is pervasive, and quid pro quo makes the system go. Legislators recognize the force of localism better than anyone. As observed by Jamie Whitten (D., MS), former chair of the House Appropriations Committee, a legislator "who handles a national program and leaves his district out had better not go home."[84]

Conventional wisdom holds that seniority in Congress really counts when it comes to the distribution of federal dollars. Is that true? Do senior members secure more federal spending for their constituents than junior members? The answer, according to Michael K. Moore and John R. Hibbing, is that states with senior House members do in fact come out somewhat better in securing federal money than states whose members have less seniority. On the Senate side, however, tenure has very little connection with the distribution of federal outlays.[85]

Research by Frances Lee adds another feature to the politics of distributing federal money. He finds that the formal arrangements of federal representation, under which all states receive equal representation in the Senate, does make a difference for public policy. Specifically, less populous states are the winners, clearly benefiting from equal representation. Although federal distributive programs are usually spliced together to benefit a majority of states, less populous states nevertheless do better (on a per capita basis) than more populous states in securing federal money, particularly when funds are allocated according to congressionally mandated formulas.[86]

Members and their staffs work tirelessly to transmit public goods to their constituencies.[87] In the conventional wisdom of members and the press, projects and federal money yield a grateful electorate and, in turn, a favorable environment for reelection.[88] Actually there is more to the story. Members seek to deliver benefits to their constituencies because they regard such activity as appropriate to their representative role and because constituents expect it. And less understood, members also search for ways to make things happen—to have an identifiable impact on government decisions. On major questions of public policy, this is ordinarily impossible.[89] Thus, in legislation to increase Social Security benefits, to alter the immigration system, or to restructure trade relations with other countries, for example, individual member contributions are almost always hidden in a bundle of collective action. But that is not true of all legislation. Narrow-gauge proposals designed for recognizable constituencies are made to order for members seeking to deliver benefits, gain satisfaction, and claim credit. "Constituency" legislation permits members to make a difference, as the late Representative Les Aspin (D., WI) observed:

Even if you're a subcommittee chairman or a full committee chairman, at the end of the process the question is, what difference have you made? That question is not easy to answer. That's why a lot of congressmen get involved in projects back home. Because at the end, there is a building that has gone up. The basic problem in this town always is, what difference did you make? The answer is you make a difference in inverse proportion to the size of the issue. A very small program, you can get on top of and ride—make it do this or that. If you want to get involved in the big issues, your impact is very hard to measure.[90]

A study of casework in four state legislatures (Colorado, Maryland, North Carolina, and Ohio) finds that this activity is more important in some states (Ohio and Maryland) than in others, that legislators from rural districts are particularly active in casework, and that the members who devote the most time to taking care of constituent problems are those who are especially concerned with career advancement.[91]

The key to constituency service is a large, industrious, and imaginative personal staff that carefully monitors individual and group requests. Currently there are nearly 12,000 persons assigned to the personal staffs of members of Congress—more than five times as many as in the late 1940s. The growth in personal staffs is the result of the growing congressional workload and the heightened demands on members for constituency services, especially the latter. The importance of the constituency factor is evident in the fact that many personal staff now work in district or state offices—about 40 percent for the House and more than one-third for the Senate.[92] The Washington staff also gives substantial time to handling constituent requests. The resourcefulness of personal staff in dealing with constituency problems is an important element in each member's design for increasing visibility and support and, ultimately, for winning reelection.[93] The resources of the typical congressional challenger pale by comparison.

Viewed broadly, the legislator's representative role also encompasses the requirement of mobilizing popular consent for new public policies and maintaining consent for continuing policies. Legislators not only monitor the claims of their constituents but also help to create conditions under which governments can better govern. Publics, like institutions, have their own inertia and intractability. When a government adopts significant new policies, average citizens find that their steadfast landmarks have moved. Old ways of doing things have been supplanted by new ways. New policies are often difficult to understand, and citizens may have to consult new agencies as well. Uncertainty and frustration are therefore likely to accompany sharp departures in public policy. Consequently, from the standpoint of the government, there may be as great a need to gain understanding and political support for measures newly adopted as for those under consideration or those still on the drawing boards. The need to breathe new life into old policies also confronts all governments. The policy process, in other words, does not stop with the passage of a law. The complexities of modern government make it essential that continuing consultation and interchange occur between those who hold and exercise political power and those who are affected by it.

A final function of representation to be noted is not, in a strict sense, a legislative function but rather a legislative *party* function, well understood by members and carried on by them with singular resourcefulness. This is the function of using legislative power to advance or safeguard the interests of the party and its members.

In the classic model of party government, parties compete with one another for power, appealing to the electorate on the basis of principles and programs, with the victorious party pledged to translate its campaign commitments into public policy and a course of government action.[94] In American practice the model is seldom if ever approximated even in two-party states because of the breakdown of party lines in the legislature; in one-party states the model bears no resemblance to the actual political process, unless we read "factions" to mean "parties."

Nevertheless, if not in their attitudes toward party programs and broad questions of public policy, legislators in at least one respect feel the pull of party loyalty. A fundamental function of the legislative party organization is to protect, solidify, and enhance the welfare of the organization, both in and out of the legislature. Legislative power offers an important means for transmitting benefits to the party organization, and on matters of organizational interest legislators ordinarily maintain a steady allegiance to their parties.

Consider the state legislature, in which the quest for party advantage in legislation is perennial. The aims of party appear in legislative proposals and tactics designed to embarrass the administration, to convey special advantage through election law, to offset election defeats in city government, and to increase access to the fruits of government—patronage in all of its forms.

A favorite gambit of the "out" party to embarrass the administration is to sponsor dramatic pay-raise bills for state employees without, of course, providing for the increased funds required to meet the new salary scales. The onus for blocking such bills invariably is placed on the governor. The call for a committee investigation of the highway or the public welfare department can be another approach to harassing governors and their parties.

Revision of election law carries many opportunities for improving party fortunes. Reapportionment legislation is an obvious example. But there are also advantages to be won, for example, by changing local elections from nonpartisan to partisan (a change that Republican legislators in Illinois have long sought for the election of aldermen in Chicago, in the belief that party identification would assist their cause), or vice versa. Illinois Republicans have also attempted to remove the requirement that party challengers must reside in the precinct or ward in which they perform their functions since they have long suspected that powerful Democratic ward organizations in Chicago control Republican watchers.

Rural-urban disputes in northern legislatures are, in some respects, illusory. In addition to those rural-urban divisions that seem to reflect distinctive values of the areas, there are the more common disputes rooted in party ideology and party interest. Urban legislators (mainly Democratic) share an ideology of liberalism, whereas rural legislators (mainly Republican) share an ideology of conservatism; some conflict is inevitable. But there are also frequent divisions along nonideological, party-interest lines. Dominant in rural and suburban areas in northern states, Republican legislators have no desire to see Democratic city administrations make good records or enjoy political security with their constituents. Suburban Republicans are especially sensitive to the politics of the nearby city and ordinarily have little difficulty in rallying the support of party colleagues who represent districts in the countryside. Where home rule is lacking, the legislature can place numerous impediments in the way of city administrations. It may turn a deaf ear to city requests for legislation to empower it to levy new or higher taxes; it may specify that the city real estate tax levy can be increased but that the additional revenue can be used only for the payment of salaries of firefighters and police officers; it may require the city to pay several hundred dollars per year to each police officer and firefighter to help them defray the costs of uniforms and other equipment; it may abolish a city department of public welfare and transfer its functions to a similar county agency, thereby shifting control over public assistance programs from one party to the other; it may transfer the power to appoint members of local redevelopment and housing authorities from the mayor to the governor. In sum, there are endless opportunities for the dominant party in the legislature to make harassing incursions into the government and politics of city administrations, and on legislative proposals that give advantage to one party and threaten the other, each party exhibits a remarkable cohesiveness.

### The Judicial Function

Several powers lead to the legislature's assumption of functions that are authentically judicial in character, that is, that call for the legislative body to resolve disputes concerning individuals and to apply appropriate law to their cases. In this category are the functions of judging the election and qualifications of its members, punishing and expelling members for contempt or for disorderly behavior, and impeaching and removing from office members of the executive and judicial branches.

From a constitutional standpoint, the most important judicial function of the legislature involves the power to impeach and to remove officials. The impeachment process set forth in state constitutions closely resembles that found in the national Constitution. Under provisions in the U.S. Constitution, the House of Representatives may impeach ("indict") the "President, Vice-President, and all civil officers" accused of "treason, bribery or other high crimes and misdemeanors." Individuals impeached by the House must be tried by the Senate, with conviction and removal from office dependent on a two-thirds vote of the members present. To date, only twelve officers have been subjected to impeachment trials, four of whom, all judges, were convicted and removed from office by the Senate. A few officials have resigned from office when threatened by impeachment; the most spectacular case of this sort was that of Richard M. Nixon, who resigned the presidency in 1974 after the House Judiciary Committee had adopted several articles of impeachment.

In late 1998, President Bill Clinton became the second American president to be impeached. The first was Andrew Johnson, whose conviction and removal by the Senate in 1868 failed by a single vote. Amid extraordinary rancor and raw partisanship, Clinton was impeached by the House in party-line voting for his sexual affair with former White House intern Monica Lewinsky. Two of four articles of impeachment were approved by the House. The first found that he had committed perjury before a federal grand jury by lying about his relationship with Ms. Lewinsky, and the second held that he had been guilty of obstruction of justice by using his powers to cover up his involvement in the affair. After a five-week trial, the Senate voted to acquit the president, with moderate Republicans voting in league with all Democratic members. Neither article garnered a simple majority of the Senate.

Impeachment proceedings are rare in the states, although some ten governors have been removed from office by such means, most recently in Arizona in 1988.

## Leadership Selection

Congress assumes certain functions of leadership selection under constitutional mandates. Under the terms of the Twelfth Amendment, the electoral vote of each state for president and vice-president is transmitted to the president of the Senate, who, in the presence of members of both houses, opens the certificates and counts the votes. Ordinarily this task is discharged perfunctorily, albeit with appropriate ceremony, since the winning candidates are known in a matter of hours or days after the polls have closed on election day. Occasionally, however, the electoral college has failed to produce its customary majority of votes for one of the party tickets. The Twelfth Amendment provides that if no candidate obtains a majority of the electoral votes, the choice of the president shall be made by the House of Representatives from among the three candidates having the largest number of electoral votes. When selection of the president is thrown into the House, each state may cast one vote, and a majority is required for election. Since 1804, when this amendment was adopted, the House has chosen one president, John Quincy Adams in 1824; in that year electoral votes were split among four presidential candidates.

The close election of 1876 between Rutherford B. Hayes and Samuel Tilden again brought Congress into the selection of the president. Several southern states transmitted to Congress conflicting sets of electoral votes. To resolve the dispute over their validity, Congress created a commission of fifteen members, which ultimately awarded all of the contested votes, and thereby the election, to Hayes.

If no vice-presidential candidate garners a majority of the electoral votes, a choice is made between the two top contenders by the Senate. Each senator casts one vote, with a majority specified for election. Only once, in 1836, has the Senate chosen the vice-president.

The Constitution also devolves on Congress the power to determine the order of presidential succession to be followed in the event that both the offices of the presidency and vice-presidency are vacant. Provisions for presidential succession have been changed several times since the early days of the republic. A statute enacted in 1947 shortly after Vice-President Truman was made president provides that the order of succession to the presidency, if both offices are vacant, shall be the Speaker of the House; the president pro tem of the Senate; and the secretaries of the executive departments, beginning with the Department of State. Following President Kennedy's death in 1963, new interest developed in the order of succession, in part because of the advanced age of Speaker John W. McCormack (D., MA).

Adoption of the Twenty-fifth Amendment to the Constitution in 1967 brought clarity to the question of presidential succession. Under its terms, the vice-president shall become president if the president dies, resigns, or is removed from office. Whenever a vacancy occurs in the office of vice-president, the president shall nominate a vice-president, subject to approval by a majority vote of both houses of Congress. The first person to become president under the provisions of the Twenty-fifth Amendment was Gerald R. Ford, selected by President Richard M. Nixon to be vice-president following Spiro Agnew's resignation. With the subsequent resignation of Nixon, Ford became president. Should a president conclude that he is unable to discharge the powers and duties of his office, he informs Congress, and the vice-president is empowered as acting president until the president is again able to assume his responsibilities. Other provisions of the amendment establish procedures to be followed in the event the president is unable to inform Congress of his disability or in the event there is disagreement over his ability to discharge the powers and duties of his office.

## A BILL BECOMES A LAW

Skillful management of legislation in committee and on the floor at times appears to be as much an occult art as anything else. There are no certainties and few unbendable rules for putting together majorities at various stages. No one understands any better than a bill's sponsors and managers that its life en route to becoming a law is never safely predictable. Opportunities to delay and to kill proposals are built into virtually all points of the legislative compass. Opportunities to change proposals in respects so fundamental as to destroy their original purposes are similarly numerous. And, of course, proposals may simply languish along the way, whether from the indifference of their sponsors, from the hopelessness of their cause, or from some other reason. No fact stands out more clearly than that it is never easy to get fast results in the legislature; all of the important advantages rest with those who are in favor of minimal change, marking time, and the status quo.

Perhaps the fundamental characteristic of the lawmaking process is that it takes place in stages, which in turn require "displays of agreement reached along the way." Charles O. Jones captures the essence of the activity that, when it works well, contributes to gaining majority support for a proposal:

> An agreement is reached in a subcommittee; the results are displayed for participants in subsequent stages in the sequence; further changes are made as new interests are represented; an agreement is reached and the results are published; previously nonparticipating interests may try for an advantage in the rules for floor debate; an agreement is reached on how the proposal will be debated and that is published; and still further interests may require representation in the settlement on the floor. The media play an important role for important legislation in advertising the agreements reached along the way, and this in turn contributes to the number of interests participating at each stage.[95]

Because the lawmaking system is highly complex, as well as partially hidden from any public audience, the process by which a bill becomes a law in American legislatures is not only difficult to understand but also difficult to sketch without resort to numerous qualifications. The *obvious* features of the system, however, can be shown in a diagram, though care should be taken not to place too much weight on the structure. The process, except perhaps for routine measures, is not as symmetrical as Figure 1.2 shows. Nor do the arrows that mark the route fix all the stray possibilities whereby legislation is considered, shaped, or rejected. The contours of power and the structure of priorities that are natural to political institutions resist plotting on the diagram. Moreover, the diagram is silent about the larger political system of which the legislature is a part and about the extralegislative actors who press their claims insistently on the members and who are, in turn, influenced by

**FIGURE 1.2   A bill becomes a law: A generalized version**

HOUSE OF REPRESENTATIVES                                        SENATE

Origination of bill (resolution, joint
resolution, concurrent resolution)
• By executive agency, political
  interest group, individual member,
  bill drafting agency

Referral to standing committee by
leadership and parliamentarian

Committee action
• Alternatives similar to those of
  House, including closed and
  open hearings, amendment,
  pigeonholing, passage, or defeat

Introduction of bill by member
• Constitution specifies revenue bills
  originate in House; custom dictates
  appropriations bills originate in House

Calendars (less elaborate than House)

Referral to standing committee by
leadership and parliamentarian

Floor action
• Alternatives similar to those of
  House, including rejection or
  acceptance of committee
  amendments, other amendments
• "Unlimited" debate

Committee action
• Possible referral to subcommittee
• Hearings customary on major bills
  Open hearings for testimony (invite or
    subpoena witnesses)
  Possible closed hearings for
    deliberation, amendment, and decision
  Committee decisions
    Disregard ("pigeonhole")
    Defeat
    Accept and report
    Amend and report
    Rewrite

(Privileged)

Conference committee
• May be requested if House and
  Senate versions differ; composed
  of managers from each house
  who vote separately; each house
  must concur in the conference
  report

Calendars
• Union (revenue and appropriations)
• House (public)
• Private (claims)
• Consent (minor, noncontroversial)
• Discharge (remove bills from committee)

Bill signed by Speaker and
Vice-President

Conference report

President
• Approve
• Veto
• "Pocket veto"
• Permit bill to become law
  without his signature

Rules committee (major bills)
• Hearings
• Closed rules
• Open rules (predominant form)

Floor action
• Committee of the Whole
    General debate
    Second reading
    Amendment
    Report to the House
• Advance to third reading
• Passage or defeat

the legislature's actions. The nature and impact of leadership, of legislative parties, and of formal rules of procedure all remain to be explored. Figure 1.2 thus may best be seen as representing in a general way the major stages and points of access in the legislative process (using Congress as an example); subsequent chapters seek to explain and place them in perspective.

## NOTES

1. Congress both leads and follows public opinion. See a study of the relationship between Congress and public opinion on women's rights issues by Anne N. Costain and Steven Majstorovic, "Congress, Social Movements and Public Opinion: Multiple Origins of Women's Rights Legislation," *Political Research Quarterly*, XLVII (March 1994), 111–35.

2. *Davis v. Bandemer*, 106 S. Ct. 2810 (1986).

3. *Congressional Quarterly Weekly Report*, January 9, 1999, p. 97.

4. For evidence that divided government produces a confused public (whereas unified control enhances public knowledge about Congress), see Stephen Earl Bennett and Linda L. M. Bennett, "Out of Sight, Out of Mind: America's Knowledge of Party Control of the House of Representatives, 1960–1984," *Political Research Quarterly*, XLVI (March 1993), 67–80. Also see a study that focuses on divided state delegations by Thomas L. Brunell and Bernard Grofman, "Explaining Divided U.S. Senate Delegations, 1786–1996: A Realignment Approach," *American Political Science Review*, XCII (June 1998), 391–99. The incidence of split Senate delegations is not simply a product of the modern era of divided government. The authors find a relationship between divided delegations and periods of electoral realignment. "As a realigning trend begins, the number of divided delegations increases and peaks in (or near) some critical election. As the realigning wave works its way through the six-year senatorial election cycle, the number of divided delegations declines, as one party begins to dominate electoral politics" (p. 398).

5. E. E. Schattschneider, *Party Government* (New York: Holt, Rinehart & Winston, 1942), pp. 30–31.

6. Molly Ivins, "Inside the Austin Fun House," *Atlantic Monthly*, March 1975, p. 55.

7. *Valley News Dispatch* (New Kensington, PA), May 13, 1983.

8. *Washington Post* (National Weekly Edition), December 10, 1984, p. 13.

9. Press release, Federal Election Commission, December 29, 1998.

10. Ibid. PAC money given to open-seat candidates is not included in this analysis.

11. *Congressional Quarterly Weekly Report*, March 12, 1983, p. 504.

12. *The Perverted Priorities of American Politics* (New York: Macmillan, 1971), p. 123.

13. Paul J. Quirk, "Structures and Performance: An Evaluation," in *The Postreform Congress*, ed. Roger H. Davidson (New York: St. Martin's Press, 1992), p. 322.

14. David R. Mayhew, *Congress: The Electoral Connection* (New Haven, CT: Yale University Press, 1974), pp. 97–99.

15. Charles O. Jones, *The Presidency in a Separated System* (Washington, DC: Brookings Institution, 1994), pp. 17–18.

16. *The Power Elite* (New York: Oxford University Press, 1959), p. 251.

17. *The Public Philosophy* (New York: New American Library, 1956), p. 28.

18. Eric Lane, "Albany's Travesty of Democracy," *City Journal*, VII (Spring 1997), 55.

19. *Congressional Quarterly Weekly Report*, September 12, 1981, p. 1740.

20. Quoted by Dotson Rader, "Tip O'Neill: He Needs a Win," *Parade*, September 27, 1981, p. 5.

21. *Congressional Quarterly Weekly Report*, September 4, 1982, p. 2177.

22. Ibid.

23. *Washington Post,* May 9, 1999.

24. Alan Ehrenhalt, "PAC Money: Source of Evil or Scapegoat?" *Congressional Quarterly Weekly Report,* January 11, 1986, p. 99. (Italics added.)

25. The statements were made by Senator Charles Mathias (R., MD) and Lowell P. Weicker (R., CT), *Washington Post,* December 11, 1985, and *Congressional Quarterly Weekly Report,* October 5, 1985, p. 1975.

26. *Bowsher* v. *Synar,* 106 S. Ct. 3181 (1986). The Court held that the provision giving budget-cutting authority to the comptroller general violated the principle of separation of powers because it placed executive powers in a legislative official.

27. The 1987 Gramm-Rudman version gave the Office of Management and Budget, an executive agency, authority to calculate the cuts necessary to reach the deficit target for the year.

28. *Congressional Quarterly Weekly Report,* July 20, 1991, pp. 1955–56.

29. Twice a year, members can accept a free ticket from a lobbyist to a basketball or hockey game at the MCI Center in the capital, where "club seats" cost $49.50, but they are not permitted to use the parking service or have waiters bring them refreshments, since these additions would put them over the $50 gift limit. A lobbyist cannot pay for any meal for a member if it exceeds $50, even if only by a penny or two; the member must pay the entire bill if it drifts above $49.99. *New York Times,* February 27, 1999.

30. *Congressional Quarterly Weekly Report,* January 14, 1995, p. 137.

31. *Congressional Quarterly Weekly Report,* June 4, 1994, p. 1451.

32. James N. Miller, "Hamstrung Legislatures," *National Civic Review,* LIV (April 1965), 186.

33. Paul Simon, "The Illinois Legislature: A Study in Corruption," *Harper's Magazine,* September 1964, pp. 74–75.

34. Wes Barthelmes, "Corruption in High Places in Maryland," *Washington Post,* August 22, 1975, p. 25.

35. "Pennsylvania's Assembly: Out of Control," a special publication by the *Philadelphia Inquirer* (first published as a series of newspaper articles), September 10–17, 1978, p. 2.

36. *State Legislatures,* April 1998, p. 11.

37. Richard F. Fenno, Jr., *Home Style: House Members in Their Districts* (Boston: Little, Brown, 1978), p. 168.

38. *Congressional Quarterly Weekly Report,* April 2, 1994, p. 787.

39. Richard Morin and David S. Broder, "Why Americans Hate Congress," *Washington Post* (National Weekly Edition), July 11–17, 1994, pp. 6–7.

40. Richard F. Fenno, Jr., "If, as Ralph Nader Says, Congress Is 'The Broken Branch,' How Come We Love Our Congressmen So Much?" in *Congress in Change: Evolution and Reform,* ed. Norman J. Ornstein (New York: Praeger, 1975), p. 278. But see the evidence of Richard Born that constituents' evaluations of Congress's performance strongly affect their assessments of their own representative. Ironically, it is the less educated voters who are most likely to link institutional and legislator evaluations. "The Shared Fortunes of Congress and Congressmen: Members May Run from Congress, but They Can't Hide," *Journal of Politics,* LII (November 1990), 1123–41.

41. See Glenn R. Parker and Roger H. Davidson, "Why Do Americans Love Their Congressmen So Much More Than Their Congress?" *Legislative Studies Quarterly,* IV (February 1979), 53–61. Also see an article by Timothy E. Cook, "Legislature vs. Legislator: A Note on the Paradox of Congressional Support," *Legislative Studies Quarterly,* IV (February 1979), 43–52. Cook finds evidence that suggests that voters view their Congress member primarily as a state or local politician, at the same time viewing Congress as a national institution. Members of Congress, accordingly, tend to be evaluated not in terms of their performance within the institution but in terms of their district activities. A study of the reputations of U.S. senators by Sarah Binder, Forrest Maltzman, and Lee Sigelman finds that the most highly regarded senators tend to come from smaller and more culturally homogeneous states and that, most important, to reflect accurately the policy preferences of their constituents. Moreover, suggestive of a halo effect, those senators who are about to retire enjoy a more favorable reputation. "Senators' Home-State Reputations: Why Do Constituents Love a Bill

Cohen So Much More Than an Al D'Amato?" *Legislative Studies Quarterly*, XXIII (November 1998), 545–60.

42. Arthur H. Miller has shown recently that voters evaluate U.S. House and Senate candidates on somewhat different bases. Their evaluations of House candidates focus on personal appeal and responsiveness to constituency. In evaluating Senate candidates, voters pay more attention to issues and the qualities of competence and integrity. "Public Judgments of Senate and House Candidates," *Legislative Studies Quarterly*, XV (November 1990), 525–42. Voters in lightly populated states are more likely than voters in populous states to evaluate the performance of their senator in terms of pork-barrel politics. See John R. Hibbing and John R. Alford, "Constituency Population and Representation in the U.S. Senate," *Legislative Studies Quarterly*, XV (November 1990), 581–98. A study of how Ohio voters evaluate their U.S. representatives finds that (1) constituents who have been in contact with their representative have more positive evaluations than constituents who have had no contacts or lack information; (2) evaluations are typically shaped by partisan attitudes and affiliations; and (3) favorable attitudes toward Congress shape citizen evaluations of their own representative. See Randall B. Ripley, Samuel C. Patterson, Lynn M. Maurer, and Stephen V. Quinlan, "Constituents' Evaluations of U.S. House Members," *American Politics Quarterly*, XX (October 1992), 442–56. Also see Samuel C. Patterson, Randall B. Ripley, and Stephen V. Quinlan, "Citizens' Orientations Toward Legislatures: Congress and the State Legislature," *Western Political Quarterly*, XLV (June 1992), 315–38.

43. David Kimball and Samuel C. Patterson, "Living Up to Expectations: Public Attitudes Toward Congress," *Journal of Politics*, LVIX (August 1997), 701–28 (quotation on p. 723).

44. For further discussion of the functions of *state legislatures,* see William J. Keefe, "The Functions and Powers of the State Legislature," in *State Legislatures in American Politics,* ed. Alexander Heard (Englewood Cliffs, NJ: Prentice Hall, 1966), pp. 37–69.

45. Woodrow Wilson, *Congressional Government* (New York: Meridian Books, 1956; first published 1885), p. 195.

46. One way to improve a bill's prospects for adoption is to attract multiple sponsors. See the evidence at the state legislative level in William P. Browne, "Multiple Sponsorship and Bill Success in U.S. State Legislatures," *Legislative Studies Quarterly*, X (November 1985), 483–88. For the development of a model of legislative success, see a study by Mark C. Ellickson, "Pathways to Legislative Success: A Path Analytic Study of the Missouri House of Representatives," *Legislative Studies Quarterly*, XVII (May 1992), 285–302. Ellickson examines institutional, personal, and environmental factors associated with passing bills into law. Institutional factors, such as party and seniority, play a particularly important role in the adoption of legislation.

47. See this key argument of Charles O. Jones in *The Presidency in a Separated System,* p. 288 and elsewhere.

48. See an interesting analysis of the costs and benefits of bill sponsorship by Wendy J. Schiller, "Senators as Political Entrepreneurs: Using Bill Sponsorship to Shape Legislative Agendas," *American Journal of Political Science*, XXXIX (February 1995), 186–203. By introducing a bill a legislator can strengthen his or her reputation as an expert, confer benefits on constituents, and contribute to the development of good public policy. But there are also costs to be considered: resource (time and energy), opportunity (less time for other issues), and political (incurring political opposition).

49. *Congressional Quarterly Weekly Report,* August 6, 1977, p. 1651.

50. *Congressional Quarterly Weekly Report,* July 24, 1993, p. 1943.

51. *Congressional Record,* 99th Cong., 2nd sess., September 10, 1986, p. H6598. (Daily edition.)

52. David E. Price, "Congressional Committees in the Policy Process," in *Congress Reconsidered,* ed. Lawrence C. Dodd and Bruce I. Oppenheimer (Washington, DC: Congressional Quarterly Press, 1985), pp. 163–64.

53. Louis Henkin, "A More Effective System for Foreign Relations: The Constitutional Framework," *Virginia Law Review,* LXI (May 1975), 757–58.

54. *Book of the States, 1990–1991 Edition* (Lexington, KY: Council of State Governments, 1991), pp. 42–43.

55. For an analysis of the factors that influence the way in which Congress conducts its oversight function, see Morris S. Ogul, *Congress Oversees the Bureaucracy* (Pittsburgh: University of Pittsburgh Press, 1976).

56. Alton Frye, *A Responsible Congress: The Politics of National Security* (New York: McGraw-Hill, 1975), p. 221.

57. Malcolm E. Jewell, *The State Legislature* (New York: Random House, 1962), pp. 126–27.

58. *The English Constitution* (first published in 1867), especially Chap. 6.

59. Wilson, *Congressional Government*, p. 195.

60. *Congressional Record*, 94th Cong., 1st sess., March 5, 1975, p. 3045. (Daily edition.)

61. Francis E. Rourke, *Secrecy and Publicity: Dilemmas of Democracy* (Baltimore: Johns Hopkins University Press, 1961), p. 118.

62. Fenno, *Home Style*, p. 164.

63. Roland Young, "Woodrow Wilson's *Congressional Government* Reconsidered," in *The Philosophy and Policies of Woodrow Wilson*, ed. Earl Latham (Chicago: University of Chicago Press, 1958), p. 205.

64. As quoted by Stephen K. Bailey, *Congress Makes a Law* (New York: Columbia University Press, 1950), p. 215.

65. John R. Johannes, "The Distribution of Casework in the U.S. Congress: An Uneven Burden," *Legislative Studies Quarterly*, V (November 1980), 519. For evidence that casework has an electoral payoff (but nevertheless does not eliminate the need for issue responsiveness), see George Serra and David Moon, "Casework, Issue Positions, and Voting in Congressional Elections: A District Analysis," *Journal of Politics*, LVI (February 1994), 200–213. George Serra and Albert D. Cover offer evidence that casework increases the popularity and salience of representatives in "The Electoral Consequences of Perquisite Use: The Casework Case," *Legislative Studies Quarterly*, XVII (May 1992), 233–46.

66. The use of office perquisites appears to increase a member's popularity and salience, according to an in-depth study of a single member's casework activity by George Serra and Albert D. Cover. See their article, "The Electoral Consequences of Perquisite Use: The Casework Case," *Legislative Studies Quarterly*, XVII (May 1992), 233–46. Contrast this study with the research of John C. McAdams and John R. Johannes, "Congressmen, Perquisites, and Elections," *Journal of Politics*, L (May 1988), 412–39. They find no support for the perquisite thesis—that is, that casework loads affect the vote.

67. See a study by Barbara Sinclair of the effects of national prominence on how well known and how well liked a senator is among his or her constituents. Interestingly, senators who are legislative activists are not regarded as highly by their constituents as less activist members. "Washington Behavior and Home-State Reputation: The Impact of National Prominence on Senators' Images," *Legislative Studies Quarterly*, XV (November 1990), 475–94.

68. Walter Lippmann, *Public Opinion* (New York: Macmillan, 1960), p. 247.

69. Lynette Palmer Perkins, "Member Goals and Committee Behavior: The House Judiciary Committee," Ph.D. dissertation, University of Pittsburgh, 1977, p. 37.

70. Sidney Wise, *The Legislative Process in Pennsylvania* (Washington, DC: American Political Science Association, 1971), pp. 7–8. A study of Ohio legislators finds that their dominant role orientation is that of ombudsman—the member preoccupied with providing constituency service. See Marshall R. Goodman, Debra S. Gross, Thomas A. Boyd, and Herbert F. Weisberg, "State Legislator Goal Orientations: An Examination," *Polity*, XVIII (Summer 1986), 707–19.

71. For interesting evidence that members of Congress are not as parochial as conventional wisdom holds, see James M. Lindsay, "Parochialism, Policy, and Constituency Constraints: Congressional Voting on Strategic Weapons Systems," *American Journal of Political Science*, XXXIV (November 1990), 936–60. In voting on strategic weapons systems, such as MX or SDI, most members are more likely to vote in line with their policy views than with their constituency's economic interests. Lindsay points out that congressional parochialism influences other parts of the defense budget and dominates decision making on military bases.

72. *Congressional Record,* 94th Cong., 1st sess., October 1, 1975, p. 9147. (Daily edition.)

73. *Congressional Record,* 103rd Cong., 2nd sess., August 21, 1994, p. H8977. (Daily edition.)

74. *Congressional Quarterly, Special Report, Weekly Report,* May 24, 1968, p. 1158, as quoted by John C. Donovan, *The Policy Makers* (New York: Pegasus, 1970), p. 142. But also see a study by Gary W. Copeland and Kenneth J. Meier, "Pass the Biscuits, Pappy: Congressional Decision-Making and Federal Grants," *American Politics Quarterly,* XII (January 1984), 3–21. Although political factors such as position and influence in Congress do affect the allocation of *federal grant funds,* the authors find that, on the whole, this money is allocated on the basis of population (or equal share).

75. Robert M. Stein and Kenneth N. Bickers, "Congressional Elections and the Pork Barrel," *Journal of Politics,* LVI (May 1994), 377–99. Also see this article for an analysis of earlier studies of the relationship between the allocation of particularized benefits and reelection margins.

76. Kenneth N. Bickers and Robert M. Stein, "The Electoral Dynamics of the Federal Pork Barrel," *American Journal of Political Science,* XL (November 1996), 1300–26.

77. R. Michael Alvarez and Jason L. Saving, "Deficits, Democrats, and Distributive Benefits: Congressional Elections and the Pork Barrel in the 1980s," *Political Research Quarterly,* L (December 1997), 809–31.

78. Patrick J. Sellers, "Fiscal Consistency and Federal District Spending in Congressional Elections," *American Journal of Political Science,* XLI (July 1997), 1024–41.

79. *Congressional Quarterly Weekly Report,* March 26, 1994, p. 714.

80. Diana Evans, "Policy and Pork: The Use of Pork Barrel Projects to Build Policy Coalitions in the House of Representatives," *American Journal of Political Science,* XXXVIII (November 1994), 894–917.

81. *New York Times,* August 17, 1994.

82. *Congressional Quarterly Weekly Report,* June 18, 1994, p. 1670.

83. *New York Times,* April 2, 1998. Also see *Congressional Quarterly Weekly Report,* April 4, 1998, pp. 882–88. Diana Evans shows the importance of including demonstration projects in general highway legislation in order to increase members' support of the committee leaders on floor votes pertaining to that legislation. "Policy and Pork: The Use of Pork Barrel Projects to Build Policy Coalitions in the House of Representatives," *American Journal of Political Science,* XXXVIII (November 1994), 894–917.

84. *U.S. News & World Report,* May 2, 1983, p. 21.

85. Michael K. Moore and John R. Hibbing, "Length of Congressional Tenure and Federal Spending," *American Politics Quarterly,* XXIV (April 1996), 131–49.

86. Frances E. Lee, "Representation and Public Policy: The Consequences of Senate Apportionment for the Geographic Distribution of Federal Funds," *Journal of Politics,* LX (February 1998), 34–62.

87. See an analysis by John A. Hird of congressional influence on the allocation of Army Corps of Engineers' construction projects. This study offers evidence that members of Congress are driven by both *pork-barrel considerations* (allocating projects to their constituencies that presumably will improve their reelection prospects) and *public interest concerns* (as reflected in standards of efficiency and equity). "The Political Economy of Pork: Project Selection at the U.S. Army Corps of Engineers," *American Political Science Review,* LXXXV (June 1991), 429–56.

88. The electoral benefits of local federal spending may be an illusion. See Paul Feldman and James Jondrow, "Congressional Elections and Local Federal Spending," *American Journal of Political Science,* XXVIII (February 1984), 147–64.

89. Mayhew, *Congress: The Electoral Connection,* pp. 59–60.

90. *Washington Post,* June 7, 1981.

91. Patricia A. Freeman and Lilliard E. Richardson, Jr., "Explaining Variation in Casework Among State Legislators," *Legislative Studies Quarterly,* XXI (February 1996), 41–56.

92. Norman J. Ornstein, Thomas E. Mann, and Michael J. Malbin, *Vital Statistics on Congress,*

*1997–1998* (Washington, DC: Congressional Quarterly, 1998), pp. 134–35. See an analysis of the role of congressional staff in district offices by John D. Macartney, "Congressional Staff: The View from the District," in *Congress and Public Policy*, ed. David C. Kozak and John D. Macartney (Homewood, IL: Dorsey Press, 1987), pp. 100–115.

93. The growth of personal and committee staff in Congress has been so substantial that it is useful to think of the individual member as running an "enterprise" that he or she must manage. See an insightful essay on the effects of staff expansion on members by Robert H. Salisbury and Kenneth A. Shepsle, "U.S. Congressman as Enterprise," *Legislative Studies Quarterly*, VI (November 1981), 559–76.

94. See a study by Gerald C. Wright that finds that in casting votes, same-state senators from different parties are particularly responsive to their respective state party elites, which in turn tend to be ideologically extreme. This finding helps to explain the polarized representation one finds among this group of senators. "Policy Voting in the U.S. Senate: Who Is Represented?" *Legislative Studies Quarterly*, XIV (November 1989), 465–86.

95. Jones, *The Presidency in a Separated System*, p. 187.

# 2

# Legislative Structures
# and Powers

The preeminent feature of American government is the division of power among three independent but interrelated branches: legislative, executive, and judiciary. Each constitution reflects the preferences of its drafters concerning the allocation of the major shares of power and responsibility. In purely constitutional terms, Congress is positioned at the center of national policymaking, having been assigned the main tasks of government and a major share of the powers presumed necessary to perform them. Congress, in other words, is the first branch of government. From a constitutional standpoint, state legislatures generally have reason to envy Congress.

The reality is that no constitutional document can provide precise statements about where power lies, how it is to be managed, or for what purposes it is to be used. Power conferred on the legislature is not easily stored or easily protected. The legislature is steadily challenged and influenced by others, including the chief executive, the bureaucracy, the courts, and political interest groups, mainly because the legislature is a remarkably open and accessible institution. It is steadily nudged, pushed, pressured, and sometimes captured because of its openness. Demands are made on it from every quarter. Consistent with this view of the legislature, much of this book is concerned with the way in which this institution relates to its environment.

This chapter seeks to describe how the legal-constitutional system establishes the legislature and lays out its main tasks and how legal-constitutional arrangements affect the way the legislature goes about its business.[1] It also raises questions concerning the impact of legislative structure on public policy. Later chapters will consider the critical question of power allocation within the legislative institution itself.

## THE CONSTITUTIONAL STATUS
## OF THE AMERICAN LEGISLATURE

Congress

The constitutional primacy of the legislative branch is unmistakable at the national level. Notwithstanding the separation-of-powers principle and the checks-and-balances network, the role and activities of government are determined by the decisions of Congress. It is Congress that sets broad policies and creates the administrative units to execute them, that develops standards for administrative action and for the appointment and removal of administrative officials, that appropriates funds for government functions, and that, in varying degrees, supervises and reviews the work of administrative establishments. Whether Congress in fact is supreme, or ought to be, is not the main question; nor is the matter of how well it does its job. The key point is that the Constitution is unambiguous in allocating the central responsibilities of government to the representative assembly.

The status of Congress is established primarily in Article I, Section 8, of the Constitution. This section enumerates the formal powers of Congress. Ranging the gamut, they include the power to levy and collect taxes; borrow money; regulate commerce; coin money; regulate standards of weights and measures; establish post offices; create courts; declare war; create an army and navy; provide for a militia; set up a government for the capital district; and adopt laws concerning bankruptcy, naturalization, patents, and copyrights.

These specified powers are known as *delegated* powers because they represent a delegation of authority by the people to the national government. In addition, the final clause in Section 8 of Article I confers upon Congress the power "to make all laws which shall be necessary and proper for carrying into execution the foregoing powers, and all other powers vested by this Constitution in the government of the United States, or in any department or officer thereof." This clause is the taproot of the doctrine of *implied* powers, an interpretation that holds that Congress has a broad authorization to use the means "necessary and proper" to carry into execution its delegated powers. As reasoned by Chief Justice Marshall in *McCulloch v. Maryland* (1819), "Let the end be legitimate, let it be within the scope of the constitution, and all means which are appropriate, which are plainly adapted to that end, which are not prohibited, but consist with the letter and spirit of the constitution, are constitutional."[2] A related, but more abstruse or inferential, band of powers is termed *resulting* powers. A resulting power cannot be traced directly to a specific authorization in the Constitution but results, or is fairly deduced, from a circumstance in which certain delegated powers are associated.

Broad and inclusive as a result of numerous court decisions, Congress's legislative power is expanded by another constitutional clause that declares that the laws of Congress "made in pursuance" of the Constitution "shall be the supreme law of the land." The supremacy clause, set forth in Article VI, Section 2, has been interpreted to mean that state constitutions or laws in conflict with the national Constitution or the acts of Congress are null and void and, additionally, not only makes federal laws superior to those of the states but also obligates state judges, no less than federal ones, to enforce their provisions.

The powers of Congress are by no means unlimited. For example, Congress may not delegate its powers to any other body or authority. The Supreme Court has insisted that in formulating policy Congress must adopt clear standards to guide the executive officials who will administer it. An act that grants too large a measure of discretion to the executive may be invalidated as an unconstitutional delegation of legislative power.[3] In addition, Congress cannot delegate its powers to the people in the form, say, of a nationwide referendum, though some states have made provision for direct legislation of this sort.

Because the lines separating legislative from judicial and executive functions are blurred and tenuous, occasional cases have arisen concerning congressional arrogation of executive and judicial powers. For example, an act of Congress requiring Senate agreement to the president's removal of certain executive officials has been held unconstitutional since it represented legislative encroachment on a purely executive power.[4]

Furthermore, congressional authority is contained by a number of constitutional provisions. First among them is the Tenth Amendment, stipulating that "powers not delegated to the United States by the Constitution, nor prohibited by it to the States, are reserved to the States respectively, or to the people." In addition, the Bill of Rights contains a wide range of prohibitions concerning civil liberties: Congress, for example, may not adopt laws respecting an establishment of religion; abridging freedom of speech, press, or assembly; depriving people of life, liberty, or property without due process of law; requiring excessive bail or denying trial by jury. And, finally, Article I, Section 9, specifically prohibits Congress from passing bills of attainder and ex post facto laws. None of these limitations, of course, represents an absolute standard, and the Supreme Court often has been involved in filling in their meanings and in judging the validity of congressional acts that touch on them.

### State Legislatures

The basis of American federalism is established in the Tenth Amendment. Under its provisions, national powers are delegated, whereas state powers are *reserved* or *residual*. Specifically, powers not delegated to the national government or denied to the states are retained by the states and the people.

Since state powers are residual rather than simply enumerated, it is difficult to mark precisely the dimensions of state legislative authority. But several points should be kept in mind. First, the national Constitution places certain limitations on the states. For example, Article I, Section 10, prohibits states from entering into treaties, from coining money, or from passing bills of attainder; in addition, it outlaws ex post facto laws and laws impairing the obligation of contracts. States may not levy import duties or enter into agreements or compacts with other states except with the consent of Congress. Moreover, the Fourteenth Amendment ("No State shall make or enforce any law which shall abridge the privileges and immunities of citizens of the United States; nor shall any State deprive any person of life, liberty, or property, without due process of law; nor deny to any person within its jurisdiction the equal protection of the laws"), as interpreted by the Supreme Court in recent decades, has served to place new and significant limitations on state action. As a result of the Court's elaboration of the "due process" clause in this amendment, certain important protections guaranteed to the citizen in the Bill of Rights against the national government now apply equally to state and local governments.

Second, provisions in state constitutions not only divide power among the three branches but also divide it by creating numerous independent and popularly elected officers, such as the attorney general, secretary of state, auditor of public accounts, treasurer, and superintendent of public instruction. Where these offices have certain constitutional powers and responsibilities, directly or by implication, the courts will invalidate legislative acts that diminish or restrict such authority.[5] Constitutional provisions regarding county government and municipal home rule place additional restrictions on legislative power, though in most states very little authority is reserved for municipal governments, whose governing process is regulated in detail by state constitutional and statutory provisions.

Third, the doctrine of "implied limitations" also affects the power of the legislature. As applied by some state courts, it means that legislative authority extends simply to the direct grants of power made by the constitution, and therefore by implication the legislature's authority over other (nonspecified) activities is narrowed or denied. Judicial inference thus has sometimes made the presence of detailed constitutional grants to the legislature a limitation on general legislative authority.

Fourth, some constitutions place specific restraints on legislative authority. These detailed prohibitions are largely a product of the last half of the nineteenth century, having been written into constitutions in order to curb a variety of abuses then flourishing in the legislatures. Before examining the limitations introduced during this reform period, it will be instructive to glance backward at the early state constitutions, adopted at a time when legislatures and legislators ranked high in public esteem. James Willard Hurst comments on this early era of legislative supremacy:

The early constitutions gave the legislature broad power. There they bore witness to its high public standing. The first state constitutions simply vested "legislative" power in described bodies. The grant implied the historic sweep of authority that [the English] Parliament had won, except as this was limited by vague implications to be drawn from the formal separation of powers among legislature, executive, and courts.

. . . Typically, the early constitution makers set no procedural requirements for the legislative process. They wrote a few declarations or limitations of substantive policy making. But these generally did no more than declare what contemporary opinion or community growth had already so deeply rooted as to require no constitutional sanction. . . .[6]

The beginning of the end of legislative preeminence came with a series of disclosures of widespread graft and corruption in the legislatures during the early and middle years of the nineteenth century. Evidence that venality had uprooted the public trust appeared in state after state. Public funds were wasted recklessly, outright bribery of legislators was all too common, charters and contracts were granted to the highest bidders, spoils systems ran riot, and special legislation in the interest of a privileged few was distinguished by its prevalence. All in all, it would be difficult indeed to catalogue the variety of peculations, barefaced and ingenious, that colored this scandalous era.

Public anxiety over the pernicious operations of the legislature, if sometimes slow to be aroused, everywhere culminated in a demand for reform. Another look at the legislature's role was in order, and in the process of review, belief grew that popular control might be made more effective and that corruption might be mitigated by placing rigorous constitutional shackles on legislative action. One careful study of this period describes what took place during the reassessment of the legislature:

Between 1864 and 1880, thirty-five new constitutions were adopted in nineteen states. Distrust of the legislature was the predominant characteristic of all of them. Records of these conventions contain pages on pages of vigorous denunciation of state legislatures by the most outstanding members of the conventions. In the constitutions they drafted, they sought to prevent a recurrence of the evils they denounced, by incorporating not only new proscriptions on what the legislature might do, but also extensive legislation regulating and controlling the new economic interests to which earlier legislators had fallen victim. Hence these constitutions added provisions defining and regulating railroads, business practices, trusts, monopolies and interlocking directorates, corporations, the marketing and watering of corporate securities, and the regulation of banking and financial institutions. New prohibitions on the passing of local and special legislation were added. By 1880 the pattern for state constitutions as legal codes, and as obstructions to the free exercise of legislative power, was clearly set.[7]

State constitutions bear a strong resemblance to one another in style, in length, in dogma, and especially in the battery of explicit limitations they fasten on the legislative branch. A brief examination of these restrictions will help us to gauge further the range of legislative powers.[8]

All state constitutions have limitations on the legislature (and other branches) in the form of a bill of rights. Normally these rights are of the "inalienable" or "fundamental" variety found in the national Constitution, but this traditional statement has not sufficed in all states. Some states, for example, have amended their constitutions to protect special economic and social rights, such as the right of labor to organize or, in other cases, not to organize (the "right to work"). Each constitutional settlement of a social or economic issue represents a further diminution of legislative power, a narrowing of alternatives for the representative assembly.

In addition, state constitutions commonly prohibit the enactment of local or special legislation—bills that affect a single person, a single corporation, a single local government. Constitutional limitations on special or local legislation, found in most states except some in New England and the South, were introduced to combat legislative preoccupation with dispensing favors to private individuals and organizations, launching special projects for particular localities, and interfering in local conditions. In some legislatures in the latter part of the nineteenth century, perhaps half to three-quarters of all bills passed during a session were special acts. Not surprisingly, where special legislation was emphasized, less attention was given to public business or to general priorities. When the states adopted constitutional provisions prohibiting special or local legislation, they specified that the legislature could pass only *general* laws, for example, those affecting not simply one local government but a whole class of local governments.

Much less private and local legislation is passed today than in the past, but the practice has not been eliminated by any means—even in states with lengthy lists of constitutional prohibitions. For example, where a multiple-category system for classifying local governments is used, the legislature has no difficulty in legislating for particular types of communities, perhaps for even a single political subdivision. Moreover, no extraordinary ingenuity is required to camouflage local and special legislation, making it appear to be general in scope. Finally, where state courts have not been rigorous in enforcing constitutional enjoiners concerning special legislation, the practice has flourished.

Another major category among constitutional restrictions involves the financial powers of the legislature, circumscribed in three principal ways in many states. The first limitation is placed on the taxing power and may include provisions setting maximum tax rates, providing exemptions for certain kinds of institutions (for example, educational, religious, and charitable), or requiring taxes to be uniform (the effect of which has been, often, to rule out *graduated* income, inheritance, and other taxes). In response to the "tax revolt" that began in the late 1970s, more and more states have adopted laws or constitutional amendments that limit state taxes and expenditures; such "caps" obviously restrict the legislature's budgetary powers. Legislative fiscal authority may also be limited by imposing a state debt limit in the constitution. Some state constitutions carry provisions that earmark certain revenues for specific state functions, such as public education or highways. In many states, continuing or earmarked appropriations and special funds make up 50 percent or more of total expenditures, thereby reducing legislative control over the state budget. In Alabama, during the mid-1980s, an extraordinary 88 percent of all revenues were earmarked for particular purposes, virtually eliminating the legislature's discretion in spending.[9] Earmarking may rest on either constitutional or statutory mandates. In either case it contributes to the erosion of the legislature's fiscal powers.

The penchant for including large quantities of "statutory" law in constitutions has enfeebled the legislature. Not only has this practice stretched the length of state constitutions to unmanageable proportions, but it has also sharply reduced the range of public policy alternatives available to legislative majorities. In constitution after constitution, one finds minute details governing corporate structure and management (especially for banks and railroads), public utilities, common carriers, toll bridges, judicial procedure, stock issues, salaries for public officers, control and management of schools, penalties for the misuse of public moneys, and so on. Of great variety and complexity, these provisions are generally anachronistic; worse yet, they encumber the legislature unnecessarily and make it difficult for it to respond rapidly to new circumstances and problems.

Another type of specific limitation results from provision in the constitution for the direct participation of voters in lawmaking. Present in one form or another in about one-half of the states, the two devices of direct legislation are the *initiative* and the *referendum*.

The initiative consists of a procedure whereby a certain percentage of voters may by petition propose a law (or constitutional amendment) to be placed on the ballot for voter approval or rejection. Circumventing the legislature, the voters draft the proposal (in practice, a pressure group usually sparks interest in the idea and does the work), circulate petitions (to be signed normally by 5 percent to 10 percent of the registered voters), and campaign for its adoption. In certain states the legislature is given an opportunity to adopt the initiated measure, in which case no further step is required. Otherwise, voters may express themselves on the question in a coming election. It is interesting to find that limitations on taxing and spending are particularly common in those states that have initiative provisions.[10]

Although the initiative was introduced as a means of empowering citizens to make their own laws, increasingly it has become an instrument of special interests (including individual businesses and narrow-gauge associations) that organize "pay-per-signature" drives. In 1994, for example, the

Washington Denturists Association (with only twenty-nine members) spent $160,000 to pay petition workers to obtain signatures for an initiative that would permit denture makers to sell false teeth directly to people without going through dentists. In California, similarly, the Philip Morris tobacco company spent about $2 million in a paid-petition drive to get an initiative on the ballot that would ease smoking regulations in the state. Paid-signature drives are now common everywhere, and attempts to ban them have had little success. According to the executive director of California Common Cause, they "send a message to wealthy corporations that if you don't like the laws, you can buy yourself an initiative."[11]

In some states, such as California, major public policies are regularly made through initiatives. "Big money" typically dominates the process of getting a proposal on the ballot. A successful 1998 initiative to end bilingual education in California, for example, was financed largely through the contributions of a single Silicon Valley entrepreneur, who contributed $640,000 of the $900,000 spent to put the measure on the ballot. Voters adopted it by a comfortable margin. Another major initiative, to require union members to approve the use of union dues in elections, was heavily financed by *national* conservative groups and only narrowly defeated. The truth of the matter is that California state legislators can easily evade decisions on controversial issues because they know that some groups will take up the cudgels for them and qualify the questions for the ballot. At other times, the legislature is helpless to resist vigorous initiative campaigns. So important is this lawmaking process that, according to one analysis, more money is spent in lobbying California voters on initiatives than in lobbying the legislature on all bills.[12]

For state politicians frustrated by the ease with which complex and controversial questions can be slid onto the ballot through the initiative process, the courts offer little relief. The Supreme Court has made it clear that it will not accept state restrictions on political conversations (even if organized and managed by out-of-state political consultants.) In a 1999 case, *Buckley* v. *American Constitutional Law Foundation,* decided by a 6–3 vote, the Court invalidated several relatively modest Colorado restrictions on the initiative process that required persons who circulate petitions to be registered voters in the state and to wear name badges and, in the case of organizations, to disclose the compensation of individuals hired to circulate petitions. The First Amendment's free-speech guarantee, the Court held, prevents "undue hindrance to political conversations and the exchange of ideas."[13]

From the standpoint of both public policy and group influence, it makes a difference whether the legislative process or the initiative process is involved. The choice of institutions can be critical. Elisabeth R. Gerber writes:

Groups that advocate policies with broad majoritarian support such as the cigarette tax increase may be more effective working through the initiative process. Groups that advocate policies associated with major contributors of campaign finance (such as the construction industry) may be more effective working through the legislative process. . . . [It] is important to recognize that most political issues have powerful groups aligned on both sides, and often the interests each side represents lead them to be more effective working through different institutions.[14]

The referendum, an ancient device, has several variants. It provides for the submission of legislative and constitutional measures to the voters for their acceptance or rejection. In nearly all states a referendum is required to approve constitutional amendments; in many states it is required for bond issues and for changes in liquor regulations. In some states provision is made for optional referendums: Questions are submitted to the voters on the judgment of the legislature. Where this option exists, there is a temptation for legislators to get out from under a nettling problem by calling for a referendum. Another variant of this device is known as the "protest" referendum; in states where it is authorized, voters have the power to prevent a measure already adopted by the legislature from taking effect. Petitions bearing the requisite number of signatures are filed with the proper state authority, and the question is then submitted to the voters. Should a sufficient vote (usually a majority) be cast against the enactment, it becomes null and void.

The argument over the initiative and referendum—valuable instruments of popular government in the opinion of some people and transparent nostrums in the opinion of others—has been carried on sporadically for over half a century. Much has been published about the details of these devices. Our point will be confined simply to the view that they are cut out of the same cloth as other restrictions, that they encroach on legislative authority, that they are vulnerable to manipulation by special interests, and that they may lead to legislative timidity and irresponsibility. Manifestly, they add nothing to *legislative* initiative or autonomy.

## ORGANIZING THE LEGISLATURE

### Congress

The first task of Congress when it assembles in each odd-numbered year is to organize itself for the consideration of business. The way the chambers go about this organization differs to some extent because of the differences between their election calendars. Since two-thirds of its membership carries over from Congress to Congress, the Senate traditionally has been regarded as a "continuing body." This "continuous" feature reduces most problems of organization to routine tasks, although disputes may arise over whether the rules continue intact from one Congress to the next.

After the Senate has attended to its organizational housekeeping, it is ready to proceed with the business of the session. It informs the House that it is assembled and ready to hear the president's annual message.

The ritual of organizing the House is more elaborate and time-consuming. It begins when the clerk of the preceding Congress calls the assembly to order and reads the names of the members who have been certified as elected. The next step is to call for the election of a Speaker, which follows after each party has made its nomination. The vote is taken and the defeated candidate escorts the newly elected Speaker to the chair, where the oath of office is administered. The other members-elect are then sworn in, except those whose election is under challenge. The majority party's candidates for the various offices of the chamber—clerk, sergeant-at-arms, doorkeeper, postmaster, and chaplain—are then presented, elected, and given the oath of office. The final step is the adoption of the rules of the chamber, normally identical to those that have previously been in force. The routine of organization is terminated, and the House apprises the Senate of its readiness to join with it for the purpose of hearing the president's message.

What has been described up to now is, as much as anything, the view from the galleries. The real work of organizing, the substance rather than the reflection, is a function of the party organizations, especially of the majority party. Preceding the formal organization of Congress, each party in each chamber caucuses to select its candidates for legislative offices—Speaker of the House, president pro tem of the Senate, floor leaders, and whips. Selection of party leaders is ordinarily run through without much controversy, with party hierarchs from the previous Congress being returned to power as expected. As a rule, the caucus plays an important role in choosing legislative leaders only when death, retirement, or election defeat has removed a member from the hierarchy. The selection of committee chairs, however, is another matter. Although seniority usually dictates their selection, the parties occasionally ignore it. At the opening of the 104th Congress (1995–96), for example, senior Republicans were bypassed in the selection of the committee chairmanships of Appropriations, Energy and Commerce, and Judiciary.

### State Legislatures

More by custom than by intent, or because problems of organization are everywhere about the same, the typical legislature goes through about the same motions as Congress in organizing for work. Hence, rather than to plow ground now familiar or to explore unique arrangements found here and there among the states, we may summarize state practice generally.

The key element in organizing the legislature in most states, as in Congress, is the majority party and its leadership—with perhaps a considerable amount of nudging from an interested governor. It is the majority party—or at least a majority of the majority party—that makes the decisions on leadership, shapes the committee structure and the party ratio within the committees, selects or reaffirms committee leadership, appoints officers, reaffirms or transforms the rules, and settles the chamber into its job.[15] Ordinarily the decisions that count have been taken before the session is convened, though it is by no means rare for intraparty conflict over the choice of the Speaker, the president pro tem, or the majority or minority floor leaders to be settled after the session has begun—perhaps on the floor rather than in the caucuses.

As a general rule, organizing the legislature is simple and mechanical, something that has to be done in order to get other things moving. New members are administered the oath of office, old members are welcomed back, election results are canvassed, quorums are ascertained, nominating speeches are made, and elections are concluded. Finally, amid other festivities, a resolution is adopted appointing a committee "to wait upon his [her] Excellency, the Governor, and inform him [her] that the Senate [or House] is convened and organized and ready to receive any communication he [she] may be pleased to make."

## PRESIDING OFFICERS

Political power in the legislature, its origins and dimensions, is neither easily identified nor easily evaluated. Elusive and transient, it may lie at one time with the presiding officers; at another time with committee chairs, a party caucus, or a nonparty bloc; and at still another time with the executive, an interest group, or an alliance of interest groups. It scarcely exaggerates the problem to say that where power starts and where it leaves off in the legislature nobody knows. Formal and conventional powers—those made "legitimate" by constitutions, statutes, rules, or customs—are recognized without difficulty, however, and we shall examine certain of them here as they pertain to the role of the presiding officers.

### Congress

The Speaker of the U.S. House of Representatives, it may be said, wears two hats: the presiding officer of the chamber and, at the same time, the acknowledged leader of the majority party. Chosen by the majority party caucus and elected by a party-line vote on the floor, the member will, normally, have become Speaker after a tour of party duty as floor leader.

Inevitably Speakers are old hands in the House, though seniority is only one factor in their selection. Very few offices are as "permanent" as the Speaker's—once elected to it they have reason to expect reelection as long as they are in Congress, whenever their party holds a majority of the seats. (But note that the Republican majority in 1995 voted to limit a Speaker's tenure to no more than four consecutive two-year terms; it is rare, however, for a Speaker to hold the office even that long.) In the role of presiding officer, the Speaker interprets and enforces the rules of the chamber, recognizes members who wish to speak, calls for votes on questions, refers bills to committees, and appoints select and conference committee members. Though Speakers' formal powers are no longer as awesome as in an earlier day (see Chapter 9), their influence is great, extending to and beyond the farthest reaches of Congress. Indeed, Speakers who lead a cohesive majority party are a compelling presence in Washington, whether or not their party holds the presidency.

The presiding officer of the Senate is the vice-president. The position is something of an anomaly since, unlike the Speakers, vice-presidents are not members of the body over which they preside and do not participate in debate. Moreover, they may vote only in case of a tie and, strangest of all, may be a member of the minority party in the chamber. Such influence as they have in the Senate is largely derived from their link to the White House. In addition, the majority party honors one of its members by electing that person president pro tempore, in which role he or she presides in the absence of the president of the Senate (the vice-president). Usually the senior member of the majority party, the president pro tem acquires no distinctive power as a result of holding this position.

### State Legislatures

In general, the presiding officers in the state legislatures have powers and duties similar to those of their counterparts in Congress, and they are selected in about the same fashion. The difference is one of degree. The speakers of the lower houses at the state level usually have greater influence on committee organization and legislation than does the Speaker of the U.S. House of Representatives. Their authority in and out of the legislature is sufficient to rank them next to the governor in the list of leading state politicians.

The presiding officer of the upper house in about three-quarters of the states is the lieutenant governor, elected at the same time as the governor by statewide vote. In contrast to the Speaker, the powers of lieutenant governors are narrowly circumscribed; they do not take part in debate and have a vote only in the case of a tie. In about a third of the states they are given authority, nominal in most cases, to appoint standing committees. In sum, the net impact of the lieutenant governor on senate decisions and state public policy is slight. Where state constitutions make no provision for this office, the senate selects a presiding officer from its membership. As in the case of the U.S. Senate, a president pro tempore is chosen, who ordinarily becomes the chief spokesperson for the majority party in the chamber.

## RULES OF PROCEDURE

A rudimentary requirement for any legislature is a set of formalized rules for governing the style and substance of internal organization, the choice of officers, and the mode of procedure to be followed by the assembly.[16] The national Constitution provides that each house is free, with a few exceptions (for example, the Constitution requires a journal to be kept), to draw up its own rules of procedure. Many state constitutions, as we have seen, specify in detail procedures to which the legislature is expected to adhere.

The basic set of rules used by Congress, and to some extent by state legislatures, is *Jefferson's Manual of Parliamentary Practice*. These rules are buttressed by standing rules in each house. Gradually evolving over the years, rules have a tenacious quality and are neither easily nor frequently changed.

Rules serve a multiplicity of purposes. They establish the order of business and provide for priorities and regularity in its consideration; they dilute opportunities for arbitrary and capricious treatment of the minority; they offer customary and traditional ways for settling disputes and for coming to decisions; and in their perpetuation from year to year and decade to decade, they impart continuity to the life of the chamber. Their essence is *systematization*, their major contribution *orderliness*.

Rules are designed to cover both routine and special questions that arise in the course of considering and enacting legislation. Thus there are rules that relate to the call of committees, quorums, recess and adjournment, calendars, appointment of conference committees, consideration of conference reports, offering of amendments, procedure in the committee of the whole, disposal of unfinished business, debate, consideration of veto messages, discharge of committees, and the readings to be given a bill. Formal rules are refined and elaborated by the rulings of the presiding officers.

Today's rules are the residue of earlier political settlements and as such are more than a means of facilitating and expediting the consideration of public business in a legislative body. They need to be understood in their *political* context, as instruments in the exercise of political power.[17] A good case can be made that the political function of rules is vastly more significant than the function of "regularizing" or "ordering" legislative processes.

Efforts to modernize legislative rules of procedure have resulted generally from two related complaints: (1) that many rules are tipped in favor of the minority, serving to put the majority in a legislative straitjacket, and (2) that many rules foster delay and inaction and tend to serve the interests of those who cling to the status quo. As Lewis A. Froman has observed, there are important implications in the fact that the rules tend to favor those legislators who are more likely to resist change than to sponsor it:

> One is that those congressmen and senators who wish to change the *status quo* are forced, by the rules, to do a considerable amount of bargaining, not only on the differences which occur among themselves but also with those who favor the *status quo*. The alternative to bargaining will often be defeat, since those who wish to protect the *status quo* are often numerous, intense, and in strategic positions.
>
> A second implication of the fact that rules and procedures, generally speaking, favor those who prefer the *status quo* over change, has to do with attempts to change the "rules of the game." Looking at rules and procedures as not being neutral in the congressional contest, proposals to change the rules, in many cases, are attempts to change the ability of certain members, and hence certain interests, to prevail in future contests. In other words, changes in the rules may change the advantage of one group of players over others.
>
> In this sense, some rules changes redistribute power. Because this is so, certain proposals to change the rules are the most bitterly fought contests in congressional politics.[18]

A former Speaker of the House, Jim Wright, once offered this observation about Congress's rules: "Senate rules are tilted toward not doing things. House rules, if you know how to use them, are tilted toward allowing the majority to get its will done."[19]

Legislative rules are significant because the methods used to reach decisions often shape the decisions themselves; procedure and policy, in other words, are often interlaced. This fact accounts for the controversy inherent in all rules of procedure. Never wholly neutral, rules are beneficial to some groups and disadvantageous to others. They are, commonly, one of the many faces of minority power.

## THE LEGISLATIVE BODY:
## SIZE, TERMS OF MEMBERS, AND SESSIONS

### Size

When the first Congress was called to order in 1789, there were eleven states in the Union and, therefore, twenty-two members in the Senate. The first House of Representatives had a total of sixty-five members. Both houses grew steadily in size until 1911, when the House membership was fixed by law at 435 and the Senate membership was set at ninety-six. With the admission of Hawaii and Alaska to statehood in the late 1950s, the Senate was increased to 100 members and the House, temporarily, to 437. Following the 1960 reapportionment of seats, the House reverted to its former population of 435.

Consensus on the proper size of state legislatures is very thin, as shown by the differences in the size of their memberships. At the summit is New Hampshire with an immoderate total of 400 members in its lower house—a number nearly seventeen times as large as its upper house. In contrast, the lower house of Alaska has 40 members, that of Delaware 41, and that of Nevada 42. More than one-third of the states have lower houses that range between 100 and 125 members. In addition to New Hampshire, states with large lower houses are Pennsylvania (203), Georgia (180), Missouri (163), and Massachusetts (160). A member of the New Hampshire lower house represents a constituency of about 2,000 people; a member of the California lower house (total membership of 80) represents a constituency of more than 300,000 people.

Minnesota leads all state senates with 67 members, followed by New York with 61, Illinois with 59, and Georgia with 56. At the bottom of the order are Alaska with 20 members and Delaware and Nevada with 21. Commonly, state senates range between 30 and 39 members. Populous California has a senate of only 40 members. On the whole, there is not a very strong relationship between state population and the size of the legislature.

**Terms of Members**

Members of the lower house of Congress are elected for a two-year term of office, members of the upper house for a six-year term. Terms of legislative office in the states are variable. In thirty-eight states, senators serve a four-year period; in the remainder the term is two years. Lower house members in forty-five states hold office for two years; in four southern and border states—Alabama, Louisiana, Maryland, and Mississippi—the term is four years.

In about one-half of the states, senate terms are staggered; that is, half of the membership comes up for election every two years. This system contributes to continuity in the life of the chamber. Since legislation covers a broad band of complex affairs, it is useful to have a number of experienced lawmakers on hand; thus the provision for staggered terms has become a standard prescription for improving legislative organization. Obviously there is a case for staggered terms, though there is at least one reason for rejecting the principle or at least for viewing it as something less than an outright advantage. The flaw is that staggered terms contribute to the problem of divided party control in the legislature. The electorate is unable to effect a complete change in the makeup of the legislature at any one time. Although a party may win the governorship and the lower house handily, the senate often is beyond its reach because of staggered terms. The possibility of party rule and party responsibility, to an extent at least, is sometimes the price paid for the continuity fostered by staggered terms of office; whether it is worth it is open to question.

A major shortcoming of legislatures, it has long been argued, is the two-year term of office provided for members of the lower house of Congress and for members of the lower houses of all but a few states. Legislators have no more than settled into their jobs before it is time to begin their campaign for reelection. Indeed, their short term of office prompts most representatives to engage in more or less continuous campaigning. A lengthened term of office—four years is usually suggested—undoubtedly would permit members to devote more time to public business. The two-year term carries important policy consequences, as Charles O. Jones has noted:

> First, the President's party usually suffers losses at the mid-term election and he will, therefore, have less support for his program in Congress. Second, frequent campaigning does take time from other activities. Indeed, a few members find it necessary to run twice and sometimes three times (if there is a runoff primary) in one year to retain their seat. Third, House members' staffs tend to become very constituency-service oriented in their work and they, too, must divert some of their energies to campaigning. The result of frequent campaigning, it is argued, is a campaign-constituency orientation in the House of Representatives, particularly in election years, which has definite policy effects (though these cannot be measured with any degree of precision). It is also argued that controversial legislation is avoided during election years. While probably true in certain cases, it is difficult to demonstrate that this is a widespread phenomenon.[20]

The proposal for a four-year term for members of Congress has often been discussed, though seldom seriously considered. Conservative newspapers and many members have been fearful that four-year terms that coincided with presidential elections would erode the power of Congress, creating a permanent "coattail Congress." A major reason why prospects for a four-year House term appear remote is the opposition of many senators. A member of the House explains why:

> We will never get a four-year term. The Senate will never go along with the idea because senators will not want to have congressmen free to run against them without having to relinquish their House seats should they lose. As it now stands, congressmen hesitate to risk everything by challenging a senator.[21]

The political environment of the late twentieth century makes it wholly unlikely that support could be won for longer terms of legislative office. Indeed, the most popular proposals today call for limiting the length of time a member may serve.

## Term Limits

In 1990, Oklahoma, California, and Colorado became the first states to adopt term limits. The California and Oklahoma voter initiatives were limited to their state legislators, while Colorado set terms for both federal and state legislators. The term-limits movement then spread rapidly. By 1995, twenty-one states had approved term limits for their state legislators and twenty-three for their U.S. representatives and senators.

From the outset, legal scholars doubted that *federal* term limits imposed by states would pass constitutional muster. They were proved right when the Supreme Court ruled in 1995, by a surprisingly close 5–4 vote, that neither the states nor Congress may limit the number of terms served by members of Congress. The Court held that the states could not add qualifications for membership in Congress to the exclusive ones set forth in the Constitution: age, citizenship, and residency in the state of election. The Court made clear that the only way by which federal term limits could be enacted would be through the adoption of a constitutional amendment.[22] This prospect is unlikely in the foreseeable future. A congressional term-limits amendment was the only proposal in the Republicans' Contract with America that failed to win House approval in 1995. The options of supporters of term limits have thus been reduced simply to making term limits an issue in congressional races in the hope of electing members who will press for the necessary constitutional change. Limitations on terms for state legislators, of course, were not affected by the Court's decision.

Currently, eighteen states have term limits for their *state* lawmakers. (Between 1995 and 1998, term limits were held unconstitutional by state supreme courts in Massachusetts, Nebraska, and Washington.) Limitations range from six to twelve years, with the most common being eight years for both chambers. Western states have been particularly attracted to the idea of limiting legislative tenure (Arizona, California, Colorado, Idaho, Montana, Nevada, Oregon, South Dakota, Utah, and Wyoming). Southern states rank second (Arkansas, Florida, Louisiana, and Oklahoma). Among eastern states, only Maine now restricts the terms of its legislators. No state had adopted this device since 1995, the year of the *Thornton* decision, which ruled term limits for U.S. representatives and senators unconstitutional.[23]

Voters' support for term limits is an outgrowth of popular disillusionment with government and politics. Supporters of term limits see them as a device for eliminating a professional political class, improving the quality of legislators, making legislatures more accountable, breaking up cozy incumbent-lobbyist relationships, purging incumbents, restoring competitive elections, reducing the influence of PACs, replacing careerists with "citizen legislators," freeing members to cast unpopular votes, checking abuses of power, and gaining control over the bureaucracy. For leaders of this conservative movement, it appears, term limits represent an opportunity to attack big government, big programs, and big budgets. For Republicans in general, term limits have been a made-in-heaven issue for getting votes and attacking Democratic incumbents—doubtlessly, in fact, contributing to a number of their House victories in 1994 (including the ouster of the Democratic Speaker, Thomas S. Foley, an outspoken opponent of term limits).

The opponents of term limits contend, among other things, that these restrictions will diminish the professional expertise available in legislatures, limit the effectiveness of legislative oversight of bureaucracy, increase the influence of professional staffs and lobbyists (on less experienced members), weaken legislative leadership,[24] and lead to the overall weakening of the legislature vis-à-vis the executive. They view voter choice as an inviolable right and believe that the proper way for voters to limit the terms of legislators is simply to vote them out of office. What is more, they see no reason to believe that term limits will reduce the influence of special interests, curb the influence of money in elections, help the legislature to control the bureaucracy, or improve the quality of legislators.

Controversy and conjecture surround the issue of term limits. A comprehensive assessment of the effects of term limits cannot be made until some time following their date of impact (i.e., the date at which incumbents are prevented from running for reelection to the same chamber). For a majority of the states that now have term limits, this will occur between the years 2000 and 2008. For California, one of the first states to adopt this device, good evidence on the impact of term limits on careers and the legislative institution itself should be available around the turn of the century.[25]

A 1995 survey of nearly 3,000 state legislators in term-limit states and non-term-limit states by John M. Carey, Richard G. Niemi, and Lynda W. Powell provides early evidence on the impact of term limits on state legislatures. The data show that term limits did not produce a new breed of legislator. Virtually no differences emerge between legislators in term-limit and non-term-limit states in comparisons of members' ideologies, income levels, education levels, or professional backgrounds. The electoral success of African-American candidates is comparable in both types of states. In terms of member composition, the only difference is that women are somewhat more likely to be elected in term-limit than in non-term-limit states. More important differences, however, are reflected in legislative behavior and institutions. Legislators in term-limit states appear to be less concerned with securing pork for their districts and to be more concerned with statewide interests than with district interests—arguably beneficial characteristics. On the other hand, in a redistribution of power, majority party leaders in term-limit states report that they have lost influence to the governor and possibly to legislative staff as well—both outcomes anticipated by opponents of term limits. Weakening of the legislative institution and the elected leaders has never been advanced as a goal of the term-limits movement.[26]

## Congressional Sessions

Several provisions in the Constitution relate to sessions of Congress. Article I, Section 4, requires Congress to "assemble at least once in every year." The Twentieth Amendment, ratified in 1933, provides that sessions shall begin at noon on January 3, unless otherwise provided. Article II, Section 3, gives the president authority to convene Congress on "extraordinary occasions," a power he has not hesitated to invoke in the past. The same section provides that should the houses be unable to agree on the time of adjournment, the president "may adjourn them to such time as he shall think proper. . . ." This latter power has never been used.

Each Congress covers a two-year period, with a new session beginning each January. Prior to World War II, sessions were relatively short. In recent decades, however, the press of business has forced Congress to operate on virtually a full-time basis. The first session of a new Congress begins in January of each odd-numbered year, and the second session begins in January of the following (even-numbered) year. The life of a bill is the life of a Congress; that is, bills introduced in the first session survive adjournment and may be taken up for action during the second session at the point where their consideration ended in the first session. A new Congress, of course, begins with the introduction of new bills.

## State Legislative Sessions

In the early state constitutions, legislatures held a privileged position. A strong legislature that met annually, it was believed, could effectively check the power of the executive. At the same time, it would provide better representation for the public. Hence few constitutional restrictions were placed on the legislature, and it soon became the dominant branch of government. The scandals in the mid-nineteenth century, however, led to the institution's undoing.

Popular confidence in the legislature gave way to popular obloquy. One manifestation of this change was the substitution of biennial for annual sessions and the provision for rigorous limitation on the length of sessions. By the turn of the twentieth century, all but a handful of states had abandoned yearly meetings of the legislature. A legislature not in session could not very well get into new trouble. Moreover, an enfeebled legislature meeting infrequently and for short sessions was not as great a threat to the status quo and to the new holders of vast economic power. This simple "solution" brought fundamental change to the political systems of the states.

Today the position of the legislature is much improved, and fewer restrictions are present than at any time in the twentieth century. Even so, one can find many examples of limitations on legislative power. Seven state legislatures, for example, continue to meet only on a biennial basis. (See Table

**TABLE 2.1   Legislative sessions in the states**

| | Years in Which Sessions Are Held | | Limitations on Length of Regular Sessions | | Special Sessions | | | |
|---|---|---|---|---|---|---|---|---|
| | | | | | Legislature May Call | | Legislature May Determine Subject | |
| | Annual | Biennial | Yes | No | Yes | No | Yes | No |
| Number of states | 43 | 7 | 38 | 12 | 30 | 20 | 36 | 14 |

SOURCE: *Book of the States, 1998–1999* (Lexington, KY: Council of State Governments, 1999), pp. 64–66.

2.1.) Constitutional limitations on the length of sessions are present in more than two-thirds of the states, with a typical provision calling for regular sessions of no more than 60 calendar days. In Wyoming, sessions are limited to 40 legislative days in odd years and 20 legislative days in even years, and in Alabama the legislature may meet for no more than 30 legislative days within 105 calendar days. The most populous state to convene biennially is Texas, whose regular session is limited to 140 calendar days. The biennial arrangement, in fact, does not work well in Texas, and special sessions are frequently called (for example, three in 1989 and three in 1990).[27] In 40 percent of the states, the legislature is not given the power to call special sessions. In sixteen states, the governor alone determines what subjects shall be taken up in special sessions. Thus, in many ways legislatures cannot control their own affairs.

## BICAMERALISM

Familiar and conventional arrangements, no less than familiar and conventional ideas, have an extraordinary capacity for perpetuating themselves. Such is the case with bicameralism.

The earliest colonial legislatures, developed out of stockholders' meetings, were unicameral in form. Deputies elected by the freemen of the towns and the appointed assistants of the colonial governors sat together in a single house. Conflict between these two disparate groups was inevitable and led to plans for the creation of two chambers. First to adopt the bicameral form was the Massachusetts Bay Colony in 1644. Many other colonies followed Massachusetts' lead, though the flight from unicameralism was not complete until the state of Vermont switched to a two-house legislature in 1836. Part of the stimulus to bicameralism in the states had come from the formation of a national legislature of two houses, replacing the single house under the Articles of Confederation.

Since the early nineteenth century, only Nebraska, in 1934, has adopted a one-house legislature. Today, there is no lively debate over the issue of unicameralism versus bicameralism, and there is not much prospect that other states will revert to the older unicameral form.

## STRUCTURE, POWERS, AND POLICY

A knowledge of the legislature's legal-constitutional structure, its formal powers, and its methods of organization and operation is basic to understanding the legislative process. These "situational landmarks"[28]—the major features of structure and organization—intrude on the behavior of the legislators and affect the output and effectiveness of the legislature. Furthermore, they offer certain analytical material useful in accounting for the emergence and development of the legislature and are suggestive concerning the relationship between the legislature and the social system.[29]

Yet there is much this body of information fails to disclose. Analysis of the formal structural-organizational arrangements may be of only modest value in accounting for action taken within the legislature; it provides no certain assistance in locating power within the institution, it cannot show how agents of parties and of private organizations influence decisions, and it may be of only marginal help in explaining why legislators behave as they do. Finally, it offers only vague clues concerning the biases of the institution or the ways by which it maintains itself. We begin a more complete answer to these questions by considering the theory and practice of representation as it relates to the legislative system.

## NOTES

1. See an instructive analysis of the literature on the organizational characteristics of legislatures by Ronald D. Hedlund, "Organizational Attributes of Legislatures: Structure, Rules, Norms, Resources," *Legislative Studies Quarterly*, IX (February 1984), 51–121.
2. *McCulloch v. Maryland*, 4 Wheaton 316 (1819).
3. *Panama Refining Co. v. Ryan*, 293 U.S. 388 (1935); *Schechter v. United States*, 295 U.S. 495 (1935).
4. *Myers v. United States*, 272 U.S. 52 (1926).
5. The fragmentation of power among several independent administrative officials also tends to stultify the governor's efforts to coordinate and to integrate the activities of the administrative branch. Because these statewide elective offices are independent sources of power, their occupants may be tempted to challenge the governor openly. Also, a good many campaigns for the governor's chair have begun in these elective offices.
6. *The Growth of American Law: The Law Makers* (Boston: Little, Brown, 1950), p. 24.
7. Byron R. Abernethy, *Constitutional Limitations on the Legislature* (Lawrence: University of Kansas, Governmental Research Center, 1959), p. 15.
8. The following paragraphs on state legislative powers lean heavily on Abernethy, ibid., especially Chap. 3.
9. Susan B. Hansen, "The Politics of State Taxing and Spending," in *Politics in the American*

*States,* ed. Virginia Gray, Herbert Jacob, and Robert B. Albritton (Glenview, IL: Scott, Foresman/Little, Brown Higher Education, 1990), p. 337.

10. Ibid., pp. 367–68.

11. *New York Times,* August 21, 1994. Concerning the denturist's initiative, the president of the state dental association remarked, "If you gave me $200,000, I could get an initiative passed that would allow electricians to practice neurosurgery."

12. *New York Times,* March 31, 1998.

13. *Buckley* v. *American Constitutional Law Foundation,* 119 S. Ct. 636, 642 (1999).

14. Elisabeth R. Gerber, "Legislatures, Initiatives, and Representation: The Effects of State Legislative Institutions on Policy," *Political Research Quarterly,* XLIX (June 1996), 263–86. Also see an article by John F. Camobreco that finds no evidence that states that use the initiative process are more likely to adopt public policies that reflect the preferences of citizens than states that do not have the initiative. "Preferences, Fiscal Policies, and the Initiative Process," *Journal of Politics,* LX (August 1998), 819–29.

15. See an article by Ronald D. Hedlund and Keith E. Hamm on the importance of party in organizing legislatures: "Political Parties as Vehicles for Organizing U.S. State Legislative Committees," *Legislative Studies Quarterly,* XXI (August 1996), 383–408.

16. See a study by Kenneth A. Shepsle and Barry R. Weingast, "When Do Rules of Procedure Matter?" *Journal of Politics,* XLVI (February 1984), 206–21.

17. This point is well documented in a study by John Bibby and Roger Davidson of the passage of the Area Redevelopment Act during the Kennedy administration. They conclude that although rules influence legislative outcomes, they "are not independent of the power struggle that lies behind them. There is very little that the houses cannot do under the rules—so long as the action is backed up by votes and inclination. Yet votes and inclination are not easily obtained; and the rules persistently challenge the proponents of legislation to demonstrate that they have both resources at their command. Thus, there is little to prevent obstruction at every turn except the tacit premise that the business of the house must go on." In addition, their study points out that rules must be used with a degree of caution. "If they are resorted to indiscriminately or flagrantly, there is the risk that they will be redefined and the prerogative taken away or modified." *On Capitol Hill: Studies in the Legislative Process* (New York: Holt, Rinehart & Winston, 1967), p. 217.

18. *The Congressional Process: Strategies, Rules and Procedures* (Boston: Little, Brown, 1967), p. 191.

19. *Congressional Quarterly Weekly Report,* July 11, 1987, p. 1486.

20. *Every Second Year: Congressional Behavior and the Two-Year Term* (Washington, DC: Brookings Institution, 1967), pp. 98–99.

21. Charles L. Clapp, *The Congressman: His Work as He Sees It* (Washington, DC: Brookings Institution, 1963), p. 330.

22. *U.S. Term Limits* v. *Thornton,* 115 S. Ct. 1842 (1995).

23. The data in this paragraph were furnished by the National Conference of State Legislatures.

24. See Timothy Hodson, Rich Jones, Karl T. Kurtz, and Gary Moncrief, "Leaders and Limits: Changing Patterns of State Legislative Leadership under Term Limits," paper presented at the Annual Meeting of the Western Political Science Association, Portland, OR, 1995. Their central argument is that term limits will increase turnover and therefore reduce the experience level of leaders when they take office.

25. For an interesting and instructive assortment of term-limits studies, see Gerald Benjamin and Michael Malbin, *Limiting Legislative Terms* (Washington, DC: CQ Press, 1992); Gary Moncrief, Joel A. Thompson, Michael Haddon, and Robert Hoyer, "For Whom the Bell Tolls: Term Limits and State Legislatures," *Legislative Studies Quarterly,* XVII (February 1994), 37–48; Cynthia Opheim, "The Effect of U.S. State Legislative Term Limits Revisited," *Legislative Studies Quarterly,* XIX (February 1994), 49–59; Patrick J. Fett and Daniel E. Ponder, "Congressional Term Limits, State Legislative Term Limits and Congressional Turnover: A Theory of Change," *PS,* XXVI (June 1993), 211–16; Wayne Francis, "Upward Legislative Career Mobility: Term Limit Effects upon Quality and Turnover," paper presented at the Annual Meeting of the Midwest Political Science Association, Chicago, 1993; Jeffery J.

Mondak, "Elections as Filters: Term Limits and the Composition of the U.S. House," *Political Research Quarterly,* XLVIII (December 1995), 701–27; and Hodson, Jones, Kurtz, and Moncrief, "Leaders and Limits." From an advocacy perspective, see George F. Will, *Restoration: Congress, Term Limits & the Recovery of Deliberative Democracy* (New York: Free Press, 1992); and Mark Petracca, "Term Limits Do Not 'Rob the Voters,'" *Extensions* (Summer 1992). Also see "Term Limits? Early Assessments," *Extension of Remarks* (Legislative Studies Section Newsletter) (July 1994), for articles that focus mainly on California.

26. John M. Carey, Richard G. Niemi, and Lynda W. Powell, "The Effects of Term Limits on State Legislators," *Legislative Studies Quarterly,* XXIII (May 1998), 271–300. For a study that shows the importance of modes of election for legislative responsiveness, see Sara Brandes Crook and John R. Hibbing, "The Not-So-Distant Mirror: The 17th Amendment and Congressional Change," *American Political Science Review,* LXXXXI (December 1997), 845–53.

27. Rich Jones, "The Legislature in 2010: Which Direction?" *State Legislatures,* July 1990, p. 25.

28. The term is used in a study of the legislatures of California, New Jersey, Ohio, and Tennessee. See John C. Wahlke, Heinz Eulau, William Buchanan, and LeRoy Ferguson, *The Legislative System: Explorations in Legislative Behavior* (New York: Wiley, 1962).

29. Marked and enduring changes in legislatures—those that significantly affect the institution's relations with its environment (such as the president or constituencies) or its internal characteristics (such as the leadership, legislative parties, or committee system)—rarely occur. Only a few significant breaks with the past have occurred in congressional history. See a theory of major institutional change by Elaine K. Swift, "Reconstructive Change in the U.S. Congress: The Early Senate, 1789–1841," *Legislative Studies Quarterly,* XIV (May 1989), 175–203.

# 3

# Representation
# and Apportionment

No tenets of democratic theory are grounded more firmly in American political thought and practice than that legislators are expected to look steadily to the people who elect them, to seek out their opinions, to speak to their convictions and uncertainties, to express their values, to protect their interests, and to defend or explain legislative decisions before them. The legislative process and the representative system are inseparably linked in all democratic political orders. The action of the legislature is the ultimate expression of the representative principle.

The connection between representation and the legislative process is fundamental. What the legislature does is influenced, first, by the way in which members perceive the job of the representative—whether, for example, they regard themselves as constituency agents or as free agents. Second, the standard for evaluating legislatures that seems to have made the strongest impression on both the public and the courts is that of "representativeness"; at a minimum, a representative legislature requires that legislative districts contain about the same number of people. Finally, a good indication of the significance of representation for the legislative process is that ideas concerning representation tend to shape some of the most familiar questions asked about legislators, legislatures, and legislation: Are legislators responsible to their constituents? How do they perceive their relationships to voters? How do legislators weigh their obligations to their constituents, their party, the nation, or their locality? Do majorities rule in the legislature? Can the public effectively control its representatives?

Representation is a process that seeks to foster communication and interaction between governors and governed.[1] It is based on a theory of responsible government: Those who hold political power should be accountable to those on whose behalf they exercise it. "In modern parlance," Carl Friedrich wrote, "responsible government and representative government have . . . almost come to be synonymous."[2] Elections, representation, and responsibility are all currents in the same stream. Voters choose those persons who will hold and use the community's power, and representation helps to endow the officeholder's decisions with legitimacy. Representatives must account for their actions, moreover, when running for reelection. In at least some measure, representation permits the public to express and enforce its preferences regarding public policy.

Representation has held a unique place in the history of legislative assemblies, as Friedrich observed:

> [Ever] since the sixteenth century legislation was believed to be the most striking manifestation of political and governmental power. Legislation entailed the making of rules binding upon the whole community. . . . [The] making of a rule presupposes that there is a series of events which have certain aspects in common. In other words, there must be a "normal" situation. This means that time is available for deliberation to determine what had best be done regarding such a situation. Representative, deliberative bodies require time, obviously, and therefore legislation seems to be peculiarly fitted for such bodies.[3]

Explorations of the concept of representation often focus on the nature of the electorate, relations between representatives and constituents, and the system under which representatives are elected. This chapter is concerned with the latter two questions and begins with an examination of representative-constituency linkages.

## REPRESENTATIVES AND REPRESENTED

Whom do representatives represent—their constituency, some sector of their constituency, the nation, the state, their party, some particular clientele? What forces affect the voting of legislators? If constituents hold a view opposite to that of the member, must he or she vote in line with prevailing local opinion? The classic problem of representation is this: Are representatives free to follow their own judgments on policy questions or are they merely agents of their constituents? In actual practice, this question is neither simply nor sharply drawn. The legislator must weigh other factors in addition to constituency and personal judgment. Representatives must assess their obligations to party, to chief executive, and perhaps to organized interest groups. And they may find it prudent to take into account the position of the media or that of some outside body of experts. Information flows from multiple sources, and decision making is a complex process. Each vote on an issue of consequence, moreover, carries snares as well as opportunities, and the decision that satisfies one constituency element may distress another.

### Representative as Agent of Constituency

The theory that representatives should serve manifestly as agents of their constituents, carefully mirroring their views, apparently stirs the hearts and influences the behavior of many American legislators. They see their job as that of advancing the cause of the people back home. Lewis A. Dexter quotes a congressman explaining his vote on the Reciprocal Trade Extension Act:

> My first duty is to get reelected. I'm here to represent my district. . . . This is part of my actual belief as to the function of a congressman. . . . What is good for the majority of districts is good for the country. What snarls up the system is these so-called statesmen—congressmen who vote for what they think is the country's interest. . . . Let the senators do that. . . . They're paid to be statesmen; we [members of the House] aren't.[4]

Legislators believe their records are highly visible to their constituents. One way to increase their security, they believe, is to be certain that their records show that they have been attentive to constituency interests and effective in representing them. The point is made in these comments by an Illinois congressman requesting support for an amendment to appropriate $150,000 for studies of possible public works projects in his district:

> My people are up in arms. They want at least a study made of these problems. They do not mind me voting for worthy projects all over the United States, but I can tell you, I am not much to look at, and unless I get some money to be spent down in southern Illinois, to study some of these problems, you may not be seeing me here next year. I hope all of the Members will go along with me and vote for my amendment.[5]

The members' responsiveness to district interests frequently confounds party leaders and the president. When members perceive a clear-cut constituency interest, loyalty to party and president usually are no match. Several dozen House Democrats, for example, resisted President Clinton's $30 billion anticrime bill in 1994 because among its provisions was a controversial ban on the sale of nineteen assault weapons; gun proponents, including the powerful National Rifle Association, were of course opposed to that. Among the members who voted against a rule to bring the measure to the floor was the prominent chair of the House Foreign Affairs Committee, Lee H. Hamilton (D., IN), who observed:

> It doesn't give me any joy to cast a vote against President Clinton or any other president, for that matter. Would I like to see him get a victory when he obviously needs one? Yes. Do I make that my first or my second priority? No. The basic nature of American politics has changed. I don't get elected because of what Bill Clinton thinks or what the House leadership thinks. The electorate makes up its own mind. That inevitably means that presidents have a lot less clout with Congress than they used to have. All presidents, I mean.[6]

Constituency is not by any means the only explanation for legislators' voting decisions, but it is clearly of high importance—at least in the perceptions of numerous legislators. On many issues that come before the legislature, typically members hear little or nothing from their constituency. How they vote on these questions probably makes little difference in their districts. When constituency feelings are intense, however, the legislator is under great pressure to vote according to constituency preferences. Even so, a single vote is not likely to jeopardize the member's career. Much more to be feared is the development of a "string of votes" that appears to collide with the best interests of various constituency elements. As one congressman explains,

> I suppose this one issue wouldn't make much difference. Any one issue wouldn't swing it. But you get one group mad with this one. Then another group—much more potent, by the way—gets mad about gun control. Then unions about compulsory arbitration. Pretty soon you're hurting. It doesn't take too many votes like this before you've got several groups against you, all for different reasons, and they all care only about that one issue that you were wrong on. A congressman can only afford two or three votes like that in a session. You get a string of them, then watch out.[7]

Recent research by Sara Brandes Crook and John R. Hibbing provides good evidence that the mode of election affects not only the types of people chosen as legislators but also their responsiveness to changes in public sentiment. Their study finds that adoption of the Seventeenth Amendment in 1913, providing for the direct election of senators, significantly increased the chances that Senate candidates with government experience rather than wealth and family connections would be elected. The impact of direct elections on representation was arguably more important. With its members no longer selected by state legislatures, the Senate became more responsive to the public mood. In essence, the Senate became more like the House and more closely connected to the people and their preferences.[8]

## Representative as Free Agent

The other leading theory of the role of the representative is that the member should be unfettered by constituency directives and free to express personal views on matters of public policy. In the classic form of this theory at least, legislators serve as delegates from their districts, and although they acknowledge the lines of responsibility to their constituents, they are not bound simply to reproduce local sentiments. The best-known interpretation of this position belongs to Edmund Burke, who, following his election to the House of Commons in 1774, issued these remarkable instructions to his constituents of Bristol, England:

> Certainly, gentlemen, it ought to be the happiness and the glory of a representative, to live in the strictest union, the closest correspondence, and the most unreserved communication with his constituents. Their wishes ought to have great weight with him; their opinions high respect; their business unremitted attention. . . . But his unbiased opinion, his mature judgment, his enlightened conscience, he ought not to sacrifice to you, to any man, or to any set of men living. . . . Your representative owes you, not his industry only, but his

judgment; and he betrays, instead of serving you, if he sacrifices it to your opinion. . . . If government were a matter of will upon any side, yours, without question, ought to be superior. But government and legislation are matters of reason and judgment, and not of inclination; and what sort of reason is that in which the determination precedes the discussion, in which one set of men deliberate and another decide, and where those who form the conclusion are perhaps three hundred miles distant from those who hear the arguments? . . . Parliament is not a *congress* of ambassadors from different and hostile interests, which interests each must maintain, as an agent and advocate, against other agents and advocates; but Parliament is a *deliberative* assembly of *one* nation, with *one* interest, that of the whole—where not local purposes, not local prejudices, ought to guide, but the general good, resulting from the general reason of the whole. You choose a member, indeed; but when you have chosen him, he is not a member of Bristol, but he is a member of Parliament.[9]

### Evaluation of the Representative's Role

In the lore of politics the belief is strong that legislators are heavily influenced by their constituencies. And not a few people believe that the broad purposes of government are frequently undermined by the legislators' need to placate provincial interests and insistent constituents. What does the evidence on this matter look like? Does the search for political security require legislators to be submissive to the opinions of their constituents? Are all legislators concerned with defending constituency interests? Under what circumstances is constituency influence greatest?

One assessment finds expression in the writing of Walter Lippmann, who contended that democratic politicians get ahead only if they are able to manage or mollify the interests in their constituencies.[10] In contrast, there are at least some legislators who feel that they have substantial freedom of action, as these remarks by a congressman make plain:

> You know, I am sure you will find out a Congressman can do pretty much what he decides to do and he doesn't have to bother too much about criticism. I've seen plenty of cases since I've been up here where a guy will hold one economic or political position and get along all right; and then he'll die or resign and a guy comes in who holds quite a different . . . position and he gets along all right too. That's the fact of the matter.[11]

Several empirical investigations have sought to explain the role of the legislator as representative and the nature of the relationship between the legislator and the constituency. Studies of state legislators in four states—California, New Jersey, Ohio, and Tennessee—and of a sample of members of the U.S. House of Representatives disclose that representatives may adopt one of several role orientations. In the matter of representation style, legislators may see their role as that of *trustee* (legislators who view themselves as free agents, free to use their own judgment in matters before the legislature), of *delegate* (legislators who feel a need to consult their constituents, perhaps

**TABLE 3.1** Legislators' representational role orientations

| Role Orientation | California N = 49 | New Jersey N = 54 | Ohio N = 114 | Tennessee N = 78 | U.S. House N = 87 |
|---|---|---|---|---|---|
| Trustee | 55% | 61% | 56% | 81% | 28% |
| Politico | 25 | 22 | 29 | 13 | 46 |
| Delegate | 20 | 17 | 15 | 6 | 23 |
| Undetermined | 0 | 0 | 0 | 0 | 3 |
| Total | 100% | 100% | 100% | 100% | 100% |

SOURCES: John C. Wahlke, Heinz Eulau, William Buchanan, and LeRoy C. Ferguson, *The Legislative System: Explorations in Legislative Behavior* (New York: Wiley, 1962), p. 281; and Roger H. Davidson, *The Role of the Congressman* (New York: Pegasus, 1969), p. 117.

following local instructions even though they conflict with personal judgments or principles), or of *politico* (legislators who hold both the trustee and delegate orientations, alternating between them).[12]

In light of the conventional wisdom that lawmakers are preoccupied with eliciting and responding to constituency opinions, the results of the four-state study are surprising. The data of Table 3.1 tell the story. Substantially more than half of the state legislators (81 percent of the respondents in Tennessee) held the trustee or free-agent orientation toward their role as representative. About one-quarter of this sample of legislators expressed their role orientation as that of politico, and departing from the expected, only about one-seventh viewed their role as that of delegate. For members of the U.S. House of Representatives, on the other hand, the dominant role orientation was that of politico; nearly one-half of those members interviewed were classified in this category. The trustee role orientation was held by 28 percent of the congressional sample and the delegate conception by 23 percent. The fact that so few legislators take the delegate role may be due mainly to the difficulties in learning what constituents want: One cannot be a delegate unless one understands what one has been delegated to do.

Legislators may perceive their role in terms of the *foci* of representation. Thus, legislators may be oriented primarily to the district, to the state, or to the district and state. The data of Table 3.2 illuminate the areal role orientations of legislators in relation to the political character of their districts. Members from competitive districts are clearly more attentive to district interests and problems than members from one-party districts, who are more likely to express interest in state programs and policies. It is easy to conclude that legislators who are most in jeopardy of losing office are most likely to respond to district stimuli, whereas members from safe districts have greater freedom to focus on the wider problems of the state. The areal orientations of legislators are thus substantially influenced by the competitive quality of the district they represent.

**TABLE 3.2** Legislators' areal role orientations in relation to the political character of their electoral districts in three states

| Areal Role Orientation | Political Character of District | | |
| | Competitive N = 72 | Semicompetitive N = 77 | One-Party N = 96 |
| --- | --- | --- | --- |
| District | 53% | 48% | 33% |
| District-state | 28 | 34 | 33 |
| State | 19 | 18 | 34 |
| Total | 100% | 100% | 100% |

SOURCE: John C. Wahlke, Heinz Eulau, William Buchanan, and LeRoy C. Ferguson, *The Legislative System: Explorations in Legislative Behavior* (New York: Wiley, 1962), p. 292. The three states are California, New Jersey, and Ohio. "Not ascertained" respondents are omitted.

The evidence of Table 3.3 suggests that legislators and citizens view the job of the legislator in sharply different ways. Three broad conclusions can be drawn from these survey data. First, a majority of the public (56 percent) believes that House members should be primarily concerned with promoting the interests of their districts rather than those of the nation as a whole. Second, the largest segment of the public (46 percent) believes that when House members are presented by a conflict between the preferences of the people of their district and their own conscience, they should follow the district. And third, members disagree with the public on both counts. They

**TABLE 3.3** The attitudes of the public and of House members toward representational role orientations

| *Should a congressman be primarily concerned with looking after the needs and interests of his own district or should he be primarily concerned with looking after the needs and interests of the nation as a whole?* | Public | Members | *When there is a conflict between what a congressman feels is best and what the people in his district want, should he follow his own conscience or follow what the people in his district want?* | Public | Members |
| --- | --- | --- | --- | --- | --- |
| Own District | 56% | 24% | Follow His Own Conscience | 22% | 65% |
| Whole Nation | 34 | 45 | Follow His District | 46 | 5 |
| Both Equal | — | 28 | Depends on the Issue | 27 | 25 |
| Not Sure | 9* | 3 | Not Sure | 5 | 4* |

*Totals do not add to 100 percent because of rounding.

SOURCE: *Final Report of the Commission on Administrative Review,* U.S. House of Representatives, 95th Cong., 1st sess., 1977, pp. 836, 838, 887, 890.

profess to favoring their conscience over their district (65 percent to 5 percent) and the nation as a whole over their district (45 percent to 24 percent). Lewis Dexter has suggested that members of Congress may enjoy substantial freedom from district pressures. Many of the policy questions that come before Congress do not have a direct impact on district interests. Moreover, members trying to identify the prevailing view in their districts on a particular issue, even such a major issue as reciprocal trade, may find this a difficult task, for there are few indices of community sentiment available to them. One consequence is that the views of persons around the representative carry a great deal of weight. Dexter concludes that it is less a case of the individual member responding to the opinions of the constituents than it is of representing "what he hears from the district as he interprets it."[13]

An empirical study of representation by Warren Miller and Donald Stokes adds other evidence concerning constituency control over members of the U.S. House of Representatives.[14] Their study sought to investigate the extent of policy agreement between members of Congress and their districts by comparing the policy preferences of constituents, as shown in interviews, with those of their respective members, as revealed both by interviews and roll-call voting behavior. Covering a total of 116 congressional districts, the study tests policy agreement in three fields: social welfare, American involvement in foreign affairs, and federal civil rights programs on behalf of blacks. On policy matters involving social welfare and civil rights, there is marked agreement between legislators and their districts, especially in the case of civil rights, in which legislators tend to behave in the fashion of "instructed" delegates; on questions of foreign involvement, however, legislators are inclined to follow the administration, regardless of prevailing opinion in their districts.

Although the evidence of this study is firm that a district is able to influence its representative on social welfare and civil rights legislation, there are few signs of meaningful communication between district and legislator. "The Representative has very imperfect information about the issue preferences of his constituency, and the constituency's awareness of the policy stands of the Representative ordinarily is slight." Yet the constituency's ignorance about the specific positions of its representative does not free the legislator to vote as he or she pleases. A great majority of representatives *believe* that their records are essential for their reelection. Moreover, the fact that only a small number of constituents are informed about the record of their representative nevertheless can prove to be crucial in a close election— "the Congressman is a dealer in increments and margins." In addition, voters may have acquired a general impression of the legislator's record, even though they know virtually nothing about its specific content. Finally, control results from the fact that the representative is always alert to potential sanctions by the constituency.[15]

Bruce I. Oppenheimer has discovered several key features of the representational relationships of U.S. senators and their constituents. First of all, senators' representational experience is a function of the population size of their states. Small state senators have many more personal contacts with constituents than do senators from large states, who rely more on impersonal contacts, such as the electronic media and mass mailings. What difference does this make? Constituents are less likely to communicate with their senators in large states and are more likely to feel distant from them. In contrast, constituents in small states are more likely to evaluate their senators favorably, to seek help from them on a problem, to see their help as beneficial, and to recall something they have done. Numbers plainly matter: Constituents in smaller states have a closer relationship with their senators and are better satisfied with the representation they are receiving. This nexus influences the career choices of small state senators. Sensitive to the electoral connection, they gravitate toward the constituency committees rather than the policy committees, which are preferred by large state senators. The main question raised by these findings is whether the Senate is unduly constrained by having more than one-third of its membership attuned to the parochial interests of small state constituencies.[16]

To conclude this discussion, it should be noted that representation does not necessarily have to focus on the relationship between a specific legislator and his or her constituency. As Robert Weissberg has shown, representation may also be viewed in terms of *institutions* that collectively represent the people as a whole. Thus, individual citizens may be generally satisfied with policy outcomes in a legislature even though the legislators who represent their districts have been unresponsive or have "misrepresented" district opinion.

> [It is quite likely] that representation of citizen preferences will occur independently of an electoral connection between a member of Congress and a constituent. . . . It may be impossible for one legislator to represent 400,000 people with any degree of accuracy; it may, however, be possible for 435 legislators to represent more accurately the opinions of 220,000,000 citizens. To be sure, whether or not a particular legislator follows his or her constituency is an important question, but this question is not necessarily the most appropriate one if we ask, "Do representatives represent?"[17]

## THE REPRESENTATIVE SYSTEM

The formation of a system of representation requires a method by which representatives are chosen, an apportionment formula that provides for the allocation of representatives to constituencies, and a method for reapportionment as the distribution of population changes. The first requirement is met in the United States through an electoral structure based on periodic elections and mass suffrage. The second and third requirements are central to the focus of this chapter and thus require careful consideration.

## Criteria for Apportionment

Apportionment is the act of forming constituencies or districts and allotting them units of representation. Alfred de Grazia identifies five possible criteria that can be employed in devising a method of apportionment: (1) territorial surveys, (2) government boundaries, (3) official bodies, (4) functional divisions of the population, and (5) free population alignments. The fourth method, which has never been used in the United States, calls for the representation of certain nonterritorial functional interests of a social or economic character—as in the Chamber of Corporations created by the fascist regime in Italy. The fifth method is central to proportional-representation schemes and has been used sparingly in the United States, principally in local elections. Method three, apportionment by official bodies, was used for the selection of U.S. senators until adoption of the Seventeenth Amendment in 1913. This amendment removed the choice of senators from state legislatures and vested the power in the people.[18]

The apportionment plan utilized most commonly is that of the territorial survey, which is designed to distribute the population into relatively equal, albeit artificial, districts. Analysis of population shifts is necessarily related to this method since a new apportionment (that is, reapportionment) must in some way take account of the movement of people in and out of areas. This problem will be discussed subsequently.

Government boundaries, the final criterion to be noted, figure in all schemes of apportionment. Precincts, wards, cities, counties, states, and the nation—the boundaries of each exist as a potential apportionment base. Some cities constitute their city councils through election of members from wards, and other cities provide for election of all council members at large. A group of wards may constitute a state legislative district, and several counties may make up a congressional district. Each state, of course, selects two U.S. senators from within its boundaries. In each case the unit of apportionment directly utilizes at least one formal government boundary.

The ideal apportionment based on territorial surveys produces districts equal to one another in population. To those people accustomed to the idea that one vote should equal one vote, such mathematical accuracy is appealing; it is also difficult to achieve and to maintain. Shifts in population steadily erode the parity gained through the last reapportionment. There is always a certain amount of "catching up" to be done.

## The Legal Framework for Apportionment: Congress and the States

The apportionment of seats in the U.S. House of Representatives and in the state legislatures is affected by constitutional and statutory provisions, on the one hand, and by court decisions, on the other. Constitutions lay down the general guidelines for apportionment—for example, the maximum size of legislative assemblies is prescribed by the constitutions of the states—and statutes embody the decisions of a specific apportionment. Strictly speaking, apportionment combines two distinct processes, the allocation of seats to districts and the drawing of district lines. Under the federal system, the national government and the states cooperate in providing for the election of representatives: The Bureau of the Census determines the number of seats to be awarded to each state (apportionment), and the states perform the critical task of shaping congressional districts. The apportionment and districting of state legislative seats are formally functions of the legislature, though its discretion may be circumscribed by specific constitutional provisions or, as in recent years, by the courts.

When the normal political process fails to produce new electoral lines—perhaps because of a stalemate in the legislature or a governor's veto of a redistricting bill—the task of redistricting may be assigned to a reapportionment commission or to a special panel of judges. Redistricting is quintessentially political regardless of the arena in which it takes place.

The most important agency in the apportionment process in recent years has been the Supreme Court, supported by other federal and state courts. In 1962 the Court held in the Tennessee case, *Baker* v. *Carr*, that courts could hear suits brought by qualified voters to challenge legislative apportionments that failed to provide "equal protection of the laws" for all citizens.[19] Apportionment thus became a "justiciable" question. In a series of opinions two years later (the principal opinion appears in *Reynolds* v. *Sims*), the Court held that *both* houses of state legislatures must be apportioned on the basis of equality of population among districts.[20] In *Wesberry* v. *Sanders*, also in 1964, the Court declared that *congressional* districts must be made up of approximately the same number of people.[21] Although some legislatures were slow to comply with the Court's "one man–one vote" decisions, the great majority acted with dispatch.

The history of congressional apportionment begins with the Constitutional Convention in Philadelphia in 1787. The convention settled a central question of apportionment when it approved the "Connecticut compromise," providing for equal representation of the states in the Senate and for representation on the basis of population in the House. Article 1, Section 2, of the Constitution specifically enjoined Congress to apportion representatives among the states according to population and to reapportion after each census. The Constitution made no mention of congressional districts, and in the early years many states chose to elect their representatives at large.

For many years Congress took the easy way out in meeting the requirements for reapportionment: It simply chose to increase the size of the House. Rapidly growing states could be awarded additional seats without penalizing the slowly growing states by cutting their quotas of seats. Finally, in 1911, Congress put a lid on its membership, setting it at 433, with the total to go to 435 upon the admittance of Arizona and New Mexico to the Union. When Hawaii and Alaska were admitted to statehood in 1959, the number was increased temporarily to 437; following the 1960 census it returned to 435.

Congress took no action to infuse criteria for apportionment into law until 1842. Beginning with the apportionment act of that year and supplemented through the acts of 1862 and 1872, Congress set forth certain specifications for state redistricting; representatives should be elected from single-member districts, and such districts should be compact,[22] contiguous, and as nearly as possible, of equal population. Congress continued to impose these standards on the states in many subsequent acts, including the one adopted in 1911. However, these specifications were not included in the next apportionment act, thereby freeing state legislatures to draw congressional district lines to suit their purposes. Given this free rein, the boldness of their strokes as well as their ingenuity scarcely could be exaggerated.

When Congress failed to pass an apportionment act following the 1920 census, interest developed in a plan to provide a permanent solution to the problem. In 1929 Congress adopted an act providing for "automatic" reapportionment. Under the terms of this act, as later amended, a redistribution of seats takes place automatically after each decennial census, using the computation method of "equal proportions." The Bureau of the Census is charged with the responsibility of calculating the number of seats to be allotted to each state; this information is then relayed to Congress by the president. The clerk of the House of Representatives must then notify the governor of each state of the number of representatives allotted to the state for the next session of Congress.

Prior to the key reapportionment decisions, a major obstacle to the development of equitable systems of representation was the typical state constitution. As of 1960, for example, there were only ten states whose constitutions specified that representation in both houses should be based on population. It was common to find states in which area (for example, town or county) representation counted fully as much as population in the allocation of legislative seats. Today, however, the picture has changed radically as a result of the *Reynolds* v. *Sims* decision. Apportionment provisions of state constitutions are invalid if they prohibit the legislature from basing district lines in both houses on population. Thus, states can no longer provide for representation of population in one house and representation of area in the other. The reapportionment cases represent a massive commitment to the principle of equality of representation for all citizens. State constitutions must now reflect this fact.

## THE MALAPPORTIONMENT ISSUE

The assault on the theory of representation according to population began at the Philadelphia Constitutional Convention, when agreement was reached to allot to each state two senators.[23] Today, Alaska's population of 550,000 entitles it to two members of the Senate as surely as does California's population of 30 million. Be that as it may, equal representation of states in the Senate is such a conventional fact of civics that it is never seriously challenged.[24]

The apportionment of the lower house of Congress, however, is entirely another matter. The fact that the Senate rests on an apportionment that bears no relationship to population is a good reason why the House should be apportioned to represent the distribution of population. It is plain that this was the intention of the members of the Philadelphia convention, even though the Constitution does not contain an exact prescription for it.

Prior to the major reapportionment decisions of the 1960s, maldistricting among congressional and state legislative districts was the dominant characteristic of apportionment patterns throughout the country. It was common to find districts with populations two or three times as large as the smallest districts within a state. A study at that time revealed that of the forty-two states that had more than one congressional district, twenty-one had constituencies in which the smallest district was less than one-half of the population of the largest district. In effect this discrepancy made the vote of each resident of the smallest district at least twice as valuable as the vote of each resident of the largest district.[25] The principal beneficiaries of skewed representation were the residents of small town, open-country districts, and the principal victims of it were the residents of populous, urban districts. In retrospect, it seems clear that the failure of Congress and the great majority of state legislatures to deal with serious problems of malapportionment made judicial intervention inevitable.

### The Gerrymander

"First they took away some Democratic stuff, next they added more Democrats than they took away. And finally they gave him some new Republican stuff. But the net result was just a small Democratic gain, and the district's still safe for a Republican."[26] This description of a Pennsylvania congressional district after it had been refashioned by a Republican majority in the state legislature suggests the central characteristic of a gerrymander. No stratagem of American politics serves more unabashedly political aims than the gerrymander, a device employed by the dominant legislative party to maximize its strength and to minimize the strength of the minority party. State legislative majorities show remarkable ingenuity in laying out legislative districts that will lead to partisan advantage in elections.

To guide redistricting decisions, the majority party uses the statistics of past voting behavior of the state's political subdivisions.[27] Under skillful hands, bolstered by sophisticated computer analyses, precinct, ward, and other political subdivisions can be spliced together in district designs calculated to produce the greatest number of legislative victories for the majority party. One technique is to *concentrate* the opposition party's voting strength in as few districts as possible, conceding the opposition these districts by wide margins but preventing it from winning other neighboring districts: The majority is always willing to forfeit one district if by doing so, it can win three others. The other main technique calls for the majority to draw district lines in such a way as to *diffuse* the minority's strength, making it difficult for it to bring its popular support to bear effectively in the election. Skillful gerrymandering is likely to be worth a number of legislative seats to the architects of the district lines.

The majority party is not greatly concerned if it finds it necessary to create districts of bizarre dimensions. Nor, ordinarily, do party leaders lose sleep over the usual newspaper criticisms that attend the disclosure of gerrymandered districts. As one New York politico observed following the Supreme Court's decision holding unconstitutional the state's congressional districting plans, "Now it's just a question of slicing the salami, and the salami happens to be in our hands."[28] Whatever may be the explanation, reapportionment acts are not easily transformed into critical campaign issues.

### A Ranking of Interests in Reapportionment

The preeminent characteristic of reapportionment is its political aspect. Political interests are served through reapportionment—but whose interests and in what ways? Why is the struggle over reapportionment so strenuous and the resolution of the problem so difficult? We begin to answer these questions when we recognize that apportionment legislation leads to a convergence of political pressures on the members. In an instructive study of Illinois redistricting, Steiner and Gove suggest that there are "informal limits" (as well as constitutional directives) that govern the formulation of redistricting bills:

> (1) Individual preservation, the desire of each legislator to be in a "safe" district. (2) Mutual preservation, the willingness of members to cooperate with each other in protecting incumbents against potential challengers. (3) Political party preservation, the desire of the leaders of each political party organization to maximize its strength in the legislature. (4) Bloc preservation, the desire of members of voting blocs—whether based on geographic, economic, or ideological cohesion—to retain existing personnel and strength. Such blocs are often bipartisan, and their membership is relatively small.[29]

An analysis of a recent reapportionment in Pennsylvania by Ken Gormley, executive director of the state's reapportionment commission, identifies incumbency as the dominant factor in redistricting decisions:

Preservation of jobs is the most powerful driving force behind reapportionment; even more powerful than political rivalries or personal hatreds. The fact is, Democrats and Republicans rally 'round the common goal of preserving each others' political necks first. Only then, after most members' jobs are safe and secure, will the knives be sharpened for occasional raids on the opposing political party, or attacks on hated personalities.[30]

Every incumbent interest, no matter how trifling, takes on importance in drawing district lines:

The appetites of incumbents, when given a chance to draw their own maps, are boundless. One legislator from northwestern Pennsylvania fought violently when he discovered that Punxsutawney (home of "Punxsutawney Phil," world's most famous groundhog) had been drawn out of his district. The impassioned argument presented by political staffers during closed-door conferences—how could this legislator be deprived of the privilege of delivering the annual Ground Hog's Day speech, when he had exercised that honor for decades? Punxsutawney went back in. And there was the legislator whose cousin owned a farm that was an ideal spot for campaign cookouts—couldn't it be moved back into the district? Just a quick squiggle of the lines did it.[31]

A study of congressional reapportionment in the 1980s by Q. Whitfield Ayres and David Whiteman shows that four factors compete in the design of state plans: incumbency, party, race, and ideology. Typically, one of these priorities comes to dominate the process. Of most importance during the 1980s was incumbency—the attempt to protect incumbents of both parties. This was the dominant priority in eighteen of thirty-six states (the remaining fourteen states were made up of those with only one congressional seat or those in which the plans sought merely to protect the status quo). Plans that were shaped to promote the interests of one party over another were next in importance, characterizing redistricting in thirteen states. Race was the controlling factor in four states; in these states, in other words, efforts were made to give an electoral advantage to a particular racial group (in response to intervention by the Department of Justice or the federal courts). Finally, ideological considerations dominated redistricting in one state.

The type of reapportionment plan adopted appears to vary by circumstance. Party-dominant plans were most likely to emerge in states losing congressional seats. Incumbency was the main priority in states gaining seats or experiencing no change in number. From an overall standpoint, party-dominant plans were no more likely to be produced in states in which one party controlled the state government than in states with split-party control; in states losing congressional seats, however, single-party control did tend to produce partisan plans. Generally, the authors conclude, there is less resistance to plans designed to protect incumbents than to those designed to promote partisan advantage.[32] For members of Congress, one can be certain, that observation has a pleasant ring to it.

Another study of congressional redistricting in the 1980s by Janet

Campagna and Bernard Grofman found that at the national level the outcome was virtually a wash, culminating in only a marginal pro-Democratic bias. Significant partisan bias in districting plans—reflected in marked discrepancies between votes and seats—occurred only in certain states in which one party controlled the districting process. Overall, the authors conclude, what is most striking is how little partisan bias affected election outcomes in this decade.[33]

Similarly, a study of fifteen state legislatures following the 1980 redistricting found that partisan gains tend to be short term and, in fact, to evaporate after two or three elections. The broad conclusion of this study by Harry Basehart and John Comer is that the electoral fortunes of the parties are not significantly affected by partisan redistricting. Whether the redistricting plan is partisan or bipartisan, moreover, incumbents are likely to be reelected.[34]

A recent study of redistricting in thirty state lower houses, covering the years 1968 to 1988, by Andrew Gelman and Gary King finds that redistricting has two major, somewhat surprising effects: First, it increases the electoral responsiveness of legislatures (i.e., as the vote proportion received by a party increases, following redistricting, so does its proportion of legislative seats) and second, it reduces partisan bias (defined as the extent to which one party is favored in the translation of statewide votes into legislative seats). Put another way, the authors contend that the chief effect of redistricting, whether partisan or bipartisan, is to make the electoral system fairer than it would have been if there had been no redistricting.[35]

Although redistricting legislation carries some risks for incumbents, it is particularly discomforting for members of the U.S. House of Representatives. They ordinarily find it more difficult than state legislators do to defend their districts in a showdown over redistricting. First, U.S. representatives are not directly involved in making the decisions, nor are they steadily on the scene; the state capital may be a long way from Washington. The views of House members may be solicited by a reapportionment committee of state legislators or perhaps by party leaders outside the legislature, and if their seniority records are impressive, their districts may be changed only marginally—to meet the standard of population equality. But members who lack friends in high places in the party organization or in the legislature may find their preferences ignored so that other, more powerful claims can be satisfied.

Redistricting is critical for incumbents when a state has lost seats in Congress. Congressional delegations hope that the legislature will change individual districts no more than necessary, unless such changes strengthen their partisan coloration. If several seats have been lost, a number of major changes in districts may have to be made. In many cases House members occupy the uneasy role of spectator as state legislators and state party leaders tinker and toy with their districts, balancing their convenience and welfare against the convenience and welfare of the party, other incumbents, and other regions, perhaps removing friendly blocs of voters in one area and adding hostile blocs in another. The lines that are drawn can prompt a member to retire from office or threaten defeat in the next election. Understandably, from the vantage point of an incumbent, a congressional redistricting bill that serves the party's interest is not nearly so attractive as one that serves the member's personal interest. House members of one party ordinarily are quite willing to see the districts of opposition party members made more secure if, in the process, their own positions can be made safer. The party, they feel, can take care of itself; and when their party fails to protect them, they look for allies in the opposition party. In sum, everything about redistricting, whether legislative or congressional, suggests the triumph of self-interest.

The threat that redistricting poses for House members may be more apparent than real. Research has shown that incumbents who run in redrawn districts fare virtually the same as members who run in districts left intact.[36] No doubt members who must run for reelection in altered districts suffer some apprehension. The evidence suggests, however, that their anxieties are misplaced. Incumbents rarely lose (see Chapter 4).

## THE STRUGGLE FOR EQUITABLE APPORTIONMENT

For decades equitable apportionment was something of an anomaly in American legislatures. Not until the 1960s did the outlook brighten for significant reapportionment at the congressional and legislative levels. Several reasons help explain why the principle of representation according to population was so late in visiting American legislatures.

In the first place, the general public seems never to have mustered much interest in the issue, perhaps because of its preoccupation with other, more tangible matters or because of its conservative instincts or simply because of its inertia and indifference. Understandably, most legislators were inclined to ignore the need for reapportionment. Finally, neither chief executives nor judges were anxious to become involved in a reapportionment dispute, to challenge legislatures on a matter that their memberships regarded as peculiarly within legislative jurisdiction. Over the years, the combination of these factors—indifferent public, self-interested legislators, cautious chief executives and judges—appeared to place out of reach the achievement of equitable districting. Accordingly, apportionment on the basis of rigorous population standards characterized very few legislatures in the early 1960s.

### Judicial Intervention

Past experience is not always a reliable guide, as shifting court doctrines testify. In 1946, the U.S. Supreme Court held in *Colegrove* v. *Green*, a case concerned with flagrant inequalities in the population of Illinois congressional districts (one district had nine times as many inhabitants as another), that apportionment was, for several reasons, a "political question," one that properly should be settled outside the judicial process. Writing for three justices (only seven took part in this case), Justice Frankfurter contended that "Courts ought not to enter this political thicket. The remedy for unfairness in districting is to secure state legislatures that will apportion properly, or to invoke the ample powers of Congress."[37] The suit was dismissed by a four-to-three decision. Although the *Colegrove* verdict technically left malapportionment undisturbed, the narrowness of the decision offered at least some prospect that no lasting precedent had been established.

A new phase in the struggle for equitable apportionment was opened by several state and federal courts in the late 1950s. In 1956, a federal district court ordered at-large elections for the territorial legislature of Hawaii, a state whose last reapportionment had taken place in 1901.[38] As it turned out, this sanction was never applied because Congress was moved to redistrict the legislature. Of comparable importance was the 1958 action of a federal district court involving the Minnesota legislature, which was then functioning under a 1913 apportionment act.[39] The defendants sought to have the case dismissed on the grounds of *Colegrove* v. *Green*. Instead, the court accepted jurisdiction but stated that it would defer its decision until the next session of the legislature, a postponement that would give the lawmakers another chance to draw up a new apportionment act. The outcome was that the legislature heeded the court's advice and redistricted the state, in general submitting to the demands for population parity among districts. The upshot of these decisions, supported by several others by state courts, was that the judicial power came to be considered the principal hope for inducing reapportionment in the 1960s.

The breakthrough in the struggle for fair apportionment came in a court case involving the Tennessee legislature. Despite a state constitutional requirement that required decennial reapportionment, the legislature had not done the job for more than sixty years; as a result, there were extraordinary variations in the populations of legislative districts. The vote of a resident of sparsely populated Moore County, for example, was worth nineteen times as much as the vote of a resident of populous Shelby County in the election of members of the lower house. Discrepancies of this sort led a group of Nashville voters to bring suit, contending that the 1901 apportionment act deprived them of equal protection of the laws, as guaranteed by the Fourteenth Amendment, and asking that the act be held unconstitutional and that subsequent elections be held on an at-large basis. The case was dismissed by a federal district court in 1959 on the ground that it brought up a "political question," and hence the court lacked jurisdiction, as in *Colegrove* v. *Green*. The Supreme Court agreed to hear the case in 1961, however, and announced its decision in March 1962.

*Baker* v. *Carr,* the Tennessee reapportionment case, has been widely interpreted as a turning point in the struggle for equitable apportionment.[40] By a vote of six to two, the Court held that the case was justiciable (that is, that a court might suitably consider a case involving this subject matter), that the federal courts had jurisdiction in the case, and that the plaintiffs had standing to challenge the act's constitutionality. Interestingly, in remanding the case to the district court for further consideration, the High Court did not offer any guidance in making its decisions nor propose any remedies. Instead, much of the majority opinion, written by Justice Brennan, centered on the question of whether reapportionment was a "political question" and thus beyond the reach of the court.

Like many court decisions, *Baker* v. *Carr* answered some relevant questions and avoided some others. By making it clear that reapportionment was not a "political question," the majority opinion opened the possibility that judicial remedies could be proposed to correct inequitable districting arrangements. It served notice that citizens can seek judicial redress if they believe that apportionment debases the value of their votes, thereby depriving them of their right to "the equal protection of the laws" under the Fourteenth Amendment. In effect, the decision recognized that without outside help a majority within a state may be powerless to bring about changes in the apportionment system; many earlier state and federal court decisions had advised that relief from malapportionment could be won by the voting power and political effectiveness of an aroused and insistent citizenry. In essence, the outcome of *Baker* v. *Carr* indicated that the courts could provide a means by which underrepresented urban and suburban forces could gain a fair share of representation in state legislatures.

But there were many critical questions the *Baker* decision left dangling. (1) Did equal protection of the laws require *both* houses of the legislature to be apportioned on the basis of population? Since at that time approximately one-third of the states employed the so-called federal plan—one house based on population, the other on a nonpopulation factor such as political subdivisions (for example, counties)—the question obviously was of major significance. (2) At what point would divergence between population and representation become "invidious discrimination," hence prohibited by the equal-protection-of-the-law clause? The *Baker* case provided no clues; in fact, the justices declined to say that apportionment must rest on districts of equal population. (3) If nonpopulation apportionment was produced by state *constitutional* provisions that discriminated against centers of population, were these arrangements incompatible with equal protection for all citizens? (4) How would gerrymandering be affected by the Court's equal-population doctrine? In *Gomillion* v. *Lightfoot,*[41] the Court held that an Alabama statute that set municipal boundaries in a way designed to deprive blacks of their right to vote was in violation of the Fifteenth Amendment. Would a racial gerrymander differ from a party gerrymander? (5) And finally, how would *congressional* districts be affected by the judiciary's new role in the reapportionment struggle?

The impact of court decisions is never wholly evident in the short run. Yet in *Baker* v. *Carr,* it is plain that the stage was set for a sustained attack on malapportionment. Subsequent cases yielded answers to some of the questions left unanswered in *Baker.* Thus, in February 1964, *congressional* districting finally became the subject of a Supreme Court ruling. In *Wesberry* v. *Sanders,* a Georgia case, the Court held that "... the command of Art. 1, Section 2, that Representatives be chosen 'by the people of the several states,' means that as nearly as is practicable one man's vote in a congressional election is to be worth as much as another's."[42] Within four days of the Court's decision, the Georgia legislature had redrawn district lines; Atlanta was awarded a second congressional seat and other districts were brought more nearly in line with the equal-population doctrine. It was not long before legislators in other states were queuing up to deal, in their fashion, with the new problem of congressional districting.

Additional reapportionment business came to state legislative agendas in June 1964. Then, in *Reynolds* v. *Sims,*[43] the Court ruled that *both houses* of state legislatures must be apportioned in accordance with population thereby rejecting the "federal analogy" and extending the principle of "one man–one vote," which it had applied to congressional districts in *Wesberry.* In the case of *Lucas* v. *The Forty-fourth General Assembly of the State of Colorado,* announced on the same day, the Court ruled unconstitutional an apportionment plan that had been approved by the state's voters in 1962. This plan, which had been launched through the initiative process, fell before the Court because it failed to provide for apportionment in both houses on a population basis. "A citizen's constitutional rights can hardly be infringed," the Court declared, "simply because a majority of the people choose to do so."[44] Opinions in still other cases decided that day made it clear that state constitutional provisions that deny representation on a population basis are not sustainable under the equal-protection clause.[45]

Building on the critical decisions of the 1960s, the Supreme Court further refined the meaning of fair apportionment in the 1970s and 1980s. In the case of congressional districting, the Court has made it clear that it will tolerate virtually no population variation among districts. In *Kirkpatrick* v. *Preisler,* a congressional districting plan in Missouri was found wanting even though the maximum deviation from the norm was only 3 percent.[46] In *Wells* v. *Rockefeller,* a case involving congressional districts in New York, the Court nullified a districting plan in which the maximum deviation from the norm was 6 percent.[47] And in 1983, in *Karcher* v. *Daggett,* the Court ruled five to four that New Jersey's congressional reapportionment following the 1980 census was unconstitutional, even though the population difference between the largest and smallest districts was less than 1 percent.[48] It reaffirmed its position in the Missouri case that states must make "a good faith effort to achieve precise mathematical equality"; if this is not attained, each population variance must be justified. "Adopting any standard other than population equality, using the best census data available," Justice William J. Brennan wrote for the Court, "would subtly erode the Constitution's ideal of equal representation." The essence of these rulings is that any congressional districting plan that *can* be made more equitable *must* be made more equitable, or the state must provide an acceptable defense for deviating from the one-person–one-vote standard. Some variance might be justified, the opinion stated, in order to form compact districts, respect municipal boundaries, preserve the core of existing districts, or avoid contests between incumbents.[49] The New Jersey legislature had sought to justify district variance in terms of the need to protect the state's black vote, but it failed to show how the new district lines served that (acceptable) objective.

The Supreme Court's decision in *Mahan* v. *Howell* (1973) established the position that the states have greater latitude in legislative than in congressional districting. Upholding a state legislative reapportionment act in Virginia, even though the deviation between the largest and smallest districts was 16.4 percent, the majority opinion found it legitimate to form districts along political subdivision lines: "The policy of maintaining the integrity of political subdivision lines in the process of reapportioning a state legislature, the policy consistently advanced by Virginia as a justification for disparities in population among districts that elect members to the House of delegates, is a rational one."[50] Consistent with that decision, the Court in 1983 upheld a Wyoming districting plan that awarded the state's smallest county one seat in the lower house even though its population was less than half of that demanded by the equality standard. The deviation was justified, in the Court's view, by the state's geography and its "long-standing and legitimate policy of preserving county boundaries."[51]

The distinctions drawn by the Court in *Mahan* and *Brown*, along with other decisions,[52] suggest that the Court will be reluctant to strike down a state legislative plan if the overall range in district size is less than 10 percent—unless invidious discrimination can be demonstrated. If the range is more than 10 percent, as in the Virginia and Wyoming cases, the state will have to prove that the plan reflects a rational state policy, such as providing for the representation of political subdivisions.

Reflecting another facet of the struggle for fair apportionment, the Court has examined the use of multimember districts in state legislative elections. These districts have been challenged on the ground that they diminish the possibility that minorities can gain representation in the legislature. In the first case of this type, decided in 1971, the Court held that the multimember district used in the election of twelve representatives and five senators in Hinds County, Mississippi, had to be divided into single-member districts.[53] The Court's order made it inevitable that several black candidates would be elected to the Mississippi legislature from Hinds County.

Of no particular surprise, the Mississippi case did not settle the issue. In *Whitcomb* v. *Chavis,* a case involving the residents of a black community in Indianapolis, the Court held that "experience and insight have not yet demonstrated that multimember districts are inherently invidious and violative of the Fourteenth Amendment."[54] Since the Democratic party in particular had regularly slated candidates from this black community, "the failure of the ghetto to have legislative seats in proportion to its population emerges more as a function of losing elections than of built-in bias against blacks."[55] The key factor thus appears to be the circumstances of a given case. The Court's position is that "the challenger [must] carry the burden of proving that multimember districts unconstitutionally operate to dilute or cancel the voting strength of racial or political elements."[56]

Another case involving minority representation came before the Supreme Court in 1973. In *White* v. *Regester,* the Court upheld a district court decision ordering the creation of single-member districts out of two Texas multimember districts, one that discriminated against blacks and the other against Mexican-Americans.[57]

Racial representation again came to the fore in a major case decided in 1977. In *United Jewish Organizations* v. *Carey,* the Court upheld a New York State apportionment act that had used race as the primary consideration in drawing certain district lines. To create several substantially nonwhite legislative districts, the legislature had divided a large community of Hasidic Jews, moving half of them into an adjoining district, thereby reducing their collective voting strength. In the lawsuit brought by this group, the Court ruled that a state that seeks to diminish discrimination in voting may consider the voters' race when redrawing political boundaries. The use of racial criteria in this instance, the Court observed, did not violate either the Fourteenth or Fifteenth Amendment.[58] In a sense, the redistricting plan legitimized by the Court was a form of "affirmative action gerrymandering."

### Current Issues: Vote Dilution and Gerrymandering

By the early 1980s, the drive to equalize the vote—to provide through population-based districting that one person's vote would weigh just as much as any other person's—was essentially complete. Probably no concept of representation, in fact, was ever incorporated so rapidly and completely into American national and state political systems.

Acceptance of the principle of the equally weighted vote, and its institutionalization, did not bring an end to controversy and problems involving legislative and congressional redistricting. But the emphasis changed. Fair apportionment has come to include the idea that everyone is entitled to a meaningful or undiluted vote—and population equality among districts does not necessarily ensure it. Vote-dilution cases involve two kinds of gerrymandering: racial and partisan.[59]

Adopted in 1965, the Voting Rights Act delivered what the Fifteenth Amendment (1870) promised: that the right to vote cannot be denied to anyone because of race, color, or previous condition of servitude. Amendments to this act in 1982 have become a major factor in redistricting, particularly in cases involving the representation of minority voters. Section 2 prohibits the use of any voting arrangement that results in the denial of the right to vote. Specifically, a state districting plan is in violation of Section 2 if the members of any group do not have an equal opportunity "to participate in the political process and to elect representatives of their choice."[60] Section 5 requires that "covered" states (currently some sixteen states that have had a history of discriminatory voting practices and low turnout) must receive preclearance from the attorney general or the U.S. District Court for the District of Columbia for any proposed change in their election laws and practices including redistricting plans. Preclearance is required to prevent changes that would lead to a loss in minority voting strength.

The 1982 amendments made a significant change in the burden-of-proof requirement for challenging electoral structures and practices. Before the amendments, a plaintiff had to demonstrate that a redistricting plan had been intentionally shaped to dilute the minority vote. Abandoning that standard, the amendments substituted a "results" test under which a plan can be found unconstitutional if the plaintiffs can show that their political participation was hindered in such a way as to prevent them from electing candidates of their choice.

The first interpretation of the 1982 amendments by the Supreme Court occurred in 1986 in *Thornburg* v. *Gingles,* a case involving multimember state legislative districts in North Carolina. The Court unanimously affirmed a lower court decision that the voting strength of blacks in these districts had been impermissibly diluted. Although multimember districts are not inherently discriminatory, the Court held, they violate the Voting Rights Act when, "under the totality of the circumstances," the result of using the device is to deny a group "equal access to the electoral process." The Court went on to establish three tests for determining the existence of vote dilution: (1) The minority group is sufficiently large and geographically compact to enable it to form a majority in a single-member district, (2) the minority group votes cohesively, and (3) the white majority ordinarily casts a bloc vote sufficient to defeat the minority's preferred candidate.[61]

The thrust of these changes was aptly described by Bruce E. Cain and David Butler: "In sum, minorities originally had to show that lawmakers were diluting their voting power. Now mapmakers must show that they have done all they can do to maximize minority voting strength."[62]

The vigorous enforcement of the Voting Rights Act under the Bush administration led to dramatic gains in black and Hispanic legislative representation following the 1990 census. Between 1990 and 1993, 52 congressional districts were created with either black (32) or Hispanic (20) population majorities. Under these more favorable conditions, with districts drawn specifically to assure victories by minority candidates, the number of black members of the House increased from 26 to 39 and the number of Hispanics from 13 to 18.[63] The most striking change occurred in the South, where the number of black members of Congress increased from 4 to 17; in some of these states, such as Alabama and South Carolina, blacks were elected to the House for the first time since Reconstruction.

The constitutionality of majority-minority districts was quickly challenged in a spate of lawsuits. The Supreme Court entered the picture with its decision in *Shaw* v. *Reno* (1993), a case involving North Carolina's congressional districts. The Court ruled that a state's redistricting plan can be an unconstitutional racial gerrymander if it contains districts of a "bizarre" or "irrational" configuration, even though the plan's central purpose was to increase the representation of blacks. Writing for the majority, Justice O'Connor observed that "reapportionment is one area in which appearances do matter. A reapportionment plan that includes in one district individuals who belong to the same race, but who are otherwise widely separated by geographical and political boundaries, and who may have little in common with one another but the color of their skin, bears an uncomfortable resemblance to political apartheid. . . ."[64] *Shaw* thus opened the door to legal challenges of majority-minority districts; in particular, those with "extremely irregular" shapes became constitutionally suspect.[65]

Race-conscious districting came to the fore again in a 1995 Supreme Court case involving Georgia's 11th congressional district. To satisfy the Justice Department's preclearance demand for an additional black majority district, the Georgia legislature, following the 1990 census, carved out a plan that concentrated black voters in three districts, including the 11th, an imaginative, sprawling 260-mile district stretching from suburban Atlanta to Savannah—and having 64 percent black population. In *Miller* v. *Johnson*, decided by a 5–4 vote, the Court invalidated this district, saying that race cannot be a "predominant factor" in drawing district lines. Justice Kennedy, who wrote the majority opinion, observed: "Just as the state may not, absent extraordinary justification, segregate citizens on the basis of race in its public parks, buses, golf courses, beaches and schools, so did we recognize in *Shaw* that it may not separate its citizens into different voting districts on the basis of race."[66] (See Figure 3.1.)

The *Miller* case makes it clear that identification of an impermissible racial gerrymander does not depend simply on evidence of a district's bizarre shape. Rather, districts become questionable when "race for its own sake" becomes "the legislature's dominant and controlling rationale in drawing its district lines." Put another way, race can be considered along with other factors in districting decisions; it is invoked illegitimately when it crowds out all other customary factors, including ethnicity, geography, and partisanship.

**FIGURE 3.1.** **Black majority districts in Georgia and North Carolina**

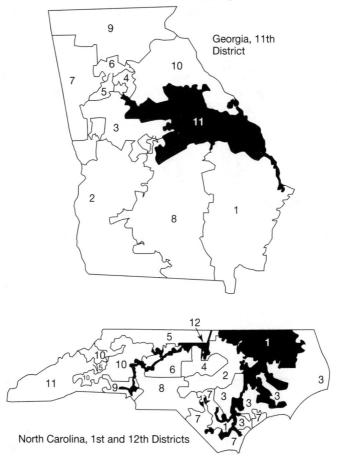

Georgia, 11th
District

North Carolina, 1st and 12th Districts

Shown here are the congressional districts fashioned by Georgia and
North Carolina following the 1990 census. In 1995, in *Miller* v. *Johnson,*
the Supreme Court struck down Georgia's 11th district, finding that race
was the "predominant factor" in placing voters in this district and that
this rationale violated constitutional guarantees of equal protection. In
*Shaw* v. *Hunt,* decided in 1996, the Supreme Court held that North Carolina's 12th district was an unconstitutional racial gerrymander; the 1st
district survived on a technicality. In 1998, a three-judge federal panel
approved a redistricting plan that made the 12th district wider and more
compact and, at the same time, cut the percentage of blacks in the district from 47 percent to 36 percent. See an account in the *Congressional
Quarterly Weekly Report,* January 27, 1998, p. 1751.

SOURCE: *Congressional Quarterly Weekly Report,* July 1, 1995, p. 1945.

Two major cases challenging race-conscious redistricting were decided in 1996. In *Bush* v. *Vera,* a sharply divided (5–4) Court struck down three Texas congressional districts: a black-majority district and a Hispanic-majority district in Houston and a black-majority district in Dallas.[67] In *Shaw* v. *Hunt,* the same majority threw out North Carolina's 12th district, also a black-majority district (described as "the least geographically compact district in the nation").[68] "The decision to create a majority-minority district" is not "objectionable in and of itself," Justice O'Connor wrote in the Texas case. The problem arises, as *Miller* held, when race becomes the predominant factor: "Significant deviations from traditional districting principles, such as the bizarre shape and non-compactness demonstrated by the districts here, cause constitutional harm insofar as they convey the message that political identity is, or should be, predominantly racial."[69]

In a 1999 decision, *Hunt* v. *Cromartie,* the Supreme Court added an interesting wrinkle to the question of racial gerrymandering by focusing on North Carolina's version of the 12th district created following *Shaw* v. *Hunt.* By a 9–0 vote, the Court held that consciously placing a large number of black voters in a district does not necessarily make race "the predominant factor" in drawing the lines—and hence impermissible. Rather, the key element is the *motivation* of those who do the redistricting. Their design might be influenced as much by political considerations as by racial considerations. Writing for a unanimous Court, Justice Clarence Thomas observed:

> . . . a jurisdiction may engage in constitutional political gerrymandering, even if it so happens that the most loyal Democrats happen to be black Democrats and even if those responsible for drawing the district are *conscious* of that fact. . . . Evidence that blacks constitute even a supermajority in one congressional district while amounting to less than a plurality in a neighboring district will not, by itself, suffice to prove that a jurisdiction was motivated by race in drawing its district lines when the evidence also shows a high correlation between race and party preference.[70]

Although it will take some time to sort out the implications of this decision, it appears to open the way for state politicians to safeguard the election of black representatives in some districts while at the same time serving the interests of the parties in making their districts more secure by larding them with loyal party voters. *Hunt* v. *Cromartie* is an invitation to district line-drawers to exercise a special ingenuity—and people should be surprised if they are not up to it.

The guidelines set forth in the *Miller, Bush,* and *Shaw* (1996) decisions, as refined by *Hunt* v. *Cromartie,* fall well short of definitiveness. The gist of these decisions is that, to pass constitutional muster, race-based districting must yield districts that are reasonably compact and "narrowly tailored" to advance a compelling governmental interest—that is, protecting the voting strength of blacks and Hispanics. Maximizing the representation of minorities, however, has gone by the boards. Districts where traditional race-neutral principles are plainly subordinated to race seem destined to come under "strict scrutiny" by the courts. At the same time, districting schemes that reflect *political* as well as *racial* motives may in fact satisfy the courts.

Substantial litigation will be required to spell out the significance that can be attached to race in redistricting. The redistricting dilemma was aptly described by Justice O'Connor in *Bush* v. *Vera:*

> The Voting Rights Act requires the States and the courts to take action to remedy the reality of racial inequality in our political system, sometimes necessitating race-based action, while the Fourteenth Amendment requires us to look with suspicion on the excessive use of racial considerations by the government. But I believe that the states, playing a primary role, and the courts, in their secondary role, are capable of distinguishing the appropriate and reasonably necessary uses of race from its unjustified and excessive uses.[71]

Majority-minority districts owe a great deal to the relentless pressure of a Republican-controlled Justice Department on state legislatures. It insisted that they squeeze out the maximum possible number of minority districts; geography, compactness, and other factors were all but ignored in drawing district lines. And a number of voting-rights lawsuits were initiated by alliances of black Democrats and Republican party officials. Concentration gerrymanders became the order of the day—where the potential for them was present. In partisan terms, the net result of creating new black (heavily Democratic) districts was to weaken the Democratic base in surrounding areas—making them both more white and more Republican.[72] (The Georgia delegation in the 106th Congress, for example, was composed of eight white Republicans and three black Democrats.) And as L. Marvin Overby and Kenneth M. Cosgrove have shown, those white incumbents whose districts became "whiter" became less sensitive to the interests of African-Americans.[73]

The Supreme Court's rulings have changed the terrain of race-conscious districting. In doing their redistricting business, state legislators will need to search for balance—reflecting the need to give minority voters an equal opportunity to elect representatives of their choosing (thus complying with the Voting Rights Act) while at the same time creating reasonably compact districts whose lines are not excessively influenced by racial statistics. That is a tall order. How provision for minority representation will play out is not at all clear. Some reduction in the number of seats held by blacks and Hispanics, however, seems inevitable. As for state legislatures, their role in redistricting is now more challenging than ever.

The second vote-dilution issue involves partisan gerrymandering. Such gerrymanders are about as old as the nation itself, but only recently have they come under the direct review of the courts. In a 1986 case concerning state legislative districts in Indiana, *Davis* v. *Bandemer*, the Supreme

Court warned that redistricting plans will be held unconstitutional "when the electoral system is arranged in a manner that will consistently degrade a voter's or a group of voters' influence on the political process as a whole."[74] This decision thus made partisan gerrymanders justiciable. Although the Court declined to invalidate the Indiana (Republican-devised) plan, since it appeared to be not so overwhelmingly partisan as to be unconstitutional, its ruling opened the door for litigation in which the losing party in reapportionment struggles can contend that it has been egregiously disadvantaged by partisan redistricting.

The importance of the *Bandemer* decision, however, is still far from clear. In 1989, the Supreme Court affirmed a lower court's decision in *Badham v. Eu*, a case involving California's 1981 (Democratic-devised) congressional redistricting. Following *Bandemer*, the lower court found that the case was justiciable, but refused to overturn the plan, holding that California Republicans had failed to prove that their party had been "'shut out' of the political process" since it held the governorship, a U.S. Senate seat, and 40 percent of the congressional seats.[75] Although affirming the lower court's ruling, the Supreme Court offered no reasons for its action.[76] Whatever else may be said about the current status of partisan gerrymanders, it would appear that successful challenges to them will require substantial evidence (probably involving more than one election) of substantial discrimination. With this new entry on their agenda, the courts will find it necessary to develop manageable guidelines for identifying significant partisan vote dilution—a task that promises to be both difficult and drawn out in the case of sophisticated districting strategies and schemes.

### The Impact of the Reapportionment Cases

Estimating the permanent importance of the reapportionment cases—their bearing on structures of political power, political careers, and public policy—is not an easy matter. Those who have searched for the consequences flowing from reapportionment have found themselves in the midst of a jumble of crude facts, for the changes attributable to reapportionment have not been easy to sort out from those whose origins trace from other sources. Hence the observations that follow deal more with the broad contours of the question than with the specific details.

Since the reapportionments of the 1960s and 1970s, the greatest gains in representation have been achieved by the suburban areas of the nation. This development ranks among the principal outcomes of the reapportionment cases. As expected, the heaviest losses in seats have been suffered by rural areas. Big cities in some states have increased their representation, but not to as great a degree as their surrounding suburbs. In recent years, of course, suburbs have been at the center of population growth in all sections of the country, and thus the new apportionments according to population have carried striking rewards for these areas. A number of central cities, in contrast, actually have declined in population. No city today holds as much as 50 percent of the population of a state. The longtime fear that reapportionment would bring big-city domination of the legislatures has proved to be groundless. The new strength of suburbs places them in a critical position to advance or retard the multiple claims of the central cities, as well as to promote the welfare of their own districts.

In conventional discourse on politics, reapportionment was often celebrated as a way by which urban Democrats might wrest political power from rural Republicans—at least in the North. It was anticipated that if rural areas were cut back in representation, the populous urban areas would inevitably profit. Power would shift from rural to urban and, *pari passu*, from Republicans to Democrats. Although reapportionment appears to have had some effect on partisan divisions in the legislatures, the changes have not been dramatic. A study of thirty-eight northern legislative chambers found that reapportionment led to a Democratic gain of fewer than 3 percent of the legislative seats.[77] One reason for this is that Republicans have gained more than Democrats from the increase in representation awarded to suburbs; rural Republicans have been replaced, to be sure, but often by suburban members of the same party.

The loss of rural seats does not mean that a league of urban and suburban interests can now dominate the state legislatures or Congress. Political interests are far too complex to be grouped neatly within geographic sectors or statistical abstractions. Neither urban nor suburban nor rural areas are now, or are likely to become, monolithic. Each houses a variety of interests; each is vulnerable to internal cleavages. The easing of rural power is likely to mean that no bloc will be sufficiently powerful, even when firmly united, to control legislative decisions.

Perhaps the most important question to be answered, and also the most difficult, is whether reapportionment has had a discernible effect on the public policy questions that come before the legislatures. A raft of studies in the middle 1960s suggested that there was little or no relationship between malapportionment and public policy—that is, that fairly apportioned legislatures did not make significantly different policy choices than malapportioned legislatures.[78] More recent studies, however, cast doubt on this conclusion. It has been shown, for example, that equity in apportionment has led to a generally higher level of direct state expenditures and to an increase of state spending for such urban-related activities as public welfare, public health, and hospitals. At the same time there has been a decrease in spending on highways, a longtime preoccupation of rural legislators. There is evidence in Florida that equitable apportionment led to an increase in party competition and to the adoption of regulatory legislation that fostered environmental interests and women's rights.[79] Certain kinds of nonfiscal policy decisions, such as firearms control policies and voting rights legislation, also appear to have been affected by reapportionment. Overall, disparities in the treatment of metropolitan and nonmetropolitan areas have been reduced, as central cities and suburban counties are now receiving proportionately larger amounts of state aid.[80] The significance of this last development should be obvious: Few decisions that governments make are more important than those that involve the allocation of money.

A change in the concept of representational equality led to the election of many new black and Hispanic legislators in the early 1990s. Nonetheless, both groups continue to be underrepresented in Congress and the state legislatures (see Chapter 5). The main questions now are, first, whether the Court's recent decisions will lead to the invalidation of only a few majority-minority districts judged extreme or whether they will open to challenge a broad range of districts where minorities enjoy clear or marginal advantage, and second, how state legislatures will respond to the Court's invitation to recalibrate the role of race in crafting legislative and congressional districts.

Under the aegis of the courts, the principle of representation according to population has become a reality in American legislatures. Today, no apportionment plan is likely to survive judicial scrutiny unless it provides that all legislators will represent districts "as nearly of equal population as is practicable."[81] Moreover, the courts will be sensitive to any electoral plan that has the effect of diluting the minority vote. The bottom line is that citizens, "protected classes" (racial, color, and language minorities), and political parties (since *Bandemer*) are entitled to an equal opportunity to participate in the political process and to elect candidates of their choice.

One fact above all others stands out in this prolonged struggle over political power, the democratization of politics, and the principle of representation: Great progress toward the goal of equalizing the voting power of all citizens was made in the last several decades. Considering the complexity of the problem, the most remarkable feature of the reapportionment era may be simply the speed with which substantial equality of representation was achieved.

## NOTES

1. Perhaps the best contemporary book on the general problem of representation is Hanna F. Pitkin, *The Concept of Representation* (Berkeley: University of California Press, 1967).

2. Carl J. Friedrich, *Constitutional Government and Democracy* (Boston: Ginn, 1950), p. 264.

3. Ibid., pp. 268–69.

4. Quoted in Lewis A. Dexter, "The Representative and His District," in *New Perspectives on the House of Representatives*, ed. Robert L. Peabody and Nelson W. Polsby (Chicago: Rand McNally, 1977), pp. 5–6. See also R. Bauer, I. Pool, and L. Dexter, *American Business and Public Policy* (New York: Atherton Press, 1963), especially Part 5.

5. *Congressional Record*, May 22, 1956, p. 7862.

6. *New York Times*, August 17, 1994. Ultimately, Representative Hamilton voted for the bill.

7. John W. Kingdon, *Congressmen's Voting Decisions* (New York: Harper & Row, 1981), p. 42.

8. Sara Brandes Crook and John R. Hibbing, "A Not-So-Distant Mirror: The 17th Amendment and Congressional Change," *American Political Science Review,* XCI (December 1997), 845–53.

9. Edmund Burke, *Works* (Boston: Little, Brown, 1866), II, 95–96.

10. Walter Lippmann, *The Public Philosophy* (Boston: Little, Brown, 1955), p. 27.

11. Quoted in Dexter, "The Representative and His District," p. 5.

12. This discussion of representational role orientations is based on two studies: John C. Wahlke, Heinz Eulau, William Buchanan, and LeRoy C. Ferguson, *The Legislative System: Explorations in Legislative Behavior* (New York: Wiley, 1962), especially Chaps. 12 and 13; and Roger H. Davidson, *The Role of the Congressman* (New York: Pegasus, 1969), pp. 110–42. For a study that finds a strong relationship between *prelegislative* life experiences (in particular, political experiences) and the representational roles assumed by freshman legislators in the state senate of California, see Charles G. Bell and Charles M. Price, "Pre-Legislative Sources of Representational Roles," *Midwest Journal of Political Science,* XIII (May 1969), 254–70.

13. Dexter, "The Representative and His District," p. 12. Also see David C. Kozak, "Contexts of Congressional Decision Behavior," Ph.D. dissertation, University of Pittsburgh, 1979. This study shows that communications from individual constituents vary according to the nature of the issue. Issues such as abortion, saccharin ban, legislative ethics, legislative pay raise, dolphin protection, and common situs picketing produce a substantial volume of constituent mail. Complex and technical issues with low-profile characteristics, in contrast, generate communications from narrow segments of the population, in particular organized groups. See especially Chapter 4 of this dissertation. For evidence concerning the extent to which legislators can accurately judge their constituents' preferences, see Ronald D. Hedlund and H. Paul Friesema, "Representatives' Perceptions of Constituency Opinion," *Journal of Politics,* XXXIV (August 1972), 730–52.

14. "Constituency Influence in Congress," *American Political Science Review,* LVII (March 1963), 45–56.

15. Ibid., pp. 53–56 (quotations on pp. 56 and 55, respectively). Constituency control or influence over legislators may derive from electing a legislator who shares the views of the constituents—in which case the legislator's policy preferences are directly related to those of the constituents—or from having a legislator who seeks to learn what the constituency wants in order to satisfy those elements that might otherwise turn him or her out of office—in which case the legislator's policies presumably relate to his or her perceptions of constituency objectives. This survey also reports that even among the *voting* sector of the public, only about one-half of the voters had read or heard something about either congressional candidate. "Information" usually consisted of nothing more than an evaluation such as "he's a good man" (see pp. 50–51).

16. Bruce I. Oppenheimer, "The Representational Experience: The Effect of State Population on Senator-Constituency Linkages," *American Journal of Political Science,* XL (November 1996), 1280–99.

17. Robert Weissberg, "Collective vs. Dyadic Representation in Congress," *American Political Science Review,* LXXII (June 1978), 535–47 (quotation on p. 547).

18. This opening discussion of the *criteria* for apportionment is based on an analysis by Alfred de Grazia, "General Theory of Apportionment," *Law and Contemporary Problems,* XVII (Spring 1952), 256–67.

19. 369 U.S. 186 (1962).

20. 377 U.S. 533 (1964).

21. 376 U.S. 1 (1964).

22. H. P. Young argues that "compactness" lacks the precision necessary to be used as a legal requirement for districting plans. See "Measuring the Compactness of Legislative Districts," *Legislative Studies Quarterly,* XIII (February 1988), 105–15. Guidelines for using compactness as a districting criterion are offered by Richard G. Niemi, Bernard Grofman, Carl Carlucci, and Thomas Hofeller, "Measuring Compactness and the Role of a Compactness Standard or a Test for Partisan and Racial Gerrymandering," *Journal of Politics,* LII (November 1990), 1155–81.

23. Frances E. Lee and Bruce I. Oppenheimer have shown that equal apportionment in the Senate has affected partisan competition for seats. States with larger populations are more competitive than those with smaller populations. At times, one party or the other has won a disproportionate share of seats, given its overall support in the country, because of its electoral successes in those (less competitive) states with smaller populations. "Senate Apportionment: Competitiveness and Partisan Advantage," *Legislative Studies Quarterly,* XXII (February 1997), 3–24.

24. Equal representation of the states in the Senate does make a difference in public policy. Frances E. Lee finds that, on a per capita basis, less populous states tend to receive more federal money than more populous states for a wide range of domestic spending programs. "Representation and Public Policy: The Consequences of Senate Apportionment for the Geographic Distribution of Federal Funds," *Journal of Politics,* LX (February 1998), 34–62.

25. Andrew Hacker, *Congressional Districting: The Issue of Equal Representation* (Washington, DC: Brookings Institution, 1963), p. 2. See also *Reapportionment in the 1970s,* ed. Nelson W. Polsby (Berkeley: University of California Press, 1971).

26. Chalmers Roberts, "The Donkey, the Elephant, and the Gerrymander," *The Reporter,* September 16, 1952, p. 30.

27. For an instructive interpretation of how gerrymandering is accomplished through systematic shifting of voters to and from districts, see John D. Cranor, Gary L. Crawley, and Raymond H. Scheele, "The Anatomy of a Gerrymander," *American Journal of Political Science,* XXXIII (February 1989), 222–39.

28. As quoted in William J. D. Boyd, "High Court Voids States' Districts," *National Civic Review,* LVIII (May 1969), 211.

29. Gilbert Y. Steiner and Samuel K. Gove, *The Legislature Redistricts Illinois* (Urbana: University of Illinois, Institute of Government and Public Affairs, 1956), p. 7.

30. Ken Gormley, "Reapportionment: Tales from the Trenches," *Pennsylvania Law Weekly,* October 16, 1995, p. 28.

31. Ibid.

32. Q. Whitfield Ayres and David Whiteman, "Congressional Reapportionment in the 1980s," *Political Science Quarterly,* IC (Summer 1984), 303–14.

33. Janet Campagna and Bernard Grofman, "Party Control and Partisan Bias in 1980s Congressional Redistricting," *Journal of Politics,* LII (November 1990), 1242–57. For other assessments of the impact of redistricting during this decade, see Alan I. Abramowitz, "Partisan Redistricting and the 1982 Congressional Elections," *Journal of Politics,* VL (August 1983), 767–70; Peverill Squire, "Results of Partisan Redistricting in Seven U.S. States During the 1970s," *Legislative Studies Quarterly,* X (May 1985), 259–66; Richard Born, "Partisan Intentions and Election Day Realities in the Congressional Districting Process," *American Political Science Review,* LXXIX (June 1985), 305–19; Bruce E. Cain, "Assessing the Partisan Effects of Redistricting," *American Political Science Review,* LXXIX (June 1985), 320–33; and Bruce E. Cain and Janet Campagna, "Predicting Partisan Redistricting Disputes," *Legislative Studies Quarterly,* XII (May 1987), 265–74.

34. Harry Basehart and John Comer, "Partisan and Incumbent Effects in State Legislative Redistricting," *Legislative Studies Quarterly,* XVI (February 1991), 65–79. See the evidence of Donald Ostdiek that partisan gerrymanders weaken both the majority's and minority's safe districts. "Congressional Redistricting and District Typologies," *Journal of Politics,* LVII (May 1995), 533–43.

35. Andrew Gelman and Gary King, "Enhancing Democracy Through Legislative Redistricting," *American Political Science Review,* LXXXVIII (September 1994), 541–59.

36. Charles Bullock III, "Redistricting and Congressional Stability, 1962–72," *Journal of Politics,* XXXVII (May 1975), 569–75.

37. 328 U.S. 549, at 556 (1946).

38. *Dyer* v. *Kazuhisa Abe,* 138 F. Supp. 220 (1956).

39. *Magraw* v. *Donovan,* 163 F. Supp. 184 (1958).

40. 369 U.S. 186 (1962).

41. 364 U.S. 399.

42. *Wesberry* v. *Sanders*, 376 U.S. 1 (1964).

43. 377 U.S. 533 (1964). For a comprehensive examination of the *Baker* v. *Carr* and *Reynolds* v. *Sims* cases, see Richard C. Cortner, *The Apportionment Cases* (Knoxville: University of Tennessee Press, 1970).

44. *Lucas* v. *The Forty-fourth General Assembly of the State of Colorado*, 377 U.S. 736–37.

45. *Maryland Committee for Fair Representation* v. *Tawes*, 377 U.S. 656 (1964); *Roman* v. *Sincock*, 377 U.S. 695 (1964).

46. *Kirkpatrick* v. *Preisler*, 89 S. Ct. 1225 (1969).

47. *Wells* v. *Rockefeller*, 89 S. Ct. 1234 (1969).

48. *Karcher* v. *Daggett*, 103 S. Ct. 2653 (1983).

49. Interestingly, research has shown that voters have a greater knowledge of congressional candidates when there is congruence between natural community lines and congressional districts. Hence, there is good reason to take account of community boundaries in the redistricting process. But the Supreme Court thus far has given little attention to this factor. Rather, it views population equality as the sine qua non of congressional district plans. See a study by Richard G. Niemi, Lynda W. Powell, and Patricia L. Bicknell, "The Effects of Congruity Between Community and District on Salience of U.S. House Candidates," *Legislative Studies Quarterly*, XI (May 1986), 187–201.

50. *Mahan* v. *Howell*, 93 S. Ct. 979 (1973).

51. *Brown* v. *Thomson*, 103 S. Ct. 2690 (1983).

52. See *Gaffney* v. *Cummings*, 412 U.S. 735 (1973); and *Connor* v. *Finch*, 431 U.S. 407 (1977).

53. *Connor* v. *Johnson*, 91 S. Ct. 1760 (1971).

54. *Whitcomb* v. *Chavis*, 91 S. Ct. 1858 (1971), at 1877.

55. Id. at 1874.

56. Id. at 1869. See also *Fortson* v. *Dorsey*, 379 U.S. 439 (1965).

57. 93 S. Ct. 2332 (1973). Although multimember districts appear to contribute to the underrepresentation of racial or linguistic minorities, they do not dilute the strength of the minority party in state legislatures. See the evidence presented by Richard G. Niemi, Jeffrey S. Hill, and Bernard Grofman, "The Impact of Multimember Districts on Party Representation in U.S. State Legislatures," *Legislative Studies Quarterly*, X (November 1985), 441–55.

58. *United Jewish Organization* v. *Carey*, 97 S. Ct. 996 (1977).

59. Two studies were particularly useful in developing the analysis in this section: *Reapportionment Law: The 1990s* (Denver: National Conference of State Legislatures, 1989); and Bruce E. Cain and David Butler, "Redrawing District Lines," *The American Enterprise*, II (July/August 1991), 29–39.

60. 42 U.S.C. Sec. 1973 (a) 1982.

61. 106 S. Ct. 2572 (1986).

62. Cain and Butler, "Redrawing District Lines," p. 32. See an instructive case study of the reapportionment process in Pennsylvania by Ken Gormley, *The Pennsylvania Legislative Reapportionment of 1991* (Harrisburg, PA: Bureau of Publications, Commonwealth of Pennsylvania, 1994) in which the creation of majority-minority districts was a particularly difficult and controversial problem faced by the Legislative Reapportionment Commission.

63. Frank R. Parker, "*Shaw* v. *Reno*: A Constitutional Setback for Minority Representation," *PS: Political Science and Politics*, XXVIII (March 1995), 47.

64. *Shaw* v. *Reno*, 113 S. Ct. 2816 (1993).

65. See an interesting array of articles on *Shaw* v. *Reno* by Paula D. McClain and Joseph Stewart, Jr., Bernard Grofman, Timothy G. O'Rourke, Susan A. McManus, Frank R. Parker, Pamela S. Karlan, and Dianne M. Pinderhughes in *PS: Political Science and Politics*, XXVIII (March 1995), 24–56.

66. *Miller* v. *Johnson*, 115 S. Ct. 2486 (1995).

67. *Bush* v. *Vera*, 116 S. Ct. 1941 (1996).

68. *Shaw* v. *Hunt,* 116 S. Ct. 1894 (1996).

69. *Bush* v. *Vera,* 116 S. Ct. 1961.

70. *Hunt* v. *Cromartie,* 119 S. Ct. 1551 (1999).

71. *Bush* v. *Vera,* 116 S. Ct. 1941.

72. Kevin A. Hill found that four of the nine congressional seats won by Republicans in eight southern states in 1992 were the result of the formation of majority black districts. In addition, several other districts that had been won easily by Democrats in the past became closely contested by the creation of majority black districts. "Does the Creation of Majority Black Districts Aid Republicans? An Analysis of the 1992 Congressional Elections in Eight Southern States," *Journal of Politics,* LVII (May 1995), 384–401. See an analysis of majority-minority districts developed within the framework of the "politics of commonality" (where black candidates campaign for white as well as black votes) and the "politics of difference" (where they do not). For a politics of commonality to emerge, a diversity of candidates within the black community is needed, encouraging biracial coalitions of moderate whites and blacks to form to choose a candidate acceptable to each group. Each side thus wins something. David T. Canon, Matthew M. Schousen, and Patrick J. Sellers, "The Supply Side of Congressional Redistricting: Race and Strategic Politicians, 1972–1992," *Journal of Politics,* LVIII (August 1996), 846–62. Also see a study by David Lublin that finds that it is very difficult for African-American and Latino representatives to win elections in white-majority districts. His evidence is that "race, rather than socioeconomic factors highly correlated with race, accounts for racial polarization in congressional elections." "The Election of African Americans and Latinos to the U.S. House of Representatives, 1972–1994," *American Politics Quarterly,* XXV (July 1997), 269–86 (quotation on p. 269).

73. L. Marvin Overby and Kenneth M. Cosgrove, "Unintended Consequences? Racial Redistricting and the Representation of Minority Interests," *Journal of Politics,* LVIII (May 1996), 540–50. Also see a study by Charles Cameron, David Epstein, and Sharyn O'Halloran that analyzes the influence of majority-minority districts in enacting legislation that promotes minority interests. Do these districts diminish the overall influence of minorities on public policy? The authors find intriguing evidence that "past a certain point, an increase in the number of minority representatives comes at the cost of [congressional] votes in favor of minority-sponsored legislation." "Outside the South, substantive minority representation is best served by distributing black voters equally among all districts. In the South, the key is to maximize the number of districts with slightly less than a majority of black voters." "Do Majority-Minority Districts Maximize Substantive Black Representation in Congress?" *American Political Science Review,* XC (December 1996), 794–812 (quotations on pp. 809 and 810). Also see a critique of this study by David Lublin, "Racial Redistricting and African-American Representation: A Critique of 'Do Majority-Minority Districts Maximize Substantive Black Representation in Congress?' " *American Political Science Review,* XCIII (March 1999), 183–86; and a rejoinder by Epstein and O'Halloran, "A Social Science Approach to Race, Redistricting, and Representation," *American Political Science Review,* XC (March 1999), 187–91.

74. *Davis* v. *Bandemer,* 106 S. Ct. 2810 (1986).

75. 694 F. Supp. 664 (N.D. Cal. 1988).

76. 109 S. Ct. 839 (1989).

77. Robert S. Erikson, "The Partisan Impact of State Legislative Reapportionment," *Midwest Journal of Political Science,* XV (February 1971), 55–71.

78. See a critique of the skeptics' literature by William E. Bicker, "The Effects of Malapportionment in the States—A Mistrial," in *Reapportionment in the 1970s,* ed. Nelson W. Polsby (Berkeley: University of California Press, 1971), pp. 151–210.

79. Michael A. Maggiotto, Manning J. Dauer, Steven G. Koven, Joan S. Carver, and Joel Gottlieb, "The Impact of Reapportionment on Public Policy: The Case of Florida, 1960–1980," *American Politics Quarterly,* XIII (January 1985), 101–21.

80. Yong Hyo Cho and H. George Frederickson, "The Effects of Reapportionment: Subtle, Selective, Limited," *National Civic Review,* LXIII (July 1974), 357–62.

81. *Reynolds* v. *Sims,* 377 U.S. 577.

# 4

# Legislators and the Electoral Process

The systems used for choosing public officials in the United States call for an enormous investment of time, effort, and money. No other country so emphasizes its nomination and election devices. Rooted in law and in custom, American practices are exceedingly complex. Moreover, there are substantial differences between the states in their electoral arrangements and political cultures. This chapter sketches the main features of the political process leading to the election of state legislators and members of Congress. Three principal topics come under consideration: recruitment, nominations, and elections.

## RECRUITMENT OF LEGISLATORS

The election of candidates to office is easily the most visible stage in the process of selecting political decision makers. But it is not necessarily the most important stage. First, candidates must be recruited—that is, in some way induced to stand for office or else, in the case of multiple potential candidates, screened out.[1] Despite its significance, there is little comprehensive evidence on legislative recruitment patterns; such evidence as exists deals mainly with state legislators in a small group of states.[2]

The most instructive studies of the career lines of state legislators suggest four principal conclusions concerning recruitment.[3] First, the social characteristics of the constituency sharply constrict the list of potential candidates. Race, religion, and ethnic and national backgrounds tend to be "givens in the availability formulas to which candidates must conform." The mainstreams of American constituencies, rather than the eddies, give rise to the vast majority of legislative candidacies. The following observations by Frank Sorauf concerning the recruitment of Pennsylvania state legislators accurately reflect the norms of legislative constituencies throughout the country:

The dominant values of the community result from its social characteristics, and these values are in turn imposed on all who would rise to positions of community leadership. The candidates for public office must reflect, at least in basic social affiliations, the constituency if they are to win its confidence and support. It is this fact rather than any systematic party policy that accounts, for instance, for the relation between Catholic candidates and the Democratic Party. The outsider, the stranger to the way of life of the community, stands little chance of breaking into any political elite. No matter how long he lives in the district, the atypical remains a newcomer. So the community stamps its image on its candidates for public office by demanding that they have absorbed the majority values from a background similar to that which predominates in the district.[4]

Second, many state legislators get elected to office without previous government experience—perhaps one-third to one-half of the members. An even larger number make their way to the legislature without holding any party position along the way.[5] A study of the legislatures of Connecticut, Pennsylvania, Minnesota, and Washington finds that the nature of the nominating system has a strong bearing on the recruitment of candidates. In states with "restrictive" nominating systems (Connecticut, convention system; Pennsylvania, closed primary), the prospects are much greater that legislators will have held previous public office than in states with "nonrestrictive" systems (Minnesota, nonpartisan primary; Washington, blanket primary). When nominations are made by convention or closed primary, party leaders tend to dominate the nominating process and to select or promote candidates with substantial political experience.[6] Nevertheless, apprenticeship in lower office, an especially congenial idea in democratic theory, is plainly not essential for recruitment or election to the legislature. Its incidence appears to be highest in those states that have competitive parties and/or restrictive nominating systems.

Third, there are a number of procedures by which candidates may launch their legislative careers. A study of Oregon state legislators by Lester Seligman describes four ways: conscription, self-recruitment, cooptation, and agency. Conscription of candidates ordinarily is associated with the minority party in districts where its prospects for victory in the general election are dim or nonexistent. Self-recruitment refers to those candidates who are self-starters, those who enter the contest without waiting for a nod from party officials. Cooptation describes a recruitment pattern in which party leaders seek out and persuade individuals who are not active party members to run for office; the candidate is often a well-known person of high social status. The mechanism of agency refers to those candidacies generated by political interest groups, with a view to transforming "a lobbyist into a legislator without much apparent change in role."[7]

Fourth, the leading variable associated with legislative recruitment and career patterns appears to be the structure of party competition within the state or district. The study of Oregon legislators discloses, for example, that for the majority party in one-party areas, individuals and groups, rather than party officials, tend to instigate and promote candidates; conversely, the minority party officialdom in one-party areas often is required to conscript candidates. In competitive districts the "candidacy market place" is most open; here groups, factions, party officials, and the self-recruited vie with one another over nominations.[8]

In certain constituencies potential candidates jump at every opportunity to run for the legislature, whereas elsewhere party recruiters have to beat the bushes to flush out any sort of candidate. James D. Barber identifies three factors that appear to be related to potential candidates' willingness to run and the readiness of recruiters to enlist them: *motivation, resources,* and *opportunity*—all interlinked. Motivation includes at least two elements: the potential candidate's personal needs that might be satisfied through political participation and a positive predisposition toward politics. Resources include such items as the candidate's skills, finances, and capacity to make time available for politics. Candidacies are generated when political opportunities become available; opportunity is governed to some significant extent by how recruiters evaluate the motives and resources of candidates. The kinds of candidates to whom recruiters devote a friendly ear undoubtedly vary from state to state and even from district to district. Everywhere, it would seem, the recruiter's test is political feasibility rather than any abstract standard. Finally, it should be remembered that candidates are not invariably recruited for their vote-getting power. Other considerations may be more important:

> A candidate may be chosen because he will gain a substantial number of votes ("make a respectable showing"), add prestige to the party, work hard for other candidates, satisfy some important party faction, contribute money to the campaign, offer special skills useful in campaigning, be the best man for the job regardless of his actual chances, accept a nomination as reward for his past sacrifices for the party, take training in this campaign for one he may win later, or be sufficiently innocuous to leave a delicate intraparty balance undisturbed. Calculations along these dimensions will depend a great deal on the peculiarities of the political system within which the candidate is to be selected, including the community's population, stability, party balance, and political values.[9]

The patterns of recruitment for members of Congress have varied over time, from jurisdiction to jurisdiction, and from party to party. But several general observations, based on Paul S. Herrnson's research, are in order. First, the decision by congressional candidates to run for office is "extremely personal." Family and friends play a major role in shaping the decision. Second, candidates report that party organizations have modest influence on the decision (though Republican organizations are more active than Democratic in recruitment). Third, the parties work harder to recruit candidates in competitive than in noncompetitive districts. Fourth, the most active party units in congressional recruitment are the congressional and senatorial campaign committees.[10]

A study by Thomas A. Kazee and Mary C. Thornberry of several dozen candidates for the House in competitive districts reported that 61 percent were self-starters, 17 percent were recruited by their parties, and 22 percent were of a "mixed" variety (self-starters encouraged to some extent by party activists). Since many self-starters had participated in party activities before their decision to run, the party role in congressional recruitment is somewhat more important than the percentages suggest.[11]

Partisan reality plays a major role in the decision to run for office. L. Sandy Maisel and Walter J. Stone have shown that the willingness of potential candidates to run for the U.S. House is related to their assessment of the prospects for winning. Bleak chances stifle their interest. Moreover, aware of their disadvantages, potential candidates are reluctant to challenge an incumbent. Interestingly, potential candidates are more influenced by their estimated chances of winning the primary rather than by their estimated chances of winning the general election.[12] The truth is that potential candidates are rational actors. Not many run "just for the hell of it."

The recruitment of quality candidates for Congress, even for winnable seats, has become more difficult. A variety of 1998 interviews by the *New York Times* of formidable, prospective candidates uncovered substantial reluctance to run for a House seat. Not even the president's personal pledge to campaign with them in their districts and to help them raise political cash made a great deal of difference. "Rising stars" did not want to upset family arrangements, commute long distances, give up their present positions, or confront the stern reality of raising huge amounts of campaign money. The perception of a corrosive political environment in Washington also entered their calculations. Virtually every potential candidate had something to say about the relentless pressure of fund-raising. A Wisconsin state senator comments:

> I would have to engage in some things that I don't find very tasteful. Like cold calling. Like asking current contributors to give me ten times more than they have in the past. Not only do you raise that kind of money now, but as soon as the election is over you turn around and do it all over again. I can't even see doing it once. But to do it over and over again is something I just wouldn't be able to do.[13]

Research by Linda L. Fowler and Robert D. McClure helps to answer the question of what makes a strong congressional candidate. The first requirement is simply that the candidate must "fit" the district—possess those personal attributes that inspire public confidence. A good fit is thus more than partisan or ideological compatibility with the voters. Second, the strong candidate must have a burning desire to be elected to Congress.

Ambition for a seat in the House, more than any other factor—more than money, personality, or skill at using television, to name just a few examples—is what finally separates a visible, declared candidate for Congress from an unseen one. Even among the declared candidates, it is the force of ambition that most often turns up as the critical difference between the winners and the losers, because only intense motivation can overcome the high political, personal, and financial hurdles that law and custom impose in a politician's path to a seat in the U.S. Congress.[14]

## THE NOMINATING PROCESS

### The Direct Primary

Most of the basic law governing nominations and elections for both state and federal office is written by the state legislature. Originally, nominations for office were private or party affairs, made by caucuses and conventions, unnoticed and unregulated by the legislature. Gradually states began to adopt laws prescribing a framework for the conduct of nominations; the trend toward more government regulation was sped along by several U.S. Supreme Court decisions concerning voting rights and corruption in primary elections. Today, nomination and election systems are regulated in detail by batteries of state laws and a few major acts of Congress.

Very early in the twentieth century, states began to adopt the direct primary for the nomination of state and local officials. The attractiveness of this method was attributable in large measure to popular disaffection with party conventions, which were believed to be instruments easily manipulated by "bosses" and "special interests." Heightened popular control over government was required, ran the incantation of the progressive-era reformers, and the device best suited to ensure it was the direct primary, which provided for an election to designate nominees for office. The reformist proposal shortly won statutory expression in many states, becoming in time the dominant method for making nominations; today it is used in all fifty states.

The spread of the direct primary ended the party organization's formal control over the choice of nominees. Through the use of preprimary endorsements, here and there countenanced by state law but practiced in any case, and through its campaign apparatus, a strong party organization can still dominate the nominating process.[15] But this is probably more the exception than the rule. In states and localities where the parties are weak or torn by factions, legislative (and other) nominations may go to the individual who has managed to build a personal following, who can finance his or her own campaign, who has spliced together factional support, who has the support of key interest groups, or who has a name that sounds "right." As V. O. Key's investigations revealed, a "bewildering variety of party structures exist behind the facade of the direct primary."[16] Nominations are made under circumstances that range from those in which the public typically ratifies candidates slated by the dominant organization to those in which the primary is a tumultuous free-for-all.

Several aspects of the direct primary are worth noting. In certain predominantly one-party districts and states, the primary is the "real" election; that is, the primary winner is virtually assured of winning in the general election. Moreover, belying one critical assumption—that it would lead to greater competition for nominations—the primary has often been "deserted," with only one candidate contending for the office.[17] Finally, legislative nominations are generally made under conditions of local autonomy; the choice of congressional nominees, for example, is seldom influenced by national party leaders.

### Congressional Nominations

The manner in which congressional nominations are made profoundly affects the American political system. Some observers believe, in fact, that the loose, decentralized character of the nominating process is a major explanation for the weakness of the congressional party organizations, reflected in an inability to maintain cohesion on major policy questions.

The keys to congressional nominations are kept in the constituencies, where individual candidates, interest groups, party organizations and party leaders, and the media vie for power. The ultimate result of local control over nominations is that any brand of Democrat or Republican may be nominated and elected to Congress. With substitution of current issues for those of the 1920s, Senator William E. Borah's statement of the problem would be fully appropriate today:

> Any man who can carry a Republican primary is a Republican. He might believe in free trade, in unconditional membership in the League of Nations, in states' rights, and in every policy that the Democratic party ever advocated; yet, if he carried his Republican primary, he would be a Republican. He might go to the other extreme and believe in the communistic state, in the dictatorship of the proletariat, in the abolition of private property, and in the extermination of the bourgeoisie; yet, if he carried his Republican primary, he would still be a Republican.[18]

All states now use some form of primary for the nomination of members of Congress. Congressional primaries are not necessarily competitive. Contests for House nominations are most likely to occur in those districts in which the victor will have a good chance of winning the general election. If the prospects for winning in November appear slight, the primary is frequently uncontested: Politicians do not struggle to win nominations that are unlikely to lead to public office.

An important factor in explaining the absence of competition in congressional primaries is incumbency. When a primary contest for a House seat fails to develop, even though the district is promising for that party, the explanation often lies in the fact that the incumbent is seeking renomination. Incumbency clearly diminishes primary competition. A study of House elections between 1956 and 1974, for example, found that 55 percent of all Democratic primaries were contested when no incumbent was running and only 37 percent when an incumbent was in the race; the percentages for Republican primaries were 44 and 20.[19]

The ability of incumbents to discourage candidates standing in the wings is not surprising. The longer representatives stay in office, the more time they have to establish personal followings among public, party, and interest-group elements. Representatives tend to feel that there is slight excuse for losing any election, so great are the advantages of incumbency—prestigious office, staff assistance, franking privilege, and numerous opportunities for distributing benefits to constituents and for attracting publicity both at home and in Washington.

Despite the advantages of incumbency, primary battles may have to be fought from time to time.[20] Even so, there is statistical comfort for members in knowing that very few incumbents fail to win renomination. In 1998, for example, out of 403 seeking renomination, only 2 House members were defeated in primaries. No senators lost their bids for renomination.

### National Party and Congressional Nominations

National party leaders are rarely involved in discussions with state and local party leaders over congressional nominations. By and large, the national party neither attempts to recruit candidates for congressional office nor intervenes in primary elections by backing one candidate over another. Experience has shown that national intervention in primaries is fraught with difficulties. President Franklin D. Roosevelt's attempt in 1938 to "purge" anti–New Deal incumbent Democrats—southerners in the main—by publicly supporting their primary opponents, ended in disaster, with nearly all of the victims singled out for elimination winning handily. A similar fate befell President Truman's efforts when he endorsed a candidate for the Senate in the 1950 Missouri Democratic primary. Although the presidential "purge" occasionally has met with success—Roosevelt, for example, initiated actions leading to the primary defeat of the Democratic chair of the House Rules Committee in 1938—the overall record is marked mainly by failure.

Even though there are good grounds for claiming that national authorities have a legitimate interest in the nomination of congressional candidates, there are few signs today of national activity in the primaries. The usual denouement of the "purge" undoubtedly has produced a cautious attitude among national leaders, for the most part discouraging them from even such a mild form of intrusion as helping to recruit candidates when no incumbents are in the running. Congressional nominations are not regarded as much different from other nominations, and state and local political leaders show no enthusiasm for interference by Washington. For lack of a good alternative, Washington goes along with the folkway of local control. This awkward fact of American politics makes matters difficult for the party in Congress, for the presence of members of Congress who are discovered locally and who owe virtually nothing to the national party confounds attempts to develop coherent party policies. Rampant parochialism, the frequent rupture of party lines, the evasion and confusion of national issues, and a possible loss of legislative talent—in the judgment of one school of writers—are the concomitants to the selection of congressional candidates on an almost exclusively local basis.

## CONGRESSIONAL AND LEGISLATIVE ELECTIONS

### Congressional Elections

Table 4.1 provides a point of departure for examining major features of congressional elections. The most important fact highlighted by the data for the House is that the typical election is not closely contested. "Marginal" elections—those in which the winning candidate receives less than 55 percent of the vote—usually make up about 15 percent of all House elections. In 1994, however, in the midst of a nationwide Republican surge, 23 percent of House

**TABLE 4.1**  Marginal, safer, and uncontested seats in off-year elections, U.S. House of Representatives and Senate, 1986–98, by percentage of total seats

|  | House | | | | Senate | | | |
|---|---|---|---|---|---|---|---|---|
|  | 1986 | 1990 | 1994 | 1998 | 1986 | 1990 | 1994 | 1998 |
| *Marginal seats (won by less than 55% of the vote)* | | | | | | | | |
| Democratic | 4.3 | 7.0 | 11.0 | 5.7 | 29.4 | 11.4 | 18.2 | 17.7 |
| Republican | 5.0 | 5.8 | 11.9 | 5.7 | 11.8 | 14.3 | 21.2 | 11.7 |
| *Safer seats (won by 55% or more of the vote)* | | | | | | | | |
| Democratic | 42.6 | 43.5 | 34.1 | 38.9 | 29.4 | 31.4 | 18.2 | 35.3 |
| Republican | 31.5 | 25.3 | 35.7 | 39.1 | 29.4 | 28.6 | 42.4 | 35.3 |
| Uncontested seats | 16.6 | 18.4 | 7.3 | 10.6 | 0.0 | 14.3 | 0.0 | 0.0 |
| Total | 100.0 | 100.0 | 100.0 | 100.0 | 100.0 | 100.0 | 100.0 | 100.0 |

NOTE: Uncontested elections also include a few elections in which a major party candidate is challenged by a minor party or independent candidate.

SOURCE: Computed from data drawn from various issues of *Congressional Quarterly Weekly Report*.

elections ended up in this closely contested category. Reverting to form in 1998, only 11 percent of House elections ended up in this category.

Since so many House seats are safe, winning by less than 55 percent may no longer be an accurate measure of marginality. If a marginal district is defined as one carried by less than 60 percent of the vote, the overall picture is somewhat different. Under this relaxed definition, 20 percent of all House elections were marginal in 1990, 38 percent in 1994, and 27 percent in 1998.

Surprises are few and victory is rarely in doubt in most House districts.[21] A landslide such as Roosevelt's in 1936 and Johnson's in 1964 may of course upset allegiances of long standing. A dramatic shift in voter preferences in an off-year election, as in 1994, can produce similar results. Nevertheless, the typical House seat in the typical election is virtually impervious to even the most sweeping of national election tides. Even in turbulent 1994, nearly half (46 percent) of all House seats were won by at least 65 percent of the vote or were uncontested.

Though more competitive than those of the House, Senate elections usually result in control by the same party. Typically, about 30 to 40 percent of Senate elections are won by less than 55 percent of the vote.

It is difficult to pinpoint the reasons for the decline in the number of competitive seats. Among the hypotheses that have been advanced are an increase in redistricting efforts designed to protect incumbents; the development of better "advertising" by incumbents, which leads to name recognition in elections; an increase in federal grant programs, for whose local manifestations members of Congress can claim credit; a greater sophistication among legislators in position taking on issues of importance to their districts; and changes in voter behavior under which incumbency becomes a more important voting cue than party affiliation.[22] The expansion of the federal role in delivering public goods and services has also increased the opportunities for legislators to engage in constituency service, thereby building goodwill among voters who need their assistance.[23]

Another reason for the success of incumbents is the so-called "sophomore surge"—the sharp increase in voting support typically garnered by members in their initial bid for *reelection*. For freshman classes in the 1970s and 1980s, this increase averaged between 7 percent and 9 percent. Put another way, the average freshman during these years was reelected with 65 percent to 70 percent of the vote. With two years to solidify their electoral followings, even freshmen elected by a marginal vote have reason to expect a lesser challenge the second time around—that is, unless they face a troubled or hostile electorate such as confronted Democratic freshmen in 1994.[24]

Competition between the parties for congressional seats apparently has never been particularly high. In the great majority of districts, the same party wins election after election. The data of Table 4.2 show the extent of interparty competition for congressional seats during six different intervals, beginning in 1914. The data reflect two measures of party competitiveness. One

TABLE 4.2    Interparty competition for congressional seats

| Time Period | Percentage of Fluidity | Percentage of No-Change Districts | Number of Changes |
|---|---|---|---|
| 1914–26 | 11.8 | 62.1 | 308 |
| 1932–40 | 10.6 | 69.9 | 184 |
| 1942–50 | 11.9 | 74.0 | 199 |
| 1952–60 | 7.8 | 78.2 | 135 |
| 1962–70 | 8.2 | 76.5 | 136 |
| 1972–80 | 9.1 | 68.7 | N.A. |

SOURCE: Charles O. Jones, "Inter-Party Competition for Congressional Seats," *Western Political Quarterly*, XVII (September 1964), 465. The data for the 1962–70 time period are drawn from Charles Bullock III, "Redistricting and Congressional Stability, 1962–72," *Journal of Politics*, XX–XVII (May 1975), 575; and for the period 1972–80, from Harvey L. Schantz, "Inter-Party Competition for Congressional Seats: The 1960s and 1970s," *Western Political Quarterly*, XL (June 1987), 373–83.

measure shows whether there was any change in party control over the time period studied; for example, in the five elections between 1972 and 1980, 68.7 percent of all congressional districts were won by the same party. The second measure registers a "percentage of fluidity"—how many alterations were made in party control during any period. In all House elections between 1972 and 1980, only 9.1 percent culminated in changes of party. The broad picture is one of limited competition between the parties for seats in Congress. By and large, each party wins where it is expected to win.

The data of Table 4.3 portray the regional patterns of party strength in Congress at certain intervals since the early 1960s. Several trends stand out. First, the importance of the South to the Democratic party has declined significantly. In 1961–62 (the Kennedy presidency), 42 percent of the House Democrats and 37 percent of the Senate Democrats were southerners. By the 106th Congress (1999–2000), the percentages had slipped to 26 in the House and 18 in the Senate. The contemporary Democratic party is more of a northern party than at any time in the last century. Its gains in Senate seats have been particularly impressive in the East. Second, the Republican party has dramatically increased its strength in southern and western states. More than one-third of the House Republicans are now elected from the South—a far cry from the 1950s, when the party often failed to run candidates in about half of the southern districts.[25] In the 106th Congress (1999–2000), nearly two-thirds of the Republican senators were from southern and western states.

Another way to explore competitiveness between parties is pictured in Figure 4.1. Developed by Joseph Schlesinger, this illustration employs two measures of competitiveness: The horizontal axis depicts the extent to which the parties have divided control of each state office, while the vertical axis shows the rate of turnover in control of the office between the parties. The

TABLE 4.3    The geographical basis of party strength in Congress—
percentage of each party's members by region, selected years

|  | East | Midwest | South | West |
|---|---|---|---|---|
| **House Democrats** |  |  |  |  |
| 1961–1962 (87th Congress) | 26 | 19 | 42 | 13 |
| 1971–1972 (92nd Congress) | 29 | 22 | 34 | 15 |
| 1979–1980 (96th Congress) | 28 | 24 | 31 | 17 |
| 1987–1988 (100th Congress) | 26 | 24 | 33 | 17 |
| 1991–1992 (102nd Congress) | 25 | 25 | 32 | 18 |
| 1995–1996 (104th Congress) | 27 | 22 | 31 | 20 |
| 1999–2000 (106th Congress) | 29 | 24 | 26 | 21 |
| **House Republicans** |  |  |  |  |
| 1961–1962 | 35 | 45 | 5 | 15 |
| 1971–1972 | 27 | 39 | 17 | 17 |
| 1979–1980 | 25 | 35 | 21 | 19 |
| 1987–1988 | 24 | 29 | 25 | 22 |
| 1991–1992 | 25 | 27 | 26 | 22 |
| 1995–1996 | 19 | 26 | 32 | 23 |
| 1999–2000 | 17 | 24 | 37 | 22 |
| **Senate Democrats** |  |  |  |  |
| 1961–1962 | 14 | 18 | 37 | 31 |
| 1971–1972 | 18 | 23 | 32 | 27 |
| 1979–1980 | 24 | 24 | 32 | 20 |
| 1987–1988 | 25 | 24 | 33 | 18 |
| 1991–1992 | 27 | 25 | 30 | 18 |
| 1995–1996 | 30 | 22 | 22 | 26 |
| 1999–2000 | 33 | 27 | 18 | 22 |
| **Senate Republicans** |  |  |  |  |
| 1961–1962 | 43 | 34 | 6 | 17 |
| 1971–1972 | 32 | 25 | 18 | 25 |
| 1979–1980 | 24 | 24 | 17 | 35 |
| 1987–1988 | 22 | 24 | 18 | 36 |
| 1991–1992 | 20 | 23 | 20 | 37 |
| 1995–1996 | 19 | 19 | 30 | 32 |
| 1999–2000 | 16 | 22 | 33 | 29 |

NOTE: *East:* CT, DE, ME, MD, MA, NH, NJ, NY, PA, RI, VT, WV.
*Midwest:* IL, IN, IA, KS, MI, MN, MO, NB, ND, OH, SD, WI.
*South:* AL, AR, FL, GA, KY, LA, MS, NC, OK, SC, TN, TX, VA.
*West:* AK, AZ, CA, CO, HI, ID, MT, NV, NM, OR, UT, WA, WY.

figure demonstrates convincingly that individual state offices vary sharply in competitiveness. Some offices regularly shift back and forth between the parties, whereas others are controlled for long stretches of time by the same party. For the country as a whole, excluding southern states ordinarily dominated by the Democrats, the least competitive office has been that of representative, the most competitive offices those of governor and senator.[26]

An important understanding is illuminated by this evidence: The

**FIGURE 4.1    Party competition for individual offices in selected states, 1914–58**

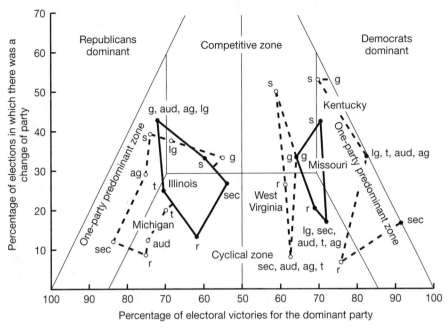

Office key:

| | | |
|---|---|---|
| g | : | Governor |
| s | : | Senator |
| r | : | Congressmen |
| lg | : | Lieutenant Governor |
| sec | : | Secretary of State |
| ag | : | Attorney General |
| aud | : | Auditor |
| t | : | Treasurer |

"... the more centrally located on the horizontal axis the more competitive an office was in over-all terms; the higher on the diagram the more rapid the rate of turnover; and correspondingly, the lower on the diagram an office falls, the longer the cycles of one-party control, regardless of the degree of over-all competition."

SOURCE: Joseph A. Schlesinger, "The Structure of Competition for Office in the American States," *Behavioral Science,* V (July 1960), 203.

American political party is a pastiche of disparate national, state, local, and personal organizations brought together for limited purposes. For reasons that are not easy to fathom, a party's candidates may run very well for some offices and very poorly for other offices—in election after election. The "structure of competition" for state and national offices is such that candidates are loosely affiliated with one another and with their parties. The dominant impression conveyed is that the candidates are on their own, a fact that requires them to develop their own campaign strategy, to siphon off financial support where they can find it, and to seize on transitory circumstances to put together their own electoral majority. How the party as a whole fares in an election is not of first importance to individual candidates; nor is it likely that party automatically will be of first importance once they have taken office. Following the evidence of this study, it seems plain that some major part of the explanation for party disunity in government, and perhaps especially in Congress, is found in the fragmentation of the electoral parties, marked by an inability of the parties to control a range of offices and by the necessity for candidates to develop their own personal organizations.

Once the relatively "permanent" character of the House is recognized, it is easy to understand why presidential legislative programs often encounter so much difficulty there. The popular impulses to which many members of Congress must respond are far from identical to those which spur the president. Moreover, many members have discovered how to maintain themselves securely in office, insulating their careers from national election tides and the vagaries of presidential elections. Presidents come and go; the House goes on and on.

### Members of Congress and the President's Coattails

The degree to which the voting strength of presidential candidates influences voting for congressional offices has long been a matter of interest and of speculation. It has often been assumed that the popularity of the victorious presidential candidate rubs off on his party's congressional candidates, swelling their votes and pulling some candidates into office who might not make it on their own. Congressional candidates, in other words, "ride" into office on the president's "coattails."

Although there are undoubtedly elections in which certain congressional candidates profit from the vote-amassing ability of the presidential candidate, it appears that the influence of the president's coattails is exaggerated. First, successful presidential candidates typically do not run ahead of their party's congressional candidates. Consider these recent examples. In 1984, Ronald Reagan ran behind his party's successful House candidates in 68 percent of the districts. The vote differential was even greater in 1988, when George Bush trailed his party's winning House candidates in 85 percent of the districts.[27] And in 1992, Bill Clinton ran behind winning Democratic congressional candidates in 71 percent of the districts (if only the major party vote is included, but 98 percent of the districts if the Perot vote is included).[28] A great many voters obviously split their tickets when voting for president and representative.[29]

A second difficulty with the coattail theory is that it makes no allowance for the capacity of congressional incumbents to withstand adverse presidential outcomes. Plainly, President Lyndon Johnson's coattails helped a number of Democratic congressional candidates to win office in 1964; the party increased its margin in the House by thirty-eight seats. And in 1980, Ronald Reagan's impressive victory over Jimmy Carter was accompanied by Republican gains of thirty-four seats in the House and twelve in the Senate.

But other presidential elections show much different outcomes. Although President Dwight Eisenhower won a lopsided victory in 1956, the Republican party actually lost two seats in the House. Richard Nixon's close election in 1968 was accompanied by a gain of only four Republican seats in the lower house, and his extraordinary margin over George McGovern in 1972 resulted in a gain of only twelve seats. George Bush's comfortable victory in 1988 was accompanied by a Republican loss of eight seats in the House. And although Bill Clinton easily won a second term in 1996, Democrats lost two seats in the Senate and gained only nine in the House. On the whole, congressional incumbents have been remarkably successful in insulating themselves from the vicissitudes of presidential contests, even in landslide years.

Third, the coattail theory ignores the losing presidential ticket. When the presidential candidate of the winning party does better than his congressional candidates, the presidential candidate of the losing party is bound to do worse than his congressional candidates. Finally, there are a great many districts wholly dominated by one party; here the presidential race has negligible impact on the fortunes of congressional candidates. About the most that can be said is that the impact of the president's coattails is felt mainly in two kinds of districts: marginal and open-seat.[30] That fact, of course, may be critical. For every additional percentage point of the two-party vote captured by the party's presidential candidate, one study has shown, the party can expect to win three additional House seats.[31] Some members from marginal districts do have reason to worry about the strength of their presidential ticket. A recent study by James Campbell and Joe Sumners finds that the effects of presidential coattails on Senate election results is "fairly modest." Much of the relationship between presidential and Senate votes stems from the fact that both votes come from the same partisan electorate.[32]

### Midterm Congressional Elections

Midterm congressional elections are characterized by four main patterns. First, voter participation declines sharply in the absence of a presidential contest—typically, in recent years, by about 16 percent. In all midterm elections from 1974 to 1994, turnout was below 40 percent of the eligible electorate. Second, the great majority of voters cast their ballots in keeping with their party identification. Although the rate of defection among party identifiers has increased significantly during the past two decades, party continues to be a major factor in voting decisions in both off-year and presidential elections. In all elections from 1956 to 1992, the proportion of votes cast by party identifiers for the House candidate of their party was never less than 69 percent; during most of these years about three-fourths of all voters in House elections were party-line voters. (See Table 4.4.) Third, when party defections occur in either off-year or presidential elections, they strongly favor incumbents.[33]

**TABLE 4.4   Party-line voting in House elections, 1960–96 (in percentages)**

| Year | Party-Line Voters | Defectors | Independents | Total |
|------|------|------|------|------|
| 1960 | 80 | 12 | 8 | 100 |
| 1962 | 83 | 12 | 5 | 100 |
| 1964 | 79 | 15 | 5 | 100 |
| 1966 | 76 | 16 | 8 | 100 |
| 1968 | 74 | 19 | 7 | 100 |
| 1970 | 76 | 16 | 8 | 100 |
| 1972 | 75 | 17 | 8 | 100 |
| 1974 | 74 | 18 | 8 | 100 |
| 1976 | 72 | 19 | 9 | 100 |
| 1978 | 69 | 22 | 9 | 100 |
| 1980 | 69 | 23 | 8 | 100 |
| 1982 | 76 | 17 | 6 | 100 |
| 1984 | 70 | 23 | 7 | 100 |
| 1986 | 72 | 22 | 6 | 100 |
| 1988 | 74 | 20 | 7 | 100 |
| 1990 | 72 | 22 | 5 | 100 |
| 1992 | 70 | 22 | 8 | 100 |
| 1994 | 77 | 17 | 6 | 100 |
| 1996 | 77 | 17 | 6 | 100 |

NOTE: Party-line voters are those who voted for the party with which they identified. (Those who considered themselves independents but stated that they leaned toward the Democratic or Republican party are treated as party-line voters.) Defectors are those who voted for the party other than that with which they identified. Independents are those who identified themselves as such and who voted for either candidate. Data may not add to 100 because of rounding.

SOURCE: Thomas E. Mann, *Unsafe at Any Margin: Interpreting Congressional Elections* (Washington, DC: American Enterprise Institute for Public Policy Research, 1978), p. 14; as updated by data in Norman J. Ornstein, Thomas E. Mann, and Michael J. Malbin, *Vital Statistics on Congress, 1997–1998 Edition* (Washington, DC: American Enterprise Institute for Public Policy Research, 1998), p. 75.

Fourth, and of most significance, the administration party at midterm nearly always loses seats in Congress, occasionally even its majority; the most recent examples of the latter are the Republican party's loss of its House majority in 1954 and its Senate majority in 1986, and the Democratic party's loss of both chambers in 1994. (See the evidence on midterm elections from 1922 to 1998 in Figure 4.2.) Only twice in the last century, in 1934 and 1998, has the party in control of the administration increased its representation at midterm. In 1934, in the first off-year election following Franklin D. Roosevelt's election, the Democrats increased their representation in the House by nine seats and in the Senate by ten seats. In 1998, the Democrats picked up five seats in the House and broke even in the Senate as voters rejected the Republican campaign focus on the impeachment of President

**FIGURE 4.2    Off-year gains and losses in Congress by the president's party, 1922–98**

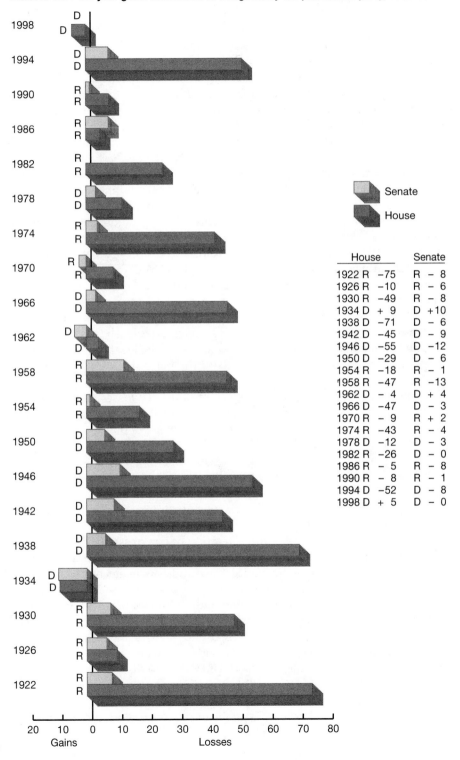

| House | | Senate | |
|---|---|---|---|
| 1922 R | −75 | R | − 8 |
| 1926 R | −10 | R | − 6 |
| 1930 R | −49 | R | − 8 |
| 1934 D | + 9 | D | +10 |
| 1938 D | −71 | D | − 6 |
| 1942 D | −45 | D | − 9 |
| 1946 D | −55 | D | −12 |
| 1950 D | −29 | D | − 6 |
| 1954 R | −18 | R | − 1 |
| 1958 R | −47 | R | −13 |
| 1962 D | − 4 | D | + 4 |
| 1966 D | −47 | D | − 3 |
| 1970 R | − 9 | R | + 2 |
| 1974 R | −43 | R | − 4 |
| 1978 D | −12 | D | − 3 |
| 1982 R | −26 | D | − 0 |
| 1986 R | − 5 | R | − 8 |
| 1990 R | − 8 | R | − 1 |
| 1994 D | −52 | D | − 8 |
| 1998 D | + 5 | D | − 0 |

Clinton. The most prominent casualty of the 1998 election reversal was Speaker Newt Gingrich (R., GA), who was forced out of his leadership position by disgruntled members of his own party.

The rise and fall of party fortunes, in presidential and midterm elections, affects both parties alike. No president has reason to count on improving his party's congressional position at midterm; on the contrary, he has every reason to fear the worst.

It is not a simple matter to explain why the president's party nearly always loses seats in midterm elections. The *Washington Post* once lamented, "The only conclusion that one can safely draw from American congressional elections is that the voters show a preference for the winners instead of for the losers."[34] Beguiling as that proposition is, there is more to the story.

The dominant interpretation of midterm losses holds that they are the result of the electorate's return to "normal"—in particular, to its normal partisan equilibrium—following the strains and dislocations of the previous presidential election. Although this view helps to explain why the president's party suffers losses at the midterm, it does not account for the magnitude of the shift in seats. It does not, in other words, explain why some presidents fare worse than others in off-year elections. Evidence offered by Edward R. Tufte discloses that two variables are closely associated with the dimensions of midterm congressional losses: the level of the president's popularity at the time of the election and the performance of the economy in the year of the election. If the president's popularity is low at midterm or if the economy is performing poorly (or both), the losses by the administration party are likely to be sharp. Conversely, the "in" party is likely to lose substantially fewer seats if the president's popularity is high or if the economy is performing well (or both). In this sense, the midterm vote is essentially a referendum, one in which members of Congress find themselves being "evaluated" by an electorate that is looking the other way—focusing on the president and assessing his administration's management of the economy.[35] Anomalies such as this, of course, are common to the lives of legislators.

A broad and compelling interpretation of congressional elections—including those in presidential as well as midterm years—is found in the "exposure thesis." Applicable for both House and Senate elections, the theory posits that at any one time each party holds a core of seats that corresponds to party loyalties and the normal vote within the electorate. These seats, in other words, are regularly won by the same party, election after election. Occasionally this equilibrium is disturbed and seats change hands. When a party becomes overexposed—that is, when it has won a number of seats that the other party traditionally has held—its vulnerability grows and it can be expected to lose seats at the next election. The reverse is also true. A party that is underexposed can be expected to gain seats in the next election, thus moving the parties back toward equilibrium. Exposure, a long-term force, is a major factor in congressional election outcomes. When the exposure factor is linked to the short-term forces of presidential popularity and the state of the economy, the resulting model yields a comprehensive explanation for the parties' fortunes in congressional races.[36]

Midterm elections provide both a brake to the development of *national* leadership centering in the presidency and an invitation to jarring stalemate between president and Congress; at the same time, they make it difficult to develop a national party system broadly responsible to the total electorate. Whatever else may be said of them, midterm elections contribute heavily to the preservation of tenaciously decentralized political parties. Abandonment of the two-year term for House members in favor of a four-year term would strengthen national party leadership, especially if all senators were elected for the same period. Political scientists, who seldom are chary about recommending change, appear to support the four-year term for House members with great enthusiasm. But this prescription, like others involving major congressional reform, has won no authentic audience among either legislators or the public. Currently, in fact, the public is clearly in favor of term limitations. (See Chapter 2.)

## The Pursuit of Reelection

Virtually all members of Congress share a common, overarching goal: reelection.[37] Nothing else matters so much, so preoccupies their attention, or so firmly shapes their behavior. If this is the members' singular goal, what can they do about it? Does what they do make a difference? Are there ways by which they can enhance their prospects for reelection? David R. Mayhew argues that there are three basic types of activities that legislators engage in, day in and day out, in order to be successful the next time around.

One activity is that of *advertising* one's name in a manner that is likely to produce a favorable image among constituents. Advertising requires no issue content. Members of Congress need to be seen as experienced, sincere, knowledgeable, and responsive. Visits to the constituency, speeches, newspaper articles, radio and television appearances,[38] and the use of the franking privilege are all devices of congressional advertising—most of them available at public expense.

Another activity may be described as *credit claiming*. Here the emphasis rests on the individual accomplishments of the legislator on behalf of specific people, groups, or the constituency as a whole. For members of Congress, taking care of business requires them to do all manner of "casework" and favors for individuals or groups, things for which they can take credit and that may be acknowledged in the voting booth. They also supply goods to the district in the form of post offices, dams, river and highway projects, and other public installations.[39] Numerous members believe that their longevity in office is due to their capacity to "deliver the goods" for "the folks back home."[40] Searching for opportunities to earn credit, or to appear to earn it, is nothing less than a vocation for most members of Congress.

A third activity of Congress is that of *position taking*, the making of judgments on matters of interest to the constituency or some sectors of it. One form of this is the roll-call vote. More important are the judgmental statements members make

> . . . prescribing American governmental ends (a vote cast against the war; a statement that "the war should be ended immediately") or governmental means (a statement that "the way to end the war is to take it to the United Nations"). The judgments may be implicit rather than explicit, as in: "I will support the president on this matter." . . . The congressman as a position taker is a speaker rather than a doer. The electoral requirement is not that he makes pleasing things happen but that he is making pleasing judgmental statements. The position itself is the political commodity.[41]

Members of Congress engage in these activities because they believe they make a difference. Measuring their effects is, of course, quite difficult. It is somewhat easier to observe the differences among members in the importance they attach to the different activities. In general, senators are more likely than House members to engage in position taking; as a group, House members appear to place greater reliance on credit taking. House members from "machine" cities are mainly concerned with the allocation of benefits to the district, whereas members from suburban, middle-class constituencies are more inclined to fasten on position taking. Senators and House members with ambitions for higher office spend more time on advertising and position taking than on credit claiming. Whatever the distinctive emphases, most members engage steadily and imaginatively in all three activities. By doing everything, they believe, the risks of losing can be diminished.[42]

Legislators stay in Congress by spending time in their constituencies and paying close attention to matters at home. It is interesting to find that constituency attentiveness does not decline with a member's increased seniority (and thus influence in Washington). Despite their additional responsibilities, committee chairs spend about as much time in their districts as the average member. An attentive home style is the norm in Congress.[43]

### Incumbents and Elections

In traditional interpretation, the great divide in American political campaigns is the factor of incumbency. Potential candidates for Congress may grow restive as the years pass by and the old hands in Washington hang on, but there is not much they can do except wait for death, retirement, or a major redistricting act to provide an opening. The members of Congress who work at staying in office and utilize the advantages that are available to them are exceedingly difficult to defeat. House members in particular often appear invulnerable. Some of the reasons for their successes are suggested in these comments by current and former members.

> I have the feeling that the most effective campaigning is done when no election is near. During the interval between elections you have to establish every personal contact you can, and you accomplish this through your mail as much as you do it by means of anything else. At the end of each session I take all the letters which have been received on legislative matters and write each person telling him how the legislative proposal in which he was interested stands.

> Personally, I will speak on any subject. I am not nonpartisan, but I talk on everything whether it deals with politics or not. Generally I speak at nonpolitical meetings. I read 48 weekly newspapers and clip every one of them myself. Whenever there is a particularly interesting item about anyone, that person gets a note from me. We also keep a complete list of the changes of officers in every organization in our district. Then when I am going into a town I know exactly who I would like to have at the meeting. I learned early that you had to make your way with Democrats as well as with Republicans. And you cannot let the matter of election go until the last minute. I budget 17 trips home each session and somehow I've never managed to go less than 21 times.[44]

> The reason I get 93-percent victories is what I do back home [in Detroit]. I stay highly visible. No grass grows under my feet. I show that I haven't forgotten from whence I came.[45]

> The newer guys keep a lot closer connections with their districts. In the old days, it was like a lifelong honor bestowed on you. In the South, it was a sacrilege to run against an incumbent congressman.[46]

Since 1900, the average advantage of House incumbents has been about two percentage points, according to research by Andrew Gelman and Gary King.[47] The superior position of incumbents stems from a number of factors. They have a public record to which they can refer, visibility gained through previous public exposure,[48] a disposition of the press to cover them rather than their challengers,[49] positions that enable them to help constituents with their problems, the franking privilege, a staff and offices, generous travel allowances, and exceptional access to campaign funds—especially from PACs. Voters are more familiar with them than with their challengers and like them better than their challengers; the public also has many more contacts with incumbents than with those who challenge them.[50] For some incumbents, the ability to scare away all challengers, thus leaving them with an uncontested election, may be their greatest advantage.[51]

The fact is that opportunities to exploit incumbency are limited only by an underdeveloped imagination. When he was serving as House majority leader, Jim Wright advised his Democratic colleagues to record "testimonials" from constituents who had received assistance from their offices. The cases should involve "at least some element of drama or human interest," he counseled. "Get about twenty of these little testimonials, schedule them for saturation broadcast in the days immediately prior to the election . . . it will sound as if the congressman has personally helped virtually everyone in town."[52]

The key factor in explaining competitiveness in House and Senate races, a large number of studies has shown, is the quality of the challenger. Incumbents typically are successful because they face weak opponents.[53] "Quality" candidates do better against incumbents, and sometimes defeat them, because they have more to offer—in particular, experience in public office (and, accordingly, experience in organizing and conducting campaigns). Governors, U.S. House members, and other officials holding state-wide offices thus are high-quality challengers to Senate incumbents. Challengers who hold less imposing offices, or no office at all, do not perform as well against incumbents.[54] Quality challengers are particularly effective in raising large sums of campaign money—the sine qua non of competitive campaigns.[55] Superior challengers are more numerous when national conditions, such as the state of the economy and the president's level of popular approval, appear to favor their party.[56]

The weakened influence of partisanship in congressional elections also has a bearing on the success of incumbents. David W. Romero and Francine Sanders have shown that voters' loosened partisan attachments increase the probability of an incumbent vote. In today's candidate-centered system, incumbents are not only better able to attract the votes of challenger party identifiers with weakened party attachments but also to retain the support of their own party's identifiers whose partisanship has been loosened.[57]

Incumbents also profit from the fact that voters are much better able to remember their names than the names of challengers—and name recall is strongly related to the vote. (But the singular fact is that candidates generally, incumbents and challengers alike, have lost salience for the voters—as judged by their ability to remember the names of candidates—over the past four decades.)[58]

Focusing on House elections in the late 1980s, Alan I. Abramowitz concludes that the most significant determinant of outcomes is the challenger's campaign spending. The low level of competition in House races results from the increasing costs of these campaigns and the declining ability of challengers to raise campaign money.[59]

The broad point, of course, is that relatively few incumbents lose their bids for reelection (see Table 4.5).[60] Incumbents rarely lose in primaries; only 8 of 1,172 House members seeking renomination were defeated in the elections of 1994, 1996, and 1998. Strange circumstances, of course, can produce strange results. In 1992, in the midst of a House banking scandal (numerous members were charged with overdrafts on the House bank), 19 House members were defeated at the primary stage.[61]

General elections carry somewhat greater risks for incumbents. Yet it is an unusual election, such as in 1994, in which fewer than 95 percent of

**TABLE 4.5**   The successes of incumbents in House and Senate elections, 1978–98

| Year | Defeated in Primary | Running in General Election | Elected in General Election | Defeated in General Election | Running in General Election Elected |
|---|---|---|---|---|---|
| | | **Total Number of Incumbents** | | | **Percentage of Incumbents** |
| **1978** | | | | | |
| House | 5 | 377 | 358 | 19 | 94.96 |
| Senate | 3 | 22 | 15 | 7 | 69.18 |
| **1980** | | | | | |
| House | 6 | 392 | 361 | 31 | 92.09 |
| Senate | 4 | 25 | 16 | 9 | 64.00 |
| **1982** | | | | | |
| House | 4 | 383 | 354 | 29 | 92.42 |
| Senate | 0 | 30 | 28 | 2 | 93.33 |
| **1984** | | | | | |
| House | 3 | 408 | 392 | 16 | 96.07 |
| Senate | 0 | 29 | 26 | 3 | 89.65 |
| **1986** | | | | | |
| House | 2 | 391 | 385 | 6 | 98.46 |
| Senate | 0 | 28 | 21 | 7 | 75.00 |
| **1988** | | | | | |
| House | 1 | 408 | 401 | 6 | 98.28 |
| Senate | 0 | 27 | 23 | 4 | 85.15 |
| **1990** | | | | | |
| House | 1 | 406 | 391 | 15 | 96.30 |
| Senate | 0 | 32 | 31 | 1 | 96.87 |
| **1992** | | | | | |
| House | 19 | 349 | 325 | 24 | 93.12 |
| Senate | 1 | 27 | 23 | 4 | 85.19 |
| **1994** | | | | | |
| House | 4 | 382 | 345 | 37 | 90.31 |
| Senate | 0 | 26 | 24 | 2 | 92.31 |
| **1996** | | | | | |
| House | 2 | 381 | 360 | 21 | 94.49 |
| Senate | 1 | 19 | 18 | 1 | 94.74 |
| **1998** | | | | | |
| House | 2 | 401 | 395 | 6 | 98.50 |
| Senate | 0 | 29 | 26 | 3 | 89.66 |

SOURCE: Various issues of *Congressional Quarterly Weekly Report.* The data for 1992–98 were provided by Eugene J. Gabler of Congressional Quarterly Inc.

incumbents are returned to Washington. "If a safe incumbent [winning by more than 60 percent in the previous election] avoids redistricting and scandal," Monica Bauer and John Hibbing contend, "chances of defeat are very close to nil."[62] Senators have more reason to worry about what the voters will do, but they also campaign from a position of strength.[63] The power of incumbency must be considered one of the most important facts to be known about the contemporary Congress. Even misologists would feel comfortable with that argument!

## State Legislative Elections

The broad facts concerning nominations and elections for state legislatures are about the same as for Congress. The important similarities are that (1) the influence of party organizations on legislative nominations has declined along a broad front; (2) in virtually all cases formal nominations are made in primaries; (3) incumbents are less likely to face opposition in primaries than nonincumbents;[64] (4) incumbents are not often defeated in either primary or general elections, and a growing number are unopposed in one or both elections;[65] (5) competition is less intense in states where members are best equipped with resources to provide constituent services;[66] (6) in running in their second election state legislative incumbents, like their congressional counterparts, greatly benefit from the "sophomore surge";[67] (7) in some states reapportionment has contributed to declining competition;[68] (8) the crucial battles for control of the legislature in competitive states take place in a relatively small number of marginal districts; (9) the proportion of marginal districts varies from one state to another and, within states, from one election to the next, but the broad trend is one of declining competition;[69] (10) the strength of gubernatorial and presidential coattails in state legislative races is about equal, and a strong race by either a gubernatorial or presidential candidate increases the party's share of legislative seats;[70] (11) the coattail effect carries particular significance for candidates in marginal districts; (12) PAC contributions decidedly favor incumbents;[71] and (13) as in the case of Congress, money plays a major role in state legislative elections.[72]

Legislative elections leave their imprint on state politics in many ways. One effect is especially important. A frequent outcome of state elections is that one party gains control of the governorship and the other party gains control of one or both houses of the legislature. The incidence of *divided government* in the states is at a high point. (See Table 4.6.) Currently the chances are better than one out of two that following each new state election the governor will face an opposition party majority in at least one of the two houses, and it is not unusual for the governor to find both houses under the control of the opposition party. Where divided party control is a common condition, it probably contributes as much to shaping the governor's legislative strategies as any other factor. The party that loses the governor's chair but wins a legislative majority, moreover, is often in the catbird seat, positioned to extract major concessions and to influence the thrust of state public policy in central ways.

Disparities between party gubernatorial and legislative victories are

**TABLE 4.6** Incidence of party division (governor versus legislature) following elections of 1994, 1996, and 1998

| Relation between Governor and Legislature | Following Election of 1994 | | Following Election of 1996 | | Following Election of 1998 | |
|---|---|---|---|---|---|---|
| | Number of States | Percent | Number of States | Percent | Number of States | Percent |
| Governor and majority in legislature not in same party | 26 | 53 | 31 | 63 | 26 | 53 |
| Governor and majority in legislature in same party | 23 | 47 | 18 | 37 | 23 | 47 |

SOURCE: Data from various issues of *Congressional Quarterly Weekly Report, World Almanac,* and *Book of the States.* Nebraska is excluded because it has a nonpartisan legislature.

due to a number of factors, including the election of legislature and executive for nonconcurrent terms, the use of staggered elections for upper and lower houses, and the separation of gubernatorial and presidential elections. The ability of some gubernatorial candidates to build nonparty personal followings by relying on their names, the media, and awesome campaign expenditures may be another explanation. Also, here and there, the distribution of safe legislative districts may give one party a distinct advantage over the other, regardless of the gubernatorial election. Deliberate electoral preference for divided executive-legislative control is perhaps another factor. Whatever the reasons, divided government undoubtedly makes it difficult to fix responsibility for decisions on either party. At worst, it gives rise to deadlock and internecine warfare between the parties.

### Vacancies in Congress and the State Legislatures

There are several methods for filling vacancies in legislative office because of the death, retirement, or (rarely) expulsion of members. The U.S. Constitution provides in the case of House vacancies that the governor of the affected state "shall issue writs of elections to fill such vacancies." In the case of the Senate, the Seventeenth Amendment stipulates that the governor "shall issue writs of election to fill such vacancies: provided, that the legislature of any state may empower the executive thereof to make temporary appointments until the people fill the vacancies by election as the legislature may direct."

House vacancies may be filled by calling for a special election,[73] or the selection of a replacement may be put off until the next regular election.[74] When a senatorial vacancy is filled by election, the senator chosen completes the term of the person he or she is replacing, instead of being elected to the usual six-year term. Unless a Senate vacancy occurs very close to an election, the governor ordinarily will appoint a new senator, who holds office until the next election. This appointment may rest on a clear understanding with party leaders in the state that he or she will serve only until the next election and not seek to win office in his or her own right: Such appointments are no more than holding operations. There are also cases in which the governor resigns, having earlier made an agreement to have a successor appoint him or her to fill the Senate vacancy. Only rarely do governors fail to appoint a member of their own political party to fill a vacancy, notwithstanding the party membership of the former senator.

Legislative vacancies occur far more frequently than might be imagined. From 1945 to 1971, only slightly more than half (51.4 percent) of the men and women who entered the U.S. Senate were elected to a regular six-year term. The remainder became senators either as a result of special elections (19.8 percent) or gubernational appointment (28.8 percent). It is interesting to find that appointed senators are especially vulnerable if they seek reelection. Over the period 1945–1971, only 40 percent of those appointed who sought reelection were successful, as compared with 80 percent of those who gained entry to the Senate through regular or special elections.[75]

The manner in which Senate vacancies are filled is obviously important since the newly appointed senator has all the legal powers of any other senator. The appointment may affect the partisan division of the Senate, the outcomes of closely contested votes, and the politics of the home state. A good case can be made that popular control of government would be enhanced if state legislatures adopted laws to eliminate the governor's role in this process and to provide for special elections to fill vacancies.[76]

Vacancies in the state legislature are filled by holding special elections; by giving the power of appointment to the governor; or by empowering a local agency, such as a party committee, county commission, or county court to appoint replacements. It is not at all unusual for legislative vacancies to be left open until the next regular election, a practice that deprives certain districts of direct representation during the interval.

## FINANCING CONGRESSIONAL CAMPAIGNS

At no time in American history has there been as much concern over the financing of political campaigns as during the current period. Scandals involving "political" money, coupled with sharply rising campaign expenditures, have heightened public awareness of this key element of American politics.

In response to growing pressure "to do something" about campaign finance, Congress passed a series of laws in the 1970s to regulate the use of money in elections. The most important were the 1974 amendments to the Federal Election Campaign Act (FECA). Under the terms of this legislation, public funds became available for the financing of both presidential *nominating* campaigns (under a private-public matching formula) and *election* campaigns (total funding). Although Congress chose to leave the financing of congressional campaigns in private hands, it adopted two important provisions regulating congressional campaign expenditures. The first restricted the *personal* campaign expenditures of Senate candidates to $35,000 and of House candidates to $25,000. The second placed restrictions on the *total expenditures* that could be incurred by congressional candidates in primaries and general elections. In a 1976 case, *Buckley* v. *Valeo*, the Supreme Court held that both limitations were unconstitutional, in violation of the First-Amendment right to free speech. It also ruled that limitations on individuals spending *independently* on behalf of a candidate were unconstitutional. Political money, the Court held, is closely associated with political speech.[77]

With congressional campaign finance left to the private domain and with no restrictions on either personal or total expenditures, campaign spending increased dramatically. Its growth is traced in Figure 4.3. In the 1998 election cycle (a two-year period including primary campaigns), candidates for Congress spent $740 million, about twice as much as spent in the campaigns a decade earlier. Plainly, campaign costs have increased at a much faster rate than inflation has.

Another perspective on campaign costs is available from evidence on spending by individual members. The data in Table 4.7 show campaign expenditures in 1994, 1996, and 1998 by House candidates in varying electoral circumstances. Several facts stand out. First, the typical House incumbent currently spends about half a million dollars on his or her reelection campaign, with Republicans generally spending more than Democrats. Second,

**TABLE 4.7**   Campaign expenditures of U.S. House candidates, 1994–98

|  | 1994 | 1996 | 1998 |
|---|---|---|---|
| Median expenditure by Democratic incumbents | $485,000 | $463,000 | $421,000 |
| Median expenditure by Republican incumbents | 398,000 | 589,000 | 529,000 |
| Median expenditure by Democratic open-seat candidates | 484,000 | 580,000 | 628,000 |
| Median expenditure by Republican open-seat candidates | 533,000 | 588,000 | 828,000 |
| Median expenditure by Democratic challengers | 72,000 | 122,000 | 91,000 |
| Median expenditure by Republican challengers | 132,000 | 98,000 | 160,000 |

SOURCE: Adapted from data in press release, Federal Election Commission, December 29, 1998.

**FIGURE 4.3** **Expenditures in congressional elections, 1982–98**

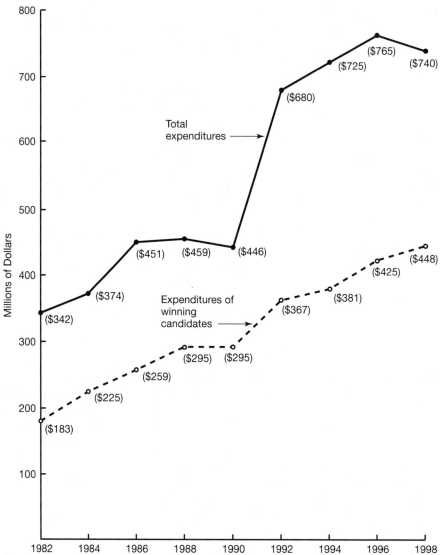

SOURCE: Federal Election Commission: http://www.fec.gov/press/canye98.htm. Primary expenditures are included.

campaigns for open seats (no incumbent) are especially expensive; the median expenditure for Republican open-seat candidates in 1998 was $828,000, and for Democrats $628,000.[78] And third, most challenger campaigns are woefully underfinanced, which helps to explain why they fare so poorly against incumbents. The one thing that winning challengers (never a large group) have in common is that invariably they are well financed. For the vast majority of challengers, about the only chance of getting to Washington is simply as a visitor.

Challengers suffer from three main financial disadvantages. First, incumbents outhustle them for money from the campaign's inception to its end, and as the election draws near their fund-raising advantages become even more pronounced. Second, challengers need contributions to secure more contributions; disappointing results in the early and middle stages of the campaign frustrate efforts to raise money near its end. And third, few challengers have fund-raising reserves to respond either to opportunities or to the incumbent's sudden funneling of unexpectedly large sums of money into the campaign. Well-financed, incumbents are poised to react rapidly to campaign events, while challengers are not.[79]

The data in Table 4.8 are particularly instructive because they show how expensive House campaigns have become in marginal districts. In 1998, the typical Democratic or Republican incumbent spent about $1 million to win reelection in a competitive district. The median expenditure for five Democratic challengers who won was about $1.3 million. The most expensive campaigns, on the whole, took place in open-seat districts, where the median expenditure for the candidates of both parties was roughly $1.1 million.[80] In closely contested districts, it is apparent, both parties pull out all the stops in raising and spending money.

Some spending bursts in House campaigns are astonishing. The 1998 campaign of Speaker Newt Gingrich (R., GA) reported disbursements of $7.3

TABLE 4.8   **The cost of winning a House seat in closely contested districts: Median expenditures in 1994, 1996, and 1998**

|  | | *1994* | | *1996* | | *1998* |
|---|---|---|---|---|---|---|
| Democratic incumbents who won | (40) | $642,000 | (19) | $ 847,000 | (11) | $ 977,000 |
| Republican incumbents who won | (7) | 741,000 | (38) | 918,000 | (16) | 1,061,000 |
| Democratic challengers who won | (0) | 0 | (14) | 826,000 | (5) | 1,226,000 |
| Republican challengers who won | (10) | 414,000 | (3) | 1,164,000 | (1) | 823,000 |
| Democrats who won open seats | (8) | 568,000 | (12) | 782,000 | (8) | 1,133,000 |
| Republicans who won open seats | (13) | 440,000 | (11) | 712,000 | (7) | 1,129,000 |

NOTE: These data are for districts where the winner received 55 percent or less of the vote. The number of districts is shown in parentheses.

SOURCE: Adapted from data in press release, Federal Election Commission, December 29, 1998.

million, whereas Minority Leader Richard Gephardt (D., MO) spent $3.1 million. A Democratic House candidate in New Mexico spent $5.3 million in losing narrowly to a Republican incumbent who spent $1.1 million. A former Republican congressman in California spent $3.7 million in losing to a Democratic congresswoman who spent $2.4 million. Altogether, ninety-four House candidates spent more than $1 million in their 1998 campaigns.[81] The fact of the matter is that million-dollar House campaigns are now commonplace.

Getting elected to the Senate is even more expensive. In the 1998 election cycle, twenty-one candidates spent more than $4 million and twenty-nine more than $3 million. The median expenditure for winning Senate candidates was $3.8 million. The costliest Senate campaign in 1998 was that of New York, where Charles Schumer spent $16 million in defeating Alfonse D'Amato, who spent $24 million.[82] The most expensive Senate campaign in history took place in California in 1994, when Dianne Feinstein spent nearly $15 million to win reelection over her Republican opponent, Michael Huffington, who spent $30 million.

Campaign funds are derived from several sources. Contributions of individuals are most important. In 1998, these contributions (limited to $1,000 per election) made up 62 percent of the funds raised by all Senate candidates and 53 percent of the funds raised by all House candidates. Ranking next are the campaign gifts of political action committees (PACs). In 1998, PAC contributions made up 37 percent of the receipts of all House candidates and 19 percent of the receipts of all Senate candidates. In all, individual and PAC contributions accounted for about 81 percent of the funds collected by Senate candidates and about 90 percent of the funds collected by House candidates.[83] The other sources are party contributions, loans, and candidate contributions.

One of the major developments in congressional campaign finance is the heightened involvement of political interest groups. (See Figure 4.4.) Operating through their PACs, labor, corporate,[84] trade, membership, health, and other groups gave $83.6 million to congressional campaigns in 1982 and a whopping $206.8 million in 1998.

Virtually all candidates for Congress are assisted by PAC contributions, but the funds are by no means distributed indiscriminately. Labor PACs, for example, gave 91 percent of their funds to Democratic candidates in 1998, and business PACs contributed 70 percent of their funds to Republican candidates.[85] The important factor in PAC contributions, however, is not party but incumbency. Eighty percent of all PAC money contributed to House candidates in 1998 was given to incumbents, eight times as much as contributed to challengers (10 percent); another 10 percent was funneled to candidates for open seats. Senate incumbents received almost six times as much PAC money as challengers.[86] Among incumbents, the leading beneficiaries are always party leaders, committee chairs, and members of major committees.

The data of Table 4.9 illuminate the importance of PAC gifts to

**FIGURE 4.4    PAC contributions to House and Senate candidates, 1982–98**

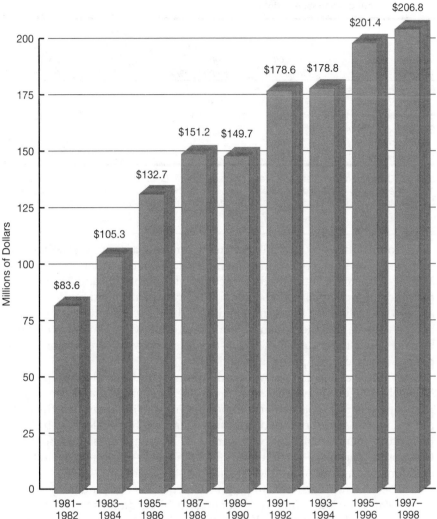

SOURCE: Federal Election Commission: http://www.fec.gov/press/canye98.htm.

incumbents. House members in particular depend on interest-group money. In 1998, 47 percent of all campaign money raised by House Democrats came from PACs, and for House Republicans, 39 percent. The average Democratic incumbent accepted $308,000 from PACs, the average Republican incumbent $304,000. Sixty-four House incumbents had PAC receipts in excess of $500,000. Minority leader Richard Gephardt (D., MO) led the way with PAC gifts totaling nearly $1.2 million.[87]

**TABLE 4.9**   **The relative dependence of incumbents on PAC funds, by party, 1998 congressional elections**

|  | Net Receipts (in millions) | Receipts from PACs (in millions) | Percent of Receipts Contributed by PACs | Average PAC Contributions per Member |
|---|---|---|---|---|
| House Incumbents |  |  |  |  |
| Democrats (194) | $126.5 | $59.8 | 47 | $ 308,000 |
| Republicans (211) | 162.5 | 64.1 | 39 | 304,000 |
| Senate Incumbents |  |  |  |  |
| Democrats (15) | 66.3 | 15.5 | 23 | 1,030,000 |
| Republicans (14) | 68.0 | 17.8 | 26 | 1,271,000 |

SOURCE: Calculated from data in a press release, Federal Election Commission, December 29, 1998. The number of candidates in each category is shown in parentheses. Other sources of funds include individual contributions, loans, party contributions, and candidate contributions.

Contributions by PACs to Senate incumbents are sizable, though they represent a smaller proportion of members' total receipts than in the House. Twenty-six percent of the funds of incumbent Republicans and 23 percent of the funds of incumbent Democrats in 1998 were contributed by PACs, averaging $1.3 million for the former and $1 million for the latter. Four incumbents each accepted more than $1.9 million from PACs.[88] Whatever else may be said about the infusion of interest-group money in congressional campaigns, it arrives in impressive quantities.

A study of the campaign contributions of PACs by Kevin Grier and Michael Munger shows that the committee assignments and seniority of House members are particularly important in enabling them to attract PAC money, whereas most of the contributions garnered by senators are based on their party membership and voting record. This pattern is consistent with traditional interpretations that stress the importance of committees in House decision making and of individualism in Senate behavior.[89]

The Federal Election Campaign Act regulates how much money the parties can contribute directly to congressional candidates and how much they can spend on their behalf. Direct contributions by party committees are not of large consequence—for *both* parties in 1998, the total was only about $4 million—but party spending on behalf of candidates, so-called *coordinated expenditures*, is clearly important. In 1998, Democratic committees allocated $18.6 million for coordinated spending, and Republican committees about $15.7 million.[90] Although these are sizable amounts (about eight times as large as direct contributions), they do not stack up well with overall PAC contributions, which amounted to $206.8 million in 1998. Nevertheless, coordinated spending may well be critical in some congressional campaigns.

The central role of interest groups in financing congressional campaigns stems from several factors.[91] First, the number of PACs has increased significantly, from about 700 in the mid-1970s to about 4,000 by the year 2000. Second, presidential candidates who accept public financing of their campaigns cannot accept private contributions (though groups and individuals can spend unlimited sums on *behalf* of presidential candidates); this limitation doubtlessly has encouraged groups to focus on congressional races. Third, no limits exist on the amount of money that can be collected and spent by candidates for Congress, making them as anxious to receive campaign money as PACs are to provide it—a marriage of convenience if ever there was one. What is more, incumbents are encouraged to raise funds because they believe that a large campaign treasury tends to discourage potential challengers. Some prominent members of Congress have in fact created their own PACs to raise campaign funds to assist allies and to promote themselves.[92] And finally, heavy interest-group involvement in this phase of politics owes something to the dramatic increase in campaign costs as candidates make greater use of television and as charges for television time have soared.[93] Other sophisticated techniques, such as polling and targeted mailings, have also become major items in many campaign budgets. The result of these new costs and opportunities is that congressional candidates hustle money as never before.

There are two central issues posed for Congress involving campaign finance. One is whether to extend public financing, linked to expenditure limits, to congressional campaigns. This proposal is seen, from one perspective, as a way of limiting runaway campaign costs, attracting small contributors, curtailing corrupt practices, and diminishing the reliance of congressional candidates on the contributions of "special interests."[94] Others see it as an incumbent-protection device as well as a waste of "taxpayer's dollars." Republican members in particular are dubious about the merits of any public financing bill with low spending ceilings, the effect of which might be to limit the capacity of their party's candidates to challenge Democratic incumbents.[95] And there are members in *both* parties who are apprehensive about changes that might make it easier for challengers to mount campaigns against them. Legislation to provide for the public financing of congressional campaigns, in sum, encounters opposition from all those members who, for varied reasons, are more comfortable with the apparent predictability that accompanies private financing.

The other major issue that troubles more and more members of Congress, as well as many outside observers, is the heavy flow of PAC money into congressional campaigns. The root of the matter is a suspicion that donor groups gain policy preferments of one kind or another, thereby undermining popular control of the representative system. Some members of Congress stress the need for reform because raising campaign funds requires so much of their time and energy. Former Senator Brock Adams (D., WA) makes this point:

I never imagined how much of my personal time could be spent on fundraising. Whether it was personal phone calls asking for a contribution, meeting
with potential donors, fundraising receptions in and out of the state, I spent at
least 50 percent of my time asking for money. . . . When I was traveling the state
my mornings began with fundraising calls and my evenings ended with
fundraising calls. . . .

I do not think a candidate for the U.S. Senate should have to sit in a motel room
in Goldendale, Washington, at 6 in the morning and spend three hours on the
phone talking to political action committees. . . . I was not talking to individual
contributors. . . . I was talking to professional politicians, the folks who make a
living figuring out the odds on each race and betting the percentages. . . . They
were not only afraid of the incumbent, they were trying to decide how much
money I had. It became an endless circle, the chicken and the egg. "If you do
not have it, you cannot get it. If you get it, you get more." Those political pros
told me again and again I could not win because I had not raised either enough
early money or enough late money or enough middle money, but it always
came down to I had not raised enough money. Well, I did win. What bothers
me most of all is I wish I had been able to win by debating the issues with my
opponent rather than debating my political prospects with political banks.[96]

Proposals to overhaul the system for financing congressional campaigns have received substantial attention in Congress in recent years. The
best known of these is the McCain-Feingold bill, named for its sponsors, Senators John McCain (R., AZ) and Russell D. Feingold (D., WI). Illustrative of
current mainstream thinking about reform, McCain-Feingold would ban soft
money (money that cannot be used in connection with federal elections),
constrict PAC contributions, and provide incentives for candidates to adhere
to voluntary spending limits. Senate spending limits would be based on each
state's voting-age population, ranging from $1.5 million in a small state like
Wyoming to $8.5 million in a large state like California. House spending lim-
its would be set at $600,000. Candidates who voluntarily comply with these
limits would be entitled to thirty minutes of free prime broadcast time, dis-
counts on additional broadcast time, and reduced postal rates. Moreover, if a
candidate's opponent exceeded the spending limit, the complying candidate
could accept larger individual contributions and exceed the limit as well.

Under the McCain-Feingold legislation, PAC contributions would be
cut from $5,000 to $1,000 in primary and general elections, with the additional proviso that House candidates could not accept more than 20 percent
of the spending limit from PACs and Senate candidates no more than 25
percent from this source. Another feature would provide that 60 percent of
all contributions must come from home-state residents. Bundling of contributions would be outlawed. (A party committee can evade spending limits
by getting donors to write checks directly to candidates; the party then bun-
dles them together and delivers them. These contributions are not recorded
as party receipts or expenditures. PACs do the same thing.) In addition, candidates in compliance with the spending limits would be permitted to

exceed them if necessary to counterattack ads financed through independent expenditures.

Whatever the motives that underlie members' attitudes toward campaign finance reform, it is plain that this issue bears peculiarly on congressional careers. Members are tempted to evaluate all proposals for reform in personal and political terms, favoring or opposing legislation in light of its probable impact on their electoral security and the welfare of their party. At the same time, members feel pressure to do something in view of the runaway costs of recent years and the heavy involvement of PACs in campaign spending.

Despite the partisan conflict that has smothered campaign finance legislation in recent years, as in 1999, Congress may be coming closer to passing some type of reform bill. Campaign finance scandals, such as those of 1996, highlight the need for tighter regulations. Members feel the heat. What is more, members of both parties now profess the need to reduce out-of-state funding, to rein in soft-money contributions and spending, to diminish candidates' excessive reliance on PAC money, and to make the playing field at least somewhat more level for challengers. And there is broad support on both sides of the aisle for legislation that would cut the cost of television time for candidates and require broadcasters to make available for campaign messages the best time slots in their advertising schedules. Whatever changes ultimately are made, one should expect the legislation to contain a number of provisions that benefit the members who adopted it.

## ELECTIONS AND THE LEGISLATURE

Decisions made at the recruitment and election stages of the American political process are as likely to shape legislative behavior as decisions made by legislators themselves once in office. The selection of legislators settles a great many matters in advance of sessions.[97] Who runs, who wins, who loses—all help to form the boundaries within which the legislative process takes place.[98] The appearance of slack, options, or room for maneuver in the legislature may be more illusory than real. Recruitment determines whether the legislature will be populated by "lawmakers" or "spectators," by those who take their work seriously or by those who sit around watching others. The early decisions concerning who is to be recruited for legislative office are of critical importance because once members are established in office they are exceedingly difficult to dislodge. Old legislators may die, but they rarely fade away.

Similar observations may be made of legislative elections. They may constitute a sharp break with the past, and thereby contribute to different policy outcomes in the legislature, or they may duplicate the previous election, and thereby impose continuity on legislative decision making.[99] Losses by the president's party in off-year elections, for example, usually do more to define the character of congressional decisions (and executive-legislative relations) than any amount of resourcefulness on the part of legislative leaders of his party or of unity among the rank-and-file members. To a striking degree, legislative decisions are tailored to the measure of earlier election victories and losses.

Two concluding observations may help to fill out the argument. First, when legislators are largely on their own, as is the case generally in the American political system, there is scant reason to expect them to take cues from sources that have slight bearing on their careers. Some legislators live with risk and insecurity. Others thrive in safe districts. Party support is not necessarily critical to the careers of legislators from either marginal or safe districts. The independence of the American legislator is a fact of extraordinary significance for understanding the performance of legislative parties. More will be said about this in later chapters.

Second, when the membership of the legislature is generally *stable*, as in the case of Congress, there is scant reason to expect it to come forth with legislative proposals that depart sharply from previous settlements. Old policies have a tendency to look strictly modern to those who originally made them. Moreover, newcomers to the system, who might be more inclined to abandon past policies and practices, ordinarily lack the political resources to make their preferences count. Finally, what sometimes impresses outsiders as curious or irresolute legislative response to new demands or nagging problems may appear to legislators themselves as both appropriate and necessary. The stakes are rarely quite the same for nonmembers as for members. Left mainly to their own devices, legislators stay in office by viewing large questions in a parochial light and by making self-preservation one of their chief priorities.

## NOTES

1. For a comprehensive inventory and analysis of research on legislative recruitment in both American and non-American systems, see Donald R. Matthews, "Legislative Recruitment and Legislative Careers," *Legislative Studies Quarterly*, IX (November 1984), 547–85.
2. See an instructive review essay on the recruitment and retention of legislators by Gary F. Moncrief, "Recruitment and Retention in U.S. Legislatures," *Legislative Studies Quarterly*, XXIV (May 1999), 173–208.
3. Lester G. Seligman, "Political Recruitment and Party Structure: A Case Study," *American Political Science Review*, LV (March 1961), 77–86; and "A Prefatory Analysis of Leadership Selection in Oregon," *Western Political Quarterly*, XII (March 1959), 153–67; John C. Wahlke, Heinz Eulau, William Buchanan, and LeRoy C. Ferguson, *The Legislative System: Explanations in Legislative Behavior* (New York: Wiley, 1962), Chap. 5; Frank J. Sorauf, *Party and Representation: Legislative Politics in Pennsylvania* (New York: Atherton Press, 1963), Chap. 5.
4. Sorauf, *Party and Representation*, p. 89.

5. Wahlke et al., *Legislative System,* pp. 95–97.

6. Richard J. Tobin, "The Influence of Nominating Systems on the Political Experiences of State Legislators," *Western Political Quarterly,* XXVIII (September 1975), 554–59. The percentages of legislators who had held previous public office were Connecticut, 79.6; Pennsylvania, 59.7; Minnesota, 41.3; and Washington, 40.7. (Since 1973, Minnesota legislators have been elected on a partisan ballot.)

7. Seligman, "Political Recruitment and Party Structure," 85–86.

8. Ibid., 84.

9. James D. Barber, *The Lawmakers: Recruitment and Adaptation to Legislative Life* (New Haven, CT: Yale University Press, 1965), pp. 10–15 (quotation on p. 13).

10. Paul S. Herrnson, *Party Campaigning in the 1980s* (Cambridge, MA: Harvard University Press, 1988), pp. 49–50, 86.

11. Thomas A. Kazee and Mary C. Thornberry, "Where's the Party? Congressional Candidate Recruitment and American Party Organizations," *Western Political Quarterly,* XLIII (March 1990), 61–80.

12. L. Sandy Maisel and Walter J. Stone, "Determinants of Candidate Emergence in U.S. House Elections: An Exploratory Study," *Legislative Studies Quarterly,* XXII (February 1997), 79–96. Also see Walter J. Stone, L. Sandy Maisel, and Cherie Maestas, "Candidate Emergence in U.S. House Elections," paper delivered at the Annual Meeting of the American Political Science Association, Boston, September 3–6, 1998. This paper stresses the importance of incumbency in deterring potential candidates from running for the House.

13. *New York Times,* March 15, 1998.

14. Linda L. Fowler and Robert D. McClure, *Political Ambition: Who Decides to Run for Congress* (New Haven, CT: Yale University Press, 1989), p. 2. Also see Linda L. Fowler, "Congressional Recruitment and Political Context," in *Home Style and Washington Work,* ed. Morris P. Fiorina and David W. Rohde (Ann Arbor: University of Michigan Press, 1989), pp. 47–69.

15. See an account of the striking success that party-endorsed state legislative candidates have in Minnesota by Joseph A. Kunkel III, "Party Endorsement and Incumbency in Minnesota Legislative Nominations," *Legislative Studies Quarterly,* XIII (May 1988), 211–23.

16. *Politics, Parties, and Pressure Groups* (New York: Thomas Y. Crowell, 1964), p. 377.

17. See an interesting literature that examines the relationship between competitive primaries and general election voting. The question is, Does a hard-fought primary hurt the party's chances for victory in the general election? The results are mixed. For research on this question, see Patrick J. Kenney and Tom W. Rice, "The Effect of Primary Divisiveness in Gubernatorial and Senatorial Elections," *Journal of Politics,* XLVI (August 1984), 904–15; Richard Born, "The Influence of House Primary Divisiveness on General Election Margins 1962–76," *Journal of Politics,* XLIII (August 1981), 640–61; Robert A. Bernstein, "Divisive Primaries Do Hurt: U.S. Senate Races, 1956–1972," *American Political Science Review,* LXXI (June 1977), 540–45; Patrick J. Kenney and Tom W. Rice, "The Relationship Between Divisive Primaries and General Election Outcomes," *American Journal of Political Science,* XXXI (February 1987), 31–44; and Patrick J. Kenney, "Sorting Out the Effects of Primary Divisiveness in Congressional and Senatorial Elections," *Western Political Quarterly,* XLI (September 1988), 765–77. For a study of this question at the presidential level, see Walter J. Stone, "The Carryover Effect in Presidential Elections," *American Political Science Review,* LXXX (March 1986), 271–79.

18. Quoted in the report of the Committee on Political Parties of the American Political Science Association, *Toward a More Responsible Two-Party System* (New York: Holt, Rinehart & Winston, 1950), p. 27.

19. Harvey L. Schantz, "Contested and Uncontested Primaries for the U.S. House," *Legislative Studies Quarterly,* V (November 1980), 545–62.

20. In primary elections, Robert A. Bernstein has shown, Democratic incumbents lose support by being too conservative, while Republican incumbents hurt themselves by being too liberal. See his article, "Limited Ideological Accountability in House Races: The Conditioning Effect of Party," *American Politics Quarterly,* XX (April 1992), 192–204.

21. Richard F. Fenno, Jr., has suggested that *subjective* assessments of marginality by members of Congress may be considerably more important in explaining their behavior than the objective electoral margin figures. Thus many members may feel that their seats are in jeopardy even though past general election results would indicate that they have nothing to worry about. In this connection Fenno finds virtually no relationship between electoral margins and the frequency of trips to the home district. In addition, the member who regularly wins by a large margin in the general election—thus apparently enjoying a "safe" seat—may have serious challenges at the primary stage. *Home Style: House Members in Their Districts* (Boston: Little, Brown, 1978), pp. 35–36. For a close examination of an individual senator's attentiveness to his constituency, see William A. Taggart and Robert F. Durant, "Home Style of a U.S. Senator: A Longitudinal Analysis," *Legislative Studies Quarterly*, X (November 1985), 489–504.

22. David R. Mayhew, "Congressional Elections: The Case of the Vanishing Marginals," *Polity*, VI (Spring 1974), 295–317.

23. See Morris P. Fiorina, "The Case of the Vanishing Marginals: The Bureaucracy Did It," *American Political Science Review*, LXXI (March 1977), 177–81. For different perspectives on the decline in the number of marginal seats, see Gary C. Jacobson, "The Marginals Never Vanished: Incumbency and Competition in Elections to the U.S. House of Representatives, 1952–82," *American Journal of Political Science*, XXXI (February 1987), 126–41; Glenn R. Parker and Suzanne L. Parker, "Correlates and Effects of Attention to District by U.S. House Members," *Legislative Studies Quarterly*, X (May 1985), 223–42; Robert S. Erikson and Gerald C. Wright, "Voters, Candidates, and Issues in Congressional Elections," in *Congress Reconsidered*, ed. Lawrence C. Dodd and Bruce I. Oppenheimer (Washington, DC: Congressional Quarterly Press, 1985), pp. 87–108; Jon R. Bond, Gary Covington, and Richard Fleisher, "Explaining Challenger Quality in Congressional Elections," *Journal of Politics*, XLVII (May 1985), 510–29; Glenn R. Parker, "Stylistic Change in the U.S. Senate," *Journal of Politics*, XLVII (November 1985), 1190–1202; John C. McAdams and John R. Johannes, "Constituency Attentiveness in the House: 1977–1982," *Journal of Politics*, XLVII (November 1985), 1108–39; D. Roderick Kiewiet and Mathew D. McCubbins, "Congressional Appropriations and the Electoral Connection," *Journal of Politics*, XLVII (February 1985), 59–82; Albert D. Cover, "The Electoral Impact of Franked Congressional Mail," *Polity*, XVII (Summer 1985), 649–63; John R. Owens, "Economic Influences on Elections to the U.S. Congress," *Legislative Studies Quarterly*, IX (February 1984), 123–50; Bruce E. Cain, John A. Ferejohn, and Morris P. Fiorina, "The Constituency Service Basis of the Personal Vote for U.S. Representatives and British Members of Parliament," *American Political Science Review*, LXXVIII (March 1984), 110–25; Larry Wade and John R. Owens, "Federal Spending in Congressional Districts," *Western Political Quarterly*, XXXVII (September 1984), 404–23; Donald A. Gross and James C. Garand, "The Vanishing Marginals, 1824–1980," *Journal of Politics*, XLVI (February 1984), 224–37; Gary C. Jacobson, "The Effects of Campaign Spending in Congressional Elections," *American Political Science Review*, LXXII (June 1978), 469–91; John R. Johannes and John C. McAdams, "The Congressional Incumbency Effect: Is It Casework, Policy Compatibility, or Something Else?" *American Journal of Political Science*, XXV (August 1981), 512–42; Melissa P. Collie, "Incumbency, Electoral Safety, and Turnover in the House of Representatives, 1952–1976," *American Political Science Review*, LXXV (March 1981), 119–31; John R. Alford and John R. Hibbing, "Increased Incumbency Advantage in the House," *Journal of Politics*, XLIII (November 1981), 1042–61; Roy A. Dawes and A. Hunter Bacot, "Electoral Career Patterns and Incumbency Advantage in the U.S. House of Representatives," *Legislative Studies Quarterly*, XXIII (November 1998), 575–83; Richard Born, "Generational Replacement and the Growth of Incumbent Reelection Margins in the U.S. House," *American Political Science Review*, LXXIII (September 1979), 811–17; Diana Evans Yiannakis, "The Grateful Electorate: Casework and Congressional Elections," *American Journal of Political Science*, XXV (August 1981), 568–80; Lyn Ragsdale, "Incumbent Popularity, Challenger Invisibility, and Congressional Voters," *Legislative Studies Quarterly*, VI (May 1981), 201–18; James L. Payne, "The Personal Electoral Advantage of House Incumbents, 1936–1976," *American Politics Quarterly*, VIII (October 1980), 465–82; Candice J. Nelson, "The Effect of Incumbency on Voting in Congressional Elections, 1964–1974," *Political Science Quarterly*, XCIII (Winter 1978–79), 665–78; John A. Ferejohn, "On the Decline in Competition in Congressional Elections," *American Political Science Review*, LXXI (March 1977), 166–76; and Albert D. Cover, "One

Good Term Deserves Another: The Advantage of Incumbency in Congressional Elections," *American Journal of Political Science,* XXI (August 1977), 523–41. For an interesting case study of why incumbents win, see John F. Bibby, "The Case of the Young Old Pro: The Sixth District of Wisconsin," in *The Making of Congressmen: Seven Campaigns of 1974,* ed. Alan L. Clem (North Scituate, MA: Duxbury Press, 1976), pp. 209–34.

24. See the freshman class (reelection) data for the elections of 1974, 1976, 1978, and 1982 in *Congressional Quarterly Weekly Report,* January 9, 1982, p. 36; and William J. Keefe, *Congress and the American People* (Englewood Cliffs, NJ: Prentice Hall, 1988), p. 74.

25. For evidence on the growing capacity of the Republican party to contest state senate elections in the South, see Joseph A. Aistrup, "Republican Contestation of the U.S. State Senate Elections in the South," *Legislative Studies Quarterly,* XV (May 1990), 227–45.

26. "The Structure of Competition for Office in the American States," *Behavioral Science,* V (July 1960), 197–210.

27. See Norman J. Ornstein, Thomas E. Mann, and Michael J. Malbin, *Vital Statistics on Congress, 1989–1990* (Washington, DC: Congressional Quarterly Press, 1990), p. 63.

28. Norman J. Ornstein, Thomas E. Mann, and Michael J. Malbin, *Vital Statistics on Congress, 1993–1994* (Washington, DC: Congressional Quarterly Press, 1994), p. 65.

29. The great bulk of the literature on presidential-congressional voting finds the coattail effect to be of declining importance. Nevertheless, some scholars attach more significance to the presidential vote than others. For differing perspectives and approaches, see James E. Campbell, "Predicting Seat Gains from Presidential Coattails," *American Journal of Political Science,* XXX (February 1986), 165–83; Albert D. Cover, "Party Competence Evaluations and Voting for Congress," *Western Political Quarterly,* XXXIX (June 1986), 304–12; Alan I. Abramowitz, Albert D. Cover, and Helmut Norpoth, "The President's Party in Midterm Elections: Going from Bad to Worse," *American Journal of Political Science,* XXX (August 1986), 562–76; Albert D. Cover, "Presidential Evaluations and Voting for Congress," *American Journal of Political Science,* XXX (November 1986), 786–801; Richard Born, "Reassessing the Decline of Presidential Coattails: U.S. House Elections from 1952–1980," *Journal of Politics,* XLVI (February 1984), 60–79; John A. Ferejohn and Randall L. Calvert, "Congressional Elections in Historical Perspective," *American Journal of Political Science,* XXVIII (February 1984), 127–46; Randall L. Calvert and John A. Ferejohn, "Coattail Voting in Recent Presidential Elections," *American Political Science Review,* LXXVII (June 1983), 407–19; and George C. Edwards III, "Impact of Presidential Coattails on Outcomes in Congressional Elections," *American Politics Quarterly,* VII (January 1979), 94–108.

30. For evidence on the impact of presidential coattails on outcomes in open-seat districts, see Jeffrey J. Mondak, "Presidential Coattails and Open Seats: The District-Level Impact of Heuristic Processing," *American Politics Quarterly,* XXI (July 1993), 307–19. The voters' need for cognitive efficiency prompts them to use their evaluations of the presidential candidates as cues for casting their votes for congressional candidates. See Jeffrey J. Mondak and Carl McCurley, "Cognitive Efficiency and the Congressional Vote: The Psychology of Coattail Voting," *Political Research Quarterly,* XLVII (March 1994), 151–75. The number of open-seat races decisively affected by presidential coattails, however, is not particularly large. Gregory N. Flemming finds that coattails perhaps made a difference between winning or losing in about 13 percent of the House open-seat contests between 1972 and 1992 (34 of 254 races). When presidential coattails are decisive, it is because the president carried the district by an unusually large margin and the race was unusually close. "Presidential Coattails in Open-Seat Elections," *Legislative Studies Quarterly,* XX (May 1995), 197–208.

31. Campbell, "Predicting Seat Gains from Presidential Coattails," pp. 180–82.

32. James E. Campbell and Joe A. Sumners, "Presidential Coattails in Senate Elections," *American Political Science Review,* LXXXIV (June 1990), 512–24. But also see a study by Jeffrey E. Cohen, Michael A. Krassa, and John A. Hamman, "The Impact of Presidential Campaigning on Midterm U.S. Senate Elections," *American Political Science Review,* LXXXV (March 1991), 165–78. They find that presidential campaign appearances mobilize nonvoters (rather than converting them), increase turnout, and help candidates to raise money—a more important role for presidents at midterm than conventional interpretations depict.

33. Albert D. Cover and David R. Mayhew, "Congressional Dynamics and the Decline of

Competitive Congressional Elections," in *Congress Reconsidered,* ed. Lawrence C. Dodd and Bruce I. Oppenheimer (Washington, DC: Congressional Quarterly Press, 1981), pp. 74–78.

34. *Washington Post,* November 5, 1962. This observation does not necessarily qualify as an enduring generalization, but it *has* been used in the previous nine editions of this book.

35. Edward R. Tufte, "Determinants of the Outcomes of Midterm Elections," *American Political Science Review,* LXIX (September 1975), 812–26. See corroboration of Tufte's referendum voting model by Robin F. Marra and Charles W. Ostrum, Jr., "Explaining Seat Change in the U.S. House of Representatives, 1950–86," *American Journal of Political Science,* XXXIII (August 1989), 541–69; and Gary C. Jacobson, "Does the Economy Matter in Midterm Elections?" *American Journal of Political Science,* XXXIV (May 1990), 400–404. An examination of Tufte's theory in House midterm elections by Alan I. Abramowitz finds that when presidential performance is salient, those who are most affected are incumbents in the president's party. See "Economic Conditions, Presidential Popularity, and Voting Behavior in Midterm Congressional Elections," *Journal of Politics,* XLVII (February 1985), 31–43; and, additionally, Alan I. Abramowitz, Albert D. Cover, and Helmut Norpoth, "The President's Party in Midterm Elections: Going from Bad to Worse," *American Journal of Political Science,* XXX (August 1986), 562–76. John R. Hibbing and John R. Alford find that the electoral margins of incumbents (especially senior ones) are affected more by economic conditions than are those of nonincumbents. See "The Electoral Impact of Economic Conditions: Who Is Held Responsible?" *American Journal of Political Science,* XXV (August 1981), 423–39. In addition, see Morris P. Fiorina, *Retrospective Voting in American National Elections* (New Haven, CT: Yale University Press, 1981); Donald R. Kinder and D. Roderick Kiewiet, "Economic Discontent and Political Behavior: The Role of Personal Grievances and Collective Economic Judgments in Congressional Voting," *American Journal of Political Science,* XXIII (August 1979), 495–527; Lyn Ragsdale, "The Fiction of Congressional Elections as Presidential Events," *American Politics Quarterly,* VIII (October 1980), 375–98; and Howard S. Bloom and H. Douglas Price, "Voter Response to Short-Run Economic Conditions: The Asymmetric Effect of Prosperity and Recession," *American Political Science Review,* LXIX (December 1975), 1240–254.

36. See Richard W. Waterman, "Comparing Senate and House Electoral Outcomes: The Exposure Thesis," *Legislative Studies Quarterly,* XV (February 1990), 99–114; and Bruce I. Oppenheimer, James A. Stimson, and Richard W. Waterman, "Interpreting U.S. Congressional Elections: The Exposure Thesis," *Legislative Studies Quarterly,* XI (May 1986), 227–47. See a modification of the Waterman, Oppenheimer, and Stimson exposure model that stresses the net exposure of the president's party in open seats by Ronald Keith Gaddie, "Congressional Seat Swings: Revisiting Exposure in House Elections," *Political Research Quarterly,* L (September 1997), 699–710.

37. This analysis is based on David R. Mayhew, *Congress: The Electoral Connection* (New Haven, CT: Yale University Press, 1974), especially Part I. For a study that finds that members are driven by four different goals—serving district interests, making good policy, making a political mark, and promoting the president's agenda—see Richard L. Hall, "Participation and Purpose in Committee Decision Making," *American Political Science Review,* LXXXI (March 1987), 105–27. For a study of the goals of state legislators (in Indiana), see David J. Webber, "The Contours and Complexity of Legislator Objectives: Empirically Examining the Basis of Purposive Models," *Western Political Quarterly,* XXXIX (March 1986), 93–103. For legislators in this state, constituent-oriented activities are most important.

38. It should be noted, however, that the *national* media focus attention on party and seniority leaders, not on the average member. Members have excellent access to the local media and on the whole are well served by this exposure, thus promoting their chances for reelection. See a study of the national media by Timothy E. Cook, "House Members as Newsmakers: The Effects of Televising Congress," *Legislative Studies Quarterly,* XI (May 1986), 203–26.

39. See a study by John A. Hird, "The Political Economy of Pork: Project Selection at the U.S. Army Corps of Engineers," *American Political Science Review,* LXXXV (June 1991), 429–56.

40. Consult a study by John R. Hibbing that offers evidence that members of Congress respond to approaching elections (and the need to be reelected) by distributing economic benefits to the voters: "The Liberal Hour: Electoral Pressures and Transfer Payment Voting in the

United States Congress," *Journal of Politics*, XLVI (August 1984), 846–65. Paul Feldman and James Jondrow find no evidence that local federal spending has any effect on an incumbent member's reelection prospects. Concretely, reduced expenditures in the districts do not threaten congressional careers. "Congressional Elections and Local Federal Spending," *American Journal of Political Science*, XXVIII (February 1984), 147–64.

41. Mayhew, *Congress*, pp. 61–62.

42. See a study that suggests that electoral pressures may in fact diminish a legislator's responsiveness to his or her constituents. John D. Wilkerson, "Reelection and Representation in Conflict: The Case of Agenda Manipulation," *Legislative Studies Quarterly*, XV (May 1990), 263–82. Election losses are not the end of the world. Harvey Palmer and Ronald Vogel have discovered that about 16 percent of House members who suffered election defeats or retired between 1961 and 1992 were given a federal appointment. If only representatives of the president's party are considered, the proportion rises to 28 percent. A good possibility of a federal appointment makes it easier for loyal House members of the president's party to run for the Senate; if they lose, the president will take care of them with a federal appointment. "Political Opportunity for Federal Appointment: Departing Members of the U.S. House of Representatives, 1961–1992," *Journal of Politics*, LVII (August 1995), 677–95.

43. Glenn R. Parker, "Is There a Political Life Cycle in the House of Representatives?" *Legislative Studies Quarterly*, XI (August 1986), 375–92. Also see his book, *Homeward Bound: Explaining Changes in Congressional Behavior* (Pittsburgh: University of Pittsburgh Press, 1986).

44. Quoted in Charles L. Clapp, *The Congressman: His Work as He Sees It* (Washington, DC: Brookings Institution, 1963), p. 332.

45. *Congressional Quarterly Weekly Report*, July 7, 1979, p. 1350.

46. Ibid., p. 1351.

47. Andrew Gelman and Gary King, "Estimating Incumbency Advantage Without Bias," *American Journal of Political Science*, XXXIV (November 1990), 1142.

48. Voters who have high levels of media exposure are more likely to vote for incumbents than for challengers. See Robert K. Goidel and Todd G. Shields, "The Vanishing Marginals, the Bandwagon, and the Mass Media," *Journal of Politics*, LVI (August 1994), 802–10.

49. See Kim Kahn, "Senate Elections in the News: Examining Campaign Coverage," *Legislative Studies Quarterly*, XVI (August 1991), 349–74. News coverage of U.S. Senate campaigns varies substantially; some campaigns get substantial press attention, while others do not. Competitive races and open-seat campaigns receive the most press coverage.

50. See Gary C. Jacobson, "Incumbents' Advantages in the 1978 U.S. Congressional Elections," *Legislative Studies Quarterly*, VI (May 1981), 183–200; Lyn Ragsdale, "Incumbent Popularity, Challenger Invisibility, and Congressional Voters," *Legislative Studies Quarterly*, VI (May 1981), 201–18; Glenn R. Parker, "Interpreting Candidate Awareness in U.S. Congressional Elections," *Legislative Studies Quarterly*, VI (May 1981), 219–33; and Barbara Hinckley, "The American Voter in Congressional Elections," *American Political Science Review*, LXXIV (September 1980), 641–50. For interesting evidence on incumbent visibility, see Charles H. Franklin, "Senate Incumbent Visibility Over the Election Cycle," *Legislative Studies Quarterly*, XVIII (May 1993), 271–90. Visibility is, of course, a substantial advantage for incumbents; however, the longer a senator is in office, the greater the number of negative evaluations with which he or she must contend. Voters "do not forgive and forget" (p. 287). For analysis of the meaning of "marginality" and "safety" in congressional elections, see James C. Garand, Kenneth Wink, and Brian Vincent, "Changing Meanings of Electoral Marginality in U.S. House Elections, 1824–1978," *Political Research Quarterly*, XLVI (March 1993), 27–48; Gary C. Jacobson, "Getting the Details Right: A Comment on 'Changing Meanings of Electoral Marginality in U.S. House Elections, 1824–1978,'" 49–54; and Garand, Wink, and Vincent, "Similar Details, Different Interpretations: A Response to Professor Jacobson," 55–65. See the evidence of Christopher Kenny and Michael McBurnett that incumbents' contact with voters through television enhances the impact of spending to a greater extent than it does for challengers. "Up Close and Personal: Campaign Contact and Candidate Spending in U.S. House Elections," *Political Research Quarterly*, L (March 1997), 75–96. Also see Stephen Ansolabehere and Alan Gerber, "Incumbency Advantage and the Persistence of

Legislative Majorities," *Legislative Studies Quarterly,* XXII (May 1997), 161–78; and Peverill Squire and Eric R.A.N. Smith, "A Further Examination of Challenger Quality in Senate Elections," *Legislative Studies Quarterly,* XXI (May 1996), 235–49.

51. Gelman and King, "Estimating Incumbency Advantage Without Bias," 1158.

52. *Congressional Quarterly Weekly Report,* June 10, 1978, p. 1463.

53. See a study of challengers that distinguishes between "experience-seeking amateurs" and "ambitious amateurs" by David Canon, "Sacrificial Lambs or Strategic Politicians? Political Amateurs in U.S. House Elections," *American Journal of Political Science,* XXXVII (November 1993), 1119–141. With previous political experience, ambitious amateurs tend to run against vulnerable incumbents and are considerably more likely to win than experience-seeking amateurs, whose chances are extraordinarily remote (5 in 1,000). The best prospect for amateurs, of course, is found in open-seat House races.

54. Gary W. Cox and Jonathan N. Katz argue that most of the advantages incumbents enjoy come from facing low-quality challengers rather than from the value of their office resources (e.g., franking privilege, staff and office allowances, committee positions). The value of having an experienced candidate has increased as candidate-centered campaigns have replaced party-centered ones. "Why Did the Incumbency Advantage in U.S. House Elections Grow?" *American Journal of Political Science,* XL (May 1996), 478–92. Steven Levitt and Catherine D. Wolfram also hold that the ability of incumbents to scare off high-quality challengers is a better explanation than office resources for incumbency success. They suggest that the dramatic increase in campaign costs is the main reason for the decline in the number of high-quality challengers; they are unwilling to pay these opportunity costs to contest well-financed incumbents. "Decomposing the Sources of Incumbency Advantage in the U.S. House," *Legislative Studies Quarterly,* XXII (February 1997), 45–60.

55. For an assortment of studies on this topic, see Peverill Squire, "Challengers in U.S. Senate Elections," *Legislative Studies Quarterly,* XIV (November 1989), 531–47; Peverill Squire and John R. Wright, "Fundraising by Nonincumbent Candidates for the U.S. House of Representatives," *Legislative Studies Quarterly,* XV (February 1990), 89–98; Donald Philip Green and Jonathan S. Krasno, "Salvation for the Spendthrift Incumbent: Reestimating the Effects of Campaign Spending in House Elections," *American Journal of Political Science,* XXXII (November 1988), 884–907; Jonathan S. Krasno and Donald Philip Green, "Preempting Quality Challengers in House Elections," *Journal of Politics,* L (November 1988), 920–36; Alan I. Abramowitz, "Explaining Senate Election Outcomes," *American Political Science Review,* LXXXII (June 1988), 385–403; John C. McAdams and John R. Johannes, "Determinants of Spending by House Challengers, 1974–1984," *American Journal of Political Science,* XXXI (August 1987), 457–83; Jon R. Bond, Cary Covington, and Richard Fleisher, "Explaining Challenger Quality in Congressional Elections," *Journal of Politics,* VL (May 1985), 510–29; and Mark C. Westlye, "Competitiveness of Senate Seats and Voting Behavior in Senatorial Elections," *American Journal of Political Science,* XXVII (May 1983), 253–83.

56. Gary C. Jacobson, "Strategic Politicians and the Dynamics of U.S. House Elections, 1946–86," *American Political Science Review,* LXXXIII (September 1989), 773–93. For additional evidence on the importance of challenger quality, see David Ian Lublin, "Quality, Not Quantity: Strategic Politicians in U.S. Senate Elections, 1952–1990," *Journal of Politics,* LVI (February 1994), 228–41. Also see a study of challenger quality at the state level by Emily Van Dunk, "Challenger Quality in State Legislative Elections," *Political Research Quarterly,* L (December 1997), 793–807. Van Dunk finds that quality challengers are strategic in their decision to challenge an incumbent. Quality challengers are most likely to emerge where previous legislative races have been competitive, where incumbents have shown previous electoral vulnerability, where a decrease in the state's real per capita income has occurred (the incumbent can be blamed for it), and where older incumbents are seeking reelection. The key is perceived vulnerability.

57. David W. Romero and Francine Sanders, "Loosened Partisan Attachments and Receptivity to Incumbent Behaviors: A Panel Analysis," *Political Science Quarterly,* XLVII (March 1994), 177–92. A recent study of congressional electorates shows that election turnout is affected by the quality of the challenger and his or her capacity to raise campaign funds. Robert A. Jackson writes: "If the challenger operates from a position of relative partisan strength, has prominent political experience, and is able to raise and spend a large amount of money, an

additional 4–5 percent of the congressional electorate may be mobilized." "The Mobilization of Congressional Electorates," *Legislative Studies Quarterly*, XXI (August 1996), 425–46 (quotation on p. 438).

58. Gary C. Jacobson, "The Declining Salience of U.S. House Candidates, 1958–1994," paper presented at the Annual Meeting of the American Political Science Association, Boston, September 3–6, 1998.

59. Alan I. Abramowitz, "Incumbency, Campaign Spending, and the Decline of Competition in U.S. House Elections," *Journal of Politics*, LIII (February 1991), 34–56.

60. The chances of defeating a House incumbent are slim indeed. Thus why do challengers run? A study of congressional challengers by Thomas A. Kazee offers these explanations: (1) Running for Congress is seen as a "personally rewarding experience"; (2) challengers feel that they have a chance to win; (3) challengers perceive congressional elections as isolated phenomena and thus believe that they can win regardless of national trends. "The Decision to Run for the U.S. Congress: Challenger Attitudes in the 1970s," *Legislative Studies Quarterly*, V (February 1980), 79–100. Strong challengers to incumbents tend to emerge when there are significant policy discrepancies between the member and district, when members are accused of ethical improprieties, and when the challenger in the previous election did relatively well. See Lyn Ragsdale and Timothy E. Cook, "Representatives' Actions and Challengers' Reactions: Limits to Candidate Connections in the House," *American Journal of Political Science*, XXXI (February 1987), 45–81. Also consult a study by William T. Bianco that finds that district-level political factors (for example, open seat or incumbent's previous electoral margin) and changes in economic conditions are the most important factors in influencing potential challengers to seek congressional office. His analysis focuses on *quality* congressional challengers (candidates who held, or previously held, elected office at the time of announcing their candidacy). "Strategic Decisions on Candidacy in U.S. Congressional Districts," *Legislative Studies Quarterly*, IX (May 1984), 351–64. Senate incumbents are most likely to be defeated when there is a discrepancy between their policy stances (as shown in roll-call votes) and the preferences of their constituents. See Kenny J. Whitby and Timothy Bledsoe, "The Impact of Policy Voting on the Electoral Fortunes of Senate Incumbents," *Western Political Quarterly*, XXXIX (December 1986), 690–700. Of related interest, see Gary W. Copeland, "Choosing to Run: Why House Members Seek Election to the Senate," *Legislative Studies Quarterly*, XIV (November 1989), 549–65. Also see Jon R. Bond, Richard Fleisher, and Jeffrey C. Talbert, "Partisan Differences in Candidate Quality in Open Seat House Races, 1976–1994," *Political Research Quarterly*, L (June 1997), 281–99. They find that experienced candidates tend to run for an open seat if their party has held the seat and if the normal vote works to their party's advantage.

61. For studies of the impact of bank overdrafts on members' careers, see Gary C. Jacobson and Michael A. Dimock, "Checking Out: The Effects of Bank Overdrafts on the 1992 House Election," *American Journal of Political Science*, XXXVIII (August 1994), 601–24; and Timothy Groseclose and Keith Krehbiel, "Golden Parachutes, Rubber Checks, and Strategic Retirements from the 102nd House," *American Journal of Political Science*, XXXVIII (February 1994), 75–90.

62. Monica Bauer and John R. Hibbing, "Which Incumbents Lose in House Elections: A Response to Jacobson's 'The Marginals Never Vanished,'" *American Journal of Political Science*, XXXIII (February 1989), 270. Also see Gary C. Jacobson, "The Marginals Never Vanished: Incumbency and Competition in Elections to the U.S. House of Representatives, 1952–82," *American Journal of Political Science*, XXXI (February 1987), 126–41.

63. The principal threat to an incumbent senator's reelection is a quality challenger—that is, a candidate who holds a high-profile office and is regarded as a good campaigner. But even higher-quality candidates face enormous obstacles in races against incumbents. See Peverill Squire, "Challenger Quality and Voting Behavior in U.S. Senate Elections," *Legislative Studies Quarterly*, XVII (May 1992), 247–63.

64. Craig H. Grau, "Competition in State Legislative Primaries," *Legislative Studies Quarterly*, VI (February 1981), 46–53; Malcolm E. Jewell and David Breaux, "Southern Primary and Electoral Competition and Incumbent Success," *Legislative Studies Quarterly*, XVI (February 1991), 129–43. See an analysis by Anita Pritchard of the conditions under which state legislative incumbents are likely to face opposition in their bids for reelection: "Strategic

Considerations in the Decision to Challenge a State Legislative Incumbent," *Legislative Studies Quarterly*, XVII (August 1992), 381–93. Gary W. Cox and Scott Morgenstern find that the incumbency advantage of state legislators doubled over the period 1970 to 1986: "The Increasing Advantage of Incumbency in the U.S. States," *Legislative Studies Quarterly*, XVIII (November 1993), 495–511.

65. It is not unusual for 80 percent to 90 percent (or more) of all incumbents on the ballot to be reelected. See Alan Rosenthal, *Legislative Life: An Analysis of Legislatures in the States* (New York: Harper & Row, 1981), pp. 22–26. Perhaps 3 percent of state legislative incumbents lose at the primary stage. See Grau, "Competition in State Legislative Primaries," 47. Also see an analysis of incumbent candidates' vote proportions by James C. Garand, "Electoral Marginality in State Legislative Elections, 1968–86," *Legislative Studies Quarterly*, XVI (February 1991), 7–28. Garand finds that although incumbents' vote proportions have increased significantly, their victory rates have increased only slightly.

66. Ronald E. Weber, Harvey J. Tucker, and Paul Brace, "Vanishing Marginals in State Legislative Elections," *Legislative Studies Quarterly*, XVI (February 1991), 29–47. Also see Gary W. Cox and Scott Morgenstern, "The Increasing Advantage of Incumbency in the U.S. States," *Legislative Studies Quarterly*, XVIII (November 1993), 495–514.

67. Thomas M. Holbrook and Charles M. Tidmarch, "Sophomore Surge in State Legislative Elections, 1968–86," *Legislative Studies Quarterly*, XVI (February 1991), 49–63. An increase in legislative resources, such as staffs and district offices, has contributed to the "sophomore surge." See Chao-Chi Shan and Jeffrey M. Stonecash, "Legislative Resources and Electoral Margins: New York State Senate, 1950–1990," *Legislative Studies Quarterly*, XIX (February 1994), 79–93.

68. Weber, Tucker, and Brace, "Vanishing Marginals in State Legislative Races," 44.

69. Ibid., 29–47; Garand, "Electoral Marginality in State Legislative Elections," 7–28; Jewell and Breaux, "Southern Primary and Electoral Competition," 129–43; Charles M. Tidmarch, Edward Lonergan, and John Sciortino, "Interparty Competition in the U.S. States: Legislative Elections, 1970–1978," *Legislative Studies Quarterly*, XI (August 1986), 353–74; and Malcolm E. Jewell and David Breaux, "The Effect of Incumbency on State Legislative Elections," *Legislative Studies Quarterly*, XIII (November 1988), 495–514. Also see Jeffrey E. Cohen, "Perceptions of Electoral Insecurity Among Members Holding Safe Seats in a U.S. State Legislature," *Legislative Studies Quarterly*, IX (May 1984), 365–69.

70. James E. Campbell, "Presidential Coattails and Midterm Losses in State Legislative Elections," *American Political Science Review*, LXXX (June 1986), 45–63. Also see a study by Thomas H. Little showing that Republican state parties that developed electoral contracts similar to the Republican "Contract with America" gained more seats in the 1994 elections than the Republican parties in those states where the advice of the national party was ignored. "On the Coattails of a Contract: RNC Activities and Republican Gains in the 1994 State Legislative Elections," *Political Research Quarterly*, LI (March 1998), 173–90.

71. Joel A. Thompson and William Cassie, "Party and PAC Contributions to North Carolina Legislative Candidates," *Legislative Studies Quarterly*, XVII (August 1992), 409–16.

72. Anthony Gierzynski and David A. Breaux, "Money and the Party Vote in State House Elections," *Legislative Studies Quarterly*, XVIII (November 1993), 515–33.

73. See an analysis of women candidates in special House elections by Ronald Keith Gaddie and Charles S. Bullock III, "Structural and Elite Features in Open Seat and Special U.S. House Elections: Is There a Sexual Bias?" *Political Research Quarterly*, L (June 1997), 459–68. The authors find no bias against women in special elections.

74. See a study of House special elections by Ronald Keith Gaddie, Charles S. Bullock III, and Scott Buchanan, "What Is So Special About Special Elections?" *Legislative Studies Quarterly*, XXIV (February 1999), 103–12. They find that special elections resemble open-seat elections in that they are heavily influenced by candidate and constituency factors; they find no evidence that special elections are referenda on the president.

75. Roger H. Marz and William D. Morris, "Treadmill to Oblivion: The Fate of Appointed Senators," paper presented at the Annual Meeting of the American Political Science Association, San Francisco, September 2–5, 1975.

76. See Alan L. Clem, "Popular Representation and Senate Vacancies," *Midwest Journal of Political Science*, X (February 1966), 52–77.

77. 424 U.S. 1 (1976).

78. Press release, Federal Election Commission, December 29, 1998.

79. Jonathan S. Krasno, Donald Philip Green, and Jonathan A. Cowden, "The Dynamics of Campaign Fundraising in House Elections," *Journal of Politics*, LVI (May 1994), 459–74. Also see the persuasive evidence on the importance of early money provided in a study by Robert Biersack, Paul S. Herrnson, and Clyde Wilcox, "Seeds for Success: Early Money in Congressional Elections," *Legislative Studies Quarterly*, XVIII (November 1993), 535–51. Contrary to conventional interpretations, Alan Gerber finds that incumbent spending in U.S. Senate elections is even more important than challenger spending. In a typical Senate election, the incumbent's spending advantage produces a 6 percent increase in his or her share of the vote. "Estimating the Effect of Campaign Spending on Senate Election Outcomes Using Instrumental Variables," *American Political Science Review*, XCII (June 1998), 401–11.

80. Press release, Federal Election Commission, December 29, 1998.

81. Ibid.

82. Ibid.

83. Ibid.

84. See an interesting study of why corporations decide to form PACs by Craig Humphries, "Corporations, PACs and the Strategic Link Between Contributions and Lobbying Activities," *Western Political Quarterly*, XLIV (June 1991), 353–72.

85. http://www.fec.gov/press/allsum98.htm.

86. At the state legislative level, the advantages of incumbents in raising funds are also substantial. See, for example, Jeffrey M. Stonecash, "Working at the Margins: Campaign Finance and Party Strategy in New York Assembly Elections," *Legislative Studies Quarterly*, XIII (November 1988), 477–93; Michael W. Giles and Anita Pritchard, "Campaign Expenditures and Legislative Elections in Florida," *Legislative Studies Quarterly*, X (February 1985), 71–88; Ruth S. Jones and Thomas J. Borris, "Strategic Contributing in Legislative Campaigns: The Case of Minnesota," *Legislative Studies Quarterly*, X (February 1985), 89–105; and Joel A. Thompson, William Cassie, and Malcolm E. Jewell, "A Sacred Cow or Just a Lot of Bull? Party and PAC Money in State Legislative Elections," *Political Research Quarterly*, XLVII (March 1994), 223–37.

87. Press release, Federal Election Commission, December 29, 1998.

88. Ibid.

89. Kevin B. Grier and Michael C. Munger, "Comparing Interest Group PAC Contributions to House and Senate Incumbents, 1980–1986," *Journal of Politics*, LV (August 1993), 615–43.

90. Press release, Federal Election Commission, April 9, 1999.

91. The PAC world is by no means monolithic. Those that seek access focus their contributions on incumbents. There are other PACs that seek to evaluate the parties' electoral prospects before deciding where to put their money. And there are adversarial PACs that concentrate their efforts on electing candidates who mirror their views. See Theodore J. Eismeier and Philip H. Pollock III, "Strategy and Choice in Congressional Elections: The Role of Political Action Committees," *American Journal of Political Science*, XXX (February 1986), 197–213.

92. See Clyde Wilcox, "Share the Wealth: Contributions by Congressional Incumbents to the Campaigns of Other Candidates," *American Politics Quarterly*, XVII (October 1989), 386–408.

93. Perhaps 70 percent to 80 percent of the campaign funds collected by U.S. Senate candidates goes to the television-station owners in their states. In the words of a senator, candidates have become "bag men for the TV operators." See a column by David S. Broder, *Washington Post*, June 15, 1987.

94. Under FECA, a PAC can contribute up to $5,000 to a candidate's campaign in each election (primary, runoff, and general elections are considered to be separate elections).

95. There is good reason for Republican concern over ceilings on campaign expenditures. Campaign money spent by challengers is more likely to affect election outcomes than that spent

by incumbents. Limitations on spending favor incumbents, who can draw on the numerous advantages of congressional office. See Gary C. Jacobson, "The Effects of Campaign Spending in Congressional Elections," *American Political Science Review*, LXXII (June 1978), 469–91; Gary C. Jacobson, "The Effects of Campaign Spending in House Elections: New Evidence for Old Arguments," *American Journal of Political Science*, XXXIV (May 1990), 334–62. Also see Donald Philip Green and Jonathan S. Krasno, "Rebuttal to Jacobson's 'New Evidence for Old Arguments,'" *American Journal of Political Science*, XXXIV (May 1990), 363–72; and Scott J. Thomas, "Do Incumbent Campaign Expenditures Matter?" *Journal of Politics*, LI (November 1989), 965–76.

96. *Congressional Record*, 100th Cong., 1st sess., June 5, 1987, p. S7723–24. (Daily edition.)

97. On the importance of elections in shaping subsequent legislative behavior—particularly in terms of the legislature's capacity for making fundamental policy changes—see Patricia Hurley, David Brady, and Joseph Cooper, "Measuring Legislative Potential for Policy Change," *Legislative Studies Quarterly*, II (November 1977), 385–98.

98. See three instructive studies of congressional campaigns and campaigners by Robert J. Huckshorn and Robert C. Spencer, *The Politics of Defeat: Campaigning for Congress* (Amherst: University of Massachusetts Press, 1971); Jeff Fishel, *Party and Opposition: Congressional Challengers in American Politics* (New York: David McKay, 1973); and Alan L. Clem, *The Making of Congressmen: Seven Campaigns of 1974* (North Scituate, MA: Duxbury Press, 1976).

99. Suzanna De Boef and James Stimson find that the U.S. House is *not* insulated from public opinion. The fortunes of the political parties in elections follow the movement of citizen policy preferences; when the public's preferences shift, as shown in opinion surveys, the party composition of the House shifts in the same direction. "The Dynamic Structure of Congressional Elections," *Journal of Politics*, LVII (August 1995), 630–48. Also see a study by William Koetzle that finds that politically diverse House districts are much more competitive than less diverse districts. "The Impact of Constituency Diversity upon the Competitiveness of U.S. House Elections, 1962–96," *Legislative Studies Quarterly*, XXIII (November 1998), 561–73.

# 5

# The Legislators

To have great legislatures a nation or state must have greatly interested citizens, the most talented of whom are willing to run for office. Critics, whatever their preferences about legislative design or function, seem to agree that the central element in the strength of any legislature is the quality of its members.[1] The kinds of individuals who are being attracted to legislative service is one of the principal topics examined in this chapter. How they adapt to the legislature—the manner in which they relate to their office and to legislative norms—is another. Whether they care to stay in office for any length of time, and are able to, is a third. Why they leave the legislature is a fourth. This chapter begins with an analysis of the backgrounds of American legislators. The pattern disclosed is much less variegated than might be expected.

## SOCIAL AND OCCUPATIONAL BACKGROUNDS OF AMERICAN LEGISLATORS

Is the American legislature made up of men and women who represent a cross section of the American population? Who are the legislators who make our laws? What groups are "overrepresented" in the legislature? What groups are "underrepresented"? What conclusions can be drawn about the caliber of American legislators?

Political scientists and sociologists have published a number of studies of the social origins and occupational backgrounds of political decision makers, a few of which have focused on legislators. Despite substantial gaps in factual knowledge about legislative personnel, as well as a number of special problems confronting such investigations, a certain degree of generalization about the individuals who serve as legislators is attainable.

*1. Most legislators are drawn from a relatively narrow social base.* The most important fact emerging from studies of the social backgrounds of legislators is that a significant (and disproportionate) number come from

155

middle- and upper-class environments. The legislature, it is apparent, is not a microcosm of the population at large. In the typical legislature no more than a handful of members come from the homes of wage earners.

Evidence on this point is sufficient to puncture the myth that all American citizens have an equal chance to be elected to legislative office. In his study of postwar senators (covering the years 1947–57), Donald R. Matthews found that 24 percent of the senators' fathers were professional men, 35 percent proprietors and officials, and 32 percent farmers. Only 2 percent of the senators were sons of low-salaried workers; 5 percent were the sons of industrial wage earners; for 2 percent the relevant facts were unknown.[2] Other studies of the membership of the lower house of Congress show a similar distribution.[3] An earlier investigation of the occupations of state legislators in thirteen states by Charles S. Hyneman established the fact that legislators are to a marked extent drawn from the more privileged classes.[4]

2. *No single profile characterizes the political socialization of American legislators—that is, legislators acquire their political interests, values, and attitudes in a variety of ways and at different periods in their life cycles.* Although research on the political socialization of legislators is limited, several generalizations appear to be warranted. First, the initial political interest of legislators may be derived from a number of sources, including *primary groups* (for example, family and friends), *political or civic participation* (for example, school politics and activity in occupational groups), *public events and circumstances* (for example, wars, elections, and economic crises), *personal predispositions* (for example, ambition, indignation, interest, and sense of obligation), and *socioeconomic beliefs.* Second, of those legislators who report that they became interested in politics at an early age, the socialization agent ordinarily responsible has been the family. The study of California, New Jersey, Ohio, and Tennessee state legislators shows, for example, a high proportion of members with relatives in politics—over 40 percent in each of the states. Political interest becomes a natural outgrowth of family associations and experiences—"I was born into a political family. . . . I grew up in politics." "I met lots of people in politics through my father." "People around home took their politics serious."[5]

A third generalization is that notwithstanding the incidence and importance of preadult socialization, a surprising number of legislators become adults before they acquire an interest in politics. In the four-state study, nearly four out of every ten legislators indicated that their initial interest in public affairs occurred during adulthood. Another study of a group of seniority and elective leaders in Congress finds roughly the same proportion of members reporting that their first interest in politics came relatively late—in college (or equivalent period) or after college.[6] Political socialization thus may occur at virtually any time in the life of the legislator. Finally, although preadult political socialization obviously has some bearing on adult attitudes and political behavior, an incumbent legislator's political behavior may not be affected significantly by the nature of the initial political socialization. Political socialization theory rests heavily on the idea that the attitudes, beliefs, and perceptions formed early in life fundamentally shape adult outlook and behavior. Wide-ranging evidence for this belief, however, is difficult to establish. Indeed, one study suggests that there may be no relationship between an individual's socialization into politics and later orientations as a legislator. Specifically, no relationship appears to exist between legislators' initial socialization and their legislative orientations toward their constituency ("representative role orientations"), toward interest groups ("group role orientation"), or toward performance of legislative duties ("purposive role orientation"). Legislators may recall their early introduction to politics vividly and enthusiastically, but these socialization experiences apparently have no distinctive impact on how they respond to their official duties. Their orientations are virtually the same as for those members whose socialization occurred as adults.[7]

3. *In educational achievement, American legislators scarcely resemble their constituents.* About one-fourth of the adult population of the United States has received some college education. In Congress, however, it is rare to find a member who has not attended college; indeed, the vast majority are college graduates and many hold advanced degrees, such as in law. The situation is similar at the state level. It seems likely that well over half of all state legislators have had some college education.

These facts are not likely to cause anyone to demur, although their significance may escape notice for they reveal more than a vagrant wisp of social class. The typical legislator is far from a typical citizen. Not only is his or her career launched from a more elevated social station than the typical citizen's, but it is also launched amid more of the social advantages conferred by education. Formal educational attainment thus appears to be one of the central criteria in the winnowing-out process under which legislative candidates are recruited and elected. An invitation to legislative candidacy is not likely to come unbidden to those whose credentials fall short.

4. *The predominant occupations found among legislators are the professions, business, education, and farming.* The U.S. Senate presents a striking example of the dominant representation of the professions and business in legislative assemblies. In the 106th Congress (1999–2000), for example, lawyers and businesspersons vastly outnumbered all other occupations. More than half of all senators (55 percent) were lawyers, and 24 percent came from careers in business or banking. In the House, the percentages for these leading occupations were 37 percent and 36 percent, respectively. Members with backgrounds in education and real estate were next most numerous in both houses.[8]

The two occupations found most frequently among state legislators are also business and law. A 1993 survey by the National Conference of State Legislatures found that 21 percent of all members had backgrounds in business (with about half classified as business owners) and 17 percent in law (down from 22 percent in 1976). Next most numerous were full-time legislators (15 percent), farmers (8 percent), and educators (6 percent). Legislators' occupations varied sharply from state to state. For example, there were only two lawyers in the Alaska legislature; in Virginia, 39 percent were attorneys. Twenty-five percent of all legislators in southern states were lawyers as contrasted with only 12 percent in western states. Interestingly, 30 percent of all legislative leaders were attorneys.[9]

Several circumstances are associated with the emergence and development of the lawyer as policymaker.[10] First, this profession, like that of the physician, outstrips most others in prestige—evidently an important factor both to party organizations in search of candidates and to voters in quest of representatives. Second, like all successful politicians, the lawyer is an adroit broker of ideas as well as of interests. Legal training, if deficient and illiberal on some counts, is extraordinarily successful in assisting its recipients to master the intricacies of human relations, to excel in verbal exchange, to understand complex and technical information, and to employ varying tactics to seize advantage. These qualities of mind and makeup serve the legislator no less than the campaigner. Third, the lawyer, unlike the usual farmer, teacher, or mechanic, ordinarily finds it convenient to link professional work to steady participation in politics; and political involvement may well bring an unearned increment by attracting, through publicity and social visibility, new clients and higher fees. Finally, whereas people in the workaday activities of other occupations stand on the outskirts of power, the lawyer, with professional knowledge and skills, is automatically the representative of power:

> The attorney is the accepted agent of all politically effective groups of the American people. As the lawyer is habitually the representative of the grasping and abused in litigation, as he is increasingly the negotiator between businessmen with conflicting interests, as he is more and more the spokesman of individual and corporation in public relations—so is the lawyer today depended upon to represent citizens in the lawmaking body.[11]

Finally, it is worth noting that in recent Congresses more than half of all House members have been former state legislators. And as Michael B. Berkman has shown, House members with experience in *professionalized* state legislatures are better able to adapt to congressional service than other members. Their earlier legislative training helps them to find their policy niches in the House and, additionally, improves their prospects for moving up the chamber's career ladder.[12]

5. *The typical American legislator is male, white, Protestant, and of Anglo-Saxon origin.* The electoral process provides no guarantee that the legislators chosen will closely resemble the people who elected them. The truth is that certain groups in the population are overrepresented whereas other groups are underrepresented in American assemblies.

If blacks were to gain representation in Congress equal to their proportion of the population, there would be more than fifty blacks in the House of Representatives and twelve in the Senate. In fact, however, only four blacks have ever been elected to the Senate, the most recent Carol Moseley-Braun (D., IL), who was elected in 1992; she was defeated in 1998. The creation of black-majority districts in redistricting plans, beginning in the 1990s, led to a marked increase in the number of black representatives. Thirty-nine blacks (including the nonvoting delegate from the District of Columbia) were elected to the House in 1994 and again in 1998, the largest number ever elected to that chamber; nearly half were elected from southern states, where the introduction of districts designed to facilitate minority representation had a particularly dramatic effect. In the 106th Congress (1999–2000), there were nineteen Hispanic House members, more than half of whom were elected from Texas and California.[13]

The story is roughly the same in state assemblies. Although blacks are underrepresented in virtually all state legislatures, significant gains have been made in recent years. In 1979, there were 285 black members in thirty-seven states; by 1986, there were 387 black members in forty-two states. Following the election of 1990, black members totaled 430 in forty-two states. And in 1997, there were 567 black members in forty-two states, or 7.6 percent of the nation's 7,424 state legislators. (See Table 5.1.) As in the case of Congress, the sharp increase in black state lawmakers stemmed from interpretations of the Voting Rights Act that required legislatures to create the greatest possible number of districts in which minorities would constitute a majority (so-called majority-minority districts).[14]

Black voter mobilization, stemming from the Voting Rights Act of 1965, has clearly heightened the responsiveness of state legislators to black interests. Mary Herring's study of three southern state legislatures (Alabama, Georgia, and Louisiana) demonstrates that the black proportion of a district has a major, positive impact on legislative support (including that of white members) for policies favored by blacks.[15]

It remains true that in most states, northern as well as southern, the underrepresentation of blacks in the legislature is an uncomfortable fact of life, one well understood by black political leaders. Blacks make up 11.8 percent of the population of the nation but only 7.6 percent of the state legislators.[16] The underrepresentation of blacks is particularly acute in state senates.

Black legislative life is not viewed in the same light by all black state legislators. Research by David Hedge, James Button, and Mary Spear finds

**TABLE 5.1   Black membership in state legislatures, nation and leading states, 1997**

|  | Total Number of Legislators | Number of Black Legislators | Percent Black Legislators | Percent Black Population |
|---|---|---|---|---|
| Nation | 7,424 | 567 | 7.6 | 11.8 |
| Mississippi | 174 | 45 | 25.9 | 33.3 |
| Alabama | 140 | 35 | 25.0 | 23.9 |
| Louisiana | 144 | 33 | 22.9 | 29.6 |
| South Carolina | 170 | 34 | 20.0 | 27.8 |
| Maryland | 188 | 36 | 19.1 | 26.6 |
| Georgia | 236 | 45 | 19.0 | 26.5 |
| North Carolina | 170 | 24 | 14.1 | 20.5 |
| Ohio | 132 | 18 | 13.6 | 10.5 |
| New York | 211 | 27 | 12.8 | 16.8 |
| Florida | 160 | 20 | 12.5 | 13.4 |
| Illinois | 177 | 22 | 12.4 | 13.9 |
| Tennessee | 132 | 16 | 12.1 | 15.0 |
| Michigan | 148 | 17 | 11.5 | 13.2 |
| New Jersey | 120 | 13 | 10.8 | 13.6 |
| Virginia | 140 | 14 | 10.0 | 19.0 |
| Arkansas | 135 | 13 | 9.6 | 14.3 |
| Texas | 181 | 16 | 8.8 | 11.8 |
| Indiana | 150 | 12 | 8.0 | 7.6 |
| Missouri | 197 | 15 | 7.6 | 10.1 |
| Connecticut | 187 | 14 | 7.4 | 8.4 |
| Pennsylvania | 253 | 18 | 7.1 | 8.8 |
| Delaware | 62 | 4 | 6.4 | 18.0 |
| Rhode Island | 150 | 9 | 6.0 | 4.4 |
| California | 120 | 7 | 5.8 | 7.1 |

SOURCE:   Joint Center for Political and Economic Studies, Washington, DC, 1998.

that those who assess it most favorably tend to be more senior members, leaders, males, those from outside the Deep South, and those who live in states where race relations are perceived to be better.[17] Interestingly, African-American legislators who represent majority-white districts have a more benign view of the legislative process than those black members who represent districts with large black populations.[18]

At the congressional level, African-American lawmakers are significantly overrepresented among the most senior Democrats in the House. In the not too distant future, when Democrats control the House, Alan Gerber suggests, black legislators are likely to hold one-quarter of the most important committee and subcommittee chairmanships.[19] Thus, the seniority system seems destined to make a larger contribution to the advancement of minority interests in Congress. For much of the twentieth century, by contrast, seniority had a deleterious impact on minority policy concerns, since it favored elderly and conservative white southern Democrats.

The election of Hispanic legislators in significant numbers occurs in only a few states. Following the 1998 elections, Hispanic legislators made up 36 percent of the New Mexico legislature, 20 percent of the California legislature, 19 percent of the Texas legislature, 12 percent of the Arizona legislature, and 9 percent of the Florida legislature. Altogether, in 1999, there were 186 Hispanic state legislators in twenty-seven states.[20]

The composition of legislatures may also be examined in terms of the religious affiliation of members. Consider Congress. First, religious affiliation itself is overrepresented in the legislature. Although 60 percent of the American people are members of some denomination, more than 90 percent of the members of Congress profess a religious affiliation. Affiliants of some denominations are much more successful than others in being elected to office. Denominations of high social status, such as Episcopalian and Presbyterian, are invariably overrepresented in the chambers. In the 106th Congress (1999–2000), Episcopalians numbered about 8 percent of the membership and Presbyterians about 9 percent; each denomination made up less than 2 percent of the population. The leading Protestant denomination in Congress, Baptist, made up 13 percent of the membership; next came Methodist, with 12 percent.

Catholics and Jews are now winning seats in Congress in excess of their shares of the population. In the 106th Congress, Catholics made up 28 percent and Jews 6 percent of the membership; they are 25 percent and 2 percent of the population, respectively. Both groups were substantially underrepresented in Congress as recently as the 1960s.[21]

Although its political significance is lessening, religious affiliation is nevertheless a factor in the recruitment and election of legislative candidates. Year in and year out, Alabama, Mississippi, and South Carolina will send to Congress delegations largely made up of Baptists and Methodists; New York City will thrust up a delegation almost solidly Catholic and Jewish; Minnesota will have a significant number of Lutherans in its delegation; and the "silk-stocking" districts in urban and suburban areas will dispatch to Washington a large proportion of Episcopalians and Presbyterians.

The election of large numbers of women to legislative office is a relatively recent development. About 600 women were elected to the state legislatures in 1974, doubling the number who were elected a decade earlier. By 1999, the number had grown to 1,652, or 22.3 percent of the nation's 7,424 state legislators.[22] The state with the highest number of women legislators was Washington, with 41 percent, followed closely by Nevada with 37 percent and Arizona with 36 percent. Other states in which at least one-fourth of the legislators were women were Colorado, Kansas, New Hampshire, Vermont, Arizona, Connecticut, Maryland, Minnesota, Nebraska, Rhode Island, California, and Massachusetts. Lowest on the rung was Alabama, where only 8 percent were women. Women made up 10 percent of the membership of the Oklahoma legislature. At the national level, 65 women were members of the 106th Congress (1999–2000)—record numbers for both the House (56 or 12.9 percent) and Senate (9 or 9 percent).[23] On the whole, women are most likely to be elected to the state legislature in states in which the population is better educated and per capita income is higher.[24] Conventional wisdom holds that women are more likely to be elected in multimember districts than in single-member districts, but a study by Susan Welch and Donley T. Studlar finds only limited support for that notion.[25]

A study of press coverage of women candidates for the U.S. Senate by Kim Fridkin Kahn finds that women candidates receive less coverage than male candidates and that the coverage itself tends to be negative, in the sense that it frequently stresses their poor prospects for winning. Moreover, in addition to focusing on the women candidates' viability rather than issue positions, coverage also gives disproportionate attention to the "horse-race" (who's winning?) aspect in campaigns where there are women candidates.[26]

Briefly, what we have gained from this discussion is this: No American legislature comes close to housing a cross section of the population it serves. The political system inevitably has built-in biases, numerous devices for the containment of minority-group aspirations for office and for the advancement of dominant segments of the population. Some groups win often; others lose often. Although the data on social-class attachments of legislators are fragmentary, they support the view that national and state legislators speak mainly in the idiom and accents of the middle and upper classes.

The facts of social class in legislative representation, however, must be treated warily. They may conceal as much as they disclose and may invite misinterpretation. In the first place, they do not show that the legislature succumbs to upper-class pressures or that it is only a transmission belt for moving along benefits to privileged groups. Moreover, there is the matter of representing the interests of social groups as well as of representing the groups themselves. It is one thing to say that few people of working-class background ever make it to the legislature and quite another to say that the interests of the working class are treated unsympathetically by legislators not of this class. It is one thing to point to the ascendant position of the lawyer-legislators and quite another to say that they are preoccupied with improving the fortunes of the legal profession or any other special group. Nevertheless, we might have greater confidence that value allocation by the legislature would approximate more closely the interests of all segments of the public if political and electoral processes produced a more nearly representative set of decision makers.[27]

At the least, this glance at the characteristics of American legislators ought to show sufficiently that they are not run-of-the-mill citizens. Their formal education, more than anything else, argues that they have had much better preparation for legislative service than the ordinary citizen. But what no social background study has shown is whether they are usually men and women of integrity—persons who reckon in terms of the general well-being of the social system, persons in whom the public has reason to impart trust. Very little can be stated with certainty about the presence or absence of these qualities among the legislators as a whole. Nor, for that matter, can much be said with certainty about the presence or absence of these qualities among bankers, labor leaders, or college professors.

## LEGISLATIVE EXPERIENCE: TENURE AND TURNOVER

Although some differences between Congress and the typical state legislature are no more than minor subsurface variations, this is far from the case with respect to the tenure and turnover of their memberships. The membership of Congress is substantially more stable than that of the typical state legislature.

### Congress

There is no sure-fire formula for wrestling a seat from a congressional incumbent. Indeed, it has been a rare election when significant numbers of incumbents were removed by the voters. Even the extraordinary Republican victory in the 1994 midterm election did not take a particularly heavy toll of incumbents; more than 90 percent in both houses were reelected. Republican success stemmed mainly from the party's ability to win open seats; Republican candidates captured 22 Democratic-held open seats, while losing only four of their own.

The impressive tenure of House members is shown by the data of Table 5.2. In the 105th Congress (1997–98), for example, 13.2 percent of the members of the lower house had been elected to ten or more terms, about eight times as many as had been elected this many times in the 58th Congress (1903–04).[28] More than one-third of the House members of the 105th Congress had been elected to six or more terms. Members bent on a career in

**TABLE 5.2** Distribution of membership of the U.S. House of Representatives, by terms of service, selected Congresses

| | Percentage of Members | | | | |
|---|---|---|---|---|---|
| Terms of Service | 105th Congress (1997–98) | 104th Congress (1995–96) | 100th Congress (1987–88) | 88th Congress (1963–64) | 58th Congress (1903–04) |
| 10 or more | 13.2 | 13.5 | 14.9 | 17.0 | 1.8 |
| 6–9 | 20.6 | 22.1 | 23.5 | 28.7 | 11.4 |
| 3–5 | 32.4 | 22.3 | 41.4 | 26.5 | 38.2 |
| 1–2 | 33.8 | 42.1 | 20.2 | 27.8 | 48.6 |

SOURCE: Adapted from data in T. Richard Witmer, "The Aging of the House," *Political Science Quarterly* LXXIX (December 1964), 538 (as updated).

TABLE 5.3 One-sided congressional elections: Percentage of incumbents winning by more than 60 percent of the vote, selected years, 1960–98

| Year | House | Senate |
|------|-------|--------|
| 1960 | 59 | 41 |
| 1962 | 64 | 26 |
| 1964 | 59 | 47 |
| 1966 | 68 | 41 |
| 1968 | 72 | 38 |
| 1970 | 77 | 31 |
| 1972 | 78 | 52 |
| 1974 | 66 | 40 |
| 1976 | 69 | 40 |
| 1978 | 77 | 32 |
| 1980 | 71 | 31 |
| 1986 | 85 | 47 |
| 1990 | 74 | 63 |
| 1994 | 60 | 36 |
| 1996 | 64 | 32 |
| 1998 | 77 | 63 |

SOURCE: Data drawn from various issues of the *Congressional Quarterly Weekly Report.*

Congress have an excellent chance of achieving one. Numerous House and Senate candidates win by lopsided margins, even in unusually turbulent years (see Table 5.3). In 1998, 77 percent of House incumbents and 63 percent of Senate incumbents received more than 60 percent of the vote.

Even so, turnover in congressional membership is higher today than it was a couple of decades ago. Like other people, and of no surprise, incumbents die or retire. Retirements have become more common.[29] Departing members cite a variety of reasons for leaving, including family sacrifices, the "fishbowl factor," the public's disrespect for public officials, the unpleasantness of fund-raising, better salaries in the private sector, the declining value of seniority, and a range of legislative frustrations.[30]

A systematic analysis of voluntary departures from Congress between 1960 and 1996 by Michael K. Moore and John R. Hibbing concludes that "the motivation to remain in Congress is diminished when members feel isolated from their party, from large portions of their voting constituents, and from the opportunity to occupy positions of influence within the Congress." Thus, "ideological misfits" are more likely to leave voluntarily than their colleagues who are lodged in the party's mainstream. A precarious electoral situation may prompt members to retire. And members who see slim prospects for gaining influence within the institution are prime candidates for voluntary departure. Circumstances thus play a key role in decisions to leave Congress.[31]

In addition, some members abandon their seats to run for other offices. A few lose primaries; others lose general elections. The result is that over several elections, the membership of Congress can change substantially.[32]

The power of incumbency is the critical factor in the stability of Congress. But the broad significance of a high degree of stability is more difficult to establish. The fact is plain that contemporary Congresses are weighted heavily on the side of experience. Whether the current mixture of newcomers and veterans is more conducive to effective legislative performance than mixtures of half a century ago is impossible to say. Some consequences of stability, however, can be identified. The member of Congress today is more of a professional than the member elected around the turn of the century. Increased tenure affords members a much better opportunity to become familiar with legislative procedures and the multiple roles of the legislator. Moreover, the "survival" trend accentuates the importance of achieving seniority as a means of gaining influence in Congress since it takes much longer to rise to a chairmanship in a veteran-dominated institution. In addition, the increasing tenure of members probably serves to strengthen the House's position in its relations with the Senate; House committee chairs now have service records that are at least the equal of those of Senate chairs. Finally, the power of the House vis-à-vis the executive would appear to be strengthened as a consequence of the growing tenure of members; presidents and bureaucrats alike must contend with committee and subcommittee chairs who have accumulated singular experience in their special fields. The stability of congressional membership may be a partial explanation for the conflict that sometimes dominates executive-legislative relations. The time perspectives of the president and members of Congress are far from identical—the president, limited to two terms, is necessarily in a hurry to fashion a program, whereas veteran members of Congress from safe districts can afford to take their time. No one is ringing a bell for them—what is urgent for the president is not necessarily urgent for them.

The virtues of stability are often extolled, perhaps with good reason. Continuity, experience, expertise, and prudence—all are associated with a membership that continues relatively intact from Congress to Congress. But stability may also be seen in a light that illuminates its disadvantages. Somnolence sometimes settles over stable institutions. Opportunities for introducing major changes in policy or organization tend to be small, for changes often pose risks for those who profit from traditional structures and practices. The price of continuity may be a low level of adaptability and a timidity toward experimentation. The ironic byproduct of a stable institution, made that way partly by the public itself, may be popular disaffection over the institution's reluctance or inability to come to terms with new demands and new conditions. Insofar as Congress is concerned, the evidence is less than persuasive on either side of the tenure-turnover equation.

## In the States

One of the long-term features of twentieth-century state legislatures has been a high rate of turnover among members. During the 1930s, for example, the turnover rate (proportion of first-term members to total membership) for the fifty state senates (including unicameral Nebraska) was 50.7 percent; the rate for the forty-nine state houses was 58.7 percent. The turnover rate remained quite high through the 1960s—typically averaging about 40 percent. A significant drop in the rate took place in the 1970s. And during the 1980s average turnover fell to 24.1 percent for state senates and 28.0 percent for state houses—less than half their levels in the 1930s.[33] Most recently, eighteen state houses and twenty-three state senates had turnover rates in excess of 25 percent between 1992 and 1994. Newcomers made up 55 percent of the Kansas Senate, 46 percent of the Alabama Senate, 45 percent of the Maine House, and 43 percent of the Maine Senate, Maryland Senate, and Maryland House. In contrast, the turnover rate for the Louisiana House and Mississippi House was less than 1 percent and only 2 percent in the Mississippi Senate and South Carolina Senate.[34] Taking the states as a whole, there is clearly less turnover today than in the past. Life in the legislature has improved, as reflected in a range of inducements to remain in office, such as better salaries for members, the availability of professional staff, and an overall enhancement of working conditions.[35]

Charles S. Hyneman, whose initial studies of legislative tenure and turnover posed the problem of legislative experience, observed:

> Each program of public policy must root itself in a mass of existing legislation; and each body of lawmakers, whether eager to push forward or concerned to preserve the *status quo,* will profit from a thorough acquaintance with the procedures and ways of the agencies, private and governmental, that put so much of legislative policy into execution. Old-timers in the legislature are more likely than newcomers to possess this needed familiarity with existing legislation and with the ways of these persons and groups that transform the black words of a statute into patterns of action.[36]

A recent study by Peverill Squire of the lower houses of twenty-five states finds a strong relationship between membership stability, on the one hand, and salary and prospects for political advancement, on the other hand. Specifically, turnover is less in states in which legislators are relatively well paid and where they enjoy ample opportunities to advance their political careers (for example, by running for the upper state house or the U.S. House of Representatives). Legislatures vary considerably in the extent to which they offer these incentives to remain in office. Some can be classified as "career legislatures" (those that offer members financial incentives to make legislative service a career), others as "springboard legislatures" (those that offer significant opportunities for advancement), and still others as "dead end legislatures" (those that offer neither financial incentives nor prospects for advancement). Membership stability is greatest in career legislatures.[37]

It seems safe to say that most voters are not troubled in the slightest about membership turnover in American legislatures. If it has thought about it at all, the public has apparently dismissed the argument that becoming an effective legislator requires years of experience in lawmaking. Moreover, the notion that term limits are "the dumbing down of democracy," as Representative Henry J. Hyde (R., IL) described them in 1995, has not caught on with the general public.[38] Quite the contrary: Public opinion surveys in the mid-1990s found that more than three out of four voters were in favor of them.

## PAY AND PERQUISITES

### In the States

State legislators traditionally have been among the lowest-paid public officers found at any level of American government. Although in recent years many states have improved legislative salaries, the new pay levels, with some exceptions, tend to preserve the doubtful tradition that individuals should not make legislative service a career. The idea of the citizen as part-time legislator has an uncommon virility in American politics; it helps sustain the practice of paying woefully inadequate salaries to legislators in many states.

Two basic salary-payment plans are used. The oldest method, which is still used in six states, provides for payment on a per diem basis. (In a slight variation, Vermont legislators are paid by the week.) Forty-three states pay their lawmakers an annual salary.

Of the states that pay a fixed salary, California leads (as of 1998) with a yearly salary of $75,600, followed by New York ($57,500), Pennsylvania ($57,367), Michigan ($51,895), Illinois ($47,039), Massachusetts ($46,410), Ohio ($42,427), Wisconsin ($39,211), New Jersey ($35,000), Hawaii ($32,000), and Oklahoma ($32,000). At the bottom of the list of states using the salary plan are New Hampshire ($100) and South Dakota ($4,267). In 1998, the median for states with fixed salaries was $17,500. In all but five states, legislators receive a per diem payment to cover living expenses while the legislature is in session.[39]

Legislators paid on a per diem basis fare much worse than those paid according to a salary plan. Alabama's per diem is $10 (plus an expense allowance of $2,280 per month) for 105 calendar days; Montana's per diem is

$58 for 90 days (plus an expense allowance of $70 per day). At the top of the heap in this group of states are Nevada, whose lawmakers are paid $130 per day, and Wyoming, where the per diem is $125.[40]

Morris P. Fiorina has found that the professionalization of state legislatures—marked by higher salaries and accompanying full-time service—has made the legislative career a more attractive option to Democrats and a less attractive one to Republicans. The reason for this is that Republicans have better opportunities than Democrats for lucrative careers in the private sector and are less likely to sacrifice them for a full-time job as legislator. On the whole, legislative service is more attractive to potential Republican candidates in less professional legislative settings, where short sessions make the job of legislator less time-consuming; in these "amateur" states, it is easier for them to combine legislative office with an outside career. Professionalization thus has been an advantage for the Democratic party and the pool of potential candidates from which it draws its legislators. Overall, Fiorina finds that every $10,000 increase in legislative salary is associated with approximately a 1 percent increase in the number of Democratic legislators.[41]

State legislative salaries in many states, according to observers, are clearly inadequate. If here and there some state legislators are under the thumb of lobbyists who buy their meals and drinks or otherwise favor them, or of interest groups that place them on their payrolls in the interim between sessions, should such waywardness be surprising? If the legislatures are failing to attract outstanding persons, if they are unable to retain most members for more than one or a few sessions, if their members are low on imagination—the familiar assertions—is there reason to believe that low salaries have something to do with it? As a member of the Idaho legislature observed, "When the gardener working around the state house is paid more than the legislators, you'll never be able to attract the caliber of people you need to run state government."[42]

What constitutes a reasonable standard of remuneration for state legislators is difficult to decide for many reasons, not the least of which are the variations between the states in length and frequency of sessions and in the demands of the job during and between sessions. But this fact does not leave us without a solution. A general prescription would call for states to pay legislators salaries that meet "the cost of their election campaigns and [assure] them, during the period of their service, approximately the kind of living which they are confident they could win in other pursuits."[43] Beyond a doubt, a majority of states would fail this test.

### Congress

Unlike some state legislatures that must receive popular approval of constitutional amendments to raise salaries, Congress is master of its own salary.[44] And although low salary is not the same disabling feature in Congress that it is in many state legislatures, a decent case can be made that congressional pay is far from exceptional in view of the expenses that confront the typical member. The salary of a member of Congress in 1946 was $12,500. In 1999, the salary for members was $141,300.

A major side benefit for members is a substantial allowance for hiring personal staff. Each House member may hire a personal staff of up to twenty-two employees (four of whom must fit into one of several part-time categories, such as interns). In the Senate, staff allowances are made on the basis of state populations, with no limits on the number of employees that may be hired. For a senator from California, the most populous state, the staff allowance is about $2 million. The average member of the Senate has a personal staff of about forty.[45] In one way or another, personal staffs are drawn into the reelection efforts of members. They represent one of the large advantages of incumbents over their challengers.

Fringe benefits of great variety are available to members of Congress. These include a generous pension system, life and health insurance, a certain amount of free medical care from a full-time staff of physicians and nurses, liberal travel allowances, and special tax considerations based on the fact that members require a residence not only in Washington but also in their home district. Hidden "fringe" benefits became news in 1991 when it was disclosed by the General Accounting Office that more than 100 members had bounced (without penalty or interest charge) some 8,000 personal checks on the House's private bank during a one-year period ending June 1990. And before the journalistic and talk-show frenzy over "interest-free loans" could subside, it was disclosed that House members owed more than $300,000 in tabs for meals and catering services provided by restaurants in the Capitol and House office buildings. Self-serving practices, even if not of large significance, do incalculable damage to Congress's image while at the same time fueling campaigns to unseat incumbents by imposing term limits.

An additional perquisite for members should be noted: the franking privilege, the right to send official mail postage-free. Members use the frank not only to respond to constituents' inquiries and requests but also to mail copies of speeches, questionnaires, baby books, and other literature to them—communications that undoubtedly increase the members' visibility and promote their reelection fortunes. Although the franking privilege is widely employed to build electoral support, there are certain restrictions on its use. The ethics code of each house, for example, prohibits the use of the frank for a mass mailing within sixty days of a primary or general election in which the member is running.

The salary of a member of Congress is not as spectacular as it looks to the average voter. Members are subject to a great variety of special expenses that cut a swath through their incomes. Most members maintain houses in their home states as well as in Washington. Social life is expensive: Numerous constituents must be entertained at lunch and at dinner, and there are a great many social gatherings that legislators feel compelled to attend. Local charities and fund drives find members an easy mark, and many members feel pressure to make political contributions of one sort or another. Such reasons help to explain why members of Congress do not grow rich on their salaries, why some go into debt, why others retire, and why still others seriously contemplate retirement.

## PRIVILEGES AND IMMUNITIES

Buttressed by the Constitution and parliamentary conventions, members of Congress enjoy a considerable measure of freedom of speech as well as immunity from arrest. State legislators enjoy similar protection under state constitutions. The national Constitution provides in Article I, Section 6, that senators and representatives "shall in all cases, except treason, felony, and breach of the peace, be privileged from arrest during their attendance at the session of their respective Houses, and in going to and returning from the same; and for any speech or debate in either house, they shall not be questioned in any other place." The proviso granting immunity from arrest is not of major importance today, but the language concerning "speech or debate" is highly significant. In effect, this clause means that there are no formal limits to what a senator or representative may say in Congress (in committee as well as on the floor), no limits to charges he or she may choose to make, no danger of being sued for libel or slander for allegations that he or she has made. Nevertheless, the Supreme Court has made clear, the protection afforded by the "speech or debate" clause does *not* extend to newsletters or press releases of members.[46]

Still another aspect of this constitutional grant was expanded in 1966 when the Supreme Court ruled unanimously that the "speech or debate" clause prohibits the executive and judicial branches from inquiring into a legislator's official acts or the motives that support them. The Court reversed the conviction of a congressman who had accepted $500 to make a floor speech in support of savings and loan institutions; the congressman's assistance came at a time when several of these associations in his state had been indicted on mail fraud charges. The opinion in *U.S.* v. *Johnson* makes it clear that members of Congress enjoy wide-ranging protection from official inquiry concerning their remarks and behavior in Congress.[47]

## LEGISLATORS' ADAPTATION TO THE LEGISLATURE

Legislators are recruited, nominated for office, and elected in a variety of ways. In some jurisdictions, political parties are either the chief or the exclusive sponsor of legislative careers. Elsewhere, parties may count for little or nothing in generating candidacies. Where parties are weak, candidates may be "self-starters," launching their careers apparently on their own initiative. Candidates may be induced to run by former officeholders, friends and associates, or interest groups. Here and there factions appear among the explicit sponsors of legislative careers. A panoramic study of how individuals make their way out of private life or other public position and into the legislature would be certain to show a number of alternative routes or strategies available to candidates. Selection of an appropriate route to winning legislative office is perhaps the first critical decision that faces aspiring candidates. Their second critical decision, obviously of enduring significance for the legislature, involves selection of the role they will play in the system. Vastly different models are open to them.[48] How legislators relate to their office and adapt to the legislative environment determines, in great part, the nature of their contribution to the work and effectiveness of the legislature.

A seminal study of the Connecticut legislature by James D. Barber identifies four major role orientations[49] among freshman legislators: Spectator, Advertiser, Reluctant, and Lawmaker. Spectators do not come to terms with the matters that are central to the legislature. They attend sessions of the legislature regularly, listen to debate, but rarely participate. They like the idea of being in the legislature. Legislative activities, they find, are "tremendously interesting" and legislative service is "a wonderful experience." But they sit and watch. Although their role is passive, legislative service carries rewards for them, including recognition and prestige. These remarks by a Spectator invited to the Governor's Tea are instructive:

> We were very impressed. I mean you couldn't help but be impressed. It's a beautiful home. The Governor and his wife met us graciously and gave us the full roam of the house—"Go ahead, look at anything you want. Make yourself at home. We'll see you later on." And we wandered around. It's a beautiful home. Everything in it is beautiful. And, ah, then tea was served—so we had coffee (laughs). So we were sitting around, or standing there, and the Governor came by and he talked to everybody, and his wife talked with everybody. So—before that, we drove up in front of the house and a state trooper, there, he opened the car door. The passengers got out. I got out. The state trooper took the car, parked it for me. And, ah . . . so we had tea, and the Governor talked with us. His wife talked with us. And when it came time to leave, we departed. And again, why—a warm handshake. None of this fishy handshake, but a warm handshake. And, ah, they thanked us for coming—whereas normally we should have thanked them for being invited. They thanked us for coming. And we got out there, the state trooper, he opened the car door. And off we go. Well, as I say, we had a wonderful afternoon there. As I say, we were only there an hour, hour-and-a-half. It was very impressive. You couldn't help but be impressed. . . .

Advertisers, many of whom are ambitious young lawyers, view the legislature in the harsh light of personal opportunity. One of the main reasons that they decide to run for the legislature is that they may be able to use the office for their own advancement. The legislature is a good place to meet people, make contacts, and gain publicity. As legislators, they are active, aggressive, disdainful of other members, impatient, and often unhappy and frustrated over their inability to accomplish their objectives.

Their stay in the legislature is likely to be brief. Motivation for legislative service is shown clearly in these comments by a legislator classified as an Advertiser:

> But—that's law—a lawyer cannot advertise. The only way that he can have people know that he is in existence is by going to this meeting, going to that meeting, joining that club, this club, becoming a member of the legislature—so that people know that there is such a person alive. And they figure that—"Oh, X, I heard of him. He's a lawyer. Good. I need a lawyer. I don't know one. I'll call him." Otherwise you're just in your cubbyhole waiting for someone to come in off the street. And it doesn't happen.

Reluctants are in the legislature in spite of their attitudes toward it and the nagging problems of adjustment that confront them. These are legislators who are not really interested in politics and who were probably pressured into accepting the nomination by party leaders in their communities. Reluctants usually lack interest in political advancement, dislike political controversy, and are tempted to withdraw from legislative life. To avoid the "politics" and other unpleasant aspects of the legislature, Reluctants are likely to concentrate on mastering the formal rules and procedures that govern deliberation and decision making. The chances are strong that they agreed to serve in the legislature out of a sense of duty:

> Well, of course, my father lived in this town all his life, and the town has been good to him and, well, he's been good to the town. And I thought to myself— of course, father's dead and all that—but I said to myself, Dad would say, "You've got the time, you ought to do it." So that's about the way I felt, that I was doing what was really set out for me to do, that I should do. I felt a, well, I felt duty bound to it, that's all. It wasn't a great hankering that I had. . . .

A legislature populated only by Spectators, Advertisers, and Reluctants would be a remarkably bland and unimaginative institution. Missing would be those legislators who carry the main burdens of the legislature: the Lawmakers. Legislators with this role orientation are highly interested in elective politics, hold positive sentiments toward the legislature, and take an active part in all phases of the legislative process. Deeply interested in issues and confident of their capacity to persuade others, their principal concern is to achieve concrete legislative results. Lawmakers recognize the need for compromise and bargaining and believe that the job of the legislator is to make decisions on bills. The key to understanding Lawmakers is found in their concern over legislation, illustrated in the following comments by two members who were asked to rate their own performances:

Well, I think I've done pretty well. For this reason, that I supported several issues. I served on two important committees, and I supported many main issues—when I say supported, I mean not only voted, but took an actual part in promoting and speaking for them. Appeared before many committees on subjects that were important to my constituents and to the projects that I mention. So I was successful in getting bills that our town needed, and also other bills.

Well, I feel that I've done a big thing in being able to vote on the X bill. I think that was simply tremendous. And of course there are other bills in which I'm very interested. I introduced the bill for Y. And then the bill for Z will be heard tomorrow morning. That would be a big step forward.

Table 5.4, drawn from the Connecticut study, categorizes the four types of legislators according to their *activity* in the legislature (measured by bills introduced and participation in committee and floor discussions) and their *willingness to return* for at least three future sessions. Each variable provides evidence concerning the manner in which members relate to their office. Surprisingly, the variables are not correlated. Thus, the two types of legislators who are most active in the legislature—Lawmakers and Advertisers— differ sharply on the question of returning to the legislature for subsequent sessions. Similar mixing occurs among Lawmakers and Spectators, who differ strikingly in activity but agree in terms of willingness to stay in the legislature.

Legislatures are hospitable to almost all kinds of members. Apart from a few legal qualifications, the only tests of entry are political, and these may be far from rigorous. Recruitment practices and "availability" criteria differ so widely that men and women with markedly different orientations wind up in the legislature—those who watch and applaud, those who advertise their wares, those who serve out of a sense of duty, and those who legislate. Each orientation, it may be argued, contributes something to either the work or the morale of the institution. Spectators, conciliatory and appreciative, doubtless help to reduce tension; Advertisers, aggressive and cynical, may help to illuminate issues and rationalize debate; Reluctants, motivated by a stern moral sense, work to keep "the rules of the game" observed and to keep conflict within tolerable limits. Whatever the occasional or special impacts these legislators may produce, however, it is the Lawmaker who

**TABLE 5.4   Patterns of adaptation among legislators**

|  |  | Activity | |
| --- | --- | --- | --- |
|  |  | High | Low |
| Willingness to return | High | Lawmakers | Spectators |
|  | Low | Advertisers | Reluctants |

SOURCE: James D. Barber, *The Lawmakers: Recruitment and Adaptation to Legislative Life* (New Haven, CT: Yale University Press, 1965), p. 20.

supplies the central energy, ideas, and vision of the legislature. The permanent importance of the Lawmaker is that his or her work is located at the authentic center of the legislative process. Other roles, though functional for limited purposes, are peripheral.

Although hard evidence is lacking, it seems probable that these general role orientations are found in all state legislatures. The types have an authentic ring for students of the legislative process. Perhaps the important question to be distilled from this analysis concerns the recruitment of legislators. There is no reason to believe that the present mixture of these four types in the legislatures is one of harmonious equilibrium or that it is conducive to effective legislative performance. Rather, it is a fair surmise that American legislatures today are overrepresented by legislators who opt for or sink into "secondary" roles, and underrepresented by legislators who fulfill the expectations of the Lawmaker role. The question, then, is whether there are ways by which Lawmakers can be identified and recruited.

Men and women who turn into effective legislators may always be in short supply, their recruitment at best uncertain. Endless statistics could be assembled to prove that business and the professions siphon off considerable talent that might otherwise be available for public office. This is one obstacle to the recruitment of more Lawmakers. A second is that not enough is known about the personal endowments of those individuals who become Lawmakers, and hence there is uncertainty about the qualities to be sought. On the basis of the Connecticut evidence, Barber believes that Lawmakers are characterized by a basic expectation of success, a strong and realistic sense of personal identity, a quest for personal goals, and a disposition to engage in cooperative efforts—confidence, recognition, achievement, and sharing.[50] A third obstacle is simply that there is no assurance that party recruiters regard the identification and selection of Lawmakers as a matter of high urgency; abundant evidence exists, in fact, to suggest that other availability criteria may outweigh that of potential effectiveness as a legislator.

Yet assuming for the moment that some, perhaps many, party recruiters are interested in obtaining the best possible talent for the legislature, are there outward signs that provide clues to potential Lawmakers? The Connecticut study shows that the prelegislative careers of Lawmakers are distinguished by *active* memberships in organizations, *persistent* involvement in organizational work, abiding interest in *political issues,* and a strong measure of *personal security.* In addition, their *careers* have been sufficiently successful that movement to the legislature is not merely an adventure for the purpose of rescuing a precarious business or profession. Whether, once recruited and elected, Lawmakers will make a career of legislative service appears to depend on the nature of the legislature and the nature of the job. For Lawmakers the preeminent requirement is that the legislature be engaged in important work and that individual members be permitted to focus their energy and intelligence on the resolution of issues and the development of legislation.[51]

## LEGISLATORS AND LEGISLATIVE NORMS

All human institutions seek to maintain and to guarantee their survival by establishing norms of conduct that apply to their members. These norms, folkways, or rules of the game govern a variety of situations and practices, both prescribing and proscribing certain kinds of behavior. "For the legislator they set the approximate limits within which his discretionary behavior may take place."[52] They contribute to the continuity of the legislature and carry great significance for the established power structure, plainly helping to support it. The "unwritten rules" keep new members from breaking away from familiar and conventional ways of doing things and offer veteran members comfortable justifications for the way the system governs itself. To the extent that the norms are observed, they are a residual source of power for those members who receive advantage from a stable political institution.

The most authoritative study of congressional norms has been made by Donald R. Matthews in *U.S. Senators and Their World*. Although this study examines only the Senate, there is abundant impressionistic evidence that House norms are distinctly similar. Matthews identifies six main "folkways," or norms: apprenticeship, legislative work, specialization, courtesy, reciprocity, and institutional patriotism.[53]

Until recently, *apprenticeship* was an especially powerful norm in Congress. New members were expected to serve an apprenticeship before entering fully into legislative activity. The newcomer who entered debate too soon, spoke too often, or discussed too many different subjects was likely to be criticized by other members. He or she was likely to be advised that "No congressman has ever been defeated by a speech he didn't make on the floor of the house."[54] Newcomers were also counseled on the importance of learning rules and procedures. A former Speaker of the House, John W. McCormack (D., MA), put the matter this way:

> If I might make a suggestion to new members, going back myself thirty-five years when I came here as a new member, study the rules of the House of Representatives. That's the legislators' Bible. Study the interpretations of the rules as made by the various Speakers. Watch and study older members participating and putting into execution the rules. Learn from them through their experiences. It will be very, very helpful to you. . . . [Those congressmen] who devote themselves to [study] and become conversant with the rules of the House and the interpretation of the rules will . . . become model members of the House.[55]

Freshmen who grew impatient with the apprenticeship norm sometimes ran into difficulty with the leadership:

The very ingredients which make you a powerful House leader are the ones which keep you from being a public leader. It is analogous to the fable that when you go over the wall you are speared; when you go underneath you end up with the fair lady. The yappers just won't get to be leaders. Take————[a freshman] for example. He is a very able individual, but because he persists in getting on the floor and discussing the issues he'll never have any power around here. The structure of power in the House is based on quietude and getting along with the leadership. Freshmen who are vocal and want to exercise initiative and leadership are confined to the cellar, merely because they have been speaking too often.[56]

Today the norm of apprenticeship is less important. New members may become full-fledged participants in the legislative process quite early in their careers. They also move up to important positions, such as a subcommittee chairmanship, earlier in their careers. The greater freedom of new members owes something to the times—to the weakness of the parties, to the independence of voters, to the candidate-centeredness of campaigns, to congressional reforms, and to the greater dispersal of power in Congress. New members find less reason to defer to senior members. At the same time, leaders have found their tasks far more difficult. Senator Mark Hatfield (R., OR) comments on the problems of protecting a committee bill on the floor:

It's terribly frustrating. You come out of a committee with some kind of a proposal that seems to be rather reasonable and then all of a sudden it's like a dog in heat trotting down the street. You attract every conceivable idea, wild, weird and otherwise, that ever penetrated the mind of a human being. . . . When I came to the Senate, you almost waited for the senior members to speak first. You weren't really so audacious as to speak first, let alone challenge on the floor or elsewhere.[57]

Yet whatever members may say about the apprenticeship *norm*, the fact is that apprenticeship continues to be related to significant forms of behavior in Congress. A recent study of House career patterns by John Hibbing finds that senior members are the most active in making speeches, offering amendments, and sponsoring bills. They are also the most specialized and the most efficient (in terms of having their bills both reported out of committee and passed). In other words, they "make the legislative process go":

Actual involvement in legislative matters (in terms of raw activity levels, promoting a focused legislative agenda, and shepherding bills through the legislative process) is more strongly related to tenure than ever before. . . . Senior members, more than any time in the last 40 years, are carrying the legislative burden in Congress. . . . Constituency service operations hum along from the start to the end of the modern congressional career. But legislative involvement, even though opportunities are now available for junior members, is primarily the province of their senior colleagues.[58]

Similarly, an analysis of the House Committee on Education and Labor (re-named Economic and Educational Opportunities in 1995) by Richard Hall finds that freshman members participate in committee decision making much less than experienced members. Participation costs are particularly high for newcomers:

> While group pressures may no longer restrain a new member's behavior, the freshman is more likely to be uninformed about the substance of a bill, naive about committee politics, and dependent on staff who are themselves inexperienced and inefficient. Overcoming such disadvantages requires a substantial investment of the member's scarce time and energy, an investment not likely to be sustained across a range of bills.[59]

A second folkway insists that members should give substantial attention to *legislative work,* even though much of it is tedious and politically unimportant. But someone has to do it, and members are expected to carry their fair share. A former congressman points out that members sometimes ignore the fact that they have two constituencies—"the voters back home and the other members of the House":

> There are three groups of members who either cannot or will not recognize their House constituency. The first group are the nonentities, the members who make no effort to acquire or exert influence in the House. They could be expected to have rather brief House careers, but some last a surprisingly long time. The second group are the demagogues. The term may be strong, but it is the one commonly applied in the House to the member who plays to the press gallery and the home folks on every possible occasion, in full knowledge that everything he says and does is recognized, and discounted, by his colleagues for exactly what it is. The third group who ignore the House constituency are the "pop-offs." Their behavior may occasionally be demagogic, but most of the time it is based on the sincere but greatly exaggerated notion that their colleagues and the world in general need their good advice. Their opinions are quite often sound, but because of their attitude, the "pop-offs" have no influence on the House at large.[60]

*Specialization* is a classic norm. It too is less potent than in the past. When observed, it restricts the interests of members; they are expected to concentrate on limited fields of legislation, ordinarily those that fall within their committee assignments or those that have major significance for their states or districts. As a congressman once argued,

> If [a member] does speak when he is not on the committee concerned with the legislation, the subject matter should relate to a matter of vital importance to his district. Even if a man is exceptionally able there is resentment if he seeks to be an expert on a matter not related to his district or his committee work. ⸺ was one of the most able speakers on almost any subject that

came up, and he usually spoke on every subject before us. Yet members resented the fact he was in on every discussion.[61]

As members acquire increasing expertise in certain substantive fields, the specialization norm predicts, their influence increases. When education or social security or defense policies are under consideration, specialists in these fields are the persons singled out by other legislators in search of information and counsel. "[The] decision to specialize in some legislative field," a former member of Congress has written, "is automatic for the member who wants to exercise any influence. The members who are respected in the House are the men who do their committee chores and become able exponents of the legislative programs in which they have specialized."[62] Although specialization, like certain other norms, has slipped in importance, there are still a number of members whose reputations and influence rest primarily on their knowledge of a substantive field of legislation. Many House members, moreover, continue to see specialization as important to their careers.

Legislatures struggle over matters that count. The stakes are often massive—for parties, interest groups, the executive, bureaucracy, and individual legislators. If it were not for the folkway of *courtesy*, conflict over major issues might easily extend beyond tolerable limits, jeopardizing the ability of members to work together in any fashion. The courtesy rule helps to keep political disagreements and personal aspirations from corroding relations between members.

> The selection of committee members and chairmen on the basis of their seniority neatly by-passes a potential cause of grave dissension in the Senate. The rules prohibit the questioning of a colleague's motives or the criticism of another state. All remarks made on the floor are, technically, addressed to the presiding officer, and this formality serves as a psychological barrier between antagonisms. Senators are expected to address each other not by name but by title. . . . Personal attacks, unnecessary unpleasantness, and pursuing a line of thought or action that might embarrass a colleague needlessly are all thought to be self-defeating—"After all, your enemies on one issue may be your friends on the next."[63]

But this norm is also breached more often in the contemporary Congress. Civility cannot be taken for granted, as these observations by Senator Joseph Biden, Jr. (D., DE), indicate:

> There aren't as many nice people as there were before. It makes working in the Senate difficult. Ten years ago you didn't have people calling each other sons of bitches and vowing to get each other. The first few years, there was only one person who, when he gave me his word, I had to go back to the office to write it down. Now there's two dozen of them. As you break down the social amenities one by one, it starts expanding geometrically. Eventually you don't have any social control.[64]

The norm of *reciprocity* is an outgrowth of the need of both individual legislators and legislative blocs to aggregate support for their positions. Reciprocity activates the legislature, prompts members to examine problems from the vantage point of their colleagues, underlies bargains of all kinds, helps members to extricate bills from legislative bogs, promotes state delegation unity, and explains voting behavior on numerous proposals. Under the rule of reciprocity, members help one another with their problems—ordinarily the most significant exchange occurs in trading votes. Although this folkway is not perfectly observed by any means, there are numerous examples of its use every day legislatures meet:

> ———'s reclamation project carried by just a few votes. One thing that broke the liberal and big city line against it was the fact that all the boys who played poker and gin rummy with him voted for it. And they took some of the rest of us with them. They said he wasn't going to be so difficult in the future.[65]

> It depends on the importance of the bill. On local bills, I think I would [be willing to trade votes]. For example, I am interested in a potato referendum bill . . . and I'm sure that my good friend ——— of New York couldn't care at all about the bill, but he'll probably support it because we're friends. And I'd do the same for him.[66]

> Over the years, House members come to know how most of the other members will react to any given issue, and it is natural that the closest relationships, working and personal, are developed among those men who face common problems and have compatible points of view. The influential member is not the man who limits himself to these natural associations: he is, rather, the man who takes time to study the problems of other groups of members, to seek among them the areas of compatible short-term interest, and who capitalizes on those interests by working with such groups in temporary alliances to mutual benefit.[67]

> I always say, when you're west of the Rockies, there's northern and southern California. When you're east of the Rockies, there's only California.[68]

> We all support anything that's for Pennsylvania no matter where it goes. You have to in this place with its logrolling.[69]

> If a member of Congress representing that district supports [a water project], it generally is funded.[70]

> We can be in the middle of a philosophical battle with strong feelings on both sides, but in the midst of that battle, we can come together on Texas issues.[71]

A final congressional norm is that of *institutional patriotism.* Members are expected to display loyalty to the institution. When thoroughly imbued with the norm, members see the institution and their colleagues as possessing exceptional qualities: "Nowhere else will you find such a ready appreciation of merit and character. In few gatherings of equal size is there so little jealousy and envy."[72] Consider the Senate: "the most remarkable group that I have ever met anywhere," "the most able and intelligent body of men that it has been my fortune to meet," "the best men in political life today."[73] But institutional patriotism is one thing in Washington and another in the constituencies. When the members are back home, campaigning, they are often severely critical of Congress. "Members of Congress," Richard F. Fenno, Jr., has pointed out, "run *for* Congress by running *against* Congress."[74]

The vitality of traditional norms in Congress clearly has declined. A study of decision making on the Senate floor leads Barbara Sinclair to conclude that the apprenticeship norm and the intercommittee reciprocity norm (not reciprocity in general) are dead. Freshman members today are much more active in offering floor amendments than freshmen in the 1950s—thus suggesting the demise of the apprenticeship norm. And with respect to intercommittee reciprocity, it is now standard behavior for members to propose floor amendments to bills from committees on which they do not sit—also an uncommon practice in the 1950s. Members also flout the specialization norm by their practice of offering amendments to bills from a variety of committees. The floor style of senators two or three decades ago was one of restrained activism; today it is one of unrestrained activism. This new style of behavior, interestingly, distinguishes a large share of the membership, regardless of seniority, section, ideology, or party. Among the forces that have contributed to it are the growing openness in institutions, the proliferation of groups, the emergence of highly contentious issues, the independence of members, the weak position of party leaders, the increased importance of the national media, and a heightened concern among members about electoral politics (including the emergence of the Senate as a source of presidential and vice-presidential nominees). In the midst of these changes, the outward-directed activist style has proved irresistible to most senators, and thus restraining norms have given way.[75]

The modern Senate obviously is not the same as the Senate of the 1950s and 1960s, as described so well by Matthews in *U.S. Senators and Their World*. But how much has it changed? An intriguing study by John R. Hibbing and Sue Thomas of how members' activities affect their status within the institution suggests that, in certain important respects, the Senate has changed very little. They find that the members who currently are accorded the most respect exhibit many of the same traits and behavioral patterns that characterized those senators who were most esteemed a generation ago. As in the 1950s and 1960s, those who currently are held in high regard place the institution first and have a reputation for being steadily involved in substantive legislative activities. Because they come closest to observing the classic norms, their description looks familiar:

> . . . a senior member who perhaps possesses a party or committee leadership position, who is a legislatively successful specialist, who is not sycophantic with regard to the president or ideologically extreme interest groups, and who does not devote a disproportionate share of time and resources to constituency

mailings, constituency travel, and legislatively irrelevant floor speeches. [In contrast] those who focus extreme amounts of attention on the constituency, or are overly submissive to the wishes of the president at the expense of effective and focused legislative work, have a more difficult time earning respect.[76]

Expectations concerning appropriate behavior in the modern Senate are different in two aspects, this study shows. Members who make a bid for the presidency and who are successful in gaining media exposure do not suffer any loss of respect from the congressional community. These actions apparently are perceived as enhancing the prestige of the institution rather than detracting from it.[77]

Unwritten rules that influence the behavior of members, in one degree or another, are characteristic of all legislative institutions. Conventional interpretation holds that these norms contribute to the overall effectiveness of the legislature by defining appropriate behavior, rewarding compliance, and diminishing opportunities and incentives for interpersonal conflict. Additionally, norms are expected to make legislative relationships more predictable and to enhance the capacity of members to cooperate with one another. But as we have noted, "going along" to "get along" has not seemed a matter of high urgency to many members in recent years.

The norms that tend to characterize Congress are also found in state legislatures. Other rules also apply. The four-state study (California, New Jersey, Ohio, and Tennessee) discloses that a large number of norms, or "rules of the game," are generally understood and widely accepted by members. Considering the states as a group, the most widely noted rules are that members should perform their obligations (that is, keep their word and abide by commitments), respect other members' legislative rights, show impersonality in their legislative actions, exhibit self-restraint in debate, and observe common courtesies.[78]

There is some evidence of "payoffs" for legislators who behave responsibly and moderately, who strive for accommodation with other members, and who subordinate their own political and policy objectives to that of maintaining institutional harmony. A study of four state legislatures (California, Illinois, Michigan, and New York) finds that legislators whose behavior is "nonprogrammatic" (adaptive or accommodative) have significantly greater influence in the legislature—as measured by their seniority and their selection for top committees and leadership positions—than their more "programmatic" (issue-oriented) colleagues.[79]

In counterpoise, members who bridle at the norms run the risk of alienating their colleagues and incurring sanctions. Among other things, they may lose out on choice committee assignments, be denied special legislative privileges, or find their legislation bottled up in committee or opposed on the floor. For the typical member who wishes to get ahead in the legislature, the "rules of the game" are usually taken into account.

## LEGISLATOR AND LEGISLATURE

Complaints against the legislature come together at two familiar locations. One stream of criticism, centering on the weaknesses in structure and organization of the legislature, finds fault with the fragmentation of legislative parties; with the fact of committee hegemony; and with all the institutional devices that divide power, smother majorities, and make it difficult to fix responsibility. The other finds fault with the quality of members, the "perks" they enjoy, and their apparent failure to observe strict standards of rectitude.

Congress is indicted on both counts. Critics contend that it has failed to organize itself—to organize its power—in a way that will permit it to act responsibly and with dispatch. The decentralization and fragmentation of power, the weakness of the party apparatus and leadership, the power of committees and subcommittees (and their chairs), the custom of seniority, the opportunities for minority and biparty control over public policy formation, and the network of interlocking rules that sometimes immobilizes the decision-making process—these are among the structural-organizational attributes that expose Congress to a steady stream of criticism. Members are also hit with a barrage of criticisms concerning their behavior—charges involving their preoccupation with pork-barrel projects, particularized benefits, local advantage, constituency service, horse trading and vote swapping, short-term policy fixes, serving the organized, protecting incumbents, and other forms of self-serving activity (while at the same time ignoring fundamental matters of reform and ethical conduct).

The organizational logic of the state legislative process attracts relatively little attention. Though it is hard to document, at least in any systematic way, popular uneasiness over state legislatures appears to derive from estimations of the quality of the men and women who serve as legislators. The belief that state legislatures are populated by mediocre men and women is an old complaint, at least as old as the allegations of venality among state legislators in the middle of the nineteenth century.

The criticisms of state legislators are more or less familiar to any newspaper reader: Nominations for state legislative office all too often go to "party hacks" and to persons too long accustomed to making their living from public jobs; legislative elections too frequently involve choices between greater and lesser evils; legislators and their parties are too devoted to individual, factional, or party gains; patronage is the sine qua non for holding office, and at those rare moments when legislators are not working to protect this interest, they are busy "playing politics" with the public's business; legislators are, on the one hand, subservient to local bosses and, on the other hand, vulnerable to the blandishments and the mischief of lobbyists; legislators are indifferent to their duties and attach the greatest urgency to their private and career interests outside the legislature; and election to legislative office becomes a sinecure for jobs well done in party vineyards, an advertisement for fledgling lawyers, or an interlude for some persons of talent on the way up. To sum up all the disparate accounts of legislative incompetence and waywardness, state legislatures are made up of too many persons of second-rate ability, too many persons anxious to serve the private interests of party, too many persons actuated by base motives, and too many persons likely to be caught in this or that peccadillo. If this is not the public image of many legislators, then much of the discussion one hears about state legislators and much of the newspaper comment one reads about the institution and its members are simply unintelligible.

Does this appraisal—shared, it seems, about equally by the wider public, the various attentive publics, the press, and a good many of the press's political writers—have good standing in fact? Unfortunately, available data neither sustain nor invalidate these assessments, although the study of Connecticut legislators shows a large number of members (Spectators, Advertisers, and Reluctants) who are not seriously oriented to the main tasks of the legislature. What comprehensive data do show beyond any doubt is that the men and women who win seats in the legislature generally represent nonlegislative occupations of high social status and that they have attained a high level of formal education; on both counts they rank well above the voters who send them to office. In these respects, then, they are anything but "representative"; in certain other respects, especially in religious and ethnic affiliations, they tend to resemble their constituents.

Yet the belief that many state legislators are persons of modest talents, persons not especially suited to meet the responsibilities of the legislature, has had a long life. If this evaluation is largely erroneous, as it could be, it is one that no legislature easily can afford; if this evaluation is largely accurate, as it could be, it is one that no political system easily can afford. Finally, if prevailing notions about state legislators could be shown to be accurate, they would lead to many salient questions about the public itself since the typical legislator is in several major respects clearly superior to the voters who elect him or her to office.

## NOTES

1. On the importance of attracting and retaining talented and ambitious politicians to the maintenance of an independent Congress, see a provocative essay by Kenneth A. Shepsle, "Representation and Governance: The Great Legislative Trade-off," *Political Science Quarterly*, CIII (Fall 1998), 461–84.
2. *U.S. Senators and Their World* (Chapel Hill: University of North Carolina Press, 1960), p. 20.
3. Donald R. Matthews, *The Social Background of Political Decision-Makers* (New York: Random House, 1954), p. 23.
4. "Who Makes Our Laws?" *Political Science Quarterly*, LV (December 1940), 556–81.
5. John C. Wahlke, Heinz Eulau, William Buchanan, and LeRoy C. Ferguson, *The Legislative System: Explorations in Legislative Behavior* (New York: Wiley, 1962), pp. 77–94, quotations on p. 83.

6. Allan Kornberg and Norman Thomas, "The Political Socialization of National Legislative Elites in the United States and Canada," *Journal of Politics*, XXVII (November 1965), 761–75.

7. Kenneth Prewitt, Heinz Eulau, and Betty H. Zisk, "Political Socialization and Political Roles," *Public Opinion Quarterly*, XXX (Winter 1966–67), 569–82.

8. *Congressional Quarterly Weekly Report*, January 9, 1999, p. 63.

9. *State Legislators' Occupations* (Denver: National Conference of State Legislatures, 1994). See a study of the relationship between political culture and occupational status in state legislatures by John R. Baker, "Exploring the 'Missing Link': Political Culture as an Explanation of the Occupational Status and Diversity of State Legislators in Thirty States," *Western Political Quarterly*, XLIII (September 1990), 597–611.

10. Many citizens disapprove of Congress because it does not conform to their expectations. As the public sees it, Congress is too partisan and too driven by the career orientations of its members; in addition, as the public sees it, it has too many lawyers. David Kimball and Samuel C. Patterson, "Living Up to Expectations: Public Attitudes Toward Congress," *Journal of Politics*, LIX (August 1997), 701–28.

11. Hyneman, "Who Makes Our Laws?" 569.

12. Michael B. Berkman, "Former State Legislators in the U.S. House of Representatives: Institutional and Policy Mastery," *Legislative Studies Quarterly*, XVIII (February 1993), 77–97.

13. *Congressional Quarterly Weekly Report*, January 2, 1999, p. 62.

14. Bernard Grofman and Lisa Handley, "The Impact of the Voting Rights Act on Black Representation in Southern State Legislatures," *Legislative Studies Quarterly*, XVI (February 1991), 111–28. Also see Bernard Grofman and Lisa Handley, "Black Representation: Making Sense of Electoral Geography at Different Levels of Government," *Legislative Studies Quarterly*, XIV (May 1989), 265–79. The election of black legislators is facilitated by the use of single-member districts, especially in urban areas. See the evidence of Gary F. Moncrief and Joel A. Thompson, "Electoral Structure and State Legislative Representation: A Research Note," *Journal of Politics*, LIV (February 1992), 246–56. The critical importance of majority-minority districts to the election of African-American and Latino candidates for Congress is shown by the research of David Lublin, "The Election of African Americans and Latinos to the U.S. House of Representatives, 1972–1994," *American Politics Quarterly*, XXV (July 1997), 269–86.

15. Mary Herring, "Legislative Responsiveness to Black Constituents in Three Deep South States," *Journal of Politics*, LII (August 1990), 740–58. For divergent evidence on voting in Congress, see Kenny J. Whitby, "Effects of the Interaction Between Race and Urbanization on Votes of Southern Congressmen," *Legislative Studies Quarterly*, X (November 1985), 505–17; and Charles S. Bullock III, "Congressional Roll Call Voting in a Two-Party South," *Social Science Quarterly*, LXVI (November 1985), 789–804. Also see Vincent L. Hutchings, "Issue Salience and Support for Civil Rights Legislation Among Southern Democrats," *Legislative Studies Quarterly*, XXIII (November 1998), 521–44.

16. Peverill Squire finds a positive relationship between the percentage of legislators who are black and the state legislature's level of professionalization (as indicated by higher salaries, days in session, and ampleness of staff). "Legislative Professionalization and Membership Diversity in State Legislatures," *Legislative Studies Quarterly*, XVII (February 1992), 69–79.

17. David Hedge, James Button, and Mary Spear, "Accounting for the Quality of Black Legislative Life: The View from the States," *American Journal of Political Science*, XL (February 1996), 82–98.

18. James Button and David Hedge, "Legislative Life in the 1990s: A Comparison of Black and White State Legislators," *Legislative Studies Quarterly*, XXI (May 1996), 199–218.

19. Alan Gerber, "African-Americans' Congressional Careers and the Democratic House Delegation," *Journal of Politics*, LVIII (August 1996), 831–45.

20. http://www.naleo.org/CivicEducation/resultstables.htm.

21. *Congressional Quarterly Weekly Report*, January 9, 1999, p. 63.

22. Women serving in the state legislatures of the 1990s are significantly different from women who served in previous decades. They are younger, better educated, and more likely to come from professional backgrounds. Men serving in the legislatures of the 1990s have about the same characteristics as those who served earlier. See the evidence of Kathleen

Dolan and Lynne E. Ford, "Change and Continuity Among Women State Legislators: Evidence from Three Decades," *Political Research Quarterly*, L (March 1997), 137–51.

23. In earlier years a majority of congresswomen were the widows of former members of Congress. The matrimonial connection is no longer quite so important. See Irwin N. Gertzog, "Changing Patterns of Female Recruitment to the U.S. House of Representatives," *Legislative Studies Quarterly*, IV (August 1979), 429–45. Also see Diane D. Kincaid, "Over His Dead Body: A Positive Perspective on Widows in the U.S. Congress," *Western Political Quarterly*, XXXI (March 1978), 96–104; and Irwin N. Gertzog, "The Matrimonial Connection: The Nomination of Congressmen's Widows for the House of Representatives," *Journal of Politics*, XLII (August 1980), 820–31. The main reason why so few women are elected to Congress, one study finds, is that relatively few enter the race. Evidence also suggests that the more winnable the seat, the harder it is for women candidates to capture the nomination. See Raisa B. Deber, "'The Fault, Dear Brutus': Women as Congressional Candidates in Pennsylvania," *Journal of Politics*, XLIV (May 1982), 463–79. Robert A. Bernstein finds that the prospects for women to be elected to the U.S. House are limited because they receive the wrong kind of nominations—nominations to challenge incumbents instead of nominations for open seats. See the development of this argument in "Why Are There So Few Women in the House?" *Western Political Quarterly*, XXXIX (March 1986), 155–64. The gender gap in congressional representation is not the result of a gender gap in raising campaign funds, according to a study by Barbara C. Burrell, "Women's and Men's Campaigns for the U.S. House of Representatives, 1972–1982: A Finance Gap?" *American Politics Quarterly*, XIII (July 1985), 251–72. Barbara Burrell also finds that female candidates do as well as male candidates in open-seat primaries for the U.S. House of Representatives. The failure of women to hold more seats in the House is primarily the result of a paucity of female candidates. "Women Candidates in Open-Seat Primaries for the U.S. House: 1968–1990," *Legislative Studies Quarterly*, XVII (November 1992), 493–508. The representation of women in legislatures is important, Beth Reingold has shown, because women legislators are attitudinally more inclined to represent women's interests than are their male colleagues. Women legislators are particularly likely to see female constituents as a very important element in their reelection constituency. "Concepts of Representation Among Female and Male State Legislators," *Legislative Studies Quarterly*, XVII (November 1992), 509–37. A study of female members of Congress by Arturo Vega and Juanita M. Firestone finds that their voting behavior resembles that of their male counterparts, although they do emerge as somewhat more liberal. "The Effects of Gender on Congressional Behavior and the Substantive Representation of Women," *Legislative Studies Quarterly*, XX (May 1995), 213–22. Research by Edith J. Barrett shows that black women state legislators, unlike other race and gender groups, are in solid agreement on agenda priorities in the states: education, health care, economic development, and employment. "The Policy Priorities of African American Women in State Legislatures," *Legislative Studies Quarterly*, XX (May 1995), 223–44. According to a study by Kirsten la Cour Dabelko and Paul S. Herrnson, the campaigns of men and women for the U.S. House of Representatives have more similarities than differences. One difference is that women are more likely than men to stress social issues, such as children's welfare, poverty, and education. "Women's and Men's Campaigns for the U.S. House of Representatives," *Political Research Quarterly*, L (March 1997), 121–35.

24. Carol Nechemias, "Changes in the Election of Women to U.S. State Legislative Seats," *Legislative Studies Quarterly*, XII (February 1987), 125–42. In all probability, more women would be elected to state legislatures if more women were candidates for open seats. See Susan Welch, Margery M. Ambrosius, Janet Clark, and Robert Darcy, "The Effect of Candidate Gender on Electoral Outcomes in State Legislative Races," *Western Political Quarterly*, XXXVIII (September 1985), 464–74. Also see Wilma Rule, "Why Women Don't Run: The Critical Contextual Factors in Women's Legislative Recruitment," *Western Political Quarterly*, XXXIV (March 1981), 60–77. Where incumbent reelection rates are high, the entry of women into state legislatures is retarded. R. Darcy and James R. Choike show that the growth in the number of women in state legislatures depends to an important extent on keeping women incumbents in office. But that poses a dilemma because women legislators are the primary source of candidates for higher office. "A Formal Analysis of Legislative Turnover: Women Candidates and Legislative Representation," *American Journal of Political Science*, XXX (February 1986), 237–55. Also see Wilma Rule, "Why More Women Are State

Legislators," *Western Political Quarterly*, XLIII (June 1990), 437–48; and Sue Thomas and Susan Welch, "The Impact of Gender on Activities and Priorities of State Legislators," *Western Political Quarterly*, XLIV (June 1991), 445–66.

25. Susan Welch and Donley T. Studlar, "Multi-Member Districts and the Representation of Women: Evidence from Britain and the United States," *Journal of Politics*, LII (May 1990), 391–412. A recent study by Gary F. Moncrief and Joel A. Thompson finds that women are more likely to be elected from multimember districts than from single-member districts. "Electoral Structure and State Legislative Representation: A Research Note," *Journal of Politics*, LIV (February 1992), 245–56. Similarly, Richard E. Matland and Deborah Dwight Brown find that in North Carolina and New Hampshire there is a positive relationship between multimember districts and the more equitable representation of women. "District Magnitude's Effect on Female Representation in U.S. State Legislatures," *Legislative Studies Quarterly*, XVII (November 1992), 469–92. Also see a study of the Colorado legislature by Lyn Kathlene that finds that "as the proportion of women increases in a legislative body, men become more verbally aggressive and controlling in hearings." This study of "conversational dynamics" shows that "the more women on a committee, the more silenced women become." "Power and Influence in State Legislative Policymaking: The Interaction of Gender and Position in Committee Hearing Debates," *American Political Science Review*, LXXXVIII (September 1994), 560–76.

26. Kim Fridkin Kahn, "The Distorted Mirror: Press Coverage of Women Candidates for Statewide Office," *Journal of Politics*, LVI (February 1994), 154–73. Also see Kim Fridkin Kahn, "Does Being Male Help? An Investigation of the Effects of Candidate Gender and Campaign Coverage on Evaluations of U.S. Senate Candidates," *Journal of Politics*, LIV (March 1992), 497–517.

27. See evidence that the presence of women legislators does make a difference in shaping state abortion policy: Michael B. Berkman and Robert E. O'Connor, "Do Women Legislators Matter? Female Legislators and State Abortion Policy," *American Politics Quarterly*, XXI (January 1993), 102–24. A study of Colorado state legislators finds that gender matters in the formation of public policy dealing with crime. Women legislators stress long-term preventive strategies and intervention measures, whereas male legislators prefer to address the crime problem in terms of stricter sentencing and increased prison space. See Lyn Kathlene, "Alternative Views of Crime: Legislative Policymaking in Gendered Terms," *Journal of Politics*, LVII (August 1995), 696–723. On the other hand, strategies for getting bills passed, Beth Reingold finds, are about the same for male and female lawmakers. In the Arizona and California legislatures, institutional norms, such as compromise and consensus building, are stressed by men and women members alike. Both report that they are reluctant to participate in "hard-ball" politics (e.g., intimidation, coercion), stereotypically associated with masculine behavior. "Conflict and Cooperation: Legislative Strategies and Concepts of Power Among Female and Male State Legislators," *Journal of Politics*, LVIII (May 1996), 464–85. Also see a study by Michele L. Swers that finds that although ideology best predicts voting on women's issues, "congresswomen are more likely to vote for women's issue bills than are their male colleagues even when one controls for ideological, partisan, and district factors." "Are Women More Likely to Vote for Women's Issue Bills Than Their Male Colleagues?" *Legislative Studies Quarterly*, XXIII (August 1998), 435–48.

28. See T. Richard Witmer, "The Aging of the House," *Political Science Quarterly*, LXXIX (December 1964), 526–41.

29. The legislative behavior of members who decide to retire differs from the behavior of those who are running for reelection. With electoral pressures eliminated, retiring members introduce fewer bills, miss more roll-call votes, pass fewer bills, make fewer trips home, and have fewer contacts with their constituents than members seeking reelection. In a word, their legislative activity declines. On the other hand, they tend to have a more focused legislative agenda, since they no longer feel the need to introduce bills on all kinds of topics as a way of satisfying diverse constituency elements. Consult Rebekah Herrick, Michael K. Moore, and John R. Hibbing, "Unfastening the Electoral Connection: The Behavior of U.S. Representatives When Reelection Is No Longer a Factor," *Journal of Politics*, LVI (February 1994), 214–27.

30. See John R. Hibbing, "Voluntary Retirement from the U.S. House: The Costs of

Congressional Service," *Legislative Studies Quarterly*, VII (February 1982), 57–74; Paul Brace, "A Probabilistic Approach to Retirement from the U.S. Congress," *Legislative Studies Quarterly*, X (February 1985), 107–23; John R. Hibbing, "Voluntary Retirement from the U.S. House of Representatives: Who Quits?" *American Journal of Political Science*, XXVI (August 1982), 467–84; Joseph Cooper and William West, "The Congressional Career in the 1970s," in *Congress Reconsidered*, ed. Lawrence C. Dodd and Bruce I. Oppenheimer (Washington, DC: Congressional Quarterly Press, 1981), pp. 83–106; Stephen E. Frantzich, "Opting Out: Retirement from the House of Representatives," *American Politics Quarterly*, VI (July 1978), 251–73; Steven G. Livingston and Sally Friedman, "Reexamining Theories of Congressional Retirement: Evidence from the 1980s," *Legislative Studies Quarterly*, XVIII (May 1993), 231–53; D. Roderick Kiewiet and Langche Zeng, "An Analysis of Congressional Career Decisions, 1947–1986," *American Political Science Review*, LXXXVII (December 1993), 928–41 (Kiewiet and Zeng point out that "knowing the age of a member of the House tells you virtually nothing about the likelihood that he or she will run for reelection, that formal committee and party leadership positions and previous vote margins do not appear to figure into House members' career decisions, and that House Republicans exhibit no higher a level of progressive ambition than do Democrats." Quotation on p. 939.); and Richard L. Hall and Robert P. Van Houweling, "Avarice and Ambition in Congress: Representatives' Decisions to Run or Retire from the U.S. House," *American Political Science Review*, LXXXIX (March 1995), 121–36. The authors find that, among other things, majority party members who are well positioned in the committee power structure are less likely to retire than others and that electoral insecurity increases the probability of retirement.

31. Michael K. Moore and John R. Hibbing, "Situational Dissatisfaction in Congress: Explaining Voluntary Departures," *Journal of Politics*, LX (November 1998), 1088–1107 (quotation on p. 1105). Also see the evidence of Sean M. Theriault that "strategically disadvantaged members," disappointed over their prospects for moving up in the congressional system, are more inclined to depart Congress than their colleagues who are better positioned for advancement. "Moving Up or Moving Out: Career Ceilings and Congressional Retirement," *Legislative Studies Quarterly*, XXIII (August 1998), 419–33.

32. See interesting studies of political amateurs in Congress (members who are elected without prior political experience) by David T. Canon, *Actors, Athletes, and Astronauts: Political Amateurs in the United States Congress* (Chicago: University of Chicago Press, 1990); and by L. Marvin Overby, "Political Amateurism, Legislative Inexperience, & Incumbency Behavior: Southern Republican Senators, 1980–1986," *Polity*, XXV (Spring 1993), 401–20.

33. Richard G. Niemi and Laura R. Winsky, "Membership Turnover in U.S. State Legislatures: Trends and Effects of Districting," *Legislative Studies Quarterly*, XII (February 1987), 115–23. This study updates one by Kwang S. Shin and John S. Jackson III, "Membership Turnover in U.S. State Legislatures: 1931–1976," *Legislative Studies Quarterly*, IV (February 1979), 95–104.

34. *Book of the States, 1996–1997* (Lexington, KY: Council of State Governments, 1997), p. 70.

35. Alan Rosenthal, *The Decline of Representative Democracy* (Washington, DC: Congressional Quarterly Press, 1998), p. 62.

36. Charles S. Hyneman, "Tenure and Turnover of Legislative Personnel," *The Annals*, CXCV (January 1938), 22.

37. Peverill Squire, "Career Opportunities and Membership Stability in Legislatures," *Legislative Studies Quarterly*, XIII (February 1988), 65–82. For additional evidence that turnover is lower in career opportunity states, see Gary F. Moncrief, Joel A. Thompson, Michael Haddon, and Robert Hoyer, "For Whom the Bell Tolls: Term Limits and State Legislatures," *Legislative Studies Quarterly*, XVII (February 1992), 37–47. This study provides good evidence that term limits would not have much impact in most states because relatively few legislators stay in office as long as twelve years. But also see Cynthia Opheim, "The Effect of U.S. State Legislative Term Limits Revisited," *Legislative Studies Quarterly*, XIX (February 1994), 49–59. Opheim finds that a substantial majority of state legislators' careers would be affected by term limitations. Norman R. Luttbeg concludes that the most striking fact about state legislative careers is their *brevity*; what is more, most legislative careers end by voluntary retirement rather than electoral defeat. "Legislative Careers in Six States: Are Some Legislatures More Likely to Be Responsive?" *Legislative Studies Quarterly*, XVII (February 1992), 49–68. And see a study by Jeffrey M. Stonecash of the New York legislature that finds that

the increasing tenure of legislators in that state is *unrelated* to either higher salaries or the members' advantages in resources (staffs, offices, and the like). "The Pursuit & Retention of Legislative Office in New York, 1870–1990: Reconsidering Sources of Change," *Polity*, XXVI (Winter 1993), 301–15.

38. See excerpts from a floor speech by Representative Hyde in the *New York Times*, March 30, 1995.

39. *Book of the States, 1998–1999* (Lexington, KY: Council of State Governments, 1998), pp. 80–81.

40. Ibid.

41. Morris P. Fiorina, "Divided Government in the American States: A Byproduct of Legislative Professionalism?" *American Political Science Review*, LXXXVIII (June 1994), 304–16. Also see Peverill Squire, "Another Look at Legislative Professionalization and Divided Government in the States," *Legislative Studies Quarterly*, XXII (August 1997), 417–32. Squire contends that the increased incidence of divided government is more a function of changes in the behavior of legislators than changes in the characteristics of the institution.

42. Quoted by Carl D. Tubbesing, "Legislative Salaries: The Debate Continues," *State Legislatures*, I (November–December 1975), 19.

43. Hyneman, "Tenure and Turnover," 30.

44. See a study by John A. Clark on the politics of passing a bill to increase congressional salaries: "Congressional Salaries and the Politics of Unpopular Votes," *American Politics Quarterly*, XXIV (April 1996), 150–68. Senior members from safe districts are typically the core supporters of pay-raise bills; they can better tolerate these risky votes than their more junior colleagues.

45. For a variety of data on congressional staffs, see Norman J. Ornstein, Thomas E. Mann, and Michael J. Malbin, *Vital Statistics on Congress, 1993–1994 Edition* (Washington, DC: Congressional Quarterly, 1994), pp. 121–46. Also see Harrison W. Fox, Jr., and Susan Webb Hammond, *Congressional Staff: The Invisible Force in American Lawmaking* (New York: Free Press, 1977); Kenneth Kofmehl, *Professional Staffs of Congress* (West Lafayette, IN: Purdue University Press, 1977); and Michael J. Malbin, *Unelected Representatives: Congressional Staff and the Future of Representative Government* (New York: Basic Books, 1980).

46. *Hutchinson v. Proxmire*, 99 S. Ct. 2675 (1979).

47. 383 U.S. 169 (1966). See also "The Bribed Congressman's Immunity from Prosecution," *Yale Law Journal*, LXXV (December 1965), 335–50.

48. This discussion of legislators' adaptation to the legislature is based on James D. Barber, *The Lawmakers: Recruitment and Adaptation to Legislative Life* (New Haven, CT: Yale University Press, 1965). The statements by members are from pp. 31, 69, 141, and 164–65.

49. "Role orientation," as it is used here, refers to the kind of behavior that legislators themselves believe to be appropriate for fulfilling the duties of legislative office.

50. Barber, *Lawmakers*, pp. 251–54.

51. Ibid., pp. 256–57.

52. David B. Truman, *The Governmental Process* (New York: Knopf, 1951), pp. 348–49.

53. Matthews, *U.S. Senators and Their World*, pp. 92–117.

54. Quoted in Charles L. Clapp, *The Congressman: His Work as He Sees It* (Washington, DC: Brookings Institution, 1963), pp. 126–27.

55. Quoted in Donald G. Tacheron and Morris K. Udall, *The Job of the Congressman*, 2nd ed. (Indianapolis: Bobbs-Merrill, 1970), pp. 200–201.

56. Clapp, *Congressman*, p. 21.

57. *USA Today*, March 28, 1983, p. 8A.

58. John R. Hibbing, "Contours of the Modern Congressional Career," *American Political Science Review*, LXXXV (June 1991), 405–28 (quotation on pp. 425–26). Also see a study of the different types of former state legislators who are elected to Congress: Michael B. Berkman, "Former State Legislators in the U.S. House of Representatives: Institutional and Policy Mastery," *Legislative Studies Quarterly*, XVIII (February 1993), 73–104. Recently about half of all House members have been former state legislators; those members coming from states with professionalized legislatures, such as California and New York, adapt more easily to

the House than members coming from states with the least professionalized legislatures, such as New Hampshire and Wyoming.

59. Richard L. Hall, "Participation and Purpose in Committee Decision Making," *American Political Science Review,* LXXXI (March 1987), 105–27 (quotation on p. 114).

60. Frank E. Smith, *Congressman from Mississippi* (New York: Pantheon Books, 1964), pp. 130–31.

61. Quoted in Clapp, *Congressman,* p. 24.

62. Smith, *Congressman from Mississippi,* p. 130.

63. Matthews, *U.S. Senators,* pp. 97–98.

64. *Congressional Quarterly Weekly Report,* September 4, 1982, p. 2176.

65. Quoted in Clapp, *Congressman,* p. 15.

66. Quoted by Herbert B. Asher, "The Learning of Legislative Norms," *American Political Science Review,* LXVII (June 1973), 503.

67. Smith, *Congressman from Mississippi,* p. 131.

68. Quoted by Barbara Deckard, "State Party Delegations in the United States House of Representatives—An Analysis of Group Action," *Polity,* V (Spring 1973), 329. Also see Richard Born, "Cue-Taking Within State Party Delegations in the U.S. House of Representatives," *Journal of Politics,* XXXVIII (February 1976), 71–94.

69. Ibid., 330.

70. *Congressional Quarterly Weekly Report,* March 4, 1978, p. 566.

71. *Congressional Quarterly Weekly Report,* January 3, 1987, p. 25.

72. Quoted in Clapp, *Congressman,* p. 16.

73. Quoted in Matthews, *U.S. Senators,* p. 102.

74. Richard F. Fenno, Jr., *Home Style: House Members in Their Districts* (Boston: Little, Brown, 1978), 168.

75. Barbara Sinclair, "Senate Styles and Senate Decision Making, 1955–1980," *Journal of Politics,* XLVIII (November 1986), 877–908. In research on the House of Representatives, Rebekah Herrick and Michael K. Moore find that members with "progressive ambition" (those who want to obtain a more important office) are less likely to follow House norms than members with "intrainstitutional ambition" (those who aspire to a leadership position in the House). Seeking visibility, legislators with progressive ambition introduce more legislation and are more active on the floor than members with intrainstitutional ambition. "Political Ambition's Effect on Legislative Behavior: Schlesinger's Typology Reconsidered and Revisited," *Journal of Politics,* LV (August 1993), 765–76.

76. John R. Hibbing and Sue Thomas, "The Modern United States Senate: What Is Accorded Respect," *Journal of Politics,* LII (February 1990), 126–45.

77. Ibid., p. 143. Also see a study by Laura I. Langbein and Lee Sigelman that finds no evidence to support the conventional interpretation that some members of Congress are "show horses" (those who concentrate on gaining publicity) whereas others are "work horses" (those who actually do legislative work). "Show Horses, Work Horses, and Dead Horses," *American Politics Quarterly,* XVII (January 1989), 80–95.

78. Wahlke et al., *Legislative System,* Chap. 7.

79. Corey M. Rosen, "Legislative Influence and Policy Orientation in American State Legislatures," *American Journal of Political Science,* XVIII (November 1974), 681–91.

# 6

# The Committee System

National and state constitutions vest supreme lawmaking power in the legislative branch of government. Such grants of legislative power are set down in broad terms and awarded to the representative body as a whole. Constitutions, however, cannot satisfactorily provide for the management or conservation of this power. In practice, legislative committees have come to occupy positions of great and often crucial importance in the American legislature's decision-making process.

This observation on committee power is far from new. Political scientists have long had a heavy intellectual investment in it, in some part because of its early sponsor. Writing near the end of the nineteenth century, Woodrow Wilson described the committees of Congress as "little legislatures," comprising a "disintegrate ministry."

> The House sits, not for serious discussion, but to sanction the conclusions of its Committees as rapidly as possible. It legislates in its committee-rooms; not by the deliberation of majorities, but by the resolutions of specially-commissioned minorities; so that it is not far from the truth to say that Congress in session is Congress on public exhibition, whilst Congress in its committee-rooms is Congress at work.

> It would seem, therefore, that practically Congress, or at any rate the House of Representatives, delegates not only its legislative but also its deliberative functions to its Standing Committees. The little public debate that arises under the stringent and urgent rules of the House is formal rather than effective, and it is the discussions which take place in the Committees that give form to legislation.

> The privileges of the Standing Committees are the beginning and the end of the rules. Both the House of Representatives and the Senate conduct their business by what figuratively, but not inaccurately, might be called an odd device of *disintegration*. The House virtually both deliberates and legislates in small sections.[1]

## THE ROLE OF COMMITTEES

Tens of thousands of bills and resolutions are introduced in the fifty state legislatures each session (probably 175,000 bills alone in a biennium),[2] and perhaps 10,000 during both sessions of Congress. With a torrent of proposals flooding the legislatures each time they assemble, no chamber can consider all the individual measures put before it. Committee organization, a means for screening the legislature's business, has proved unavoidable.

The key feature of executive-legislative relations in the United States—a system of separated powers with considerable independence for each branch—makes it unlikely that the committee system could have developed much differently. In formal terms, Congress is master of its own house; its committees are its creatures. Over the years, however, committees have steadily accumulated powers vis-à-vis the chambers as a whole. Hence, there are times at which Congress seems to be little more than the sum of its committees. In clear contrast is the position of committees in the British Parliament, where committee powers are carefully circumscribed. As Herman Finer put it so well,

> The British Parliament differs from Congress in this one tremendous practical feature: *it is in the full assembly of the House, not in its committees, that the center of authority over political principle and action is located.* The House of Commons does not delegate to its committees the power of life and death over laws and the conduct of investigation as the House of Representatives and the Senate do. The principle of a bill, its main theory, the great lines of its enacting clauses, are decided by open debate in the House of Commons itself with the social passions, the party emotions, the flow of information and the contending interests, focussed in the one body open to the public view.[3]

The importance of committees in American legislatures does not stem from the legislature's willingness to divest itself of power, to turn the crucial phase of decision making over to smaller units. Nor is it the result of the legislature's prolonged neglect of its internal processes. There are rather a number of good reasons for the prominence of committees. An obvious one, first, is simply the volume of proposals introduced—so great is it that it would be impossible for the assembly as a whole to consider each proposal. A second reason emerges from the complexity of legislation. To the outsider, legislation may seem to flow placidly along, as Wilson observed; a closer look, however, shows that this is not the case. Because it is complicated and almost invariably technical in detail, legislation demands a measure of expertise from those who consider it. Proposals need examination in light of existing statutes, details need to be fashioned, and estimates and decisions regarding the requirements for passage have to be made. To these tasks committees are able to bring specialization.

Policy specialization is also important to the members at large. The thrust and implications of legislation are frequently not clear. Nonspecialists in particular need information and cues, which committee and subcommittee experts can provide. As observed by a senior subcommittee member, "I didn't go to any of my colleagues for the purpose of getting information. Actually, other members come and talk with me. On this issue, I probably know more than most of them because of my position on the subcommittee."[4]

Many years of experience in dealing with a policy domain are wrapped up in a committee's members, especially in Congress. With committee experience comes the opportunity for specialization, which in turn enhances the member's and the legislature's effectiveness—so run certain assumptions. But for several reasons, there is more to the story. First, years of legislative seasoning provide no guarantee of a member's expertise or effectiveness; its principal contribution may be to sharpen the legislator's instinct for conserving that which is familiar and comfortable. Second, committees are made up of both "formal" and "efficient" parts. A committee's formal element comprises the chair and the party majority; a committee's efficient element is made up of the men and women who do the real work of the committee, who guide the hearings, pose the main options, shape the amendments, and steer the legislation when it is considered on the floor. The formal and efficient parts of a committee do not necessarily coincide, though they may. Holbert N. Carroll, who makes this distinction, believes that the efficient element ordinarily is less than a majority of a congressional committee.[5] Third, contemporary members simply find it more difficult to specialize because of the time they must give to constituency service and to the quest for reelection (including the oppressive demands of raising campaign funds). And fourth, multiple committee assignments detract from the attention that members can give to the policy questions of any one committee. All this suggests that the contribution of committees to specialization may be somewhat less than is usually presumed; nonetheless, it is still substantial and, doubtlessly, a stronger norm in some committees than in others.

A third reason that helps to account for the prominence of committees arises from the decentralization of American politics. The separation of powers, the difficulties that attend executive efforts to influence the legislature, the absence of a central agenda for the legislature, and the relative weakness of legislative party organizations—each contributes to the creation of a legislature with multiple and diffuse points of access. One specific outcome is a strong, sometimes independent, committee system. A fourth reason is that the committee process facilitates negotiation and logrolling. Congress turns most of its work over to committees, writes John Fischer, "simply because the committee room is the only place where it is possible to arrange a compromise acceptable to all major interests affected."[6]

A fifth reason that committees loom so important in the legislative process, and particularly in Congress, is that they are an essential element in the strength of the institution as a whole. Nelson W. Polsby makes the case succinctly:

> Any proposal that weakens the capabilities of congressional committees weakens Congress. Congressional committees are the listening posts of Congress. They accumulate knowledge about the performance of governmental agencies and about the effects of governmental programs and performance on private citizens. They provide incentives to members of Congress to involve themselves in the detailed understanding of governmental functioning. They provide a basis—virtually the only well-institutionalized basis in the House of Representatives—for understanding and for influencing public policy.[7]

Finally, though some lawmakers chafe under committee rule, it seems clear that most view sympathetically the role that committees have come to play in the legislative process. Committee and subcommittee chairs, of course, have a stake in protecting the power of committees.

The functions of committees resemble those of the legislature itself. A committee's lawmaking function involves studying, sifting, sorting, drafting, and reporting legislation that has been referred to it. In their "executive" capacity, committees are concerned with matters of presidential nominations, treaties, and executive agreements. As investigative bodies, committees hold hearings, invite and subpoena witnesses to testify and to be interrogated, call for records, inquire into the operations of executive agencies and policies, and issue reports. Cast in the role of consultants, some committees meet and confer regularly with administration officials; among the committees dealing with foreign policy this attempt to improve executive-legislative relations is most highly developed. Finally, in a capacity of liaison, committees provide not only a link with the executive branch but also, through hearings and other meetings, a bridge to public opinion; a point of access for groups and private individuals; and in the case of the foreign relations committees, a forum for contact and consultation with visiting foreign officials.

Kenneth Shepsle and Barry R. Weingast provide a different perspective on the prominence of committees in the legislative process. Committee power is viewed as a function of *gatekeeping* (deciding which measures will reach the floor), *information advantage* (committees as repositories of policy expertise), and *proposal power* (committees as policy incubators and shapers of legislation). In addition, the norms of *deference* and *reciprocity*, under which members tend to defer to committee judgments, further bolster the committees' strategic position in the legislative process. (These norms, of course, are less powerful today than in the past.) But the key element in committee power, in this interpretation, is the ex post veto. Most major bills are put in final form by a conference committee. Since conference committee members are drawn from the relevant committees, these members get a "second crack" at their bill; if it has been amended in unacceptable ways they can refuse to agree to a conference settlement, thus killing the bill. The existence of the ex post veto and the take-it-or-leave-it quality of conference reports gives credibility to the committee when its legislation is under consideration on the floor.[8]

The power of committees is, of course, not immutable. Steven S. Smith has shown that congressional policymaking has become increasingly influenced by floor decisions. Committee decisions are more likely to be challenged on the floor today than they were in the 1950s and 1960s. Specifically, more floor amendments are offered and more are adopted—leading to a Congress in which floor politics has become more important and decision making more collegial. The heightened influence of the floor in decision making affects both the committees' *positive* powers (their capacity to bring about a policy change when confronted by a floor majority opposed to it) and their *negative* powers (their capacity to prevent change when confronted by a floor majority in favor of it).[9]

On the whole, negative power (such as the power to kill legislation by refusing to report it to the floor, the ex post veto, or the committee advantage conferred by closed rules) is almost as decisive today as it was several decades ago. The committees' positive powers, however, have suffered some attrition. The power to propose measures does not guarantee that floor leaders will schedule the legislation or that floor majorities will consider it. Although the advantage still rests with committees, their edge in information over nonmembers has declined. "Open meetings, larger personal staffs, the availability of experts in the congressional support agencies, assistance from more interest groups and other factors have multiplied the source of information, both political and substantive, to which rank-and-file members have access." The growth in subcommittee power and the ebbing significance of the apprenticeship and deference norms have also taken a toll on committee cohesiveness and positive power. The net result is that committees are now less successful in resisting unfriendly amendments on the floor. The committees that are most likely to experience floor-amending activity are those with large and controversial agendas, such as the money and foreign policy committees.[10]

Notwithstanding the growing importance of floor politics, committee power is still substantial. The same party that controls the committees controls the floor. Moreover, the policies favored by committee majorities typically are not in conflict with the preferences of floor majorities.[11] Thus Smith concludes, "The vast majority of the policy provisions enacted into law each year still are put in legislation at the committee stage. The pattern of change in floor amending activity therefore reflects a change in degree, rather than kind. Committees remain powerful, even if not as dominant as they once were."[12]

Another line of research seeks to account for the substantial success of committees. Forrest Maltzman asks why members support committee recommendations. He tests three explanations:

1. *Institutional:* Members support committee recommendations because they derive power from the committee system (because in deferring to other committees, they protect their influence within their own committees or because they have been socialized to support committee decisions).

2. *Policy:* Members support committee recommendations because their recommendations are consistent with members' policy preferences.

3. *Majority party:* Members support committee recommendations out of partisan loyalty; that is, majority-party members defer to committees because their party controls the committee system.

Based on an analysis of roll-call data from three recent Congresses (98th through the 100th), the study finds relatively little evidence that supports the institutional explanation and substantial evidence for the other two. Specifically, committees can expect a high level of floor support because party loyalty is at work and because they report only bills that are consistent with members' policy preferences. Committees, in other words, are constrained in important respects.[13]

## THE REPRESENTATIVENESS OF COMMITTEES

The powers that committees exercise contribute to a concern over their representativeness. At the root of the problem is the process by which members are assigned to committees. Among the factors that are taken into account are the members' own preferences. Legislators quite naturally attempt to gain seats on those committees that are most likely, for one reason or another, to enhance or safeguard their careers.

Research by E. Scott Adler and John S. Lapinski demonstrates that a number of House committees are "outliers"—that is, committees whose memberships are distinctly unrepresentative of the chamber as a whole in terms of the characteristics of their districts. The members of these outlier committees represent districts with high demand for the policy benefits that can be transmitted through committee decisions. The most "extreme" or unrepresentative committees, when compared to the floor, are Agriculture (members from agriculturally oriented districts); Armed Services (districts with military installations and/or high levels of military employment); Banking, Finance, and Urban Affairs (poor urban districts or those with major banking/finance activities); Education and Labor (districts with strong union interests); Foreign Affairs (districts with large foreign-born populations that are especially interested in foreign aid or foreign policy programs); Interior and Insular Affairs (rural districts with large land areas controlled by the Interior Department); Merchant Marine and Fisheries (coastal districts, particularly those with large ports and/or maritime academies); and Public Works and Infrastructure (districts with high levels of interest in large public works projects, particularly those that protect against natural disasters).[14] It is not surprising that "private goods" committees, such as Agriculture and Interior, have unrepresentative memberships, but it is confounding to find that "public goods" committees such as Foreign Affairs and Banking have so many members from districts with compelling policy needs. From a public policy standpoint, of course, unrepresentative committees and members' preoccupation with particularized benefits go hand in hand.[15]

Committees convey important benefits to their members. The "pork" and "interest" committees—for example, Resources (formerly Interior and Insular Affairs), Transportation and Infrastructure (formerly Public Works and Transportation), and Agriculture in the House—have a particular attraction for those legislators seeking direct payoffs for their constituencies. The House Armed Services Committee regularly contains a disproportionate number of members representing constituencies with military installations; in addition, as Bruce A. Ray has shown, new members recruited for this committee are more supportive of the military than their colleagues.[16]

The results of skewed representation are not unexpected. First, some committees (and subcommittees) become overrepresented by liberals, others by conservatives. In the House, the memberships of Armed Services, Agriculture, and Veterans Affairs are distinctly conservative. In contrast, the memberships of Education and Workforce (formerly Education and Labor), International Relations (formerly Foreign Affairs), and Judiciary are more liberal than average. Differences of this type also appear in the makeup of Senate committees.[17] Nevertheless, Senate committees overall are more ideologically representative today than they were in the 1960s.[18] A study of the committee assignment process in the House suggests that ideological imbalance results more from the distribution of members' committee preferences than from systematic and calculated favoritism.[19]

Second, certain committees tend to become the special pleaders for legislation designed to promote the interests of their clienteles. As put by a member of the House:

> It has generally been regarded . . . that the members of the committees should almost be partisans for the legislation that goes through the committee and for the special interest groups that are affected by it.[20]

Third, some committees are closely linked to the representation of distinctive state interests. Barry Rundquist and his colleagues have shown, for example, that the defense committees of the House and Senate (including the relevant subcommittees of the appropriations committees) consistently overrepresent large and conservative states with major economic interests in defense spending. The defense committees are not only outliers in terms of ideology but also in terms of military payrolls and contracting.[21]

Committees that are out of touch with the full house may, of course, find their proposals modified or defeated on the floor. Nevertheless, controls by the parent chamber can only partially counteract biases in committee representation. Committee members possess much greater expertise and information on subjects within their jurisdiction than the average member. When a committee refuses to take action, moreover, the full house cannot do much about it. The advantages built into the legislative process favor the committees rather than the chamber.

The development of a more representative committee structure is no easy task. The goal of balanced committees collides with the hard realities of politics, including the members' own aspirations. Just as urban members do not flock to the Agriculture Committee, farm-belt members do not strain for ways to serve on the Economic and Educational Opportunities Committee. "The way in which committee assignments are made," writes Richard L. Hall, "guarantees that these groups are deep in 'interesteds' and unrepresentative of the regional, ideological, and seniority patterns evident in the parent chamber."[22]

The concern of this chapter, to this point, has been to introduce legislative committees by marking their principal characteristics, noting their activities, and suggesting the general dimensions of their authority. We can now turn to an examination of committee organization and the principal kinds of committees found in legislative bodies.

## KINDS OF COMMITTEES

### Standing Committees

Standing committees are the permanent units established in the rules of each house. They continue from one session to the next, though the parent house may of course choose to augment or decrease their number from time to time. Organized along policy lines, they are the real draft horses of the legislature, their power sufficient to prompt Woodrow Wilson to describe the American system as "a government by the Standing Committees of the Congress."[23] Their importance traces from the fact that all legislative measures, with an occasional exception, are sent to appropriate standing committees for consideration.

Standing or permanent committees have been used since the earliest Congresses, though in the formative years reliance was placed chiefly on the select or special variety.[24] One early Congress created more than three hundred select committees to deal with ad hoc problems. To bring order and save time, Congress soon turned to the further development of standing committees. During the 14th Congress (1816), for example, the Senate adopted a resolution that provided for the appointment of eleven additional standing committees each session, some of which, such as Foreign Relations, Finance, and the Judiciary, have continued to the present day. Standing committees were also firmly established in the House by then, and before long each chamber had brought to life more permanent committees than in fact it knew what to do with.

By 1913 there were seventy-three permanent committees in the Senate, almost one to a senator. Congress finally chose to do something about it, and eliminated a number of committees in 1921. Writing in 1926, Congressman Robert Luce described the situation: "In Congress the Senate has 34 committees, nearly all functioning, for it has reformed its organization. The House has 61, about two thirds of which get something to do, the rest being superfluities, sustained for ulterior but not altogether useless purposes. A score of the House Committees do nine tenths of the work."[25] In 1946 Congress made a concerted effort to rationalize the committee structure by passing the Legislative Reorganization Act, just about as well known under the names of its sponsors, Senator Robert M. La Follette, Jr., and Congressman Mike Monroney.

With the passage of this act Congress had, for the first time in over a century, organized itself in what appeared to be a reasonable number of standing committees. The House cut its roster of permanent committees from forty-eight to nineteen, the Senate from thirty-three to fifteen. Committees that had led a furtive, somnolent existence for decades were now merged with others or, in a few cases, abolished outright. (See Table 6.1.)

A switch in party control can lead to sharp changes in the committee system. Following their sweeping victory in 1994, House Republicans eliminated three standing committees: District of Columbia, Merchant Marine and Fisheries, and Post Office and Civil Service; their jurisdictions were assumed by other committees. Currently, there are nineteen standing committees in the House and seventeen in the Senate.

In quest of improved organization, state legislatures have also reduced the number of their standing committees. Several decades ago it was common to find state lower houses with forty or fifty standing committees. Today the average lower house has less than twenty such committees, while state senates have even fewer.

### Select Committees

Select committees are limited, episodic bodies created by resolution for the purpose of undertaking a particular task, such as an investigation or a study. Members are ordinarily appointed by the presiding officer, and when the committee has made its report to the chamber, it is disbanded. Although

TABLE 6.1  Standing committees of the House and Senate

| House | Senate |
|---|---|
| Agriculture | Agriculture, Nutrition and Forestry |
| Appropriations | Appropriations |
| Armed Services | Armed Services |
| Banking and Financial Services | Banking, Housing and Urban Affairs |
| Budget | Budget |
| Commerce | Commerce, Science and Transportation |
| Education and the Workplace | Energy and Natural Resources |
| Government Reform | Environment and Public Works |
| House Administration | Finance |
| International Relations | Foreign Relations |
| Judiciary | Governmental Affairs |
| Resources | Health, Education, Labor and Pensions |
| Rules | Indian Affairs |
| Science | Judiciary |
| Small Business | Rules and Administration |
| Standards of Official Conduct | Small Business |
| Transportation and Infrastructure | Veterans Affairs |
| Veterans Affairs | |
| Ways and Means | |

they resemble standing committees, and sometimes are transformed into them, they are rarely empowered to originate legislation.

Any one of several reasons may underlie the establishment of a select committee. In the House of Representatives they have been formed to accommodate interest groups wanting special attention to their claims, to reward a legislator by giving him or her the chairmanship of a committee, to evade the jurisdiction of a standing committee considered unsuitable for an assignment, and to undertake a particular task when two or more standing committees might contest jurisdiction in the matter. Select committees in the House generally have had slight influence on public policy. One study of House select committees established during six Congresses (80th–85th) concludes that a majority "did not perform as legislative committees but functioned as institutions for the self-education of the House and the education of American publics, and also as forums and service centers for interest groups that claimed to have inadequate access to the regular standing committees."[26]

Select committees have lost favor in recent years. Amid charges that they represent wasteful government spending, four House select committees (Aging, Children, Hunger, and Narcotics) were abolished in 1993. And only four select committees were funded in the 106th Congress (1999–2000)—Ethics, Intelligence, and Special Aging (in the Senate) and Intelligence (in the House).

## Joint Committees

Joint committees, formed through concurrent resolution or legislative act, get their names from the nature of their membership since they are made up of legislators from each house. There are three principal subtypes: *conference* (which has the temporary status of a select committee), *select* (generally charged with very minor joint administrative functions), and *standing*. Congress has made some use of joint standing committees, and in a few states—Connecticut, Maine, and Massachusetts—they constitute the predominant form of committee organization. Joint committees are used in thirteen additional states, but their activities not only are limited but also are usually of low urgency.

As of 1996, there were four joint committees in Congress: Economic, Taxation, Library, and Printing. The chairmanship of a joint committee is usually rotated between the chambers at the beginning of each Congress. If the chair is a member of the House, the vice-chair is usually a senator, and vice versa.

Joint committees traditionally have been prescribed as a means of achieving coordination in a bicameral legislative system. Some of the claims made for them are clearly verifiable, as the following list should indicate, whereas others rest chiefly on the impressions offered by observers and legislators themselves. The advantages of joint committees, as estimated by the Committee on American Legislatures of the American Political Science Association, are that

1.  They avoid the necessity for dual consideration of bills, which is both time-consuming and expensive.

2.  They provide the means for better coordination of the work of the two houses, avoiding much of the usual friction and misunderstanding.

3.  They facilitate the expeditious consideration of legislation and afford some of the advantages of a unicameral legislature while retaining a bicameral system.

4.  They provide, as a rule, for more thorough consideration of legislation and the better utilization of qualified staff than is possible with separate committees.

5.  They reduce the use of companion bills, as well as the need for conference committees.[27]

Despite the apparent advantages of joint committees, many legislators view them with much less than unbridled enthusiasm. Political rivalries and concern over political advantage undermine their attractiveness. Zealous in guarding the jurisdictions of committees of which they are members, legislators are reluctant to create other centers of power and prestige. Rivalries between the House and Senate similarly inhibit the formation of joint committees. House members in particular are offended by the practice of some senators in sending members of their staffs to represent them in meetings.

### Conference Committees

Among the run of joint committees, one kind in particular stands out—the conference committee. These committees, preeminent examples of committee power, hold the key to the fate of many major legislative proposals. "[They] are the ultimate high for legislators," observes a House member. "They are the Supreme Court of legislation. If you don't get it here, there's no other place to go." Also, as discussed earlier, conference committees are a prime example of ex post power. Since these committees generally are more important in Congress than in the state legislatures, our discussion begins at the national level.

A conference committee is an ad hoc committee created to adjust differences between the chambers when a legislative proposal passes one house in one form and is amended in the other, with the second chamber unwilling to recede from its amendment(s) and the originating house unwilling to accept the alteration. On some measures amendments are shuttled back and forth between the houses as members search for common ground. When agreement cannot be reached, the chambers ordinarily agree to form a conference committee to seek resolution of the conflict. A bill or resolution cannot be transmitted to the executive unless it has passed both houses in identical form.

The number of members appointed by each house to a conference committee is variable. During the 1950s and 1960s, the usual conference had a membership of five representatives and five senators. Reflecting the growing concern for the democratization of intracommittee politics, the average conference today has a membership of twelve representatives and ten senators.[28] To handle major, omnibus legislation, extremely large conferences have become common, with members drawn from a dozen or more different committees. The larger the conference, some members contend, the greater the likelihood that the key compromises will be worked out by a small group of House and Senate leaders. The growing size of conference delegations, coupled with the requirement for open meetings, appears to have heightened the accountability of conferees.[29] There is no requirement that each house appoint the same number of managers. A majority of managers representing each house must agree to the provisions of a conference report before it can be sent to the chambers.

Conference committee members, termed managers or conferees, are appointed by the Speaker of the House and by the presiding officer of the Senate. In practice, the chair and ranking minority members of the committee having jurisdiction over the bill select the conferees. Seniority may or may not be followed in the selection of members. It is expected that the conferees will represent the position of their respective houses in conference deliberations, but not to such an extent that compromise is impossible. Since the mid-1970s the House has had a rule that instructs the Speaker, "to the fullest extent feasible," to name members who are the chief supporters of the key provisions of the chamber's bill.[30]

Conference committees have been the object of heavy criticism over the years, the principal charge being that they exceed their authority, writing virtually new legislation rather than adjusting differences in the separate versions. But the reality is that conferees need to be given considerable discretion since major compromises are often required to reach an acceptable agreement. Thus rules that restrict conferees are difficult to enforce. And note the problem when one house amends a proposal originating in the other house by striking out everything following the enacting clause and substituting provisions that make it an entirely new bill; the versions are now sharply different, thus giving the conferees considerable room for maneuver. A study by Gilbert Steiner of two decades of conference committee action on major bills, however, found that it was rare for conferees to produce completely new bills.[31] The controversy over conference committees stems largely from the fact that major congressional measures often wind up being routed through these committees.

The conference process is well illustrated in this account by Richard F. Fenno, Jr., of negotiations over appropriations:

> The Appropriations Committee, or, rather, a few of its members act as the spokesmen for the House in these negotiations. They are expected to drive as hard a bargain as possible on behalf of those provisions approved by the House. House expectations may be registered in different ways and with different degrees of intensity. In some instances the House may, by special roll call vote, "instruct" its conferees, i.e., bind them, to a certain position. Ordinary roll calls may also register House expectations. In these cases, the more lopsided the roll call votes the more firm is the House expectation that its position should be upheld. In other cases, individual Members will simply exhort the Committee to "stand hitched" or to "fight until the snow comes if necessary to maintain the position of the House in effecting reduction in these bills." The House expects, however, that the Committee will have to compromise if a bill is to be produced. They hope that Appropriations Committee conferees will draw upon a sufficient reservoir of institutional patriotism and skill to produce compromises which they can claim as "victories" over "the other body." But House members do not expect to fix the terms of the compromise themselves. Again, within certain guidelines, the specifics of decision-making are left to the Committee.[32]

A number of studies have been made of conference committee decision making. For the most part they show that the Senate is more likely than the House to dominate conference outcomes. For example, Fenno has shown that of 331 appropriations conferences occurring between 1947 and 1962, the "dollar outcome" in the final bill was closer to the Senate version than to the House version in 187 cases. House conferees won 101 times, and the two groups "split the difference" in 43 cases. The Senate thus won almost twice as many contests in conference as the House.[33] In a study of 596 conferences in five Congresses over a twenty-year period, David Vogler found that of those conference outcomes marked by a "victory" for one or the other house, the House prevailed 35 percent of the time, as against 65 percent for the Senate.[34]

Several explanations for Senate dominance have been advanced. One is that the Senate tends to be the "high house"—that is, it usually comes to a conference supporting higher appropriations than the House. When demands for appropriations overcome sentiments for economy, as they often do, the Senate wins. Yet this explanation suffers from the fact that the Senate wins about as often when it supports the *lower* figure as when it supports the higher figure. Fenno believes that Senate influence is stronger in conference "because the Senate [Appropriations] Committee and its conferees draw more directly and more completely upon the support of their parent chamber than do the House [Appropriations] Committee and its conferees. . . ." "When the Senate conferees go to the conference room," he writes, "they not only represent the Senate—they are the Senate. The position they defend will have been worked out with a maximum of participation by Senate members and will enjoy a maximum of support in that body." Chamber support for House conferees, in contrast, is more tenuous, probably because House members as a whole are not as "economy-minded" as the members of the Appropriations Committee. Given less than firm support by members of their own chamber, House conferees may be tempted to yield at critical junctures in conference negotiations.[35] Another explanation for Senate dominance is that, more often than not, the Senate acts second to the House on legislation. More legislation originates in the House than in the Senate. In the conference bargaining process, "the conferees from the first acting chamber have an incentive to exchange marginal amendments in the bill with conferees from the second acting chamber to obtain the latters' support for the major aspects of the bill their chamber has passed."[36]

Whether the House or Senate "wins" in conference may well depend on the policy questions at stake. For example, John Manley has shown that the final settlements on tax and trade legislation tend to be closer to Senate versions than to House versions, whereas social security legislation is more likely to find the House getting its way. The study suggests that in the case of both tax and trade legislation, on the one hand, the Senate does better "because politically Senate decisions are more in line with the demands of interest groups, lobbyists, and constituents than House decisions." On the other hand, the House has tended to dominate social security legislation through its capacity to insist that such legislation be sound from an actuarial stand-point—that is, that liberalized benefits be accompanied by increases in the social security tax and/or in the wage base subject to the tax.[37]

The "who wins–who loses" argument is invariably difficult to settle, not only because of the complexity of legislation but also because "the process is not a zero sum situation." Gains derived in one respect may be off-set by losses in another:

> The overriding ethic of the conference committee is one of bargaining, give-and-take, compromise, swapping, horse-trading, conciliation, and malleability by all concerned. Firm positions are always taken, and always changed. Dead-locks rarely occur to the degree that the bill is killed. Someone gives a little, per-haps after an impressive walkout, in return for a little; compromise is the cardinal rule of conference committees. Small wonder that each side claims vic-tory; because almost everyone does win—something, somehow, sometime.[38]

At the state level, one survey has shown, the most common method of reconciling conflicts between the chambers is through consultation among legislative leaders. In about one-fourth of the states, however, conference committees are the principal method for resolving differences between the chambers. On the whole, conference committees play a more important role in those states in which there are significant conflicts over policy.[39] It is quite unlikely that conference committees are as important in any state as they are in Congress. A few states make no provision for them.

### Subcommittees

In some respects the most noteworthy development in committee organiza-tion and management in Congress since the Legislative Reorganization Act of 1946 has been the growth of subcommittees. In the typical Congress of the 1980s, for example, there were more than 225 subcommittees in operation. One of the first acts of the new House Republican majority in 1995 was to cut the number of subcommittees by about 25 percent. The total for both houses in the 106th Congress (1999–2000) was about 140.

Although subcommittees create problems of coordination in shaping legislation, they are a boon to individual members, permitting them to lay claim to a "piece of the action." The wry observations of a member of the House are worth quoting:

> We've got committees, select committees, permanent select committees. When we get to a problem like energy, about ten different subcommittees have juris-diction, so we set up a select committee and then what it does has to be redone by the subcommittees. I think there are almost a hundred and fifty chairmen of committees and subcommittees in the House. When you walk down the halls and you don't know a member's name, if you say "Hello, Mr. Chairman" you come out right one out of three times.[40]

One of the key questions concerning congressional subcommittees is their power vis-à-vis parent committees and chambers. The broad facts appear to be that, ordinarily, there is limited control over subcommittees by the parent chambers and that the relative independence of committees varies from committee to committee. Under Democratic control of the House in the 1970s, the powers of committee chairs to create subcommittees, establish their size, name their membership, hire their staff, and regulate their meeting times were sharply constricted. In many committees, subcommittees gained substantial control over their own affairs. And it became common to find subcommittee chairs managing legislation on the floor, making arrangements for conference committee meetings, and negotiating with the Rules Committee for a rule—powers previously in the hands of the committee chairs. Some observers began to speak of "subcommittee government" in much the same way as, in an earlier day, they spoke of "committee government."

A recent investigation of subcommittee power in three House committees (Agriculture, Education and Labor, and Energy and Commerce) by Richard L. Hall and C. Lawrence Evans confirms the importance of subcommittees in shaping legislation. As shown by interviews with committee and subcommittee staffs, subcommittee members generally dominate committee decision making, from the drafting of bills through the full committee markup (when legislation is put in final form). Subcommittee members are largely responsible for negotiating compromises and for the amendments to measures adopted in full committee. Despite the unmistakable importance of subcommittees in influencing committee decisions, the authors conclude that the "government by subcommittee" generalization may be too sweeping since the influence of subcommittees varies from committee to committee and even from bill to bill.[41]

In all probability, subcommittee independence and influence peaked under successive Democratic majorities in the 1970s, 1980s, and early 1990s. Elections, of course, affect institutions. The emergence of Speaker Newt Gingrich (R., GA) as the undisputed leader of his House party in 1995 led to a general tightening of party control over the committee system. The importance of seniority in the selection of committee and subcommittee chairs eased, and the Republican leadership made it clear that committees and subcommittees were expected to work cooperatively to advance the party's agenda, including its celebrated "Contract with America." This experiment with party responsibility, centering in the Speaker's office, did not last long. Under Speaker Dennis Hastert (R., IL), who replaced Gingrich in 1999, party-committee relations returned to normal, which is to say that the balance of power between party leaders and committees shifted to favor the committees (see Chapter 7 for an analysis of the leader activist and committee autonomy models).

Although division of labor and specialization are major attributes of committee and subcommittee systems, they nevertheless count for less today than formerly. Kenneth A. Shepsle writes:

> Final legislation today is less the result of specialized consideration by experts than it is the product of whomever is skilled at assembling floor majorities. On some occasions, as in olden times, this may in fact be a wily committee or subcommittee chair; but on other occasions it may well be an agent of the Speaker, of the majority party caucus, of external interest groups, or even of the president. Extreme decentralization, in effect, threatens to destroy legislative independence without substituting compensating safeguards. The Congress becomes vulnerable to penetration from outside. . . .[42]

## COMMITTEE JURISDICTION

After a bill has been introduced, it is referred to committee for consideration. Although bills often deal with subjects that might be considered by any of several committees, they are usually acted on by a single one. As a result, policy interrelationships may be missed, emerging policies may begin or come to work at cross purposes, and committees may wrangle with one another over the custody of measures and activities.

Jurisdictional problems crop up frequently—on all kinds of legislation. Richard Bolling (D., MO) described the jurisdictional dilemma involving aid to education measures:

> Committee jurisdiction is now a maze that confounds even veteran members. For example, as many as eighteen committees have jurisdiction over one or more programs of aid to education. In any one Congress, only one-third to one-half of the education bills are referred to the Education and Labor Committee itself. Interstate and Foreign Commerce Committee, for an obscure historical reason, has jurisdiction over education bills affecting physicians and dentists; Veterans' Affairs over education programs for veterans; Armed Services over programs for servicemen and women; Ways and Means over legislation to give tax credits to parents with children in college; Banking and Currency has had bills relating to college classroom construction; and Science and Astronautics over science scholarships. The power and importance of a committee and its chairman can have an almost 1-to-1 relationship to its jurisdiction. Consequently, no matter how clear the need for rationalization in respect to jurisdictions, the *status quo* has sensitive, powerful allies outside the Congress. Inside, the condition persists by means of a mutual protection society. Members defend their own committee's entrenched preserve by telling the members of other committees, "You may be the 'victim' the next time."[43]

To promote intercommittee cooperation and to reduce jurisdictional conflict, the House instituted a multiple referral procedure in 1975 under which bills and resolutions could be processed by two or more committees.[44] Three types of multiple referrals were made available to the Speaker: joint, split, and sequential. Under joint referral, a measure is simultaneously referred to two or more committees. Under split referral, which is rare, different titles or sections of a bill are referred to two or more committees. When sequential referral is used, a measure that is reported by a committee is sent to one or more additional committees. The use of multiple referral reflects the fact that bills commonly cover several different topics and that the committees' traditional jurisdictional boundaries may not coincide with the substantive provisions of measures.

Critics contend that the multiple referral procedure has promoted jurisdictional rivalries, led to duplication in hearings, contributed to delays in processing legislation, and afforded groups additional opportunities to delay or defeat legislation. It has also enhanced the Speaker's control over legislation. One of the early actions of the House Republican majority in 1995 was to eliminate joint referrals, while retaining sequential and split referral procedures.

Jurisdictional squabbles are difficult to avoid when important and complex legislation is at stake, particularly in the House. When President Clinton's health care overhaul bill was introduced in 1994, for example, it was formally referred to a total of nine House committees. Ways and Means laid claim to substantial jurisdiction because its purview included taxes and Medicare, Energy and Commerce because it dealt with Medicaid and health insurance, and Education and Labor because it dealt with employee benefits. Other committees that were able to establish limited jurisdiction were Judiciary (malpractice, antitrust), Post Office and Civil Service (health benefits for federal employees), Armed Services (health insurance for military retirees), Government Operations (privacy issues related to health care), Natural Resources (health care for American Indians), and Veterans Affairs (VA hospital system).[45] Committees fight tooth and nail for important shares of major bills, such as health care, because jurisdiction can make a huge difference—affecting leadership success, the policy alternatives presented, the influence and publicity accruing to committees and their members, the access of lobbies, and the future oversight of the policy. What is more, the members of committees that win out in a major policy area are likely to become beneficiaries of campaign contributions from affected interests.[46]

David C. King makes a key distinction between statutory jurisdiction and common law jurisdiction. Statutory jurisdictions are set down formally in the rules of the House and the Senate; ordinarily, a committee will have ten to fifteen specific issues within its purview. Common law jurisdictions develop out of the precedents established by House and Senate parliamentarians when they refer jurisdictionally ambiguous bills. These decisions establish binding precedents that will govern referrals on future bills on the same subjects. Legislative "turf" is extremely valuable, and it produces numerous "border wars" between committees seeking to expand their influence over legislation. In the words of a committee staff member,

"Jurisdiction boils down to whether you'll have a seat at the table when important decisions are being made. If you're not at the table you're a nobody."[47] King finds that jurisdiction is up for grabs and that it is acquired through common law advances rather than through formal rules changes adopted in "reforms." "The relentless pursuit of turf," he writes, "has left the House and Senate committee systems highly fragmented."[48]

Jurisdictional fragmentation nevertheless carries benefits as well as costs. It contributes to heightened communication between committees (thus promoting consensus before a bill reaches the floor), reflects the concerns of a broader and more representative set of members, and disrupts issue monopolies under which an interest-group community simply focuses on a single committee. In addition, jurisdictional fragmentation may well enhance the influence of the leadership. Jurisdictional squabbles invite leaders to step in. King writes: "Given a choice between no jurisdictional fragmentation and the patchwork quilt of conflicts we have today, House and Senate leaders would likely prefer fragmentation. Solving the problems they create give those leaders more power to shape policy outcomes."[49]

In general, committee jurisdictions are considerably more ambiguous in state legislatures than in Congress. Rules governing assignment of bills to state legislative committees are rarely detailed, and presiding offices (or committees on the assignment of bills) are likely to enjoy a large measure of discretion in bill referral. A decision about which committee a measure will be referred to may well decide its fate.

Practice and rules often conspire to define jurisdictions so broadly as to give a few committees a disproportionate share of the legislative workload. It is not unusual for a single committee, such as Judiciary or Ways and Means, to process 20 percent or more of all bills introduced in a session. Other committees may receive scarcely more than a handful of bills in a session. Time for the careful consideration of legislation is obviously limited in those committees that process an unduly large number of measures.

## COMMITTEE MEMBERS AND COMMITTEE CHAIRS

"Congress is an institution in which power and position are highly valued. Seniority is not only a rule governing committee chairmanships, it is also a spirit pervading the total behavior."[50] There are few features of congressional life that elude a brush with seniority, extending as it does not only to the selection of committee chairs but also at times to the assignment of members to committees and to the choice of subcommittee chairs and conference committee members. "It affects the deference shown legislators on the floor, the assignment of office space, even invitations to dinner."[51] Before we consider the seniority system and its ramifications, however, an explanation of the methods for assigning members to committees is required.

## The Machinery of Congressional Committee Assignment

Committee assignments are made by party committees in each chamber. In the House, the Republicans use a Steering Committee, chaired by the Speaker, to make assignments. Democrats employ a Steering Committee chaired by the minority leader. Committee assignments in the Senate are made by a Republican Committee-on-Committees and a Democratic Steering and Coordinating Committee. Party leaders play a prominent role in making assignments, particularly in the House. To promote party harmony and to help new members secure good assignments, the parties in both chambers observe rules and practices that limit the members of certain key committees to only one assignment.[52]

Members of the Senate typically have about twice as many committee assignments as members of the House. In the 105th Congress (1997–98), for example, the mean number of standing committee assignments for a senator was 3.1, and for a congressman, 1.8; for subcommittees, the mean numbers were 6.5 and 3.2. Counting select, special, and other committee assignments, the mean number for senators was 10.3, and for House members, 5.1.[53] Under the right circumstances, the committee system can sometimes be streamlined. But ordinarily, committee assignments are treated as member turf, and there is little enthusiasm to cut their number, even though numerous assignments dilute the attention that members can give to any one.

## Factors in Assignment

The criteria used in making committee assignments include such factors as the member's party loyalty, electoral situation, seniority, state, region, type of district represented, special competence and experience, prestige, policy views, sense of responsibility, ideology, previous political experience, and endorsements.

Few if any goals are more important to members of Congress than desirable committee assignments. The main factor that influences a member's chances of receiving a preferred assignment is the level of competition for seats on the committee requested.[54] Some seats are coveted much more than others. The money committees (dealing with appropriations, taxation, and budget) and commerce committees in both houses invariably are much sought after—by veteran members seeking transfers as well as by newly elected members. To promote harmony, party leaders in recent years have frequently expanded the size of committees to accommodate the requests of their members, although this is less likely to be done in the case of prestigious committees. Many assignments are made on a routine basis, under which requests are simply accommodated.[55]

Personal and political factors affect assignment calculations when competition is present, as it always is in the case of prestigious committees. The need to provide representation on a committee for a particular state or

region can be an important consideration. Supported by their state delegations and prominent political leaders, members actively campaign for seats
on major committees. Interest groups may lobby on their behalf. Party leaders have sometimes made party support a key factor in selecting members
for the top committees. Occasionally, leaders postpone filling a vacancy on a
particularly attractive committee as a way of inducing contenders for the
seat to support party positions on upcoming legislation.[56] Among leadership
resources, influence over committee assignments ranks particularly high—
that is, if they choose to use it. Senate Republicans, for example, follow seniority rather closely in resolving contests for the same seat.[57]

Ordinarily, the most important factor in making committee assignments is the electoral position of the member. Committee makers try to make
assignments that will help the members of their party to be reelected. And
members let them know what they want:

> I got on the Agriculture Committee by request. I wanted it. I lobbied most of
> the Steering and Policy Committee and I told them that I really needed to be on
> that committee—that my reelection to Congress depended on whether I got a
> seat on the committee.[58]

The members' own goals have a strong bearing on the assignment process. Members may be primarily concerned with gaining reelection, influence within the House, or good public policy and thus seek committee
assignments that are consistent with their particular goals. Members who actively sought membership on the Appropriations or Ways and Means Committees, Fenno discovered some years ago, were primarily concerned with
achieving increased influence in the House. Members who desired seats on
the Interior and Post Office Committees were preoccupied with "district interests" and "projects"—concerns that seemed likely to attract constituency
interest and to promote the members' reelection. Still other members were
concerned with certain public policy objectives, prompting them to seek assignments to such committees as Education and Labor and Foreign Affairs.[59]

Committees are a key component in distributive politics and policymaking. The fortunes of individual states are often linked to their representatives' committee assignments. States that have representation on the
defense committees, for example, benefit by garnering more military contracts than other states. When they lose representation, moreover, they lose
contracts. States that lose senior members are particularly likely to suffer a
loss of military contracts.[60]

Members and committees change. Committees that in an earlier year
seemed to promise influence within the House now have substantial reelection benefits—and the reelection goal of members is never much below
the surface. Members of the Ways and Means Committee, for example, do

especially well in attracting PAC campaign gifts.[61] When health care legislation became a major issue in the 1992 Clinton campaign, members of several relevant committees (House Energy and Commerce and Ways and Means, Senate Finance and Labor and Human Resources) were inundated with PAC funds; members of these committees averaged $52,000 in contributions from health interests (health care, health insurance, pharmaceutical firms) in the 1992 election cycle, with some key committee and subcommittee leaders garnering three or four times that much.[62]

A committee's influence may also decline. House Appropriations, for example, has lost ground, as evidenced by the growing number of floor amendments made to its measures; similarly, the budget process introduced in the 1970s has also shaved the committee's influence over spending. The broad point is that members seek assignments to committees for distinctive goal-related reasons.

The attractiveness of committees and subcommittees for members changes in response to events, political opportunities and risks, and the emergence of distinctive issues. The House Banking Committee, for example, lost much of its cachet with members when it became saddled with the savings and loan scandal (including the Whitewater affair) in the 1980s and 1990s. And scarcely anyone wants to serve on the immigration subcommittees, since there is no national consensus on immigration policy, but a great many groups with insistent, conflicting views. Representative Romano L. Mazzoli (D., KY), former chair of the House immigration subcommittee, made these observations on the difficulties of recruiting members:

> A member would have to take two or three long gulps before they would say yes and take the subcommittee on immigration. You have to virtually shanghai people to get them onto this thing. You've got to dragoon them. . . . Since my race for reelection in 1981, it's been used against me every time. "Why am I wasting time on immigration instead of helping Louisville?"[63]

Trade-offs underlie some committee assignments. No one is anxious to serve on an ethics committee, for example, and thereby become involved in cases of colleagues' alleged misconduct. An ethics committee assignment, observes a House member, is "to some degree a payback for a prestigious committee assignment." Nine of the fourteen members who sat on the House ethics committee (Standards of Official Conduct) in the 103rd Congress, for example, also held seats on Appropriations, Ways and Means, or Rules.[64]

The preeminent position of committees in Congress makes the assignment process of great significance. Members cannot be indifferent to their fortunes. Winning a seat on the "right" committee may give a member an electoral advantage. Ultimately at stake in this process, of course, are important questions of public policy.[65]

## Committee Assignments in the State Legislature

At the state level, a long tradition supports the prerogative of the Speaker to appoint committee members in the lower house. Party, political, factional, and personal considerations often influence the Speaker's selections, but only a handful of states provide for an alternative mode of selection or formally limit the Speaker's discretion. In Alaska, Kentucky, and Pennsylvania, committee members are selected by a committee-on-committees. In Hawaii, the party caucus is given this authority.

The methods of selecting committee members in state senates are more diverse than in the lower houses. The dominant method entrusts the selection to the president of the senate; this method is used in about two-fifths of the states. A committee-on-committees is the next most common method; it is used in about one-quarter of the states. Another one-quarter of the states vests this authority either in the president pro tem or in the floor leader. Finally, committee assignments are made by the Committee on Rules in California, by the Committee on Senate Organization in Wisconsin, by a subcommittee of the Rules Committee in Minnesota, by the party caucus in Hawaii, and by seniority in South Carolina.[66]

Party leaders clearly play a major role in the committee assignment process at the state level. The evidence of a recent study suggests, however, that they exercise their authority in a moderate way, typically seeking to accommodate the interests of members. Throughout the country, the great majority of members of *both* parties receive assignments that satisfy them. The effort by leaders to satisfy members' preferences leads them to increase the membership of particularly attractive committees and even to increase the number of committees (thus increasing the number of chairmanships to be conferred).[67] Nevertheless, there are some state chambers where leaders are accustomed to "stacking" certain committees in the interests of factions, groups, and ideologies. A conservative leadership, for example, can use its influence to make sure that conservatives dominate certain key committees. A liberal leadership can do the same. Organized interest groups may enter the committee assignment process by pressing for the appointment of members who are disposed to favor their claims. What makes the politics of committee assignment important everywhere is of course that committee decisions usually are upheld on the floor.

## The Committee Caste System

A paramount fact about legislative committees is that there are major differences in their relative attractiveness and prestige. Some legislators serve their entire careers on the committees to which they were initially assigned. But it is more common for members to transfer from one committee to another, moving from less prestigious to more prestigious assignments.

The prestige patterns are about the same in both houses. Committees with national-issue domains, such as Finance (Ways and Means in the House), Appropriations, Budget, Rules (House), and the commerce and foreign policy committees in each house ordinarily dominate the list of prestige committees. About 60 percent of committee assignment requests in the Senate are for seats on one of the "big four": Appropriations, Foreign Relations, Finance, and Commerce.[68]

Prestige differentiation among committees contributes to several conditions.[69] Newly elected legislators constitute a disproportionate component of the less prestigious committees. Party and seniority leaders gravitate toward the elite committees and avoid the less desirable ones. Indeed, the most important factor in assignment success in the Senate is the seniority of the member. Members from highly competitive states (or districts in the case of the House), whose careers may be tenuous, find it more difficult to gain chairmanships or senior positions on major committees. The principal fact to recognize is that committee prestige is one of the main structural features of each house and an important clue to the distribution of power within the institution.

## Seniority in Congress

The seniority system in Congress is controversial because it is inextricably bound up with privilege and power. Although it confers both prestige and advantages on the individual members, its principal significance lies in its impact on public policy.[70] The seniority system has never found expression in the rules of either house of Congress; yet its philosophy has been firmly embedded in legislative practice for well over a century. The form it assumes is simple and predictable, which in part explains its lasting power. When assigned to a committee, a member's name is placed at the bottom of the party's list. With reelection and the passage of time, the member's stake in the committee—seniority—increases. Inevitably, death, retirement, and the vicissitudes of elections remove those members above. The moment arrives in some session when his or her name rests at the top of the party's list for that committee. Should the member's party be in the majority at the time, the chairmanship is very likely to be awarded to that person.

The process of selecting committee chairs, nevertheless, is no longer automatic. At the opening of the 92nd Congress (1971), both parties in the House of Representatives agreed to modify their seniority rules to provide that seniority would not be the only factor taken into account in the selection of committee chairs or ranking minority members. House Republicans now vote by secret ballot on whether to accept the nominations for ranking minority members (or chairs) made by their committee-on-committees. The current Democratic rule provides for a secret vote in caucus on their

Steering Committee's nomination for any chairmanship or on the seniority of any committee member. Should the caucus reject a nominee for committee chair, the Steering Committee is required to advance another name from the list of remaining committee members. Although the Senate thus far has relied exclusively on seniority in the choice of committee leaders, the Democratic caucus in 1975 altered its procedures to provide for a secret ballot on any committee chairmanship if requested by 20 percent of the caucus members.

Breaches of the seniority rule are becoming more common in the House. In 1975 the Democratic caucus voted to remove three standing committee chairs from their positions. In 1977 the caucus voted to remove the chair of the Military Construction Subcommittee of the Appropriations Committee, a southern legislator who had been censured the previous year for conflict of interest. In 1985 the caucus removed the aging chair of the Armed Services Committee and selected as his successor a member ranking seventh on the committee seniority list. In the organizing meetings before the opening of the 102nd Congress (1991–92), the House Democratic caucus again struck, removing the elderly chairs of the Public Works and House Administration committees. The seniority system was breached in 1992 when the ill and elderly chair of the House Appropriations Committee was replaced and in 1994 when the Democratic caucus chose David R. Obey of Wisconsin to head the Appropriations Committee instead of the member next in line.

Seniority was brushed aside again in organizing the 104th Congress (1995–96). The Republicans' new leader, Newt Gingrich, passed over three senior Republicans in order to name aggressive conservatives to head Appropriations, Energy and Commerce, and Judiciary; his selections were later ratified by the party's Committee-on-Committees and the Republican Conference.

Under the seniority tradition, subcommittee chairmanships ordinarily are awarded to the senior member of the majority party on each subcommittee. But as in the case of committee chairmanships, the process is no longer automatic. Subcommittee chairmanships are settled by secret balloting among majority-party committee members.

These changes in seniority practices significantly affect the structure of congressional power. First, they reestablish the control of party leaders and the party caucus (or conference, in the case of Republicans) over committee leaders. Second, they eliminate the automatic succession to these positions afforded by seniority. Third, they warn committee chairs that they can be removed if they are insufficiently responsive to committee members and to their party colleagues at large. Fourth, they dictate that committee chairs must be cooperative and prudent in their relations with party leaders and members.

Despite the recent violations of seniority in picking committee and subcommittee chairs, there is no reason to believe that the seniority system will be set aside. Modifications are more likely. At the opening of the 104th Congress, for example, House Republicans, joined by more than half of the Democrats, voted to impose a six-year term limit on committee and subcommittee chairs.

The power of committee chairs—their critical impact on public policy—prompts much of the controversy over seniority. Opponents of the seniority system are able to muster an impressive indictment of the practice. Among their arguments are the following: (1) Seniority is incompatible with responsible party government since the party, rather than committee chairs, should be able to control the disposition of legislation. (2) Adherence to the seniority rule does not ensure the appointment of chairs of ability and special competence; similarly, it may stymie the advancement of promising younger legislators. (3) Seniority tends to favor one-party areas since the tenure of members coming from two-party constituencies is sometimes short-lived; chairs may represent a minority view within the party. (4) Once elevated to the office, committee chairs are likely to hold the position for the rest of their congressional career, even though they may become increasingly inadequate for the task.

Although seniority poses certain problems for the congressional parties, observers find prudent reasons for keeping it (more or less) intact. Seniority does involve "gambler's chances," as George H. Haynes remarked, but it also has a logic: "It usually brings to the headship of a committee a man who has had many years of experience in handling the special problems in its domain."[71] It has also been argued that the seniority system "avoids the waste implicit in instability of committee composition and management."[72] Moreover, the seniority system increases the attractiveness of congressional service. Nelson W. Polsby writes,

> The House's major career incentive is the opportunity accorded [many of] its members to possess the substance of power in the form of a committee or subcommittee chairmanship or membership on a key committee. At present seniority acts as a bulwark of this incentive system, by guaranteeing a form of job security at least within the division of labor of the organization. Without decentralization of power there would quite likely be no incentive for able men to stay in the House; without able men (there are few enough of these at any rate) there would be no expertise. Without subject-matter mastery, initiatives and modifications in public policy are capricious, responsive largely to prejudice, ineffective, and failing that, detrimental.[73]

Another assessment of the seniority system is offered by Kenneth Shepsle:

> The pecking order quality of the seniority system, for all its warts, assures a modicum of continuity and institutional memory. Positions of authority are

held by those who have waited in the queue for an extended period, are familiar both with the players and the plays, current and past, and have long-term relationships with those above and below them in the queue. To the extent that a committee established an institutional existence separate from the individual legislators in its queue at any one time, especially in terms of stability of jurisdiction and staff, seniority contributes to continuity in decision making and to the development of an institutional memory that economizes on wheel-reinventing activity.[74]

The emergence and consolidation of the seniority system is closely linked to the rise in careerism. Seeking to protect their careers and knowing that the parties by themselves could not ensure their reelection, rational legislators developed the seniority system to reduce uncertainties and to regularize career advancement. Seniority lets members know where they stand and limits the discretion of party leaders over them.[75]

### Seniority in the State Legislatures

Seniority does not reign in the states as firmly as it does in Congress, and apparently it never has. On the basis of scattered studies and informed judgments, it is evident that seniority is simply one factor among several in the selection of committee members *and* committee chairs. In the Illinois Legislature, for example,

> Committee chairmen . . . are not chosen in accord with any regularly established practice, although, other things being equal, the incumbent can usually expect reappointment. In at least one recent session, however, an influential veteran of fourteen sessions was without a chairmanship, a House member serving his second term became chairman of an important committee, and a senator was refused reappointment as head of a committee by way of discipline for lack of party regularity.[76]

Similarly, in California, "all existing committee assignments . . . are subject to change at the beginning of each session. Assembly and Senate leaders can—and frequently do—shift chairmanships and other standing committee assignments of members, even against their wishes."[77] "The [California] speaker rewards his friends and punishes his enemies through the use of his power to make committee assignments."[78] In the Iowa House, "a primary consideration in the chairman selection process . . . is whether or not an individual legislator supported the speaker at the majority party organizational caucus."[79] In the Texas House, over a period of twenty-six years, only 11 percent of the committee chairs had served on their committees two or more sessions.[80] In the lower house of Connecticut, "there is little evidence of a systematic seniority system, or of much stability in committee leadership."[81] In Mississippi, Pennsylvania, and Rhode Island, veteran members appear to be given preference in the assignment of chairmanships, but there is no established seniority rule.[82] In the New York Assembly, seniority counts for more than in most states, as it and loyalty to the party leader are the two main factors in the selection of committee chairs.[83]

Committee chairs in lower houses are appointed by the Speaker in forty-five states. In the remaining states they are selected by a committee-on-committees, by party caucus, and by election. State senates employ a variety of methods. Nineteen states vest their authority in the senate president, nine states in the president pro tempore, six states in a committee-on-committees, and six states in the majority leader. In the remaining states, the appointive power is awarded to a particular committee (such as rules), or to the party caucus, except in Nebraska and South Carolina, where they are elected, and in Virginia, where the senior member of a committee is automatically made chair.[84]

Despite the absence of a large reservoir of studies covering practices in other states, it is still much better than a guess to say that state legislatures in general do not attach great importance to seniority. A questionnaire survey conducted by the American Political Science Association received estimates that seniority was a prominent factor in the selection of committee chairs in fourteen senates and twelve houses and was not important in twenty-three senates and thirty-six houses.[85] A survey in the 1980s found that seniority was "only one of many factors taken into account" in the appointment of committee chairs.[86] Writing in 1996, Ronald D. Hedlund and Keith E. Hamm observe, "Only a few state legislative chambers restrict via rules the committee appointment powers of political parties. In many additional states, [party leaders say] that although they consider member seniority to some degree in their appointment choices, seniority does not serve as the constraining factor on party power in the appointment process as it does in Congress."[87] What is more, turnover among chairs is high, even on key committees such as appropriations, ways and means, and finance.[88]

Committee chairs in state legislatures ordinarily are not as powerful as those in Congress. If the powers of the chairs were more formidable, undoubtedly there would be a greater insistence that seniority should be the principal consideration in making appointments. The position of the chair in the Illinois legislature would seem to be broadly representative of most states:

> Committee appointments, and particularly appointments to committee chairmanships, are valuable as indications of confidence by legislative leaders. Virtually no actual legislative power attaches to a chairmanship, but legislators regard chairmen of particular committees as part of an influential circle. Being a chairman is not a source of power but being designated a chairman very well may be a source of informal power.[89]

## COMMITTEE STAFFS

### Congress

The enormous volume of work set before committees, the quest for technical knowledge, and the pressure of time have combined to crystallize the need for professional staffs to serve committees. This development was a long time in the making, however, and in fact it was not until the turn of the twentieth century that specific funds were set aside for staffs for the standing committees. Congress placed the employment of committee personnel on a firmer basis in 1924. Finally, in the La Follette-Monroney Act of 1946, professional staffs came of age, with provision made for the employment of up to four staff members and six clerks by each standing committee of Congress. Certain committees, most notably the appropriations committees, were empowered to appoint larger staffs.

The size of committee staffs has grown significantly over the years, especially in the House. In 1971, there were 729 committee staff members in the House and 711 in the Senate. In 1987, the numbers stood at 2,024 in the House and 1,074 in the Senate.[90] Somewhat smaller by 1994, House committee staff numbered about 1,850 and Senate committee staff about 1,200. In keeping with the party's promise to reduce government spending, the new Republican majorities in 1995 made much sharper cuts; the staff of House committees was pared to about 1,250 and the staff of Senate committees to about 950.[91]

The central reason for creating professional staffs was to free committees from excessive reliance on research studies produced by executive agencies. "For Congress to function as a coequal partner with the executive in the legislative process," Gladys Kammerer observed, it was essential "that Congress empower itself to obtain its own independent staff services and that it pay adequately for them."[92]

The augmentation of the staff function since 1946 has not altogether met the pristine purposes of that year's Legislative Reorganization Act, although improvement in the caliber of staff members has been substantial. Today's congressional staffer is young and well educated; those with advanced degrees, in fact, are common. Many are policy experts, and they are often a part of a Washington "issue network." A recent study of a cross section of House committee staff finds that about one-fourth come to their jobs from executive agencies and one-fourth from members' offices. And many move to Washington from the academic community and the private sector. Staff turnover is relatively high. Commonly, staffers regard their positions as steppingstones to other opportunities rather than as a career.[93]

A competent professional staff can improve the general efficiency and quality of the legislative process through a variety of contributions: by collecting, winnowing, and analyzing data; by identifying problems of relevance for members and suggesting alternative courses of action; and by preparing studies and committee reports on legislation.[94] Responsible committee decisions and imaginative legislation usually rest on a foundation of intelligent staff work.

Committee staffs also help to integrate committees, subcommittees, the two chambers, and the legislative and executive branches. For the most part, committee staffs work closely together, exchanging information and tasks. But more than that, they often work closely with staff members of the counterpart committee in the other house and with the staffs of agencies and departments, contributing to both communications and cooperation. It is quite common to find committee staff members with previous experience in executive agencies and agency staff members with previous staff experience in Congress.

The functions performed by committee staffs make it inevitable that they will have substantial influence on the legislative process.[95] New legislation cannot be adopted or existing law altered without the information that is collected and analyzed by committee staffs. It is the staffs, moreover, that arrange public hearings and investigations, draft legislation, and prepare committee reports.

The extraordinary growth of professional staffs has not been altogether salutary. In a word, staffs create problems as well as solve them. In his instructive study of congressional staffs, Michael J. Malbin writes,

> Congress has failed utterly to cope with its workload. If anything, the growth of staff has made the situation worse. First, on the level of sheer numbers, more staff means more information coming into each member's office, with more management problems as different staff aides compete for the member's time to present their own nuggets in a timely fashion. The member, under these conditions, is becoming more of a chief executive officer in charge of a medium-sized business than a person who personally deliberates with his colleagues about policy. Second, the problems created by large numbers are exacerbated by the staffs' new roles. Increasingly, the members want aides who will dream up new bills and amendments bearing their bosses' names instead of helping the bosses understand what is already on the agenda. The result is that the new staff bureaucracy and the workload it helps create threaten to bury Congress under its own paperwork, just as surely as if the staff never existed.[96]

### Staffs and Politics

Under the terms of the 1946 Legislative Reorganization Act, appointments to committee staffs were to be made without regard to political affiliation. Many committees have followed this prohibition, but others have not. Not surprisingly, partisan staffs tend to develop in those committees characterized by major ideological conflicts among members. The partisan role of committee staffs is a natural outgrowth of the staff selection process. As long as staff members owe their loyalty to the committee or subcommittee chair or to the ranking minority member, their own security may require them to adopt a partisan orientation toward committee business. The existence of partisan staffs is a recognition of at least two facts—that public policy alternatives are often laden with significance for the parties and that there is a need for different kinds of experts. Taking Congress as a whole, there are few committee staffs that adhere to strict standards of nonpartisanship.

Committee staff members do more than committee work. Although the practice violates the spirit if not the letter of the law, many legislators use committee staff members in much the same fashion as they use their personal staffs—for working in members' offices, handling "case work," doing political chores in the constituencies, and in some cases promoting the members' ambitions for higher office.

A recurrent plaint is that staffs have encroached on the members' role in policymaking. The staff contribution to shaping committee positions and legislation, it is argued, has thrust it forward as virtual spokesperson for committee members. The problem this creates can be estimated from the following critical paragraphs found in the individual views appended to a Senate Judiciary Committee report on juvenile delinquency. Contending that the report should be described as a "staff study" rather than as a report on the committee itself, two minority members state,

> Staff help is indispensable. It is skilled and experienced in its specialty. It knows what to look for, where to find it, and how to reduce the information collected to usable form.
>
> But it also has its own jurisdiction in which to work and limitations which should be observed. Its province is investigation and the assembling of source material. At this point it is normal procedure for members of the subcommittee to familiarize themselves with the subject and source material at hand. In this manner they will be able to direct, if not actually produce, the end products and especially that portion of it which contains general policy, conclusions, and recommendations. . . . The instant report follows an all too common pattern for investigative activities by this body. It embraces the practice of abdicating committee responsibility and relying totally upon a professional staff which, however competent and authoritative, lacks certain basic qualifications. It is not composed of elected representatives of the people who are the true policy-deciding officials.[97]

Minority-party members are often skeptical concerning the information provided by the majority party's committee staff. When the Democratic leadership's health care bill was being developed in the House Ways and Means Committee in 1994, Representative Nancy L. Johnson (R., CT) offered these observations on the staff:

> They are very smart, very competent, but they do come at the subject with a strong ideological bias. The way that bent affects minority members of Congress, particularly members who take a different view, is this: They are not

anxious to give you information that undercuts the bill their boss is trying to get through the committee. Unless you ask exactly the right question, you don't necessarily get the information that you and the public need.[98]

The role a committee staff assumes in the formation of public policy is affected by several considerations. A study by John Manley of the Joint Committee on Internal Revenue Taxation discloses four principal variables that shape staff influence in this committee. Of leading importance is the subject matter handled by the committee. "As the complexity of decisions facing legislators increases so too does the likelihood that the staff will exert influence on the outcomes." Moreover, staff influence tends to be constricted on those issues that are important to a large number of participants. Another factor involves the personal relations between the staff and leading committee members. Finally, the influence of the staff will depend on the extent to which staff judgments are congruent with the judgments of the committee majority. Although staff experts undoubtedly play an important role in the legislative process, on the whole "they take more cues from the formal policy-makers than they give."[99] A recent study of subcommittee staff directors by Christine DeGregorio supports that interpretation. Staff directors, she concludes, "characteristically work as human extensions of their bosses," and when they seek to promote particular policies, "they generally do so at the behest of the chair."[100]

## In the States

A leading objective in the drive to improve state legislatures has been the development of professional staffs. For many years, about the only source of expert advice for legislators (apart from outside sources) was a central research agency, such as a legislative council or legislative reference service. Today, all states provide some form of professional staff assistance to standing committees. Nevertheless, committee staffing at the state level is much less developed than at the congressional level. In some states, staff aid is available only to certain major committees, such as finance, appropriations, and judiciary. In other states, committees are provided staff only on a pool basis. The principal result of limited professional staffing for committees is that they are required to look elsewhere for information and assistance. Executive agencies and interest groups are usually anxious to provide it—in order, of course, to strengthen their own positions.

The importance of committee staffs in the policymaking process of state legislatures is growing, according to a recent survey of state legislators by Gary F. Moncrief, Joel A. Thompson, and Karl T. Kurtz. Veteran legislators from fifteen states reported that during their tenure in office the influence of committee staffs had grown significantly; only the media's influence had outpaced that of committee staffs. In contrast, the big losers, in their perceptions, were the party leadership and the governor. Most of the respondents in this survey viewed the heightened influence of staff as positive and necessary (while lamenting the growing influence of the media).[101]

The capacity of legislatures to make intelligent, independent judgments is sharply influenced by expert staff assistance. A study of the Wisconsin legislature has shown that the addition of research analysts to each party caucus in the Assembly and Senate has had notable effects on legislative decision making, integration, and performance. Among the consequences have been a strengthening of the caucus system at the expense of the committees, a greater visibility for legislative party leaders, a growth in party cohesiveness and in interparty conflict, and a new capacity for the development of legislative alternatives to executive proposals and for legislative control of the administration.[102]

The availability of professional staff for legislators may be particularly important in those eighteen states that have term limits, and hence fewer experienced lawmakers in party leadership and committee positions. The newcomers that dominate these legislatures need information. If they choose to do so, they can lean on professional staff for "institutional memory," as well as for instruction on procedures, organization, chronic issues, and policy development. How the influence of staff will be affected in term-limited legislatures remains to be seen, but it would be surprising indeed if it did not increase markedly.[103]

Staff support in state legislatures is every bit as important as it is in Congress. It is crucial for the development and maintenance of legislative autonomy. In broad terms, the chief contribution of staff is to diminish the lawmakers' dependence on the chief executive, executive agencies, and lobbyists for information on policy choices.

## NOTES

1. These paragraphs were taken from *Congressional Government* (New York: Meridian Books, 1956; first published 1885), pp. 69, 71, 62, respectively.

2. Alan Rosenthal and Rod Forth, "The Assembly Line: Law Production in the American States," *Legislative Studies Quarterly*, III (May 1978), 270–71.

3. "Congressional Investigations: The British System," *University of Chicago Law Review*, XVIII (Spring 1954), 523. (Italics in original.)

4. As quoted by Robert Zwier, "The Search for Information: Specialists and Nonspecialists in the U.S. House of Representatives," *Legislative Studies Quarterly*, IV (February 1979), 31–42 (quotation on p. 35). Zwier finds that in their search for information, specialists themselves tend to rely on congressional staffs and the executive branch, whereas nonspecialists are inclined to consult colleagues and constituency elements. Broadly similar findings are reported by Paul Sabatier and David Whiteman in their study of legislative information flow in the California legislature. See "Legislative Decision Making and Substantive Policy Information: Models of Information Flow," *Legislative Studies Quarterly*, X (August 1985), 395–419. Also see a study by Carol S. Weissert that analyzes the role and impact of policy entrepreneurs—experts who invest substantial effort to achieve the adoption of certain policies—in the North Carolina legislature. "Policy Entrepreneurs, Policy Opportunists, and Legislative Effectiveness," *American Politics Quarterly*, XIX (April 1991), 262–74.

5. Holbert N. Carroll, *The House of Representatives and Foreign Affairs* (Pittsburgh: University of Pittsburgh Press, 1966), pp. 27–29.

6. "Unwritten Rules of American Politics," *Harper's Magazine,* November 1948, p. 31.

7. *Hearings on Committee Organization in the House Before the Select Committee on Committees,* U.S. House of Representatives, 93rd Cong., 1st sess., 1973, III, p. 9.

8. Kenneth A. Shepsle and Barry R. Weingast, "The Institutional Foundations of Committee Power," *American Political Science Review,* LXXXI (March 1987), 85–104. See a critique of their argument, particularly concerning the ex post veto concept, by Keith Krehbiel, "Why Are Congressional Committees Powerful?" *American Political Science Review,* LXXXI (September 1987), 929–35, followed by a rejoinder by Shepsle and Weingast, pp. 935–45. See a modification of the Shepsle and Weingast model that depicts committee influence as dependent on the behavior of the Speaker and the members of the majority party: Jonathan Nagler, "Strategic Implications of Conferee Selection in the House of Representatives: It Ain't Over Till It's Over," *American Politics Quarterly,* XVII (January 1989), 54–79.

9. Steven S. Smith, *Call to Order: Floor Politics in the House and Senate* (Washington, DC: Brookings Institution, 1989), especially Chap. 6.

10. Ibid., pp. 171–77 (quotation on p. 175).

11. Ibid., p. 170.

12. Ibid., p. 195.

13. Forrest Maltzman, "Maintaining Congressional Committees: Sources of Member Support," *Legislative Studies Quarterly,* XXIII (May 1998), 197–218.

14. Some of these House committees have had their jurisdictions altered and their names changed since the Republicans won control of Congress in 1994. Banking, Finance, and Urban Affairs is now Banking and Financial Services; Education and Labor is now Education and the Workforce; Foreign Affairs is now International Relations; Interior and Insular is now Resources; and Public Works is now Transportation and Infrastructure.

15. E. Scott Adler and John S. Lapinski, "Demand-Side Theory and Congressional Committee Composition: A Constituency Characteristics Approach," *American Journal of Political Science,* XLI (July 1997), 895–918.

16. Bruce A. Ray, "The Responsiveness of the U.S. Congressional Armed Services Committees to Their Parent Bodies," *Legislative Studies Quarterly,* V (November 1980), 501–15.

17. See the evidence in Norman J. Ornstein, Thomas E. Mann, and Michael J. Malbin, *Vital Statistics on Congress, 1993–1994* (Washington, DC: Congressional Quarterly Press, 1994), pp. 206–16.

18. Barbara Sinclair, *The Transformation of the U.S. Senate* (Baltimore: Johns Hopkins University Press, 1989), p. 110.

19. Timothy E. Cook, "The Policy Impact of the Committee Assignment Process in the House," *Journal of Politics,* XLV (November 1983), 1027–36.

20. This section leans heavily on an article by Roger H. Davidson, "Representation and Congressional Committees," *The Annals,* CDXI (January 1974), 48–62 (quotation on p. 55).

21. Barry Rundquist, Jungho Rhee, Jeong-Hwa Lee, and Sharon E. Fox, "Modeling State Representation on Defense Committees in Congress, 1959–1989," *American Politics Quarterly,* XXV (January 1997), 35–55.

22. Richard L. Hall, "Participation and Purpose in Committee Decision Making," *American Political Science Review,* LXXXI (March 1987), 105–27.

23. Wilson, *Congressional Government,* p. 56.

24. For a wide-ranging study tracing the development of standing committees in the U.S. House of Representatives, see Joseph Cooper, *The Origins of the Standing Committees and the Development of the Modern House* (Houston: Rice University Studies, 1970). Also see Elaine K. Swift, "Reconstructive Change in the U.S. Congress: The Early Senate, 1789–1841," in *The Changing World of the U.S. Senate,* ed. John Hibbing (Berkeley: Institute of Governmental Studies, 1990), pp. 9–37; and a study by Gerald Gamm and Kenneth Shepsle that seeks to explain the institutionalization of standing committees through rational choice and organization theory: "Emergence of Legislative Institutions: Standing Committees in the

House and Senate, 1810–1825," *Legislative Studies Quarterly*, XIV (February 1989), 39–66. Also see Jeffrey A. Jenkins, "Property Rights and the Emergence of Standing Committee Dominance in the Nineteenth-Century House, *Legislative Studies Quarterly*, XXIII (November 1998), 493–519. Jenkins treats committee assignments as a form of "property right" under which members might better serve their constituents' interests.

25. Robert Luce, *Congress: An Explanation* (Cambridge, MA: Harvard University Press, Copyright 1926, by The President and Fellows of Harvard College), p. 6.

26. See V. Stanley Vardys, "Select Committees of the House of Representatives," *Midwest Journal of Political Science*, VI (August 1962), 247–65 (quotation on p. 265), on which this discussion is based.

27. Belle Zeller, ed., *American State Legislatures* (New York: Thomas Y. Crowell, 1954), pp. 100–101. See also David B. Ogle, "Joint Committee Operations and Budget Procedures in Connecticut," *State Government*, XLVII (Summer 1974), 170–74.

28. Smith, *Call to Order*, p. 209.

29. Ibid., p. 211.

30. Ibid., p. 200.

31. Gilbert Y. Steiner, *The Congressional Conference Committee, Seventieth to Eightieth Congresses* (Urbana: University of Illinois Press, 1951), pp. 170–72.

32. Richard F. Fenno, Jr., *The Power of the Purse: Appropriations Policies in Congress* (Boston: Little, Brown, 1966), p. 19.

33. Ibid., p. 663.

34. David J. Vogler, "Patterns of One House Dominance in Congressional Conference Committees," *Midwest Journal of Political Science*, May 1970, pp. 303–20.

35. Fenno, *Power of the Purse*, pp. 666–70 (quotation on p. 669).

36. Gerald S. Strom and Barry S. Rundquist, "A Revised Theory of Winning in House-Senate Conferences," *American Political Science Review*, LXXI (June 1977), 448–53 (quotation on p. 452).

37. *The Politics of Finance: The House Committee on Ways and Means* (Boston: Little, Brown, 1970), pp. 269–94 (quotation on p. 279).

38. Ibid., p. 271.

39. Jeanie Mather and Glenn Abney, "The Role of Conference Committees in State Legislatures," paper delivered at the Annual Meeting of the Southern Political Science Association, Memphis, TN, 1981. Judging which chamber wins in conference is a complicated process. In Georgia, for example, the Senate usually wins in the appropriations conference committee, but its success is due less to its independent strength vis-à-vis the House than to its alignment with the governor. See Thomas O. Lauth, "The Governor and the Conference Committee in Georgia," *Legislative Studies Quarterly*, XV (August 1990), 441-53.

40. As quoted by Elizabeth Drew, "A Reporter at Large," *New Yorker*, April 9, 1979, p. 104.

41. Richard L. Hall and C. Lawrence Evans, "The Power of Subcommittees," *Journal of Politics*, LII (May 1990), 335–55.

42. Kenneth A. Shepsle, "Representation and Governance: The Great Legislative Trade-off," *Political Science Quarterly*, CIII (Fall 1988), 480.

43. Richard Bolling, *Power in the House* (New York: Dutton, 1968), pp. 262–63.

44. This discussion of multiple referral is based on an article by Roger H. Davidson, Walter J. Oleszek, and Thomas Kephart, "One Bill, Many Committees: Multiple Referrals in the U.S. House of Representatives," *Legislative Studies Quarterly*, XIII (February 1988), 3–28. Also see Roger H. Davidson, "Multiple Referral of Legislation in the U.S. Senate," *Legislative Studies Quarterly*, XIV (August 1989), 375–92; and Roger H. Davidson and Walter J. Oleszek, "From Monopoly to Management: Changing Patterns of Committee Deliberation," in *The Postreform Congress*, ed. Roger H. Davidson (New York: St. Martin's Press, 1992), pp. 129–41.

45. See *Congressional Quarterly Weekly Report*, October 9, 1993, pp. 2734–737, and Supplement to the *Weekly Report* issue of March 5, 1994, p. 8.

46. Ibid.

47. David C. King, "The Nature of Congressional Committee Jurisdictions," *American Political Science Review*, LXXXVIII (March 1994), 48–62 (quotation on p. 48).

48. Ibid., p. 60. Also see a study by Jeffrey C. Talbert, Bryan D. Jones, and Frank R. Baumgartner that finds that entrepreneurial chairs use nonlegislative hearings (investigations and oversight hearings) as a way of laying claim to future jurisdiction over a certain issue. These hearings may also force rival committees to take actions they would prefer to avoid. "Nonlegislative Hearings and Policy Change in Congress," *American Journal of Political Science*, LXXXIX (May 1995), 383–406.

49. David C. King, *Turf Wars: How Congressional Committees Claim Jurisdiction* (Chicago: University of Chicago Press, 1997), especially pp. 139–47 (quotation on p. 146).

50. Ernest S. Griffith, *Congress: Its Contemporary Role* (New York: New York University Press, 1951), p. 19.

51. George Goodwin, Jr., "The Seniority System in Congress," *American Political Science Review*, LIII (June 1959), 412.

52. See a study by Sally Friedman that finds that women elected to the U.S. House of Representatives are receiving better committee assignments than in the past; in addition, their assignments have been more impressive than those received by African-American newcomers. "House Committee Assignments of Women and Minority Newcomers, 1965–94," *Legislative Studies Quarterly*, XXI (February 1996), 73–82.

53. Norman J. Ornstein, Thomas E. Mann, and Michael J. Malbin, *Vital Statistics on Congress, 1997–1998* (Washington, DC: Congressional Quarterly Press, 1998), pp. 122–23.

54. Steven S. Smith and Christopher J. Deering, *Committees in Congress* (Washington, DC: Congressional Quarterly Press, 1984), p. 240.

55. See Irwin N. Gertzog, "The Routinization of Committee Assignments in the U.S. House of Representatives," *American Journal of Political Science*, XX (November 1976), 693–712.

56. *Congressional Quarterly Weekly Report*, May 28, 1994, p. 1430.

57. Smith and Deering, *Committees in Congress*, pp. 240–43.

58. Robert P. Weber, "Home Style and Committee Behavior: The Case of Richard Nolan," in *Home Style and Washington Work*, ed. Morris P. Fiorina and David W. Rohde (Ann Arbor: University of Michigan Press, 1989), p. 82.

59. Richard F. Fenno, Jr., *Congressmen in Committees* (Boston: Little, Brown, 1973), especially pp. 1–14. For a study of a "mixed goal" committee, see Lynette P. Perkins, "Influences of Members' Goals on Their Committee Behavior: The U.S. House Judiciary Committee," *Legislative Studies Quarterly*, V (August 1980), 373–92.

60. Barry S. Rundquist, Jeong-Hwa Lee, and Jungho Rhee, "The Distributive Politics of Cold War Defense Spending: Some Level Evidence," *Legislative Studies Quarterly*, XXI (May 1996), 265–82.

61. House committee assignments are much more valuable in attracting PAC contributions than Senate committee assignments. Virtually no relationship exists between a senator's committee and his or her ability to secure PAC money. See Kevin B. Grier and Michael C. Munger, "Comparing Interest Group PAC Contributions to House and Senate Incumbents, 1980–1986," *Journal of Politics*, LV (August 1993), especially pp. 637–40.

62. *Congressional Quarterly Weekly Report*, July 31, 1993, p. 2048.

63. *New York Times*, September 15, 1994.

64. *Congressional Quarterly Weekly Report*, January 14, 1995, p. 139.

65. See a study by Richard L. Hall and Bernard Grofman that posits the conditions under which committees are most likely to be unrepresentative of their parent chambers: "The Committee Assignment Process and the Conditional Nature of Committee Bias," *American Political Science Review*, LXXXIV (December 1990), 1149–166. Also see Keith Krehbiel, "Are Congressional Committees Composed of Preference Outliers?" *American Political Science Review*, LXXXIV (March 1990), 149–63.

66. *Book of the States, 1990–1991* (Lexington, KY: Council of State Governments, 1991), p. 125.

67. Wayne L. Francis, "Leadership, Party Caucuses, and Committees in U.S. State Legislatures," *Legislative Studies Quarterly*, X (May 1985), 243–57. For additional evidence on the accommodation explanation for committee appointments, see Ronald D. Hedlund, "Entering the Committee System: State Committee Assignments," *Western Political Quarterly*, XLII (December 1989), 597–625. Minority party organization and a sense of partisanship tend to develop in one-party legislatures when the minority party's members perceive that they are being treated unfairly, particularly in such a matter as committee assignments. See a study by Robert Harmel, "Minority Partisanship in One-Party Predominant Legislatures: A Five-State Study," *Journal of Politics*, XLVIII (August 1986), 729–40. Conventional wisdom holds that a major factor in the allocation of committee seats is whether a particular assignment will help a member to win reelection. A recent study of four lower houses (Iowa, Maine, Pennsylvania, and Wisconsin) by Ronald D. Hedlund and Samuel C. Patterson finds no significant linkage between close election margins and the success of members in getting their preferred committee assignments. In fact, safe-seat members have a better chance of getting desirable committee assignments. "The Electoral Antecedents of State Legislative Committee Assignments," *Legislative Studies Quarterly*, XVII (November 1992), 539–59.

68. Charles S. Bullock III, "U.S. Senate Committee Assignments: Preferences, Motivations, and Success," *American Journal of Political Science*, XXIX (November 1985), 789–808.

69. Michael B. Berkman has shown that U.S. House members who are former state legislators are more likely to serve on policy and prestige committees than members without political experience, who gravitate toward committees with distinctive constituency foci. "Former State Legislators in the U.S. House of Representatives: Institutional and Policy Mastery," *Legislative Studies Quarterly*, XVIII (February 1993), 77–97.

70. See an inventive study that confirms the hypothesis that seniority influences the distribution of federal benefits: Brian E. Roberts, "A Dead Senator Tells No Lies: Seniority and the Distribution of Federal Benefits," *American Journal of Political Science*, XXXIV (February 1990), 31–58. U.S. senators are permitted to chair only one committee in a Congress. See a study by Melissa P. Collie and Brian E. Roberts of the choices made by senators when they have had the opportunity to chair two or more committees. Two factors dominate. As a rule, senators choose the more prestigious committee or the one where the heir apparent's policy interests are less compatible with their own. "Trading Places: Choice and Committee Chairs in the U.S. Senate, 1950–1986," *Journal of Politics*, LIV (February 1992), 231–45. See a comprehensive study of the relative value of seats on Senate committees by James W. Endersby and Karen M. McCurdy, "Committee Assignments in the U.S. Senate," *Legislative Studies Quarterly*, XXI (May 1996), 219–34.

71. George H. Haynes, *The Senate of the United States* (Boston: Houghton Mifflin, 1938), I, pp. 296–97.

72. Emanuel Celler, "The Seniority Rule in Congress," *Western Political Quarterly*, XIV (March 1961), 164.

73. "Strengthening Congress in National Policymaking," *Congressional Behavior*, ed. Nelson W. Polsby (New York: Random House, 1971), pp. 6–7.

74. Shepsle, "Representation and Governance," p. 470.

75. David Epstein, David Brady, Sadafumi Kawato, and Sharyn O'Halloran, "A Comparative Approach to Legislative Organization: Careerism and Seniority in the United States and Japan," *American Journal of Political Science*, XLI (July 1997), 965–98. A study of committee tenure patterns from the reconstruction era to the New Deal by Jonathan N. Katz and Brian R. Sola finds a significant relationship between the adoption of the Australian (secret) ballot in the 1890s and the emergence of the norm of committee assignments as a "property right" (with members retaining their assignments from one Congress to the next). The secret ballot gave voters the opportunity to reward or punish their representatives individually. The effect was to sensitize members to the importance of claiming credit for their individual accomplishments and thus to strengthen their electoral connection; predictable committee tenure contributed to members' policy expertise and influence over the distribution of pork. Committee assignment as property right became a key component in the

reelection calculus of members. "Careerism, Committee Assignments, and the Electoral Connection," *American Political Science Review,* XC (March 1996), 21–33.

76. Gilbert Y. Steiner and Samuel K. Gove, *Legislative Politics in Illinois* (Urbana: University of Illinois Press, 1960), pp. 14–15.

77. Joel M. Fisher, Charles M. Price, and Charles G. Bell, *The Legislative Process in California* (Washington, DC: American Political Science Association, 1973), p. 50.

78. Peverill Squire, "Member Career Opportunities and the Internal Organization of Legislatures," *Journal of Politics,* L (August 1988), 735.

79. Charles W. Wiggins, *The Iowa Lawmaker* (Washington, DC: American Political Science Association, 1971), p. 37.

80. William E. Oden, "Tenure and Turnover of Recent Texas Legislatures," *Southwestern Social Science Quarterly,* XLV (March 1965), 371–74.

81. Squire, "Member Career Opportunities," 737.

82. C. N. Fortenberry and Edward H. Hobbs, "The Mississippi Legislature," in *Power in American State Legislatures,* ed. Alex B. Lacy, Jr. (New Orleans: Tulane University Press, 1967), p. 82; Sidney Wise, *The Legislative Process in Pennsylvania* (Washington, DC: American Political Science Association, 1971), p. 49; and Elmer E. Cornwell, Jr., Jay S. Goodman, William J. DeNuccio, and Angelo A. Mosca, Jr., *The Rhode Island General Assembly* (Washington, DC: American Political Science Association, 1970), p. 85.

83. Squire, "Member Career Opportunities," p. 734.

84. *Book of the States, 1998–99* (Lexington, KY: Council of State Governments, 1999), p. 114.

85. Zeller, *American State Legislatures,* p. 197.

86. Wayne L. Francis, "Leadership, Party Caucuses, and Committees in U.S. State Legislatures," *Legislative Studies Quarterly,* X (May 1985), 245.

87. See the evidence of Ronald D. Hedlund and Keith E. Hamm, "Political Parties as Vehicles for Organizing U.S. State Legislative Committees," *Legislative Studies Quarterly,* XXI (August 1996), 404.

88. Alan Rosenthal, *Legislative Performance in the States: Explorations of Committee Behavior* (New York: Free Press, 1974), pp. 174–80. Also see Hubert Harry Basehart, "The Effect of Membership Stability on Continuity and Experience in U.S. State Legislative Committees," *Legislative Studies Quarterly,* V (February 1980), 55–68. Something of an informal seniority system may be developing in some states as legislative leaders increasingly permit members to retain their committee assignments from one session to the next. See Keith E. Hamm and Ronald D. Hedlund, "Accounting for Change in the Number of State Legislative Committee Positions," *Legislative Studies Quarterly,* XV (May 1990), 201–26.

89. Steiner and Gove, *Legislative Politics in Illinois,* p. 82.

90. Norman J. Ornstein, Thomas E. Mann, and Michael J. Malbin, *Vital Statistics on Congress, 1993–1994* (Washington, DC: Congressional Quarterly Press, 1994), p. 132.

91. *Congressional Quarterly Weekly Report,* March 11, 1955, p. 735; January 28, 1955, p. 265.

92. "The Record of Congress in Committee Staffing," *American Political Science Review,* XLV (December 1951), 1126.

93. This paragraph is based largely on a study by Beth M. Henschen and Edward I. Sidlow, "The Recruitment and Career Patterns of Congressional Committee Staffs; An Exploration," *Western Political Quarterly,* XXXIX (December 1986), 701–708.

94. See an essay by David E. Price that distinguishes between two types of staff aides: "professionals" and "policy entrepreneurs." Whereas "professional" staff aides are distinguished by "neutral competence," "policy entrepreneurs" are inclined to use their positions to advance their own policy preferences, even though it requires them to play a political role in the committee. Both staff orientations, the author contends, are essential. "Professional and 'Entrepreneurs': Staff Orientations and Policy Making on Three Senate Committees," *Journal of Politics,* XXXIII (May 1971), 316–36.

95. See a study by David C. Kozak, "Contexts of Congressional Decision Behavior," Ph.D. dissertation, University of Pittsburgh, 1979, especially Chap. 4. Kozak finds that the influence

of various forces (staffs, party leaders, constituents, fellow members, and so on) varies *according to issues*. On some issues the influence of personal staffs on the members' decision is substantial, whereas on other issues it is scarcely perceptible. Overall, the study shows that the personal staffs of members have a major impact on congressional decision making. The influence of committee staffs in influencing voting behavior is much less important. At the state legislative level, specialist legislators rely heavily on staffs for policy information. See Paul Sabatier and David Whiteman, "Legislative Decision Making and Substantive Policy Information: Models of Information Flow," *Legislative Studies Quarterly*, X (August 1985), 395–419.

96. Michael J. Malbin, *Unelected Representatives: Congressional Staff and the Future of Representative Government* (New York: Basic Books, 1980), pp. 6–7. Also see a comprehensive analysis of congressional staffs by Harrison W. Fox, Jr., and Susan Webb Hammond, *Congressional Staffs: The Invisible Force in American Lawmaking* (New York: Free Press, 1977); and an inventory and analysis of the literature on legislative staffing by Susan Webb Hammond, "Legislative Analysis," *Legislative Studies Quarterly*, IX (May 1984), 271–317.

97. Senate Committee on the Judiciary, *Juvenile Delinquency*, Senate report no. 1593, 86th Cong., 2nd sess., 1960 (Washington, DC: U.S. Government Printing Office, 1960), pp. 127–28.

98. *New York Times*, August, 5, 1994.

99. Congressional Staff and Public Policy-Making: The Joint Committee on Internal Revenue Taxation," *Journal of Politics*, XXX (November 1968), 1046-67 (quotations on pp. 1066 and 1067).

100. Christine DeGregorio, "Professionals in the U.S. Congress: An Analysis of Working Styles," *Legislative Studies Quarterly*, XIII (November 1988), 459–76.

101. Gary F. Moncrief, Joel A. Thompson, and Karl T. Kurtz, "The Old Statehouse, It Ain't What It Used to Be," *Legislative Studies Quarterly*, XXI (February 1996), 57–72.

102. Alan Rosenthal, "An Analysis of Institutional Effects: Staffing Legislative Parties in Wisconsin," *Journal of Politics*, XXXII (August 1970), 531–62.

103. For emerging evidence on the importance of staff in term-limited legislatures, see several articles in *State Legislatures*, July/August 1998.

# 7

# Committees at Work

Congress and state legislatures are beset by much the same irritation: a nagging doubt about their self-sufficiency. The reasons for this doubt are many and complex, ranging from those that reflect problems largely internal to any legislature to those that arise from the pressure of external agencies and events. Public policy today is complicated beyond comparison; it changes at a rate that tends to make last year's information inappropriate to this year's understanding, it grows steadily as a result of the new ventures of government, it suffers from contingencies policymakers can never fully estimate, and it imposes a heavy burden on legislators who attempt to meet their responsibilities conscientiously.

Legislators' restiveness over how well they are doing their jobs is linked in part to their perceptions of the advantages held by the executive branch. Legislators are generalists; their frequent antagonists, the bureaucrats, are typically specialists. In broad terms, legislators view the executive branch as a vast organization better equipped to collect and process information and to generate policy options. While serving in the Senate, Walter F. Mondale sketched the problem in these terms:

> I have been in many debates, for example, on the Education Committee, that dealt with complicated formulas and distributions. And I have found that whenever I am on the side of the Administration, I am surfeited with computer print-outs and data that comes within seconds, whenever I need it to prove how right I am. But if I am opposed to the Administration, computer print-outs always come late, prove the opposite point, or always are on some other topic. So I think one of the rules is that he who controls the computers controls the Congress, and I believe that there is utterly no reason why the Congress does not develop its own computer capability, its own technicians, its own pool of information. I would hope that we do so.[1]

The main response of legislatures to the presumed research and informational advantages of the executive branch has been to expand their own resources, particularly personal and committee staffs. Between 1957 and

1997, members' personal staffs in the U.S. House of Representatives grew from 2,441 to 7,282 and in the Senate from 1,115 to 4,410. House committee staffs increased from 329 in 1955 to 1,250 in 1997; in the Senate they increased from 386 to 1,002.[2] Over the years, Congress has also increased its research capacity by expanding its support agencies, including the Congressional Research Service, the General Accounting Office, the Office of Technology Assessment, and the Congressional Budget Office. (In the drive to "downsize" government in 1995, OTA was abolished.)

The other response of legislatures, and particularly of Congress, has been to focus on data collection, the use of expert witnesses, and the processing of all kinds of information useful for legislating and for strengthening the legislature's position.[3]

The committee is the principal agency of the legislature for gathering information and the principal instrument by which the legislature can defend and maintain itself in struggles with the chief executive and the bureaucracy. "A committee is commissioned not to instruct the public, but to instruct and guide the House."[4] A major technique for carrying out this task is the hearing.

## COMMITTEE HEARINGS

The practice of committee hearings is associated historically with the right of citizens to petition Parliament, either in support of or in opposition to a proposed action. In the English experience, limits were clearly defined. In assessing the value of *public* measures, Parliament became the sole judge, and citizens' opinions were neither sought nor entertained except when measures were thought to have adverse consequences for private rights and interests. The principal opportunity for witnesses to appear before committees developed with private bills, those involving the claims of individuals, companies, or local authorities.

American experience with hearings has been mixed. Writing in the 1920s, Robert Luce observed that "on this side of the water it has generally been held that no right exists in any case, whether public or private."[5] Many state legislatures make only limited use of hearings. Congress, however, has long been inclined to open its doors to nonmembers and in recent years has actively solicited their testimony. David Truman writes that the development of the public hearing in the United States, in the period since 1900, "was a consequence of the proliferation of interest groups and of the challenge to established interests that their claims constituted."[6] Today few major bills emerge from congressional committees without having proceeded through the hearing stage.

## The Functions of Hearings

The advantages of legislative hearings, particularly the public (or open) variety, are steadily extolled by American legislators. Hearings, their litany insists, present an opportunity to "get at the facts," to "hear all sides" (and "interested parties"), to educate the member to the provisions of a bill and their probable consequences, and to inform the representative of the "wishes of the people." In sum, the public face of hearings, the one immediately described by legislators, shows lawmakers educating and warming themselves in the glow of the active citizen's opinions and intelligence. The only trouble with this description is that it does not completely square with the facts.

David Truman describes the functions or purposes of public hearings as three in number. The initial purpose, defined by the preceding glossy accounts, is to provide "a means of transmitting information, both technical and political, from various actual and potential interest groups to the committee." The second function "is as a propaganda channel through which a public may be extended and its segments partially consolidated or reinforced." Third, public hearings serve "to provide a quasi-ritualistic means of adjusting group conflicts and relieving disturbances through a safety valve."[7]

Purposes two and three rank well above one in importance. If the principal purpose of hearings were to transmit information to committee members, the major groups would make better use of expert staff personnel as witnesses because they are better equipped to testify on technical points. The fact is that organizations tend to use ("parade" may be a better word) their most distinguished members as spokespersons, individuals whose names command committee respect and newspaper print. The very appearance of the representative "is a subtle reminder that it might cost precious votes or support in the next campaign if the measure under consideration is not dealt with 'properly.' "[8] The propaganda function is achieved through coverage by the news media, including television and radio. "At some points in the development of a measure, in fact, the primary purpose of hearings lies in their propaganda value."[9]

The safety-valve function involves a further dimension of committee hearings. Legislators recognize its utility, though they do not publicize it. Even witnesses may understand this function, as shown in the statement by a South Carolina attorney testifying on civil rights legislation: "I appreciate the fact that you have been sitting all day, but I have come about 500 miles to get something off my chest and I hope you gentlemen will let me do it."[10] "In my own opinion," wrote Luce, "not the least, and perhaps the greatest, of the advantages of public committee hearings is their service as a safety-valve. If the wild reformer, the crank, can but be heard, he is often content and thereafter for a while will do little mischief. Bottle him up and he will explode."[11]

In traditional interpretation, the committee member usually has been described as an impartial judge, expected to study the facts, listen, weigh the evidence, and decide the case. The committee members' standards, this interpretation held, were those of the "public interest," and their role was that of guardian. A more realistic generalization proposes that the members themselves are usually willing and active participants in the political struggle and that their interests in the outcome are far from neutral.

Ralph Huitt examined the suitability of these generalizations in explaining the behavior of members of the Senate Committee on Banking and Currency in hearings on the question of extending price controls, an explosive controversy in which the leading antagonists were the National Association of Manufacturers (NAM) and the Congress of Industrial Organizations (CIO) among the organized interest groups, and the Republican senators and the administration among officialdom. This study's findings accent the political function of hearings: (1) Committee members tended to identify with particular interest groups—the supporters of price control with the administration, labor spokespersons, and the National Farmers Union; the opponents, with NAM, the American Farm Bureau Federation, and other business groups. (2) "Each group [of senators] seemed to come into the hearings with a ready-made frame of reference. Facts which were compatible were filled into it; facts which were not compatible, even when elaborately documented, were discounted, not perceived, or ignored." (3) "The members of this Committee did not sit as legislative judges to discover an abstract general interest, nor did they seem concerned with presenting a balanced debate for public consideration. On the contrary, most of them did take sides."[12] In a word, most of the members were involved in the price-control squabble as participants. The likelihood is great that this behavior is characteristic, especially in the case of legislation having major socioeconomic implications.

### Testimony and Interrogation of Witnesses

Committee witnesses begin their presentation by reading or summarizing a statement of their views. As a rule, committee members appear more interested in questioning the witnesses than in listening to them read a statement.[13] "We just hope the witness will keep in mind that there are many more witnesses to be heard and much of the testimony is cumulative," the chair is likely to caution. As a result, formal statements tend to be brief, merely recording the salient points of the written statement, which will be incorporated into the record. A surprisingly large amount of testimony is taken with only a small contingent of the committee members present. This practice may be partly attributable to the fact that the committee is concerned with simply going through the motions of hearing out witnesses, but it also occurs because other activities vie for the members' time. Important witnesses—cabinet members, governors, the heads of major pressure groups —are likely to attract a full complement of committee members.

Testimony given in committee ranges widely. At times it has a distinctly authentic ring, with witnesses introducing new and relevant information, identifying clearly the positions of their organizations, and helping to bring the issue into sharp focus. But there is no avoiding the fact that much of what is said in formal statements and in response to questioning is designed mainly to win propaganda advantage, to intensify old loyalties, and to fill out the record. This cuts both ways: Legislators often are just as anxious as witnesses to establish their orthodoxy. They can be of immense help to witnesses or they can go a long way toward making their committee appearances uncomfortable, even unpleasant. On the one hand, witnesses who can claim a personal friend, or whose organization has gained a sympathetic ear among the members, start with an advantage worth having, regardless of the legislation under consideration. If they get into a jam, there is someone to help extricate them. The committee reception to a witness, on the other hand, may try the patience of the witness and fray the nerves of some committee members. Questioning by a hostile committee member is apt to be prolonged, dilatory, and involved, and may call for specific data the witness is unlikely to have. Stated and repeated answers rarely satisfy. Doggedness, sometimes brusqueness, and a mixture of irony and humor may serve to keep the witness off balance.

An often dominant impression conveyed by hearings is that witnesses are questioned in such a way as to elicit statements that buttress the views of one or more members of the committee. The questioning is calculated to help a witness plead a point of view and make all the "right" arguments. During the 1998 impeachment proceedings of President Bill Clinton, the following exchange occurred between David P. Schippers, chief investigative counsel for the House Judiciary Committee, and Kenneth Starr, the Independent Counsel:

MR. SCHIPPERS:   Now, Judge, there has been a lot of talk in the public domain and on the television and things that this is—that all the President did was deny sex, deny a sexual relationship with an intern. He went a lot further than that, didn't he? For an example, with Mr. Blumenthal?

MR. STARR:   Yes.

MR. SCHIPPERS:   As a matter of fact, before Mr. Blumenthal came in to testify, he was subjected to an elaborate, elaborate lie by the President concerning the relationship with Monica Lewinsky.

MR. STARR:   Yes, he was.

MR. SCHIPPERS:   If I may, the President told Mr. Blumenthal that Monica made sexual demands upon him which he rebuffed. Is that right? And that was not true, was it?

MR. STARR:   That was not true.

MR. SCHIPPERS: He also said that Monica Lewinsky threatened to claim an affair and he wouldn't go along with it; that he had been threatened by Monica Lewinsky; is that right?

MR. STARR: Yes.

MR. SCHIPPERS: Now, this is at a time when the President thought that it was a one-on-one with Monica Lewinsky, didn't he?

MR. STARR: I believe that is what he thought at that time.

MR. SCHIPPERS: And this would have been a perfect answer. "She threatened to say I had sex with her if I didn't do something for her. I didn't do something, therefore, everything she is saying is a lie."

MR. STARR: It would be a very good answer.

MR. SCHIPPERS: It has been suggested that your people used the young lady and betrayed the young lady. Wouldn't that more properly belong to the President of the United States?

MR. STARR: Well, I am not sure I should be the one to pass judgment, but we certainly did not betray Ms. Lewinsky. We were doing our job, and we certainly never took any steps other than to vindicate the interests of the criminal law. . . .

MR. SCHIPPERS: There has been some suggestion, Judge, that this was merely a private crime. The United States Constitution provides for three branches of government, does it not, co-equal branches?

MR. STARR: That is correct.

MR. SCHIPPERS: And the judiciary is coequal with the executive?

MR. STARR: Absolutely.

MR. SCHIPPERS: Did I understand you earlier to say that lying under oath, perjury, and obstruction of justice strikes at the very heart of the judicial system of the United States?

MR. STARR: Absolutely, and I think every judge would agree with that, that this is absolutely inimical to the judicial functioning. It is inimical to our court system.

MR. SCHIPPERS: And under the Constitution of the United States, if the judicial system is destroyed, that is destroying one of the constitutional portions of our government; isn't it?

MR. STARR: No question that from the founding of the Republic, the importance of our judiciary as an enforcer of rights and the vindicators of rule of law is absolutely critical.

MR. SCHIPPERS: So when the President of the United States lies under oath, a civil or criminal case, grand jury or other, and obstructs justice, civil or criminal, grand jury or other, he is effectively attacking the judicial branch of the United States constitutional government, isn't he?

MR. STARR: That is the way I would view it.[14]

Bias in the committee-hearing process occurs because committee members typically are interested parties, concerned about how committee decisions will affect their interests and those of their constituencies. A recent study of nearly 10,000 witnesses who testified on pesticides issues between 1900 and 1988 and on smoking-and-tobacco issues between 1945 and 1986 offers substantial evidence of committee bias in the selection of witnesses. Jones, Baumgartner, and Talbert write,

> When an agriculture committee has hearings on pesticides topics, its members are three times more likely to listen to testimony from representatives from the pesticides industry or from others likely to have a favorable view on pesticides than from health or environmental representatives. When a health committee holds hearings on a similar topic . . . almost three quarters of the witnesses appearing before these committees are health or environmental experts, rather than agricultural officials. . . . Agricultural and trade committees, when considering tobacco questions, simply do not schedule witnesses who could be expected to attack the industry. Congress specializes. When pesticides are to be attacked, one group of committees holds these hearings, and one group of members hears their testimony. When pesticides are to be defended, another committee holds those hearings and schedules a different group of experts to give testimony. Committees use hearings to garner support for the views they already have.[15]

Policy bias is mitigated, this study finds, by the breakdown of committees' monopolistic control over issues. As an issue becomes more controversial, other committees will lay claim to a piece of the action—that is, some part of the issue. They in turn use their hearings as venues to air views that challenge the existing policy subsystem and its clients' interests. Bias in one part of the congressional system, in other words, may offset bias in another part.[16]

There is considerable variation in the extent to which committee chairs seek to dominate the hearing process, carefully managing both the agenda and the selection of witnesses as a way of supporting their own policy preferences. An interview study of high-ranking staff aides and subcommittee chairs by Christine DeGregorio finds that although some chairs consistently use hearings to advance their own views, the dominant leadership style is one of accommodation in which the chairs regularly defer to the wishes of their colleagues in setting the agenda. About three-fourths of the staff in this study reported that they made an effort to select witnesses who would provide a full range of views, whereas only one-fourth sought to pick witnesses who would simply support their bosses' point of view. The chair's accommodating behavior toward colleagues is well illustrated by the observations of a staff aide on scheduling hearings by the House Committee on Agriculture:

> Sometimes a member comes up to him (the chair) and says, "I need to have a hearing on . . . in my district. Five hundred growers want to burn me at the stake." He'll tell me to check it out in the district. If it's within reason, we'll do it. Also, there is a lot of trading between members. One member may have (commodity) in his district and he needs us to get in there and alleviate political pressure, give the people an opportunity to express themselves. My boss

may say to him: "Well, I have terrible credit problems, will you hold a hearing on that?" There is a pretty good network here on Agriculture; members of different subcommittees will help each other out like that.[17]

Most committee hearings are open to the public. Occasionally, however, testimony is taken in executive or closed session. The principal justification for holding closed hearings is that the information to be disclosed may be of such a nature that it should not be released to the public—for example, certain military, diplomatic, and scientific data. The principal route to classified information in the executive branch is through closed hearings, permitting greater freedom of testimony for government witnesses. A common practice is to ask each witness to review his or her testimony to make as much of it as possible available for public inspection. Given the complex regulations regarding publication of executive information, this often is a frustrating task; not surprisingly, there may be disagreement between legislators and administrators concerning what information may safely be released.

From what ranks are congressional committee witnesses drawn? No general answer to this question can be given since the character of the legislation at hand is the governing factor. Major legislation will invariably call forth witnesses from three main sources: the administration, Congress, and private organizations. The testimony of "citizen" witnesses is also not uncommon. Nothing in the rules of either house insists that committees must listen to the arguments of all prospective witnesses; yet it is a rare instance in which a representative of any organized group is denied an opportunity to appear and testify. The doors are, of course, virtually wide open to legislators and administration officials.

## Hearings in the State Legislatures

Unlike Congress, whose attachment to the use of hearings is only slightly less than its attachment to the flag, most state legislative committees are both inclined and geared to act on measures without bothering to gather testimony. Apart from a few states that make considerable use of the device, public hearings are regarded either as rarities or as a special treatment to be accorded only major or controversial bills. For a majority of states, the use of public hearings is probably similar to that found in Pennsylvania:

> Public hearings by committees in either house are an infrequent occurrence, are used to permit airing of controversial issues, but are held entirely at the discretion of the committee concerned. Although there is advance notice of such meetings, there does not appear to be any regularized procedure to keep the general public informed on forthcoming hearings. Joint hearings by committees of both houses are even less frequent and, in fact, have been used only sparingly by the two appropriations committees.[18]

Public hearings in the state legislatures are often spectacular, boister-ous, and entertaining, and indeed traveling circuses would be hard put to compete with some of them. Let a state legislature schedule a hearing on a bill to license chiropractors and hundreds of them will be in attendance, con-veniently, because the annual convention happened to be held in the state capital the week of the hearing. Let a joint committee on sports and physical fitness schedule hearings to consider fitness programs, and among those present to "testify" will be a representative of a physical culture studio, clad appropriately in a black leotard, to demonstrate "body rhythms" for atten-tive committee members. And should a bill to furnish medical schools with unclaimed dogs and cats for research be up for a hearing, it is a foregone conclusion that dog and cat lovers from hundreds of miles around will be there, carrying gory, colored photographs of vivisections and testifying, among other things, that *dog* spelled backwards is *God*.

Few people who watched the legislatures in the 1950s will ever forget the titanic battles waged in public hearings to permit the sale of precolored oleomargarine. Seldom have so many owed so much to so few as to the hero-ic housewives who, under the kindly eyes of the soybean farmers and the big oleo manufacturers, happily splattered oleo throughout the state com-mittee rooms of the nation as they demonstrated the tedious method by which it is hand-colored. Last to drop the bar against precolored oleo was Wisconsin (in 1967), a legislature that has always had an abnormal affinity for butter and cheese, not to mention a good many legislators from dairy counties.

### Evaluation of Committee Hearings

No student of the legislature describes committee hearings as models of effi-ciency or of objectivity. The assessment usually is just the reverse. The most serious charges deal with misinformation, unrepresentative opinions, bias, and staging. Robert Luce, for example, evaluated committee hearings in the Massachusetts legislature in this way:

> The value of the opinion brought out by hearings is as uncertain as that of the information. The opinion is the more dangerous, for misinformation can be cor-rected, but there is no test for opinion. Ponder it for a moment, and you will see the risk in drawing inference as to the opinion of two million or so of adult human beings in a State like Massachusetts, from the views expressed by five or fifty persons in a committee room. It may be said that these are the persons most interested, which may or may not be true. Unfortunately the persons at-tending are usually extremists, biased, uncompromising. Therefore no cautious legislator refrains from having at hand, metaphorically speaking, a bag of salt from which he may take many grains when he listens to speakers addressing a committee. The most to be said for opinion so furnished is that it may help.[19]

Julius Cohen attacks committee hearings on many points, but perhaps his sharpest criticism is reserved for the committee staff, among whose tasks, he says, "critical investigation" is not numbered. The political dimensions of committee hearings may be revealed as clearly by the behavior of the staff as by that of the members themselves. The job of committee aides may be

> . . . the delicate one of slanting the hearing, of manipulating the hearing machinery in such a way that a previous commitment on a bill would be made to appear as a decision reached by rational, detached deliberation. . . . This the staff can do by several means: by inviting the strongest, most persuasive witnesses to testify on behalf of the measure, by endeavoring to limit the number of strong opposition witnesses to a minimum; by asking "proper" questions of "friendly" witnesses and embarrassing ones of witnesses who are "unfriendly"; by arranging to close the hearing at a propitious time; by writing a report which brings out the best features of the testimony in favor of the bill and the most unfavorable features of that offered by the opposition; by subduing or discarding facts which do not fit the pattern of preconceived notions, opinions, or prejudices. In addition, the bill might be given the "killed-with-kindness" treatment—that is, given so lengthy a hearing that no time is left prior to adjournment to consider the measure on the House or Senate floor, thus assuring its defeat.[20]

It is not unfair to characterize Congress as preoccupied with the hearing process. Outside critics are persistent in questioning this activity, which consumes inordinate time, harasses legislators, and yields an uncertain product. Nevertheless, this is not the full story. It is true, if hackneyed, that there is educational value to hearings—if not consistently to the legislators, at least to sectors within the public that follow the well-reported hearings on major bills. Quite apart from the intrinsic value of information conveyed by interest groups, an important function of instruction is served. Whether the testimony of interest-group representatives or administration spokespersons is partisan, factual, or superficial is not the main point. Hearings may be justified in terms of the American public, which look to group testimony both for policy cues and for an extension of their own outlooks—hearings may be considered a useful stage in the representative process.

No critic contends that all hearings are a waste of time. Some hearings cover immense ground, yielding data and opinions of significance. As for interrogations, if they are sometimes banal, niggling, and obsessively partisan, they are also, in counterpoise, sometimes illuminating and productive. Major policies occasionally trace their origin directly to the attention of the press and the public. Whatever the verdict on hearings, they represent an ambitious attempt to blend the legislature's requirements for information with the member's and party's requirements for influence and advantage.

## INVESTIGATING COMMITTEES

Congress, wrote Woodrow Wilson in 1885, "may easily be too diligent in legislation. It often overdoes that business."[21] "What is quite as indispensable as the debate of problems of legislation," he contended, "is the debate of all matters of administration." Moreover,

> It is the proper duty of a representative body to look diligently into every affair of government and to talk much about what it sees. It is meant to be the eyes and the voice, and to embody the wisdom and will of its constituents. Unless Congress have and use every means of acquainting itself with the acts and the disposition of the administrative agents of the government, the country must be helpless to learn how it is being served; and unless Congress both scrutinize these things and sift them by every form of discussion, the country must remain in embarrassing, crippling ignorance of the very affairs which it is most important that it should understand and direct. *The informing function of Congress should be preferred even to its legislative function.*[22]

The instrument for looking "into every affair of government" is the legislative committee. To conduct an investigation, Congress may create a special committee or entrust the task to one of its standing committees (or subcommittees). Although there is no precise accounting of the number of investigations that have been held since the initial one in 1792—the House investigation concerned with General St. Clair's abortive campaign against the Indians—it is likely that more investigations have been conducted in the last two or three decades than in all previous congresses put together.[23]

### Legislative Investigations and the Courts

The power of Congress to conduct investigations was well established before it was ever examined carefully by the judiciary. In the early decades of the national government, the House authorized many more investigations than the Senate. The Senate's initial investigation was approved in 1818; its initial investigation specifically designed as an aid to legislating did not take place until 1859, when it set out to learn the facts "attending the late invasion and seizure of the armory and arsenal at Harper's Ferry." By this time congressional investigations had become commonplace. Congress was using its power to compel witnesses to testify and to produce their records; witnesses who refused to cooperate were cited for contempt and, on occasion, committed to jail. Although there were occasional disputes in Congress over the wisdom of certain inquiries, few if any members questioned the legislature's power to authorize investigations.[24]

In 1881, however, the scope of the investigative power was whittled down by the Supreme Court. In the case of *Kilbourn* v. *Thompson*, the Court upbraided Congress for having confined Kilbourn to jail following his refusal to produce papers concerning the bankruptcy of Jay Cooke & Co. The investigation was held to be improper on several counts: The resolution authorizing the investigation was indefinite, the House had undertaken a "clearly judicial" function, and the inquiry was not directly concerned with producing information relevant to the function of legislating.[25] The lasting significance of the *Kilbourn* case was that it brought the Supreme Court directly into the controversy over congressional investigations; its immediate impact was to throw into doubt the dimensions of the investigative power. Nevertheless, Congress, not extraordinarily impressed, continued its investigations in about the same fashion as before.

The right of Congress to investigate was given firm legal support in 1927 by the Supreme Court in *McGrain* v. *Daugherty,* a case arising out of an investigation of the administration of the Department of Justice. The Court held unanimously that Congress had the power to investigate in order to secure information relevant to its lawmaking function:

> We are of opinion that the power of inquiry—with process to enforce it—is an essential and appropriate auxiliary to the legislative function. . . .
>
> A legislative body cannot legislate wisely or effectively in the absence of information respecting the conditions which the legislation is intended to affect or change; and where the legislative body does not itself possess the requisite information—which not infrequently is true—recourse must be had to others who do possess it.[26]

A 1957 case involving the House Un-American Activities Committee (HUAC), *Watkins* v. *United States,*[27] renewed the challenge to congressional investigations launched in *Kilbourn.* In this case the Court refused to uphold a conviction of a witness who had declined to answer questions about individuals he believed were no longer associated with the Communist party. Although the Court recognized the importance and the sweep of the investigatory power of Congress, it held that the power was not without limits: "There is no general authority to expose the private affairs of individuals without justification in terms of the functions of the Congress. . . . No inquiry is an end in itself; it must be related to, and in furtherance of, a legitimate task of the Congress."[28]

A decision on the same day concerned the conviction of Paul Sweezy by a New Hampshire court.[29] The state legislature had empowered the attorney general of New Hampshire to investigate subversive activities and persons, and in the course of the investigation Sweezy was summoned to appear before the attorney general and to answer questions concerning a lecture he had given at the University of New Hampshire. His refusal to answer the questions led to a citation for contempt, and as in the *Watkins* case, the Supreme Court set aside the conviction.

The 1957 decisions established the fact that witnesses could not be punished for contempt unless the *pertinency* of questions asked them was unmistakably clear and the inquiry itself was related to a valid legislative purpose; moreover, the Court ruled in the *Watkins* case that a committee's jurisdiction must be spelled out in sufficient detail to permit a witness to judge whether questions put to him or her were pertinent. The *Watkins* case was especially notable for its sharp censure of the investigatory practices of HUAC.

The immediate reaction to these decisions by most observers was that the Court had put a tight rein on investigating committees. This evaluation was soon proven erroneous. In 1959 a sharply divided Court upheld the contempt conviction of Lloyd Barenblatt, a former college professor, who refused to state before a subcommittee of HUAC whether he was or ever had been a Communist party member. Barenblatt contended that the committee's authority for the investigation was vague, that the pertinency of the questions asked him was not made clear, and that the First Amendment supported his refusal to answer the questions. The Court held that the committee had been duly authorized and that the relevance of the questions had been established. Coming to the constitutional issue, the Court invoked the "balance-of-interest" test and concluded that "the balance between the individual and the governmental interest . . . must be struck in favor of the latter. . . ."[30]

In 1961, again dividing five to four, the Court upheld HUAC and its procedures in two cases in which outspoken critics of the committee had been cited for contempt.[31] Both witnesses had refused to answer questions concerning possible Communist party membership, contending that the questions asked were not pertinent and that the inquiry did not serve a valid legislative purpose. The Court ruled otherwise.

Later cases involving investigating committees have yielded decisions based on fairly narrow grounds. By a five-to-two vote in 1962, in *Russell* v. *United States,* the Court set aside the convictions of six men who had declined to answer questions concerning Communist associations that had been asked by subcommittees of HUAC and the Senate Internal Security Subcommittee. The Court held that the indictments against the men were "defective in failing to identify the subject which was under inquiry at the time of the defendants' alleged default or refusal to answer."[32] Henceforth, indictments for contempt of Congress must show specifically the subject of the committee investigation; it is not sufficient simply to state that the questions asked witnesses were "pertinent" to the inquiry. In 1963 the Court held, by a five-to-four vote, that a state legislative investigating committee must have hard evidence concerning Communist infiltration of an organization before it can ask questions of its members. In this case (*Gibson* v. *Florida Legislative Investigation Committee*) the Court reversed the contempt conviction of the president of the Miami branch of the NAACP (National Association for the Advancement of Colored People), who had refused to provide information to a state investigating committee concerning the membership of the local NAACP organization.[33] The Court held that the contempt conviction violated the free-speech and free-association provisions of the First and Fourteenth Amendments since evidence was insufficient to show a substantial connection between a local branch of this organization and Communist activities. In *Yellin* v. *United States* (1963), the Court again split five to four while reversing the conviction of a witness who had refused to answer questions asked by HUAC. The witness, Edward Yellin, had challenged his conviction on the ground that the committee had violated one of its own rules when it failed to consider his request to be heard in executive session before being questioned in a public hearing. The rule provides that "if a majority of the Committee or Subcommittee . . . believes that the interrogation of a witness in a public hearing might endanger national security or *unjustly injure his reputation*, or the reputation of other individuals, the Committee shall interrogate such witness in an Executive Session for the purpose of determining the necessity or advisability of conducting such interrogation thereafter in a public hearing."[34] The committee's failure to observe this rule led the Court to upset the conviction.

Another major case involving the investigative power of Congress was decided in 1975. The case involved an investigation by the Senate Subcommittee on Internal Security to determine whether the activities of a servicemen's organization were potentially harmful to the morale of the armed forces. In the course of the inquiry, a subpoena was issued to a bank, ordering it to produce all records involving the organization's account. The organization then sought a court order barring implementation of the subpoena on the grounds that it was an invasion of privacy and a violation of the First Amendment. In a sweeping defense of legislative independence and congressional immunity, the Supreme Court, by an eight-to-one vote, held that "once it is determined that Members are acting within the 'legitimate legislative sphere' the Speech or Debate Clause [Article I, Section 6, of the Constitution] is an absolute bar to interference."[35] Furthermore, the Court held, "in determining the legitimacy of a congressional act we do not look to the motives alleged to have prompted it."[36]

In sum, several court cases have held that the investigative power is not unlimited and that reasonable procedures must be followed. Yet it is equally clear that the boundaries of this power are very wide. The Court plainly recognizes the legitimacy of legislative investigations and is reluctant to interfere with them.

## Purposes of Congressional Investigations

There are four widely accepted purposes of investigations.[37] First, Congress can investigate for the purpose of securing information relevant to its responsibility for the enactment of legislation. This power is implied by the specific grants of power awarded to the legislature by the Constitution, "and each time that Congress' power of legislation is broadened, it follows that the power of investigation is similarly expanded."[38]

Second, Congress can investigate the management of executive departments, and it has done so persistently from the earliest administrations. The legitimacy of these inquiries was made clear in *McGrain v. Daugherty* and reaffirmed in *Watkins v. United States*. These investigations usually are difficult to conduct. "At the heart of the problem of congressional investigation of the executive branch is executive resistance to congressional probing."[39] Often these investigations become struggles over information—Congress needing it, the executive branch reluctant to disclose it.

The need for Congress to inform the public is the third reason advanced in support of investigations—a justification that seems presumptively valid. Although the Supreme Court has never specifically upheld this use, there is probably no necessity that it do so since any investigation for the purpose of informing the public would not be "utterly devoid of legislative possibilities."[40] The lengthy investigation of the assassinations of President John F. Kennedy and Martin Luther King, Jr., in the late 1970s, for example, were designed as much to inform the public as to produce recommendations for new legislation. At the same time, of course, the nature of the investigation—examining the possibility of conspiracy—yielded substantial publicity for members of the House Select Committee on Assassinations. The investigation of the Iran-Contra affair by House and Senate select committees late in the Reagan administration was an effort not only to expose unlawfulness and duplicity but also to provide instruction for the public on the need for the rule of law and the accountability of elected officials. The prolonged hearings also presented the Democratic majority with an opportunity to highlight disarray in the inner workings of the Reagan administration and to gain political advantage. One concrete outcome of this inquiry was the development of tighter controls over the government's covert actions and procedures for informing Congress of them. Finally, the Waco and Whitewater investigations in 1995 by Republican majorities doubtlessly were designed as much to embarrass President Clinton as to provide some kind of public instruction on the events themselves.

The fourth purpose of investigations is to permit Congress to resolve questions concerning its membership. This authority stems directly from Article I of the Constitution, which makes each house "the judge of the Elections, Returns and Qualifications of its own members. . . ." Under this provision, congressional committees have investigated such matters as campaign expenditures in congressional elections, attempts by interest groups to influence improperly or illegally members of the legislature, and members' use of political contributions to pay personal bills. A growing concern with legislative ethics in the 1970s and 1980s led to a number of investigations of members' conduct—involving such cases as the acceptance of money and gifts from influence peddlers, payroll kickback schemes, bribery, perjury, improper expense reimbursements, acceptance of illegal corporate political contributions, diversion of campaign funds for personal use, evasion of rules on outside income and speaking fees, and intervention with executive branch regulatory officials in return for campaign contributions (the Keating Five episode).

Periods of intense investigation wax and wane. Party interest is often just below the surface. During the Speaker Newt Gingrich era (1995–99), a spate of investigations of the Clinton administration occurred, including major House inquiries into alleged fund-raising abuses in the president's 1996 campaign, alleged campaign finance abuses by the Teamsters Union, and the administration's dealings with China involving technology transfers by U.S. satellite companies. On the Senate side, nearly $200 million was spent on investigations between 1995, when the Republicans took control, and 1998;[41] the most prominent ones, in addition to the Whitewater and Waco controversies, involved alleged abuses by the Democratic party in fund-raising and by the Internal Revenue Service in dealing with taxpayers. Nothing much came of the highly partisan campaign finance investigations. The IRS investigation, however, contributed to a substantial restructuring of the agency and the adoption of an array of taxpayer rights and protections.

### State Legislature Investigating Committees

In general, our previous judgment regarding the use of hearings by state legislatures applies equally well to investigating committees, for the states devote less energy and resources to investigations than Congress does. There is no argument concerning whether state legislatures have the investigative power; clearly they do, deriving it from the implied and auxiliary power to gather information held relevant to the enactmet of future legislation. State investigating committees may be created by statute, joint resolution, or the resolution of one house. Ordinarily, committees that are intended to function in the interim between sessions are created by statute.

State legislative investigations are justified on the same grounds as congressional investigations: to secure information needed for the enactment of legislation, to inquire into the management of administrative agencies, to inform the public, and to examine the qualifications of members of the legislature. The activities of state investigating committees are comparable to those of congressional committees. They hold hearings; take testimony; issue subpoenas commanding the presence of persons and the production of books, papers, and records; administer oaths; and report to the parent body their findings together with recommendations for remedial legislation.

Almost any incident or rumor is likely to spur a resolution to create a special investigating committee. A turnpike attendant treats a patron discourteously and the act is witnessed by a legislator, who immediately introduces a resolution to investigate the personnel policies of the turnpike commission. A sportsman's club in a rural district tells its representative that rabbits imported from out of state to replenish the native stock are carriers of communicable diseases, and the legislator promptly calls for an investigating committee to learn the facts. The committee on fisheries may be asked to investigate the reason for the decline in the sale of fishing licenses. A special committee may be set up to inquire into the adequacy of measures for protection of schoolchildren against fire. A rumor circulates that peculiar circumstances surround a pardon made by the governor, and a committee is formed to investigate the incident, and probably the board of pardons as well.

The investigations that count involve highly political subjects rather than the communicable diseases of out-of-state rabbits or the ennui of anglers. An investigation handled skillfully, with "proper" attention to the potential of publicity, may be worth a good many thousands of votes in the next election. Two kinds of investigations are especially commonplace. One is an inquiry into the administration of election law and alleged examples of vote frauds, which almost invariably makes the big cities the object of investigation. The other, doubtless more prevalent, is an investigation of state agencies and the management of state institutions of one type or another. Many begin with a rumor elevated to the initial "whereas" of a resolution for an investigating committee. The highway and public welfare departments, both major spending agencies, are great favorites for investigating committees.

Obviously, it is hazardous to ascribe motives to the investigators, but it is very difficult to escape the impression that partisan advantage, the desire to harass and embarrass governors and perhaps to wring accommodations from them, is at the root of many investigations. However, it is true that the public interest is sometimes served equally with the party interest.

## COMMITTEE SESSIONS

In its struggle over secrecy with the executive branch, Congress's claims have become more persuasive as a result of sharp modifications of its own practices concerning open committee meetings. Although some committee meetings continue to be closed, the prevailing spirit is one of openness. Under a rule adopted in 1973, House committee sessions must be open to the public (including, of course, the press and interest groups) unless a majority of a committee votes, in open session, to close the meeting. After much foot-dragging, a similar rule change was adopted in late 1975 by the Senate. Under the "sunshine" rules in effect in both chambers, even markup sessions (held for the purpose of working out the final details of bills) and meetings of conference committees are open to the public—unless committee members vote, publicly, to close them.

Voting to close meetings will be more difficult under a rule adopted by House Republicans in the 104th Congress (1995–96). Committee majorities voting to close a meeting are required to give a specific explanation for their action; meetings can be closed only under quite limited circumstances— when an open meeting would compromise national security or law enforcement or damage a person's reputation.

The main reason for holding private meetings, members testify, is to reduce the pressure of lobbyists. As a member of the Ways and Means Committee who regularly votes against closed meetings observed, "I hate to say it, but members are more willing to make tough decisions on controversial bills in closed meetings. In a closed meeting, you can come out and say, 'I fought like a tiger for you in there, but I lost.'"[42] To quote Representative Dan Rostenkowski, former chair of Ways and Means,

> One of my members is sitting there looking at some labor skate and thinking, "Oh, well, how does he want me to go on this one?" Or the labor guy is running around and pulling him out to say, "Wait a minute, you can't do this." It's just difficult to legislate. I'm not ashamed about closed doors. We want to get the product out. . . .[43]

Lobbyists naturally see closed meetings in another light, but they are not all equally frustrated. A lobbyist for the AFL-CIO remarks,

> We would prefer to have the meetings open. A lot of lobbyists really complain about closed meetings. It tends to be less the men or women on the Hill every day working than the folks from the law firms and the accounting firms who come up here to take notes and go back and write up a newsletter and charge their clients $250 an hour. They scream and yell like crazy because they don't know what's going on. They have fewer contacts and they don't feel comfortable with grabbing a member as they go in and out and asking them what in the world is going on. We can find out. I can find out who rolled me and let them know that we weren't pleased with that. And when they come around to us for funds or for support on something, we can let them know, "You banged me on that one, don't look to us on this."[44]

## COMMITTEE DECISIONS

### Committee Reports

It is a fact of legislative life that not all bills become law. Those that fail—and normally these are a majority in any session of any legislature—often meet their demise in committee. Bills seldom die as a result of wounds inflicted in battle. Instead, they die of neglect because nobody, or at least not very many, cared sufficiently one way or another. Among the tidy-minded in committees, the proper thing called for in the case of unwanted bills is euthanasia, followed by silent interment. Except for its possible impact on the sponsor and maybe a friend of the idea here and there in the assembly, the whole operation is rather painless. If this description is too extravagant, the process at least is quite simple: Committees eliminate far more bills by ignoring them than by voting them down.

In thirteen states, however, committees are required to report out to the floor all bills referred to them, although this requirement may receive only technical compliance. Congress and the rest of the states are not hobbled by this provision and, consequently, are able to eliminate a large number of proposals simply by pigeonholing them. At least 90 percent of all bills introduced in Congress die in committees without action having been taken on them, a proportion unquestionably higher than in the state legislatures. In the absence of a large number of studies, it is risky to generalize regarding the extent of pigeonholing in those legislatures where it is permitted. Nevertheless, it is common to find states in which 50 percent or more of all bills introduced never emerge from the committees to which they were referred.[45]

In some states, it is clear, committee decisions are largely perfunctory. Pennsylvania provides an example. In this state the authentic center of decision making is the party caucus. To quote the House majority leader, "What takes place on the floor is a postscript. By then everything has been decided [in caucus] and we know what the vote will be." A Pennsylvania state senator makes a related point: "We'll call a committee meeting, walk off the floor for a few minutes and then return and report out a dozen bills. It's a sham, and everybody knows it."[46]

There are three principal courses of action open to a committee in deciding the fate of a proposal, apart from the pigeonholing option already mentioned.[47] Committees may report a bill (1) as committed with a recommendation that it pass; (2) together with committee amendments, with the recommendation that it pass; (3) with the recommendation that it "do not pass." In addition, committees sometimes recommend that the chamber adopt a committee substitute in place of the original proposal. Finally, provisions may exist for reporting a measure without a recommendation of any sort. The latter alternative is used on very rare occasions by Congress and the states and comes close to being an adverse report.

The usual response of state legislative committees, except where rules require them to report all bills, is either to report a bill with a "do pass" recommendation or to make no report at all. In most states there is infrequent resort to the "do not pass" recommendation, probably in less than 5 percent of all referrals. Some chambers avoid it entirely. It is much easier simply to keep an unwanted bill bottled up in committee, thereby serving the same purpose and diminishing the likelihood of controversy. Although legislators do not shrink from controversy, neither as a rule do they promote it if an alternative is available. Nevertheless, an adverse report occasionally is brought out, and a bill so recommended limps onto the floor more dead than alive. The sponsor may move that the house nonconcur in the committee report, but it is unusual for the motion to be adopted.

It is a curious fact that in many state legislatures a favorable committee recommendation may not at all represent the sense of the committee members; indeed, a majority of the members may be plainly opposed to a measure to which "do pass" is affixed. This action occurs because committees are hesitant to take on the responsibility for weeding out bills. Sponsors may contend that in the interest of "fair play" their bills should be permitted to go before the chamber as a whole, and members who intend to oppose them on the floor may agree and recommend accordingly. Legislatures may have a tradition of letting bills slide out of committee despite the presence of strong opposition to them. Legislators who work hard enough have a good chance of moving their bills to the floor, even though they have no chance of acceptance by the chamber. There is nothing unusual about hearing committee members say, "I'll vote to send it out but I reserve the right to help vote it down on the floor."

The height of committee detachment, of unwillingness to kill a bill, is the occasional practice of reporting out two diametrically opposed bills, such as gasoline tax bills with vastly different apportionment formulas, each carrying a recommendation of "do pass." Action of this type usually placates those sponsors who might lose in committee and helps to avoid committee wrangles; unfortunately, it also adds new work and new problems to an already heavily burdened chamber. A former speaker of the Illinois House of Representatives illustrates the problem: "I think we would be able to conduct more business more efficiently if the committees would find a bad bill bad and say so at the committee level."[48]

Committees devote considerable time to considering amendments to bills, some of which have emerged from the hearings. Amendments may include only slight changes or be so extensive as to involve a substitution for the original measure. As a general rule, amendments, if not emasculatory, are best accepted at the committee stage because if proposed and adopted on the floor, they may stimulate the introduction of other amendments that would imperil the bill's purpose.[49] A great many amendments are proposed at the floor stage, even though the chambers are generally chary about accepting amendments that have not been given prior committee study. Committee amendments must be accepted by the parent chamber, but this is usually not a major problem since the houses tend to defer to the decisions of their committees.

Although a proposal may not have clear sailing once out of committee, it has at least surmounted the major obstacle in the legislative process. This is notably true of Congress, where about nine out of ten bills die in committee; moreover, a bill that is reported from a congressional committee has an

**TABLE 7.1** **The centrality of committee decisions: Number of bills introduced, reported, and passed in the U.S. House of Representatives, 91st–105th Congresses***

| Congress | Introduced | Reported | Percent Reported | Passed† |
|---|---|---|---|---|
| 91st | 21,436 | 1,137 | 5.3 | 1,130 |
| 93rd | 18,872 | 906 | 4.8 | 923 |
| 95th | 15,587 | 1,044 | 6.7 | 1,027 |
| 97th | 8,094 | 601 | 7.4 | 704 |
| 99th | 6,499 | 631 | 9.7 | 973 |
| 101st | 6,683 | 640 | 9.6 | 964 |
| 103rd | 8,544 | 1,083 | 12.7 | 1,431 |
| 105th | 5,014 | 768 | 15.3 | 710 |

*Includes joint resolutions
†Measures may be taken up on the floor without having been referred to or reported from committee; this practice occurs frequently in the case of joint resolutions

SOURCE: Arthur G. Stevens and Sula P. Richardson, *Indicators of Congressional Workload and Activity* (Washington, DC: Congressional Research Service, 1981), p. 11; and *Congressional Record-Daily Digest,* January 25, 1983, p. D17; December 20, 1985, p. D1565; October 18, 1986, p. D1343; January 23, 1990, p. D1; November 2, 1990, p. D1453; December 20, 1994, p. D1275; and January 19, 1999, p. D29.

excellent chance of being passed by the chamber. (See Table 7.1.) Similarly, a bill that emerges from a state legislative committee is very likely to win acceptance on the floor. Scattered studies suggest that between 65 percent and 85 percent of favorable committee reports are accepted on the floor in the house of origin.[50] Having survived committee action in one house, a bill has a good chance of being accepted in the other house; some of those that fail in the second house are identical to or close approximations of bills already passed by that chamber. In short, committee action in American legislatures is often decisive. Plainly, committees do more than advise and recommend to their parent chambers. Nevertheless, committee decisions everywhere are challenged on the floor; in Congress, in particular (see the following), floor activity is considerably greater today than in the past.

The reports of congressional committees are substantially more elaborate and have a greater utility than those of the states. Whereas a state legislative committee will simply record its decision, which constitutes a recommendation to the body, a congressional committee will submit a written explanation of the bill and a justification for the recommendation. Evidence considered by the committee in arriving at its decision is summarized and evaluated. Some reports go into extraordinary detail in recapitulating facts and opinions brought out in the committee's study of the proposal, including the arguments that may prove useful on the floor. Reports also may serve as campaign documents. "Individual views" of committee members are sometimes appended to the body of a report. The position of members not in accord with the majority may be submitted separately in the form of a minority report.

State legislative committees operate under a number of handicaps, some of which are self-imposed and all of which tend to drain off their efficiency. First, there is a shortage of trained staff members; in many cases, committees carry a heavy workload without staff assistance in any form. Second, committees are generally so numerous and individual assignments so heavy that even the more conscientious committee members find it difficult to keep abreast of their work. Committee members come late to meetings and leave early, not for lack of interest but for lack of time; there are always other things they should be doing and other meetings they should be attending; there is scarcely any relaxation from the pressures of constituents and lobbyists.

Nonetheless, state legislators in most states see the committee system as highly important. In a recent nationwide survey, state legislators were asked to identify the most important decision-making arenas in their legislatures. Seen as most important were the presiding officers or majority leaders. Committee meetings ranked a close second, followed by the party caucus, the governor's office, and the floor. What is more, legislators reported that they spent about half of their time on committee work. As expected, there were substantial differences among the states. Among those in which committees were evaluated as especially significant in decision making were Nevada, South Carolina, Oregon, Virginia, Louisiana, Mississippi, and Arkansas. The committee system received its lowest ranking in California, Alaska, New Jersey, Delaware, Iowa, Illinois, and Pennsylvania. Taking the nation as a whole, committees tend to be viewed as most important in states (and chambers) dominated by one party.[51]

## COMMITTEE POWER

### Committee-Floor Relations

Congressional policymaking long has been heavily influenced by the preferences and decisions of House and Senate committees and their leaders, and that statement continues to be true today.[52] But it is also apparent that congressional committees have lost some degree of autonomy and that the floor stage has become more important in policymaking than it was a generation ago.[53] The decline in the influence of committees and committee chairs arises in part from the weakening of the norms of apprenticeship and deference—traditional supports for committee power—and in part from reforms designed to redistribute influence and democratize the legislative process. Several House reforms in particular stand out in this regard. Subcommittees became increasingly important in the 1970s as they gained their own staffs, predictable jurisdictions, and increased control over legislation. (See Chapter 6.) The influence and integration of committees accordingly declined to some extent. Centralization was also fostered and the Speaker's influence enhanced by the authority to nominate the Democratic members of the Rules Committee and to refer bills to more than one committee. Additionally, other changes such as recorded teller votes and electronic voting served to focus attention on the floor, encourage floor attendance, and heighten accountability.

The long and the short of it is that during the 1970s and 1980s, it became much more common for House committee recommendations to be questioned on the floor and sometimes to be changed through amendments. Recorded votes became more frequent, floor activity more burdensome and unpredictable (in the face of flurries of amendments), and partisanship more likely to develop. Decisions that were once taken in committee and later ratified by the floor were now more likely to be challenged by rank-and-file members, including minority party members, and altered by the actions of transient floor majorities.

The dramatic increase in floor-amending activity eventually prompted House Democratic leaders in the 1980s to take action to protect committee policy decisions, and to a large extent their efforts were successful. As an arm of the leadership, the House Rules Committee became a major player in designing intricate special rules to curtail unrestrained floor activity, particularly on controversial legislation. Budget resolutions and reconciliation bills, for example, invariably came to be accompanied by special rules to limit opportunities for floor amendments. The net result of these party-driven changes was that a good measure of committee autonomy was restored and a greater measure of certainty reintroduced in floor decision making. Nevertheless, committee-floor relations has surely been changed from the days in which committees and their leaders thoroughly dominated policymaking.

Committee-floor relations in the contemporary Senate are not unlike those found in the House. Floor decision making, in fact, is even more important in the Senate. Barbara Sinclair observes:

> Senate decisionmaking is less committee-centered than it used to be; committees are no longer autonomous. Senators are much less willing to accept committee decisions with only perfunctory review. The floor has become a significant decisionmaking arena, one in which legislation is subjected to scrutiny and, frequently, to alteration. . . . Committees perforce are more open to influence by nonmembers than formerly.[54]

### Committee Leaders and Party Leaders

Another way to examine committee power is to focus on relations between committee leaders and party leaders. Several studies help to clarify this relationship.

David Truman's groundbreaking book, *The Congressional Party,* was the first to question the traditional interpretation of legislative politics that stressed the primacy of standing committees and their chairs. Within each legislative party, Truman pointed out, there are two sets of leaders: "elective leaders" and "seniority leaders." The first set, which includes the floor leaders, obtains its position through election by the party caucus, and the second set, made up of committee chairs and ranking minority members, comes to its position through continuous tenure on a committee. Agreement between them at the floor roll-call stage obviously is not always present. When they differ on a vote, whose position usually prevails? Truman's data show that the floor leader is usually on the winning side, especially in the case of the majority leader. On questions in which the committee chair voted opposite the leader, members of the chair's own committee voted more frequently with the leader than with the chair. The floor leaders, Truman states, "were not at the mercy of the seniority leaders and they did, with varying degrees of effectiveness, act as if they were the trustees of the party's record."[55] In other words, this study finds that the "formal" and "real" leadership of the party coincide much of the time.

Randall Ripley has shown that there are variable patterns of interaction between party leaders and standing committees, based on the extent to which leaders intervene in the activities of committees. The *leader-activist* pattern of interaction is facilitated when four conditions are met:

1. When the personalities involved (of the party leaders and committee leaders of the same party) are congenial and the party leaders are the more aggressive individuals

2. When there are relatively few serious policy or ideological disagreements between the party leaders and committee leaders

3. When committee traditions permit (or even demand) a relatively large degree of partisanship

4. When the majority party is involved—particularly a new majority that has come to power in Congress and is full of programmatic zeal.[56]

Conversely, a pattern of near *committee autonomy* emerges if these conditions are reversed—that is, if there are personal strains and ideological conflicts between the party leaders and the committee leaders, if the committee has a nonpartisan climate, and if the minority party is involved. In Ripley's judgment, the leader-activist (centralized) model is more likely than the committee autonomy (decentralized) model to promote coherence in a legislative program, restrictions on the influence of "subgovernments" (that is, key bureaucrats, key interest-group representatives, and key committee members), oversight of administration, representation of broad national interests, and the possibility that Congress as a whole can maintain its independence and exert maximum influence over a range of policy.[57]

A study of congressional committees by Steven Smith and Christopher Deering finds evidence for these conclusions concerning party leader-committee relations:

1. The dominant goal of enhancing party harmony typically prompts party leaders to give committee members considerable leeway to do what they want to do.

2. When leaders do become involved in intracommittee politics, they are more likely to be concerned with the pace of committee action than with the substance of legislation.

3. Contacts between committee leaders (including subcommittee chairs) and party leaders are typically initiated by committee leaders (and usually involve scheduling).

4. Leadership attention tends to focus on the budget and tax committees rather than the general run of committees.

5. Party leaders are limited in what they can do to control committees and their members and committee leaders are similarly limited in controlling committee members.

6. Leadership intervention is not necessarily a matter of high urgency since committee members and party leaders are often in general agreement.[58]

Although committees still control the contents of the vast majority of bills, with relatively little intervention by the party leadership, some legislation is simply too far-reaching and controversial to be handled in the normal committee process. When committees are immobilized or unable to produce a bill that can attract a majority on the floor, party leaders are now more likely to become involved in working out provisions that will get the bill moving. In fact, nothing stands out more about the 104th Congress (1995–96), under GOP control for the first time in forty years, than the vigor and activity of Republican party leaders in the House and the high levels of party unity among rank-and-file members.

Much else could be said about committees in relation to legislative leadership, political interest groups, and the bureaucracy. We shall return to these topics in later chapters.

Following committee action, measures proceed to the floor for decision. The flow of legislation from the committees to the floor, unlike water over the dam, is neither steady nor predictable. The next chapter begins with an analysis of how the flow is regulated, how the floor may attempt to

control its committees, and the way in which proposed legislation is scheduled for consideration by the parent chamber.

## NOTES

1. Quoted in Charles O. Jones, "Why Congress Can't Do Policy Analysis," *Policy Analysis,* II (Spring 1976), 256.
2. Norman J. Ornstein, Thomas E. Mann, and Michael J. Malbin, *Vital Statistics on Congress, 1997–1998* (Washington, DC: Congressional Quarterly Press, 1998), p. 139.
3. See an analysis of the ways in which Congress uses policy analysis by David Whiteman, "The Fate of Policy Analysis in Congressional Decision Making: Three Types of Use in Committees," *Western Political Quarterly,* XXXVIII (June 1985), 294–311.
4. Woodrow Wilson, *Congressional Government* (New York: Meridian Books, 1956, first published 1885), p. 71.
5. Robert Luce, *Legislative Procedure* (Boston: Houghton Mifflin, 1922), p. 143. The preceding paragraph is based on Luce's work.
6. David Truman, *The Governmental Process* (New York: Knopf, 1953), p. 373.
7. Ibid., p. 372.
8. Julius Cohen, "Hearing on a Bill: Legislative Folklore?" *Minnesota Law Review,* XXXVII (December 1952), 39.
9. Truman, *Governmental Process,* pp. 373–74.
10. *Hearings on Civil Rights—1957, Before the Subcommittee on Constitutional Rights of the Committee on the Judiciary,* Senate, 85th Cong., 1st sess., 1957, p. 727.
11. Luce, *Legislative Procedure,* p. 146.
12. The Congressional Committee: A Case Study," *American Political Science Review,* XLVIII (June 1954), pp. 354 and 365.
13. A study of House committee hearings by James L. Payne finds that the collegial questioning of witnesses has been largely replaced by a "lone wolf" pattern in which a member pursues an independent line of questioning without interacting with other members. Payne hypothesizes that this individualistic pattern is a function of members' growing concern with self-promotion. "The Rise of Lone Wolf Questioning in House Committee Hearings," *Polity,* XIV (Summer 1982), 626–40.
14. *Impeachment Inquiry: William Jefferson Clinton, President of the United States, Hearing Before the Committee on the Judiciary,* House of Representatives, 105th Cong., 2nd sess., 1998, pp. 199–200.
15. Bryan D. Jones, Frank R. Baumgartner, and Jeffrey C. Talbert, "The Destruction of Issue Monopolies in Congress," *American Political Science Review,* LXXXVII (September 1993), 657–71.
16. Ibid., 666–69.
17. Christine DeGregorio, "Leadership Approaches in Congressional Committee Hearings," *Western Political Quarterly,* XLV (December 1992), 971–83 (quotation on p. 977).
18. Sidney Wise, *The Legislative Process in Pennsylvania* (Washington, DC: American Political Science Association, 1971), p. 40.
19. Luce, *Legislative Procedure,* pp. 145–46.
20. Cohen, "Hearing on a Bill," 38.
21. Wilson, *Congressional Government,* p. 199.
22. Ibid., p. 198. (Emphasis added.)
23. This is the informed estimate of M. Nelson McGeary, who has researched the question as thoroughly as anyone. See his book, *The Development of Congressional Investigative Power* (New York: Columbia University Press, 1940), and also his summary article, "Congressional Investigations: Historical Development," *University of Chicago Law Review,* XVIII (Spring 1951), 425–39.

24. McGeary, "Congressional Investigations," 425–27.

25. *Kilbourn v. Thompson*, 103 U.S. 168, 190 (1881).

26. *McGrain v. Daughtery*, 273 U.S. 135, 174–75 (1927).

27. 354 U.S. 178 (1957).

28. Ibid., 187.

29. *Sweezy v. New Hampshire*, 354 U.S. 234 (1957).

30. *Barenblatt v. United States*, 360 U.S. 109, at 134.

31. *Braden v. United States*, 365 U.S. 431 (1961); *Wilkinson v. United States*, 365 U.S. 399 (1961).

32. *Russell v. United States*, 369 U.S. 749 (1962).

33. *Gibson v. Florida Legislative Investigation Committee*, 372 U.S. 539 (1963).

34. *Yellin v. United States*, 374 U.S. 109 (1963). (Emphasis added.)

35. *Eastland et al. v. United States Servicemen's Fund et al.*, 95 S. Ct. 1813, 1821 (1975).

36. Ibid., 1824.

37. Harold W. Chase, "Improving Congressional Investigations: A No-Progress Report," *Temple Law Quarterly*, XXX (Winter 1957), 138–44.

38. McGeary, "Congressional Investigations," 435.

39. J. Leiper Freeman, "Investigating the Executive Intelligence: The Fate of the Pike Committee," *Capitol Studies*, V (Fall 1977), 105.

40. Robert K. Carr, *The House Committee on Un-American Activities, 1945–50* (Ithaca, NY: Cornell University Press, 1952), p. 411.

41. *Congressional Quarterly Weekly Report*, January 10, 1998, p. 84.

42. *Congressional Quarterly Weekly Report*, May 23, 1987, p. 1059.

43. Ibid.

44. Ibid., p. 1060.

45. See Keith E. Hamm, "U.S. State Legislative Committee Decisions: Similar Results in Different Settings," *Legislative Studies Quarterly*, V (February 1980), 32.

46. Jack H. Morris, "A State Legislature Is Not Always a Model of Ideal Government," *Wall Street Journal*, July 28, 1971, p. 16.

47. Even within a single chamber there is likely to be substantial differences among committees in the extent to which they screen legislation. Some committees are quite "permissive," that is, inclined to give favorable action to bills referred to them. Others recommend relatively few bills for passage without change or commonly give "do not pass" recommendations. In this connection, see a study of the New Hampshire House of Representatives by David Ray, "Assessing the Performance of State Legislative Committees: A Case Study and a Proposed Research Agenda," *Western Political Quarterly*, XXXIX (March 1986), 126–37.

48. Quoted in Gilbert Y. Steiner and Samuel K. Gove, *Legislative Politics in Illinois* (Urbana: University of Illinois Press, 1960), p. 62.

49. Bills subjected to major alterations in committee often become "clean bills" before submission to the floor. This procedure involves incorporating committee amendments into the original bill and treating the product as a brand new bill to the point of giving it a new number. The advantage is that the alterations become a fundamental part of the bill and are no longer treated as amendments. Hence, they are not considered separately on the floor.

50. See Joel M. Fisher, Charles M. Price, and Charles G. Bell, *The Legislative Process in California* (Washington, DC: American Political Science Association, 1973), p. 49.

51. Wayne L. Francis and James W. Riddlesperger, "U.S. State Legislative Committees: Structure, Procedural Efficiency, and Party Control," *Legislative Studies Quarterly*, VII (November 1982), 453–71. For additional evidence on the importance of committees in shaping state legislative outcomes, see William P. Browne and Delbert J. Ringquist, "Sponsorship and Enactment: State Lawmakers and Aging Legislation, 1956–1978," *American Politics Quarterly*, XIII (October 1985), 447–66.

52. Diana Evans finds that one of the important powers of committee leaders is their capacity to build coalitions for broad national legislation by adding particularistic district benefits onto

this legislation, making it more attractive for legislators whose districts are benefited. The judicious use of targeted pork by leaders thus improves the prospects for passage of general benefit legislation. "Policy and Pork: The Use of Pork Barrel Projects to Build Policy Coalitions in the House of Representatives," *American Journal of Political Science*, XXXVIII (November 1994), 894–917.

53. The analysis in this section on committee-floor relations is based largely on a study by Steven S. Smith, *Call to Order: Floor Politics in the House and Senate* (Washington, DC: Brookings Institution, 1989), especially Chaps. 2 and 3.

54. Barbara Sinclair, *The Transformation of the U.S. Senate* (Baltimore: Johns Hopkins University Press, 1989), p. 138.

55. *The Congressional Party* (New York: Wiley, 1959), p. 246.

56. Randall B. Ripley, "Congressional Party Leaders and Standing Committees," *Review of Politics*, XXXVI (July 1974), 401.

57. Ibid., 403–409.

58. Steven S. Smith and Christopher J. Deering, *Committees in Congress* (Washington, DC: Congressional Quarterly Press, 1984), pp. 246–49.

# 8

# Debate and Decision Making
# on the Floor

The decisions of Congress usually reflect the choices of its committees and subcommittees. For the most part, legislation that provokes a stir in committee provokes a stir on the floor; legislation that eludes controversy in committee eludes controversy on the floor. In the contemporary Congress, committee members have come to expect that their recommendations on major bills will be challenged, at least to some extent, on the floor. The underlying reason for this practice is simply that many members want to be part of the action, whether or not they sit on the committee that produced the legislation. What is more, new rules and practices invite them to participate.

First among all congressional committees in the authority to frame the dimensions of floor discussion and action is the Rules Committee of the House of Representatives. Its role is analyzed following a brief discussion of the House calendar system.

## FROM COMMITTEE TO FLOOR

### The Calendars

Bills that succeed in running the committee gauntlet are reported to the floor and placed on a calendar. The most complex calendar arrangement is that of the U.S. House of Representatives, which has five distinct calendars: union, House, private, discharge, and corrections day. The union calendar receives bills that provide for revenue or appropriations, and the remaining public bills go on the House calendar. Bills of a private character (for example, an individual's claim against the government) are placed on the private calendar and considered on the first and third Tuesdays of each month. The discharge calendar, taken up on the second and fourth Mondays, lists motions to "discharge" bills from committee. Also, in a procedure designed to expedite floor action, bills that are not highly controversial may be called up and considered by unanimous consent.

An idea advanced by Speaker Newt Gingrich (R., GA), the corrections day calendar was adopted by House Republicans in 1995 to provide a fast-track method for voting on the elimination of federal rules and regulations deemed unnecessary, excessive, or simply "dumb." The Speaker selects the bills (reported from committee) that are placed on the corrections day calendar, which is held on the second and fourth Tuesdays of each month. Legislation brought up under this procedure requires a three-fifths majority for approval, as contrasted with the two-thirds requirement for suspension of the rules (see below), another method for the House to act with dispatch. Democrats who opposed this innovation were fearful that it would be used to pass bills to undo environmental and consumer regulations.[1]

Two additional provisions in the House scheduling system require comment. Under the first of these, the District of Columbia day, the second and fourth Mondays in each month are set aside for the consideration of measures called up by the Committee on the District of Columbia. The committee determines the order in which it wishes to present bills. The second special day is Calendar Wednesday, which permits standing committees to call up for immediate floor consideration proposals listed on the House or union calendars that have been sidetracked for lack of privileged status or a special rule of the Rules Committee. Privileged bills, such as appropriations, are not eligible for action on Calendar Wednesday.

## THE RULES COMMITTEE OF THE HOUSE OF REPRESENTATIVES

The calendars, though not without use, tell very little about the order in which bills are brought before the House, for two main reasons. First, certain bills from a few committees, Appropriations and Ways and Means among others, are accorded privileged status and can be reported at any time for prompt consideration; this rule also applies to conference-committee bills and measures vetoed by the president. Second, the Rules Committee has the authority to regulate the flow of legislation from the standing committees to the floor and to prescribe the conditions under which it will be considered.

To begin the analysis of this committee, we need to point out that it does not control all bills and resolutions reported from the legislative committees. The great majority of measures brought to the floor each session of Congress are mainly free from controversy and are handled in routine fashion by any of several devices, such as the consent or private calendars; the Rules Committee takes no part in their disposition. Rather, its role in shaping the consideration of legislation is confined to more important and controversial proposals—those that will receive at least a moderate amount of debate on the floor.

Acting as an agent of the majority-party leadership, the Rules Committee lays out the central paths that the House takes by controlling its agenda. Favorable action on a bill by a legislative committee is only the initial step toward passage. Committee reports that lack privileged status require a rule from the Rules Committee to be brought up for floor consideration. A majority vote on the floor is needed for adoption, and rules set the terms for debating and amending legislative measures. They can encourage floor participation or constrain it. Because special rules often reflect the leadership's political and policy objectives, particularly in the case of closed and restrictive rules (see the following), it is common for the minority-party members to vote against them. When partisanship enters the picture, the leadership must make a special effort to satisfy its own party members on provisions both in the bill and in the rule that governs its consideration on the floor.

Special rules represent a good example of the discretionary authority of the party leadership, working in consultation with the majority members of the Rules Committee. A comprehensive study of the contemporary House by Stanley Bach and Steven Smith describes six types of special rules.[2] *Open* rules permit the House to amend measures in any fashion the members prefer as long as the amendments are germane. Infrequently used, *organizing* rules are a form of open rule establishing the sequence in which certain amendments will be offered but not otherwise limiting members' options to propose amendments. A third type of open rule is described as *expansive*—one that expands the opportunities for floor amendments by waiving points of order that might be lodged against noncommittee amendments. Setting aside the germaneness rule is an example of this type.

The other three types of special rules restrict the right of members to propose amendments on the floor. *Closed* rules completely prohibit floor amendments or specify that they may be offered only by the committee that handled the measure. These rules usually involve more controversial matters than open rules and often accompany legislation that would be especially vulnerable to "special-interest" or "politically irresistible" amendments. *Restrictive* rules limit floor or amending activity but do not preclude it altogether. Ordinarily, restrictive rules either limit amendments to those enumerated in the rule or else permit amendments to be offered only to certain provisions of the bill; restrictive rules thus vary in their restrictiveness. *Complex* special rules contain features present in restrictive, expansive, or organizing rules. A particularly good example of this type is the "king-of-the-mountain" rule under which alternative versions of a bill ("substitutes") are voted on in an order set by the Rules Committee; if more than one version receives a majority, only the last one is adopted. Usually the leadership's preferred alternative is voted on last. Reflecting the leadership's position, these rules permit the Rules Committee to accommodate various factional interests by enabling them to secure clear-cut votes on their policy options.

Deciding on the rule to be employed and the sequence for the consideration of amendments are major components of the majority party's floor strategy since the provisions may well be critical in shaping the outcome.

Until fairly recently, the vast majority of special rules were open. In the 95th Congress (1977–78), for example, 85 percent of all rules (179 out of 211) were open; by the 103rd Congress (1993–94), only 31 percent (31 out of 99) were open.[3] Major bills in particular are likely to be brought to the floor under restrictive rules. Bach and Smith explain the attraction of these rules:

> At various times . . . restrictive rules have served the interests of the committees reporting legislation by making prospective floor developments more predictable and manageable, the interests of the majority party and its leaders by preventing unwelcome amendments from reaching the floor, and the interests of the House as an institution by keeping the amendment process within constructive bounds.[4]

Restrictive rules are important for the majority party in structuring debate and in curtailing votes on highly charged issues. When the Republicans took control of the House in the 104th Congress (1995–96), after decades of Democratic domination, they promised to institute a more open way of doing business, which would include only limited use of restricted rules and the elimination of such innovations as the "king-of-the-mountain" rule.[5] To take the place of the king-of-the-mountain rule, the new Republican majority adopted a "most-votes-wins" rule, under which the proposal that receives the most votes wins, irrespective of the order in which it is considered.

Open rules are an invitation to the minority party to introduce numerous floor amendments, not only to make a record and to highlight party differences but also to confront the majority with difficult political choices. Despite the problems that open rules create for the majority, the Republicans have made somewhat more use of them since gaining a House majority. In the 104th Congress (1995–96), 46 percent (69 of 151) of the rules were open, and for the 105th Congress (1997–98), 40 percent (57 of 142).[6]

### Controversy over the Rules Committee

The Rules Committee has played a major role in the House since the days of Speaker Thomas B. Reed of Maine in the 1890s. "Czar" Reed was succeeded by Charles Crisp, an aggressive Georgian who piled new and greater powers on the Rules Committee. The zenith of Rules Committee power was reached under the speakership of Joseph G. Cannon of Illinois shortly after the turn of the century.

In the heyday of Reed and Cannon, the Rules Committee was a powerful instrument for control of the House and its agenda. "The right of the minority," Speaker Reed is reported to have lectured House Democrats, "is to draw its salaries and its function is to make a quorum."[7] As Speaker and as chair of the Rules Committee, Cannon used the full power of the offices to determine which proposals would be enacted and which defeated. Eventually, his heavy-handed rule got him into trouble. A successful revolt against "Cannonism" in 1910–11, directed by insurgent Representative George W. Norris of Nebraska, sharply constricted the Speaker's powers and removed him from his position as chair of the Rules Committee.

There are two things of main significance in this episode of "revolution." The first is that the revolutionaries did not touch the powers of the Rules Committee itself. The second is that their action severed the link between the committee and the elected leadership of the House. Comparing the Cannon regime with its successors, Robert Luce argued that "the most striking difference between the old and the new methods is that, whereas leadership was then in the open, it is now under cover. Then the Speaker was the recognized center of authority. Now nobody knows who in the last resort decides."[8]

The 1910–11 revolution laid the groundwork for the Rules Committee to establish itself as an *independent* center of power. From the late 1930s until the 1960s, many House sessions (especially in the later years) were dominated by a conservative coalition of southern Democrats and northern Republicans. This coalition held sway in the Rules Committee, making many critical decisions and at times holding the assembly in "parliamentary thralldom," as one critic put it.[9] Throughout this period, members from urban, industrial states of the North, East, and West were underrepresented on the Rules Committee; their power was slight even when one of their number held the chairmanship. The ruling coalition on the committee was sometimes in harmony with the House leadership and sometimes indifferent to it; at times it could be moved aside when the Speaker could secure the vote of a moderate Republican member. Rarely was the committee sympathetic to the legislative requests of the president. Year in and year out, its hue was distinctly conservative, regardless of significant changes in the House membership produced by elections. But all that has changed.

In 1973, the Democratic caucus added the Speaker, majority leader, and caucus chair to the membership of the committee-on-committees, thus giving the leadership greater influence over the selection of committee members, including, of course, the Rules Committee. In 1975, the caucus transferred the authority to make committee assignments from the Democratic members of the Ways and Means Committee to the Steering and Policy Committee (which had been created in the previous Congress). Most important, the caucus empowered the Speaker to nominate the Democratic members of the Rules Committee, subject only to acceptance by the caucus. In short, the committee came under the firm control of the majority-party leadership. Under Republican control since 1995, the Rules Committee continued to function as a reliable arm of the party leadership, in particular the Speaker.

The Rules Committee is clearly a prestigious committee. Members know that it can be a springboard to a party leadership position. And just as important, Rules members "get to do things for other members" and for themselves. Because they know that their bills must win the approval of the Rules Committee, committee chairs take pains to include provisions in their legislation that benefit the members of this key committee. "You have leverage with the committee chairmen," a member of Rules observes. "Those guys are always looking to please us."[10]

### The Discharge Rule and Calendar Wednesday

The parliamentary weapons that House members may call on in attempting to bring obdurate committees to heel are not impressive. There are two principal means by which the floor can gain possession of a measure pigeonholed in a legislative committee or sidetracked by the Rules Committee: the discharge rule and Calendar Wednesday.

The discharge rule was adopted in 1910 when the House was warring with Speaker Cannon and the Rules Committee. Floyd Riddick records that the rule has been changed half a dozen times since first adopted, with each party at intervals having shaped it to its purposes.[11] The present provision, adopted in the 74th Congress (1935), enables a majority of the members of the House (218) to compel a committee to release its hold on a bill or resolution and to send it to the floor. The liberal rule in the 72nd Congress (1931) required only 145 signatures. Discharge days occur on the second and fourth Mondays. Discharge petitions can be readied after a bill has been in a legislative committee for thirty days or after a resolution has been held up by the Rules Committee for seven days. Motions to discharge bills must be listed on the calendar seven days before they can be brought up for consideration, an interval that permits committees to report bills likely to be pried out from under them by the House. Simply because a majority of the members have signed a discharge petition, however, does not ensure the bill's removal from committee; it must be accepted by a majority vote on the floor when the formal motion is offered.

The discharge rule ordinarily is not a major threat to committee positions. From 1931 to 1994, only forty-six discharge petitions gained sufficient signatures to force measures to the floor. Of this total, eighteen were passed by the House, and two eventually became law, the Wage and Hour Act of 1938 and the Federal Pay Raise Act of 1960.[12] Thus, in practical terms, the rule has not been very useful for frustrated House members attempting to pry a bill out of committee. Occasionally the threat of a discharge has been sufficient to force a committee to release a measure to the floor.

This device for harnessing committees may become more important in the future as a result of a change introduced in 1993. Until then, the names on petitions were kept secret until 218 signatures had been obtained. Secrecy doubtlessly benefitted the leadership intent on keeping certain bills bottled up, while at the same time keeping pressure off of the members. In 1993 a united Republican party (173 out of 175 members), bolstered by forty-five Democrats, succeeded in discharging a measure from the Rules Committee to change the discharge rule itself. Soon adopted, the new rule provides that the names of members who sign petitions are made public as soon as they sign. House conservatives regarded the change as a means of pressuring members to sign petitions for such "popular" bills as those providing for term limits, the line-item veto, and the balanced-budget amendment. Their successful antisecrecy drive was greatly aided by the relentless attention given to the issue by conservative talk-show hosts and the mobilization efforts of the Perot organization.[13]

Calendar Wednesday, in use since 1909, is simple in form but has been difficult to invoke in practice. It may be used to call up nonprivileged bills or those denied a rule by the Rules Committee. Under its terms, each Wednesday is to be set aside for calling the roll of the standing committees, in alphabetical order, with each committee permitted to bring forth any bill it has earlier reported that lacks privileged status. In earlier years, a number of successive Calendar Wednesdays might be taken up with the consideration of a single bill brought before the House. Progress down the alphabetical list of committees was slow, and an entire session could go by without reaching all the committees. Eventually, this problem was met through a limitation of debate to two hours on any measure called up on Calendar Wednesday, permitting more committees to get their turn. Nevertheless, Calendar Wednesday is cumbersome and largely ineffective. Theoretically, minorities are protected under this rule by the requirement that a two-thirds vote is needed to set aside this procedure. In practice, however, it is common for the majority leader to request each week that Calendar Wednesday for the following week be dispensed with, and this motion is usually accepted by the House. Since 1950, Calendar Wednesday has been used only three times, most recently in 1984, to bring measures to the floor.

### Suspension of the Rules

Many relatively noncontroversial proposals are brought before the House through a procedure known as suspension of the rules. Currently, about one-third of all bills and joint resolutions receive floor consideration under this procedure, which is firmly controlled by the Speaker. Stanley Bach of the Congressional Research Service describes how this expeditious method for handling legislation works:

> On any Monday or Tuesday the Speaker has discretionary authority to recognize representatives (usually committee or subcommittee chairs) to make motions to suspend the rules and pass a bill, even if the bill has not yet been reported from committee. The House then debates both the motion and the bill

for no more than 40 minutes, during which members cannot offer any floor amendments. After the debate, they cast a single vote on suspending the rules and passing the bill, with a two-thirds vote required for passage. The suspension motion also has the effect of waiving any points of order that members otherwise could make during the bill's consideration.[14]

### Screening the Senate's Legislative Program

The responsibility for screening bills and resolutions for floor consideration in the Senate is held by the majority floor leader and the majority policy committee. Ordinarily, the decisions about which measures will be called up for floor consideration are made by the majority-party leadership. "Quite often the floor leader simply brings in a legislative agenda for the ensuing week and asks the policy group if it has any questions. Members may then ask to have certain items included."[15]

Senate procedure in scheduling legislation is less complicated than in the House. With its much smaller size, it has less need for rigidly defined schedules such as both guide and limit the activities of the House. Moreover, Senate leaders take great pains to schedule important measures to suit the convenience of its members. The Senate has only two calendars and no system of special days. Bills and resolutions reported from committee are routed to the calendar of business, and treaties and nominations go to the executive calendar. Much of the Senate's work is accomplished under an arrangement of unanimous consent. This agreement, subject to the veto of any member, limits the time to be allotted for debate on the bill and on amendments and motions and sets the time for voting. Noncontroversial legislation is easily handled by unanimous consent. On complex legislation, however, the floor leaders are likely to be involved in lengthy negotiations to gain rank-and-file support for agreements that necessarily limit their parliamentary prerogatives. In the increasingly individualistic Senate, Steven S. Smith and Marcus Flathman argue, the leaders' capacity to manage and expedite floor business depends heavily on their creativity in accommodating their colleagues. "The necessity of obtaining unanimous consent creates political leverage for all senators, regardless of seniority, party, committee assignment, and state of origin."[16]

### Scheduling the Legislative Program in the State Legislatures

All states use calendars for listing bills ready for floor action. In about 60 percent of all state chambers, bills of minor importance are placed on special (or "consent") calendars so that they can be handled expeditiously—in other words, with a minimum of attention and debate. By expediting the passage of uncontested bills, the legislature is able to give more time to legislation regarded as important.[17]

Typically, the party leadership plays a major role in screening and arranging the legislative program. In the lower house the speaker ordinarily dominates the process of scheduling major proposals. In states in which parties are weak, control over the agenda may rest with calendar committees, rules committees, factions, or a leadership that pays slight attention to partisan considerations.

In legislative houses in which the rules committee bears an important responsibility for scheduling legislation, it ordinarily derives its power from its role as a party agency, as a steering committee for the majority-party leadership and caucus. A common arrangement provides for the speaker of the house to serve as chair of the rules committee and to appoint its members. The number of members on the committee ordinarily is quite limited, and some states emphasize its party function by stipulating that appointees are to be drawn exclusively from the majority party.

The significance and the functions of the rules committee vary from legislature to legislature. It is doubtful, however, whether any rules committee at the state level matches in power its counterpart in the lower house of Congress. Ordinarily, rules committees in the state legislatures either deal with miscellaneous "housekeeping" matters of secondary importance or become screening agencies for legislation only in the turbulent closing days of the session. The latter function is common. With the calendars bulging with measures whose priority is ambiguous and the session rapidly coming to an end, most state houses use the rules committee (or create a special sifting committee) to identify those measures to be given floor consideration and those to be consigned to the wastebasket. At this juncture, the rules committee, operating under the direction of the majority leadership, has enormous power over the fate of bills. Since legislatures pass an inordinate number of proposals the last week of the session, particularly on the last day, the sifting committee may gain a decisive voice in molding the legislature's record.

The power to discharge bills from committees, customarily present in the rules of state legislative houses, is not in practice very useful in diminishing committee control over legislation. In the states, unlike Congress, it is an easy matter to gain a vote on a discharge resolution since usually a handful of legislators is sufficient to file a motion and to bring it to a vote, whereas in Congress a majority of the total membership is required. Yet the net result is about the same. One survey found that the discharge rule was ineffective or infrequently employed in at least one-half of the houses.[18] Even this appraisal may exaggerate the potency of the rule in the states. Individual studies show that except in those states where committees must report all bills by a certain date or automatically lose them, there are few instances in which they lose control of measures referred to them. Bottled up in committee, a controversial bill stays bottled up.

In the vigorous two-party states, the principal function of the discharge rule is to permit the minority party to place its position on a bill or resolution on record in a formal floor vote. Discharge resolutions often become party issues, and when party lines hold, as they invariably do on matters of this sort, the motions are lost. Thus, this rule has utility as a campaign weapon, a technique for recording party policy and principle. Even here, however, the issue may be blurred or blunted since in opposing a discharge motion the majority leadership usually contends that the vote is not on the substance of the bill but on the issue of protecting orderly procedures and preventing committee powers from becoming enfeebled. The wry observations of a former West Virginia state legislator illuminate the point:

> The oddest debate on the food tax occurred on a motion to remove the bill from the reluctant Finance Committee and bring it to the floor for a vote. Several delegates who favored the food exemption nevertheless rose to their feet to denounce this "attack on the committee system." In trying to understand how they could favor the tax relief bill but oppose the only motion which realistically might bring it to a vote, I conjured up a picture of a couple sitting on a front porch. "Ethel," the husband might say, "I'd sure like to see the tax off food." "Yes, Homer," the wife replied, "but, you know, we've got to uphold that committee system up there."[19]

A discharge resolution is also a handy device for mollifying a lobby group whose measure is tied up in committee, for it demonstrates that something is being done, even though it usually comes to naught.

The typical legislature operates at a bewildering pace in the closing days of the session. Few things are more common in the course of legislative affairs, especially in the states, than the last-minute rush to wind up business for another year or another biennium. It is not unusual to find 30 percent to 40 percent of all bills passed during a session receiving final approval in the last week before adjournment. And occasionally the proportion exceeds 50 percent.

The severity of end-of-session logjams varies from state to state. A study by Harvey J. Tucker finds that logjams are a lesser problem in states that have provisions for the prefiling of bills, bill passage deadlines, and longer legislative sessions. Legislatures with ample staff assistance may also be less subject to the logjam problem. Institutional arrangements thus have a bearing on the size of legislative logjams. But the hoary and intuitively attractive generalizations that logjams are most likely to occur in states that have biennial sessions and limitations on session length are simply not borne out by this study.[20]

End-of-session logjams may well be the fallout from political maneuvering. What separates legislative leaders from rank and file in the closing days of the session is that the leaders control the contingencies—they can cause things to happen if certain conditions are met. For example, leaders may find it expedient to stall the consideration of minor or noncontroversial bills until the major program bills have been voted on.[21] A member whose pet bill is pigeonholed in committee or lost on an overcrowded calendar knows the folkway well; if the member votes against a major bill desired by the leadership, his or her own bill may never be moved toward passage. After the big bills have been brought to a vote, leaders clear the way for the rapid disposition of other bills. In some legislatures, control over the schedule is the principal weapon of discipline available to the leaders. Possibly no other device is so successful in wringing accommodations out of skeptical or stubborn opponents.

The New York state legislature provides a particularly good example of how the logjam contributes to the leadership's tight control over the agenda. Eric Lane, former counsel to the New York Senate minority leader, describes the waning days of a typical legislative session:

> With no legislation yet on the table for a vast range of "must" issues, the leaders of the Assembly and Senate hold a flurry of meetings with each other and with the governor; leadership staffers work round the clock, hammering out agreements acceptable to their bosses. And ordinary members? They wait in the wings for a signal to show up on the floor. Finally, clerks appear to distribute printed bills, each accompanied by a message of "necessity" from the governor, allowing the legislature to ignore the state constitution's requirement—meant to promote deliberation—of three days between the printing of a bill and the vote on it. Within 24 hours the legislative leader or his designee mounts the rostrum. He calls for a vote, and in short order, the bills pass without comment, their contents largely unknown to the members.[22]

A second political factor that contributes to the closing rush involves logrolling—a mutual-assistance pact by which legislators combine to pass one another's bills. Often, logrolling alliances cannot be negotiated until a number of bills have been sidetracked, usually near the end of a session. When a number of legislators are involved and enough pressure has been built up, it is not overly difficult to form logrolling combinations sufficient to give proposals new momentum. In the practice of logrolling, what helps one legislator eventually helps all who join the club.

One final political factor that contributes to the problems of legislative scheduling needs identification. This is the budget bill—"key log in the jam." In state after state the budget bill is introduced long after the session has started; then begins a round of hearings marked by tedious negotiations between the parties, between the chambers, and between the legislature and the governor. Compromises are elusive, and the working out of amendments that will pull a majority vote takes time. The delay is thus considerable, and although negotiations proceed, most of the other bills are left on the shelf. As is true of all good things, negotiations finally end. Sufficient support for the budget bill is won; legislators have been convinced, mollified, or dragooned, and the bill is cleared for passage. A quickening of the legislative tempo results, and the countless little bills clogging the calendars or bottled up in committee are rushed through to passage.

All in all, political factors make up the principal obstacles to improving legislative scheduling. Legislators themselves are not greatly troubled by how the press and public view legislative behavior in the tumultuous closing days of the session. By the time the next legislature is ready to convene, most observers will have forgotten how the last one came to a close.

## THE AMENDING PROCESS

An amendment is a proposal to make a change in a bill, resolution, or motion under consideration. In addition, existing law is changed through the passage of "amendatory" bills. The legislative process contains several junctures at which measures may be amended: in committee, on second reading, in the committee of the whole, or on third reading. Committee amendments are actually more in the nature of recommendations since they do not become a part of the bill until adopted by the house to which they have been reported. The amending process is most important in committee, on second reading, or—in those legislatures that make extensive use of the device—in the committee of the whole.

On many measures the key vote occurs not on final passage but at the amending stage. Major bills often invite a raft of amendments, many of which will be offered in committee, with others to follow on the floor. Bill management on the floor is the responsibility of either the committee chair or the relevant subcommittee chair of the committee reporting the bill. Although it is risky to predict the fate of a bill on the floor, it appears that an influential chair or subcommittee chair of a prestigious committee has a reasonably good chance of defeating amendments that would significantly alter the committee bill. But the most important variable in accounting for the fate of floor amendments is committee unity. If committee members vote in agreement, the committee position nearly always wins. When a committee's members are divided, the probability that a floor amendment will be accepted is greatly increased.[23]

Overall, bills are much more likely to be amended on the floor today than in the past. The weakening of the office of chair, the presence of many newcomers, and the erosion of norms (apprenticeship, deference to senior members, and reciprocity among committees) have combined to make floor decisions much less predictable. Anything can happen there, now that members find less reason to defer to committees. The House, Congressman Morris Udall (D., AZ) once observed, has become a "fast breeder reactor" for amendments. "Every morning when I come to my office, I find that there are twenty new amendments. We dispose of twenty or twenty-five amendments and it breeds twenty more amendments." Former Senator Paul Simon (D., IL) put it this way: "We are in the process of moving from a time in the history of the House when committees had too much power, and we are moving to a point where the floor itself becomes a large, unwieldy committee."[24] What is more, floor amendments offered by noncommittee members are increasingly likely to be accepted. This practice may reflect either a decline in the value of expertise or a belief that it is not particularly associated with the membership of the committee that reported the bill.[25]

Amendments are not always what they seem. They represent ways both of perfecting bills and of undermining them. Weeks and months of study and planning may precede their introduction, or in the case of occasional floor amendments, only a few minutes may have been spent. The alterations they impose may be so slight as to involve nothing much more than a change in language or so drastic as to effect total substitution. The damage that an amendment will do to a bill is not always apparent, as an Iowa state legislator observes:

> Some amendments are innocent looking as the dickens, but in reality they will ruin your bill. You've got to be sharp enough to determine what an amendment really does to your bill, even if some fellow looks you straight in the eye and says that he is proposing a "friendly amendment" to it.[26]

Amendment sponsors may number one or a dozen or more, perhaps representing both parties, and may include members who fully intend to vote for the bill on final passage and those who intend to oppose it.[27] Every now and then a bill is amended to such an extent that sponsors are forced to vote against their "own" bill. The reverse of this development are sponsors who are willing to accept virtually any alterations to get their bills passed, unmindful of the changing substance of their proposals.

Despite the frequency with which amendments are offered on the floor, the amending process is subject to many limitations. The Rules Committee of the U.S. House of Representatives, as we have seen, frequently employs closed and restrictive rules to foreclose or limit the options of members on the floor. Such rules are particularly likely to be used when major legislation is under consideration. Majority-party interests frequently underlie them.

A favorite gambit in attacking a bill is to "perfect," or amend, it to death. Under this plan, amendment after amendment is submitted to the bill, ostensibly to make it a "better" bill. With each amendment a new group can be antagonized and brought into opposition to the bill. Nor is it very difficult to make a bill unworkable, even ridiculous. Thus the president of the Illinois Retail Merchants Association succeeded in getting a committee in the Illinois House to adopt an amendment to a minimum-wage bill, a measure he vigorously opposed, setting up a $500,000 fund to be used in enforcement of the law. This move was calculated to stimulate new opposition to the bill.[28] Another example of this common practice occurred in the struggle to prevent repeal of prohibition in Oklahoma, when "dry" leaders in the lower house almost succeeded in amending a repeal referendum, hoping to kill it by adding a provision that put the state itself into the liquor-store business.[29]

Many a bill has been threatened or emasculated by a carefully drawn and skillfully maneuvered amendment.

Amendments may also be resisted because they would "improve" a bill and thus make it less likely to be vetoed. Thus in 1990 conservative senators, mainly Republican, were able to block certain amendments to a civil rights bill designed to help victims of job discrimination; their success made it certain that the bill would remain unpalatable to President Bush. Senator Dale Bumpers (D., AR) observed, "You do not have to be a rocket scientist to figure out that the whole goal is to make the bill as bad as possible or to try to make it as bad as possible to give the president more cover in vetoing the bill."[30]

When a major campaign finance bill (Shays-Meehan) was before the House in 1998, numerous "poison pill" amendments were voted on and defeated. Designed to make the bill unacceptable, and thus to scuttle it, these amendments included such extraneous matters as changing the motor voter law to eliminate mail-in registration and to require prospective voters to provide photo identification and evidence of citizenship and social security participation. Another amendment would have prohibited states from providing voters with voting information in any language other than English. And still another "killer" amendment would have required House candidates to raise at least half of their campaign funds from within their home states. As it turned out, the reform bill passed the House more or less intact but was filibustered to death in the Senate.[31]

A recurrent and vexatious problem posed for sponsors is to determine when to accept amendments and when to resist them. An effective floor manager needs to be able to anticipate, and incorporate if possible, those amendments likely to pull a majority vote since a defeat on one amendment sometimes leads to an avalanche of additional amendments, each one difficult to overcome. New support for a measure or consolidation of initial strength is often to be won by the prudent acceptance of an amendment—a "sweetener," as it is sometimes called. Usually a "sweetener" amendment provides for the exclusion of some group from the provisions of a bill, such as exempting a certain group of workers from coverage under minimum-wage legislation. Moreover, a good strategy may at times dictate the acceptance of an amendment even though the sponsor has the votes to defeat it, "for in the long run the friendship and good will of the opposition may be more valuable than securing a legislative victory. . . ."[32]

An additional quirk of the amending process requires discussion: the legislative rider. As its name hints, it refers to an irrelevant amendment—one that is tacked onto a bill well on its way to passage. Unlikely to make it on its own for one reason or another, the amendment rides into law as part of another measure. Typically, a rider is attached to an appropriation bill, and there is good reason for this choice. The chief executive who lacks the item veto—as do about a dozen governors and the president—must accept the whole bill, including the rider, or accept none of it. In the case of a rider attached to an agency appropriation bill, enormous pressures are generated to accept the bill, rider and all, rather than to jeopardize a program. Under such circumstances, it is an unusual chief executive who thinks twice about rejecting the bill, despite a repugnant and irrelevant rider.

Congress, of course, is mindful of the abuses associated with riders, and the House in particular is likely to quash an amendment that is not germane to a bill under consideration. The temptation to resort to a rider is strong, however, when no other possibility seems likely to succeed. The familiar interpretation of riders characterizes them as evasive, underhanded, and to some degree, even dangerous; however that may be, Congress has given its tacit consent to their use, and they appear in session after session.

## DEBATE

### The U.S. Senate

In the traditions of the Senate, no rule or practice has seemed more firmly rooted or drawn more discussion, much of it contentious, than that of "unlimited" debate. This tradition—perhaps the most distinguishing characteristic of the Senate—insists on the right to free and unlimited debate for members, even at the cost of freedom to act and to govern. The extreme of unlimited debate is the filibuster, the tactical efforts employed by a minority to prevent the majority from making a decision. Its essence is obstruction; its tactics, delay. Weapons are also available in the parliamentary arsenal to slow down action. Quorum calls are particularly handy weapons of obstruction, as are amendments introduced in great quantity.

The first major controversy involving freedom of debate in the Senate occurred in 1841, when Henry Clay's fiscal bills were thwarted by a Democratic filibuster. Clay sought to have the Senate adopt the hour rule for limiting debate, an innovation in the House at the time, but his efforts were unproductive. A few more attempts were made to limit Senate debate in the late decades of the nineteenth century, but none was successful in the slightest and few were even considered seriously.[33] Throughout this period (indeed to the present day), the Senate rules carried the admonition "No one is to speak impertinently, or beside the question, superfluously or tediously." But virtually all members on occasion did, and filibusters grew in volume and disputatiousness. Slowly the lines were being drawn for a battle over talk in the Senate.

Prefaced by preliminary sparring in the first decade of the twentieth century, the main battle over unlimited debate was fought in 1917. At stake was President Wilson's proposal to arm merchant ships. The bill passed the House handily but ran into opposition and a well-organized filibuster in the

Senate. Stymied by the filibuster of a hostile band of eleven senators, President Wilson strongly attacked the Senate. It is, he said, "the only legislative body in the world which cannot act when its majority is ready for action. A little group of willful men, representing no opinion but their own, have rendered the great government of the United States helpless and contemptible." The way out of this impasse, President Wilson continued, "is that the rules of the Senate shall be so altered that it can act. The country can be relied on to draw the moral. I believe that the Senate can be relied on to supply the means of action and save the country from disaster."[34]

With a large majority of the Senate in favor of the president's recommendation to arm merchant ships, and with public resentment against the filibusterers running high, the Senate moved to adopt its first cloture rule since 1789. Less than a week following Wilson's statement, it had fashioned a rule to limit debate, but its concession was one of expediency and of little consequence. Henceforth, the new rule (rule 22) provided, debate could be brought to an end when certain conditions were met: (1) Sixteen senators must sign and present a petition calling for termination of debate, (2) a period of two days should elapse prior to a vote, and (3) two-thirds of the senators *voting* would have to agree that further debate on the question be foreclosed. Having adopted the motion, no senator could speak more than one hour on the measure, dilatory motions and amendments were ruled out, and points of order would be decided without debate. Debate ended following the last one-hour presentation.

The filibuster rule has been formally changed three times since its adoption. In 1949, the rule was altered to provide that the two-thirds voting requirement be based on total membership rather than on those present and voting. A second provision, of at least as much importance, stipulated that cloture would not apply to any motion to consider a change in rules; a motion to take up such a resolution would thus become an invitation to filibuster. Plainly, the 1949 amendment strengthened the conservative hand in the Senate.

During the 1950s, pressure grew steadily for a change in rule 22. Efforts were unsuccessful until the "liberal tide" running in the 1958 congressional elections brought a new group of Democratic senators to Washington. The antifilibuster bloc in the 86th Congress (1959–60) based its strategy on the holding that each new Senate has the right to adopt new rules by a simple majority vote. Conservative opponents, mainly southern Democrats and northern Republicans, were equally insistent that the Senate is "a continuing body" since two-thirds of its membership carries over to each new Congress. If the membership carries over, their argument ran, the rules of the preceding Congress similarly carry over, and hence a motion to adopt a new set of rules would not be in order.

The outcome of the 1959 hassle was unsatisfactory to the antifilibuster forces, though a revised rule was adopted. Bearing a strong resemblance to the 1917 rule, the amended rule carried three provisions: (1) As in the original rule, two-thirds of the senators present and voting could order cloture; (2) cloture could be brought to bear on motions to change the rules, thereby removing the "perpetuity" feature of the 1949 amendment; and (3) the Senate was designated "a continuing body." The first two provisions made it slightly easier to break a filibuster, whereas the last, a concession to the South, made it more difficult.

Despite repeated efforts by liberals to fashion a new cloture rule in subsequent Congresses, it was not until 1975 that their efforts met with any success. After weeks of bitter wrangling (and filibustering), agreement was reached to substitute "three-fifths of the entire membership" for "two-thirds of those present and voting." The new rule thus requires sixty votes to cut off debate, assuming that there are no vacancies in the body. Future attempts to terminate debate on rules changes, however, will continue to require a two-thirds majority of the members present and voting. The holding that the Senate is "a continuing body" was reaffirmed.

In 1979, the Senate further tightened its rules on debate, this time to prevent "postcloture" filibusters. Under rule 22, each senator was permitted to talk for one hour after cloture had been voted, but time spent on parliamentary requirements, such as quorum calls and roll-call votes, was not included in this limitation. This loophole, once discovered, was an invitation to another form of filibustering. Members bent on delaying or defeating legislation began the practice of demanding frequent quorum calls and of introducing dozens, even hundreds, of amendments to a bill after cloture had been voted on it. These "postcloture" delays were sometimes substantial. To eliminate this tactic, a "debate cap" was adopted in 1979 stipulating that once cloture is voted, a final vote on a bill must be taken after no more than 100 hours of debate, including time spent on quorum calls, roll calls, and other parliamentary procedures. In 1986 this provision was modified to limit postcloture debate to 30 hours.

### Evaluating Unlimited Debate

Many famous filibusters have caught the attention of the nation, particularly those that involved spectacular achievements in individual endurance. In the tour de force class are Robert La Follette's eighteen-hour speech against a currency bill in 1908, Huey Long's wild and irrelevant filibustering of over fifteen hours in 1935 on the National Recovery Administration, Wayne Morse's speech of twenty-two hours and twenty-six minutes on the offshore oil bill in 1953, and J. Strom Thurmond's record-making denunciation (twenty-four hours and eighteen minutes) of a civil rights bill in 1957. Long's speech, which was sometimes germane to the subject, is best remembered for the recipes he gave for southern-style cooking and "potlikker."

Although one-person filibusters are effective in dramatizing an issue and focusing attention on Washington, they rarely accomplish very much. Much more significant is the effort of a team of senators intent on bringing the legislative process to a halt unless their demands are met, which probably means the abandonment of a bill or its significant alteration. With proper attention to organization, a determined, cohesive, and resourceful group can obstruct Senate action for days and weeks on end. Often as effective as a filibuster in frustrating majority intentions is the threat to start one. Knowing the difficulty of breaking a filibuster and under pressure to handle other legislation, the leadership may make significant policy concessions to members who are threatening to filibuster.[35] And it is not unusual for them simply to drop an "offensive" bill in order not to jeopardize other proposals.

Senate action can also be impeded by the use of a "hold"—the request of a member to the floor leader that as a matter of courtesy, action on a bill be delayed. At a minimum, a hold identifies a measure as being of concern to a member. Although it is not expected to delay the consideration of legislation indefinitely, a hold is sometimes tantamount to a veto. "As long as members are willing to back their holds with actual extended debate," Barbara Sinclair writes, "the leaders are faced with an impossible situation when floor time is short. Assuming that the bill at issue is not 'must' legislation, calling it up is likely to consume scarce time unproductively, time for which the leaders have multiple and clamorous requests."[36] Leaders try to accommodate members' requests for holds because they will need not only their votes on legislation in the future but also their support for unanimous consent agreements.[37] Overall, the prerogatives that individual senators enjoy sharply constrain the opportunities of leaders to shape debate, deliberation, and decision making.

The practice of holds has become more common and more controversial in recent years. As Senator Ron Wyden (D., OR) observed recently, holds come "pretty close to legislative blackmail."[38]

Efforts to invoke cloture over the last seventy years are shown by the data in Table 8.1. Few attempts to cut off debate were made between 1930 and 1960, and none was successful. In the last two decades, many more attempts to vote cloture have been made, with greater success. Still, only about one out of three cloture motions is successful today.

The character of filibusters has changed over the years. From the late

**TABLE 8.1  Senate cloture votes, 1919–97**

|  | 1919–39 | 1940–49 | 1950–59 | 1960–69 | 1970–79 | 1980–89 | 1990–97 |
|---|---|---|---|---|---|---|---|
| Number of cloture votes | 13 | 6 | 3 | 23 | 99 | 137 | 179 |
| Number successful | 4 | 0 | 0 | 4 | 34 | 56 | 57 |

SOURCE: Various issues of *Congressional Quarterly Weekly Report* and *Congressional Quarterly Almanac* (Washington, DC: Congressional Quarterly Press).

1930s through the 1960s, civil rights issues (for example, anti–poll tax, fair employment practices, voting rights, and open housing) were the usual fare of filibusters. With the support of conservative northern Republicans, southern Democrats typically provided the strategists and the "troops" necessary to launch and sustain filibusters. And more often than not, they won their way. Since 1970, filibusters have involved a wide range of subjects, including the military draft, creation of a consumer protection agency, voter registration, public campaign financing, trade reform, public debt ceiling, MX missile, abortion, school prayer, water rights, housing stimulus, genocide treaty, line-item veto, antiapartheid, Conrail sale, immigration reform, product liability reform, omnibus drug bill, gun control, job discrimination, elementary and secondary education reauthorization, California desert protection, striker replacement, nuclear waste storage, Food and Drug Administration overhaul, District of Columbia appropriations, right to work, unfunded mandates, lobbying disclosure, and a variety of tax proposals (such as capital gains, highway gas, and dividend withholding). Almost any type of proposal can produce a filibuster. Filibusters on procedural motions, such as requesting a conference with the House, have become more common; campaign finance reform was killed in this manner in 1994.

By those senators who have opposed attempts to curtail debate in the past, unlimited debate has often been justified as a principle of governing designed to protect *any* minority and to give each member the full opportunity to have a say. In the language of its traditional supporters, unlimited debate is not simply a parliamentary safeguard but also something of a moral principle, sustained by a validity that should not be compromised. What the cloture votes of recent years demonstrate more clearly than anything else is that for many senators unlimited debate is much less a "principle" than a weapon. Whether unlimited debate is a good thing seems to depend mainly on whose chestnuts are in the fire.

### The U.S. House of Representatives

In their treatment of time the House and Senate are quite dissimilar. On the one hand is the Senate, concerned with maintaining its tradition of unlimited debate and zealous in defense of procedures and practices that enhance the influence of individual members; on the other hand is the House, a majority-rule institution with a rigid system for handling legislation and making decisions. Measures that reach the floor of the House shortly meet their fate, for there is little opportunity to defer action or obstruct decisions. A number of House rules combine to place restrictions on debate and to limit the possibilities for rearguard delaying tactics. Major legislation normally comes to the floor by a special order of the Rules Committee specifying the time to be allocated to the measure. Special rules look like this:

*Resolved,* That upon the adoption of this resolution it shall be in order to move that the House resolve itself into the Committee of the Whole House on the State of the Union for the consideration of the bill (H.R. 5808) to amend the Act of August 24, 1966, as amended, to assure humane treatment of certain animals, and for other purposes. After general debate which shall be confined to the bill and shall continue not to exceed one hour, to be equally divided and controlled by the chairman and ranking minority member of the Committee on Agriculture, the bill shall be considered as having been read and open to any point for amendment under the five-minute rule. At the conclusion of the consideration of the bill for amendment, the Committee shall rise and report the bill to the House with such amendments as may have been adopted, and the previous question shall be considered as ordered on the bill and amendments thereto to final passage without intervening motion except one motion to recommit.[39]

By adopting the resolution, the House approves the terms under which the measure will be considered.

House debate is abridged in yet other ways. Unless exception is made, "general debate" on a measure by an individual member is confined to one hour. Under "suspension of the rules," a period of forty minutes is set aside for debate. The "five-minute" rule in committee of the whole restricts a member to a five-minute presentation on an amendment, unless consent is given for a brief extension of time.[40] The formal technique for cutting off debate in the House is to move the "previous question," a highly privileged motion. In use since 1811, the previous question permits a majority of those voting to end debate, after which the House advances immediately to a vote on the pending matter. The previous question is used to close debate on amendments and on final passage of a measure.

Opportunities to delay action on the floor of the House of Representatives are not as numerous today as they were in an earlier era, and neither are the parliamentary means as potent. An effective device to forestall action formerly used by members called for them to remain silent when a quorum call was held, and without a quorum the chamber was powerless to act. This practice was broken in 1890 when Speaker Thomas Reed, over the vigorous objections of the Democrats, began to count as present any members who sat silent in their seats. His practice was later made a part of the House rules. Also contributing to the death knell of filibustering in the House was the innovation during Reed's tenure that dilatory motions would not be entertained by the Speaker. By then, the "country at large, and the leaders of both parties, had wearied of the spectacle of a minority, of even a single member, defying the majority and effectively blocking legislation, and they were united in the belief that a radical reform must be brought about."[41] The rigorous and controversial "Reed rules" achieved such reform; at the same time, they laid the groundwork for a major shift in power to the Speaker.

Although filibustering is not unknown in the House today, it is a slim shadow of its former self. Bent on delaying a vote, members can still resort to quorum calls and demand roll-call votes; they can offer amendments designed to stall proceedings; they can seek a recess or attempt to adjourn the chamber. Such efforts, however, are of minimal avail. Delay is brief and inconclusive, and soon the House is back on schedule.

## The Nature and Function of Debate in Congress

In the judgment of a number of critics, debate in the Senate is superior to debate in the House. Whenever it is suggested that meaningful controls should be placed on Senate debate to curb filibustering, for example, the response is likely to be a variation of Lindsay Rogers' view that the Senate would "gradually sink to the level of the House of Representatives where there is less deliberation and debate than in any other legislative assembly."[42] As to the character of debate in the House, a former congressman writes, "While short tenure limits the foresight of the House, the unwieldy size of the body has muted its voice. As in most large assemblies, debate in the House is controlled to the point where much of the discussion is not debate at all but a series of set speeches."[43]

From knowledge of the "unlimited speech" tradition in the Senate, it is a natural step to conclude that debate ranges more freely and that questions of public policy are explored more fully there than in the House. Although this assertion may indeed be true, rigorous supporting evidence is hard to find. There is a great deal of talk in each house, but there is very little "debate"—in the sense of direct and immediate confrontations over issues between adversaries—in either house. Both houses devote substantial time, not to "debate," but to set speeches, and these often are poorly attended, indifferently received, and frequently interrupted. Moreover, much time is given over to questioning, often only for the purpose of assisting the speaker to emphasize a point. Colloquies on the floor may be helpful, informative, humorous, or caustic, but most do not impart a strong sense of "debate":

MR. BAUMAN (R., MD):  Mr. Speaker, my question is, does this legislation [to assure the humane treatment of animals shipped in commerce] require the sponsors of the Annual National Hard Crab Derby at Crisfield to come under the control of the U.S. Agriculture Department to obtain licenses, be inspected, and become subject to civil and criminal penalties?

MR. FOLEY (D., WA):  Mr. Speaker, will the gentleman yield?

MR. BAUMAN:  Yes, I yield to the gentleman from Washington.

MR. FOLEY:  No, the answer is no. In the first place, I do not know exactly whether crab racing is the sport of kings or not.

MR. BAUMAN:  It is in my area, I would say.

MR. FOLEY:  In any event, there is nothing to interfere, as far as I can tell, in this bill with crab racing. . . . A crab is not a mammal or a warmblooded animal, I will advise the gentleman from Maryland and there is nothing in the racing of crabs in any event that would be reached by this bill. . . .

MR. BAUMAN:    . . . In the past it has become the practice of our seafood industry to ship large quantities of oysters and clams to exhibits [in such places] as New York and Washington. . . .

MR. FOLEY:   This bill does not cover seafood. It covers no aquatic life except that which consists of warmblooded animals or mammals. The whale is a mammal. It might theoretically cover whales; but not crabs, oysters, and other examples . . .

MR. SYMMS (R., ID):    . . . I am wondering how Shamu, the trained killer whale in San Diego, would be affected by this. He is a mammal, too.

MR. BAUMAN:   I am not an expert on whales, but I would suggest there might be one political implication in this legislation that no one has considered. . . . [I know that] Republican Party officials sometimes bring in a live baby elephant [to their national convention] and Democratic Party officials bring in a live ass or two, to graphically illustrate their party symbols. I assume the respective national parties will now come under the control of the Department of Agriculture. . . .

MR. LOTT (R., MS):    The gentleman does think that something like "coon on the log" would be covered?

MR. FOLEY:   If the gentleman will yield, I am not familiar totally with the custom known as "coon on the log." But if the purpose is to force animals to fight one with the other, rather than to hunt animals, then the activity is covered, insofar as the use of interstate facilities is concerned. . . .

MR. CONTE (R., MA):   Mr. Speaker, will the gentleman yield?

MR. LOTT:   I yield to the gentleman from Massachusetts.

MR. CONTE:    . . . If I go to a field trial and I see a dog there I like and I want to buy it and if the dog is over $500, what do I have to do?

MR. FOLEY:   If the gentleman will yield, the gentleman from Massachusetts has to have $500 to buy it, I assume. . . . The dog would not be covered by the bill.

MR. CONTE:   I know that, but the gentleman from Washington was telling the gentleman from Mississippi—[44]

Senate debate, writes Donald Matthews, ordinarily "lacks drama and excitement. Since most members have already made up their minds, the audience is pitifully small and often inattentive. Moreover, the senators tend to listen to the speakers with whom they agree and to absent themselves when the opposition takes the floor. The debate is not sharply focused but skips from one subject to the next in an apparently chaotic manner. 'I wonder,' one old reporter once said, 'if in the whole history of the Senate two speeches in a row ever were made on the same subject.'"[45]

The participation of members in debate is affected by legislative folkways, or traditional norms of conduct. In the U.S. Senate the norm of apprenticeship has held that freshman members should wait some time before engaging fully in the activities of the chamber, particularly in its debate. In recent years this norm has declined in significance as freshman members have grown increasingly impatient with it. More important is the norm that a senator should not engage in a personal attack on another member.

Relations between members in public debate are impersonal, enforced through the rule that remarks be addressed to the presiding officer and not to any member. By observing this and related rules of courtesy, senators believe that partisanship can be kept within bounds, cooperation made possible, and disruptive personal enmities kept from developing. Another norm dictates that senators specialize in certain fields of legislation, and senators who range the gamut of legislative affairs may find their influence diminished even where their competence is recognized.[46]

Not all members of a legislative body share equally in debate, any more than all share equally in influence within the chamber or within their party. Party leaders, committee chairs, and ranking members set the style and contribute a disproportionate share of the talk in state legislatures and in Congress. They focus the debate on a measure and pick the principal speakers to be heard. The scheduling of speakers is most complete in the U.S. House of Representatives, though floor participation is ordered in some respects in all legislatures.

Congressional debate serves several distinct purposes. One function of floor talk is to help supporters of a bill communicate with one another: "Floor statements are often the quickest and most effective methods of passing the word around among other members of Congress, strengthening the cohesiveness of a group or fanning the enthusiasm of supporters." Strong speeches may also win additional votes. There are usually some members who are undecided on major bills, and "a well-oriented speech or series of speeches can often directly influence fence sitters to jump in one direction or another." Speeches may serve a strategy of delaying the vote, permitting leaders to bargain for additional support. Finally, floor talk can be useful in establishing a record for future campaigns, and it may even be consulted by the courts later as evidence of "congressional intent."[47]

### Debate in the State Legislatures

"Debate" in the state legislatures, as in Congress, is no longer a feature of the legislative process; and oratory, in the full sense of the word, is conspicuously absent. Legislative talk is made up almost entirely of "set" speeches and interrogation—of the sponsor or, if a party measure, the majority or minority floor leaders.

What has been said about the functions of debate in Congress applies equally to the state legislature. Moreover, floor debate in the legislature, as well as in Congress, is highly useful in advancing personal interests and objectives: It is a good way for members to persuade colleagues of their competence in a public policy field; it enables them to affirm a personal position or to support or back off from a party position; it presents an opportunity to gain publicity, to consolidate old support, and perhaps to attract new followers; and it permits members to marshal evidence useful in campaigns for reelection. Nevertheless, the member who frequently engages in debate runs some risk, as these comments by a state legislator suggest:

> Guys who monopolize their chamber's time by making a lot of long speeches are considered "pains in the neck" and are in for a lot of trouble. Eventually, their colleagues are going to take it out on them by refusing to support their bills, some of which may even be good government bills. We've had legislators in the past who never could get a bill passed because they talked too much. Former Senator _____ never got a bill passed as long as he was here because he talked too much and alienated everyone in the process. Everything he was for, he just lost.[48]

Although legislators contend that floor speeches do not often sway votes, they do admit that members with expert knowledge have a continuing influence on the membership.[49] Each chamber has its battery of experts—on school legislation, banks, insurance companies, conservation, agriculture, fish and game, mental health, and other fields. When issues are of low urgency to party or factional groupings and when they do not intrude on special constituency interests, members are inclined to take their cues from other legislators whose special competence is recognized. Possibly, as one analysis shows, the expert's influence on other members is greater in the early stages, when bills are shaped and considered in committee, than "after an issue has been recognized as controversial, differences structured and sides chosen."[50]

Where there are legislatures, there are filibusters, but they are one thing in the U.S. Senate and quite another in the legislatures of the states. Lengthy filibusters in the states are almost unknown, and the little ones, if they occur at all, invariably develop in the final days or hours of the session. The rules of most state legislatures, notably those of the lower houses, are well fashioned to guard against prolixity. All but a handful of chambers have rules that limit the number of times and the number of minutes a member may speak without leave of the floor. The great majority of states authorize use of the previous question to cut off debate. Many states have supplementary cloture rules to go along with the previous question, and a few maintain a practice of setting the time for a vote. The point is that there are few opportunities for state legislators to make either immoderate incursions on the time of their colleagues or rapacious demands by threatening a filibuster. Even so, the "world record" for filibustering is a state record. A Texas state senator spoke for forty-two hours and thirty-four minutes in 1977, breaking the record set several years earlier by another Texas senator. "I don't know how we've been so lucky in the Texas Senate," the lieutenant governor observed while announcing the new record.[51]

What has been said up to now does not mean that determined minorities have no weapons at hand to snag proceedings, but the weapons are small-gauge, and timing is most important. Hence most filibusters in the states occur in the waning days or hours of the session. Tactics designed to impede majority action are about the same everywhere; as a rule, their effect is to delay decision, not to postpone it indefinitely. Roll calls, whether to establish the presence of a quorum or to settle another procedural question, can and are used to serve a dilatory objective. The demand that the journal of the previous day be read in full, instead of dispensing with the requirement in the customary fashion, may be used to hold up proceedings. More effective as a weapon of the minority is the right to insist that all rules be strictly followed, including the reading of bills in their entirety. This filibustering device occasionally has been broken by hiring a battery of clerks to read different sections of a bill simultaneously, resulting in a cacophony of sounds wholly unintelligible to anyone. Finally, as in Congress, a bill may be filibustered by offering numerous amendments and then debating each one as long as time permits. In sum, dilatoriness is a conventional weapon of the minority everywhere; its effectiveness varies from legislature to legislature, depending on the willingness of the majority to acquiesce.

## Recording Debate

An account of debate in Congress that aims to be "substantially a verbatim report of proceedings" is recorded each day in the *Congressional Record*. Bound volumes appear on a semimonthly basis. Actually the *Record* extends well beyond the debate of the day since it also contains a wide variety of other materials, some valuable and some not, in its appendix and daily digest. The panorama of members' interests is revealed in the appendix, for virtually anything that comes to their attention, and meets with their approval, is apt to wind up as an entry in its pages. Speeches, articles, and editorial comment—typically, coincidental with the sponsoring member's views—appear in quantities guaranteed to discourage the most avid reader of congressional fare. As a current index to Congress, the daily digest is highly valuable. Appearing as the final section of each issue of the *Record*, it summarizes and reports the principal activities of Congress and is particularly useful for its record of committee work.

Although congressional debate is recorded in full, a good deal of its original purity has been lost by the time it appears in the cold pages of the *Record*. Its transformation in the course of moving from floor to printed page often has been an issue. Two things happen to it en route. In the first place, both houses permit members to revise their remarks before being printed, and although such revision is not supposed to alter the substance of statements, it is often so extensive that floor statements become unrecognizable in print. "This privilege has been abused to the extent that even in a colloquy which has occurred in debate the remarks of one of the debaters has been so changed as to render meaningless the printed remarks of his opponent which remain unrevised."[52] Adulteration of the transcript takes place in yet another way, by the House practice of authorizing its members to "extend" their remarks. What occurs is that members gaining the floor will speak for perhaps a minute, or possibly five, and then seek the consent of the House to have their remarks entered in full in the *Record* ("leave to print" is the argot of the request). The House readily assents, thereby creating doubt about what was said on the floor. Every now and then a member attempts to expose this practice:

> Having received unanimous consent to extend my remarks in the record, I would like to indicate that I am not really speaking these words. . . . I do not want to kid anyone into thinking that I am now on my feet delivering a stirring oration. As a matter of fact, I am back in my office typing this out on my own hot little typewriter, far from the madding crowd and somewhat removed from the House chamber. Such is the pretense of the House that it would have been easy to just quietly include these remarks in the record, issue a brave press release, and convince thousands of cheering constituents that I was in there fighting every step of the way, influencing the course of history in the heat of debate.[53]

As it goes into the *Record,* House debate is thus a curious mélange of the opening lines of many speeches never heard on the floor, coupled with revised, sometimes totally new, remarks. Senate debate in the *Record,* in contrast, is closer to what was actually said on the floor, if for no other reason than that an individual senator has a greater allotment of floor time and can ordinarily deliver his or her speech in full. Nevertheless, members in both houses rearrange the facts and rewrite bits and chunks of historical record. That, at least, has been the case—for about as long as anyone can remember. In 1995, however, the Republican majority adopted a rule to confine members' changes in their floor remarks to corrections of a technical or grammatical nature. How this effort to turn the *Congressional Record* into a verbatim account would work out remained to be seen.

Consistent with the drive to increase the "openness" of state legislative processes, a number of states now require debate to be recorded and minutes or summaries of all public meetings to be kept. Transcripts of debate not only serve an informational function for the public, newspapers, and scholars but also contribute to a measure of political control. Recorded speeches may serve to keep legislative talk more responsible and to discourage the use of bogus data in debate. The record of deliberations, the ways in which decisions were reached, and the votes themselves become a part of the public domain, open to study and evaluation. Recorded debate may also be used to help clarify legislative intent at the time a measure was passed. In the interpretation of statutes, courts will sometimes turn to the legislative history of an act to seek the meaning of certain language or to learn the intention of the majority that passed it.

## CASTING THE VOTE

The legislative act of casting a vote is not taken lightly, at least when major legislation is at stake. A permanent record, hardened, irretrievable, available for public inspection—these are the qualities of the vote. Of all the facts that might be recorded about voting, none seems more necessary to emphasize than its complexity. A vote on a major measure is rarely made easy for the legislator; reasons for voting yea shade into those for voting nay. Robert Luce, with experience in both a state legislature and Congress, describes the matrix of influences that shape voting:

> Assuming that it is best for constituents to be informed of each act of their representatives, yet it is far from certain that records of roll-calls disclose the votes adequately or that they accurately inform. There are such things as half truths, and often the record of a vote is in effect a half truth. Often it fails to show the real nature of the matter decided. Titles of bills are necessarily brief and rarely tell the whole story. Again and again a legislator will sympathize with a measure, will desire what its title purports to give, and yet be compelled to vote against it because he knows it is improperly drawn or because he thinks it will not accomplish its ostensible purpose or because it will also accomplish some other purpose of more harm than enough to offset the good. Every legislator has seen a wise bill, for which he has voted at one stage, ruined by amendments at the next, forcing him to reverse his vote. Or again the time may not be ripe for the measure; or some other step ought to be taken first; or a measure may be undesirable unless some other measure goes with it. Any one of a score of perfectly legitimate reasons the public will never know may lead a conscientious and honorable lawmaker to record his vote in a way that will put him in a false light, and may bring him political ruin.[54]

T. V. Smith points to the problem for the legislator of understanding the dimensions of a vote:

> The predicament of the legislator is that every vote is a dozen votes upon as many issues all wrapped up together, tied in a verbal package, and given a single number of this bill or that. To decide what issue of the many hidden in each bill one wants to vote upon is delicate, but to make certain that the vote will be actually on that rather than upon another issue is indelicate presumption.[55]

Voting is essentially a contextual act—to be more precise, how a member decides to vote depends on the kind of issue that is presented. On complicated issues, David C. Kozak has shown, members engage in an extended search for information, often taking cues from committee members or members of their state delegation who have similar constituencies. On hot issues, such as abortion or tax reform, members already have a high level of information; their votes may be based on personal values, ideology, campaign promises, or constituency opinion. Many issues are seen as routine, having come up before, and members thus have little difficulty in deciding how to vote. Overall, the nature of the issue influences how extensively members search for information, the sources from which they seek it (for example, staff, other members, or party intelligence), how carefully they weigh constituency interests, and the time (early or late) of their decision.[56]

Legislators exhibit a high degree of consistency in their voting on recurrent policy questions.[57] Maintaining a consistent voting history has definite advantages for members. First, it simplifies the task of making decisions on complex matters. Second, legislators who vote the same way each time a certain issue arises find it easier to justify their position to constituents and colleagues. And third, consistency appears to cut electoral risks since there is a presumption that the member's constituency has approved previous votes. Nevertheless, some legislators do change their positions over time. A shift in party control of the administration may induce a member to change long-standing attitudes on certain policy questions. It is undoubtedly easier, for example, for members to support an increase in the debt ceiling when their party controls the presidency than when the other party controls it. The nature of the policy conflict itself may change under the press of new forces or altered world conditions, thus attenuating the member's ties to previous positions. Finally, legislators' own environments may be transformed as a result of their advancement to positions of leadership or the radical alteration of their constituencies. Hence, although legislators have numerous "standing decisions" on issues, they occasionally develop new postures in response to external or internal forces.[58]

Voting may carry fewer risks for legislators than ordinarily is supposed—particularly if their behavior back in the district is pleasing to constituents. Richard F. Fenno, Jr., argues convincingly that

> ... all House members can use their home styles to give themselves a great deal of voting leeway in Washington if they so desire. . . . House members are not tightly constrained in their legislative votes by the necessities of constituent support. So long as members can successfully explain a vote afterward, their constituent support depends—except for one or two issues—more on what they do at home than on what they do in Washington.[59]

Legislatures have devised a variety of voting methods: viva voce, division, tellers (including recorded tellers), and roll calls (or yeas and nays). The first three methods have in common the fact that no formal record is made of the votes of individual members, though sharp-eyed observers can gain a fair impression of supporters and opponents when division or tellers are used. Under viva voce, the chair simply calls for a voice vote of yeas and nays and then estimates which chorus constitutes the prevailing side. A close voice vote may lead to utilizing one of the other methods. A division vote is held by having members rise and be counted, first those in favor and then those in opposition. Vote by teller, such as used by the U.S. House of Representatives, requires the members to pass down the center aisle and be counted, the yeas first and then the nays. In each case, it is the outcome or total vote that counts, and the chamber makes no record of individual positions. Under the Legislative Reorganization Act of 1970, provision was made for recording teller votes if demanded by twenty members. This reform has not only given greater visibility to members' votes at the crucial stage of the amending process but has also induced far larger numbers of members to be present for voting in the committee of the whole.

The success of party leaders in convincing members to follow their lead may depend on the voting method used. On votes that are not highly visible to the public, the press, or others—as in the case of committee voting and division and voice voting on the floor—party leaders can often count on a high measure of support from rank-and-file members. Roll-call votes on final passage of controversial bills, however, are another matter. Members cannot quietly go along with the party, relatively assured that their votes are hidden from critical eyes. A roll-call vote is the most visible vote of all, and visibility tends to attenuate the influence of party leaders and to strengthen the hand of those opposed to the leadership.

Both houses of Congress make use of voting "pairs," a form of proxy voting for the record. Under this practice, a member who cannot be present for a roll-call vote, or simply wants to avoid it, agrees to "pair" with another member on the question, one to be recorded as voting for and the other against. Pairs may also be "general" in character, which means that the arrangement holds until the two members agree to cancel it. A convenient device when members find it necessary to be absent at the time a vote is scheduled, pairing is also a means of dodging a controversial vote. The votes of pairs are not counted in the official tally, serving nothing more than to identify the intentions of the contracting members. Pairs are often arranged simply by having the clerks match names, with no overtures between individual members having preceded the coupling. "The system is for the most part farcical. . . . The assumption is that every vote is a party vote, and that every absentee if present would vote with the leaders of his party, both of which things are far from true. Therefore the printed list has no real significance."[60] The practice of pairing has been used in the state legislatures but is unimportant today.

The business at hand determines the voting requirements in Congress. In most cases the vote demanded is a majority of a quorum. Interestingly, in the House committee of the whole, where numerous major decisions are taken and where a quorum is only 100 members, amendments can be adopted or defeated by as few as fifty-one votes. Some matters require extraordinary majorities, as in the case of the two-thirds vote needed in both houses to override a veto and the two-thirds vote in the Senate to ratify a treaty. In yet other cases, as we have seen earlier, unanimous consent is a prerequisite for taking a particular action.

The number of votes needed to pass a bill in the legislature varies somewhat from state to state. About two-thirds of the states require a majority of the members elected, whereas most of the rest call for a simple majority of those present and voting. The requirement of a "constitutional majority"—majority of the members elected—has come to present a convenient and evasive way of killing a bill without going on record against it. An absent or nonvoting member becomes in effect an opponent of the bill; if enough members decline to vote, the bill is certain to fail. Individual legislators can, if they choose, argue that they were meeting with constituents or that they did not hear the bell or that they were otherwise detained. Legislative devices for evasion, for escaping pressures and avoiding records, are numerous; most of them are maintained by plausible, if not altogether convincing, reasons.

Commonly, the states require extraordinary majorities, perhaps two-thirds of all members elected, to override vetoes and to pass emergency legislation or special kinds of appropriation measures. In about two-thirds of the states, roll-call votes are required on the final passage of all measures. Even in those states where this requirement is absent, it is usually a simple matter to demand a roll call on final passage—only a few members needing to make the request. The average state legislature conducts many hundred more roll-call votes than Congress does.

Legislative voting is not necessarily an act based on serious reflection. On many bills, legislators find it hard to learn all they need to know in order to cast an "intelligent" vote. The problem may be particularly acute at the state level. In the search for information, even at the last minute, cues of all kinds become important:

> As the bills came up, many delegates looked around the room for indications on how to vote. Some looked to a floor leader or committee chairman for a thumbs up or thumbs down. Others bent their ears to a colleague who might know something about the bill. On any given topic, probably about a third of the membership is familiar with the bill, another third knows the issue generally, and another third is playing follow the leader.[61]

## THE MULTIPLE POINTS OF DECISION MAKING

A central theme of this book is that there are multiple points in the legislative process at which critical decisions are made. Frequently, they are made in committees and subcommittees, where party and leadership preferences may or may not be reflected in the outcome. Sometimes the key decisions are taken by screening panels, such as the leadership-dominated Rules Committee in the U.S. House of Representatives, or by conference committees formed to adjust interchamber differences. Party leaders and caucuses may play a major role in shaping policies. And critical decisions also may be made in response to the initiatives and influence of interest groups, bureaucrats, or the chief executive. At bottom, of course, it is the generalized demands of special publics and the wider public that spur legislatures to act—that is, to work out proximate solutions to public policy issues and problems.

## NOTES

1. *Congressional Quarterly Weekly Report*, June 17, 1995, p. 1712; *New York Times*, June 21, 1995.

2. Two studies were particularly useful in developing the analysis of this section: Stanley Bach and Steven S. Smith, *Managing Uncertainty in the House of Representatives* (Washington, DC: Brookings Institution, 1988); and Steven S. Smith, *Call to Order: Floor Politics in the House and Senate* (Washington, DC: Brookings Institution, 1989).

3. *Congressional Record*, 103rd Cong., 2nd sess., September 29, 1994, p. H10297. (Daily edition.)

4. Bach and Smith, *Managing Uncertainty*, p. 70.

5. *Congressional Quarterly Weekly Report*, November 19, 1994, pp. 3319–323.

6. See House Committee on Rules, *Survey of Activities of the House Committee on Rules*, House report 104-868, 104th Cong., 2d sess., 1996 (Washington, DC: U.S. Government Printing Office, 1996), pp. 30, 90, and House Committee on Rules, *Survey of Activities of the House Committee on Rules*, House report 105-840, 105th Cong., 2d sess., 1999 (Washington, DC: U.S. Government Printing Office, 1999), pp. 20, 64.

7. Hubert Bruce Fuller, *The Speakers of the House* (Boston: Little, Brown, 1909), p. 231.

8. Robert Luce, *Congress: An Explanation* (Cambridge, MA: Harvard University Press, 1926), p. 117.

9. Tom Wicker, "Again That Roadblock in Congress," *New York Times Magazine*, August 7, 1960, p. 14.

10. *Congressional Quarterly Weekly Report*, August 24, 1985, p. 1673. The remarks are those of Representative David E. Bonior (D., MI).

11. *The U.S. Congress: Organization and Procedure* (Manassas, VA: National Capitol Publishers, 1949), p. 237.

12. *Congress and the Nation*, III (Washington, DC: Congressional Quarterly, 1973), p. 363; *Congressional Quarterly Weekly Report*, May 7, 1983, p. 879.

13. *Congressional Quarterly Weekly Report*, September 11, 1993, pp. 2369–370.

14. Stanley Bach, "Suspension of the Rules, the Order of Business, and the Development of Congressional Procedure," *Legislative Studies Quarterly*, XV (February 1990), 49.

15. Hugh A. Bone, "An Introduction to the Senate Policy Committees," *American Political Science Review*, L (June 1956), 349–50.

16. Steven S. Smith and Marcus Flathman, "Managing the Senate Floor: Complex Unanimous Consent Agreements Since the 1950s," *Legislative Studies Quarterly*, XIV (August 1989), 349–74. Also see a bargaining model developed by Scott Ainsworth and Marcus Flathman that argues that unanimous consent agreements can be used by majority leaders to strengthen their bargaining position. "Unanimous Consent Agreements as Leadership Tools," *Legislative Studies Quarterly*, XX (May 1995), 177–93.

17. Harvey J. Tucker, "Legislative Calendars and Workload Management in Texas," *Journal of Politics*, LI (August 1989), 631–45.

18. Belle Zeller, ed., *American State Legislatures* (New York: Thomas Y. Crowell, 1954), p. 198.

19. Larry Sonis, "'O.K., Everybody. Vote Yes': A Day in the Life of a State Legislator," *Washington Monthly*, June 1979, p. 25.

20. Harvey J. Tucker, "Legislative Logjams: A Comparative State Analysis," *Western Political Quarterly*, XXXVIII (September 1985), 432–46.

21. See a discussion by John J. Pitney, Jr., of the use of the logjam as a leadership weapon in the New York Senate. "Leaders and Rules in the New York State Senate," *Legislative Studies Quarterly*, VII (November 1982), 495.

22. Eric Lane, "Albany's Travesty of Democracy," *City Journal*, VII (Spring 1997), 51.

23. Richard Fleisher and Jon R. Bond, "Beyond Committee Control: Committee and Party Leader Influence on Floor Amendments in Congress," *American Politics Quarterly*, XIII (April 1983), 131–61.

24. Barbara Sinclair, "The Speaker's Task Force in the Post-Reform House of Representatives," *American Political Science Review*, LXXV (June 1981), 397–410 (quotations on p. 399).

25. Barbara Sinclair, "Senate Styles and Senate Decision Making, 1955–1980," *Journal of Politics*, XLVIII (November 1986), 902.

26. Charles W. Wiggins, *The Iowa Lawmaker* (Washington, DC: American Political Science Association, 1971), p. 70.

27. See an interesting study by James M. Enelow and David H. Koehler of "sophisticated voting"—voting designed to "save" or "kill" a bill by adding an amendment—in "The Amendment in Legislative Strategy: Sophisticated Voting in the U.S. Congress," *Journal of Politics*, XLII (May 1980), 396–413.

28. *Chicago Sun-Times*, April 10, 1957, p. 35.

29. Robert S. Walker and Samuel C. Patterson, *Oklahoma Goes Wet: The Repeal of Prohibition* (New York: McGraw-Hill, Eagleton Cases in Practical Politics, 1960), p. 17.

30. *Congressional Quarterly Weekly Report*, July 21, 1990, p. 2316.

31. *Congressional Quarterly Weekly Report*, August 8, 1998, p. 2198.

32. Roland Young, *The American Congress* (New York: Harper & Row, 1958), p. 143.

33. Lindsay Rogers, *The American Senate* (New York: Appleton-Century-Crofts, 1931), pp. 165–67.

34. Quoted in George H. Haynes, *The Senate of the United States* (Boston: Houghton Mifflin, 1938), p. 403.

35. See a discussion of filibustering and cloture in Smith, *Call to Order*, especially pp. 94–99.

36. Barbara Sinclair, *The Transformation of the U.S. Senate* (Baltimore: Johns Hopkins University Press, 1989), p. 131.

37. Smith, *Call to Order*, p. 111.

38. *Congressional Quarterly Weekly Report*, March 6, 1999, p. 543.

39. *Congressional Record*, 94th Cong., 2nd sess., February 9, 1976, p. H819. (Daily edition.)

40. A member who wishes to secure the floor for five minutes to discuss a section of a bill may utilize a pro forma amendment, a parliamentary move under which a member can record his or her views. Thus a member will rise and say, "I move to strike out the last word," after which he or she is permitted to talk for five minutes. Normally, an opponent will then obtain the floor by stating, "I rise in opposition to the pro forma amendment," and deliver a five-minute talk. The pro forma amendment is a device for entering debate and has no substantive significance.

41. Fuller, *Speakers of the House*, p. 230.

42. Rogers, *The American Senate*, p. 6.

43. Stewart L. Udall, "A Congressman Defends the House," *New York Times Magazine*, January 12, 1958, p. 69.

44. *Congressional Record*, 94th Cong., 2nd sess., February 9, 1976, pp. H820–21. (Daily edition.)

45. *U.S. Senators and Their World* (Chapel Hill: University of North Carolina Press, 1960), p. 246.

46. See Donald R. Matthews, "The Folkways of the United States Senate: Conformity to Group Norms and Legislative Effectiveness," *American Political Science Review*, LIII (December 1959), 1067–71.

47. Bertram Gross, *The Legislative Struggle: A Study in Social Combat* (New York: McGraw-Hill, 1953), pp. 366–67.

48. Wiggins, *Iowa Lawmaker*, pp. 68–69.

49. A study of the Michigan House of Representatives finds that members in search of information on legislation are much more likely to turn to other legislators than to depend on discussion or debate in committees, on the floor, or in caucus. H. Owen Porter, "Legislative

Experts and Outsiders: The Two-Step Flow of Communications," *Journal of Politics*, XXXVI (August 1974), 709. In Nevada, by contrast, legislators in search of information rely most heavily on committee hearings and the staff of the Legislative Counsel Bureau. See Robert B. Bradley, "Motivations in Legislative Information Use," *Legislative Studies Quarterly*, V (August 1980), 393–406. A recent study of the California legislature affirms the key importance of staff in transmitting policy information. See Paul Sabatier and David Whiteman, "Legislative Decision Making and Substantive Policy Information: Models of Information Flow," *Legislative Studies Quarterly*, X (August 1985), 395–419. For good evidence on the importance of experts (subcommittee members) in transmitting information on legislation to rank-and-file members of the South Carolina House of Representatives, see Donald R. Songer, "The Influence of Empirical Research: Committee vs. Floor Decision Making," *Legislative Studies Quarterly*, XIII (August 1988), 375–92. In a study of the Indiana, Massachusetts, and Oregon legislatures, Christopher Z. Mooney finds that legislators tend to be "closed-minded rationalizers" who rely heavily on information with a political component; moreover, they usually use only information with which they agree. See his article, "Putting It on Paper: The Content of Written Information Used in State Lawmaking," *American Politics Quarterly*, XX (July 1992), 345–65.

50. William Buchanan, Heinz Eulau, LeRoy C. Ferguson, and John C. Wahlke, "The Legislator as Specialist," *Western Political Quarterly*, XIII (September 1960), 649. This observation is made specifically with reference to the California legislature.

51. *Washington Post*, May 5, 1977.

52. Statement by Representative Curtis of Missouri, *Congressional Record*, CIV (1958), 6594.

53. The remarks were those of Ken Hechler, a former member of the House from West Virginia, *Congressional Quarterly Weekly Report*, March 15, 1975, p. 527.

54. Robert Luce, *Legislative Procedure* (Boston: Houghton Mifflin, 1922), p. 361.

55. "Custom, Gossip, Legislation," *Social Forces*, XVI (October 1937), 31.

56. David C. Kozak, "Decision Settings in Congress," in *Congress and Public Policy*, ed. David C. Kozak and John D. Macartney (Homewood, IL: Dorsey Press, 1982), pp. 313–28.

57. Legislators are also largely consistent in their voting behavior from committee to floor; that is, with relatively few exceptions they vote the same way on the floor on a bill or amendment as they had earlier in committee. See the evidence on the U.S. House of Representatives by Joseph K. Unekis, "From Committee to the Floor: Consistency in Congressional Voting," *Journal of Politics*, XL (August 1978), 761–69. At the state level, see a study by Keith E. Hamm, "Consistency Between Committee and Floor Voting in U.S. State Legislatures," *Legislative Studies Quarterly*, VII (November 1982), 473–90. This study of seven state legislative chambers finds that votes cast on the floor are consistent with committee votes more than 90 percent of the time.

58. Herbert B. Asher and Herbert F. Weisberg, "Voting Change in Congress: Some Dynamic Perspectives on an Evolutionary Process," *American Journal of Political Science*, XXII (May 1978), 391–425. In addition, see John W. Kingdon, *Congressmen's Voting Decisions* (New York: Harper & Row, 1981); Aage R. Clausen, *How Congressmen Decide: A Policy Focus* (New York: St. Martin's Press, 1973); and Keith T. Poole, "Dimensions of Interest Group Evaluation of the U.S. Senate, 1969–1978," *American Journal of Political Science*, XXV (February 1981), 51–67. But also see a study by Richard C. Elling, which finds that as U.S. senators near the end of their terms, their voting behavior shifts to become more conservative and more moderate. "Ideological Change in the U.S. Senate: Time and Electoral Responsiveness," *Legislative Studies Quarterly*, VII (February 1982), 75–92. See another study of the voting behavior of reelection-seeking senators whose findings are broadly consistent with Richard Elling's. Martin Thomas finds that about one-fourth of all senators running for reelection change the ideological cast of their roll-call voting to improve their reelection prospects. "Election Proximity and Senatorial Roll Call Voting," *American Journal of Political Science*, XXIX (February 1985), 96–111. For a study of how ambition influences behavior on the House side, see John R. Hibbing, "Ambition in the House: Behavioral Consequences of Higher Office Goals Among U.S. Representatives," *American Journal of Political Science*, XXX (August 1986), 651–65. His study shows that House members who decide to run for the Senate change their behavior as the election nears, seeking to bring their voting records into line with the

prevailing ideology of the state as a whole. Voting behavior also shifts in response to redistricting. Members respond to their new political environment. As a district becomes more liberal (because of its altered composition), Democratic members of Congress vote along more liberal lines; as a district becomes more conservative, Republican members vote along more conservative lines. See Amihai Glazer and Marc Robbins, "Congressional Responsiveness to Constituency Change," *American Journal of Political Science*, XXIX (May 1985), 259–72.

59. Richard F. Fenno, Jr., *Home Style: House Members in Their Districts* (Boston: Little, Brown, 1978), pp. 231–32.

60. Luce, *Legislative Procedure*, p. 381.

61. Sonis, "'O.K., Everybody. Vote Yes,'" p. 26.

# Political Parties
# and the Legislative Process

The stark fact about American legislatures is that total power is seldom, if ever, concentrated in any quarter.[1] This is the chief truth to be known about the legislative process, and if it is well understood, a lot of other things may be safely forgotten. A certain quantity of political power, variable according to people and circumstance, is lodged within each of the legislature's principal parts. Committees, committee chairs, seniority leaders in general, officers of the chambers, sectional and ideological spokespersons, and agencies of the parties cooperate and compete with one another in the exercise of legislative power. Executive agencies and private organizations, from vantage points within and without the legislature, contribute varying measures of content and thrust to legislative decisions. On occasions more rare, the court slips into the struggle as acts of the legislature fall under its scrutiny. In a word, numerous centers of power in and out of the legislature negotiate for the right to have a say on public policy. This chapter examines the role of political parties in the legislative process.

## LEGISLATIVE PARTY ORGANIZATION

### Party Conferences

One of the oldest agencies of party, used for choosing legislative leaders and developing party policy, is the legislative party caucus or conference. Membership in one or the other of the party conferences is automatic for the party member upon election to the legislature.

The high point of caucus power in Congress was reached in the second decade of the twentieth century. The earlier eras of Reed and Cannon saw the House so dominated by the Speaker—through control of the Rules Committee—that the majority caucus had no independent voice. Following the Speaker's loss of power in the 1910–11 revolution, the majority-party caucus waxed strong and, during the Wilson administration, was notably effective.

Loyalty to the party was expected, binding caucuses were frequent, and steady efforts were made to translate party platforms into congressional programs. After World War I, the power of the caucus dropped sharply, mainly because of the growing unpopularity of its compulsory features.

From this early period until the late 1960s the caucuses of Congress were all but moribund. Their most important activity was the selection of the party leadership. In 1969, largely as a result of the initiatives of the Democratic Study Group, the House Democratic caucus began to stir. Regular meetings of the caucus were scheduled, at which various legislative reforms were discussed. This led ultimately to major modifications of the seniority rule. Currently, the House Democratic caucus and the Republican conference hold secret ballots on all nominations for chairmanships.

Committee chairs in the postreform Congress are now dependent on caucus (or conference) support and accountable to the party membership. If chairs fall out of step with committee members, disregard their interests, and fail to meet their expectations concerning committee leadership, they run a good risk of being deposed from office.

The revitalization of the parties represents an important shift in power in the House. Caucus power has weakened the grip of seniority, reduced the influence of committee chairs, and strengthened the position of the party leadership. But these changes should be kept in perspective. The realities of congressional politics are such that the caucus has not been a reliable agency for shaping the behavior of members on major policy proposals. Members who think seriously about maintaining their seats in Congress think first and last about their constituencies, especially about those elements that can return them to or dismiss them from office.[2] This is the first principle of congressional life, one to which party leaders are adjusted and inured.[3] The claims of party, as a result, ordinarily take on significance only when they can be accommodated by the legislators in their general design for maintaining the support of their constituents.

The place of party caucuses in decision making varies from state to state. A recent investigation by Wayne L. Francis finds that in the view of legislators themselves, committees rank most important in shaping decisions in state legislatures. Next in line are party leaders, followed by party caucuses. The caucus and leadership appear to be particularly powerful in such states as New York, New Jersey, Pennsylvania,[4] Indiana, Illinois, and Connecticut. In contrast, the caucus is of limited significance in southern states.[5] Connecticut is a good example of a state in which caucus deliberations and decisions are taken seriously, as these comments by a member of the Assembly illustrate:

> A lot has been said about the importance of parties in the Assembly and by and large what they say is true. I was a little amazed that I really didn't have the freedom to vote as I wanted on some legislation. It wasn't that I found myself

in disagreement with my party very often but it was assumed after the caucus that I would fall in line and there were implied sanctions that might be imposed if I didn't. Actually though, it's not as bad as it sounds. You do have the opportunity to speak in the caucus. If you have good reasons, and you are honest about it, you can vote in opposition to a party position. There are also many issues where there is no party position and you are completely free. In retrospect I think that strong party organizations in the legislature are a good thing. It is an efficient way of running the legislature, it facilitates the process of compromise, and it enables you to run on a party record. It takes a little while to get used to the fact that you seem to be subordinate to some higher force within the Assembly. But eventually most of us come around to the view that we can't operate as 177 individuals and parties are the best way to get the job done.[6]

It should be emphasized that even in states where the caucus is an important party instrument, its decisions are usually not binding on the member, who may claim that the proposed action would run counter to the best interests of his or her district or that it would contravene a pledge made to constituents.

A major controversy over party caucuses is whether they should be open to the public (and thus to the press and lobbies as well) or restricted to members. In ten states (Hawaii, Idaho, Indiana, Missouri, Ohio, Oregon, Pennsylvania, Texas, Washington, and West Virginia) party caucuses are always closed in both houses. They are always open in five states (Arizona, Colorado, Kansas, Montana, and North Dakota). Taking the country as a whole, 56 percent of legislative chambers currently have caucuses that are always or usually closed and 35 percent are always or usually open. In urban, industrial states with strong party systems—for example, Illinois, Indiana, New Jersey, New York, Pennsylvania, Ohio, and Connecticut (House)— party caucuses are always or usually closed. In a few states, such as Colorado and Montana, court decisions forced the legislatures to open their caucuses.[7]

### The Policy Committees of Congress

The need for greater party responsibility in legislative chambers has been a persistent theme in the literature of political science during the last two decades. Legislative party organization should be tightened up, runs this view, so that the majority party can be held accountable for the conduct of government, especially for the formulation of public policy. Invariably, proposals directed toward the reform of Congress have included steps to be taken to shore up the party leadership committees. The Joint Committee on the Organization of Congress in its 1946 report recommended the creation of policy committees "to formulate over-all legislative policy of the two parties." Subsequently, the provision was placed in the La Follette-Monroney reorganization bill and accepted by the Senate, only to be stricken in the House. In an independent action in 1947, the Senate set up its own policy committees. Two years later House Republicans converted their steering committee into a policy committee. In 1973, in the midst of a reform wave, the House Democratic caucus established a Steering and Policy Committee to develop and shape legislative strategy.

Currently, House Republicans have both a Steering Committee, chaired by the Speaker and responsible for committee assignments, and a Policy Committee to advise on party actions and policy. On the Democratic side, the minority leader serves as chair of both the Steering Committee and the Policy Committee, which have responsibilities similar to those of the Republican party committees. The corresponding party committees in the Senate are for the Republicans, the Policy Committee and the Committee on Committees, and for the Democrats, the Policy Committee and the Steering and Coordination Committee.

A review of the experience of the Senate policy committees is not reassuring to those who hoped these agencies might serve to enhance party responsibility in Congress. The name "policy committee" itself is illusory. "They have never been 'policy' bodies, in the sense of considering and investigating alternatives of public policy, and they have never put forth an over-all congressional party program. The committees do not assume leadership in drawing up a general legislative program . . . and only rarely have the committees labeled their decisions as 'party policies.' "[8] Issues seldom are resolved by votes being taken, and decisions are never binding. "The Democratic Policy Committee is sometimes described as the counterpart to the House Committee on Rules," writes Robert L. Peabody, "but this comparison is misleading. The Senate committee has no authority to issue rules governing floor debate, imposes no limits on time, and seldom delays a bill from being scheduled."[9]

In the view of one of the most skillful Democratic floor leaders of the twentieth century, Lyndon B. Johnson, neither the policy committee nor the party conference should make policy; this responsibility belongs rather to the standing committees. He contended that members should make their influence felt "in committees of which they are members. . . . If they cannot get a majority vote there, how do they expect me to get a majority vote out here?"[10]

The failure of the policy committees to fulfill the expectations of those who have sought a more meaningful party performance in Congress is not hard to explain.[11] At bottom, the dilemma is based on a conflict between irreconcilables. The stark simplicity of the plan—a centralized party body to shape legislative policy—could not overcome the many problems that have repeatedly confounded attempts to gather and store legislative power in a central place. A policy committee worthy of its name necessarily would intrude on the traditional arrangements of power and authority. Inevitably, seniority leaders would be forced to relinquish some share of their considerable power over legislation, for an independent committee system and central party leadership are incompatible. Similarly, individual power would be threatened by the party. There is nothing novel in the finding that powerful members of Congress greatly prefer the customary allocation of power. Moreover, those outside Congress who secure policy advantages from existing legislative arrangements obviously have an aversion to change.

The policy committees have not provided a significant departure from the past because they could not go to the root of the problem, party disunity, nor as Ralph Huitt has argued, could they accommodate the relationship between the individual members and their constituencies. Many lawmakers have cultivated "careers of dissidence." Closely attuned to the interests and aspirations of their constituents, they know that what counts is pleasing the voters who elect them, not satisfying a legislative party agency.[12] Moreover, the party is unable to exert effective discipline over them. "The American legislator," Clinton Rossiter wrote, "is uniquely on his own, and he lives and dies politically through the display of talents more numerous and more demanding than party regularity. He must therefore make his own adjustment among the forces that play upon him, even if this means defiance of his party's leadership."[13]

## The Floor Leaders

The chief spokespersons of the parties in the legislature are the floor leaders. Majority and minority floor leaders are chosen by party caucuses in each house. Customarily, the majority leaders have greater influence in the legislature than anyone save the Speaker of the House.

The majority leaders' role is much easier to describe than are the elements that combine to shape their influence. Their task, in general, is to plan the work of their chamber, which they do as leader of the majority party. Depending on their skills, personality, and support, they may have a decisive voice in formulating the legislative program as well as in steering it through the house. In the course of developing and scheduling the legislative program, majority leaders work closely with committee chairs and other key leaders in their party. Their relations with the committees are basic: "You must understand why the committee took certain actions and why certain judgments were formed," stated Lyndon Johnson.[14] Or as Mike Mansfield, his successor, has said, "I'm not the leader, really. They don't do what I tell them. I do what they tell me. . . . The brains are in the committees."[15] Jim Wright, a former majority leader (and former Speaker), described the leader's role in this way: "The majority leader is a conciliator, a mediator, a peacemaker. Even when patching together a tenuous majority he must respect the right of honest dissent, conscious of the limits of his claims upon others."[16] Former Senate majority leader Robert C. Byrd had this to say about his position: "a traffic cop, babysitter, welfare worker, minister, lawyer, umpire, referee, punching bag, target, lightning rod and . . . the cement that holds his party together."[17]

Effective leadership grows out of continuing communication between the majority leader and the rest of the party; the leader must be especially sensitive to the interests of those who hold power in their own right. The importance of keeping the lines of communication open can scarcely be exaggerated, for certain kinds of intelligence can keep the majority leader from being caught on the short end of a floor vote.

The floor leader has few formal powers. David Truman observes that leaders must construct their influence out of "fragments of power":[18] their influence over committee assignments, ability to help members with their special projects, control over the legislative schedule, role as leader in debate, ties to the administration if their party is in control, links to the leadership of the other chamber, skill as a parliamentarian, and position as party spokesperson through the media of communication.

What makes the post of floor leader so important is that it is located at the center of things in the legislature. Only the floor leader can gather together the partial powers scattered throughout the legislature and forge them into an instrument of leadership. By using these powers skillfully and judiciously, the floor leader can hold them intact. "The only real power available to the leader is the power of persuasion," Lyndon Johnson, an extraordinarily effective Senate leader, once observed. "There is no patronage; no power to discipline; no authority to fire Senators like a President can fire his members of Cabinet."[19]

To a significant extent, leaders lead by facilitating and accommodating the interests of members. Steven S. Smith and Marcus Flathman describe how the constraints that confront the Senate leadership in managing floor activity have changed since the 1950s:

> The task of managing floor activity became far more difficult. Majority leaders faced the necessity of adjusting floor practices to the needs of more senators, to the complexity of more issues, and to the burden of more amendments. They did so with no significant change in their formal authority or informal resources. To the contrary, majority leaders' primary parliamentary instrument, the unanimous consent agreement [used to expedite business and limit debate], became even more difficult to design and get approved. By the early 1960s, the majority leader could no longer assume that consultation with the minority leader and the two senior committee leaders would be sufficient. As rank-and-file senators became more concerned about the implications of the agreements for their own opportunities to participate in floor debate, they more frequently questioned leaders about proposed agreements and demanded consultation. Thus, on top of everything else, the process of negotiating unanimous consent agreements became more complex and time-consuming just as the importance of achieving agreements was increasing.[20]

Members' expectations regarding the role of the floor leader, especially in relationship to the chief executive, present another perspective of the office. Writing of the U.S. Senate, William S. White contends that although there is no unified view of what a leader is or what a leader ought to do, "there is general agreement on what he is *not* and what he ought *not* to do." In the first place, except in extraordinary circumstances, the Senate expects that its floor leader, if a member of the party of the president, "will not so much represent the President as the Senate itself." Second, if the floor leader is a member of the party that lost the presidency, the leader should "represent not so much that party as the Senate itself." Finally, the floor leader should "consider himself primarily the spokesman for a group in the *Senate* and not so much for any group in the country or any non-Senatorial political organism whatever, not excluding the Republican and Democratic National Committee organizations."[21] The floor leader's "constituency," in this view, is the "institution" itself: It, not the president, provides the cues for its leaders; its prerogatives, not the president's, must be protected. The effective leader, then, is one who puts first things first: the interests of the senatorial group. Or as a member of the House put the matter, "I don't look for leadership that I help elect to be a parrot for the White House. If they're just going to listen to the White House and come back and tell us what the White House wants, they aren't our leadership."[22]

David Truman offers a counterinterpretation, which asserts that a close tie between the majority leader and the administration is necessary for effective leadership. He holds that "elective leaders are, and probably must be, both the president's leaders and the party's leaders. . . . [In] order to be fully effective as leaders of the Congressional parties, they must above all be effective spokesmen for the President; or at least, excepting the most unusual circumstances, they must appear to be his spokesmen."[23]

The floor leader must be a "middleman in the sense of a broker."[24] Prominent identification with an extreme bloc within the party, Truman hypothesizes concerning Congress, is likely to jeopardize the leader's effectiveness. Leaders' voting records generally locate them close to the center of the legislative party. Moreover, members on the ideological edges of the party structure are often ruled out for the position as leader since problems of communication, difficult at best, might prove insurmountable if the leader were drawn from the extreme reaches of the party.[25] While he was serving as House minority leader, Congressman John Rhodes (R., AZ) observed, "Everyone has a different idea as to how the leadership is supposed to operate. I think that's perfectly healthy. But I think everybody also understands that you can't please everybody on everything. To please the majority, you have to keep from going too far to the left or to the right."[26] Location within the party, as well as relative skills and personality, is thus a factor affecting choice of the floor leader.[27]

Selecting leaders from the party "middle" is not, of course, etched in stone. Exceptions occur. And sometimes it appears that the party middle itself has shifted. When House Republicans chose Newt Gingrich (R., GA) to replace Robert H. Michel (R., IL) in 1994 as party leader, they not only followed the "routine advancement" tradition (from the number-two whip position to floor leader), but selected one of the party's most partisan, ideological, and combative members. "With each election," said Vin Weber, a former Republican representative from Minnesota, "the party in the House has become more populist and more with a conservative edge, and Newt used his skill to mobilize them."[28]

Recent evidence on leadership selection patterns in the U.S. House of Representatives points to differences between the parties. Studying the period 1876–1987, Brian D. Posler and Carl M. Rhodes find that potential leaders "signal" their partisan and ideological credentials for a leadership position:

> Democratic leaders move away from the opposing party throughout their pre-selection careers, demonstrating ever-increasing levels of party fidelity as their moment of selection draws near. . . . Republican leaders consistently align themselves within the core of their party, never differentiating themselves from the party's median member.[29]

The Democratic party may prefer leaders who are "polarizers" because, as the more heterogeneous of the two parties, it needs to maintain its distinctiveness from the Republicans.[30]

The properties of party leadership in the U.S. Senate are aptly characterized by Samuel C. Patterson as *situational* (limited formal powers), *personalized* (shaped by leaders' personal styles), *partisan* (the leaders' special responsibility), *collegial* (inevitable in a body of equals), and *mediating* (contributing to the leaders' role as broker and compromiser). These key features of Senate leadership help to explain why party management of the chamber is extremely difficult and unusually problematic.[31]

The role of congressional party leaders in responding to and shaping public opinion has been little examined, despite its significance. What emerges from a recent study is that rank-and-file members tend to view public opinion polls skeptically and to discount the importance of public opinion; they claim not to be greatly influenced by it. In contrast, leaders are steadily involved in assessing public opinion and they seize any opportunity to manage it. An analysis of health care reform and public opinion in the 103rd Congress by Lawrence Jacobs, Eric Lawrence, Robert Shapiro, and Steven Smith makes this interesting argument concerning the key role played by leaders:

> Motivated by collective party goals and taking advantage of the resources associated with their positions, party leaders have become instrumental to the process by which Congress responds to and directs public opinion on major issues. Even when public opinion is but a marginal concern of most rank-and-file members, leaders' pursuit of party goals can under particular circumstances sway the public to adopt their preferred policies. Leaders' attention to shaping

opinion may explain public opinion's correspondence with congressional decisions, even if its effect on most members is hardly detectable.[32]

The central question concerning congressional party leadership would appear to be this: "What difference does it make whether or not the individual party leaders of the Senate and the House of Representatives are strong or weak, change-oriented or defenders of the status quo, liberal, moderate, or conservative?" The answer, Robert L. Peabody states, is that "it all depends":

> It depends on who the leader is, what vitality and skills he possesses, what position he holds, under what institutional constraints he operates, how cohesive a majority of his party is behind him, his relationship to the President—in short, the impact of a wide range of fluctuating and interacting factors. . . . The outputs of Congress, especially its legislative accomplishments, remain largely systemic. That is to say, a major proportion of its achievements, perhaps as much as 80 per cent, is stimulated from outside—constituents, interest groups, the executive branch. . . . The party leadership's contribution to most of these legislative endeavors is marginal at best; they schedule legislation, work out appropriate floor strategy, and corral a few votes here and there. This is not to say that their contributions have no import. Indeed, the leaders' involvement or noninvolvement may be critical to the success or failure of many important bills that are held or passed by a given Congress. A party leader may be instrumental in securing for a valued colleague a committee assignment or an appointment to a joint committee, which he, in turn, may parlay into national prominence. Party leaders may create or spur on a select committee to important legislative findings. Party leaders' support or opposition to an amendment or bill may mean its life or death. Although leadership contributions may be marginal, most important political choices are made at the margins. . . .[33]

The more individualistic and decentralized legislative assemblies become, the more difficult it is for the party leadership to play an important role. As former Senator James B. Pearson (R., KS) observed, "It's every man for himself. Every Senator is a baron. He has his own principality. Once you adopt that as a means of doing business, it's hard to establish any cohesion." Former Senator Alan Cranston (D., CA) put it this way: "A lot of leadership is just housekeeping now. Occasionally you have an opportunity to provide leadership, but not that often. The weapons to keep people in line just aren't there."[34] Or, to quote David T. Canon, "representatives pursuing individual goals, without a strong party system as an anchor, will continually press toward service-oriented, weak leadership."[35]

The individualistic bent of members is particularly likely to compress opportunities for developing party initiatives in the U.S. Senate, as these observations make clear:

> Party positions usually are not articulated in the Senate, even for major legislation. . . . [Senators] take great pride in their independence, which limits the

pressure leaders can apply to rank-and-file members without antagonizing members. Senate individualism is grounded in formal rules and informal practices. Senate leaders have relatively weak formal powers, limiting the leverage they can gain by extending or withholding favors to members. And because some fellow partisans and members of the opposite party resent official party policy positions, party endorsements often are counterproductive.[36]

## The Whips

Another element in the legislative party structure is the whip organization. A whip is chosen by the party caucus (or floor leader) in each house. Whereas the "organization" is both simple and informal in the state legislatures—usually consisting of a single member—it is fairly elaborate in Congress, especially in the House. Organized in Congress around 1900, the whip system provides a communications network for the party membership. The whip is expected to keep in touch with all members of the party—to find out what, if anything, is troubling them; to discover their voting intentions; to relay information from party leaders; to round them up when a vote is being taken; and in the case of the administration party, to apply pressure on members to support the president's program. The large size of the U.S. House of Representatives necessitates the appointment of numerous assistant whips, who are selected to provide regional representation.

When a crucial vote on a major administration bill is scheduled, the whip's office is likely to go all out to ensure maximum attendance of party members known to be friendly to the bill. Telegrams and telephone calls will be made to members, urging them to be on the floor when the vote is to be taken. Efforts will be undertaken to persuade members at home in their districts to return to Washington. The effectiveness of the whip organization depends ultimately on the quality of the information that it collects concerning the preferences and intentions of members.[37] One assistant whip has noted,

> On some whip checks where we have asked people how they will vote, we ask what their objection is if they indicate opposition to a bill the leadership wants. If you can determine that there are enough members objecting to one feature of the bill and that elimination of that feature might move the bill, it can be a very valuable piece of intelligence.[38]

The main source of intelligence is the poll, which the whip's office conducts if the leadership decides one is required. Randall Ripley's study of the whip system has shown that these polls are remarkably accurate. Their principal value is that they help the leadership decide where to apply pressure. On the basis of poll information, wavering members may be brought back into line and some opponents may even be converted to the leadership's position.[39]

The significance of the whip organizations doubtless varies according to the style and preferences of the leadership. At times the whip organizations (particularly in the Democratic party) "are at the core of party activity" and "the focus of a corporate or collegial leadership in the House." Some speakers and floor leaders, however, have made limited use of the whip organization. In general, those leaders with fewer resources have tended to augment the role of the whip.[40] Where party languishes, of course, whips function indifferently and sporadically.

The growing independence of new members of Congress has made the whip's job of garnering votes for the leadership much more difficult. A veteran Democratic whip observes,

> At one time you'd blow a whistle and say this is what the party wants and the members would line up and say, "Yes sir, yes sir, yes sir." Today they get elected on Monday and they are giving a [floor] speech on Tuesday.[41]

### The Speaker in Congress

The development of the office of Speaker of the U.S. House of Representatives provides good evidence of the growing "institutionalization" of that chamber.[42] In earlier times, it was not uncommon for members who had served only one or two terms in the House to rise to the speakership. Henry Clay, for example, was elected Speaker at the age of thirty-four, a mere eight months after he was first elected to the House. His rapid rise to power was by no means unusual. A typical Speaker during the nineteenth century would have served six years in the House before his election to the speakership; in contrast, during the twentieth century, a Speaker would have served a remarkable twenty-six years prior to election. Speaker Thomas P. "Tip" O'Neill (D., MA) served twenty-three years in the House before his election to the office in 1976. Elected Speaker for the 100th Congress (1987–88), Jim Wright (D., TX) had served twenty-two years in the House and ten years as majority leader during O'Neill's speakership. Chosen Speaker in mid-1989, Thomas S. Foley (D., WA) had served twenty-four years in the House. Newt Gingrich (R., GA) had served sixteen years before becoming Speaker in 1995. By way of contrast, J. Dennis Hastert (R., IL) had served only twelve years before becoming Speaker in 1999; his selection, however, occurred during a particularly turbulent period that saw mutinous House Republicans force Gingrich out of office.[43]

The truth is that the speakership has become a "singular occupational specialty." Many prominent members of Congress doubtlessly aspire to the office and try to get on track to be considered for it. But it is open only rarely and then, ordinarily, only to those members who have amassed considerable seniority.[44]

There have been times in the history of Congress, such as in the first decade of the twentieth century, when the Speaker of the House has appeared virtually as powerful as the president. The Speaker's primacy in House affairs came about not by original design but with time, circumstance, and the contributions of those who held the office. The first Speaker of the House was hardly more than a presiding officer and a moderator of debate; in no way was the office distinguished as a source of independent power. Gradually, however, the Speaker accumulated powers, first that of appointing committee members. More important, with the development of distinct legislative parties, the Speaker became more and more a party leader, a role firmly established during the tenure of Henry Clay, six times elected to the office.

By the turn of the twentieth century, the Speakers' powers were almost complete, their hegemony virtually unchallenged. Their power of recognition was unlimited; they appointed committee members as they saw fit and named committee chairs; the Rules Committee, of which they were the chair, had become their personal domain; they interpreted House rules according to their and their party's interests; they entertained such motions as suited their aims. The architects of this structure of power were many, though Speakers Reed and Cannon are singled out for special acknowledgment. Eventually, Cannon's overweening exercise of power led to the office's undoing. Democrats and dissident Republicans joined forces in 1910, under the leadership of George W. Norris, to shear the prerogatives of Speaker Cannon. "It was 'Uncle Joe' Cannon's economic and social philosophy that first aroused the western Congressmen against his autocracy. The question of power in itself did not greatly excite the average Congressman; but power exercised for reactionary economic and social ends seemed downright pernicious."[45]

The 1910–11 imbroglio ended with the Speakers' powers diminished in three important respects. Their power to appoint members and chairs of standing committees was eliminated, their position on the Rules Committee was taken away, and their power over the recognition of members was cut back. As a result of this upheaval, a number of individuals secured keys to the House leadership: the committee chairs, the Rules Committee, the seniority leaders, and the sectional spokespersons. To a considerable extent, the reforms of the 1970s corrected the extreme fragmentation of power brought about by the revolt against Speaker Cannon. Democratic Speakers, for example, were given the power to nominate Democratic members of the Rules Committee, thus making this formidable committee an arm of the leadership (see Chapter 8), and also the authority to refer bills and resolutions to more than one committee, thus increasing their capacity to coordinate the House's workload.[46] And when the Republicans captured the House in 1994, the first steps of the new leadership were directed toward centralizing power in the Speaker's office. (In a largely symbolic gesture, the new Republican majority also placed an eight-year term limit on the speakership.)

In the view of Richard Bolling, a prominent member of the House for many years, the influence of the Speaker rests largely on personal capabilities:

A strong Speaker is necessary if the House of Representatives is to regain its proper place in government. The only officer of the House mentioned in the Constitution, the Speaker is both coach and quarterback. Under such Speakers as Henry Clay, Thomas Reed, Nicholas Longworth and Sam Rayburn, the House of Representatives received firm leadership. Goals were set, strategy devised and tactics employed. The result was a record of achievement, a sense of purpose and public recognition for the whole House. No institution can obtain these results without such leadership.

Currently, the Speaker lacks the institutional tools of leadership. He must rely upon personal persuasiveness, as Longworth and Rayburn did. The Speaker cannot establish an agenda for the House. He cannot nominate—much less designate—its lieutenants, the committee chairmen. He cannot discipline the unfaithful, and he has little with which to reward the deserving. The Speaker is but titular head of the organization. His power is personal; thus, House leadership is dependent upon the rare fortune of finding an exceptional man.[47]

In a similar vein, Barbara Sinclair writes,

Members of Congress are elected on their own: they build their own organizations, they raise their own money and, to a considerable extent, they manage to cultivate their constituencies to insulate themselves from national tides. Consequently, party leaders cannot influence whether members attain their reelection, power or policy goals to the extent that the pre-1910 party leadership could. To be sure, current leaders do have resources that can be employed to influence their members, but, for most members, most of the time, what the leadership can do for them or to them is not critical for their goal attainment. Current leaders must rely upon persuasion-based strategies; they do not possess the resources necessary to command.[48]

As Congress changes, the character and practices of its leadership change. The position of Speaker has attracted more than its share of problems and frustrations. Former Speaker "Tip" O'Neill saw the leadership problem in this way:

You talk about *discipline!* Where discipline should be is in the Democratic caucus! The very fellas who criticize the fact that we don't have discipline, when they have the opportunity to display discipline in the caucus, they don't display it. All the years I've been here, there's only been three chairmen who've ever been ousted. Listen, when I was Speaker of the Massachusetts legislature, I removed a fella from a committee. I had that power. Here, I don't have that power. Here, he's elected by the caucus, and then he's elected by the House. Here, you got conservatives and moderates and liberals! You can't discipline that! I heard [a congressman] on the radio saying we ought to discipline. There'd be *five* parties here if we tried to do that.[49]

Despite the extraordinary loss of power in the 1910–11 revolution, Speakers remain the most influential officials in Congress. But they now share power once lodged almost exclusively within the office. Although they continue to control the parliamentary machinery much as before, their overall influence is much less than in the era of Cannon, primarily because the institutional context is vastly different today. Members are far more individualistic,[50] sources of leverage for leaders are limited, and the legislative parties are far from united. Hierarchy has been replaced by bargaining. In addition, there is evidence that a strategy by the Speaker of including more junior members in the decision-making process (the "politics of inclusion") increases the likelihood that their level of party support will increase. The effect may be to socialize newer members toward becoming more loyal party members.[51] This strategy is consistent with the changing role of the Speaker. "Even if a Speaker wanted to impose an agenda, he doesn't have the tools to do it," a House member recently observed. "[The Speaker] must consult in a way that gives members the feeling that his agenda is the product of those consultations."[52] Or as Thomas S. Foley (D., WA), former Speaker of the House, put the matter, "You don't get support for these programs by routine arm-twisting. It's mythical to think that members can be forced to do something they don't want to do."[53] In the contemporary House, Joseph Cooper and David W. Brady write, the Speaker and other party leaders "function less as the commanders of a stable party majority and more as brokers trying to assemble particular majorities behind particular bills."[54] In their study of the organizational life of the congressional parties, Thomas H. Little and Samuel C. Patterson conclude that today's party leaders "are reactive consensus-builders more than they are policy-innovators."[55]

While the preceding observations capture the Speaker's position over most of the twentieth century, they do not explain the speakership of Newt Gingrich (R., GA), beginning in 1995. Few leaders have ever moved more rapidly or resolutely to consolidate power in the Speaker's office. Buttressed by a cohesive party (including seventy-three loyal freshmen), Gingrich bypassed seniority in the selection of several committee chairs, named new members to the party's Committee-on-Committees (thus centralizing party control over assignments), directed an overhaul of the committee system that included sharp cuts in committee staffs and the elimination of three standing committees, introduced a variety of changes in House procedures, and moved a "Contract with America" policy agenda through the House in the first 100 days of the session.

The impact of these singular ventures was problematic at the time. Did they reflect a profound, sustainable advance toward centralization of power in the House or merely an interlude of leader-centered party responsibility? The answer was not long in coming. The reelection of President Bill Clinton in 1996 damaged the morale of Republican House members and led to the questioning of Gingrich's leadership by his own party. And when the Republicans lost five House seats in the 1998 election (contrary to expectations for a significant gain), his days were numbered. He was successfully challenged by Robert L. Livingston (R., LA), who, not long after becoming Speaker-designate, dropped his bid for office after admitting to past extramarital affairs. The Republican conference then quickly chose J. Dennis

Hastert, a traditional conservative from Illinois, as Speaker-designate. Hastert's choice reflected the party's disposition to select a leader who was more accommodating and pragmatic than Gingrich in dealing with Democratic members, one more attuned to the need for healing rifts between conservatives and moderates in his own party, and one more likely to settle for traditional institutional arrangements that devolve power in the House.

The truth of the matter is that the House's low toleration for hierarchy and its preferences for committee autonomy, parochialism, and constituency-driven representation sooner or later put it on a collision course with a party leadership bent on aggregating power. It is not surprising that most leaders of both parties end up viewing the House as intractable.

## The Speaker in the State Legislature

In the typical state government the Speaker's powers are very great, second only to those of the governor. Although state legislatures often have emulated congressional organization and style, there has been no counterpart in the states to the 1910 revolution in the U.S. House of Representatives. Ties between the Speaker and the committee system, wrenched in the national House during the revolt against Cannonism, are firm in the states—thus helping to centralize decision making. For example, in all but a handful of states the Speaker continues to be responsible for committee appointments, naming the members of standing committees as well as members of special, select, and conference committees. The Speaker's influence in the committee structure is reinforced through the power to name committee chairs in a great many states. Massachusetts, for example, is a state in which the Speaker exerts significant influence on legislative decisions. A study by David Ray finds that the party leadership is clearly the most important source of voting cues for House members in this state. Comments by two representatives offer insight into the leader-member relationship:

> The Speaker holds all the power. He hands out the chairmanships, the office space, and everything else that everyone wants and needs. If you join the Tank early, you move up fast. That's how the game is played.

> Before a certain vote, the leadership will send someone around to all of the reps, and try to get your vote. Going against the leadership makes everything a lot more difficult. Believe me, guys line up outside the Speaker's door to jump in the Tank. But they don't even bother asking for my vote any more.[56]

Peverill Squire describes the power of the Speaker in the lower house of New York:

> The speaker in the New York Assembly is the most powerful member of the assembly for many reasons: he appoints all committees and names their chairmen, controls all legislative floor activity, and allocates office space, committee

budgets, and other resources. . . . The power to appoint all committees and party leaders allows the speaker to determine members' progression to positions of influence.[57]

The Speaker is frequently a member of the committee on rules—which often plays a critical role near the end of the session in screening proposals—and may be an ex officio member of all committees. Ordinarily, Speakers do not take an active part in committee deliberations, though their presence may be felt. When they do appear at committee meetings, it may be a good sign that the administration is unusually interested in a bill up for consideration.

The Speaker is the principal leader and grand strategist of the majority party in the lower house. Both the majority- and minority-party caucuses nominate candidates for the office (as well as for other positions), but ordinarily this is only a perfunctory gesture by the minority since it will not have the votes to elect its candidate. Following the floor vote, the majority's candidate is declared Speaker, the minority moves to make it unanimous, and the minority's candidate for Speaker becomes that party's floor leader—such is the public record of Speaker selection in the typical legislature. But politics is rarely so bland. This account tells too little about how the Speaker in fact is chosen and, moreover, ignores the occasions when the minority party enters the fray and is able to determine the outcome.

When the same party controls both administration and house, the Speaker is often the governor's choice. In theory the house is free to choose its leadership as it pleases; in practice it often defers to the wishes of the governor. Obviously, there are states where executive "interference" would be resented, and there are governors who are reluctant to risk a quarrel with legislators over a charge of aggrandizement. Nevertheless, if governors hope to play a key role in fashioning the legislative program and if conditions are propitious for such action, they are unlikely to resist an opportunity to offer their own candidate for presiding officer. To some extent at least, this is a matter of self-defense: On the one hand, a hostile Speaker has a vast array of powers that can be used to hamstring the administration's legislative program. A friendly Speaker, on the other hand, can do much to facilitate passage of the governor's bills.

The selection of the leadership sometimes opens up opportunities for the minority party to gain influence. Although there is only one case in the history of Congress in which a Speaker was chosen by a combination of majority and minority votes (the 4th Congress in 1795), a number of states can point to such events—among them Alaska, California, Connecticut, Florida, Illinois, Massachusetts, New Mexico, New York, North Carolina, Oklahoma, Tennessee, and Vermont. In 1989, for example, dissident Democrats in the Connecticut House, in league with minority Republicans, ousted a liberal Democratic Speaker and replaced him with a more conservative one. Also in

1989, a similar combination toppled the long-time Democratic Speaker of the North Carolina House; in return for the Republicans' support, the new Democratic Speaker awarded the minority party better offices, bigger staffs, and nearly half of all subcommittee chairmanships. And in California in 1995, Democratic Speaker Willie Brown resigned the speakership, which he had held since 1980, and engineered the election of a lame-duck Republican who won without getting a single vote from her own party; she became the first woman Speaker in California history, while Brown ran for mayor of San Francisco. The truth is that party, faction, and coalition machinations are typically more dramatic in state legislatures than in Congress. They rest on a system of barter and inducements that enhance the influence of the minority party. Coalition politics, in fact, appears to be on the rise.[58]

The politics of leadership selection in state legislatures often involves the committee system. Committee chairmanships and assignments to major committees are the dominant currency in the exchange between aspiring candidates for the speakership and fellow members of the caucus. A former West Virginia legislator comments on the leadership selection process in his state: "A lot of it depends on who promises what to whom. The supporters of one candidate for speaker offered me a committee chairmanship and a Finance Committee slot if only I would vote for their guy."[59]

The selection of committee chairs is also a key power of leaders in the New York legislature:

> While there is very little incentive for a lawmaker to challenge Albany's leadership culture, going along with it brings real rewards. The Assembly speaker and Senate majority leader hand out committee chairs and other leadership posts at their pleasure, and these jobs mean extra pay for members. The two chambers have also seen fit to give their leaders full control over the office budgets of individual legislators—an extraordinary power virtually unheard of in other legislatures. Favorites of the leaders can count on plenty of money for hiring staff, purchasing computers, and so forth.[60]

As in Congress, Speakers in state legislatures engage only rarely in floor debate. On those few occasions when they do take the floor, it is usually to defend an administrative action or to support a major administration bill. Their floor appearance is not a casual decision. By not "going to the well too often" they can command greater attention for their views and preserve to some degree the "principle" that the Speaker serves the pleasure of the whole House and is not merely the leader of the majority party.

In summary, the Speakers' influence in the states is compounded of numerous elements. They are the guardian of party fortunes and policies. Moreover, they are charged with many official duties, nearly all of which hold implications for the party interest. Thus, typically they appoint the members of standing, special, and conference committees; they chair the rules committee; they refer bills to committee; they preside over house sessions, decide points of order, recognize members, and put questions to a vote; they have the power to assist a member with a pet bill or to sandbag it; they can ease the way for new members or ignore them; they can advance the legislative careers of members or throw up roadblocks before them. In some states, such as California, the Speaker is a major fund-raiser for his or her party's legislative candidates.[61] All these prerogatives contribute to a network of influence. And finally, if Speakers have the strong support of the governor, if they meet with him or her regularly and are privy to administration plans and secrets, new measures of power and influence come their way. Of all the legislative posts, the one most sought after is the speakership.[62]

### Change in Party Leadership

The selection of legislative leaders has great significance for the distribution of power and the representation of interests in legislatures. When a change occurs in a leadership position, some members (and the constellation of interests they represent) gain influence in the system while others lose ground. About the same thing may be said for public policy: A change in leadership may improve the prospects for the passage of some legislation and dim the prospects for the passage of other legislation. Although a concern for continuity probably affects all new legislative leaders, they nevertheless have significant opportunities to influence the careers of other members and the course of public policy. It is thus surprising that political scientists have given so little systematic attention to change in the composition of legislative party elites.

A conspicuous exception to this observation is a study by Robert Peabody of change in party leadership in Congress between 1955 and 1974.[63] A change in party leadership may result from *interparty turnover* (that is, the minority, through an election, displaces the majority), *intraparty change* (new leaders supplant old leaders in the same party), or *institutional reform* (powers of an existing office are altered or a new position is created). As would be expected, most leaders continue in their posts from Congress to Congress. When changes occur, the most common method is that of intraparty change.

Intraparty change, according to Peabody, may take any of five forms: (1) routine advancement, (2) appointment or emergence of a consensus choice, (3) open competition, (4) challenge to the heir apparent, and (5) revolt or its aftermath. Routine advancement occurs when the ranking and "logical" successor moves into a vacated position, as in the traditional practice of elevating the majority leader to fill a vacancy in the office of Speaker. When there is no pattern of succession (for example, in the appointment of whips), contests may be avoided through the emergence of a consensus choice. Open competition occurs in still other cases in which a vacancy has appeared and a succession pattern has not yet developed. Under the fourth type of intra-party change, the heir apparent to an office may be challenged by dissident elements within the party. Finally, the most intense intraparty struggles occur when no vacancy exists, opposition is present, and the incumbent is determined to retain the office.

Members weigh numerous factors in choosing leaders. Some believe it is essential to select a party spokesperson who can communicate effectively with the public and the media; for them "outside" politics is as important as "inside" politics. Others may prefer an aggressive partisan, a skillful coalition-builder, a conciliator, a savvy legislative manager, a reformer, or an energetic campaigner and fund-raiser for members. They want someone they can trust and, usually, someone who promises a collegial leadership style. "There's no one factor," Senate majority leader George J. Mitchell (D., ME) observed shortly before leaving office in 1994. "I think some of it is personal, some of it is regional, some of it is philosophical, some of it is none of the above." "It's all of those things," said Robert C. Byrd (D., WV), Senate leader from 1977 to 1987. "Some senators will vote for you because they play tennis with you. I didn't play tennis; I didn't pick up any votes on the sports side. . . . I had some tell me when I was running for leader that they'd like to be for me, wished they could be for me, but their wives were friends and went out shopping together, got together on Saturday nights. . . . Some would tell me yes, some would tell me no, and some wouldn't tell me whether they'd vote for me. Those who wouldn't tell me, I always counted them on the other side."[64]

### Conditions for Party Leadership

At times it appears as if the only thing that some congressional Democrats have in common with other congressional Democrats (and some congressional Republicans with other congressional Republicans) is the same language.[65] Each congressional party is a bundle of interests, orientations, and ideologies. On certain kinds of issues party lines are likely to bend or break, and bipartisan coalitions perform as if they had been empowered as the majority. As a result of intraparty cleavages and the resultant decentralization of power in Congress, party leaders rarely find it an easy matter to assemble their troops behind them when major legislation is at stake.

Internal divisions within the parties invariably come to the fore in the budget process. Money questions really matter. For the Republicans, passing a budget resolution that will satisfy the conservative, tax-cutting wing as well as the party's moderates and pragmatists tests the skills of the leadership to the utmost. To quote Richard May, the former Budget Committee chief of staff under chairman John R. Kasich (R., OH), "If you satisfy the concerns of the CATs (Conservative Action Team), you create problems with the

Tuesday Group (Republican moderates). And every time you satisfy the Tuesday lunch bunch, you create problems with the CATs."[66]

Whether a legislative party is an empty promise or a cohesive unit depends on a number of conditions. Research by Lewis Froman and Randall Ripley helps to identify the conditions under which party leadership is likely to be relatively strong or relatively weak, and party members relatively responsive or relatively indifferent to the call of party. Their study of the Democratic leadership in the House of Representatives describes six conditions that bear on the success of party leaders: the commitment, knowledge, and activity of the leadership; the nature of the issue (procedural or substantive); the visibility of the issue; the visibility of the action; the existence of constituency pressures; and the activity of state delegations. In general, the prospects that the leadership will prevail are best when the principal leaders are active and in agreement, when the issue is seen as procedural rather than substantive, when the visibility of the issue and of the action to be taken is low, when constituency opposition is slight, and when the state delegations are not involved in bargaining for specific provisions. As a rule, members prefer to support their party, and they will do so if they believe that their careers will not be jeopardized.[67] The less visible the issue and the action to be taken on it, the easier it is for members to go along with the leadership. The stern test of leadership comes when the party's interest appears to be incompatible with the constituency interests of members—and the matter at stake is highly visible to press and public.[68]

The House Democratic leadership, Barbara Sinclair wrote in the late 1980s, was expected to perform two key functions: to assemble winning coalitions on major bills and to promote harmony within the party. Neither was easy to accomplish because of the independence of members and the relatively limited powers of the leadership. In this constrained environment, the leadership pursued three strategies to augment its influence. First, leaders and their aides gave considerable time and attention to providing services to members—helping them, for example, to secure projects for their districts or desirable committee assignments. Second, leaders sought to structure the choices of members—for example, by ensuring that the key roll-call vote would occur on a procedural rather than a substantive question and thus increasing the likelihood of a proleadership vote. And third, the leadership attempted to involve as many Democrats as possible—the strategy of inclusion—in splicing together winning coalitions. Widespread participation, the argument runs, increases the prospects for support of leadership positions. In the individualistic Senate, the leaders' role in providing services and favors is especially important since their powers are so limited and the powers of the rank-and-file members are so extensive.[69] All this suggests that the natural limits of party in Congress make it imperative that party leaders be persons of singular imagination and determination.[70]

# PARTY INFLUENCE ON LEGISLATION

Popular political thought seldom has taken account of the virtues of party or of the potential of party government. The vices of party, in contrast, are persistently deplored; it is not too much to say that American parties have grown up in an atmosphere of general hostility.[71] Independence from party, in the public mind, appears often to be the mark of a good person, the justifiable claim of a good legislator. Yet there is little evidence to suggest that the obloquy that hangs over the party system is the result of a careful assessment of the workings of political parties or of their contributions to representative government. One point of departure in assaying the importance of parties is to evaluate their role and potential in the legislative process.

## Party Voting in Congress

In the ritual and practices of Congress, as of nearly all American legislatures, the party can perform a variety of functions. In varying degrees and with varying success, the parties organize the legislature, select the leadership, shape the ground rules for negotiation and decision making, rationalize the conduct of legislative business, monitor the activities of the executive branch, and assist in familiarizing the public with the work of government. The parties' tasks in representative government are formidable and their functions indispensable.

One phase of the party role in the legislative process is especially vague: the direct contribution of the party in shaping legislation. The parliamentary machinery is, of course, controlled by majority-party members. But to what extent does legislation bear the imprint of party qua party, to what extent is it simply the product of transient nonparty majorities or of persistent coalitions? Do the parties present genuine policy alternatives in Congress—that is, do the parties differ? Can the voting behavior of a Republican representative be distinguished from that of a Democratic representative, the voting behavior of a Republican senator from that of a Democratic senator? How much party responsibility for a legislative program do we want? How much do we have? If party performance falls short, is it reasonable to expect otherwise—given the milieu in which parties function?

Comprehensive answers to these questions are hard to develop, even though an impressive number of studies of legislative parties have been published in the last several decades.[72] This analysis is mainly concerned with the relationship between party and public policy.

There are two principal views of the raison d'être of political parties. The first argues that parties have ideological roots and that principle undergirds their organization. In the classic definition of Edmund Burke, "Party is a body of men united, for promulgating by their joint endeavors the national interest, upon some particular principle in which they are all agreed."[73] The other view finds party preoccupation with winning elections as the fundamental basis of organization. James Bryce put it this way:

> [Legislation] is not one of the chief aims of party, and many important measures have no party character. [The] chief purpose [of political parties] is to capture, and hold when captured, the machinery, legislative and administrative, of the legal government established by the constitution.[74]

Conflicting claims such as those of Burke and Bryce have often been investigated. The pioneering study traces to A. Lawrence Lowell, who in 1901 published *The Influence of Party upon Legislation in England and America.*[75] Lowell assumed that the main test of party influence lay in the behavior of party members on roll-call votes. He defined a "party vote" as one in which 90 percent of the voting membership of one party was opposed to 90 percent of the voting membership of the other party. His analysis disclosed that party rivalry of this order was much less in evidence in Congress than in the British House of Commons in the nineteenth century. Legislative proposals before Congress were not frequently passed or lost in party votes. The "influence" of party on legislation in the state legislatures was even less than in Congress. Party affiliation, it was plain to Lowell, did not often affect the deliberations of American legislators, and party lines were not often drawn.

Party voting in Congress was reexamined by Julius Turner in 1951. Using Lowell's "90 percent versus 90 percent" test, he found that in various congressional sessions between 1921 and 1948 about 17 percent of the roll-call votes in the House were party votes.[76] An updating of this study by Edward Schneier found that in various House sessions during the period 1950 to 1967, between 2 percent and 8 percent of all roll-call votes were party votes. How these percentages compare with those in the British House of Commons—the model invoked in the argument for disciplined, responsible parties—is shown in Table 9.1. The differences are obviously substantial.[77]

Another measure of party voting in Congress is presented in Table 9.2. In this analysis the party-vote definition is relaxed from "90 percent versus 90 percent" to "majority versus majority." Plainly, party voting is not as common in the modern era as in the nineteenth century. During the Nixon, Ford, and Carter administrations about 40 percent of all recorded votes had party majorities in opposition. Conflict between the parties became more common during the Reagan, Bush, and Clinton administrations. Currently, about half of all recorded votes show a majority of one party in opposition to a majority of the other party; partisan conflict is usually greater in the House than in the Senate. It is worth noting that this level of interparty cleavage, or partisanship, is not particularly impressive since it is not based on a high level of party cohesion. The fact of the matter is that the

**TABLE 9.1** Party unity as reflected in proportion of party votes cast in selected twentieth-century legislative sessions, Great Britain and the United States

| Britain, Commons | | United States, House | |
| --- | --- | --- | --- |
| Year | % Party Votes | Year | % Party Votes |
| 1924–25 | 94.4 | 1921 | 28.6 |
| 1926 | 94.8 | 1928 | 7.1 |
| 1927 | 96.4 | 1930–31 | 31.0 |
| 1928 | 93.6 | 1933 | 22.5 |
| | | 1937 | 11.8 |
| | | 1944 | 10.7 |
| | | 1945 | 17.5 |
| | | 1946 | 10.5 |
| | | 1947 | 15.1 |
| | | 1948 | 16.4 |
| | | 1950 | 6.4 |
| | | 1953 | 7.0 |
| | | 1959 | 8.0 |
| | | 1963 | 7.6 |
| | | 1964 | 6.2 |
| | | 1965 | 2.8 |
| | | 1966 | 1.6 |
| | | 1967 | 3.3 |

SOURCE: Julius Turner, *Party and Constituency: Pressures on Congress* (Baltimore: Johns Hopkins University Press, 1951), p. 24. Data for years since 1950 appear in the revised edition (Baltimore: Johns Hopkins University Press, 1970), prepared by Edward V. Schneier, Jr. (p. 17).

congressional parties have never been especially cohesive, at least not for long, and members of both parties regularly find reasons to ignore party leaders and programs.[78]

The extent of party voting in Congress varies from one period to another and, sometimes, even from one Congress to the next. What factors appear to promote interparty conflict? Examining a recent thirty-five-year period, Samuel C. Patterson and Gregory A. Caldeira found that party voting in the House increases significantly when external party conflict is high—in particular, during periods when sharp differences exist between the national parties on central issues of the economy, labor-management questions, and the distribution of wealth. Party voting also increases when the presidency and House are controlled by the same party. In the Senate, where party voting is usually less common, presidential leadership is the key factor; specifically, when the Senate majority is of the same party as the president, party voting increases. Surprisingly, in view of conventional interpretations, the election of many new members does not lead to markedly greater increases in partisan cleavages.[79]

**TABLE 9.2    Party voting in selected Congresses, 1861–1998**

| | Party Votes: Majority versus Majority (Shown as Percentage of All Roll-Call Votes) | |
| Congresses | House of Representatives | Senate |
| --- | --- | --- |
| 37th–41st (1861–71) | 74 | |
| 57th–61st (1901–11) | 74 | |
| 72nd–76th (1931–41) | 65 | |
| 93rd (1973) | 42 | 40 |
| (1974) | 29 | 44 |
| 95th (1977) | 42 | 42 |
| (1978) | 33 | 45 |
| 97th (1981) | 37 | 48 |
| (1982) | 36 | 43 |
| 98th (1983) | 56 | 44 |
| (1984) | 47 | 40 |
| 99th (1985) | 61 | 50 |
| (1986) | 57 | 52 |
| 100th (1987) | 64 | 41 |
| (1988) | 47 | 42 |
| 101st (1989) | 55 | 35 |
| (1990) | 49 | 54 |
| 102nd (1991) | 55 | 49 |
| (1992) | 64 | 53 |
| 103rd (1993) | 65 | 67 |
| (1994) | 62 | 52 |
| 104th (1995) | 73 | 69 |
| (1996) | 56 | 62 |
| 105th (1997) | 50 | 50 |
| (1998) | 56 | 56 |

SOURCE: The data for the House of Representatives during the periods 1861–71, 1901–11, and 1931–41 are from Jerome M. Clubb and Santa A. Traugott, "Partisan Cleavage and Cohesion in the House of Representatives, 1861–1974," *Journal of Interdisciplinary History,* VII (Winter 1977), 382–83. The party-vote percentages for the modern period (93rd through 103rd Congresses), from the Nixon administration to the Clinton administration, are drawn from *Congressional Quarterly Weekly Report,* December 31, 1994, p. 3658, and January 9, 1999, p. 97.

The influence of party in congressional committees has been investigated by Daniel S. Ward. His study discloses that, on the whole, parties are stronger in committee than on the floor. In some House committees, such as Education and Labor (now Education and the Workforce) and Interior (now Resources), interparty conflict is particularly high—with majorities arrayed against each other on perhaps 80 to 90 percent of all roll calls. Party voting in the Armed Services Committee, by contrast, ordinarily occurs on less than 20 percent of roll calls. The Ways and Means Committee is distinguished by a moderate amount of partisanship. Party unity and party victories also vary across committee lines.[80]

David W. Rohde finds that the level of partisanship in Congress is a product of four factors. The most important is *electoral*. When the members of one party have similar constituency preferences and they differ from those of the other party, policy partisanship increases. For example, as southern Democratic constituencies have become more liberalized—largely because of growing black political participation following passage of the Voting Rights Act of 1965—differences between northern and southern members have declined. Democratic party unity has become easier to achieve—at least on some issues—than in the past. *Institutional differences* between the House and Senate also have a bearing on partisanship. Party voting is typically higher in the House than in the Senate for a number of reasons, a particularly important one being that House leaders have substantially more formal powers than Senate leaders. A cohesive majority party, bolstered by a determined leadership, can more easily control decisions in the House than in the Senate, where power is more equally apportioned between the parties and where institutional devices, such as unlimited debate, enhance the power of the minority party. The level of partisanship is also affected by *personal factors*—in particular, the personalities, styles, and ideological orientations of party leaders. Some are simply more partisan and ideological than others. Finally, the *legislative agenda* at any one time may heighten or diminish partisanship.[81]

The member's behavior in Congress, many studies have shown, is significantly influenced by factors external to the institution. Melissa P. Collie has assembled interesting evidence on House members that suggests that growing individualism in the electoral arena (manifested in persistent incumbency advantage) has been accompanied by growing individualism in the institutional arena (manifested in a long-term decrease in party voting). "When candidates tend to win on their own outside the legislature," Collie writes, "they tend to act on their own inside the legislature. In short, the electoral politics of the candidate as independent operator appear to translate into the institutional politics of the legislator as autonomous actor."[82] Party thus has only a partial claim on the attention and voting behavior of the individual member.

Whatever the level of partisanship in Congress, important issues are frequently at stake when party lines form. In general, Democrats have been much more likely than Republicans to vote for federal programs to assist agriculture, expanded health and welfare programs, legislation advantageous to labor and low-income groups, civil rights,[83] government regulation of business, and reductions in the defense budget and military aid. Typically, Democrats have been more inclined to call for government action to remedy domestic problems or to launch new projects (for example, some form of aid to education or expanded medical care) than have Republicans. Where a choice is posed between government involvement or private action, a larger or smaller federal role, party lines have usually formed rapidly, with the

Republicans moving strongly to the defense of private means and a limited federal role.

A good test of party differences is in the voting behavior of senators on legislative issues of concern to one of the best-known liberal organizations, the Americans for Democratic Action (ADA).[84] Figure 9.1 shows the behavior of members on certain issues in the 105th Congress (Senate). Senators voting in agreement with the ADA, for example, would have supported such proposals as these: major restrictions and penalties on the tobacco industry, provision for counting postsecondary or vocational education toward work requirements for welfare parents, requirements that gun dealers sell trigger locks with each handgun, provisions to outlaw government purchases of products made by child labor, funding for expenses related to the preparation of a nuclear test ban treaty, campaign finance reforms that would ban "soft money," restrictions on employers' hiring of foreign workers, and an increase in the minimum wage.

In turn, members would have opposed "paycheck protection" (a bill to require labor organizations to obtain voluntary authorization from members before using their dues to fund political activities), the elimination of a program that reserves a portion of federal construction funds for disadvantaged business enterprises, modification of social security to provide for personal retirement accounts, NATO expansion, the development of a national missile defense shield, caps on punitive awards against businesses in product liability cases, curbs on labor union organizing, and an override of President Clinton's veto of a bill to ban certain late-term abortion procedures.

The data of Figure 9.1 and Figure 9.2 (House of Representatives) show clearly that liberal legislation produces sharp conflicts and meaningful differences between the congressional parties.

For most of the last half century, persistent divisions within the Democratic congressional party led to the generalization that northern Democrats were the liberals of the party and southern Democrats the conservatives. Although some differences remain between the party's wings, that distinction is less useful today. Increasingly, southern Democrats (a dwindling number) now join their northern colleagues on a variety of issues that used to divide them (such as those noted above). In truth, scattering within Republican ranks is now more pronounced than in the Democratic party. On the whole, eastern Republicans in both houses are much less conservative than the rest of their party. In 1998, for example, eastern Republicans in the House were five times as likely as southern Republicans to support legislation favored by the ADA. Republican senators such as James Jeffords, John Chafee, Susan Collins, Olympia Snowe, and Arlen Specter are about as likely to be aligned with Democrats on certain types of liberal legislation as they are with members of their own party, such as Trent Lott and Jesse Helms.

Nevertheless, when all the exceptions are listed, totaled, and explained, major differences still remain between the parties. Over the years a majority

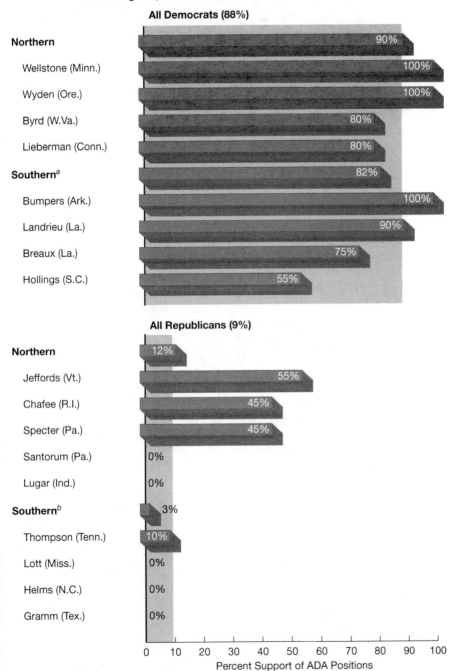

**FIGURE 9.1** Democratic and Republican support of positions held by the Americans for Democratic Action, individual members and regional party groupings, 105th Congress, 2nd Session, U.S. Senate

All Democrats (88%)

| | |
|---|---|
| Northern | 90% |
| Wellstone (Minn.) | 100% |
| Wyden (Ore.) | 100% |
| Byrd (W.Va.) | 80% |
| Lieberman (Conn.) | 80% |
| Southern[a] | 82% |
| Bumpers (Ark.) | 100% |
| Landrieu (La.) | 90% |
| Breaux (La.) | 75% |
| Hollings (S.C.) | 55% |

All Republicans (9%)

| | |
|---|---|
| Northern | 12% |
| Jeffords (Vt.) | 55% |
| Chafee (R.I.) | 45% |
| Specter (Pa.) | 45% |
| Santorum (Pa.) | 0% |
| Lugar (Ind.) | 0% |
| Southern[b] | 3% |
| Thompson (Tenn.) | 10% |
| Lott (Miss.) | 0% |
| Helms (N.C.) | 0% |
| Gramm (Tex.) | 0% |

Percent Support of ADA Positions

[a]Arkansas, Florida, Georgia, Kentucky, Louisiana, South Carolina, and Virginia.
[b]Alabama, Arkansas, Florida, Georgia, Kentucky, Mississippi, North Carolina, Oklahoma, South Carolina, Tennessee, Texas, and Virginia.
SOURCE: Calculated from voting data in *ADA Today,* January 1999, pp. 3–5.

FIGURE 9.2    Democratic and Republican support of positions held by the Americans for Democratic Action, regional party groupings, 105th Congress, 2nd Session, U.S. House of Representatives

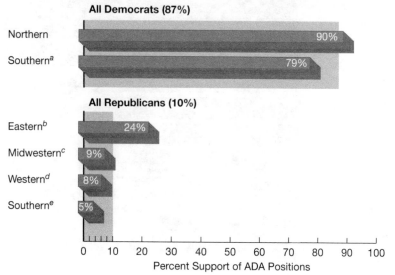

[a]Alabama, Arkansas, Florida, Georgia, Kentucky, Louisiana, Mississippi, North Carolina, South Carolina, Tennessee, Texas, and Virginia.
[b]Connecticut, Delaware, Maryland, New Hampshire, New Jersey, New York, and Pennsylvania.
[c]Illinois, Indiana, Iowa, Kansas, Michigan, Minnesota, Missouri, Nebraska, Ohio, and Wisconsin.
[d]Alaska, Arizona, California, Colorado, Idaho, Montana, Nevada, New Mexico, Oregon, South Dakota, Utah, Washington, and Wyoming.
[e]Alabama, Arkansas, Florida, Georgia, Kentucky, Louisiana, Mississippi, North Carolina, Oklahoma, South Carolina, Tennessee, Texas, and Virginia.
SOURCE: Calculated from voting data in *ADA Today,* January 1999, pp. 6–15.

of the Democratic party has favored a liberal course for the federal government on labor, defense, civil rights, and social legislation, whereas a majority of the Republican party has posed a conservative alternative.[85] The Republican choice has varied with circumstances—a smaller expenditure for the same program, a project of more modest proportions, a heightened emphasis on national defense, a reaffirmation of traditional values and arrangements, state rather than federal responsibility, and defense of the rights of property as against those of labor unions and workers.[86]

Figure 9.3 offers a somewhat different way of depicting party behavior in Congress. Members are positioned on the scattergram according to the level of their support of two distinctively ideological groups in the 105th Congress (2nd session)—the ADA and the American Conservative Union (ACU). The organizations have virtually nothing in common, and it is readily

FIGURE 9.3    Support for positions held by the Americans for Democratic Action (ADA) and by the American Conservative Union (ACU), by each senator, in percentages, 105th Congress, 2nd Session

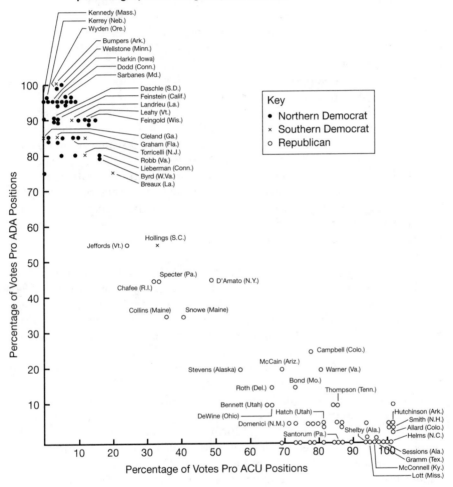

SOURCE: Calculated from voting data in *ADA Today*, January 1999, pp. 3–5, and http://www.conservative.org/98 ratings.

apparent that the issues and policies to which they are attentive resonate for the parties. The vast majority of Democratic senators score very high on ADA ratings, while Republican senators rank nearly as high on ACU ratings.

The ACU typically has a wide range of policy proposals on its agenda. Members of Congress with high ACU ratings in 1998, for example, voted to oppose the use of federal funds for national testing of students, statehood for

Puerto Rico, export of satellites to China, campaign finance reform, partial birth abortions, affirmative action, assignments of U.S. military to United Nations forces, funding for the National Endowment for the Arts, funding for the Legal Services Corporation, U.S. debt payments to the United Nations, funding for U.S. ground troop deployment in Bosnia, trigger lock requirements for guns, a minimum wage increase, a tobacco tax increase, and the transportation of minors across state lines for abortions. On the other hand, they voted to support restrictive legislation concerning labor organizing, tax cuts, tax limitation and religious freedom amendments (prayer in the public schools), abolition of the tax code, school vouchers, education savings accounts, and the implementation of a national missile defense shield.

Whatever else may be said about the ADA/ACU scattergram, it is impossible to ponder it and conclude that the parties are as alike as two peas in a pod. The parties' positions, in fact, reflect their traditional ideological moorings. Mavericks, of course, pop out of the party circle, particularly on the Republican side of the aisle, where eastern members frequently link up with the Democrats (as in the impeachment trial in 1999, when Senators Jeffords, Chafee, Specter, Collins, and Snowe all voted to acquit President Clinton).

Another way to view the linkage between party and policy is to examine the level of federal social welfare expenditures over time. Between 1949 and 1977, social welfare expenditures increased more during Republican administrations than during Democratic ones. Among the reasons advanced for this counterintuitive finding were the existence of rising unemployment during Republican administrations, the adoption of countercyclical programs to combat unemployment by Democratic Congresses, the maturation of Democratic social programs during Republican administrations (thus increasing expenditures), and efforts by Democratically controlled Congresses to increase (or bid up) benefits beyond those requested by a Republican president. Increased social spending during Democratic administrations depended mainly on the election of sufficient numbers of nonsouthern Democrats. These patterns lead to the broad and provocative conclusion that expansions of the welfare state have been most likely to occur under competitive conditions, distinguished in particular by divided party control of the presidency and Congress.[87]

### Party Fragmentation and Interparty Coalitions in Congress

The burden of the previous discussion has been to mark the policy positions that differentiate the parties in Congress. It should be clear by now that the congressional parties are by no means Tweedledum and Tweedledee, that despite the indifferent success that characterizes some party efforts, there are still important policy distinctions between the two groups.[88] No claim has been made, of course, that party performance in Congress is either "disciplined" or "responsible," in the usual sense of these words; indeed, it is quite obvious that antithetical views are present within each party.[89] The main paths along which Congress moves are not always chosen by the majority party or by a majority of the majority party, as the data of Table 9.3, depicting the level of success of the conservative coalition from 1968 to 1998, make clear.[90] Two broad conclusions can be drawn from the data. The first is that this biparty coalition has, until recently, often emerged in floor voting. During the 1960s and 1970s the coalition appeared on about one-fourth of all roll-call votes. Second, and more important, the coalition has had significant successes. In truth, over long periods of time during the last half century, this conservative bloc has been the effective majority in Congress. Between 1981 and 1986, the most productive years of the Reagan administration, the coalition appeared on about one-fifth or one-sixth of all votes and won more than 85 percent of the time. Appearing on 21 percent of the votes in 1981, the coalition won a spectacular 95 percent of the time in the Senate and 88 percent of the time in the House. Clearly, the coalition played a dominant role in the "Reagan Revolution."[91] During the late 1990s, the coalition appeared on about 10 percent of all recorded votes and won more than 95 percent of the time. On the whole, as would be expected, Republican presidents generally have had a much higher level of agreement with the policy positions of the conservative coalition than Democratic presidents.[92]

Since its emergence in the late 1930s, the conservative coalition's record has been marked by considerable success. Every president and every congressional party leader have been affected by its preferences and its power. Today, however, its vitality is more problematic than at any time in the last half century. In the first place, the coalition's composition is changing, as voters throughout the South turn to the Republican party in congressional elections (see Table 9.4). In 1955, 92 percent of all House seats and 100 percent of all Senate seats in southern states were held by Democrats. By 1985, the numbers had fallen to 64 percent in the House and 54 percent in the Senate. And by the 106th Congress (1999–2000) Democrats had become a sharply weakened minority party in the South, holding only 41 percent of the House seats and 31 percent of the Senate seats. The basic explanation for this change is that large numbers of conservative white Democratic voters switched parties, and their defections led to a sharp loss of Democratic seats, including a number held by conservative incumbents. The net result is that white Democratic members of Congress are numerically less important to the conservative coalition than previously, and their votes are less important in creating conservative majorities.

Another dramatic, closely related change that has affected the conservative coalition has been the "northernization" of southern Democratic politics. Southern Democrats have become more likely to vote with their northern party colleagues, particularly on economic issues, as their constituencies have become more similar. Urbanization and the mobilization of

**TABLE 9.3    Successes of the conservative coalition, 1968–98**

| Year | Percentage of Coalition Recorded Votes* | Percentage of Coalition Victories† | | |
|------|------|------|------|------|
| | | Total | Senate | House |
| 1998 | 6 | 96 | 100 | 95 |
| 1997 | 9 | 98 | 92 | 100 |
| 1996 | 12 | 99 | 97 | 100 |
| 1995 | 11 | 98 | 95 | 100 |
| 1994 | 8 | 82 | 72 | 92 |
| 1993 | 9 | 94 | 90 | 98 |
| 1992 | 12 | 88 | 88 | 88 |
| 1991 | 11 | 91 | 95 | 86 |
| 1990 | 11 | 82 | 95 | 74 |
| 1989 | 11 | 87 | 95 | 80 |
| 1988 | 9 | 89 | 97 | 82 |
| 1987 | 8 | 93 | 100 | 88 |
| 1986 | 16 | 87 | 93 | 78 |
| 1985 | 14 | 89 | 93 | 84 |
| 1984 | 16 | 83 | 94 | 75 |
| 1983 | 15 | 77 | 89 | 71 |
| 1982 | 18 | 85 | 90 | 78 |
| 1981 | 21 | 92 | 95 | 88 |
| 1980 | 18 | 72 | 75 | 67 |
| 1979 | 20 | 70 | 65 | 73 |
| 1978 | 21 | 52 | 46 | 57 |
| 1977 | 26 | 68 | 74 | 60 |
| 1976 | 24 | 58 | 58 | 59 |
| 1975 | 28 | 50 | 48 | 52 |
| 1974 | 24 | 59 | 54 | 67 |
| 1973 | 23 | 61 | 54 | 67 |
| 1972 | 27 | 69 | 63 | 79 |
| 1971 | 30 | 83 | 86 | 79 |
| 1970 | 22 | 66 | 64 | 70 |
| 1969 | 27 | 68 | 67 | 71 |
| 1968 | 24 | 73 | 80 | 63 |

*A coalition recorded vote is defined as any recorded vote in which a majority of voting southern Democrats and a majority of voting Republicans are opposed to a majority of voting northern Democrats. The southern wing of the Democratic party is defined as those legislators from Alabama, Arkansas, Florida, Georgia, Kentucky, Louisiana, Mississippi, North Carolina, Oklahoma, South Carolina, Tennessee, Texas, and Virginia. Members from all other states are considered "northern."
†Defined as the number of recorded vote victories achieved by the coalition when there are divisions between the coalition and northern Democrats.

SOURCE: *Congressional Quarterly Weekly Report,* January 15, 1983, p. 102; November 15, 1986, p. 2908; January 16, 1988, p. 110; December 30, 1989, p. 3551; December 22, 1990, p. 4192; December 28, 1991, p. 3794; December 19, 1992, p. 3901; December 18, 1993, p. 3435; December 31, 1994, p. 3663; January 3, 1998, p. 38; and January 9, 1999, p. 97.

**TABLE 9.4   U.S. House and Senate seats held by Democrats in southern states, in percentages, selected years, 1955–2000**

|        | 1955 | 1965 | 1985 | 1995 | 2000 |
|--------|------|------|------|------|------|
| House  | 92   | 85   | 64   | 47   | 41   |
| Senate | 100  | 85   | 54   | 42   | 31   |

The states included are Alabama, Arkansas, Florida, Georgia, Kentucky, Louisiana, Mississippi, North Carolina, Oklahoma, South Carolina, Tennessee, Texas, and Virginia.

SOURCE: Various issues of *Congressional Quarterly Weekly Report.*

black voters (plus the defections of white conservatives), Stanley P. Berard finds, have contributed to the liberalization of southern Democratic electoral coalitions and this in turn to higher levels of partisan voting by southern Democrats.[93] Additionally, the creation of black majority districts in the 1990s helped to change the shape of southern politics—enhancing liberalism in these districts while making surrounding districts increasingly white, increasingly conservative, and increasingly Republican. (The future of these districts is now in doubt as a result of a Supreme Court decision in 1995.)[94]

Although the conservative coalition comes to life less often than in the past, when it does appear, it wins—about 90 percent of the time. Its objectives are unambiguous. It can be counted on to support proposals to toughen crime legislation and to oppose gun control. Social issues increasingly find a place on its agenda: It strongly favors prayer in the public schools, strong measures to combat the drug problem, and tighter immigration controls, while opposing abortion rights and various measures perceived as soft on pornography and homosexuality (e.g., gays in the military). It tends to support nuclear energy projects, the tobacco industry, and certain kinds of defense spending (e.g., funding for the B-2 stealth bomber and Trident II missiles). It has been a friend of the balanced-budget amendment, but not of domestic partners seeking eligibility for group health insurance coverage offered to District of Columbia employees.

The conservative coalition thus continues to be successful on a limited range of issues. But it is hard to visualize the coalition's return to the prominence it enjoyed, year in and year out, for nearly half a century. The growing strength of the Republican party in the South and the corresponding liberalization of southern Democratic electoral coalitions may further erode its significance. The greater the successes of the Republican party in elections, and in governing as a party, the less political space open to this biparty coalition. On the other hand, the election of a liberal Democratic president, under the right circumstances, might well revitalize the coalition.

## Policy Changes in Congress

Under what circumstances do significant policy changes take place in Congress? There are two broad answers to this question. One holds that major policy changes are the result of *conversion*—that members switch positions, changing their votes on questions (either gradually or abruptly) in response to external forces. The stimulus to change, for example, may result from a shift in partisan control of the presidency or from members' perceptions of new signals emanating from the constituencies. The other theory asserts that significant policy changes emerge from the process of *replacement*—the election of new members disposed to vote differently from those whom they replaced.[95] Thus, elections may appear to carry a policy-change mandate. The evidence of a variety of studies suggests that some major policy changes stem largely from the conversion of members and that others stem largely from the replacement of members. In the *typical* pattern, however, both replacement and conversion seem to contribute to the new winning coalition.[96]

Do changes in constituencies significantly affect the behavior of legislators? An intriguing way to study this question is to examine the behavior of U.S. House members who are elected to the Senate. If members are responsive to their constituencies, one would expect that these members' policy views would shift to match the preferences of their new and more heterogeneous constituencies. Representing an entire state, after all, is quite different from representing some half-million people in a House district. Nevertheless, according to a new study, few House-to-Senate members change their policy positions. Only when a constituency shifts to the left do House Democratic members shift correspondingly; only when a constituency shifts to the right do Republican members shift similarly. It turns out that most House members have policy interests that are too important to them to sacrifice in the interest of vote-maximizing behavior. Moreover, members do not want to open themselves to charges of policy inconsistency.[97] And finally, most legislators sense, know, and count on what Richard F. Fenno, Jr., has demonstrated convincingly: that constituents will judge them primarily on the basis of their home style (how they present themselves) rather than on their policy decisions in Washington.[98]

## Party Voting in the States

Party politics in the legislatures varies in form and intensity from state to state. The dimensions of party conflict and of party differences are not easily compared or contrasted, for several reasons. To begin, there are wide differences in party competition among the states. There are southern states where Republican legislators are typically in a weak minority position, such as Arkansas and Louisiana, and northern states where Democrats are heavily outnumbered session after session, such as Kansas and New Hampshire. Republicans scarcely ever fare well in Rhode Island, Massachusetts, and West

Virginia, and Democrats are regularly on the losing end in North Dakota, South Dakota, Utah, and Wyoming. It is reasonable to suppose that in states where the minority party is chronically weak, the incentive for the parties to perform as cohesive groups is attenuated.

In one state, Nebraska, state legislators are elected on ballots shorn of party designations. The evidence of a study of this nonpartisan legislature suggests that in the absence of parties as sources of cues, there is no more than minimal structure in the voting behavior of members. A majority of the votes taken cannot be explained in terms of conventional party, constituency, or personal variables. These findings raise the question of whether Nebraska voters can in any real sense hold their representatives accountable for decisions taken.[99]

A second obstacle to generalization about state legislative parties is that they function in disparate environs and under variable conventions. In no two states is rural-urban cleavage of the same intensity and scope, a factor that plainly has a bearing on party behavior. In addition, the way in which legislators are chosen, their tenure and turnover, the power customarily accorded to party leaders and the criteria that govern their selection, the existence and utilization of party agencies like the caucus, and the persistence of cohesive elements within each party vary from state to state. Finally, just as party structures differ throughout the country, the legal-constitutional systems within which party processes are carried on differ from state to state.

Comparative analysis of state legislative parties is hindered most of all, however, by "the problem," the variable practices in roll-call votes in the legislatures. Where variations are significant, roll-call data are not altogether comparable. In most studies of legislative party behavior, roll calls have been the unit of analysis. In some states, however, such as Connecticut and Massachusetts, roll-call votes are not required for the passage of bills; as a result, they are not frequently taken. In most states, roll calls are mandatory on the passage of bills, whether there is controversy or not; in these states a thousand or more record votes may be taken during a session. Evaluation of the dimensions of party voting is obviously difficult where voting requirements are substantially different, and this is only one of many problems that beset roll-call vote studies.

Despite the obstacles to systematic comparison of the role of political parties in fifty state capitals, the general contour of party behavior can be sketched.[100]

1. The model of a responsible two-party system, with reasonably unified parties presenting genuine policy alternatives, is met more nearly in certain northern state legislatures than in Congress. New York, Connecticut, Massachusetts, Rhode Island, and Pennsylvania all have considerably more party voting than the usual state legislature. These

states are distinguished by a high degree of urbanization, impressive industrialization, and competitive two-party systems.[101] In states where rural-urban cleavage tends to coincide with major party divisions (rural Republicans versus urban Democrats), it is predictable (a good bet, at least) that conflict between the parties will be fairly frequent and sometimes intense. In contrast, party voting appears to be found much less frequently in rural, less populous states.[102] Party-line voting also occurs more frequently in states with unified rather than divided party control of the branches.[103]

2. As in Congress, party battles in the legislatures are episodic. A great deal of legislative business is transacted with a minimum of controversy. General consensus at the roll-call stage is common, and in many legislatures well over one-half of the roll-call votes are unanimous. Legislation having a major impact on conditions of private and public life within the state—involving schools, government organization, constitutional reform, state services, and other areas—is often shaped and adopted in actions in which the parties either are in general agreement or have taken no stands. This is true even in states where there is substantial disagreement between the parties, as in Pennsylvania. A conception of party that includes the notion that Democrats spend most of their time quarreling or bargaining with Republicans (and vice versa) over legislation is a gross distortion of reality, with perhaps the exception of a state or two.

3. Party unity fluctuates from issue to issue: Party lines are firm on some kinds of questions; rarely visible on others; and despite the appeals of party leaders, usually collapse on still other kinds. There is some evidence that legislators' support for party positions fluctuates according to the election calendar; party loyalty may be less important in a reelection year than at other times.[104] Party loyalty may also be increased by the leaders' judicious use of pork-barrel funds. In the North Carolina lower house, for example, the success of rank-and-file members in securing pork-barrel allotments for their districts (such as funds for county courthouse restoration) may depend on their party loyalty in voting and their cooperation with the leadership.[105]

4. It seems safe to say that in most states parties stay in business by being flexible about policies. They veer and tack as electoral winds dictate.

5. There is apparently no fully developed counterpart in the state legislatures to the conservative coalition of Republicans and southern Democrats that sometimes dominates Congress. Party lines are crossed in the states, to be sure, but the biparty combinations appear to lack the spirit and continuity of the congressional prototype. One can find in several states, however, small groups of liberal legislators who have created study groups, modeled after the congressional Democratic Study

Group (DSG). Their main objectives, like those of the DSG, have been to promote liberal policies through the development of staff support and a forum for strategy-making and whip organizations.[106]

6. There is evidence that the capacity of the legislative party to perform as a cohesive unit is strongly influenced by the formal powers and the political standing of the governor. Governors who fully utilize their formal powers and whose own support in the electorate is high are likely to receive substantial support from fellow party members for their legislative programs. How the legislative party performs, in other words, may be less a matter of legislative determination than of gubernatorial initiative and power in the system at large.[107] In addition, in states that have strong *electoral* parties (where preprimary endorsements are made), legislators of the governor's party will support his or her program with a high degree of loyalty; in states with weak parties, legislators of the governor's party provide less support for his or her program.[108]

7. In northern states distinguished by rigorous party competition in the legislatures, party lines are highly visible on liberal-conservative issues. The Democratic party ordinarily originates and lends considerable support to legislation favorable to the interests of labor, minorities, and low-income groups (for example, employer-liability laws, disability benefits, unemployment compensation, fair employment practices, public accommodation, open housing, and public housing). The Republican party generally is concerned with fostering the interests of the business community, and this objective is likely to take the form of resisting legislation backed by organized labor or of blocking new regulation of business. In addition, Republican legislators usually are more anxious than Democrats to devise state tax structures that are favorable to the interests of industry. Health and welfare legislation usually finds the Democratic party in the forefront to liberalize benefits or to extend state services; Republicans tend to view these questions in a fiscal context, which typically means a cautious approach to new expenditures. In a word, socioeconomic-class legislation often serves as a rallying point for each party.

8. Party conflict often is generated on issues of narrow partisan interest. In one sense, the party organizations perform essentially as interest groups, seeking to strengthen their hand in state politics and to thwart actions that would place them at a disadvantage. The welfare and survival of the party is a persistent theme in both legislation and legislative maneuvers. Accordingly, conflict is common on patronage and appointments, organizational and procedural matters in the legislatures, election law (especially reapportionment), bills and resolutions designed to embarrass the state administration, and measures to increase

state control over municipal governments (especially where the state legislature is controlled by the Republicans and the big-city administrations are controlled by the Democrats). In sum, organizational party interest cuts through a variety of public policy questions, and its presence is felt even though dissimulated in debate.

### Constituencies and Liberal-Conservative Voting Records

Political outlook in the legislature is a function of party and section, as the previous pages have shown, and also of constituency. In general, less headway has been made in evaluating the impact of constituency conditions on legislative voting than in analyzing the significance of the party factor. Here we shall be concerned briefly with examining the relationship between a high or low degree of party competition in constituencies and the voting behavior of party members in the legislature. We shall have to be content with sketching the shape of the problem since evidence is too scarce to support general propositions.

An interpretation of American politics made familiar by Schattschneider is that a two-party system tends to produce moderate parties. "A large party must be supported by a great variety of interests sufficiently tolerant of each other to collaborate, held together by compromise and concession, and the discovery of certain common interests. . . ."[109] Moderation results from the quest for a majority since neither party can make exceptional concessions to any interest without antagonizing a counterinterest. The corollary is that each party contains representatives whose voting records range the length of the liberal-conservative scale. This interpretation has been put to empirical test several times.

A study of the U.S. House of Representatives by Samuel Huntington disclosed that members coming from marginal (or closely contested) districts presented the most marked differences in liberalism and conservatism; that is, Republicans from districts where party competition was rigorous had a relatively low index of liberalism on House roll-call votes, and Democrats from comparable districts had a very high index of liberalism. In election margins, the parties were most evenly balanced in urban congressional districts, which in turn were the districts characterized by the greatest ideological cleavage between the parties. In rural areas, where "one-party" constituencies were predominant, election margins were widest and the ideological differences between the parties were smallest. Huntington hypothesized that increasing urbanization will lead to the development of sharper differences between the parties. "The parties will strive to win not by converting their opponents but by effectively mobilizing their own supporters, *not by extending their appeal but by intensifying it.*"[110]

Tests of the validity of the Huntington theory yield somewhat conflicting results. On the one hand, if analysis is confined to the behavior of marginal district members *within the legislature,* it appears that there is little support for the theory. A study of the 86th and 87th Congresses, for example, shows that representatives from close districts are most likely to develop moderate policy stances—that is, to deviate *toward* the policy positions of the other party.[111]

On the other hand, if analysis focuses primarily on congressional constituencies, a much different picture emerges. A study by Morris Fiorina of the voting behavior of legislators representing marginal-switch districts (marginal districts that switch from one party to another) offers support for the Huntington theory. The typical pattern in these volatile districts is for a liberal Democrat to replace a conservative Republican or a conservative Republican to replace a liberal Democrat. Scant evidence of moderation appears in the behavior of the winning candidate. As it turns out, Democratic winners move to Washington to represent the dominant segment of their constituencies and to ignore the remainder. Republican winners do the same. The result is that representation of these highly competitive districts alternates between extremes of Democratic liberalism and Republican conservatism.[112]

The liberal-conservative differences between Democrats and Republicans are due in some degree to the differences in the kinds of constituencies they represent. Northern Democrats tend to be elected to Congress from districts having certain pronounced characteristics: lower owner-occupancy of dwellings, higher proportion of nonwhite population, higher population density, and higher percentage of urban population. Northern Republicans tend to be elected from districts whose characteristics are the opposite.

Northern Democratic members of Congress ordinarily win out in districts whose characteristics make "liberalism" an appropriate guide to their voting behavior; their Republican counterparts ordinarily come from districts where "conservatism" is an equally appropriate response. The critical fact is that northern Democrats who represent districts with "conservative" characteristics (for example, higher owner-occupancy and a small nonwhite population) most frequently vote with conservative forces in Congress, and Republicans who represent districts with "liberal" characteristics most frequently vote liberal positions.[113] In sum, this evidence gives merit to the argument that liberalism-conservatism differences between northern members of Congress may not be so much a function of party as an expression of constituency priorities that stem from economic and demographic variables.

## Party and Separation of Powers

Effective performance by the parties, as collectivities, is hindered not only by ideological cleavages within their ranks but also by the institutional arrangements within which the parties must function. Theoretically, the majority party acts to mesh or harmonize the operations of the executive and legislative branches, permitting a common party approach to the fashioning of public policy. The one requirement essential to this function is that "electoral procedures and representative systems be so constructed that candidates of either party may capture both executive and legislature."[114] Where one party controls the executive branch and the other party controls one or both houses of the legislative branch, no opportunity exists for a party to bridge the gap created by the separation of powers. Ordinarily, indeed, the breach is widened.

Divided party control is a typical condition in many of the northern states (see Table 4.6, Chapter 4). Malapportionment has sometimes contributed to this condition. It also may be due to the weakness of the minority party's organization, which prevents it from competing vigorously in all legislative districts: "Long nourished only by the prospect of defeat, it has neither the candidates nor the campaign resources—to say nothing of a frequent lack of will—to command support at the grass roots commensurate with its gubernatorial vote." Other factors that contribute to party divisions between the executive and the legislature are staggered and nonconcurrent terms of office (for example, four-year term for governor, two-year term for lower house) and the separation of gubernatorial and presidential elections, an arrangement that serves to shield state politics from national trends. Finally, on some occasions voters appear to make a deliberate choice to give the governorship to one party and the legislature to the other. V. O. Key, Jr., and Corinne Silverman concluded that institutional arrangements and electoral procedures in the states "have been more or less deliberately designed to frustrate popular majorities."[115]

A recent study by Gary Jacobson argues that the roots of divided national government are *political* rather than structural.

> [None] of the common structural explanations for continued Democratic hegemony in the House—including, in addition to the incumbency advantage, a declining swing-ratio, gerrymandering, and campaign finance regulation—withstands serious scrutiny. . . . Republicans have failed to advance in the House because they have fielded inferior candidates on the wrong side of issues that are important to voters in House elections and because voters find it difficult to assign blame or credit when control of government is divided between the parties. . . . Divided government reflects, rather than thwarts, the electorate's will. . . .[116]

Divided government has been a persistent condition at the national level.[117] Between 1952 and 2000, less than half of the elections resulted in control of both houses of Congress and the presidency by the same party. Republican presidents are the chief victims of this incubus. One important result is that prospects for party government, in the sense that the electorate makes a decision to give the reins of government to one of the parties and to hold it responsible for the conduct of affairs, are sharply diminished when the system makes it virtually impossible for one party to win control of both the executive and legislative branches at the same time.

By one set of tests, it does not make a great deal of difference whether party control is unified or divided. David R. Mayhew finds that major laws are as likely to be adopted when party control is divided as when it is unified. Moreover, prominent, high-publicity investigations of the executive branch by congressional committees occur without regard to conditions of party control. Of thirty major investigations between 1946 and 1990, fifteen occurred when control was divided and fifteen when control was unified.[118]

## PARTY RESPONSIBILITY IN CONGRESS

Dissatisfaction over the arrangement of power in Congress and concern over the inability of the parties to legislate have been central themes in the literature of American party politics. At dead center in the controversy over American parties is the issue of an "effective" and "responsible" party system. The character such a system would have is suggested in the following statements taken from the Report of the Committee on Political Parties of the American Political Science Association:

> An effective party system requires, first, that the parties are able to bring forth programs to which they commit themselves and, second, that the parties possess sufficient internal cohesion to carry out these programs.

> The fundamental requirement [in making the parties accountable to the public] is a two-party system in which the opposition party acts as the critic of the party in power, developing, defining and presenting the policy alternatives which are necessary for a true choice in reaching public decisions.

> A stronger party system is less likely to give cause for the deterioration and confusion of purposes which sometimes passes for compromise but is really an unjustifiable surrender to narrow interests. Compromise among interests is compatible with the aims of a free society only when the terms of reference reflect an openly acknowledged concept of the public interest. There is every reason to insist that the parties be held accountable to the public for the compromises they accept.[119]

The report contains a comprehensive series of proposals designed to help achieve a more responsible party system. The main thrust of these proposals can be captured without examination of their specific details.

The congressional party system envisaged by the Committee on Political Parties would be characterized by a national party leadership that was actively involved in the congressional nominating process. "Above all, the basis of party operations in Congress is laid in the election process." National party leaders have a legitimate interest in discussing congressional nominations with local party leaders in an effort to winnow out prospective candidates who are likely to oppose the main planks in the party's program. If the national parties are unable to control the use of their party labels, candidates with all manner of policy views are likely to become party nominees; the result, inevitably, is that the congressional parties encounter great difficulty in seeking to unify their memberships on policy matters of major importance.

Party leadership in Congress is diffused and ambiguous, the report holds. A single leadership committee for each party and each house, supplanting the policy and steering committees, should be created. These committees would be responsible for placing proposals before the rank-and-file members, keeping a rein on the legislative schedule, and otherwise managing party affairs. House and Senate leadership committees of each party would need to meet together regularly, and the four leadership groups might be brought together on specific occasions—perhaps to consider the president's principal messages.

Party caucuses (or conferences) should meet more frequently, and their functions should be augmented. If party principles and programs are at stake, caucus decisions should be binding. "Rewarding party loyalty is a proper way of fostering party unity . . . [and] *when members of Congress disregard a caucus decision taken in furtherance of national party policy, they should expect disapproval.*" Members who often flout party decisions should expect their transgressions to cost them patronage and better committee assignments.

The seniority principle should be made to work in harness with the party system. Party leaders should exert their influence to keep a member who is hostile toward party aims from becoming a committee chair. Committee assignments should be recommended by the party leadership committees to the party caucuses for approval or modification; moreover, committee assignments should be reviewed at least every two years. "Personal competence and party loyalty should be valued more highly than seniority in assigning members to such major committees as those dealing with fiscal policy and foreign affairs."

Finally, the party leadership committee should control the legislative schedule. More responsible party control could be achieved if the power to steer legislation were removed from the House Rules Committee and awarded to the leadership committee of the majority party. A majority vote in the Senate should be sufficient to end debate on all matters.

The party-responsibility model[120] offered by the Committee on Political Parties has been warmly praised in some quarters and vigorously criticized in others. Analysis of the debate is quite beyond the scope of this chapter, especially since we have been concerned with only one section of the report, that which relates to party organization in Congress. The main objections to the report, however, need to be indicated.

On the whole, critics of the report have been more concerned with the broad implications of making the party system more centralized and disciplined than with the specific proposals offered by the committee. A brief condensation of the criticisms would show that one or more writers believe that the committee underestimated present party responsibility in Congress, that certain proposals are unrealistic given the cultural and social milieu in which the parties function, that the party system might be further debilitated were the report followed, that the committee failed to recognize the virtues of the present decentralized system, and that major renovation of the party system cannot be undertaken unless other basic constitutional changes are first instituted. In general, critics feel that the cost of responsible party government is too high a price to pay. Whether it is or not can be better judged after the evidence and arguments have been evaluated firsthand.[121]

## Change in the Party System

Old ideas die hard, and political blueprints are not easily transformed into political reality. Nevertheless, to a surprising degree, several leading tenets of the responsible-party model have been implemented by both parties, particularly in the House. The Democratic caucus and Republican conference have been rejuvenated, and the seniority system has become a lesser threat to party programs. Committee and subcommittee chairs no longer are automatically awarded to the senior members.

The powers of the Speaker have been significantly enlarged. For both parties, the office of Speaker is now at the center of the committee assignment process. Democratic rules, for example, empower the Speaker to nominate the members of the Rules Committee and to serve as its chair. Additionally, when the party controls the House (as it did from 1955 to 1995), the Speaker serves as the chair of the Steering Committee, the party's committee-making panel. The Republicans' capture of the House in the 1994 off-year election led to a number of incisive changes designed to centralize power and strengthen the leadership. Subcommittee independence was curbed by giving committee chairs the authority to appoint subcommittee chairs and staffs. Numerous subcommittees were abolished. Term limits were imposed on committee chairs as a way of signaling the leadership's aversion to the creation and consolidation of independent committees. Seniority was ignored in the Speaker's appointment of several committee chairs, and committee staffs were sharply reduced. A policy agenda emerged from the Speaker's office in the form of a celebrated "Contract with America"; what is more, the party adopted it almost intact. Scarcely anyone viewed these changes as cosmetic or puerile. Rather, they created conditions under which a strengthened congressional party system, centered in the office of the Speaker, could be developed and used to adopt a broad range of conservative policy proposals. Leadership, party, and hierarchy became the dominant institutional features of the House in the 104th Congress.

But this experiment was inevitably tenuous. Intraparty opposition to Speaker Newt Gingrich grew in intensity, culminating in his resignation at the opening of the 106th Congress (1999–2000). Under his successor, J. Dennis Hastert, the speakership became considerably less intrusive in House decision making. It goes without saying, of course, that members of both parties, in both chambers, find it difficult to tolerate system arrangements and decision making that unduly reflect leader preferences and a bias toward hierarchy.

## NOTES

1. See an instructive essay by Burdett Loomis, "Organizational Change and the Centrifugal Congress," *American Review of Politics*, XIV (Summer 1993), 289–305.
2. Constituency may be considered in several ways. Each member of Congress has a *geographical* constituency (the formal district), a *reelection* constituency (the representative's perceptions of his or her supporters—those who vote for this person), a *primary* constituency (the intense, rain or shine, supporters), and a *personal* constituency (the coterie of intimate friends, political advisers, and confidants). Each constituency is tucked within the previous one. See Richard F. Fenno, Jr., *Home Style: House Members in Their Districts* (Boston: Little, Brown, 1978), pp. 1–30.
3. See the exposition of this theme in David R. Mayhew's remarkable little book–big essay, *Congress: The Electoral Connection* (New Haven, CT: Yale University Press, 1974).
4. Sidney Wise, *The Legislative Process in Pennsylvania* (Washington, DC: American Political Science Association, 1971), pp. 25–38.
5. Wayne L. Francis, "Leadership, Party Caucuses, and Committees in U.S. State Legislatures," *Legislative Studies Quarterly*, X (May 1985), 243–57. Also see Robert Harmel, "Minority Partisanship in One-Party Predominant Legislatures: A Five-State Study," *Journal of Politics*, XLVIII (August 1986), 729–40.
6. Wayne R. Swanson, *Lawmaking in Connecticut: The General Assembly* (Washington, DC: American Political Science Association, 1972), p. 13.
7. Brenda Erickson, "Legislative Party Caucuses: Open or Closed?" *State Legislatures*, October/November 1998, p. 13.
8. Hugh A. Bone, "An Introduction to the Senate Policy Committees," *American Political Science Review*, L (June 1956), 352.
9. Robert L. Peabody, *Leadership in Congress: Stability, Succession, and Change* (Boston: Little, Brown, 1976), p. 338.
10. Ralph K. Huitt, "Democratic Party Leadership in the Senate," *American Political Science Review*, LX (June 1961), 343.
11. Barbara Sinclair, "Majority Party Leadership Strategies for Coping with the New U.S. House," *Legislative Studies Quarterly*, VI (August 1981), 402. A recent discussion of the policy committees describes them essentially as research and service agencies. See Samuel C. Patterson, "Party Leadership in the U.S. Senate," in *The Postreform Congress*, ed. Roger H. Davidson (New York: St. Martin's Press, 1992), pp. 99–100.
12. Huitt, "Democratic Party Leadership," 335.
13. *Parties and Politics in America* (Ithaca, NY: Cornell University Press, 1960), p. 22.
14. *U.S. News & World Report*, June 27, 1960, p. 90.
15. As quoted by James A. Robinson, *Congress and Foreign Policy-Making* (Homewood, IL: Dorsey Press, 1962), pp. 215–16.
16. *Congressional Quarterly Weekly Report*, December 11, 1976, p. 3293.
17. Quoted by Samuel C. Patterson, "Party Leadership in the U.S. Senate," in *Leading Congress: New Styles, New Strategies*, ed. John J. Kornacki (Washington, DC: Congressional Quarterly Press, 1990), p. 50.
18. David Truman, *The Congressional Party* (New York: Wiley, 1959), pp. 104–105.

19. *U.S. News & World Report*, June 27, 1960, p. 90.

20. Steven S. Smith and Marcus Flathman, "Managing the Senate Floor: Complex Unanimous Consent Agreements Since the 1950s," *Legislative Studies Quarterly*, XIV (August 1989), 350–51.

21. *Citadel* (New York: Harper & Row, 1956), p. 96.

22. *Congressional Quarterly Weekly Report*, December 15, 1973, p. 3293.

23. Truman, *The Congressional Party*, pp. 110–11 (quotation on p. 298).

24. For evaluation of the "middleman" requirement in the Senate and House, see ibid., especially pp. 106–16 and 205–208.

25. For corroboration of this finding in later Congresses, see Barbara Hinckley, "Congressional Leadership Selection and Support: A Comparative Analysis," *Journal of Politics*, XXXII (May 1970), 268–87.

26. *Congressional Quarterly Weekly Report*, July 7, 1979, p. 1345.

27. William E. Sullivan has shown, however, that the moderateness of congressional party leaders is more a product of the leadership role than a criterion involved in selecting leaders; that is, leaders move near the ideological center of their parties *after* they have assumed leadership positions. Liberals become more conservative and conservatives become more liberal. Like Truman, Sullivan finds that extreme party mavericks—highly conservative Democrats and highly liberal Republicans—are excluded from the leadership selection process. "Criteria for Selecting Party Leadership in Congress," *American Politics Quarterly*, III (January 1975), 25–44. Also see evidence by Rebekah Herrick and Michael K. Moore that House members with "intrainstitutional ambition" (those members who desire leadership positions in the chamber) are more likely to be strong supporters of the party on roll-call votes than members with "static" ambitions or members seeking higher office. "Political Ambition's Effect on Legislative Behavior: Schlesinger's Typology Reconsidered and Revised," *Journal of Politics*, LV (August 1993), 765–76.

28. *New York Times*, July 24, 1994.

29. Brian D. Posler and Carl M. Rhodes, "Pre-Leadership Signaling in the U.S. House," *Legislative Studies Quarterly*, XXII (August 1997), 351–66 (quotation on p. 364).

30. Ibid.

31. Samuel C. Patterson, "Party Leadership in the U.S. Senate," *Legislative Studies Quarterly*, XIV (August 1989), 393–413. Also see Patricia A. Hurley and Rick K. Wilson, "Partisan Voting Patterns in the U.S. Senate, 1877–1986," *Legislative Studies Quarterly*, XIV (May 1989), 225–50; and David Brady, Richard Brody, and David Epstein, "Heterogeneous Parties and Political Organization: The U.S. Senate, 1880–1920," *Legislative Studies Quarterly*, XIV (May 1989), 205–23.

32. Lawrence R. Jacobs, Eric D. Lawrence, Robert Y. Shapiro, and Steven S. Smith, "Congressional Leadership of Public Opinion," *Political Science Quarterly*, CXIII (Spring 1998), 21–41 (quotation on p. 40).

33. Peabody, *Leadership in Congress*, pp. 7–9.

34. *Congressional Quarterly Weekly Report*, September 4, 1982, p. 2181. Burdett A. Loomis finds that changes in the rules, norms, and membership of the House have substantially altered the career patterns of members. Junior members can now advance rapidly into the party leadership's expanded ranks. Members of the majority party have every reason to expect that they will hold a subcommittee chairmanship or a seat on a major committee by the time they are in their third or fourth term. Democratization, decentralization, and the breakdown of restraining norms, such as seniority and apprenticeship, have intensified the problems of the leadership. "Congressional Careers and Party Leadership in the Contemporary House of Representatives," *American Journal of Political Science*, XXVIII (February 1984), 180–202.

35. David T. Canon, "The Institutionalization of Leadership in the U.S. Congress," *Legislative Studies Quarterly*, XIV (August 1989), 415–43.

36. Steven S. Smith, "The Senate in the Postreform Era," in *The Postreform Congress*, ed. Roger H. Davidson (New York: St. Martin's Press, 1992), p. 179.

37. See Randall B. Ripley, "The Party Whip Organizations in the United States House of Representatives," *American Political Science Review,* LVIII (September 1964), 561–76.

38. Quoted in Charles L. Clapp, *The Congressman: His Work as He Sees It* (Washington, DC: Brookings Institution, 1963), p. 303.

39. Ripley, "Party Whip Organizations," 572–73.

40. Ibid., 574–75. For a study of the whip system in the Senate, see Walter J. Oleszek, "Party Whips in the United States Senate," *Journal of Politics,* XXXIII (November 1971), 955–79.

41. *Congressional Quarterly Weekly Report,* May 27, 1978, pp. 1301–1302.

42. To say that the House has become more institutionalized means that it has become "perceptibly more bounded, more complex, and more universalistic and automatic in its internal decision making." For an analysis of specific characteristics of institutionalization in the House, see Nelson W. Polsby, "The Institutionalization of the U.S. House of Representatives," *American Political Science Review,* LXII (March 1968), 144–68 (quotation on p. 145).

43. Dennis Hastert was the first Speaker ever to be elected without having held another leadership position first.

44. A tabulation of length of House service prior to becoming Speaker is instructive: Sam Rayburn (elected Speaker in 1940), twenty-seven years; Joe Martin (1947), twenty-two years; John McCormack (1962), thirty-four years; Carl Albert (1971), twenty-four years; Thomas O'Neill (1977), twenty-four years; Jim Wright (1987), thirty-two years; Tom Foley (1989), twenty-four years; Newt Gingrich (1995), sixteen years; and Dennis Hastert (1999), twelve years. *Congressional Quarterly Weekly Report,* February 27, 1999, p. 460.

45. Kenneth Hechler, *Insurgency: Personalities and Politics of the Taft Era* (New York: Columbia University Press, 1940), p. 31.

46. Roger H. Davidson, Walter J. Oleszek, and Thomas Kephart, "One Bill, Many Committees: Multiple Referrals in the U.S. House of Representatives," *Legislative Studies Quarterly,* XIII (February 1988), 3–28.

47. Richard Bolling, "Committees in the House," *The Annals,* CDXI (January 1974), 4.

48. Barbara Sinclair, "Leadership Strategies in the Modern Congress," in *Congressional Politics,* ed. Christopher J. Deering (Chicago: Dorsey Press, 1989), p. 136.

49. Dotson Rader, "Tip O'Neill: He Needs a Win," *Parade,* September 27, 1981, p. 7.

50. What contributions can party leaders make in today's increasingly member-centered Congress? See an essay on the House ("a mail drop for a group of 435 venture capitalists") by Ross K. Baker, "Fostering the Entrepreneurial Activities of Members of the House," in *Leading Congress: New Styles, New Strategies,* ed. John J. Kornacki (Washington, DC: Congressional Quarterly Press, 1990), pp. 27–34. Baker describes leadership strategies for attracting experts, directing the energies of members, providing for their political cover, and assisting them in their quest for media attention. Burdett Loomis provides an analysis of the new generation of political entrepreneurs that has been elected to Congress in *The New American Politician* (New York: Basic Books, 1988).

51. The strategy of inclusion is particularly well illustrated by the Speaker's appointment of members to task forces (ad hoc groups formed to press for the passage of a specific bill). Barbara Sinclair, "The Speaker's Task Force in the Post-Reform House of Representatives," *American Political Science Review,* LXXV (June 1981), 397–410; Burdett Loomis, "Congressional Careers and Party Leadership in the Contemporary House of Representatives," *American Journal of Political Science,* XXVIII (February 1984), 180–202; James C. Garand and Kathleen M. Clayton, "Socialization to Partisanship in the U.S. House: The Speaker's Task Force," *Legislative Studies Quarterly,* XI (August 1986), 409–28; James C. Garand, "The Socialization to Partisan Legislative Behavior: An Extension of Sinclair's Task Force Socialization Thesis," *Western Political Quarterly,* XLI (June 1988), 391–400; and James C. Garand, "Membership in Speaker's Task Forces: A Multivariate Model," *American Politics Quarterly,* XVIII (January 1990), 81–102.

52. *Congressional Quarterly Weekly Report,* July 11, 1987, p. 1483.

53. *New York Times,* February 22, 1993, as quoted by Burdett Loomis, "Organizational Change and the Centrifugal Congress," *American Review of Politics,* XIV (Summer 1993), pp. 302–303.

54. Joseph Cooper and David W. Brady, "Institutional Context and Leadership Style: The House from Cannon to Rayburn," *American Political Science Review,* LXXV (June 1981), 411–25 (quotation on p. 417).

55. Thomas H. Little and Samuel C. Patterson, "The Organizational Life of the Congressional Parties," *American Review of Politics,* XIV (Spring 1993), 39–70 (quotation on p. 67).

56. David Ray, "The Sources of Voting Cues in Three State Legislatures," *Journal of Politics,* XLIV (November 1982), 1074–1087 (quotations on p. 1083). In contrast, the party leadership does not appear as an important source of voting cues in the lower houses of New Hampshire and Pennsylvania, the other two states examined in this study. For New Hampshire legislators, "constituency" is the leading source of voting cues, and for Pennsylvania legislators, "fellow legislators." In Oklahoma and Kansas, party leaders are infrequently cited as a source of voting cues. In these states, the influence of various actors on voting decisions is a function of the issue involved; on banking issues, for example, interest groups have the greatest influence on legislators. See Donald R. Songer, Sonja G. Dillon, Darla W. Kite, Patricia E. Jameson, James M. Underwood, and William D. Underwood, "The Influence of Issues on Choice of Voting Cues Utilized by State Legislators," *Western Political Quarterly,* XXXIX (March 1986), 118–25.

57. Peverill Squire, "Member Career Opportunities and the Internal Organization of Legislatures," *Journal of Politics,* L (August 1988), 733.

58. See a series of articles on coalition politics in state legislatures in the April 1989 issue of *State Legislatures.* But see evidence that as parties become stronger in formerly one-party state legislatures, the "speaker system" (marked by the speaker's distribution of resources, such as committee positions, on the basis of personal loyalty rather than party considerations) is weakened. This nonpartisan system is inevitably challenged by the developing party system. Keith E. Hamm and Robert Harmel, "Legislative Party Development and the Speaker System: The Case of the Texas House," *Journal of Politics,* LV (November 1993), 1140–51.

59. Larry Sonis, "'O.K., Everybody, Vote Yes': A Day in the Life of a State Legislator," *Washington Monthly,* June 1979, p. 25.

60. Eric Lane, "Albany's Travesty of Democracy," *City Journal,* VII (Spring 1997), 55.

61. Richard A. Clucas, "Legislative Leadership and Campaign Support in California," *Legislative Studies Quarterly,* XVII (May 1992), 265–83. Also see Clucas, "But for Term Limits, Willie Brown Might Have Been Speaker for Life," *Public Affairs Report* (May 1995), 1, 11–12; and *The Speaker's Electoral Connection: Willie Brown and the California Assembly* (Berkeley, CA: Institute of Governmental Studies, 1995).

62. There has been little research on state legislative leaders. For a case study of a strong legislative leader, the majority leader of the New York Senate, see John J. Pitney, Jr., "Leaders and Rules in the New York State Senate," *Legislative Studies Quarterly,* VII (November 1982), 491–506. Also see an interesting study of members' expectations of party leaders in Maryland, North Carolina, and Ohio by Thomas H. Little, "Understanding Legislative Leadership Beyond the Chamber: The Members' Perspective," *Legislative Studies Quarterly,* XX (May 1995), 269–86. Little finds that young and ambitious legislators expect their leaders to focus on such external activities as public relations and campaign fund-raising as well as being skillful in managing politics in the institution itself.

63. The analysis in this section is based on Peabody, *Leadership in Congress,* especially Chaps. 1, 10, and 16.

64. *Congressional Quarterly Weekly Report,* June 11, 1994, p. 1499.

65. See Lewis A. Froman and Randall B. Ripley, "Conditions for Party Leadership: The Case of the House Democrats," *American Political Science Review,* LIX (March 1965), 52–63. For a study that examines the influence of state legislative leaders on the voting behavior of members (in Iowa), see Harlan Hahn, "Leadership Perceptions and Voting Behavior in a One-Party Legislative Body," *Journal of Politics,* XXXII (February 1970), 140–55.

66. *Congressional Quarterly Weekly Report,* May 9, 1998, p. 1218.

67. A study by David M. Olson based on interviews of members of Congress and local party leaders bears on this point. He finds that although most members prefer to support their

party's position on policy questions, very few feel much "obligation" to do so. Moreover, when party and district positions are in conflict, most members will "vote" their district. The members' willingness to side with district interests is not, for the most part, a function of communication with local party leaders. Indeed, the typical member hears very little from district party leaders concerning issues in Congress. See David M. Olson, "U.S. Congressmen and Their Diverse Congressional District Parties," *Legislative Studies Quarterly,* III (May 1978), 239–64.

68. How can Congress pass a measure that is clearly unpopular with constituents? John A. Clark argues that members have to be provided with political cover, that the issue has to be treated in such a way as to spread the blame between the two parties, and that the party leadership must use its ingenuity to protect individual members from constituents' wrath. Moreover, senior members from safe districts are expected to bear most of the burden as a way of protecting their more vulnerable junior colleagues. "Congressional Salaries and the Politics of Unpopular Votes," *American Politics Quarterly,* XXIV (April 1996), 150–68.

69. See Sinclair, "Leadership Strategies in the Modern Congress," especially pp. 144–52. Also see Barbara Sinclair, "Congressional Leadership: A Review Essay and a Research Agenda," in *Leading Congress: New Styles, New Strategies,* ed. John J. Kornacki (Washington, DC: Congressional Quarterly Press, 1990), pp. 97–162.

70. See an interesting rational choice analysis by Kathleen Bawn that argues that majority-party leaders make procedural decisions to benefit intense minorities within their party in order to serve the goal of party unity and maintenance. This incentive on procedural questions may make majority-party leaders overly responsive to organized interests rather than general interests in society. "Congressional Party Leadership: Utilitarian versus Majoritarian Incentives," *Legislative Studies Quarterly,* XXIII (May 1998), 219–43.

71. See E. E. Schattschneider, *Party Government* (New York: Holt, Rinehart & Winston, 1942), especially Chap. 1.

72. See a review of the literature on party behavior in legislative settings by Melissa P. Collie, "Voting Behavior in Legislatures," *Legislative Studies Quarterly,* IX (February 1984), 3–50.

73. *The Works of Edmund Burke* (London: G. Bell and Sons, 1897), I, p. 375.

74. *Modern Democracies* (New York: Macmillan, 1927), II, pp. 42–43.

75. *Annual Report of the American Historical Association for 1901* (Washington, DC, 1902), I, 321–543.

76. Julius Turner, *Party and Constituency: Pressures on Congress* (Baltimore: Johns Hopkins University Press, 1951), p. 23.

77. For other studies of party voting in Congress, see David W. Brady and Philip Althoff, "Party Voting in the U.S. House of Representatives, 1890–1910: Elements of a Responsible Party System," *Journal of Politics,* XXXVI (August 1974), 753–75; Barbara Sinclair, "Determinants of Aggregate Party Cohesion in the U.S. House of Representatives, 1901–1956," *Legislative Studies Quarterly,* II (May 1977), 155–75; Jerome M. Clubb and Santa A. Traugott, "Partisan Cleavage and Cohesion in the House of Representatives, 1861–1974," *Journal of Interdisciplinary History,* VII (Winter 1977), 375–401; David W. Brady, Joseph Cooper, and Patricia A. Hurley, "The Decline of Party in the U.S. House of Representatives, 1887–1968," *Legislative Studies Quarterly,* IV (August 1979), 381–407; Barbara Sinclair, "Agenda and Alignment Change: The House of Representatives, 1925–1978," in *Congress Reconsidered,* ed. Lawrence C. Dodd and Bruce I. Oppenheimer (Washington, DC: Congressional Quarterly Press, 1981), pp. 221–45; and Edward V. Schneier's revised edition of Turner's *Party and Constituency: Pressures on Congress* (Baltimore: Johns Hopkins University Press, 1970).

78. There is some evidence that members of Congress who receive the greatest financial assistance from their national parties demonstrate greater party unity on roll-call votes. See Kevin M. Leyden and Stephen A. Borrelli, "Party Loyalty and Party Unity: Can Loyalty Be Bought?" *Western Political Quarterly,* XLIII (June 1990), 343–65; and "An Investment in Goodwill: Party Contributions and Party Unity Among U.S. House Members in the 1980s," *American Politics Quarterly,* XXII (October 1994), 421–52. Also see Richard A. Clucas, "Party Contributions and the Influence of Campaign Committee Chairs on Roll-Call Voting," *Legislative Studies Quarterly,* XXII (May 1997), 179–94. Clucas finds that campaign contributions given to freshman members by the parties' congressional campaign committees

increase their support for the chairs of these committees. Money buys gratitude. But Clucas finds no indication that the contributions build support for the political parties, as reflected in freshman scores on party unity votes. Leyden and Borrelli look at all party contributions, not just those of the congressional campaign committees.

79. Samuel C. Patterson and Gregory A. Caldeira, "Party Voting in the United States Congress," *British Journal of Political Science,* XVIII (January 1988), 111–31. The authors use the "majority versus majority" definition of a party vote. For a study that analyzes how economic conditions influence party conflict, see John J. Coleman, "The Decline and Resurgence of Congressional Party Conflict," *Journal of Politics,* LIX (February 1997), 165–84. Coleman finds that party conflict declines during periods of economic stress as both parties move toward common solutions.

80. Daniel S. Ward, "The Continuing Search for Party Influence in Congress: A View from the Committees," *Legislative Studies Quarterly,* XVIII (May 1993), 211–30.

81. David W. Rohde, "Electoral Forces, Political Agendas, and Partisanship in the House and Senate." *The Postreform Congress,* ed. Roger H. Davidson (New York: St. Martin's Press, 1992), pp. 27–46. Barbara Sinclair offers an array of evidence on House floor voting that shows that the involvement of the majority-party leadership improves the prospects for the passage of legislation. What is more, the leadership is most likely to involve itself on the most difficult issues. Not surprisingly, leadership involvement is least likely to appear on issues that give rise to intraparty divisions. "The Emergence of Strong Leadership in the 1980s House of Representatives," *Journal of Politics,* LIV (August 1992), 657–84.

82. Melissa P. Collie, "Electoral Patterns and Voting Alignments in the U.S. House, 1886–1986," *Legislative Studies Quarterly,* XIV (February 1989), 107–27. Also see Melissa P. Collie, "Universalism and the Parties in the U.S. House of Representatives, 1921–80," *American Journal of Political Science,* XXXII (November 1988), 865–83.

83. See evidence of the declining level of conflict on civil rights legislation between southern and northern Democrats in Mary Alice Nye and Charles S. Bullock III, "Civil Rights Support: A Comparison of Southern and Border State Representatives," *Legislative Studies Quarterly,* XVII (February 1992), 81–94. Also see Francine Sanders, "Civil Rights Roll-Call Voting in the House of Representatives, 1957–1991: A Systematic Analysis," *Political Research Quarterly,* L (September 1997), 483–502. Sanders categorizes civil rights bills based on the extent to which the legislation stirs opposition among nonsouthern whites; as bills are perceived by nonsouthern whites as increasingly costly, House support declines sharply. Democrats are more likely to vote for civil rights bills than Republicans, but there are limits even to Democratic support. Broad support of civil rights bills by Republicans is limited to bills to end state-sponsored discrimination. Bills to attempt to ensure equality of opportunity or to ensure equality of result receive relatively few Republican votes.

84. See a study by William R. Shaffer that finds that the ADA rating is indeed a reliable and valid measure of liberalism: "Rating the Performance of the ADA in the U.S. Congress," *Western Political Quarterly,* XLII (March 1989), 33–51.

85. Ideology is a particularly potent factor in congressional roll-call voting. See Keith T. Poole and R. Steven Daniels, "Ideology, Party, and Voting in the U.S. Congress, 1959–1980," *American Political Science Review,* LXXIX (June 1985), 373–99; William R. Shaffer, "Party and Ideology in the U.S. House of Representatives," *Western Political Quarterly,* XXV (March 1982), 92–106; and Raymond Tatalovich and David Schier, "The Persistence of Ideological Cleavage in Voting on Abortion Legislation in the House of Representatives, 1973–1988," *American Politics Quarterly,* XXI (January 1993), 125–39. For a study that finds that partisanship plays "an important—if secondary" role in the congressional budgetary process, see David Lowery, Samuel Bookheimer, and James Malachowski, "Partisanship in the Appropriations Process: Fenno Revisited," *American Politics Quarterly,* XIII (April 1985), 188–99.

86. David R. Mayhew's study of party loyalty among members of Congress describes the Democratic party as a party of "inclusive" compromise and the Republican party as a party of "exclusive" compromise. His study of voting alignments in the postwar House of Representatives (1947–62) shows that the program of the Democratic party was regularly fashioned by splicing together the specific programs of various elements of the party— farm, city, labor, and western. By and large, the demands of these interests could be met

through federal aid programs; the function of the House Democratic leadership became that of working out the "inclusive" compromises (intraparty accommodations) that would permit all Democrats to back the programs of Democrats with specific interests. The Republican party, in contrast, behaved as a party of "exclusive" compromise. *"Whenever possible*, most Republican congressmen opposed federal spending programs and championed policies favored by business. Thus, whereas 'interested' minorities in the Democratic party typically supported each other's programs, each 'interested' minority in the Republican party stood alone. The Republican leadership responded to the legislative demands of each minority by mobilizing the rest of the party to oppose them." See Mayhew's book, *Party Loyalty Among Congressmen: The Difference Between Democrats and Republicans, 1947–1962* (Cambridge, MA: Harvard University Press, 1966), especially Chap. 6 (quotation on p. 155). For a study of legislative voting blocs in the U.S. Senate, emphasizing voting in different policy areas, see Alan L. Clem, "Variations in Voting Blocs Across Policy Fields: Pair Agreement Scores in the 1967 U.S. Senate," *Western Political Quarterly*, XXIII (September 1970), 530–51.

87. Robert X. Browning, "Presidents, Congress, and Policy Outcomes: U.S. Social Welfare Expenditures, 1949–77," *American Journal of Political Science*, XXIX (May 1985), 197–216.

88. The potential for fundamental policy departures in any Congress is related to decisive electoral outcomes. Landslide presidential elections, control of the presidency and the House by the same party, a large number of House districts that switch their party representation, and high membership turnover all contribute to major policy change in the new Congress. See Patricia Hurley, David Brady, and Joseph Cooper, "Measuring Legislative Potential for Policy Change," *Legislative Studies Quarterly*, II (November 1977), 385–98.

89. It is rare for any member of Congress to be disciplined for some form of disloyalty to party. But in 1983 Representative Phil Gramm (D., TX) was removed from the House Budget Committee by the Democratic Steering and Policy Committee. Gramm had led the drive to enact President Reagan's economic program in 1981. In the assessment of Ross K. Baker, however, the sanction applied to Gramm was more the result of his violation of House norms (friendly relations, moderation, trust, and honoring commitments) than his breach of party discipline. See "Party and Institutional Sanctions in the U.S. House: The Case of Congressman Gramm," *Legislative Studies Quarterly*, X (August 1985), 315–37.

90. See a recent study that finds that the conservative coalition index used by *Congressional Quarterly* is a valid measure of ideology, as demonstrated by House members' ideological self-identification and opinions on policy questions: Eric R. A. N. Smith, Richard Herrera, and Cheryl L. Herrera, "The Measurement Characteristics of Congressional Roll-Call Indexes," *Legislative Studies Quarterly*, XV (May 1990), 283–95.

91. A key element in the early success of the Reagan administration's economic program was the control of the agenda by his supportive coalition. Democratic and Republican members alike interpreted the 1980 election as a mandate for change—in particular, to reduce government spending. See Barbara Sinclair, "Agenda Control and Policy Success: Ronald Reagan and the 97th House," *Legislative Studies Quarterly*, X (August 1985), 291–314.

92. Mark C. Shelley II, "Presidents and the Conservative Coalition in the U.S. Congress," *Legislative Studies Quarterly*, VIII (February 1983), 79–96. Also see David W. Brady and Charles S. Bullock III, "Is There a Conservative Coalition in the House?" *Journal of Politics*, XLII (May 1980), 549–59. A study of the conservative coalition over a twenty-five-year period by Mary Alice Nye finds that support of the coalition by northern Democrats varies considerably over time. "Conservative Coalition Support in the House of Representatives, 1963–1988," *Legislative Studies Quarterly*, XVIII (May 1993), 255–70.

93. Stanley P. Berard, "Constituent Attitudes and Congressional Parties: Southern Democrats in the U.S. House, 1973–1992" (Ph.D. dissertation, University of Pittsburgh, 1994). M. V. Hood III and Irwin L. Morris argue that the liberalization of southern Democrats is due primarily to generational replacement. Incoming cohorts of southern Democrats have been more liberal than the incumbent Democrats whom they replaced. "Boll Weevils and Roll-Call Voting: A Study in Time and Space," *Legislative Studies Quarterly*, XXIII (May 1998), 245–69.

94. See Chapter 3. The creation of black majority districts in the South led to a considerable

success for Republican candidates in surrounding districts. See Kevin A. Hill, "Does the Creation of Majority Black Districts Aid Republicans? An Analysis of the 1992 Congressional Elections in Eight Southern States," *Journal of Politics*, LVII (May 1995), 384–401.

95. For evidence that Congress sometimes can make significant policy changes in the absence of heavy membership turnover, see Larry M. Bartels, "Constituency Opinion and Congressional Policy Making: The Reagan Defense Buildup," *American Political Science Review*, LXXXV (June 1991), 457–74.

96. The literature that considers this question is worth examining firsthand. See David W. Brady, "A Reevaluation of Realignments in American Politics: Evidence from the House of Representatives," *American Political Science Review*, LXXIX (June 1985), 28–49; David W. Brady and Barbara Sinclair, "Building Majorities for Policy Change in the House of Representatives," *Journal of Politics*, XLVI (November 1984), 1033–60; David W. Brady, "Congressional Party Realignment and Transformations of Public Policy in Three Realignment Eras," *American Journal of Political Science*, XXVI (May 1982), 333–60; Walter J. Stone, "Electoral Change and Policy Representation in Congress," *British Journal of Political Science* (January 1982), 95–115; Herbert Asher and Herbert Weissberg, "Voting Change in Congress: Some Dynamic Perspectives on an Evolutionary Process," *American Journal of Political Science*, XXII (May 1978), 391–425; David W. Brady, "Critical Elections, Congressional Parties and Clusters of Policy Change," *British Journal of Political Science*, VIII (January 1978), 79–99; Barbara Sinclair, "Party Realignment and the Transformation of the Political Agenda: The House of Representatives, 1925–1938," *American Political Science Review*, LXXI (September 1977), 940–53; and David W. Brady and Naomi Lynn, "Switched-Seat Congressional Districts: Their Effect on Party Voting and Public Policy," *American Journal of Political Science*, XVII (August 1973), 528–43.

97. Bernard Grofman, Robert Griffin, and Gregory Berry, "House Members Who Become Senators: Learning from a 'Natural Experiment' in Representation," *Legislative Studies Quarterly*, XX (November 1995), 513–29.

98. Fenno, *Home Style*.

99. Susan Welch and Eric H. Carlson, "The Impact of Party on Voting Behavior in a Nonpartisan Legislature," *American Political Science Review*, LXVII (September 1973), 854–67.

100. A variety of approaches has been used in the study of legislative party behavior in the states. For representative examples, see Glen T. Broach, "A Comparative Dimensional Analysis of Partisan and Urban-Rural Voting in State Legislatures," *Journal of Politics*, XXXIV (August 1972), 905–21; Thomas A. Flinn, "Party Responsibility in the States: Some Causal Factors," *American Political Science Review*, LVIII (March 1964), 60–71; Malcolm E. Jewell, "Party Voting in American State Legislatures," *American Political Science Review*, XLIX (September 1955), 773–91; William J. Keefe, "Parties, Partisanship, and Public Policy in the Pennsylvania Legislature," *American Political Science Review*, XLVIII (June 1954), 450–64; Hugh L. LeBlanc, "Voting in State Senates: Party and Constituency Influences," *Midwest Journal of Political Science*, XIII (February 1969), 33–57; Sarah McCally Morehouse, "The State Political Party and the Policy-Making Process," *American Political Science Review*, LXVII (March 1973), 55–72; and Charles W. Wiggins, "Party Politics in the Iowa Legislature," *Midwest Journal of Political Science*, XI (February 1967), 86–97.

101. See a study by Robert E. Entman that finds that ideology significantly influences roll-call voting in the state legislatures of Connecticut and North Carolina. Legislators from urban, industrialized areas are more likely to support liberal public policies than legislators from rural areas. "The Impact of Ideology in Legislative Behavior and Public Policy in the States," *Journal of Politics*, XLV (February 1983), 163–82.

102. David R. Derge, "Metropolitan and Outstate Alignments in Illinois and Missouri Legislative Delegations," *American Political Science Review*, LII (December 1958), 1051–65.

103. Sarah McCally Morehouse, "Legislative Party Voting for the Governor's Program," *Legislative Studies Quarterly*, XXI (August 1996), 359–82. For studies of the role of party in a "one-party" state, see Robert Harmel and Keith E. Hamm, "Development of a Party Role in a No-Party Legislature," *Western Political Quarterly*, XXXIX (March 1986), 79–92; and Robert Harmel, "Minority Partisanship in One-Party Predominant Legislatures: A Five-State Study," *Journal of Politics*, XLVIII (August 1986), 729–40.

104. James H. Kuklinski, "Representatives and Elections: A Policy Analysis," *American Political Science Review*, LXXII (March 1978), 176–77.

105. Joel A. Thompson, "Bringing Home the Bacon: The Politics of Pork Barrel in the North Carolina Legislature," *Legislative Studies Quarterly*, XI (February 1986), 91–108. Also see Joel A. Thompson and Gary F. Moncrief, "Pursuing the Pork in a State Legislature: A Research Note," *Legislative Studies Quarterly*, XIII (August 1988), 393–401.

106. Gary Keith, "Comparing Legislative Studies Groups in Three States," *Legislative Studies Quarterly*, VI (February 1981), 69–86.

107. The influence of the governor on legislation varies from state to state. See a three-state study (California, Iowa, and Texas) by Charles W. Wiggins, Keith E. Hamm, and Charles G. Bell, "Interest Group and Party Influence Agents in the Legislative Process: A Comparative State Analysis," *Journal of Politics*, LIV (February 1992), 82–100.

108. Morehouse, "Legislative Party Voting for the Governor's Program," pp. 368–72.

109. Schattschneider, *Party Government*, p. 85.

110. "A Revised Theory of American Party Politics," *American Political Science Review*, XLIV (September 1950), 669–77 (quotation on p. 677). (Emphasis added.)

111. Wayne Shannon, *Party, Constituency and Congressional Voting* (Baton Rouge: Louisiana State University Press, 1968), pp. 166–70.

112. "Electoral Margins, Constituency Influence, and Policy Moderation: A Critical Assessment," *American Politics Quarterly* (October 1973), 479–98. See an earlier study of the behavior of members of Congress from marginal-switch districts by Judith A. Strain, "The Nature of Political Representation in Legislative Districts of Intense Party Competition," B.A. thesis, Chatham College, Pittsburgh, 1963. The Strain and Fiorina tests conform more closely to the original proposition since, like Huntington, they deal with party differences within the same constituencies, not between different constituencies. Another study of the behavior of members from switched-seat districts worth consulting is David W. Brady and Naomi B. Lynn, "Switched-Seat Congressional Districts: Their Effect on Party Voting and Public Policy," *American Journal of Political Science*, XVII (August 1973), 528–43. Their analysis shows that representatives from switched districts are not only the strongest supporters of their party majority but also the strongest supporters of policy changes. The evidence is clear that representatives from switched-seat districts have voting records that are distinctly different from the members they replaced. See Patricia A. Hurley, "Electoral Change and Policy Consequences," *American Politics Quarterly*, XII (April 1984), 177–94.

113. Lewis A. Froman, Jr., "Inter-Party Constituency Differences and Congressional Voting Behavior," *American Political Science Review*, LVII (March 1963), 57–61.

114. V. O. Key, Jr., and Corinne Silverman, "Party and Separation of Powers: A Panorama of Practice in the States," in *Public Policy*, ed. Carl J. Friedrich and J. Kenneth Galbraith (Cambridge, MA: Harvard University, Graduate School of Public Administration, 1954), pp. 382–412 (quotation on p. 403).

115. Ibid., p. 398. Also see Morris P. Fiorina, *Divided Governments in the States* (Cambridge, MA: Harvard University Center for American Political Studies, 1991).

116. Gary C. Jacobson, *The Electoral Origins of Divided Government* (Boulder, CO: Westview Press, 1990), pp. 3–4.

117. See a study by Paul Frymer, Thomas P. Kim, and Terri L. Bimes on the connection between split-ticket voting and divided party government: "Party Elites, Ideological Voters, and Divided Party Government," *Legislative Studies Quarterly*, XXII (May 1997), 195–216. The authors contend that the voters who split their tickets are not doing so to create an ideologically moderate government or because they have different expectations for their House members than for their president. Rather, most split-ticket voters are ideological conservatives who cast their votes to elect conservative House members.

118. David R. Mayhew, "Does It Make Any Difference if Party Control Is Divided," *IGS Public Affairs Report* (July 1991), 10. Also see Charles O. Jones, *The Presidency in a Separated System* (Washington, DC: Brookings Institution, 1994), especially pp. 196–209 and 284–88.

119. *Toward a More Responsible Two-Party System,* published as a supplement to the *American Political Science Review,* XLIV (September 1950) (quotations on pp. 17, 18, and 20, respectively). (Italics omitted.)

120. For an analysis of the development of this concept and its key features, see Austin Ranney, *The Doctrine of Responsible Party Government* (Urbana: University of Illinois Press, 1954). The best-known exponent of the doctrine is E. E. Schattschneider. See *Party Government* and *The Struggle for Party Government* (College Park, MD: University of Maryland Press, 1948).

121. There is an impressive string of studies bearing on the party-responsibility model. The most recent analyses are Evron M. Kirkpatrick, "Toward a More Responsible Two-Party System: Political Science, Policy Science, or Pseudo-Science?" *American Political Science Review,* XLV (December 1971), 965–90; Gerald M. Pomper, "From Confusion to Clarity: Issues and American Voters, 1956–1968," *American Political Science Review,* LXVI (June 1972), 415–28; and Michael Margolis, "From Confusion to Confusion—Issues and the American Voter 1956–1972," *American Political Science Review,* LXXI (March 1977), 31–43.

# 10

# Interest Groups
# and the
# Legislative Process

The legislature is the natural habitat of political interest groups. Because interest groups are "usually engaged in getting exceptions made to established policies or in breaking down policies or preventing the creation of general policies,"[1] they are attracted to the legislature, with its many stages at which legislation can be resisted, obstructed, or sandbagged permanently. Of all groups, those concerned with defense of the status quo—as distinguished from those attempting to change government policies or to promote new ones—have found the legislative process most likely to serve their ends.[2]

Legislative politics often center on the struggle among groups. There are two principal interpretations of the nature and significance of group conflict in the legislature. Earl Latham, for example, developed this position:

> The legislature referees the group struggle, ratifies the victories of the successful coalitions, and records the terms of the surrenders, compromises, and conquests in the form of statutes. Every statute tends to represent compromises because the process of accommodating conflicts of group interest is one of deliberation and consent. The legislative vote on any issue tends to represent the composition of strength, i.e., the balance of power, among the contending groups at the moment of voting. What may be called public policy is the equilibrium reached in this struggle at any given moment. . . .[3]

However, E. E. Schattschneider argued that Latham's "referee" concept is too restrictive since it suggests that Congress "has no mind or force of its own" and hence is unable to affect the outcome of conflict among groups:

> Actually the outcome of political conflict is not like the "resultant" of opposing forces in physics. To assume that the forces in a political situation could be diagrammed as a physicist might diagram the resultant of opposing physical forces is to wipe the slate clean of all remote, general and public considerations for the protection of which civil societies have been instituted. . . . *Private conflicts are taken into the public arena precisely because someone wants to make certain that the power ratio among the private interests most immediately involved shall not prevail.*[4]

It would be arbitrary to say that one interpretation is correct and that the other is not. Many factors—including circumstance, the subject matter of legislation, and party position—help determine the impact of interest groups on public policy. At times, to be sure, group influence is decisive; at other times, and just as plainly, the legislature is master of its own house.

## INTEREST-GROUP POLITICS IN AMERICA

Neither the proliferation nor the importance of groups in American politics can be explained by recourse to a single factor, even though, at bottom, one condition is essential to their development: freedom of association. Madison put it succinctly: "Liberty is to faction what air is to fire, an aliment without which it instantly expires."[5] Given conditions that foster free association, what immediate factors serve to augment the power of private groups and to encourage their participation in politics? In the case of the United States, several reasons, associated to some degree, may be advanced.

These reasons, presumptive and familiar, may be sorted into three categories: legal-structural, political, and ideological. The structure of American government invites vigorous group action. *Decentralization* is a hallmark of the system: Federalism serves to parcel out authority and responsibility to the fifty states and a national government, and the system of separated powers has a similar impact within each level of government. Nowhere is power concentrated. The value of these structural arrangements apart, it seems obvious that they contribute to conditions under which interest groups can exert considerable influence. Battles can be fought on a variety of terrains, and one lost or hopeless on the national level, for example, may be waged vigorously in the states, as in the case of management-sponsored right-to-work laws, which were steered through about one-third of the legislatures when a national law had no chance of passage. Dispersal of power within and between branches of government carries a similar invitation to group activity. "Nothing about the system is direct and simple. Authority is perplexingly subdivided and distributed, and responsibility has to be hunted down in out-of-the-way corners."[6] Under such circumstances, it would be surprising indeed if groups were less attuned to the possibilities for gaining access to critical centers of power. From the vantage point of groups (with some exceptions), government decentralization is reason for celebration.

The American political milieu, reinforced by historic customs and outlook, also helps account for the primacy of groups in national and state politics. A principal result of our decentralized government system is a decentralized party system, one with considerably more *"pluribus"* than *unum*," in Stephen K. Bailey's choice phrase. Arguing that policy is "frequently developed by an infinitely intricate system of barter and legerdemain," Bailey observed,

The real issue is that the government, in a generation of prolific services and equally prolific regulation, has become a vast arena in which group interests and personalities struggle for power without sufficient reference to questions of the long-range public interest. These groups and personalities use the pressure points and divergent party roles and constituencies of the President, the bureaucracy, the national committees, and the two Houses of Congress as instruments of access and finagle. This produces a politics of "boodle" and accommodation, but not a politics of responsible power and clear national purpose.[7]

The absence of a unified and responsible party system magnifies the opportunities for effective interest-group action, especially in the legislative process. Organized pressures are not easily resisted by weak and undisciplined legislative parties, and it is not an excessive generalization to suggest that where parties count for little of what is done, groups count for much. Writing of Congress, Schattschneider observed that "the parties do very little to discipline or defend their members," thus permitting pressure groups to "trade on the fears and the confusion of individual members of Congress." The consequences are predictable: "In the struggle for survival in a highly chaotic political situation, the Congressman is thrown very much on his own resources, seeking support wherever he can find it and tending strongly to yield to *all* demands made on him. Any reasonably convincing demonstration of an organized demand for anything is likely to impress him out of all proportion to the real weight or influence of the pressure group."[8] The system of district representation makes members of Congress especially susceptible to appeals from groups powerful in their home constituency, from which they must win reelection.

Finally, the virility of groups is related to the low ideological content of American politics. That American voters as a whole are not moved to act on stern ideological or programmatic grounds has been well documented. What perhaps is not so well known is that the same can be said for their lawmakers. How have legislators come to acquire their political beliefs? What forces converge to shape their views of public matters? Out of several hundred legislators interviewed in a study of California, New Jersey, Ohio, and Tennessee legislators, only a handful contended that they had become interested in politics and motivated to participate as a result of socioeconomic beliefs that they had acquired. Ideological commitments, in brief, had little to do with impelling them toward a career in politics. Far more important in their political socialization (the process by which they acquired their political values, attitudes, interests, or knowledge) were primary-group influences, major events, personal predispositions (for example, a sense of obligation and admiration for politicians), and participation in certain forms of political action.[9]

Loosely or briefly linked to ideology, legislators may be particularly responsive to the demands of interest groups. Political outlook, it may be hypothesized, is something to be worked out pragmatically, as a part of the process of determining the relative weight of various factors that bear on one's career as a legislator. Under such circumstances, and in the absence of disciplined legislative party organizations, it is plausible to suppose that pressure groups are the principal beneficiaries of the low ideological content in the typical legislator's outlook. Bargains may be struck more easily—and retained as long as expedient. This interpretation, if speculative, is also consonant with Schattschneider's contention that a member of Congress "is in no good position to assess accurately the influence of minorities which make demands on him. In an extremely irresponsible political system a vote for anything looks like a cheap price to pay for the privilege of being friendly to everyone."[10]

Recent research concludes that fundamental changes have occurred in the nature of interest-group politics. Burdett A. Loomis and Allan J. Cigler identify these contemporary developments: (1) a striking proliferation of interest groups; (2) a strong tendency for groups to locate their headquarters in Washington, DC; (3) a growth in the information-processing capabilities of groups; (4) an increase in single-issue group lobbying; (5) an increase in the number of political action committees—about 4,000 in 1999; (6) an expansion of interest-group activity involving the bureaucracy, the presidency, and Congress; (7) the continuing erosion of political party activities and capabilities; (8) the growing importance of public interest groups; (9) the growing importance of lobbying by corporations, universities, state and local governments, and foreign interests; and (10) a significant increase in interest-group activity at the state level.[11]

## THE LOBBYISTS

There are many ways by which a group may communicate its views on policy matters to government officials. Since not all organizations are of equal size or possess equal resources, not all use the same techniques for advancing their claims in the lobby process. Small organizations are often forced to wage their campaigns at a distance—through telephone calls, telegrams, and the mails. Powerful interest groups, in contrast, invariably include in their pressure arsenal one or more professional lobbyists (or legislative agents) to represent their views personally to government officials. Moreover, all the main lobby groups have a headquarters in Washington and an impressive retinue of research and clerical workers. As a rule, there is nothing imposing about lobbies' headquarters in the capital cities of the states. In fact, only a few organizations have anything more than a lobbyist's hotel room to serve as a staging point for their "raids" on the legislature. Short legislative sessions (and short work weeks) make it impractical to maintain and staff a permanent headquarters.

A fairly sizable literature on lobbies and lobbying has been produced, but only limited attention has been given to the lobbyists themselves—their backgrounds, personal characteristics, careers, and role in the lobby process. A study by Lester Milbrath helps to answer some questions regarding the political party activity of Washington lobbyists. Lobbyists, the study discloses, are not as a rule active participants in party politics. In the same way that most pressure groups strive to avoid identification with either political party, believing this would imperil their access to the other party, so also most lobbyists attempt to steer clear of entangling partisan commitments. Moreover, their personal histories are notably free from partisan ties: Only about one-half of them participate in politics in any active way and fewer than one-third have held elective or appointive public office. About three-fourths of the lobbyists have received legal training, many having worked previously for the federal government. Despite a popular myth to the contrary, only a handful of the lobbyists are former members of Congress; in fact, former congressional staff assistants turn up in far greater number than former legislators. The principal way in which lobbyists participate in politics is by making financial contributions to campaigns. Plainly, the study concludes, Washington lobbyists do not feel that their role compels them to participate actively in party politics; on the contrary, most of them scrupulously avoid it in the belief that involvement cuts down their effectiveness. "Party control of the Congress shifts frequently enough to give pause to any lobbyist who might contemplate putting all his eggs in one basket and becoming closely identified with one of the parties."[12]

Several general observations about state lobbyists are in order. First, they are becoming more like national lobbyists, which is to say that they are becoming more professionalized. Lobbying is becoming more of a full-time occupation in a number of states. Second, there has been a significant increase in the number of professional lawyer-lobbyists. Third, lobbying firms that represent multiple clients have become more numerous. And fourth, there is a growing tendency for lobbyists to specialize in particular policy areas, such as agriculture, education, or labor law. Particularly in urban states, lobbying and lobbyists are coming to resemble their counterparts in Washington, DC.[13] A recent study of male and female lobbyists in California, South Carolina, and Wisconsin finds that women are considerably underrepresented in state lobbying communities (only 29 percent of lobbyists in California, 28 percent in South Carolina, and 24 percent in Wisconsin) and that they are most likely to be the agents of public interest groups. Women lobbyists behave much like their male colleagues.[14]

Former legislators who seek positions as lobbyists are likely to find their talents in demand. By hiring an ex-legislator to represent its interests, an organization acquires a certain amount of built-in access to the legislature. Such lobbyists will know most of the legislators and normally be accepted as a member of the club. A lobbyist who formerly served as a member of the U.S. House of Representatives comments:

> When you're talking to somebody you've played paddleball with or played in the Republican-Democratic golf tournament with, or seen regularly in the Capitol Hill Club, there's no question that helps. I think most sitting members go out of their way to be helpful to former members.[15]

Another indication of the value of an ex-legislator as lobbyist is shown in the experience of an oil lobbyist who formerly held a leadership position in the Colorado legislature:

> I keep close watch on the legislature on oil matters. I make it my business to visit at home each elected state legislator—or perhaps even before he is elected—to get to know him. I want to do this before he comes to Denver where my face is just one of a hundred new ones he'll have to know. If I can get him on a first name calling basis that means a lot. When he comes up to Denver, he'll be lonely, but he'll see a friendly face. I'll help him around, find out what committee he wants, explain about them, and help him get set on the committee if I possibly can.[16]

Legislators linked in a fixed or steady relationship with a particular interest group have come to be termed, somewhat pejoratively, "inside lobbyists." It is not unusual to find interest groups that have special influence, a lien of sorts, on individual legislators, causing them to respond sympathetically and predictably on certain types of legislation. Customarily the sponsors of legislation of concern to the group, they lobby their fellow members, smooth the way for favorable bills or hamstring those that are hostile, and vote according to the best interests of their affiliation. When farm legislation is at stake, for example, the agricultural lobby sometimes seems fully as evident within Congress as without. Representatives and senators regarded as spokespersons for farm, oil, labor, and environmental interests are easily found.

A principal characteristic of an effective pressure group and the stock in trade of a competent lobbyist is a large reservoir of expert knowledge concerning the legislative process, its labyrinths as well as its main paths, its vulnerability to penetration. Knowledge of the process, however, may be of little avail unless a group has access to the principal decision makers. Although procedure varies from legislature to legislature and from state to nation, the principal junctures in the legislative process where group influence can be brought to bear are everywhere the same.[17]

## MAJOR ACCESS POINTS IN THE LEGISLATIVE PROCESS

### The Introduction of Bills

Although the number of bills originating with interest groups cannot be reckoned with precision, it obviously is substantial. Many ideas for legislation are born in the offices of interest groups and later drafted there for submission in the legislature; on other occasions groups contribute their ideas to friendly members, who rely on legislative agencies or staffs for the actual drafting.

Who introduces an organization's bill may have an important bearing on the eventual outcome. The director of the national legislative commission of the American Legion testified before a congressional committee investigating lobbying:

> I attempt to get the bill introduced by the chairman of the committee. If I can't get him to introduce it I try some other member of the committee. If I can't get any member of the committee to introduce it, then we try some other congressman or senator, whichever the case may be.[18]

Groups strive to have their proposals introduced early in the session, hoping thereby to avoid losing them in the hectic closing days when the calendars may be cleared imprudently. To guard against detrimental legislation, a continuing danger, large and well-staffed organizations customarily examine all bills and resolutions introduced in order to chart a course of action; hostile bills are followed through the legislative mill as assiduously as the group's own proposals.

### The Committee Stage

The life of a bill is always tenuous, but at no time is it more vulnerable than in committee. Victory here augurs well for final passage, whereas a major setback at this point is rarely undone. Accordingly, groups usually concentrate their heaviest fire on the committees. Two lobbyists offer explanations:

> We watch the [House] Education and Labor Committee very carefully; but it's the only one we're interested in. Otherwise you would spread yourself too thin. We have to control the labor committee. It's our lifeblood. [an official of the AFL-CIO][19]

> Once a bill clears committee the battle is usually four-fifths done, because they have a habit over there of backing up their committee actions in both houses. The main battle is to get proper appropriate legislation out of the committee. . . . Once that happens, you don't have any problem. Once in ten times there'll be a floor fight. At that point you have to work with the entire Congress.[20]

The observations of a lobbyist in Massachusetts also show the centrality of committee decision making:

> You must work through committees. They have the power. If you can win in the committees you usually have your way. First you go to the committee chairman. Then you present formally to the committee hearing. Then you go to the appropriations committee. If you lose in one committee, you go to your next committee chairman to bottle it up while you push your case with the leadership.[21]

In dealing with committees, lobbyists find their tasks less formidable if sympathetic legislators are there to shepherd their interests—hence groups show keen interest in committee appointments, occasionally being able to influence them. Committee hearings afford groups an opportunity to record their positions on legislation and to submit opinions and data in support of them. Ordinarily the officers of organizations, rather than their legislative agents, are used to testify when major bills are under consideration, in the belief that their views will have greater influence among committee members. Lobbying committee staffs, Diana M. Evans has shown, can be a particularly effective technique when conflictual legislation is under consideration.[22]

Committee decisions on legislation tend to foreshadow final outcomes. Hence, committee hearings are treated as serious business by interest groups. "Great ingenuity has therefore been shown in attempts to influence committee opinion," Dayton McKean observed. "The crippled victims of industrial accidents and diseases have been paraded before committees; specimens of adulterated or misbranded foods and drugs have been displayed; where committees have consented, moving pictures of poor schools, of slums, of conditions in prisons, have been shown."[23] Veterans' groups have no qualms about producing a Medal of Honor winner for testimony and trading on his wartime valor to advance the interests of the organization. "Average" housewives, "average" businesspersons, "average" workers, "average" druggists, and "little people" are sometimes used by organizations to testify on legislation; the "plain folks" approach is more common on the state than on the national level.

The legislative activity of lobbyists, one study has shown, is shaped by the character of the issues. On issues that are relatively noncontroversial, lobbyists are primarily concerned with influencing committee decisions. This is the key stage in the consideration of "narrow" legislation. The more controversial the legislation, the greater the likelihood that lobbyists will shift their efforts to shaping decisions on the floor. Here, not surprisingly, they encounter more difficulties in protecting their interests.[24]

## Floor Action

Even though political interest groups customarily concentrate on the committee stage, they are by no means powerless on the floor. Because floor action ordinarily is more visible to the public, legislators may be more vulnerable to groups there than in committee. Every roll-call vote on an amendment or major bill is potentially dangerous to legislators since their decisions, preserved in the records of pressure groups, may cost them campaign funds and election support. Particularly hazardous is a record vote on an amendment whose purpose is to favor a certain interest by bringing it within the scope of a bill or by excluding it: The issue is sharply drawn, and to vote against the amendment is perhaps to make new enemies.

## The Conference Committee

Because House and Senate frequently disagree on legislation, the conference committee has become a conventional hurdle in the life of many bills. Major bills in Congress invariably are conference products. The reports of these committees not only carry high priority but also are closed to amendment on the floor; conference committee decisions thus tend to represent the last word of the legislature. An organization able to influence the choice of conference committee members or otherwise to inject its outlook into committee deliberations is in a strategic position to gain its ends.

## SPECIAL TECHNIQUES USED BY LOBBIES

### Inspired Communications

A lobby technique that has become increasingly common rests on appeals to the public at large—through newspapers, magazines, television, radio—or to the members of organizations or special clienteles to contact their representatives regarding legislation. All large organizations have thousands of active members who, on short notice, can be rallied to send telegrams and letters or to make telephone calls to legislators. At a decisive juncture in the legislative battle, Washington or the state capital can be rapidly flooded with communications from "the folks back home." A narrow-gauge communications campaign may be based on telegrams and calls from a select group of powerful constituents. The following paragraphs taken from a letter by the secretary of the General Gas Committee to the president of a Texas refining company, a member of the committee, illustrate how and where pressure is to be applied:

> Because this threat is so real, so immediate, we in the industry must rally to complete a legislative victory now only half won. We must carry the truth to our Senators on a ground swell of public opinion. The alternative is concession

by default to an opposition that is as well organized and active as it is misguided in its affection for regimentation.

Those Senators who are already favorable to our cause deserve the reassurance of support from their constituents. Those who are presently undecided must be given all the facts. *Those who favor keeping controls must be convinced by a flood of opinion that the ground they are on is not only fallacious but unpopular as well.*[25]

The impact of inspired communications on legislators is hard to measure.[26] Legislators often contend that they discount identical or "stock" telegrams, postcards, letters, or telephone calls. Even when different types of messages (variations on a theme) are used in an attempt to suggest spontaneity, standard clauses, repetitive and shopworn expressions, and the tendency of the messages to arrive in batches suggest that the "voice of the people" has in fact been organized by some group. A Wisconsin state legislator provides an account of such a campaign:

> There was an episode a couple of years back when the firemen were pushing through a so-called heart and lung bill. They had their lobbyists here and it looked like the bill wasn't going to go through one house. So, a lobbyist put a call back home to certain other people, who in turn put in certain other calls. Pretty soon the telephones were jammed. The firemen back home were calling their legislators and there was a constant stream of legislators to the telephone answering long-distance phone calls from constituents telling them to vote in favor of this bill. Well, when it became obvious that this was a pressure movement, I contacted the lobbyist I knew had charge of this and said, "Now look, you'd better cut those phone calls off. I'm not interested in talking to them. I know what your position is. I've already indicated that I will support this bill and I don't want to be bothered." Boom, those phone calls stopped just like that.[27]

Inspired communications take many forms. Testifying on proposed lobby legislation, the vice-president of Common Cause described the tactics of the American Trial Lawyers Association in opposing no-fault auto insurance:

> Last year the American Trial Lawyers Association set up an elaborate and devious lobbying system to oppose no-fault auto insurance. It secretly arranged for mailgrams opposing the legislation to be automatically sent to key Representatives by Western Union offices around the country. Association members needed only to call Western Union and give the names of friends and associates, and for each name given, 10 messages were sent off to Capitol Hill. The Association even arranged for Western Union's sales force to encourage local trial lawyers associations and other interested groups to use the mailgram service. The result was a deluge of messages to key congressional offices protesting no-fault insurance, all seemingly sent individually by concerned constituents. In one case, 31 sets of 100 telegrams were all sent by the same individual. The American Trial Lawyers Association was not registered at the time as a lobbying organization, although they have now done so. Moreover, new legislation should make certain that information on such devious, as well as more legitimate, lobbying tactics are the subject of public reporting requirements.[28]

Although campaigns to rally the public are often unsuccessful, on occasion they produce dramatic results. Casting about for a way to secure new revenue, the Pennsylvania legislature passed a bill to levy a 6 percent tax on insurance premiums. The response of the insurance industry was to launch a massive public opinion campaign designed to generate opposition to the tax. In a matter of days, the legislature and the governor received more than 100,000 letters, some 10,000 telegrams, and countless telephone calls. Breaking all records for dispatch, the legislature frantically adopted a "repealer" by overwhelming majorities in both houses. Explaining the debacle, the House Democratic majority leader said, "The insurance industry spent a million dollars in advertising. The industry did it very cleverly. They stirred up public indignation and scared the pants off all of us."[29]

### Campaign Contributions, Social Lobby, and Bribery

Three other forms of lobby activity clustered around the edge of the legislative process may be noted: the use of campaign contributions and campaign work, the social lobby, and outright bribery. By all odds the most important of these is the first.

Interest groups furnish what legislators need: campaign funds and political assistance. Since parties or candidates rarely judge their campaign resources to be adequate, they find it difficult to ignore an open treasury or a group of volunteer workers. Interest-group contributions to congressional candidates have soared in recent years. For the 1978 election cycle (covering a two-year period), group political action committees contributed $34.1 million to House and Senate candidates; for the campaigns of 1998, PAC contributions totaled $206.8 million. It is clear that members of Congress, particularly on the House side, have become increasingly reliant on interest-group money. In 1998, 40 percent of all the funds raised by *winning* House candidates was contributed by PACs. Democratic candidates garnered 46 percent of their funds from PACs, Republicans 39 percent. Senate incumbents (both parties) received 25 percent of their funds from PACs. For the 1998 election cycle, PACs gave nearly eight times as much money to congressional incumbents as to their challengers.[30] Money from PACs is a conspicuous element in the incumbent-protection system that flourishes in Congress.[31] Nevertheless, as John R. Wright has shown, PACs seldom contribute campaign funds to representatives from districts where they have minimal presence. "Members of Congress seldom experience financial pressures and lobbying pressures from groups that have little or no economic or organizational claims in their districts." The heightened role of PACs in financing congressional campaigns thus has not altered the members' representational focus on their geographic constituencies.[32]

Table 10.1 shows the leading PAC contributors in the 1998 election campaign, and Table 10.2 classifies PAC contributions by type of organization.

**TABLE 10.1**   Top fifteen PAC spenders in 1998 congressional elections

| Political Action Committee | Disbursements* |
|---|---|
| Emily's List | $10,295,325 |
| Democratic Republican Independent Voter Education Committee | 8,145,974 |
| NRA Political Victory Fund | 7,978,499 |
| Campaign for Working Families | 6,665,386 |
| Campaign America Inc. | 6,239,249 |
| Association of Trial Lawyers of American Political Action Committee | 5,982,021 |
| New Republican Majority Fund | 5,799,770 |
| National Education Association Political Action Committee | 5,174,228 |
| American Medical Association Political Action Committee | 4,954,043 |
| International Brotherhood of Electrical Workers Committee on Political Education | 4,396,065 |
| Leadership '98 (FKA Friends of Albert Gore, Jr., Inc.) | 3,900,983 |
| Machinists Non-Partisan Political League | 3,742,400 |
| UAW–V–CAP (UAW Voluntary Community Action Program) | 3,531,969 |
| Voice of Teachers for Educ/Cmte on Pol. Educ. of NY State UNTD Teachers (Vote/COPE) | 3,374,177 |
| Black America's Political Action Committee | 3,329,807 |

*These disbursements cover the 1997–98 election cycle.

SOURCE: Press release, Federal Election Commission, June 8, 1999, p. 18.


**TABLE 10.2**   PAC contributions (in millions of dollars) to all candidates for Congress, 1998

| PAC Type | Senate | House | Democrats | Republicans |
|---|---|---|---|---|
| Corporate | 20.9 | 50.4 | 23.0 | 48.1 |
| Labor | 6.0 | 37.3 | 39.5 | 3.7 |
| Nonconnected | 7.1 | 19.9 | 10.7 | 16.3 |
| Trade/Member/Health | 12.5 | 46.5 | 22.3 | 36.7 |
| Other | 1.5 | 4.7 | 2.8 | 3.3 |
| Totals | 48.0 | 158.8 | 98.3 | 108.1 |

NOTE: For both House and Senate, the PAC contributions shown in this table were made to 436 incumbents, 1,285 challengers, and 379 open-seat candidates. PAC contributions to all congressional candidates in the 1997–98 election cycle totaled $206.8 million.

SOURCE: Calculated from data furnished by the Federal Election Commission: http://www.fec.gov/press/canye98.htm.


Corporate PACs, which regularly top the list of donors, gave about twice as much money to Republicans as to Democrats, and, of course, most of it went to incumbents of both parties. And true to form, the funds contributed by labor PACs heavily favored Democratic members, particularly on the House side.

TABLE 10.3   PAC allocation patterns, parties and candidates, 1989–98

|  | 1997–98 | 1995–96 | 1993–94 | 1991–92 | 1989–90 |
|---|---|---|---|---|---|
| **Senate** | | | | | |
| Democrats | 43% | 36% | 51% | 57% | 49% |
| Republicans | 57 | 64 | 49 | 43 | 51 |
| **House** | | | | | |
| Democrats | 49 | 50 | 67 | 67 | 67 |
| Republicans | 51 | 50 | 33 | 33 | 33 |
| Incumbents | 78 | 67 | 72 | 72 | 79 |
| Challengers | 10 | 15 | 10 | 12 | 10 |
| Open seats | 12 | 18 | 18 | 16 | 11 |

SOURCE: Adapted from press release, Federal Election Commission, June 8, 1999, pp. 1–2.

Table 10.3 presents summary data on PAC contributions to congressional candidates in the five elections of the 1990s. It will be readily apparent that PAC gifts are heavily influenced by two key factors: majority-party status and incumbency. When the Democrats held Congress in the early 1990s, their candidates attracted considerably more PAC money than Republican candidates—about twice as much in the case of the House. The dramatic Republican victory in 1994 changed the calculus, and Republican candidates were soon receiving vastly more PAC money than previously. Recently, the parties have competed more or less evenly in the House for interest-group money, while the Republicans have won hands-down in Senate races. The story on incumbents is, of course, well known: Year in, year out, they can count on getting three-fourths of all PAC funds given to congressional candidates. Only a few challengers do well in the PAC sweepstakes. The central conclusion that emerges from Table 10.3 is that PAC money, in disproportionate amounts, tracks position and power.

Candidates for Congress spend a great deal of time raising campaign funds. Few think their treasuries are adequate, and they will accept contributions from almost any source. What is gained by those interest groups that contribute to legislators' campaigns? The conventional response looks like this:

> When the lobbyists themselves are asked to define the chief value of campaign contributions in their work, they frequently reply with one word: access. The campaign donation, they say, helps them obtain access to the legislator so they can present their case. . . . Since it would be unrealistic to expect the lobbyist to describe his campaign contributions as attempts at influence, the "access" explanation may be, in some cases, a cover story. In the majority of instances, however, it is probably the truth or close to it. Senators and Representatives are busy men, and the competition for their attention is keen. The lobbyist who

makes a campaign donation—or arranges for one to be made by his client—frequently is doing nothing more than meeting the competition and creating good will, to insure that he, too, will be heard.[33]

Legislators themselves do not agree on whether the campaign contributions of interest groups tend to undermine the legislative process:

> If you're not able to fund your campaign and keep your responsibility to the people who send you here, you don't belong in office. [Representative John D. Dingell, D., MI]

> It is fundamentally corrupting. At best, people say they are sympathetic to the people they are getting money from before they get it; at worst, they are selling votes. But you cannot prove the cause and effect. I take money from labor, and I have to think twice in voting against their interests. I shouldn't have to do that. [Representative Richard L. Ottinger, D., NY][34]

> Members are only human. You can't entirely disassociate yourself from something like a campaign contribution. How much it impacts on you and how far you're willing to move from your own principles is something each member has to decide for himself. [Former Representative Sam Gibbons, D., FL][35]

Research on PAC contributions and legislators' voting behavior has produced mixed findings. Some studies have uncovered evidence that PAC contributions do make a difference in how members vote, whereas others have been unable to detect any relationship. One study, for example, found that the campaign contributions of the National Rifle Association and Handgun Control, Inc., influenced the votes of members on gun control legislation in 1986.[36] In contrast, a study of 120 PACs concluded that "although PAC contributions may facilitate a lobby's access to a representative's time, contributions from large PACs do not generally influence members' voting patterns on issues of interest to these groups."[37]

Although systematic evidence that PACs can buy or rent votes is far from compelling, a study of PAC influence in *committees* offers support for the view that monied interests can affect members' behavior. The study of three House committees (Agriculture, Education and Labor, and Energy and Commerce) found that campaign gifts significantly increased the participation of members—reflected in such activities as attendance, voting participation, speaking, offering amendments, authoring bills and amendments, and behind-the-scenes negotiations—on the side of the groups. This study is particularly important for its findings that interest-group influence flourishes at the committee stage and that its effects appear in legislative involvement rather than in votes.[38]

PAC money is not distributed randomly. Thomas Romer and James M. Snyder, Jr., find strong evidence that PACs carefully target the members and chairs of particular committees. If a member switches from one committee to another or gains a position in the committee leadership, the pattern of his or her PAC gifts will change. A member who joins the House Committee on Agriculture, for example, is soon the recipient of contributions from various agricultural PACs; a representative who leaves this committee receives reduced support from these groups. A close relationship between membership on House Banking and banking PACs is also evident. The broad point is that PACs add or drop members depending on their committee assignments.[39]

Majority-party status also has an independent effect on the contributions of corporate PACs. When their party is in the majority in the House, Democratic incumbents receive more money from corporate PACs than when their party is in the minority. And the same is true for Republicans. Labor contributions, on the other hand, are unaffected by majority-party status. Labor simply directs its funds to Democrats.[40]

The legislator who accepts financial or other support from an interest group cannot avoid some measure of obligation to the group. The nature of the obligation undoubtedly varies from group to group and from legislator to legislator. It may involve merely the obligation to give the lobbyist a hearing about the group's interests, or it may involve much more. The observations of a lobbyist whose organization makes it a practice to contribute to state legislative campaigns show something of the character of the exchange:

> If it is an important bill, one that we just have to get passed, usually I'll go to somebody and say, "Look, this is one I have to have and I want you to vote on this bill." I am calling in a debt. However, I don't use this very often because you can only use it once in a while. And you can only use it on a legislator once during a session. It is best to avoid an overt feeling of obligation, but every lobbyist does have certain legislators that he can go to if he really needs a vote. I'll probably do this two or three times during a normal session. You just don't put on the pressure every day. You save it until you need it.
>
> I will also ask a legislator to get a vote that I can't get. This is the kind of pressure that you use, but you just don't go to a legislator and say "You do it or else." That is the poorest tactic you can use. Remember that we know most of these people very well, and in some cases have gotten them to run for office. We have worked with them in their campaigns. Even so, if I go to him and he says, "I can't do it," then I'll say, "Okay, I'll get somebody else," and forget it. You don't do it by using threats or being cute. You do not campaign against them. If they are consistently against you, they know that we would like to see them defeated, and they know that we will try to get somebody to run against them, but that is as far as it goes. I would never say to a legislator that I will try to find a candidate to oppose him, but the feeling is there.[41]

Popular perceptions that campaign contributions corrupt the legislative process doubtlessly are widespread. But the courts have not come to that conclusion. In 1998, several provisions of the Arkansas (voter-initiated) campaign finance law were held unconstitutional because, among other things, the contribution limits were set *too low* (e.g., reducing limits from $1,000 to $300 for the office of governor and to $100 for state legislators) to allow meaningful participation in the political process by individuals and PACs. The Eighth Circuit U.S. Court of Appeals held:

> If it were reasonable to presume corruption from the fact a public official voted in a way that pleased his contributors, legislatures could constitutionally ban all contributions except those from the public official's opponents, a patent absurdity. That would spell the end to the political right, protected by the First Amendment, to support a candidate of one's choice. . . . *We believe that $1,000 is simply not a large enough sum of money to yield, of its own accord and without further evidence, a reasonable perception of undue influence or corruption.*[42]

The "social lobby" refers to a practice employed by many interest groups of providing entertainment for legislators—cocktail parties, dinners, a night on the town, to mention some common forms. The impact of the social lobby on legislative decisions is probably exaggerated; nevertheless, its wide use suggests it may bear fruitful results.[43] "In its sophisticated form," according to a former member of the U.S. House of Representatives, "this activity never includes a request for a favor, but limits itself to the extension of amenities and courtesies in the form of free transportation, hospitality, and adjuncts to 'gracious living.'"[44] Both Senate and House rules provide that members cannot accept any gift or meal whose value exceeds $50, or accept more than a total of $100 in gifts and meals from any person in a year. (Between 1995 and 1999, the House had a complete ban on the acceptance of gifts, except from family members and personal friends.)

Some states have passed legislation to curtail the social lobby. In California, for example, a lobbyist is required to report monthly on each meal or drink that he or she purchased for legislators, state officials, other lobbyists, or other state employees. Moreover, lobbyists are limited to ten dollars per month in entertainment expenses for any one person. Pennsylvania's 1999 lobby law is less stringent. It requires lobbyists to identify any legislator (or state official) on whom he or she has spent $650 or more on entertainment during the year.

A popular view of legislative behavior holds that interest groups are able to gain their objectives by bribing legislators. Corrupt legislators have made their way through the pages of a good many novels and, in real life, infamous cases of venality dot the annals of Congress and state legislatures. But it is unlikely that the bribery theory explains much about legislative behavior today. As the former Speaker of the California Assembly, Jess Unruh, argued,

> Today it is rare for a legislator's vote to be corrupted by the exchange of money. Far more often the integrity of the vote is shattered by a commitment to a particular interest group, resulting from a lack of independence on the part of the legislator for a variety of nonfinancial reasons. For example, a vote may be influenced for reasons of ideology or fear of antagonizing the voting strength of a

particular group. One who is overly committed to labor or to management, or to any other interest group, whatever his reasons, can be charged with being as guilty of selling out the public interest as the man who takes money for his vote. Yet how can one search a man's mind to determine what prompted his vote?[45]

The nature of bribery diminishes its utility as a means for influencing legislators. Very simply, it is risky business, for legislator as well as lobbyist; it is costly; it is hard to conceal, for to be effective it must involve a number of lawmakers. Dark rumors about "money" or "Mae West" bills ("Come up and see me sometime") continue to float about the corridors of state capitols, and although undoubtedly such bills do crop up occasionally, their importance, indeed the prevalence of bribery in any form, is grossly exaggerated.

A pristine political state of affairs is nevertheless not easily preserved. No more than a fine line sometimes separates a campaign contribution from an outright bribe. A furor developed in 1975 when it was disclosed that the Gulf Oil Corporation had, over a period of about a decade, given several million dollars in *cash* contributions to politicians of both parties, including a number of prominent members of Congress. Passed to recipients in such places as a motel washroom in Indianapolis and behind a barn in New Mexico, the money had been "laundered" through a Gulf subsidiary, the Bahamas Exploration Company. An even more spectacular and more heavily reported scandal (marked by twenty-six days of televised hearings) made news in the early 1990s when it was disclosed that five senators who had intervened with the Federal Home Loan Bank Board on behalf of Charles Keating's failed Lincoln Savings and Loan Association had also accepted $1.5 million in political contributions from Keating and his associates. The "Keating Five" case is important for raising the question of how far members can go in pressing federal agencies for favorable action for their constituents. But it did not result in clear-cut guidelines for constituency service.[46]

### Sanctions

Lobby groups are wary in threatening the use of sanctions against legislators who refuse their demands. The threat to oppose a legislator at the polls is, of course, the most severe sanction available in the pressure arsenal. And although groups resort occasionally to this crude form, they prefer to communicate their power in subtle ways, through intermediaries, stimulated letter writing, and alliances. A pledge of support in the next election is a more circumspect way of reminding legislators of group power.[47] Yet communications that convey a vague hint of sanction, of the presence of group power, are fairly common. Thus, for instance, the chair of the Legislative Committee of the National Editorial Association, in testifying against an increase in the minimum wage, noted that his trade association spoke for 6,000 weekly, semiweekly, and small daily newspapers, and he went on to discuss the geography and operations of his clientele in what amounted to "pressure" terminology: "It is a fact," he said, "that more than 90 percent of these publications serve communities of less than 10,000 population. One or more is published in practically every congressional district and most, I think you will agree, are particularly sensitive to the needs, the demands, the habits of thinking of the people who send more than one-half of the members of both branches of this Congress to Washington."[48]

When an increase in the minimum wage bill was being considered by Congress in 1996, the chief House lobbyist for the National Federation of Independent Business (NFIB) observed:

> [Campaign contributions are] an important part of what we do, but not nearly the whole picture. We're the only group in town that can say to a member of Congress that if you're not with us, we can send letters to 15,000 of our members back in your districts saying you're an ass.[49]

A study of the way in which members of Congress evaluate interest groups suggests that groups are not necessarily perceived as applying pressure:

> Interest groups rarely have the capacity to coerce legislators. They know this and the congressmen know it. Therefore, the rules of the game have been defined, informally, so as to preclude this sort of effort. Congressmen see interest groups as having a helpful and legitimate role in the legislative process, and they appear to have no quarrel with groups so long as they do not step out of that role. When this does occur and it appears to encroach on the territory of the congressman, then the reaction on the part of that individual is apt to be negative and sharp. "When a man comes in here," one congressman said, "pounds on my desk, and tries to exact a commitment from me, I'm just liable to tell him to go to hell."[50]

## Demonstrative Lobbying

Lobby techniques that tend to the bizarre and sensational are worth a few lines since they are not uncommon, particularly in the state legislatures. For example, a bill under consideration in the New York State legislature to provide for the regulation of airways was protested by one hundred pilots who flew their planes to Albany and put them through maneuvers over the capitol; later, in pilot's garb, they appeared at public hearings.[51] Humane societies and those who travel with them can be expected to put on a flamboyant performance when a vivisection bill is before the legislature. To protest the adoption of strip-mine legislation in Pennsylvania some years back, the wives and children of several hundred strip miners marched on the capitol, bearing signs such as "Save our daddy's job." When a bill was before the Illinois legislature to regulate the interior height of taxi cabs, 150 jitney drivers from Chicago descended on Springfield, the state capital, and spent the better part of a day driving in and out of the capitol grounds, honking, blocking traffic, and otherwise making a nuisance of themselves. Their appeal, as fantastic as it was ill conceived, aroused small sympathy among exasperated legislators seeking a place to park their own cars. The net result of extravagant behavior is usually failure.

### Lobby Alliances

Pressure groups are habitually alert to possibilities for increasing and widening support for their legislative objectives, in the knowledge that backing by an additional group or two strengthens their position. Legislative combinations may be formed because groups share a common ideology and a complementary set of goals or because they are willing to engage in logrolling. Logrolling alliances are linked by quid pro quo agreements. Some of these alliances are more or less continuous, others are sporadic or spontaneous, and some are gained only with difficulty and are easily dissolved.[52]

Among veterans' organizations, the American Legion has long been linked with the viewpoint of business organizations and the Republican party. Teachers' associations have been known to undergo a quickening of interest in the objectives of other groups when teachers stand to profit in return. Thus state teacher lobbies frequently have supported the oil industry in oil states because revenues from that source contribute heavily to public education; similarly, the oil holdings and investments of some universities may cause them to look with a kindly eye on the oil industry. No organization has practiced intergroup lobbying more faithfully or effectively than the American Medical Association (AMA) in its various campaigns against national health care plans.

Richard Neuberger, who served in the Oregon legislature before becoming a U.S. senator, records his bout with an impromptu and transient alliance when he introduced a bill in the state legislature to limit the number of billboards on state highways:

> Although I had a perfect voting record on the A.F. of L. scoresheet, the head of the Signpainters' Union called me an "enemy of labor," and claimed that I wanted to throw hundreds of men out of work. Then the "widows and orphans" began to appear: forlorn families which would become public charges if they no longer could rent their roadside property to the signboard companies. The state advertising club sent an impressive delegation, which accused me of being a foe of the Bill of Rights: The advertising men would lose their "freedom of speech" if their billboards were barred from the countryside. Although the bill had been suggested to me by a wealthy old woman who loved the outdoors and did not like to see it defaced, my proposal was denounced by these delegations as being of Communist origin. . . . Put to a public referendum, I imagine the bill would have passed by at least 5 to 1. These few small pressure groups were able to induce the legislature to reject it overwhelmingly. I still marvel at the fact that the billboard owners themselves never once appeared during the entire operation.[53]

Finally, administrative agencies have learned that they can make a greater mark on the legislature if their program is supported concurrently by pressure groups; hence continuing, if sometimes subterranean, alliances between agencies and groups within their clientele have come to be common in Washington and the states. This linkage is particularly strong on matters involving veterans' affairs. Leiper Freeman observed, "The Veterans' Administration counts heavily on the American Legion and to a lesser extent on other veterans' organizations to support its recommendations to Congress. In fact, it seldom tends to make a recommendation to Congress that is not reasonably acceptable to these organizations, so strong is their partnership in all pressure politics dealing with veterans' affairs."[54]

## GRASS-ROOTS LOBBYING

Group strategies for influencing public decisions take many forms. An important form is that of seeking to mold public opinion as well as to exert immediate influence on decision makers in government. Operating on the assumption that the development and execution of public policy may be influenced by indirect ("long-distance") techniques as well as by direct methods, groups now "lobby" the public as vigorously as they lobby officeholders. They seek a favorable public attitude toward their organizations and goals; techniques for gaining public acceptance center on problems of "merchandising." Although the formal lobby organization is not ignored, its importance may be diminished. "Manipulation replaces domination or outright demands."[55]

Public relations has come a long way in politics. Formerly of small consequence among the activities of organizations, it is now recognized as a central, sometimes predominant, means by which groups seek to obtain their goals; indeed, no major organization would feel at all secure without a broadly based program for influencing public opinion. Major organizations have found it advisable to organize both short- and long-range public relations programs, the former focused to gain immediate public support in skirmishes with other groups and government, the latter aimed at molding a climate of opinion friendly to the organization and its aims. At bottom, the purpose of each "is to make the program of the group appear synonymous with the general welfare."[56] Groups have come to recognize that over the long haul, success is likely to depend on their having accumulated a reservoir of public goodwill, which in turn will have been shaped partially by widespread acceptance of their ideological positions. Merchandising an ideology or educating the public, whatever the process may be termed, is the continuing function of interest-group public relations.

A grass-roots campaign to influence public attitudes on an issue is most effective when it is successful in enlisting support from other powerful organizations. A cardinal precept followed by Whitaker and Baxter, public relations specialists, calls for mobilization of "natural allies" in campaigns. Natural allies, Stanley Kelley points out, are those organizations and associations that have a financial interest at stake, an ideological bent that coincides with the campaign's objectives, or a financial or psychological relationship to the client that impels them to join forces. "Organizations are approached not only because they represent blocs of voters but also because they can be made channels in a general system for the distribution of ideas."[57]

**FIGURE 10.1** The paths of interest-group influence

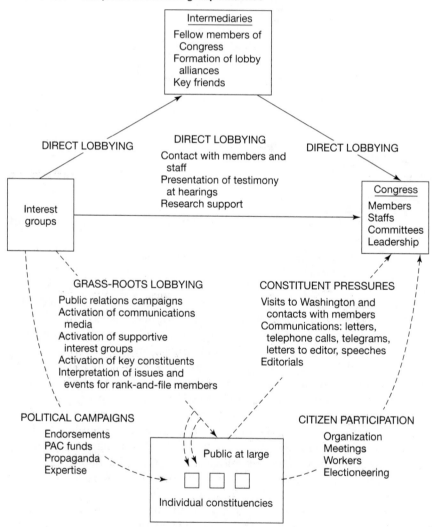

Properly instructed by the professional public relations team of an interest group, the public instinctively should favor the "right" side of an issue and do the organization's bidding, that is, communicating with its representatives in order to promote or impede the progress of legislation relevant to the group's interest. Such, at least, is the assumption on which political public relations rests. (See Figure 10.1.)

## PRESSURES ON THE PARTIES

Relations between political interest groups and political parties are variable. The nexus between groups and parties generally is weaker in the United States than in Britain, where, for example, trade unions are formally attached to a major party. Moreover, since parties count for less in the United States than they do in Britain, groups usually have not sought to establish beachheads within the parties. "Where the power is, there the pressure will be applied."[58] In Britain, therefore, groups concentrate on the administration and the parliamentary party; in the United States, groups seek to influence a variety of different institutions, using a variety of techniques. Grass-roots or public relations campaigns are joined in the United States with attempts to influence legislative committees, legislative party organizations, individual legislators, the administration, and other organizations. A realignment of the parties in the United States—resulting in a sharpening of their policy differences—probably would have an impact on the behavior of interest groups, encouraging them to seek more influence in party circles.

In those states in which legislative parties are more powerful, lobbies must pay more attention to them. Concerning Connecticut, Duane Lockard wrote, "The customary volume of pleading communications, hallway conversation, and other forms of entreaty are involved, but instances of specific effort to get legislators to ignore the caucus and the party leadership to ram a bill through are rare indeed."[59] The individual member appears to be less vulnerable to lobby pressures in party-oriented legislatures. As explained by a Republican state senator in Pennsylvania,

> I really don't get much attention from the lobbyists. They know I go along with the leadership practically all the time and so they don't really bother. The labor lobbyists don't visit me either. They don't think they can get my vote, and they're usually right on that, so they put their time to better use.[60]

Most interest groups strive to walk a line between the two parties, doing business with both if circumstances permit and avoiding deep involvement with only one. This approach gained currency in labor circles as the Gompers policy—a nonpartisan doctrine of rewarding friends and punishing enemies without regard to party affiliation. Groups continue to pay lip service to the principle today, though some have come to ignore it in practice. Several major pressure groups now identify their welfare with a single party and its program. The "alliances" formed may involve nothing more than an occasional joining of forces or perhaps a kindred feeling; in other cases, however, the development has progressed to the point of "infiltration." Examples of state party organizations heavily influenced by certain interest groups are not difficult to uncover. The Non-Partisan League in North Dakota and the Pennsylvania Manufacturers' Association (PMA) have substantial influence in the state Republican organizations; the United Automobile Workers (UAW) union in Michigan appears to have comparable influence in the state Democratic party. In states in which no group holds a commanding place in party councils, a cluster of like-minded groups may carry great weight. In the Massachusetts legislature, for example,

> Closely allied with the Republican party are the public-utility interests, the real-estate lobby, the Associated Industries of Massachusetts (the local version of the NAM), the Chamber of Commerce, the insurance companies, and the Massachusetts Federation of Taxpayer's Associations. All these groups have easy access to the leaders of the Republican party. Through shared opinions, campaign contributions, and at times common business connections, the lobbyists for these groups know they can present their arguments to attentive ears within "their" party, even as labor has similar access to the Democrats.[61]

## THE EFFECTIVENESS OF INTEREST-GROUP TACTICS

No more than a rough measure can be taken of the effectiveness of given tactics on government decision making. An interview study of over one hundred Washington lobbyists, however, affords good evidence concerning the tactics and techniques that lobbyists *perceive* to be most and least efficacious in communicating with government officials. (1) Nearly two-thirds of the lobbyists believe that the most effective tactic involves the personal presentation of their case. Testifying before hearings, included in this category, is ranked somewhat lower than personal contact with a single person. (2) An increasingly important tactic used by lobbyists, and ranked high in effectiveness, is to arrange for intermediaries—close personal friends of the legislator or a constituent—to plead the group's point of view. Lobbyists placed constituent contacts markedly higher on the scale (that is, more effective) than contact by a friend. (3) Public relations campaigns rank somewhat higher than letter and telegram campaigns; lobbyists for mass-membership organizations such as farm and labor view both approaches more favorably than lobbyists from other groups. Labor and farm group lobbyists also contend that the publicizing of legislators' voting records is moderately effective, whereas many other lobbyists view this method as worthless, even dangerous, since it may antagonize members whose records emerge as unfavorable.

(4) Of all the techniques for opening communication channels between lobbyists and legislators (entertaining, giving a party, bribery, contributing money, campaign work, and collaboration with other groups), the tactic of collaborating with other groups is most valued; campaign work and campaign contributions rank next; bribery is dismissed as both impractical and ineffective.[62]

The effectiveness of interest-group contacts with legislators can also be examined from the standpoint of the legislators, as in a study by Scott and Hunt. Among members of Congress, the interest-group techniques judged to be most effective in securing favorable congressional action are *indirect personal contacts* (individual letters, form letters, petitions, telegrams, and telephone calls) and *direct personal contacts* (office call, committee hearing, use of a personal friend as an intermediary, and conversation with a constituent). Ranked most effective among the indirect personal contacts by this sample of legislators were individual letters and telephone calls; form letters and petitions, in contrast, were held to be ineffective. In the category of direct personal contacts, testifying at committee hearings and office calls were cited as most effective, followed by contacts through friends and conversation with a constituent. *Collective personal contacts* (for example, social engagements and speeches at organization meetings) and *campaign contacts* (campaign work and campaign contributions) do not appear to most legislators to have a significant effect on legislation.[63] On the evidence of these studies, members of Congress and lobbyists do not view lobbying techniques in altogether the same light. One notable difference is that lobbyists see the personal presentation of their case as their most effective tactic, whereas members of Congress believe that committee testimony ranks above all other interest-group techniques in influencing the attitudes of members and the decisions of Congress.

Although evidence on the effectiveness of various interest-group techniques at the state legislative level is available for only a few states, the broad picture appears to be similar to that of Congress. A study of the states of Massachusetts, North Carolina, Oregon, and Utah finds that both legislators and lobbyists rank direct, personal communications (personal presentation of arguments, presenting research results, and testifying at hearings) as the most productive lobbying technique. Interestingly, in nearly all categories lobbyists regard their techniques as more effective than legislators regard them.[64]

## FACTORS IN THE EFFECTIVENESS OF INTEREST GROUPS

It is one thing to seek to influence decisions and quite another to succeed in doing it. A group may have extensive access to members of the legislature, including its key leaders, and yet have relatively meager influence on policy formation. In other words, there is a difference between the door-opening power of groups and the decision-making power. Plainly, not all groups share equally in access or in influence.

In addition, it should be noted that not all interest groups are actually concerned with gaining access to legislators and other officials. In New Jersey, for example, groups representing the interests of the aging follow a confrontational strategy in dealing with the state government. They view legislators and administrators as corrupt and inept, and their interactions with policymakers reflect this hostility as they threaten them with electoral reprisals. Aging interests elsewhere approach state policymakers in quite different fashions. In Michigan, representatives of these groups have an access orientation, and they seek to become policymaking partners with members and officials. Their counterparts in Florida and Iowa are more passive and dependent, typically inclined to await the initiatives of state officials. The important point to recognize is that there is considerable diversity in the strategies employed by similar groups in different settings. And what works in one state may not work in another.[65]

Theoretical tools for assessing the influence of political interest groups in the legislative process are not well developed. Among the factors that appear, in one degree or another, to affect the influence of groups are the following: (1) the size of the group; (2) its prestige;[66] (3) the cohesion of its membership; (4) the expertise and skills of its leadership;[67] (5) the distribution of its membership; (6) the credibility of both the organization and its advocates;[68] (7) the saliency of the issue; (8) the group's advantages in resources over its opponents; (9) the absence of countervailing interests;[69] (10) the extent of public support for the group's objectives; and (11) the group's ability to win active support of other groups and of the public at large.[70] In addition, the structural peculiarities of the government and of the political parties will tend to affect the access of certain groups to centers of power. Finally, a group's effectiveness may hinge on whether the views of the leadership are judged to represent the outlook of its rank-and-file members.

One index to the power of lobbies is the judgment of the lobbyists themselves. Not surprisingly, they are not solidly in agreement. Yet among Washington lobbyists, at any rate, there is general agreement concerning the profile of interest-group power: Those groups with large memberships—for example, certain farm, veterans', and labor organizations—are rated as the most successful in securing their objectives. The specialized groups singled out most frequently for their power are the AMA and the oil and gas lobbies. Interestingly, a noticeable number of lobbyists pick a major antagonist as the most powerful interest group.[71]

A study by Clive Thomas and Ronald Hrebenar finds a wide range of interest groups operating in the fifty states. Overall, the half dozen most influential and active interests currently are schoolteachers' organizations, general business organizations, bankers' associations, manufacturers, labor organizations, and utility companies.[72]

The overall effectiveness of interest groups in the political system appears to be related to certain economic and political variables. Table 10.4 relates the strength of pressure groups to party competitiveness, party cohesion in the legislature, and several socioeconomic variables. A profile of the data shows that pressure groups are likely to be strongest in states with these characteristics: (1) one-party political system;[73] (2) weak party cohesion in the legislature; (3) low urban population; (4) low per capita income; and (5) low index of industrialization. Although there are exceptions to this pattern, the evidence is persuasive that pressure-group strength, party politics, and the socioeconomic environment are closely related. In general, the data of this study support the hypothesis that urbanism and industrialization serve to increase group membership while at the same time decreasing group effectiveness. "The greater participation in organizations in the urban

**TABLE 10.4    The strength of pressure groups in varying political and economic situations**

| | Types of Pressure System* | | |
| | *Strong* | *Moderate* | *Weak* |
| Condition | (24 States†) | (14 States‡) | (7 States§) |
|---|---|---|---|
| **Party Competition** | | | |
| One-party | 33.3% | 0% | 0% |
| Modified one-party | 37.5% | 42.8% | 0% |
| Two-party | 29.1% | 57.1% | 100.0% |
| **Cohesion of Parties in Legislature** | | | |
| Weak cohesion | 75.0% | 14.2% | 0% |
| Moderate cohesion | 12.5% | 35.7% | 14.2% |
| Strong cohesion | 12.5% | 50.0% | 85.7% |
| **Socioeconomic Variables** | | | |
| Urban | 58.6% | 65.1% | 73.3% |
| Per capita income | $1,900 | $2,335 | $2,450 |
| Industrialization index | 88.8 | 92.8 | 94.0 |

*Alaska, Hawaii, Idaho, New Hampshire, and North Dakota are not classified or included.
†Alabama, Arizona, Arkansas, California, Florida, Georgia, Iowa, Kentucky, Louisiana, Maine, Michigan, Minnesota, Mississippi, Montana, Nebraska, New Mexico, North Carolina, Oklahoma, Oregon, South Carolina, Tennessee, Texas, Washington, Wisconsin.
‡Delaware, Illinois, Kansas, Maryland, Massachusetts, Nevada, New York, Ohio, Pennsylvania, South Dakota, Utah, Vermont, Virginia, West Virginia.
§Colorado, Connecticut, Indiana, Missouri, New Jersey, Rhode Island, Wyoming.

SOURCE: Harmon Zeigler and Hendrik van Dalen, "Interest Groups in the States," in *Politics in the American States*, ed. Herbert Jacob and Kenneth N. Vines. Copyright © 1971 by Little, Brown & Company, p. 127. Reprinted by permission.

states means that more group-anchored conflicts will come to the attention of the governmental decision makers. The greater the number of demands which come to the attention of any single decision-making agency, the less likely will be the probability that any one set of demands will be able to maintain control over the content of policy."[74]

Finally, the capacity of the legislature to resist the pressures of organized interests is likely to depend on its ability to garner and analyze information independently of other sources. Jess Unruh, former Speaker of the California Assembly, once observed,

> [Lobbyists] have influence in inverse ratio to legislative competence. It is common for a special interest to be the only source of legislative information about itself. The information that a lobbyist presents may or may not be prejudiced in favor of his client, but if it is the only information the legislature has, no one can really be sure. A special interest monopoly of information seems much more sinister than the outright buying of votes that has been excessively imputed to lobbyists.[75]

## LEGISLATOR-LOBBYIST RELATIONS

Much of the writing on political interest groups, at least until recently, has served more to adumbrate relations between lobbyists and legislators than to illuminate them. The lobbyist is commonly portrayed as a genius at dissimulation, a person virtually untouched by ethical standards, and an agent of rapacious demands. In the usual treatment, lobbies are described as extraordinarily effective in getting their way in the legislature. Legislators fit into this interpretation more as victims or as hostages than as individuals with power in their own right. All in all, this is the "theory" of the omnipotent interest group, the passive legislature, and the defenseless and harried legislator. In one form or another this theory has been transmitted tirelessly down through the years, its durability in the folklore of American politics due in part to its frequent surfacing in the popular journals and newspapers.

To set store by this thesis is to adopt a popular interpretation of American legislatures. One reason this is such a seductive thesis is that it exposes what are thought to be the ugly realities of the legislative process. The theory offers fascination for those who look for pathology in American public life and defense for those who seek to account for their own powerlessness. Popular accounts of lobby machinations, moreover, help to support the stereotype and to make interest-group power credible. Despite its popularity, however, this thesis of lobby domination of the legislatures is too simplistic to be acceptable. Put baldly, it tends to make the legislature nothing more than an arena for the joustings of interest groups, and public policy merely the expression of their preferences.

The relationships between legislators and lobbyists are in fact quite complex. Influence does not travel in one direction. A well-known study of the U.S. Senate by Donald Matthews shows that there are several important ways by which senators influence lobbyists. The first is a threat of noncooperation. "The senators have what the lobbyists want—a vote, prestige, access to national publicity, and the legislative 'inside dope.' Moreover, the lobbyist wants this not just once but many times over a number of years. The senators are in a position to bargain. They need not give these things away." The need for cooperation from senators thus tempers the actions of lobbyists. A second technique is "the friendship ploy." A senator's friendship with a lobbyist gives the senator a measure of insulation: "It makes the lobbyist indebted to him, more sensitive to his political problems, less willing to apply 'pressure,' a more trustworthy ally." "Building up credit" is a third technique open to legislators. Senators can pass on inside information to lobbyists, help publicize a group's position by delivering a speech on the floor or by inserting favorable material in the *Record*, or schedule committee hearings in order to let a lobbyist make his case—in a word, senators can help a lobbyist to "look good." A lobbyist who is indebted to a senator for favors of this kind is not in the best position to apply pressure. Finally, senators can influence lobbyists by launching or threatening to launch a public attack on them. Legislative investigations of lobbies are especially damaging; the possibility of an investigation serves to inhibit lobbyists who might otherwise be inclined to pull out all the stops in their efforts to influence legislative behavior.[76] There is, in sum, far more reciprocity in relations between lobbies and legislators than has ordinarily been suggested in the literature on legislatures.[77]

In a study of several key House decisions in a recent Congress, Christine DeGregorio describes the major properties that link legislative leaders and the advocates of organizations:

> [L]eaders and advocates need each other to pass legislation of consequence. The advocates need accommodating leaders to interject their points into the formal decision-making process. And the legislators need information, brokers, and confidants to help them arouse support within the House for passage. Because the elected officials are the only ones with the formal legitimacy to introduce and champion issues, they become the dominant partners in these mutually satisfying relationships.[78]

The impact of lobbying is more subtle and complex than commonly supposed. Lobbying may *reinforce, activate,* or convert *legislators;* clearly the most important of these is reinforcement.[79] Lobbyists know that relatively few votes are changed as a result of their efforts, and accordingly they concentrate their resources on "backstopping," or reinforcing, those members who are known to be favorable to their position. A lobbyist for the private electric-power industry explains:

There is no point in me going in and trying to change an out-and-out public-power advocate. I might try to help a person make up his mind, but there is no point in trying to convert a person who already has a strong opinion. I would be wasting my time in trying to change their minds, especially in the limited time available during a [state] legislative session. And if you've been around very long you can be pretty sure who your friends are, judging from what they have done in the past. You know who the people are who voted for your legislation. You can go down through the legislative calendar and pretty well identify individuals who will, or should, support your legislation, and you work more closely with them.[80]

The activation of members also carries high priority for lobbies—here their effort is to persuade members to work even harder on behalf of the group's interests. Hence, strange as it may appear to outsiders, most lobbyists spend most of their time lobbying members who are already friendly to their cause or else leaning in that direction. As indicated in a study of the impact of interest groups on the formation of foreign-trade policy,

Lobbyists fear to enter where they may find a hostile reception. Since uncertainty is greatest precisely regarding those who are undecided, the lobbyist is apt to neglect contact with those very persons whom he might be able to influence. . . . It is so much easier to carry on activities within the circle of those who agree and encourage you than it is to break out and find potential proselytes, that the day-to-day routine and pressure of business tend to shunt those more painful activities aside. The result is that *the lobbyist becomes in effect a service bureau for those congressmen already agreeing with him, rather than an agent of direct persuasion.*[81]

Whatever the net impact of interest groups on public policy, it seems likely that they are a prominent source of voting cues for legislators everywhere. Consider the evidence of a recent survey of legislators in the lower houses of Massachusetts, New Hampshire, and Pennsylvania. Among seven possible sources of *voting cues* (fellow legislators, committee reports, constituency, party leadership, interest groups, executive branch, and personal reading), interest groups ranked third in importance in Massachusetts, second in New Hampshire, and second in Pennsylvania. In the latter two states, interest groups were mentioned much more frequently as cue sources than either the party leadership or the governor's office (executive branch). In Massachusetts, as noted in the previous chapter, the party leadership plays a dominant role in members' voting decisions.[82]

Interest groups are functionally important to legislatures. They contribute to the definition of policy alternatives,[83] illuminate issues, marshal evidence and support, promote bargaining, and aid legislators in numerous ways that will affect legislative decisions. Some groups appear to have extraordinary influence on certain legislators. At times groups may appear to be the beneficiaries of misplaced power. On occasion their victories have been spectacular. But it is unrealistic to contend that they steadily dominate the legislative process. Legislators have minds of their own. Not all share the same orientation toward interest-group activity. They are conscious of the "mandate" under which they came into office, often zealous in achieving consistency in their voting records, and fearful of being labeled as a captive of any interest group. Moreover, they are heavily influenced by the multiple ties of party, bureaucracy, executive, and constituency. Interest groups are only one element in the bargaining process from which policies emerge.

## REGULATION OF LOBBYING

### Congressional History

The right of citizens to communicate their views to government officials is firmly protected by the First Amendment to the Constitution: "Congress shall make no law . . . abridging the . . . right of the people . . . to petition the Government for a redress of grievances." Since the earliest days of the republic, lobbies have been active in attempting to secure the passage or defeat of legislation, and occasionally their zeal has culminated in corruption and other serious abuses of the constitutional right of petition. At other times the sheer volume of lobbying has called attention to the role of interest groups in policymaking. Prompted by disclosures of venality or by uneasiness over heightened lobbying activity, Congress from time to time has investigated lobbies and lobbyists and drafted statutes to check improper or excessive activities.

Congressional regulation of lobbying has grown slowly; the steps taken invariably have been tentative, often ineffective. Initial regulation came in 1852 when the House of Representatives adopted a rule providing that House journalists employed as agents to prosecute claims pending before Congress were not entitled to seats on the House floor. In 1854 a select committee to investigate the lobbying activities of Samuel Colt was formed; its principal contribution apparently was to enhance public awareness of the nature of lobby operations. An amendment to the House rules in 1867 stipulated that former members of Congress with an interest in the outcome of any claim before Congress were to be excluded from the House floor. Further experimentation with lobby regulation occurred during the next decade when Congress passed its first law requiring lobbyists to register; adopted in 1876, the law was in effect only during that Congress, the 44th.

Increasing awareness of lobby abuses developed early in the twentieth century, chiefly as an outgrowth of a major investigation of the insurance lobby in the state of New York in 1905 and 1906. In 1913 intensive investigations were made of the tariff lobby in the Senate and of NAM in the House. Another intensive investigation of the tariff lobby by the Senate occurred in

1929, and in 1935 the lobbying methods of utility companies were examined. As a result of the latter investigation, a provision was inserted in the Public Utilities Holding Act of 1935 that required the registration of lobbyists representing holding companies before Congress, the Federal Power Commission, or the Securities Exchange Commission. Lobbyists involved with matters covered by the Merchant Marine Act of 1936 were placed under a similar enjoiner. These efforts set the stage for a more general law.

Congress passed its first comprehensive lobbying law in 1946: It was adopted as Title III of the Legislative Reorganization Act. Had it appeared as a separate bill, Congress may well have refused to approve it, for there had been no outcry over lobby abuses at the time. With members' attention riveted on other features of congressional reorganization, however, the lobbying regulations were accepted without serious challenge.

### The 1946 Regulation of Lobbying Act

The 1946 act was neither a formidable nor venturesome attempt to regulate lobbying. Its importance lay in the fact that it was the first general lobby law to be adopted. Under its terms, every person (individual, partnership, committee, association, corporation, or other organization or group of persons) who solicited or received contributions for the *principal purpose* of influencing legislation was required to keep a record, and to file reports, of all contributions and expenditures, including the name and address of each person making a contribution of $500 or more and to whom an expenditure of $10 or more was made. A lobbyist was defined as a person who solicited, collected, or received money for the *principal purpose* of influencing the passage or defeat of legislation; the law required them to register with the clerk of the House or the secretary of the Senate. Additionally, lobbyists were required to file quarterly reports concerning their employer, their salary and expenses, and their legislative interests.

The assumption underlying the national lobby law was that government can resist capture by private interests if information regarding their activities is available to officials and the public. *Identification, disclosure,* and *publicity* were the core elements of the legislation. Their importance is highlighted in the Supreme Court's 1954 decision upholding the law's constitutionality:

> Present day legislative complexities are such that individual members of Congress cannot be expected to explore the myriad pressures to which they are regularly subjected. Yet full realization of the American ideal of government by elected representatives depends to no small extent on their ability to properly evaluate such pressures. Otherwise the voice of the people may all too easily be drowned out by the voice of special interest groups seeking favored treatment while masquerading as proponents of the public weal. This is the evil which the Lobbying Act was designed to help prevent.

Toward that end, Congress has not sought to prohibit these pressures. It has merely provided for a modicum of information from those who for hire attempt to influence legislation or who collect or spend funds for that purpose. It wants only to know who is being hired, who is putting up the money, and how much.[84]

In the view of most critics, the 1946 lobby law was undermined by ambiguities and loopholes. In *U.S. v. Harriss,* the Supreme Court held that the reporting requirements applied only to those persons or organizations that solicit, collect, or receive money that is used *principally* to influence legislation, thus exempting many groups from the requirement. The Court also held that the act applied only to those persons and organizations that engage in "direct" communications with Congress; "indirect" or "grass-roots" appeals thus were not covered. Moreover, the act did not apply to individuals who engage in lobbying the executive branch, and the lobbying of congressional staff was not covered. Furthermore, no agency was established to enforce the law.

Despite intense dissatisfaction with the act, it took forty-nine years—until 1995—to overhaul it. The 1995 law tightens up registration and reporting requirements in three important ways. First, lobbyists are defined much more inclusively. Under the 1946 law, a lobbyist was defined as any person who spends a majority of his or her time lobbying members of Congress. Under the new regulations, a lobbyist is defined as any person who spends more than 20 percent of his or her time lobbying Congress (including congressional staff) or the executive branch (including the president, vice president, White House officials, cabinet secretaries, top military officials, and many others in policymaking positions). Second, a lobbyist who receives at least $5,000 from any client in a six-month period and an organization that spends at least $20,000 on lobbying in a six-month period must register with the clerk of the House and secretary of the Senate. And third, lobbyists are required to file twice-yearly reports with detailed information on the issues lobbied on during that span, the chambers of Congress and the executive branch agencies contacted, and the involvement, if any, of foreign entities.

Disclosure requires a "good faith estimate" of the amount of money spent in seeking to influence policymakers, but it does not require lobbyists to "name names"—the legislators, staff members, or executive officials who were contacted. And for the first time, lobbyists for foreign entities are required to register.

Under the broader definition of lobbyist, many more persons engaged in lobbying will be required to register and to disclose, in much greater detail, their activities regarding legislation, rules, regulations, grants, loans, permits, programs, and even presidential nominations. The "principal purpose" loophole has been closed. Prior to passage of the law, only 4,000 of the 13,500 people listed as lobbyists in the *Washington Representatives Directory* were registered with Congress.[85]

The 1995 act did not complete the full circle of lobby reform. Provisions to illuminate grass-roots lobbying (for example, to require lobbyists and organizations to disclose how much money they spend to involve the public in their campaigns) and to create an agency to enforce the law were dropped from the legislation. Their omission was part of the price of passage. Nevertheless, the public now has a better opportunity to inform itself about lobbying in Washington than ever in the past.

### Lobby Regulation in the States

Regulation of lobbies in the states, as in Congress, has had a checkered, generally unsatisfactory history. Its dim beginnings apparently trace to the Georgia Constitution of 1887, which carried a provision designating lobbying as a crime. Today, all legislatures require the registration of lobbyists. Their definitions of *lobbyists,* however, differ significantly. Most commonly, a lobbyist is defined as "anyone receiving compensation to influence legislation action." But there are also more comprehensive definitions, including one or more of the following: "anyone spending money to influence legislation," "anyone representing someone else's interest," "anyone attempting to influence legislation," and (as part of the definition in twenty states) "any executive branch employee attempting to influence legislation." In seven states the definition of a lobbyist includes elected officials.[86]

In general, state laws are aimed at increasing the visibility of groups by disclosing the identities of lobbyists and gathering information about their activities. Typically, these laws relate only to direct communications with the legislature. Nearly all states require lobbyists to file reports periodically, and the vast majority require them to report expenditures. Thirty-eight states now have independent ethics agencies to enforce their lobby laws, though their enforcement authority varies.[87]

What stands out most clearly is that some states stringently regulate lobbies whereas others do not. The states that regulate lobbies most thoroughly have laws distinguished by inclusive definitions of lobbying (for example, covering administrative as well as legislative lobbying), requirements that lobbyists report frequently and comprehensively, and significant oversight and enforcement provisions (such as giving the enforcement agency the power to subpoena witnesses and records and to impose fines and penalties).

By and large, those states that have the most comprehensive lobby laws have professional legislatures—featuring higher legislative salaries, longer sessions, and generous allowances for staff. States with "moralistic" political cultures also tend to adopt stringent lobby regulations. The more competent and capable the legislature, this analysis suggests, the greater the likelihood that the legislators will have taken steps to keep lobbies in check.

# INTEREST GROUPS AND DEMOCRATIC GOVERNMENT

The arguments on behalf of interest groups (lobbies and lobbyists) do not circulate as widely as those that are hostile to them. Nevertheless, a case can be made for pressure groups.

## The Uses of Interest Groups

American folklore to the contrary, pressure politics is not a one-way street. National and state legislators are not simply the inert victims of powerful lobbies. The truth is, rather, that legislators call for the support of lobby groups about as often as groups make claims on them. David Truman put it this way:

> The popular view is that the political interest group uses the legislator to its end, induces him to function as its spokesman and to vote as it wishes. [Although] this is not an inaccurate view . . . it is incomplete. . . . When a legislator arouses organized groups in connection with a proposal that he knows will involve them or when he solicits their support for a measure which he is promoting, the relationship becomes reciprocal. Even in connection with the development of a single bill from conception to enactment, the initiative may lie alternately with legislator and with group, including other outside influences.[88]

Political interest groups have come to be important sources of information in the legislative process. Because their own supply of technical knowledge is sometimes not as extensive as they would like, legislators regularly turn to interest groups and executive agencies for data, analysis, and opinions. The view that information conveyed by lobbyists is biased and not to be trusted is popular but probably misleading. "If the information should later prove to be false, or biased to the point of serious distortion, the decision maker is publicly embarrassed and is likely to retaliate by cutting off further access sought by the delinquent lobbyist."[89]

Policy ideas, rooted quite naturally in self-interest, are the standard equipment of interest groups. But the group contribution is not limited to advocacy of ideas or to funneling information into the legislature. Groups also contribute essential energy to assembling and sustaining support for programs. Concerning their role in shaping school aid programs in eight northeastern states, one study reports,

> [Private] interest groups perform a variety of functions beyond the support of intellectual leadership. They mobilize consent within their own organizations; they develop linkages with each other in an attempt to build a common political front; they fertilize grass roots; they exploit mass media, and develop mass media of their own; they build fires under lethargic officialdom; they lobby and

cajole legislators and governors; they provide a continuity of energy and concern in the face of temporary defeats and setbacks. Sometimes they work at cross purposes, but when they work together under strong and coherent leadership, they perform an indispensable function in the political process. State teachers' associations, teachers' unions, school boards' associations, PTA's, associations of educational administrators, other civic and professional societies—separately and as amalgams—have played essential roles in the politics of state aid to education.[90]

Finally, there is the view that not only is our anti-interest ideology fruitless, since there is no way in which a democratic society may stifle the organization of groups, but it also overlooks the vast potential of groups and their contributions to the transformation of politics: The language of politics today is the language of groups, not of individuals. We encourage groups on the one hand, suppress them on the other. "In pluralism and a national organization of interests," writes Alfred de Grazia, "can be discovered a new kind of democracy upon which a superior society may be founded. . . . It would teach groups to view themselves not as outlaws . . . but as integral parts of a whole in which they pursue their useful and dignified way. So long as we suppress rather than educate the group formations of American life, we lower the quality of their membership and activities."[91]

### A Political System Resistant to Pressure

Current controversy over pressure groups is part of a continuing debate over the proper role of private associations in the American political process. Reasonable alternatives for integrating interest groups into the social order obviously cannot include their elimination as political agencies or their regulation in such a way as to encroach on the constitutional right of petition. If difficult to resolve, the issue is easily enough stated: How can an adequate system of representation be ensured, while at the same time preventing groups from gaining undue influence in decision-making processes? What steps can be taken to check the impulse to "government by pressure group"?

By resort to the theory of "countervailing power," one may be tempted to conclude there is little reason for apprehension over the growth of interest-group power. In short, this theory holds that groups tend to restrain and offset one another, inhibiting impulses present in organizations to seek total domination over society. Thus agricultural, business, labor, veterans', professional, ethnic, and other groups in quest of particularistic goals vie with one another, thereby preventing any one interest from gaining overwhelming advantage. One group's gain imperils the position of other groups, serving to set in motion countervailing forces. In effect, then, a check-and-balance process regulates political forces as well as the government system itself.

The countervailing theory is helpful in unraveling the threads of group struggle in the legislature and elsewhere, but it has certain limitations. Most important, it neglects to allow for the tendency of interests to form alliances whereby logrolling substitutes for checks, permitting powerful combinations to press vigorously for special advantage. "In the legislative consideration of many economic measures," Walter Adams points out, "the absence of countervailing power is painfully apparent. In the enactment of tariff laws, for example, equal stakes rarely elicit equal pressures."[92] Similarly, William Cary writes, in the matter of shaping tax laws in congressional hearings,

> There is practically no one, except perhaps the Treasury, available to represent the public. Perhaps the reason is that all of the pressure group proposals are of such character that no one of them would have a large adverse effect on the tax bill of any individual. Hence counterpressure groups seldom develop. . . . A second reason why the public is not more frequently represented is the difficulty of forming pressure groups around general interests. The concentration of business organizations on appeals brought to Congress and the emphasis placed on specific and often very technical information makes it difficult even for the members of the tax committees to secure a balanced view of what is in the general interest, what the public wants or, indeed, what the public would want if it were informed as to the facts.[93]

Given the inertia of the mass of citizens and the difficulty of discovering what the public wants, it is not surprising if legislators shape their views on issues with one eye on what is most appropriate and the other on what is most expedient. Sometimes the expedient side is simply that position held by powerful and militant interest groups. A public passive or oblivious to concessions made to pressure groups is not likely to find its interest, to the extent that it can be identified at all, zealously guarded by the legislature. Countervailance demands awareness, involvement, and comparable power. A prominent former member of Congress sounds a recurrent lament: "It is disturbing to sit through legislative hearings at which the conflicting interests who should be heard are unequally represented in the presentation of their views. Worst of all . . . are those situations in which only the proponents of the suggested legislation are heard from. . . . [The congressman] is faced with a dilemma as to how far he can or should go to supply the omission."[94]

The fact of the matter is that interests are represented differentially in American politics. To put it bluntly, in terms of material resources, the pressure system is dominated by business. One study found that business organizations made up 70 percent of all organizations that had a Washington presence (reflected in the hiring of Washington-based counsel or consultants) and 52 percent of those that had their own offices. In contrast, for organizations with minimal resources (for example, groups representing minorities) the percentages fell below 10 percent in each case. The class bias in this form of representation is unmistakable. The evidence on inequality of representation, of course, does not mean that business always wins.[95]

Loomis and Cigler conclude that the success of groups makes it difficult to find solutions to complex policy problems.

The problem of contemporary interest group politics is one of representation. For particular interests, especially those that are well defined and adequately funded, the government is responsive to the issues of their greatest concern. But representation is not just a matter of responding to specific interests or citizens; the government also must respond to the collective needs of a society, and here the success of individual interests reduces the possibility of overall responsiveness.[96]

Frustrated by their inability to get the legislature to act, some groups have turned to the courts for relief. Following the lead of the states that sued the tobacco companies to pay for the treatment of their citizens who became sick from smoking, a number of cities are now (1999) suing gun manufacturers for the costs incurred for certain police protection and for treating the victims of shootings. Claims, inevitably, produce counterclaims. Thus, to meet this threat, the National Rifle Association and its allies have vigorously lobbied state legislatures throughout the country to pass legislation to make such lawsuits illegal; a number of states, including many in the South, quickly did just that. For our purposes, the importance of the cities' liability suits is that they reflect the perception that legislatures must be bypassed because they are so thoroughly dominated by lobbies. That is also part of the rationale for the use of the initiative process (see Chapter 2).

Interest groups may be kept within reasonable bounds, runs a common argument, by an effective lobby law. The argument is that politicians and the public have a right to know who is seeking what from government and how they are going about it. The most that can be said for even the best law, however, is that it may alert legislators and the citizenry to what is going on around them. Lobby law is an instrument, one of several, and it is difficult to think of it as a panacea.

Another school of thought holds that legislators can be moved to higher ground, where they will be better able to withstand the blandishments or pressures of interest groups. The vehicle is the legislature itself. Under this heading come recommendations that more substantial staff services be made available to members and to committees; that legislative reference, research, and bill-drafting services be enlarged and improved; and that salaries and retirement benefits for legislators be increased. This is the formula for legislative improvement, of making it increasingly self-sufficient, of equipping it to do many of the things for which it now looks to outside agencies.

Another answer appears in the chorus of voices advocating "a party system with greater resistance to pressure." This school places on groups the onus "for the deterioration and confusion of purposes which sometimes passes for compromise" in government policy. It states that "compromise among interests is compatible with the aims of a free society only when the terms of reference reflect an openly acknowledged concept of the public interest." It warns that the accountability of public persons for their acts can be enforced only when running the political system is the responsibility of political parties.[97] In his classic study, *Party Government,* E. E. Schattschneider made this point:

> In one way or another every government worthy of the name manages interests in formulating public policy. The difficulty is not that the parties have been overwhelmed by the interests, but that the political institutions for an adequate national party leadership able to deal with the situation have not been created. For want of this kind of leadership the parties are unable to take advantage of their natural superiority. Thus they let themselves be harried by pressure groups as a timid whale might be pursued by a school of minnows. The potentialities of adequate national party leadership in this connection have not yet been well explored in the United States, but it is a waste of time to talk about controlling the depredations of the pressure groups by other means. A well-centralized party system has nothing to fear from the pressure groups. On the other hand, aside from a strong party system there is no democratic way of protecting the public against the disintegrating tactics of the pressure groups.[98]

A final view holds that legal controls are not the best answer to controlling the lobby process. Lester Milbrath argues that "interdependence, rules of the game, power relationships, and threat of sanction against offenders that characterize the Washington policy-making system operate rather effectively" to control lobbying. Standards for the behavior of lobbyists (for example, that legislators should be able to rely on the accuracy of information communicated to them) are understood by legislators and lobbyists alike. Lobbyists who treat the norms casually, who raise doubts and anxieties among legislators, endanger their access and damage their cause. The lobbyist has no real immunity against political sanctions. Above and beyond the controls built into the legislative system, writes Milbrath, "the most effective control of lobbying, and perhaps all that is really needed, is the election of highly qualified responsible persons to public office. . . . Officials have so much power over lobbying and lobbyists that they can determine how the lobby system shall work."[99]

Virtually all writers who embark on a discussion of legislative reform feel it obligatory to tackle the lobby question—some seeing it as a nagging problem, others regarding it as a threat to representative government. It seems safe to say that in the public mind no political institution carries a more sinister image than the lobby. Because information about lobbies is partial, the case against them seems complete. There is, for example, scarcely any public awareness of the interactions between lobbyist and legislator initiated by the legislator to strengthen his or her hand. Overall, doubts and uncertainties over lobbying apparently trouble the public far more than they do the legislators themselves. This state of affairs, of course, may be due as much to the legislators' insensitivity as to the public's anxiety.

The fact is that comprehensive "solutions" to meet the problems posed by lobbies are not likely to be forthcoming. Each proposal for making the political system more resistant to pressure promises something, but none is likely to settle the matter permanently. The option of party control can be tested only when the parties are stronger and more cohesive than they are today. In the short run, the best, if unspectacular, answer may be simply to expose and highlight specific abuses by interest groups (or their lobbies) and to fashion piecemeal solutions to combat them. The dependence of members of Congress on interest groups for campaign money, for example, can be eased. One approach would be to reduce the amount that a single PAC can contribute to a congressional candidate (currently $10,000 in a primary and general election) and to limit the total amount of PAC money a candidate can accept. Another tack would be to provide for public financing of congressional campaigns. A third possibility, favored particularly by Republican members of Congress, would seek to reduce PAC influence by increasing the amount of money that parties can give to House and Senate candidates or spend on their behalf. And a fourth plan, favored particularly by congressional Democrats, would be to provide for both public financing and spending limits (with the spending limits to vary according to state population). The adoption of any of these proposals, or some combination of them, would have a significant impact on relations between interest groups and legislators. And finally, from an overall standpoint, it is useful to remember that lobby control can result from elections, which instruct and discipline parties or legislators that have fallen under the thumb of organized interests and permitted them to appropriate government power for narrow and selfish purposes.

## NOTES

1. E. E. Schattschneider, "Pressure Groups versus Political Parties," *Annals of the American Academy of Political and Social Science*, CCLIX (September 1948), 23.
2. David B. Truman, *The Governmental Process* (New York: Knopf, 1951), p. 353.
3. "The Group Basis of Politics: Notes for a Theory," *American Political Science Review*, XLVI (June 1952), 390.
4. E. E. Schattschneider, *The Semisovereign People* (New York: Holt, Rinehart & Winston, 1960), p. 38.
5. *The Federalist*, ed. Benjamin Fletcher Wright (Cambridge, MA: Belknap Press of Harvard University Press, 1961), p. 130.
6. Woodrow Wilson, *Congressional Government* (New York: Meridian Books, 1956; first published 1885), p. 214.
7. Stephen K. Bailey, *The Condition of Our National Political Parties* (New York: Fund for the Republic, 1959), p. 10.
8. Schattschneider, "Pressure Groups," 18–19.
9. See H. Eulau, W. Buchanan, L. Ferguson, and J. Wahlke, "The Political Socialization of American State Legislators," *Midwest Journal of Political Science*, III (May 1959), 188–206,

especially pp. 204–206; and also their book, *The Legislative System* (New York: Wiley, 1962), pp. 77–94.

10. Schattschneider, "Pressure Groups," 19.

11. See Burdett A. Loomis and Allan J. Cigler, "Introduction: The Changing Nature of Interest Group Politics," in *Interest Group Politics*, ed. Allan J. Cigler and Burdett A. Loomis (Washington, DC: Congressional Quarterly Press, 1991), pp. 1–2. For corroboration of these trends at the state level, see Clive S. Thomas and Ronald J. Hrebenar, "Interest Groups in the States," in *Politics in the American States*, ed. Virginia Gray, Herbert Jacob, and Robert B. Albritton (Glenview, IL: Scott Foresman/Little, Brown, 1990), pp. 123–58. A survey of veteran legislators in 1994 found that they feel that the influence of lobbyists in state legislatures has grown markedly in the last decade or two. See Gary F. Moncrief, Joel A. Thompson, and Karl T. Kurtz, "The Old Statehouse, It Ain't What It Used to Be," *Legislative Studies Quarterly*, XXI (February 1996), 57–72.

12. Lester Milbrath, "The Political Party Activity of Washington Lobbyists," *Journal of Politics*, XX (May 1958), 339–52 (quotation on p. 351).

13. See Ronald J. Hrebenar and Ruth K. Scott, *Interest Group Politics in America* (Englewood Cliffs, NJ: Prentice Hall, 1990), pp. 209–10; and Clive S. Thomas and Ronald J. Hrebenar, "Nationalization of Interest Groups and Lobbying in the States," in *Interest Group Politics*, ed. Allan J. Cigler and Burdett A. Loomis (Washington, DC: Congressional Quarterly Press, 1991), pp. 68–71.

14. Anthony J. Nownes and Patricia K. Freeman, "Female Lobbyists: Women in the World of 'Good Ol Boys,'" *Journal of Politics*, LX (November 1998), 1181–201.

15. *Current American Government* (Washington, DC: Congressional Quarterly, 1981), p. 102.

16. Robert Engler, "Oil and Politics," *New Republic*, September 5, 1955, p. 14.

17. Some groups may be more effective working through the initiative process (available in twenty-six states) rather than through the legislative process. See Elisabeth R. Gerber, "Legislatures, Initiatives, and Representation: The Effects of State Legislative Institutions on Policy," *Political Research Quarterly*, XLIX (June 1996), 263–86.

18. Quoted in *Final Report of the Special Committee to Investigate Political Activities, Lobbying, and Campaign Contributions*, 85th Cong., 1st sess., 1957, p. 43.

19. As quoted by Richard F. Fenno, Jr., *Congressmen in Committees* (Boston: Little, Brown, 1973), p. 31.

20. John M. Bacheller, "Lobbyists and the Legislative Process: The Impact of Environmental Constraints," *American Political Science Review*, LXXI (March 1977), 257.

21. As quoted by George T. Sulzner and John C. Quinn, "Lobbying in the Massachusetts Legislature," in *The Massachusetts General Court: Process and Prospects*, ed. Edwin Andrus Gere (Washington, DC: American Political Science Association, 1972), p. 52.

22. Diana M. Evans, "Lobbying the Committee: Interest Groups and the House Public Works and Transportation Committee," in *Interest Group Politics*, ed. Allan J. Cigler and Burdett Loomis (Washington, DC: Congressional Quarterly Press, 1991), pp. 270–72.

23. Dayton McKean, *Party and Pressure Politics* (Boston: Houghton Mifflin, 1949), p. 617.

24. Bacheller, "Lobbyists and the Legislative Process," 259–62.

25. *Hearings on Oil and Gas Lobby Before the Special Senate Committee to Investigate Political Activities, Lobbying and Campaign Contributions*, 84th Cong., 2nd sess., 1956, p. 545. (Emphasis added.)

26. See an interesting analysis by Jane Fritsch, "The Grass Roots, Just a Free Phone Call Away," *New York Times*, June 23, 1995.

27. Quoted in Ronald D. Hedlund and Wilder Crane, Jr., *The Job of the Wisconsin Legislator* (Washington, DC: American Political Science Association, 1971), pp. 86–87.

28. *Hearings on Lobbying and Related Activities Before the Subcommittee on Administrative Law and Governmental Relations of the Committee on the Judiciary*, 95th Cong., 1st sess., 1977, p. 132.

29. *Pittsburgh Press*, March 12, 1970, p. 10.

30. http://www.fec.gov/press/canye98.htm.

31. Congressional incumbents often contribute to the campaigns of other candidates for Congress, either through their own PACs or through their campaign committees. See a study by Clyde Wilcox, "Share the Wealth: Contributions by Congressional Incumbents to the Campaigns of Other Candidates," *American Politics Quarterly*, XVII (October 1989), 386–408. Studies of PAC contributions to state legislative candidates show that incumbents benefit disproportionally as recipients of these funds. See Joel A. Thompson, William Cassie, and Malcolm E. Jewell, "A Sacred Cow or Just a Lot of Bull? Party and PAC Money in State Legislative Elections," *Political Research Quarterly*, XLVII (March 1994), 223–37.

32. John R. Wright, "PAC Contributions, Lobbying, and Representation," *Journal of Politics*, LI (August 1989), 713–29 (quotation on p. 726).

33. James Deakin, *The Lobbyists* (Washington, DC: Public Affairs Press, 1966), p. 101.

34. *Congressional Quarterly Weekly Report*, March 12, 1983, p. 504.

35. *Washington Post*, February 11, 1997.

36. Laura I. Langbein and Mark A. Lotwis, "The Political Efficacy of Lobbying and Money: Gun Control in the U.S. House, 1986," *Legislative Studies Quarterly*, XV (August 1990), 413–40. For other studies that find that PAC money has an impact on congressional voting behavior, see James B. Kau and Paul H. Rubin, *Congressmen, Constituents, and Contributors: Determinants of Roll Call Voting in the House of Representatives* (Boston: Martinus Nijhoff, 1982); Allen Wilhite and John Theilmann, "Labor PAC Contributions and Labor Legislation: A Simultaneous Logit Approach," *Public Choice*, LIII, No. 3 (1987), 267–76; Jonathan Silberman and Garey C. Durden, "Determining Legislative Preferences on the Minimum Wage: An Economic Approach," *Journal of Political Economy*, LXXXIV (April 1976), 317–29; John P. Frendreis and Richard W. Waterman, "PAC Contributions and Legislative Behavior: Senate Voting on Trucking Deregulation," *Social Science Quarterly*, LXVI (June 1985), 401–12; and Frank L. Davis, "Balancing the Perspective on PAC Contributions: In Search of an Impact on Roll Calls," *American Politics Quarterly*, XXI (April 1993), 205–22.

37. Janet M. Grenzke, "PACs and the Congressional Supermarket: The Currency Is Complex," *American Journal of Political Science*, XXXIII (February 1989), 1–24 (quotation on p. 1). For other studies that find that contributions have scant impact on members' voting, see W. P. Welch, "Campaign Contributions and Legislative Voting: Milk Money and Dairy Price Supports," *Western Political Quarterly*, XXXV (December 1982), 478–95; Henry Chappell, "Campaign Contributions and Congressional Voting: A Simultaneous Probit-Tobit Model," *Review of Economics and Statistics*, LXIV (February 1982), 77–83; and Evans, "Lobbying the Committee," pp. 257–76.

38. Richard L. Hall and Frank W. Wayman, "Buying Time: Moneyed Interests and the Mobilization of Bias in Congressional Committees," *American Political Science Review*, LXXXIV (September 1990), 797–820. Another study that should be consulted on voting in committee is John R. Wright, "Contributions, Lobbying, and Committee Voting in the U.S. House of Representatives," *American Political Science Review*, LXXXIV (June 1990), 417–38. Studying behavior in the House Ways and Means and Agriculture Committees, Wright found that the best explanation for members' voting decisions was the number of lobbying contacts groups had with members. He found little evidence of a direct tie between money and voting, and he concluded that the main function of campaign contributions is to afford access to members. Money enters the process indirectly: "Since lobbying is significantly related to previous contributing, the political and technical information representatives receive from groups is shaped to some extent by campaign money" (quotation on p. 434).

39. Thomas Romer and James M. Snyder, Jr., "An Empirical Investigation of the Dynamics of PAC Contributions," *American Journal of Political Science*, XXXVIII (August 1994), 745–69. House candidates who run for the Senate do particularly well in attracting PAC money. See Ronald Keith Gaddie and James L. Regens, "Economic Interest Group Allocations in Open-Seat Senate Elections," *American Politics Quarterly*, XXV (July 1997), 347–62.

40. Thomas J. Rudolph, "Corporate and Labor PAC Contributions in House Elections: Measuring the Effects of Majority Party Status," *Journal of Politics*, LXI (February 1999), 195–206.

41. Quoted in Harmon Zeigler and Michael Baer, *Lobbying: Interaction and Influence in American State Legislatures* (Belmont, CA: Wadsworth, 1969), p. 116.

42. *Russell v. Burris*, 146 F. 3d 569 (8th Cir. 1998). (Emphasis added.)

43. There are no bounds to the social lobby—even academe is aware of its potential for influencing legislation. With choice football tickets and assorted hospitality looming in the background, state universities have been known to invite state legislators for a weekend visit to the campus, and if it happens that members of the appropriations committees are among those attending to inspect the institution and its plant, so much the better.

44. Emanuel Celler, "Pressure Groups in Congress," *Annals of the American Academy of Political and Social Science*, CCCXIX (September 1958), 4. (Emphasis in original.)

45. Donald G. Herzberg and Jess Unruh, *Essays on the State Legislative Process* (New York: Holt, Rinehart & Winston, 1970), p. 82.

46. See an account of the *Keating* case and the decisions of the Senate Ethics Committee in the *Congressional Quarterly Weekly Report*, March 2, 1991, pp. 517–23.

47. Lester W. Milbrath, "Lobbying as a Communications Process," *Public Opinion Quarterly*, XXIV (Spring 1960), 36.

48. *Hearings on Various Bills Regarding Minimum Wage Legislation Before the Subcommittee on Labor Standards of the Committee on Education and Labor*, U.S. House of Representatives, 86th Cong., 2nd sess., 1960, p. 278.

49. *Washington Post*, February 11, 1997.

50. Andrew M. Scott and Margaret A. Hunt, *Congress and Lobbies: Image and Reality* (Chapel Hill: University of North Carolina Press, 1966), pp. 58–59.

51. Belle Zeller, *Pressure Politics in New York* (Englewood Cliffs, NJ: Prentice Hall, 1937), p. 245.

52. Consult a study of the Iowa legislature that finds that interest groups rarely attempt to mobilize other groups to support their position. In most cases, in addition, legislators hear from only one side on a proposal. Charles W. Wiggins and William P. Browne, "Interest Groups and Public Policy Within a State Legislative Setting," *Polity*, XIV (Spring 1982), 548–58.

53. *Adventures in Politics: We Go to the Legislature* (New York: Oxford University Press, 1954), pp. 102–103.

54. "The Bureaucracy in Pressure Politics," *Annals of the American Academy of Political and Social Science*, CCCXIX (September 1958), 17.

55. Samuel J. Eldersveld, "American Interest Groups: A Survey of Research and Some Implications for Theory and Method," in *Interest Groups on Four Continents*, ed. Henry W. Ehrmann (Pittsburgh: University of Pittsburgh Press, 1958), p. 193.

56. Henry A. Turner, "How Pressure Groups Operate," *Annals of the American Academy of Political and Social Science*, CCCXIX (September 1958), 69.

57. Stanley Kelley, *Professional Public Relations and Political Power* (Baltimore: Johns Hopkins University Press, 1956), pp. 58–59.

58. Samuel Beer, "Group Representation in Britain and the United States," *Annals of the American Academy of Political and Social Science*, CCCXIX (September 1958), 138.

59. Duane Lockard, *New England State Politics* (Princeton, NJ: Princeton University Press, 1959), p. 288.

60. As quoted by Sidney Wise, *The Legislative Process in Pennsylvania* (Washington, DC: American Political Science Association, 1971), p. 64.

61. Lockard, *New England State Politics*, p. 165.

62. Milbrath, "Lobbying," 32–53.

63. Scott and Hunt, *Congress and Lobbies*, pp. 70–85.

64. Zeigler and Baer, *Lobbying*, pp. 174–75.

65. William P. Browne, "Variations in the Behavior and Style of State Lobbyists and Interest Groups," *Journal of Politics*, XLVII (May 1985), 450–68.

66. See the evidence of a five-state study that finds that state legislators view business interests as more important than labor interests. Business thus enjoys a privileged status in the legislative struggle. Margery M. Ambrosius and Susan Welch, "State Legislators' Perceptions of Business and Labor Interests," *Legislative Studies Quarterly*, XIII (May 1988), 199–209.

67. See Truman, *The Governmental Process*, Chaps. 6 and 7, for analysis of the problems of cohesion and of the bearing that leadership skills have on group effectiveness.

68. Christine DeGregorio, "Access and Advocacy in the U.S. House of Representatives," (School of Public Affairs, The American University, 1994), 5–7.

69. See Evans, "Lobbying the Committee," pp. 257–76. Intergroup conflict clearly has a negative effect on group success. What happens on issues where conflict among interest groups is missing? Diana Evans writes: "A [group] asks the committee for a benefit, the committee hears no arguments against it and gives the group what it wants." "Before the Roll Call: Interest Group Lobbying and Public Policy Outcomes in House Committees," *Political Research Quarterly*, XLIX (June 1996), 287–304. There is also evidence that the influence of an interest group varies from one stage of the legislative process to the next. See Richard A. Smith, "Advocacy, Interpretation, and Influence in the U.S. Congress," *American Political Science Review*, LXXXVIII (March 1984), 44–63.

70. Several of these variables are drawn from an inventory by Richard A. Smith, "Interest Group Influence in the U.S. Congress," *Legislative Studies Quarterly*, XX (February 1995), 89–139. Smith's critical review of the literature is particularly important for demonstrating the conflictual and problematic quality of findings on the influence of interest groups on congressional behavior.

71. Lester Milbrath, *The Washington Lobbyists* (Chicago: Rand McNally, 1963), pp. 347–51. Also see the analysis of conflict between two bank factions in the Wisconsin Assembly by Wilder Crane, Jr., "A Test of Effectiveness of Interest-Group Pressures on Legislators," *Southwestern Social Science Quarterly*, XLI (December 1960), 335–40.

72. Thomas and Hrebenar, "Nationalization of Interest Groups," p. 68.

73. See the evidence of David C. Nice showing that interest-group successes are greatest in states where political parties are weak: "Interest Groups and Policymaking in the American States," *Political Behavior*, VI, No. 2 (1984), 183–96. Additional evidence that the influence of interest groups can be offset by the governor and the legislative majority party leadership appears in Charles W. Wiggins, Keith E. Hamm, and Charles G. Bell, "Interest-Group and Party Influence Agents in the Legislative Process: A Comparative State Analysis," *Journal of Politics*, LIV (February 1992), 82–100. The states investigated are California, Iowa, and Texas, and the authors find considerable variation in the influence of these agents across state lines. Legislative party leaders, for example, are particularly important in Iowa, while the governor is the key actor in Texas.

74. Harmon Zeigler and Hendrik van Dalen, "Interest Groups in the States," in *Politics in the American States*, ed. Herbert Jacob and Kenneth N. Vines (Boston: Little, Brown, 1965), pp. 113–17 (quotation on p. 113). Also see Kenneth Hunter, Laura Wilson, and Gregory Brunk, "Societal Complexity and Interest-Group Lobbying in the American States," *Journal of Politics*, LIII (May 1991), 488–503. The authors reject the hypothesis that interest-group lobbying is associated with the growing complexity of society.

75. Herzberg and Unruh, *Essays*, pp. 17–18.

76. Donald Matthews, *U.S. Senators and Their World* (Chapel Hill: University of North Carolina Press, 1960), pp. 188–90.

77. For additional evidence that representatives are not the pawns of interest groups, see Evans, "Lobbying the Committee," pp. 257–76. Also see a game theoretical model developed by Scott Ainsworth to analyze how legislators can limit the advantages and influence of lobbyists, even in the absence of comprehensive registration and disclosure laws. "Regulating Lobbyists and Interest Group Influence," *Journal of Politics*, LV (February 1993), 41–56.

78. DeGregorio, "Access and Advocacy," pp. 24–25.

79. But see the theoretical and empirical evidence of David Austen-Smith and John R. Wright that groups also vigorously lobby unfriendly legislators, seeking to convert them. "Counteractive Lobbying," *American Journal of Political Science*, XXXVIII (February 1994), 25–44.

80. Quoted in Zeigler and Baer, *Lobbying*, p. 130.

81. Raymond A. Bauer, Ithiel de Sola Pool, and Lewis A. Dexter, *American Business and Public Policy* (New York: Atherton Press, 1963), pp. 352–53.

82. David Ray, "The Sources of Voting Cues in Three State Legislatures," *Journal of Politics,* XLIV (November 1982), 1080.

83. Interest groups may influence legislatures by limiting the policy options presented to them. The preagreement among groups on a common objective permits them to combine demands into a reduced number of policy alternatives, which effectively limits legislative choice. See W. Douglas Costain and Anne N. Costain, "Interest Groups as Policy Aggregators in the Legislative Process," *Polity,* XIV (Winter 1981), 249–72.

84. *U.S.* v. *Harriss et al.,* 347 U.S. 612 (1954).

85. *Congressional Quarterly Weekly Report,* July 29, 1995, p. 2241.

86. *Book of the States, 1990–1991* (Lexington, KY: Council of State Governments, 1991), pp. 188–92.

87. This treatment of state lobby regulation relies mainly on Cynthia Opheim, "Explaining the Differences in State Lobby Regulation," *Western Political Quarterly,* XLIV (June 1991), 405–21.

88. Truman, *The Governmental Process,* p. 342.

89. Milbrath, "Lobbying," 47.

90. Stephen K. Bailey, Richard T. Frost, Paul E. Marsh, and Robert C. Wood, *Schoolmen and Politics: A Study of State Aid to Education in the Northeast* (Syracuse, NY: Syracuse University Press, 1962), pp. 106–107.

91. "Nature and Prospects of Political Interest Groups," *Annals of the American Academy of Political and Social Science,* CCCXIX (September 1958), 120.

92. "Competition, Monopoly and Countervailing Power," *Quarterly Journal of Economics,* LXVII (November 1953), 481.

93. "Pressure Groups and the Revenue Code: A Requiem in Honor of the Departing Uniformity of the Tax Laws," *Harvard Law Review,* LXVIII (March 1955), 778.

94. Celler, "Pressure Groups in Congress," p. 7.

95. Kay Lehman Schlozman, "What Accents the Heavenly Chorus? Political Equality and the American Pressure System," *Journal of Politics,* XLVI (November 1984), 1006–1032. See a study by Benjamin Radcliff and Martin Saiz that finds that in those states where organized labor is strongest, public policy is more likely to have a liberal cast—that is, more money will be spent on education and welfare, and the tax code is more likely to be progressive. "Labor Organization and Public Policy in the American States," *Journal of Politics,* LX (February 1998), 113–25.

96. Loomis and Cigler, "Introduction: The Changing Nature of Interest Group Politics," p. 28.

97. Committee on Political Parties, *Toward a More Responsible Two-Party System* (New York: Holt, Rinehart & Winston, 1950), pp. 19–20.

98. E. E. Schattschneider, *Party Government* (New York: Holt, Rinehart & Winston, 1942), p. 197.

99. Milbrath, *The Washington Lobbyists,* p. 326.

# 11

# The Chief Executive
# as Legislator

Politics requires leadership. In the United States, legislatures and the people expect presidents and governors to provide it.[1] Chief executives provide the ideas and programs that often are at the center of the legislative agenda. What presidents and governors want, legislatures will frequently consider. In a study of executive initiatives from 1953 to 1988, Mark Peterson found that "the vast majority of presidential legislation was subjected to serious legislative attention. No political player other than the chief executive has such an impact on the legislative agenda."[2] Alan Rosenthal argues similarly for the states: "In the policy-making process of the states, the spotlight is on governors and their priorities. Any consideration of policy making in a state must begin with the governor's program, for that establishes a major agenda for the legislature and the focus for the media."[3]

Once the programs are presented, presidents and governors help build the coalitions necessary to transform the ideas into law. Executives who cannot or will not build coalitions rarely see their programs enacted. Eric Davis traced many of President Carter's difficulties with Congress to this very point. Carter, Davis suggested, did not always realize that Congress would not automatically accept his legislative proposals and that coalitions frequently had to be constructed.[4]

The quest for winning majorities pushes the executive to bargain with legislators. Negotiations often begin with members of the president's party in Congress; at times, presidents, even under unified government, require major help from the opposition party; President Clinton needed a Republican majority to push the North American Free Trade Agreement through Congress. The quest for majorities also promotes efforts outside the legislature where interest groups, other political activists, and the general public can be mobilized on occasion to further the chief executive's purposes. President Reagan could persuade Congress in 1981 to cut taxes partly because he also persuaded much of the public that his program would help them.

When the legislature enacts a law, the legislative process is not necessarily over. Legislation is often written in general terms that gain more precise meaning only when applied to specific cases. Legislation is fleshed out as laws are implemented. The importance of implementation to policy-making heightens the interest of legislators in examining how the general rules that they pass are applied in specific cases. Legislative oversight of bureaucracy is analyzed in Chapter 12.

The executive branch consists of far more than the chief executive. Nor does the executive branch speak with one voice. Bureaucratic-legislative interactions are fascinating in themselves.[5] They require more extensive analysis than can be provided here. This chapter, for purposes of clarity, will focus primarily on chief executive–legislative relations. Even this narrower topic offers a sufficient challenge to analysts.

Presidents and governors have varying impacts on their legislatures. What they can do depends on far more than who they are. Executive influence varies with four factors:

1. General conditions in society set boundaries within which politics functions.

2. The legal powers of presidents and governors channel and restrain their efforts.

3. Partisan-political factors condition executive efforts.

4. The chief executives' values, role perceptions, and personality affect what they do.

We can learn a great deal about the chief executive in the legislative process by examining these factors as they relate to presidential and gubernatorial behavior.

## SOCIETAL CONDITIONS AND EXECUTIVE INFLUENCE

Conditions in society do not determine what government will do, but they surely shape governmental behavior. Economic conditions such as inflation or high unemployment, domestic crises brought about by floods or tornadoes, the possibility or reality of war, and riots in our cities' streets affect presidential or gubernatorial success in their efforts. The environment for decision making by chief executives is vast and complex. For example, what are the consequences from data in polls showing that citizens approved of President Clinton's conduct of the presidency but yet indicated they were not too fond of him as an individual? A few aspects of the environment will be highlighted to illustrate how they affect executive behavior.

The first of these is the homogeneity of the society. The greater the degree of homogeneity in public attitudes within a society, the greater the tendency toward executive-legislative cooperation in lawmaking. A heterogeneous society means a society with conflicts. This in turn provides a breeding ground for political conflict between executives and their legislative branches. The typical system of representation in the United States (statewide or nationwide election for the chief executive and district elections for the legislative assembly) reinforces a proclivity for conflict. Industrialization and urbanization provide an environment for conflict but, at the same time, lead to additional pressures for governmental action in both the nation and the states. Such pressures may translate into increased executive influence as attention focuses on the president or governor for action.

The presence of crisis, or the appearance of it, can contribute to executive success. Many experts in 1977 agreed that the nation faced a severe energy crisis, but President Jimmy Carter, despite intense efforts, could not convince the people that the crisis was genuine. By contrast, in 1981 President Reagan did not have to labor very hard to convince the people that the nation faced difficult economic times. Lost purchasing power, no paychecks, inflation, and unemployment figures had done the job already. The legislative consequences were clear. President Carter, whatever the merits of his proposals for solving the energy crisis, faced frustration in getting Congress to act despite Democratic control of both houses. President Reagan was able to pressure Congress, one house of which was dominated by the Democrats, to pass his far-reaching economic programs. Many factors were at work in explaining this contrast. Surely one was the public perception of the immediacy and severity of the two problems under discussion. One was deep and unmistakable, the other alleged and uncertain.

Presidential influence on the legislative branch approaches its zenith in time of war. At the onset of the Civil War, President Lincoln moved beyond his constitutional powers. Congress vindicated some of his acts, however, when it met in special session some six weeks later.[6] During World Wars I and II, Presidents Wilson and Roosevelt generally found legislative acquiescence to their requests for emergency powers, as did President Bush when he sought support for military commitment in the Persian Gulf in 1991. Environmental factors, in general, and the presence or absence of war, depression, or other national disasters, in particular, provide one key to the understanding of executive influence in the legislative process. But highly visible crisis situations remain rare. What happens in more normal situations can be very different.

## THE LEGAL BASE FOR EXECUTIVE INFLUENCE

Legal powers and limits also help explain the chief executive's impact on the legislative process. Governors and presidents share many similar formal legal powers—for example, to deliver messages, to prepare budgets, to veto acts of representative assemblies, and to call special sessions of legislative bodies. However, these legal powers are not equally effective in enhancing the chief executive's impact.

## The Budget

Presidents and almost all governors can play a large role in preparing and presenting the budget. Larry Sabato described the budget as the governor's "single most important tool."[7] Most analysts agree. If the budget is conceived only as an exercise in arithmetic, then its importance cannot be understood. The budget is much more. It represents the most authoritative single measure of what the executive's program actually is. The abstract language of the political campaign provides no firm base for predicting the chief executive's program. The hard, cold budgetary item provides a better measure of what he or she wants to do.[8]

When the president or the governor (or more accurately, his or her executive subordinates and associates) prepares a budget, he or she is in effect presenting to the legislative assembly a blueprint for public policy:

> The federal government uses the budget to establish and pursue national objectives, to promote favorable economic conditions, to manage its diverse activities, to respond to the demands of citizens and groups, to assess past performance, and to plan for the future. In previous decades, the budget propelled the growth of the national government; in the 1980s it was the Reagan administration's principal weapon in reshaping national priorities and downsizing domestic programs.[9]

Because the budget is such a comprehensive plan, its complexity can be overwhelming. Even David Stockman, the architect of President Reagan's startling budget success in 1981 could assert: "None of us really understands what's going on with all these numbers."[10] Legislators realize that the columns of statistics in the budget document are the real tests of policy. Accordingly, the executive budget occupies the central position on the agenda of all legislatures. As a rule, sessions of the state legislature are unable to achieve any momentum until the governor's budget has been received; by the same token, when the critical budget decisions have been made, the legislators ordinarily are ready to return home.

The budget proposed by the executive provides not only the best single statement of the administration's program but usually the only comprehensive plan for action put before legislative assemblies. It reflects the realities of administration goals and strategies. The fiscal document provides a focus for deliberation that legislative bodies are often unable to provide for themselves. "The funds over which governors and legislatures really have discretion amount to only 5 to 15 percent of the budget. It is over these monies that the contest is waged, at the margins of the budget but still over significant amounts."[11]

**FIGURE 11.1    National government mandatory and discretionary spending, 1997–2000**

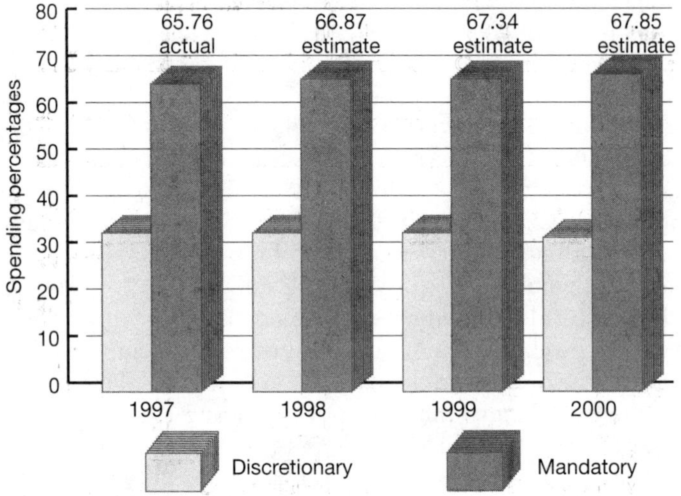

| 1997 | 1998 | 1999 | 2000 |
|------|------|------|------|
| 65.76 actual | 66.87 estimate | 67.34 estimate | 67.85 estimate |

Discretionary    Mandatory

SOURCE: Data from *Budget of the United States, fiscal year 1999*, p. 341.

At the national level, fixed payments, such as interest on the national debt, grants to the states under existing programs, and agricultural subsidies, constitute firm limits on congressional and presidential discretion in budget making. About 67 percent of the federal budget is mainly "uncontrollable" by the president and Congress on a year-by-year basis. Figure 11.1 shows the relatively "uncontrollable" portion of the budget from fiscal year 1997 to fiscal year 2000.

The familiar response of legislatures to executive budgets is to look for ways to make changes. Congress and almost all state legislatures have unlimited legal authority to alter the executive budget. How this authority is used and for what purposes vary with political environments. Congress tends to make small rather than large changes in the president's budget. Congress makes only minor changes in about 90 percent of the items. A president finding funds for a high-priority program cut may view such congressional action as more serious than for small cuts.[12]

Evidence for the states is more scattered. After an eighteen-state study, Joel Thompson contends that the budget process in the states in the 1980s still looked similar to what it was in the 1960s; governors still played a paramount role but not one as dominant as they played some twenty years before.[13]

A president who thinks that Congress has appropriated too much money may simply refuse to spend it. Presidents have impounded funds for the Air Force, for supercarriers, for flood control, as well as for other projects.[14]

President Nixon used the impoundment power with unusual vigor. He not only temporarily deferred expenditures but tried to halt permanently programs that he disliked or that he thought to be inflationary. Louis Fisher captures the essence of the situation:

> Used with restraint and circumspection, impoundment has been used for decades without precipitating a major crisis. But during the Nixon years restraint was replaced by abandon, precedent stretched past the breaking point and statutory authority pushed beyond legislative intent.[15]

The Nixon extremism led to court challenges and congressional reaction. The courts overturned some of the president's actions; Congress placed statutory limits on the president's ability to impound funds.[16] Congress has used its powers to restrict impoundments with mixed results. Congress approves almost all presidential requests for routine delays in spending. On more significant policy matters, Congress approves most of the time.[17] (See Table 11.1 for precise data.) Presidents are less successful in their requests to kill expenditures (rescissions). In its 1983 decision outlawing the legislative veto, the U.S. Supreme Court raised serious questions about the legality of a device that Congress had used to challenge presidential deferrals in spending appropriated funds.[18]

In the budgetary process, as in other policy areas, executive influence on legislative assemblies is seldom exerted on legislative bodies as a whole. Committees and subcommittees are important elements. Viewed historically, fragmented decision making has been the rule.[19]

Over the last two decades, Congress has made major alterations in the budgetary process. The goal of the Congressional Budget and Impoundment Control Act in 1974 was to achieve a more informed and coordinated review. Each house established a budget committee. A new staff resource, the Congressional Budget Office, was created and a series of deadlines was developed. The potential impact of these changes was staggering; the actual impact has been more modest.

The Budget Act of 1974 was designed to push Congress to collectively

**TABLE 11.1   Presidential proposed rescissions and congressional reactions, 1974–92**

| President | Number of Rescissions | | Percent Approved | Percent of Dollars Approved |
|-----------|-----------------------|----------|------------------|-----------------------------|
|           | Proposed              | Approved |                  |                             |
| Ford      | 152                   | 52       | 34               | 16                          |
| Carter    | 122                   | 50       | 41               | 37                          |
| Reagan    | 602                   | 214      | 36               | 36                          |
| Bush      | 169                   | 34       | 20               | 18                          |

SOURCE: Data from Allen Schick, *The Federal Budget* (Washington, DC: Brookings Institution, 1995), p. 176.

consider its decisions, to move Congress away from its traditional fragment-ed decision making where money was voted for individual programs with little regard for overall budgetary considerations. These new formal proce-dures seemed to require that Congress set and maintain spending priorities.

The full potential for centralized decision making was not realized until 1981, when a bipartisan coalition approved in essence the presidential budget proposals through a series of radically innovative techniques. The story of innovation in 1981 is the story of a strong president and a strong coalition in Congress working its will by adapting rules and procedures with effectiveness seldom matched.

The dramatic victory of President Reagan in 1981 was an exception, not an example of a new pattern of decision making. James Pfiffner points to the unusual circumstances which made that victory possible.[20] The president, in the absence of foreign policy crises, chose to make the budget fight his top priority. President Reagan's Republican party controlled the Senate, some-thing that had not happened in thirty years. The presidential victory in the 1980 election created the appearance of a public mandate for the changes that Reagan pushed. The state of the economy—high rates of inflation and unemployment—was so bad that any plausible alternative seemed attractive to many. The Democratic party controlled the House of Representatives, but that party was in such disarray that the chances for meaningful opposition were diminished. Nor should the astute strategy of the administration be forgotten. David Stockman, director of the Office of Management and Bud-get, articulated part of a strategy designed to create the appearance of equi-ty—everyone would be asked to sacrifice: "How in the world can I cut out food stamps and social services and CETA jobs . . . [and not] give up one penny for Boeing? . . . I've got to take something out of Boeing's hide to make this look right."[21]

The importance of external circumstances to the budget-making process is also stressed by Allen Schick: "Most budget outcomes are likely to turn more on external events than on operations within Congress."[22] Or put somewhat differently, "Because Congress thrives on heterogeneity and frag-mentation, . . . expanded reconciliation [the innovative technical procedure used in 1981] will not be a budget process for all legislative seasons."[23]

Subsequent budget battles in the Reagan, Bush, and Clinton adminis-trations support the thesis stressed by Pfiffner and Schick. Presidents have had visible influence in budget deliberations, but Congress has not repeated its 1981 capitulation. These oscillations would not surprise those analysts who link the budgetary process to the mood of the country, perceptions of crisis, the president's mandate, which party controls the presidency and each house of Congress, and which public policy issues are central at the time.

In recent years, Congress has made several major efforts to improve the budgetary process. In 1985, Congress passed the Balanced Budget and Emergency Deficit Control Act, the Gramm-Rudman-Hollings (GRH) Act.

The central feature of this legislation was a detailed timetable for the budget process with nearly twenty deadlines and specified amounts, until 1991, for annual deficit reductions. If the yearly deficit reduction goals were not reached, a mandatory procedure (sequestering) for across-the-board cuts made according to a formula stipulated in the legislation was required.

The Gramm-Rudman-Hollings Act was designed to give Congress increased control over budgets and deficits. By 1987, it had become clear that these goals were not being met. The anticipation of increased congressional control had proved in part to be illusory. The normal ways of doing things in Congress—fragmented decision making—had overcome the expressed desires for more coherent policy and clear priorities.

The Gramm-Rudman-Hollings Act succeeded in making members of Congress more conscious of budget deficits and of the need to relate individual budget items to overall budgetary objectives. It failed, however, to force Congress to keep a firm schedule and to move each year toward sharp reductions in the annual budget deficit.

Acknowledging the political difficulties of meeting the GRH deadlines and responding to the Supreme Court's invalidation of the automatic budget-reduction features in GRH, Congress again modified the budget process in 1987. New annual steps, less steep in their required cuts, toward a balanced budget were created, and the time period to reach that condition was lengthened. A new automatic budget-cutting procedure was established in case the president and Congress did not meet the stipulated annual reduction levels. The 1987 act again sought a structural substitute for the more difficult task of deciding budget priorities. Astutely, Schick notes, "GRH gives politicians the best of both worlds—the appearance of doing something about the deficit and the reality of not having to do very much."[24]

In 1990, Congress again confronted these intractable problems and again revised the budget process in the Budget Enforcement Act. Abandoned was a fixed calendar for balancing the budget. Added were caps for discretionary spending, shifts to adjustable deficit targets, and pay-as-you-go rules for revenues. These alterations affect budgetary decisions but do not solve the problems of how to reconcile divergent interests.

Congress continues to grope toward new answers to old problems. The very nature of the legislative process makes such efforts difficult and frustrating. Presidents cannot consistently alter this reality, but they can help modify it on occasion.[25]

Budgets make policy. The ability of Congress to implement its new budget procedures rests ultimately on its willingness to accept centralized leadership from the president, the budget committees, the party leadership, or some combination of them. Setting budget priorities is really setting policy priorities, and that should provoke caution about how much can be achieved through a modified budgetary process. Budget surpluses in the late 1990s should create no illusions about the power of budgetary reforms.

These surpluses were essentially a function of a thriving economy providing more tax revenues.

### The Veto

The executive's budget-making authority provides a broad base for the exercise of executive influence in the legislative process. In contrast, the veto is a tool for specific tasks. Essentially, the veto is a defensive weapon for the chief executive. Yet it also should be seen as one of the most powerful weapons in the arsenal of presidents and governors as they attempt to influence legislative behavior. The exercise of the veto may be interpreted as a phase of an institutional struggle for power between the executive and legislative branches—but this lessens its significance. A more appropriate interpretation describes the veto as a weapon in the making of public policy; its use, in the main, reflects the fact that the legislative and executive branches often act for strikingly dissimilar constituencies.

The power to veto acts of the legislature is held by the president and all state governors. The details of the veto power vary with each constitutional document. The president must accept or reject bills as a whole, although for a brief period, from 1996 to 1998, presidents were authorized by Congress to exercise a form of *item veto*, "enhanced rescission." President Clinton used this authority to strike down 82 "items" before the Supreme Court ruled that the Line Item Veto Act was unconstitutional.[26] During its brief life at the national government level, the item veto seemed to have had little fundamental impact on presidential relations with Congress.

The president and many governors have the power of *pocket veto*, that is, the power to prevent a bill from becoming law by not signing it if legislative adjournment prevents the chief executive from returning it for further consideration.[27]

Presidents have used the veto more than 2,500 times from 1789 to 1998, exercising the power much more frequently in the twentieth century than earlier in American history. Among nineteenth-century presidents, President Cleveland used the veto most frequently. During his long tenure in office, President Franklin Roosevelt used the veto 635 times; in a much shorter period of time, President Truman used it 250 times. President Eisenhower resorted to vetoes less frequently, 181 times in all, but used the power with great effectiveness to offset Democratic majorities in Congress. No more recent president has approached these figures. In the states, between one-half and three-fourths of all vetoes registered by governors occurred in the twentieth century.[28]

Several reasons explain the increased use of the veto: (1) the increasing number of problems confronting the American political system under the impact of industrialization, urbanization, and international crises; (2) rising public expectations and demands for governmental action; and (3) the growing scope and intensity of political conflict.

One study found significant correlation between presidential use of the veto and lateness in the term of office, serving a second term, high levels of unemployment, gaining office through succession rather than through election, and the volume of legislation passed.[29] Use of the veto can also relate to party control of Congress. After the 1986 elections gave Democrats control of the Senate, President Reagan faced a Congress with opposition party majorities in both houses. The Reagan administration then adopted a more forceful veto strategy. Unable to dominate the congressional agenda as it had, especially in its first term, the administration turned to a strategy based on blocking congressional legislative efforts. Still, few bills are victims of the executive ax. From 1789 to 1998, the average was under eleven per year. The picture has not changed visibly in the last forty years.

In the states, the data are scattered and varied. Vetoes in most states are relatively rare; overrides of vetoes by the state legislatures are even rarer. During the 1970s, Coleman B. Ransone, Jr., reports, more than 90 percent of gubernatorial vetoes were sustained by their legislatures.[30] In Pennsylvania, from 1970 to 1990, governors vetoed about eleven bills per year; of these, slightly over 3 percent were overridden.[31] See Table 11.2 for recent data for Pennsylvania.

In a comparison of vetoes in 1947 and 1973 in forty-nine states, Charles Wiggins found that governors, on the average, vetoed about 5 percent of the bills passed in each of the two years. New York and New Jersey had the highest percentage of bills vetoed in each year. In 1947, in nine states, governors vetoed less than 1 percent of legislative acts; in 1973, the figure was fifteen states.[32] In 1997, the veto was used most often in California but more

TABLE 11.2    The veto in Pennsylvania, 1987–96

| Year | No. of Bills Passed | Vetoes | Vetoes Overridden |
|------|---------------------|--------|-------------------|
| 1987 | 147 | 2 | 0 |
| 1988 | 276 | 11 | 1 |
| 1989 | 165 | 1 | 0 |
| 1990 | 290 | 13 | 0 |
| 1991 | 109 | 2 | 0 |
| 1992 | 239 | 9 | 0 |
| 1993 | 133 | 1 | 0 |
| 1994 | 223 | 9 | 2 |
| 1995 | 128 | 0 | 0 |
| 1996 | 253 | 1 | 0 |

SOURCE: Data from *The Pennsylvania Manual* for relevant years.

typical was the slight usage in Louisiana, Tennessee, and Vermont; overrides in the states in 1997 were usually less than ten.[33]

About 86 percent of the governors exercise some form of item veto. Use of the item veto also varies from state to state, as does its impact on state legislatures. In New York, the use of the item veto has been linked to the governor's authority to impound appropriated funds. Before 1932, the item veto was used regularly. With the creation of the executive budgeting system, New York governors substituted the power to impound funds. Use of the item veto dropped sharply. After the state courts in 1980 struck down the ability to impound, New York governors resumed their use of the item veto.[34] Full understanding of a particular formal power requires a grasp of its context. James Gosling studied the use of the item veto in Wisconsin over a twelve-year period. He argued that Wisconsin governors use the item veto more to strengthen partisan advantage and policy preferences than as an instrument of fiscal restraint.[35]

The veto, then, is not a power used routinely. Yet, the threat by a president or governor to veto a forthcoming bill, unless it is revised, is assuredly of significance.

Messages to accompany vetoes may be required by a constitution; at other times they are sent simply because it suits the chief executive's inclinations. Such messages range from terse, one-sentence rejections to more elaborate and colorful statements—as, for example, that of then Governor Adlai Stevenson of Illinois:

> I cannot agree that it should be the declared public policy of Illinois that a cat visiting a neighbor's yard or crossing the highway is a public nuisance. It is in the nature of cats to do a certain amount of unescorted roaming. . . . Also consider the owner's dilemma: To escort a cat abroad on a leash is against the nature of the cat, and to permit it to venture forth for exercise unattended into a night of new dangers is against the nature of the owner. Moreover, cats perform useful service particularly in rural areas, in combating rodents—work they necessarily perform alone and without regard for property lines. We are all interested in protecting certain varieties of birds. That cats destroy some birds, I well know, but I believe this legislation would further but little the worthy cause to which its proponents give such unselfish effort. The problem of the cat versus the bird is as old as time. If we attempt to resolve it by legislation who knows but that we may be called upon to take sides as well in the age-old problem of dog versus cat, bird versus bird, or even bird versus worm. In my opinion, the State of Illinois and its local governing bodies already have enough to do without trying to control feline delinquency. For these reasons, and not because I love birds the less or cats the more, I veto and withhold my approval from Senate Bill No. 93.[36]

Not all vetoes are based on executive-legislative conflict over vital questions of public policy. At the national level, vetoes based on constitutional grounds and policy differences are the norm.[37] In the states, the veto is used, in addition, because bills duplicate one another, because acts of legislatures are vague and incapable of enforcement, or because technical flaws have occurred in their drafting. The use of the veto is not an altogether accurate barometer of executive-legislative policy conflict. An attempt to assess the significance of the veto as a tool of executive influence will be deferred until we have discussed the other factors that bear on the executive's role as chief legislator.

## Messages

The obligation of the presidents and governors to deliver messages to their respective legislative bodies is a less obvious basis for influence. A chief executive, well endowed with prerequisites for influence, can translate the duty to deliver messages into a means for focusing both legislative and public attention on his or her program. About a third of all presidents have made personal appearances before Congress to deliver messages pushing their legislative programs. All presidents in the last fifty years have done so. Some chief executives may find the duty to deliver messages to be little more than a burdensome chore. The executive message, then, may be an important element in executive influence or simply something of a formality. Early in the Reagan administration, some members of Congress cringed after presidential speeches in anticipation of an outpouring of public support for the president. In 1987, under different political conditions, President Reagan continued to be forceful in his rhetoric, but the public response was essentially one of indifference.

Messages may be filled with familiar civic platitudes, requests of exceptional modesty, or bold new programs. How seriously the legislators treat executive messages depends largely on how serious they think the chief executive is in making them. In brief, it depends on how they size him up—how they evaluate the lengths to which he will go to get what he says he wants. When the executive message is part of an effective process, its delivery is merely symbolic of what legislators already have reason to anticipate—that an administration bill with administration support will soon be before the legislature.

Legislative reaction to executive messages is not likely to represent an unbiased verdict; neither is it necessarily proportional to the inherent logic of the chief executive's requests or arguments. Thus, Democratic Senate majority leader Mike Mansfield could view a message from President Kennedy as bearing "the authentic earmark of greatness," while his Republican counterpart, minority leader Everett McKinley Dirksen, could describe the same message as "a Sears & Roebuck catalogue with the prices marked up."

Richard Neustadt captures the potential of the presidential message:

> Congress can gain from the outside what comes hard from within: a handy and official guide to the wants of its biggest customer; an advance formulation of main issues at each session; a work-load ready-to-hand for every legislative

committee; an indication, more or less, of what may risk the veto; a borrowing of presidential prestige for most major bills.[38]

## Special Sessions

Of the constitutional powers that place the chief executive directly into the legislative process, the power to call special sessions is usually of least importance. The president can call a special session but, having done so, must risk legislative defiance and policy disaster. Congress is under no oblgation to act on or even to discuss the subject about which the president calls the special session. In contrast, in many states the governor not only summons the legislature into special session but indicates the session agenda as well. State legislatures cannot determine their agenda for special sessions in 25 percent of the states. In 60 percent of the states, legislatures can call themselves into special sessions. But the governor, whatever the advantage, needs to be cautious: "Experience in many states indicates that when decisions on special sessions are made on the basis of 'pushing the legislature around or embarrassing its members,' the decisions frequently backfire."[39]

In an extreme example, Governor Henry Bellmon of Oklahoma called a special session of the legislature to consider matters of tax reform only to find that no legislator would introduce his program in a bill.[40]

Despite the relative advantage of the governor, experience demonstrates that the power to call special sessions cannot be considered a critical tool for chief executives as they attempt to influence legislative behavior. The power to prepare and submit budgets, to veto legislative acts, to send messages, and to call for special sessions provides a firm legal basis for executive influence in the legislative process, for each of these powers directly involves chief executives in the lawmaking process.

Other aspects of the legal environment that do not thrust chief executives directly into legislative affairs do, however, both enhance and restrict their efforts to shape the course of public policy. The chief executives' legal relationships with the bureaucracy, their legal relationships with the electorate, and the length of their terms are all related to their leadership in the legislative process.

## Administrative Leader

Chief executives as administrative leaders gain three basic assets for legislative leadership: (1) competent professional and technical assistance in formulating programs to meet felt needs; (2) control over the appointment of personnel and over the selection and allocation of programs; and (3) awareness of imperfections in existing programs through experience gained in implementing legislative acts.

Legislative staff and information resources can seldom match those of the executive branch. The legislative branch is regularly forced to rely on information and analysis gathered and prepared by the executive. To some extent, the information that the legislature secures from pressure groups and other constituency sources serves to offset the information dominance of the executive, but this is less likely in matters of international relations and national security.

Control over the bureaucracy provides the chief executive with certain controls over personnel. The president appoints the heads of the executive departments and can remove them at his discretion. Most governors, on the contrary, do not have these extensive powers of appointment for the heads of executive departments. (See Table 11.3 for data for 1997.) Thad Beyle and Robert Dalton found that the figures on separately elected state officials did not change much from 1965 to 1980.[41] What sometimes results is that persons not in sympathy with the governor's programs win these positions; at times, they are not even of the same party affiliation as the governor. Hence it is not unusual that the top leadership of the executive branch is split both ideologically and politically, making coherent program formulation difficult. According to administrative leaders in a study of all fifty states, the primary weapon for a governor attempting to control the agencies remains the budget authority.[42]

Unlike many governors, the president is legally free to select the heads of his executive departments; in practice, the range of his choice is circumscribed. Certain appointments will be made with the view of unifying his political party; others will be designed to provide representation and to win support of groups and factions to which the president feels it necessary to appeal. Such appointees may be political strangers thrust into top executive positions. There seems to be no doubt that certain appointments serve to weaken executive unity.

Disunity in the executive branch poses difficulties for executive influence. For example, executive departments may offer legislators alternative sets of data and conflicting analyses; legislative leaders may enter into

**TABLE 11.3 Popularly elected executive department heads in the states, 1997**

| Office | Number of States |
|---|---|
| Attorney general | 42 |
| Treasurer | 39 |
| Secretary of state | 37 |

SOURCE: *Book of the States, 1998–1999* (Lexington, KY: Council of State Governments, 1998), p. 34.

alliances with particular executive subunits; and the chief executive's efforts may be blunted by prestigious subordinates who administer semiautonomous agencies.[43]

Chief executives may also win support for their programs through the judicious use of patronage. President Theodore Roosevelt put it as bluntly as possible when he stated about members of Congress, "If they'll vote for my measures, I'll appoint their nominees to federal jobs. . . . I'll play the game, appoint their men for their support of my bills."[44] The extent of patronage in appointments available to the chief executive will vary with time and environment. The rise of civil service and other merit systems for selecting personnel has slowly narrowed the patronage potential of the president to a relatively restricted portion of national government employees. At the state level, the number of patronage appointees varies tremendously. In California, Michigan, and Wisconsin, the governor has relatively few patronage positions to fill; in Pennsylvania, by contrast, the governor can make quite a few such appointments.

Appointing personnel is not the only tool of patronage available to chief executives. Support for a legislator's pet program, contracts for constituents, allocation of money for roads, and issuance of pardons are possible levers for executive influence. The essence of the patronage process was captured in a statement attributed to "an observer" by E. Pendleton Herring: "His [President Franklin D. Roosevelt's] relations to Congress were to the very end of the session tinged with a shade of expectancy which is the best part of young love."[45]

The chief executive's legislative and administrative roles are closely related. As administrative leader, the chief executive holds controls over personnel, programs, and information, which in turn enhance efforts at legislative leadership.

### Representative Character

Chief executives are more than spokesmen for their administrative departments. They possess by law a popular constituency—the state or nation—which differs from that of any legislator. The chief executive's representative character both augments and limits his potential as a legislative leader. The statewide electoral base of the governor and the nationwide electoral base of the president provide logical and political grounds for the claim that the chief executive holds a superior position in interpreting public needs and public opinion. Elected by larger numbers of people than the legislator and viewing the policy process from the heights of their broader constituency, chief executives generally see themselves advancing the state or national interest, as opposed to the more parochial orientation of the typical legislator. Their unique electoral position added to their constitutionally and legally derived powers helps chief executives draw public attention to their programs; these advantages, however, do not necessarily lead to the generation of effective political support for their programs.

Symbolically, chief executives may claim to speak for the state or the nation, but political necessity leads them to speak with special vigor for those groups who contributed most significantly to their election. A brief glance at the pattern of presidential elections provides a clear illustration. To gain election, the president must receive a majority of the electoral votes, 270 of 538. The electoral votes of eight states (New York, Pennsylvania, California, Ohio, Florida, Michigan, Illinois, and Texas) provide about 84 percent of this required total. When majorities in these states have similar problems that they wish resolved through public policy, the direction of a president's programmatic appeals is clearly channeled.

Opposed to the executive's more generalized orientation lies the more specific and more easily identifiable orientation of the legislator, the interests of whose district are comparatively clear and concrete. The legislator's concerns may contradict, or at least fail to match, the interests of the supporters of the president or governor. The necessity for some cooperation tends to bridge this gap. At the center of the problem is the fact that the legislator's roots are deep in the constituency.

The broad base of the chief executives' constituency gives them an advantage in making news and winning public attention. But the advantage is limited. The heterogeneity of their electorate is such that their attempts to translate their electoral majority into popular support for a specific program inevitably leads to antagonizing certain groups or segments of the population. To those who are antagonized must also be added those who are indifferent to the words and requests of the chief executive. "The weaker his apparent popular support," Richard Neustadt observes of the president, "the more his cause in Congress may depend on negatives at his disposal like the veto. . . . He may not be left helpless, but his options are reduced, his opportunities diminished, his freedom for maneuver checked in the degree that Washington conceives him unimpressive to the public."[46]

## Term of Office

One last aspect of the chief executive's legal environment is term of office. In about half the states, the governor's term and reeligibility are strictly limited by law. Custom promotes the same end in other states. Almost all governors have a four-year term. The president, of course, serves a four-year term and can be reelected once. Many observers assume that executive influence over legislation diminishes near the end of the final term. Malcolm Jewell, for example, states that "the consequence of his limitation [on years of service] is that during the second half of his administration the governor has declining influence in the legislature."[47] Similar assertions reverberated during debates over the Twenty-second Amendment to the United States Constitution. At the national level, Presidents Eisenhower, Reagan, and Clinton have been affected by the Twenty-second Amendment. Here the facts cast doubt on the generalization, for a good argument can be made that President Eisenhower exerted more influence on legislation in 1959 and 1960, his last two years in office, than in any previous two-year period.[48]

A catalog of the chief executives' formal powers does not serve as a reliable index of their influence in the legislative process.[49] Formal power is potential power. Its translation into actual power is a function of other elements. The influence of executives is conditioned not only by their own legal environment but also by the legal environment within which legislators act. To the extent that these formal powers are shared or overlap, a potential for conflict is present. Probably the most obvious characteristic of the legal structure within which legislators act is the dispersion of power and authority between the two houses, within the committee system, and among a number of offices such as the Speaker of the House. The argument is usually made that the presence of multiple centers of power in the legislative branch makes it more difficult for executives to mobilize support for their programs.

## Bicameralism

The clearest example of dispersion of power and authority is found in the provision for a bicameral legislature, both in Congress and in forty-nine of the fifty states. Although the presence of two houses instead of one tends to complicate the executive's political life, it is probable that the characteristics of the two bodies do more to determine the executive's influence than does the mere fact of their existence. To the extent that one house differs from the other in respect to length of term or nature of constituency, legislative bicameralism may inhibit executive influence. Another possibility, however, is that the existence of multiple access points within the legislature may enable the executive to build support initially within one house; having won it there, the executive may be able to increase his or her leverage on the second house.

## Committee Systems

The dispersion of power and authority is reflected as well in the committee system. Whether committees impede or augment executive influence depends on such things as the methods used in selection of members, the rules and traditions about reporting bills in each environment, and the prestige possessed by particular committees within the legislative system. Committee independence of executive influence seems to be directly related to the means by which members receive committee posts. Where procedures for selecting committee members, promoting them within committees, and selecting the chairs are either semiautomatic, such as through the use of seniority, or not dominated by the leadership, as in Congress, committees are more likely to constitute barriers to executive influence. In those states where the speaker appoints members of committees in the lower house, the central fact is the relationship between the chief executive and the speaker.

The method of selection of committee members and of the chairs sets the pattern for executive-committee cooperation and conflict. The legal apparatus encompassing committee work reinforces or weakens that pattern. In Congress, committee independence is a fact. A high percentage of bills die in committee. In those states where committees are important, their decisive role seems to be that of killing bills. In about 25 percent of the states, committees are required to report all bills, but this rule does not automatically augment executive influence. Discharge petitions are possible in Congress and in many states, but they are rarely used and even more rarely effective.

More elusive but still relevant in assessing committee impact on legislation is the status and prestige of each committee. The united, high-prestige committees more often generate favorable decisions in the full legislature. Legislative committees may constitute "feudal baronies" or may be subordinate dependents to other forces. Whatever their degree of freedom, they may be tools of executive leadership or impediments to it.

### Size of Legislative Bodies

Several less central aspects of the legal life of legislative bodies are relevant to the analysis of executive influence. The size of legislative bodies is one of these. Students of organizations and groups are in general agreement that any sizable body of individuals united in common tasks seldom acts spontaneously without direction. The necessity for leadership is widely recognized. Legislative bodies in the United States vary in membership from 20 in the Alaska senate to 435 in the U.S. House of Representatives. The necessity for leadership in legislative bodies can be predicted; the source of that leadership is not equally apparent. Whether the chief executive can perform this function cannot be predicted on the basis of the size of the legislature.

### Length of Sessions

The length and frequency of legislative sessions may also have a bearing on executive influence in the legislature. In many states, biennial sessions and severe time limits almost guarantee a last-minute rush. Much the same thing occurs in Congress. Whether executive programs will be pushed quickly to passage or quietly buried in the struggle of the closing days will vary from political environment to political environment.

## PARTISAN POLITICS AND EXECUTIVE INFLUENCE

Partisan politics does not determine executive influence on legislatures but it surely affects it. Competitive two-party politics characterizes the American political scene only on occasion; that the majority party runs the government is often only a myth. Conflict in one-party states is typically within the dominant party. To the extent that the governors lead, they do so by molding personal, ideological, and regional support into majority factions. In states where competitive party politics is the rule and where the governor and the legislative majority belong to different parties, party can hinder executive influence.

The president and the majority in each house of Congress usually wear the identical party label. From 1900 to 1968, the party in control of the presidency produced a majority in both houses of Congress over 60 percent of the time. From 1968 to 1998, the situation has been different. Divided partisan control of the presidency and Congress has prevailed about 76 percent of the time.

Sharing a party label is not the same as sleeping in the same ideological bed. Party lines are crossed in Congress with monotonous regularity as coalitions are formed in support of legislation. President Reagan, a Republican, won his decisive victory in the battle over the budget in 1981 despite Democratic control of the House of Representatives. In 1998, a majority of Democrats opposed a majority of Republicans on 55.5 percent of the roll-call votes in the House; in the Senate, the figure was 55.7.

Given the decentralized nature of power and authority in Congress, sympathy and support from key committee chairs can sometimes be more significant than votes from the rank-and-file party members. The importance of a chairperson to the president is illustrated by this story concerning President Kennedy and Congressman Wilbur Mills (D., AR), chair of the House Ways and Means Committee: "I read in *The New York Times* this morning," the president said in a visit to Arkansas to dedicate a new federal dam, "that if Wilbur Mills requested it, I'd be glad to come down here and sing *Down by the Old Mill Stream.* I want to say that I am delighted."[50]

In the states, a governor and a legislative majority of the same political party was the pattern from 1946 to 1976; since then, divided government has been the norm. Alan Rosenthal states that from 1950 to 1975 Democratic governors faced Democratic legislatures about two-thirds of the time, and Republican governors faced Republican legislatures about three-fifths of the time; from 1978 to 1990, Morris Fiorina notes, unified government rarely existed in more than 50 percent of the states.[51] In 1997, about 60 percent of the states had divided government.

The appeal to party meets a ready response when it reinforces other pressures on the legislator. The legislator caught in cross-pressures is more likely to pursue an independent course. Psychological pressure toward party regularity exists, but its impact is not always decisive.[52] The pull of party is illustrated in these remarks by a Republican senator:

> If the Republican party is going to stay in power it must support the President. As a result, I sometimes "hold my nose" as the saying goes—and go along with the administration, though I might personally prefer to vote the other way.[53]

If political parties make some difference for executive leadership, so must divided government where one political party holds the presidency and the other has a majority in one or both houses of Congress. Scholars continue to debate how important divided government is. To date, evidence suggests the relevance of divided government in several situations: only in some policy areas; on presidential support of legislation in Congress; on use of the veto and overrides of vetoes; on agenda setting; on aspects of the budgetary process; and on procedural questions such as the use of "fast track" in congressional deliberations on international trade agreements.[54]

Several examples are instructive. In assessing presidential support in Congress on legislation, the data indicate that presidents with their own political party in control of both houses of Congress almost always have higher support on proposals that they favor than do presidents under conditions of divided government. Under unified government during the last thirty-eight years, the average presidential support score was about 82 percent; in this same period, under conditions of divided government, this score dropped to about 60 percent.

The impact of divided government on presidential relations with Congress may be measured also by comparing presidential vetoes and overrides of vetoes in periods when unified or divided government exists. In the nearly 40-year period from 1961 to 1998, when unified government prevailed (14 years), presidents used the veto 80 times; when divided government was present (22 years), presidents vetoed 256 times. Similarly, congressional overrides of presidential vetoes occurred twice under unified government and 33 times under divided government. Which political parties control the presidency and Congress does indeed make a difference. Table 11.4 provides some evidence.

**TABLE 11.4   Unified government, divided government, and the presidential veto, 1961–98**

| | Unified Government | | | Divided Government | |
|---|---|---|---|---|---|
| | Vetoes | Overrides | | Vetoes | Overrides |
| 1961–68 | 51 | 0 | 1969–76 | 109 | 19 |
| 1977–80 | 31 | 0 | 1981–92 | 124 | 10 |
| 1993–94 | 0 | 0 | 1995–98 | 23 | 4 |

SOURCE: Data from *Congressional Record*, Daily Digest.

TABLE 11.5    Party support for Presidents Carter and Reagan (in percentages)

| | Party Support on Nonunanimous Bills | | Party Support on Nonunanimous Bills | |
|---|---|---|---|---|
| | House | | Senate | |
| | Democrats | Republicans | Democrats | Republicans |
| President | | | | |
| Carter (D) | 63% | 31% | 63% | 38% |
| Reagan (R) | 30 | 68 | 32 | 76 |

SOURCE: Data from George C. Edwards, *At the Margins* (New Haven, CT: Yale University Press, 1989), p. 43.

Which political party controls the presidency and both houses of Congress does not explain the whole story of executive-legislative relations, but it is surely an important part of any attempt at such an explanation.

The chief executive uses his party and deals with the opposition party as best he can. The ultimate test of his effectiveness rests on the extent to which his interests, those of legislative party leaders, and those of party members in the legislature become functionally interdependent.[55] For example, in 1988, more than 70 percent of the Republican senators running for election ran ahead of George Bush in their state. Presumably, this result diminishes interdependence. James McCormick and Eugene Wittkopf assert that the nature of the issue, foreign or domestic, may also affect this relationship.[56] George Edwards argues, "Party leadership is useful for the president. It often provides him an additional increment of support for his policies in Congress. Yet it is unlikely to provide the basis for the direction of major change. It is a resource operating at the margins of coalition building."[57] Table 11.5 shows how party can make a difference.

## THE PERSONAL DIMENSION OF EXECUTIVE LEADERSHIP

The influence of chief executives is enhanced or hindered by societal factors, legal rules and procedures, and the status and condition of political parties; it is not always established by them. The missing link is the chief executives themselves. Their prospects for influencing the legislature are in part a function of their personality, their conception of their office, their policy desires, and their own political skill and that of their associates. The context of political conflict does not always predetermine the results. Who the participants are can sometimes make a difference.

The importance of personal variability in decision making is a murky area of analysis. Fred Greenstein links personal impact with such factors as the ambiguity of the situation, the sanctions related to alternative acts, the active investment of effort required, and the extent of fixed expectations attached to a position.[58]

It is difficult to establish a direct connection between personal relationships and political leadership. President Roosevelt at times resorted to condemnation of Congress. On the other hand, President Eisenhower seemed to believe, at least during the early part of his first administration, that the road to executive influence was paved with bacon and eggs for visiting congressmen who attended White House breakfasts. It would be rash to state that either of these patterns is more effective in all situations.

However attractive his personality and however great his popularity, a president finds it difficult to translate these assets into favorable votes for his legislative program. Although the public opinion polls demonstrated with monotonous regularity that the people of the United States liked President Clinton, Congress demonstrated with comparable regularity that it was not anxious to support all of his programs. Presidential popularity in the nation is often assumed to mean presidential success in Congress. That relationship is not necessarily direct or clear.[59] Figures 11.2 and 11.3 illustrate this. "Approval gives a president leverage, but not control."[60] The utility and limits of presidential popularity become apparent when we see that after the U.S. military victory in the Persian Gulf in 1991 President Bush's approval rating soared to 89 percent, the highest figure in more than fifty years of measurement. Yet Bush's ability to push his domestic proposals through Congress was not notably enhanced and, of course, he was defeated in the 1992 election.

The chief executives' influence is also related to their conception of their office. The president or governor who sees his or her role essentially as that of a faithful executor of legislative policies is unlikely to be challenged in the legislature. Chief executives who see themselves as initiators or catalysts may not fare so well. Nothing is so likely to stir the legislature as a chief executive who takes an openly active role in the legislative process. Chief executives who define their office as Theodore Roosevelt did—"a bully pulpit"—or as Franklin D. Roosevelt did—"a place of moral leadership"— are not necessarily more successful in securing legislative responses. Since chief executives commonly represent a set of interests different from those of each legislator, their programs may encounter vigorous legislative opposition; in fact, the more presidents seek to do, the greater their chances of opposition in Congress. Executive vigor and executive effectiveness are not the same thing.

Each chief executive decides what behavior is appropriate to the office. In addition, chief executives bring their policy preferences into office. If a president or governor wants to preserve the status quo, or make only marginal modification of it, he is more likely to persuade his legislature than if he promotes vigorous reformist programs. By and large, legislatures are more inclined to prevent action than to promote it; accordingly, a politically

**FIGURE 11.2  Legislative support score versus presidential popularity, 1981–88**

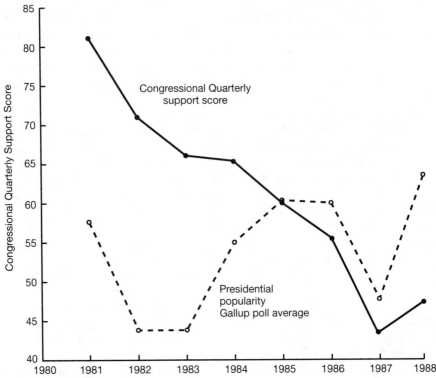

SOURCE: *The Gallup Report,* July 1988, p. 20; *The Gallup Report,* October 1988, p. 26; *Congressional Quarterly Almanac, 1989,* p. B25.

activist chief executive, except under unusual circumstances such as war, may expect to meet towering legislative roadblocks. President Carter's own words testify to this fact:

> I think I have found it is much easier for me in my own administration to evolve a very complex proposal for resolving a difficult issue than it is for Congress to pass legislation and to make that same decision. The energy legislation is one example. I never dreamed a year ago in April when I proposed this matter to the Congress that a year later it still would not be resolved. I think I have got a growing understanding of the Congress, its limitations, and its capabilities and also its leadership, which was a new experience for me altogether, never having lived or served in the federal government in Washington.[61]

The attributes of political skill are not always easy to pinpoint, but the importance of having it is agreed upon. Richard Neustadt argues persuasively that a president can muster extra margins of effectiveness through the

**FIGURE 11.3    Legislative support scores versus presidential popularity, 1993–97**

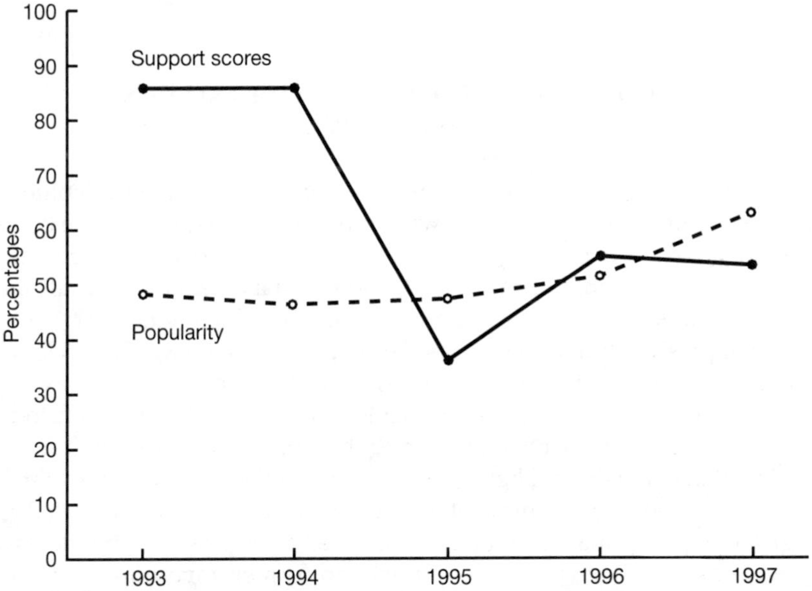

SOURCE: Approval scores from *Gallup Poll Monthly*, July 1998, pp. 7–8; support scores from *Congressional Quarterly Almanac, 1997*, p. C14.

diligent exercise of political skills. To make his colleagues in his administration and his associates in Congress see that what he wants them to do is in their own interests is the crucial task for the president.

Perhaps too much of President Carter's legislative failure and President Reagan's early success has been attributed to their political skill or lack of it. In each case, contextual factors were surely important.[62] Yet President Carter's failure to heed the advice of legislative leaders did hurt. They told him that he was "trying to do too much, too fast, and without adequate preparation."[63] The Democratic majority leader in the Senate, Robert Byrd, is reported to have told Carter, "You can't put a half gallon of water in a quart jar."[64] President Carter's ability to persuade declined to the point that one member of Congress claimed that Carter, "couldn't get the Pledge of Allegiance through Congress."[65] The relevance of contextual factors to presidential success in Congress is shown also by President Bush's ability to gain congressional support for military operations in the Persian Gulf in 1991.

Presidential efforts at persuasion depend in part on the political skills of his top assistants. Lawrence F. O'Brien, a master of legislative liaison, provided massive boosts to administration programs during the presidencies of John F. Kennedy and Lyndon B. Johnson.[66] By contrast, at least part of the Carter administration's difficulties in persuading Congress to pass its priority programs can be traced to problems in building effective legislative liaison.[67]

## THE EFFECTIVENESS OF EXECUTIVE INFLUENCE: OVERVIEW

The executives' influence in the legislative process is related to contextual factors that set boundaries within which their own personality, role conceptions, ideology, and political skills can be relevant. To what extent do attempts at executive influence succeed, and to what extent do they fall short?

On balance, when assets and liabilities are blended, most students agree that presidents and governors are very likely to be significant elements in their respective legislative processes. Alan Rosenthal notes, for example, "Officials of both the executive and legislative branches agree that today's governors are highly effective in steering their proposals through the legislatures";[68] Ransone is only slightly more restrained when he notes that "the average governor in the United States in the past fifty years has proved to be a legislative policy maker of no mean stature."[69] Success does not necessarily come easily. In a survey of governors and former governors, Thad Beyle reported that 43 percent of those who responded listed working with the legislature as their most difficult role.[70]

The president's influence with Congress tends to be significant. Most analysts see the necessity for presidential leadership in the legislative process. Some fear the enlargement of presidential power and see the possibility of such power becoming "dangerously personalized."[71]

## THE EFFECTIVENESS OF EXECUTIVE INFLUENCE: THE PROBLEM OF MEASUREMENT

If the influence of the chief executive on the legislative process is noteworthy, how is it measured? What are the standards for judging? How can we tell if a president or governor is influential? If one accepts the executive's own priority list as the standard by which to judge his or her success, then adoption of leading items on that list is meaningful. But what test is to be made of the executive with modest ambitions? Those who ask for little of consequence may in fact be quite successful but only on their own terms of measurement.

An alternative standard for gauging executive influence lies in assessing the urgency of existing problems and in comparing such lists with executive accomplishments. But this, too, is troublesome. What is an urgent priority for one person may be of only casual importance for another. Which is most important: preserving Social Security and Medicare, reciprocal trade, fighting crime, or a tax cut?

Some conceivable measures of executive influence are more easily quantifiable. How many proposals do they make? How many messages do they send to the legislature? How many television and radio speeches do they make to build support or to pacify opposition? How many conferences do they hold with legislative leaders? How many vetoes are used? The difficulty is that answers to these questions provide measures of activity rather than indices of influence.[72]

### Proposals Made and Legislation Passed

One widely used measure of influence involves analyzing the ratio of proposals made to legislation passed. Statistics seem to be on the governor's side, judging from an assortment of studies. Governors in many states regularly see their proposals passed by the legislature.[73] At the national level, since 1953 Congressional Quarterly, Inc. has compiled a "presidential support score." Figure 11.4 shows the results since 1977.[74] Variation occurs not only from year to year, but from president to president. Moreover, a president may have more support on some kinds of policy questions than on others. This is shown in Table 11.6, which contrasts congressional support given to several presidents on foreign policy and domestic policy. The difference is clear.

Drawing on such evidence, Aaron Wildavsky claimed in 1966 that presidents generally were more effective in getting congressional support on foreign policy issues than on domestic ones.[75] Scholars have continued to

**FIGURE 11.4**   One measure of presidential success: Presidential support scores, Carter (1977) to Clinton (1998)

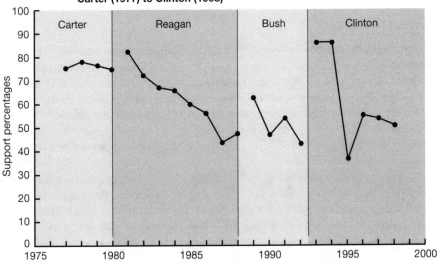

SOURCE: Data from *Congressional Quarterly Weekly Report*, January 9, 1999, p. 86.

TABLE 11.6   Presidential support in Congress on foreign and domestic policy, 1953–80

| | Success on Foreign Policy | | Success on Domestic Policy | |
|---|---|---|---|---|
| President | House | Senate | House | Senate |
| Eisenhower | 80% | 79% | 51% | 54% |
| Kennedy | 86 | 82 | 82 | 78 |
| Johnson | 71 | 79 | 72 | 76 |
| Nixon | 68 | 55 | 69 | 38 |
| Carter | 71 | 64 | 82 | 68 |

SOURCE: Data from Jon Bond and Richard Fleisher, *The President in the Legislative Arena* (Chicago: University of Chicago Press, 1989), p. 157.

debate the accuracy of the Wildavsky thesis.[76] In a study of the period 1953–84, Jon Bond and Richard Fleisher assert that the thesis holds only for Republican presidents and that the foreign-domestic distinction applies more to "normal" issues than for those that are most visible and conflictual.[77]

The preceding discussion provides hints as to executive influence. It is far from conclusive because presidential-congressional agreement does not necessarily result from presidential influence. A second reason is that no bill precisely equals any other in importance. President Clinton had impressive statistics for support from Congress in 1993 and 1994, yet he failed to push his top priority, a health care bill, through the Congress. Was he then a success or a failure? The absence of a qualitative dimension is a serious impediment to any study of executive influence on legislative voting behavior.

### Vetoes Overridden

The number of vetoes overridden provides another measure of influence. The extent to which chief executives can build support to defeat attempts to override their vetoes gives some indication of their influence among legislators. Here the governor's record is extraordinarily impressive. From 1900 to 1947, only one veto by a Pennsylvania governor was overridden.[78] In New York, no vetoes were overridden for more than one hundred years until the pattern was broken in 1975.[79] In California, no general vetoes were overridden from 1962 to 1973; a few, however, were overridden from 1975 to 1994.[80]

Very few presidential vetoes, slightly over 7 percent, have been overridden. If we include pocket vetoes in the totals (of course, they cannot be overridden), the figure is about 4 percent. The record differs dramatically for public and private bills. Of public bills subject to override, some 19 percent have been overridden; for private bills, the number is .8 percent.[81]

The veto records of presidents since World War II are detailed in Table 11.7; some data on the performance of governors are presented in Table 11.8.

**TABLE 11.7  The presidential veto record in Congress, 1945–98**

| Years | Presidents | Vetoes | Overridden | Vetoes Percent |
|-------|-----------|--------|------------|----------------|
| 1945–53 | Truman | 250 | 12 | 4.8 |
| 1953–61 | Eisenhower | 181 | 2 | 1.1 |
| 1961–63 | Kennedy | 21 | 0 | 0 |
| 1963–69 | Johnson | 30 | 0 | 0 |
| 1969–74 | Nixon | 43 | 7 | 16 |
| 1974–77 | Ford | 66 | 12 | 18 |
| 1977–81 | Carter | 31 | 2 | 6 |
| 1981–89 | Reagan | 78 | 9 | 12 |
| 1989–92 | Bush | 46 | 1 | 2 |
| 1992–98 | Clinton | 23 | 4 | 17 |

SOURCE: *Presidential Vetoes, 1789–1976,* compiled by the Senate Library, September 1978 (Washington, DC: U.S. Government Printing Office, 1978), p. ix, as supplemented by the *Congressional Record, Daily Digest.*

**TABLE 11.8  Vetoes of governors and overrides, 1947 and 1973**

| | Number of States | |
|---|---|---|
| Vetoes Overridden | 1947 | 1973 |
| Less than 5 percent | 39 | 36 |
| 5–9.9 percent | 2 | 4 |
| 10 percent or more | 8 | 9 |

SOURCE: Data compiled from table in Charles W. Wiggins, "Executive Vetoes and Legislative Overrides in the American States," *Journal of Politics,* XLII (November 1980), 1112–113.

## CONCLUSIONS AND TENDENCIES

Any of the statistics for the success or failure of the chief executive must be treated with caution. What they hide may be as important as what they show. Short-range failure, for example, may pave the path to long-range success. In his evaluation of the legislative record of the Truman administration, Richard Neustadt cites domestic programs that fell before congressional attack like tenpins. But by vigorously advocating proposals that were doomed then, Truman set the stage for future successes.[82] Innovation in policy eventually become orthodoxy in politics. On this count, the ultimate judgment concerning the influence of the chief executive has to be made many years later. Thus, whether President Reagan's legislative successes constitute a "Reagan Revolution" remains to be determined.[83]

Whatever their actual influence, presidents and governors claim superiority over members of Congress and state legislators as agents of representation. They cite the breadth of their constituency and their greater resources in information and expertise. The president or governor need not always be presented as spokesperson for the public interest, but the legislator is marked as simply the agent of narrow parochialism. Executive-legislative conflict is not necessarily a battle between heroes and villains; rather, it is a battle of advocates of different elements within the political system. Just as legislators cannot speak for all of their district, so executives cannot speak for all of the state or the nation. Their electoral bases, their party affiliations, and their personal backgrounds contribute to the pressure to which all representatives, both executive and legislative, attempt to respond.

To the extent that chief executives and legislators respond to different sets of political pressures, political conflict becomes inevitable. Yet cooperation remains a necessity.[84] Conflict among the branches of government contributes to the articulation of the many voices of society but makes it difficult to reach authoritative decisions, especially if the decisions represent a noticeable departure from past policy. Yet conflict is hardly an inherent evil. The extent to which executive-legislative conflict resolution is desirable and necessary is a function both of objective needs (such as a successful prosecution of war) and of the analyst's own ideological perspectives (such as the desirability of a system of government-run national health insurance).[85]

The phenomenon of executive influence does not lend itself easily to generalization. But there are several tendencies for which some evidence is available:

1. Crisis does tend to increase executive influence, but not always.

2. Executive influence is not confined to suggesting ideas to legislators and to receiving bills from legislative bodies. It can be and often is exerted at all stages of that process.

3. Executive influence varies with legal and environmental factors, as well as with changes in personnel or in party majorities.

4. The presence or absence of particular legal and institutional features, such as the item veto or the power to call special sessions, is probably not, in and of itself, critical in determining executive influence.

5. Successful exercise of executive influence often requires appeals based both on the inherent logic of the executive's case and on bargaining and accommodation. Conflict as to what is "good policy" is commonplace. The merits of the executive's program often are far from self-evident to all legislators.

6. Executives can and do exert considerable influence over legislatures but seldom are able to guarantee any given result. Presidents, George C. Edwards argues, are more facilitators than directors of change.[86]

Executives become legislators because their environment and formal power provide both opportunity and rationale, while their representative capacity imposes on them the obligation to do so. Representation in a democracy involves speaking for the represented, blending their disparate viewpoints, suggesting effective solutions for the problems of society, and seeking support for appropriate policies. Promoting the second and fourth functions may be the indispensable contribution of the chief executive to the legislative process.

## NOTES

1. For an excellent analysis of presidential leadership, see Bert A. Rockman, *The Leadership Question* (New York: Praeger, 1984).

2. Mark A. Peterson, *Legislating Together: The White House and Capitol Hill from Eisenhower to Reagan* (Cambridge, MA: Harvard University Press, 1990), p. 96. Edwards and Wood argue that the ability of the president to set the agenda for Congress varies across issues, within issues, and over time. George C. Edwards III and B. Dan Wood, "Who Influences Whom? The President, Congress, and the Media," *American Political Science Review*, XCIII (June 1999), 327–44.

3. Alan Rosenthal, *Governors and Legislatures: Contending Powers* (Washington, DC: Congressional Quarterly Press, 1990), p. 96. See also Thad L. Beyle and Lynn R. Muchmore, eds., *Being Governor: The View from the Office* (Durham, NC: Duke Press Policy Studies, 1983). For an analysis in Florida, see Robert E. Crew, Jr., and Marjorie Renee Hill, "Gubernatorial Influence in State Government Policy-Making," *Spectrum*, LXVIII (Fall 1995), 29–35. On governors more generally, see Coleman B. Ransone, Jr., *The American Governorship* (Westport, CT: Greenwood Press, 1982), pp. 135–42.

4. Eric L. Davis, "Legislative Liaison in the Carter Administration," *Political Science Quarterly*, XCV (Summer 1979), 301.

5. For some examples, see Joel D. Aberbach, Robert D. Putnam, and Bert A. Rockman, *Bureaucrats & Politicians in Western Democracies* (Cambridge, MA: Harvard University Press, 1981). See also R. Douglas Arnold, *Congress and the Bureaucracy* (New Haven, CT: Yale University Press, 1979).

6. For examples of President Lincoln's extraconstitutional actions, see Wilfred Binkley, *President and Congress* (New York: Knopf, 1947), pp. 110–15. A thoughtful update of the argument that contextual factors are more central to explaining presidential relations with Congress than are the skills of the participants is Barbara Sinclair, "Trying to Govern Positively in a Negative Era: Clinton and the 103rd Congress," in *The Clinton Presidency, First Appraisals*, ed. Colin Campbell and Bert A. Rockman (Chatham, NJ: Chatham House, 1996), pp. 88–125.

7. *Goodbye to Good-Time Charlie: The American Governor Transformed*, 2nd ed. (Washington, DC: Congressional Quarterly Press, 1983), p. 84. The governor has primary responsibility for budget preparation in forty-seven states.

8. For introductions to the budgetary process, see Stanley E. Collender, *The Guide to the Federal Budget, Fiscal 1997* (Lanham, MD: Rowman & Littlefield, 1996); and Allen Schick, *The Federal Budget* (Washington, DC: Brookings Institution, 1995). What the president does to congressional appropriations is discussed in Louis Fisher, *Presidential Spending Power* (Princeton, NJ: Princeton University Press, 1975).

9. Allen Schick, *The Capacity to Budget* (Washington, DC: Urban Institute Press, 1990), p. 1.

10. Quoted in William Greider, "The Education of David Stockman," *The Atlantic Monthly*, December 1981, p. 38.

11. Rosenthal, *Governors and Legislatures*, p. 132.

12. Natchez and Bupp point out that a focus on incrementalism at the agency level may obscure substantial conflict over funding specific programs within the agency budget: "Policy and Priority in the Budgetary Process," *American Political Science Review,* LXVII (September 1973), 951–63. An additional caution about incrementalism is found in Robert D. Thomas and Roger B. Handberg, "Congressional Budgeting for Eight Agencies, 1947–1972," *American Journal of Political Science,* XVIII (February 1974), 179–87.

13. Joel A. Thompson, "Agency Requests, Gubernatorial Support, and Budget Success in State Legislatures Revisited," *Journal of Politics,* XL (August 1987), 756–79. Thomas P. Lauth, "The Governor and the Conference Committee in Georgia," *Legislative Studies Quarterly,* XV (August 1990), 441–53. See also Glenn Abney and Thomas P. Lauth, "Perceptions of the Impact of Governors and Legislatures in the State Appropriations Process," *Western Political Quarterly,* XL (June 1987), 335–42. For detailed information on budget and appropriations procedures in the states, see Tony Hutchison and Kathy James, *Legislative Budget Procedures in the 50 States: A Guide to Appropriations and Budget Processes* (Denver, CO: Fiscal Affairs Program, National Conference of State Legislatures, 1988). See also *Governors, Legislatures, and Budgets,* ed. Edward J. Clynch and Thomas P. Lauth (New York: Greenwood Press, 1991). The experience in New York in 1994–95 is instructive. In his campaign for election, George Pataki promised massive improvements in the budgetary process. Private deals and budgetary gimmicks were to be eliminated. As governor, he found that gaining support to pass the 1995–96 budget forced him to accept procedures he had recently denounced. For an analysis, see *New York Times,* June 4, 1995, p. 17. See also Gerald Benjamin, "The Power to Budget in New York: The Governor Still Dominates," *Comparative State Politics,* XIX (October 1998), 3–7.

14. For examples, see Fisher, *Presidential Spending Power,* Chaps. 7 and 8.

15. Ibid., p. 201.

16. See Title X of the Congressional Budget and Impoundment Control Act of 1974. The Nixon usage is detailed in Fisher, *Presidential Spending Power,* Chap. 8.

17. See Schick, *Capacity to Budget,* p. 112. See also Christopher Wlezien, "The Politics of Impoundment," *Political Research Quarterly,* XCVII (March 1994), 59–84.

18. See Chapter 12 for a discussion of the legislative veto, its uses, and legality.

19. The traditional pattern, pre-1974, is described in Richard F. Fenno, Jr., *The Power of the Purse* (Boston: Little, Brown, 1966), especially Chap. 9.

20. "The Battle of the Budget, FY 1982: Reagan Takes Over," in *The President and Economic Policy,* ed. James P. Pfiffner (Philadelphia: ISHI Publications, 1984).

21. Greider, *The Atlantic Monthly,* p. 35. Barbara Sinclair attributes the Reagan victories in Congress in 1981 to successful agenda control. She argues that if political elites in Congress see an election (1980) as a mandate, they will accept the winner's definition of issues and policy choices. "Agenda Control and Policy Success: Ronald Reagan and the 97th House," *Legislative Studies Quarterly,* X (August 1985), 291–314.

22. Allen Schick, "The Three-Ring Budget Process: The Appropriations, Tax, and Budget Committees in Congress," in *The New Congress,* ed. Thomas Mann and Norman Orenstein (Washington, DC: American Enterprise Institute for Public Policy Research, 1981), p. 327. For related analyses, see Lance T. LeLoup, "After the Blitz: Reagan and the U.S. Congressional Budget Process," *Legislative Studies Quarterly,* VII (August 1982), 321–39; and Kim Quaize Hill and John Patrick Plumlee, "Presidential Success in Budgetary Policymaking: A Longitudinal Analysis," *Presidential Studies Quarterly,* XII (Spring 1982), 174–85.

23. Allen Schick, *Reconciliation and the Congressional Budget Process* (Washington, DC: American Enterprise Institute for Public Policy Research, 1981), p. 43. The political consequences of proposing and passing new tax measures are discussed in Susan B. Hansen, "The Politics of State Taxing and Spending," in *Politics in the American States,* ed. Virginia Gray, Herbert Jacob, and Robert Albritton (Riverview, IL: Scott, Foresman/Little, Brown, 1990), pp. 336–37.

24. Schick, *The Capacity to Budget,* p. 206.

25. An analysis of budgetary struggles in recent years can be found in Schick, *The Capacity to Budget.* See also Schick, *The Federal Budget,* pp. 56–62.

26. *Clinton President of the United States, et al.* v. *City of New York et al.*, No. 97-1374. For a brief discussion, see Robert J. Spitzer, "The Item Veto Dispute and the Secular Crisis of the Presidency," *Presidential Studies Quarterly*, XXVIII (Fall 1998), 799–815.

27. 511 F 2nd 430 (1974). Samuel B. Hoff states that presidents have used the pocket veto more than 850 times from 1889 to 1989. "The Presidential Pocket Veto: Its Use and Legality," *Journal of Policy History*, VI (n.d. 1994), 188–208. A controversy over the use of the pocket veto developed in 1971 when Congress adjourned for a Christmas vacation only to find President Nixon claiming that in its absence, he could pocket veto bills. The U.S. Court of Appeals in *Kennedy* v. *Sampson* declared that as long as Congress has established procedures to receive messages in its absence, the pocket veto cannot be legally used during a brief absence. In a related 1976 case, the U.S. District Court for the District of Columbia expanded the 1974 ruling to apply to adjournments between sessions as well as those within a session.

28. Coleman B. Ransone, Jr., *The Office of the Governor in the United States* (Tuscaloosa, AL: University of Alabama Press, 1956), p. 181.

29. Samuel B. Hoff, "Presidential Support in the Veto Process, 1889–1985," unpublished Ph.D. dissertation, State University of New York at Stony Brook, 1987, pp. 49–50. Albert C. Ringelstein finds that the veto is used more for domestic legislation than for foreign policy: "Presidential Vetoes: Motivations and Classification," *Congress and the Presidency*, XII (Spring 1985), 52. David W. Rohde and Dennis M. Simon relate public support of the president to his use of the veto: "Presidential Vetoes and Congressional Response: A Study of Institutional Conflict," *American Journal of Political Science*, XXIX (August 1985), 397–427. A useful history and analysis of the veto is Robert J. Spitzer, *The Presidential Veto* (Albany: State University of New York Press, 1988). How the veto shapes public policy is explored by Richard A. Watson, *Presidential Vetoes and Public Policy* (Lawrence: University Press of Kansas, 1993). For an argument that relates changing patterns of veto usage to structural changes in Congress and the presidency, see David McKay, "Presidential Strategy and the Veto Power," *Political Science Quarterly*, CIV (Fall 1989), 447–61.

30. Ransone, *The American Governorship*, p. 141.

31. Data from Sidney Wise, *The Legislative Process in Pennsylvania* (Harrisburg, PA: House of Representatives, Bipartisan Management Committee, 1984), as supplemented by the yearly editions of *The Pennsylvania Manual*.

32. Data from Charles W. Wiggins, "Executive Vetoes and Legislative Overrides in the American States," *Journal of Politics*, XLII (November 1980), 1112–113.

33. Council of State Governments, *The Book of the States, 1998–1999* (Lexington, KY: Council of State Governments, 1998), pp. 105–106.

34. Joseph F. Zimmerman, "Rebirth of the Item Veto in the Empire State," *State Government*, LIV, 2 (1981), 52. For an example of the role of the courts in defining the extent of the item veto, see Rosenthal, *Governors and Legislatures*, p. 181.

35. "Wisconsin Item-Veto Lessons," *Public Administration Review*, XLVI (July/August 1986), 292, 298. Gosling's conclusion is supported by Tony Hutchison, "Legislating via Veto," *State Legislatures*, XV (January 1989), 20–22. See also David C. Nice, "The Item Veto and Expenditure Restraint," *Journal of Politics*, L (May 1988), 487–99; Glenn Abney and Thomas P. Lauth, "The Item Veto and Fiscal Responsibility," *Journal of Politics*, LIX (August 1997), 822–92; and Pat Thompson and Steven R. Boyd, "Use of the Item Veto in Texas, 1940–1990," *State and Local Government Review*, XXVI (Winter 1994), 38–45.

36. *Journal of the Illinois Senate*, 66th General Assembly, p. 540.

37. Richard A. Watson analyzed the messages accompanying presidential vetoes from 1931 to 1981. He found that the primary reason offered in defense of these vetoes was unwise public policy. *Presidential Vetoes and Public Policy*, pp. 136–44.

38. "Presidency and Legislation: Planning the President's Program," *American Political Science Review*, XLIX (December 1955), 1014. Andrade and Young argue that the ability to focus attention on his policy agenda contributes to presidential influence. Lydia Andrade and Garry Young, "Presidential Agenda Setting: Influences on the Emphasis of Foreign Policy," *Political Research Quarterly*, XLIX (1996), 591–605.

39. National Governors' Association, Center for Policy Research, *Governing the American States: A Handbook for New Governors* (Washington, DC: National Governors' Association, 1978), p. 183.

40. Rosenthal, *Governors and Legislatures*, p. 8.

41. Thad L. Beyle and Robert Dalton, "Appointment Power: Does It Belong to the Governor?" *State Government*, LIV, 1 (1981), 4.

42. Data from American State Administrators Project, Deil S. Wright, Director, Institute for Research in Social Science, University of North Carolina, Chapel Hill. Reprinted in Nelson C. Dometrius, "Some Consequences of State Reform," *State Government*, LIV, 3 (1981), 94.

43. Chief executives counter these centrifugal forces with devices to promote coordination of programs before they are presented to the legislative branch. See the classic article by Richard Neustadt, "Presidency and Legislation: The Growth of Central Clearance," *American Political Science Review*, XLVIII (September 1954), 641–71. See also John H. Kessel, *The Domestic Presidency: Decision-Making in the White House* (North Scituate, MA: Duxbury Press, 1975). For the experience in Maryland, see Edward J. Miller, "The Governor and Legislation," *State Government*, LXVII (Spring 1974), 92–95. See the discussion concerning patterns of presidential-bureaucratic relations in Colin Campbell, *Managing the Presidency* (Pittsburgh: University of Pittsburgh Press, 1986).

44. Quoted in *The Autobiography of Lincoln Steffens* (New York: Harcourt, Brace & World, 1931), p. 505.

45. "First Session of the Seventy-third Congress," *American Political Science Review*, XXVIII (February 1934), 82.

46. Richard E. Neustadt, *Presidential Power* (New York: John Wiley, 1980), p. 67. The status of the presidents and governors can add to their problems. As a New York state legislator put it, "Relating to governors is like relating to the Pope, except that the only thing you have to kiss on the Pope is his ring." Rosenthal, *Governors and Legislatures*, p. 49.

47. Malcolm Jewell, *The State Legislature* (New York: Random House, 1962), p. 111. Rosenthal sees a lame-duck governor as "likely to suffer a decline in efficacy." *Governors and Legislatures*, p. 21.

48. George C. Edwards III questions the utility of the lame-duck hypothesis for presidents. "Presidential Electoral Performance as a Source of Presidential Power," *American Journal of Political Science*, XXII (February 1978), 166.

49. Joseph Schlesinger, in Chap. 6 of *Politics in the American States*, ed. Herbert Jacob and Kenneth N. Vines (Boston: Little, Brown, 1971), constructs a "General Index of the Governor's Formal Powers," but is careful not to confuse formal power with actual power. Rosenthal updates this index and finds that the high and low states are similar to those found by Schlesinger. *Legislative Life: An Analysis of Legislatures in the States* (New York: Harper & Row, 1981), pp. 236–38. An attempt to revise and improve Schlesinger's index is found in Nelson Dometrius, "Measuring Gubernatorial Power," *Journal of Politics*, XXXI (May 1979), 589–610. See also E. Lee Bernick, "Gubernatorial Tools: Formal v. Informal," *Journal of Politics*, XXXI (May 1979), 656–64. Some cautions concerning the importance of formal power are offered by Thad L. Beyle, "Governors," in *Politics in the American States*, ed. Virginia Gray, Herbert Jacob, and Kenneth N. Vines (Boston: Little, Brown, 1983), pp. 193–203. In 1987, Nelson C. Dometrius argued that the utility of the Schlesinger index was very low. "Changing Gubernatorial Power: The Measure vs. Reality," *Western Political Quarterly*, XL (July 1987), 319–43. Keith J. Mueller disagrees. He asserts that the index of formal powers remains quite useful. He would improve it by adding an informal dimension. "A Rejoinder," pp. 329–31. The use of "fast tracking" in foreign trade policy provides an interesting example of how formal powers can make a difference in executive–legislative relations. Under this procedure, Congress can only accept or reject international trade agreements made by the president; it cannot amend them. See Byron W. Daynes and Glen Sussman, "Trade Politics and the Fast Track: Impact on Congressional-Presidential Relations," *American Review of Politics*, XV (Spring 1994), 73–87.

50. *Time*, October 11, 1963, p. 26.

51. Rosenthal, *Legislative Life*, Chap. 2. Morris P. Fiorina, "Divided Government in the American

States: A Product of Legislative Professionalism?" *American Political Science Review*, LXXXVIII (June 1994), 305. Charles Wiggins suggests that more overrides of vetoes occur in the states with divided party control, "Executive Vetoes and Legislative Overrides in the American States," p. 1117. Some consequences of divided government for budgeting at the state level are discussed in James E. Alt and Robert C. Lowry, "Divided Government, Fiscal Institutions, and Budget Deficits: Evidence from the States," *American Political Science Review*, LXXXVIII (December 1994), 812–28.

52. Aage R. Clausen, *How Congressmen Decide: A Policy Focus* (New York: St. Martin's Press, 1973). David C. Kozak, *Contexts of Congressional Decision Behavior* (Lanham, MD: University Press of America, 1984); George C. Edwards III, *At the Margins* (New Haven, CT: Yale University Press, 1989); and Jon Bond and Richard Fleisher, *The President in the Legislative Arena* (Chicago: University of Chicago Press, 1990), Chap. 4. Some of the most useful research on governors and their political parties is that of Sarah McCally Morehouse. See her findings in *State Politics, Parties and Policy* (New York: Holt, Rinehart & Winston, 1981), especially Chap. 5, and in *The Governor as Party Leader* (Ann Arbor: University of Michigan Press, 1998).

53. Quoted in Donald Matthews, *U.S. Senators and Their World* (Chapel Hill: University of North Carolina Press, 1960), p. 140.

54. The impact of divided government varies with policy area according to Martha L. Gibson, "Issues, Coalitions, and Divided Government," *Congress and the Presidency*, XXII (Fall 1995), 155–66. Andrew J. Taylor argues that divided government leads to increased congressional agenda setting. "Domestic Agenda Setting, 1947–1999," *Legislative Studies Quarterly*, XXIII (August 1998), 373–97. The impact of divided government on budgeting in the states is discussed in James E. Alt and Robert C. Lowry, "Divided Government, Fiscal Institutions, and Budget Deficits: Evidence from the States," *American Political Science Review*, LXXXVIII (December 1994), 812–28.

55. The most comprehensive account of the impact of presidential elections on congressional elections is James E. Campbell, *The Presidential Pulse of Congressional Elections* (Lexington: University of Kentucky Press, 1993). Calvert and Ferejohn point out that since presidents have little effect on the election or defeat of most members of Congress, the net effect is to reduce political dependence on presidents. Randall L. Calvert and John A. Ferejohn, "Coattail Voting in Recent Presidential Elections," *American Political Science Review*, LXXVII (June 1983), 407–19. Jeffrey Cohen, Michael A. Krassa, and John Hamman suggest that the president can help senatorial candidates under the right circumstances: "The Impact of Presidential Campaigning on Midterm U.S. Senate Elections," *American Political Science Review*, LXXXV (March 1991), 165–77. Gregory Flemming argues that presidential coattails may indeed make some difference in congressional elections but not very much. "Presidential Coattails in Open-Seat Elections," *Legislative Studies Quarterly*, XX (May 1995), 197–211.

56. James M. McCormick and Eugene A. Wittkopf, "Bipartisanship, Partisanship, and Ideology in Congressional-Executive Foreign Policy Relations, 1947–1988," *Journal of Politics*, LII (November 1990), 1077–100.

57. Edwards, *At the Margins*, p. 100. In a more recent study, Edwards finds that "important legislation is more likely to fail to pass under divided government." George C. Edwards, Jr., Andrew Barrett, and Jeffrey Peake, "The Legislative Impact of Divided Government," *American Journal of Political Science*, XLI (April 1997), 545–63.

58. *Personality and Politics* (Chicago: Markham, 1969), pp. 50–57. A few efforts have been made to study this subject matter in a presidential context. James David Barber, *The Presidential Character* (Englewood Cliffs, NJ: Prentice Hall, 1972). Alexander and Juliette George, *Woodrow Wilson and Colonel House* (New York: John Day, 1956). For research linking presidential prestige to presidential influence, see George C. Edwards III, "Presidential Influence in the House: Presidential Prestige as a Source of Presidential Power," *American Political Science Review*, LXX (March 1976), 101–13.

59. In a careful review of scholarship analyzing the impact of presidential popularity on presidential legislative success, Bond and Fleisher discuss research establishing such a correlation, note some flaws and limits to this research, and then present alternative findings. They conclude that presidential popularity has a marginal impact on legislative success. Bond and Fleisher, *The President in the Legislative Arena*, pp. 23–29 and Chap. 7. Rosenthal sees

gubernatorial popularity as a useful basis for influence with the legislature. Rosenthal, *Governors and Legislatures: Contending Powers*, p. 28.

60. Edwards, *At the Margins*, p. 113. Kenneth Collier and Terry Sullivan find that public approval of the president has little impact on his influence in Congress. "New Evidence Undercutting the Linkage of Approval with Presidential Support and Influence," *Journal of Politics*, LVII (February 1995), 197–209.

61. Reprinted in *President Carter—1978* (Washington, DC: Congressional Quarterly Press, 1979), p. 92A.

62. The importance of context for understanding presidential leadership is stressed in Bert A. Rockman, *The Leadership Question*. The significance of presidential skills as compared to context is examined in George Edwards, *At the Margins;* Jon Bond and Richard Fleisher, *The President in the Legislative Arena;* and Mark Peterson, *Legislating Together*. For an argument on the centrality of context in the Bush administration, see Bert Rockman, "The Leadership Style of George Bush," in *The Bush Presidency, First Appraisals,* ed. Colin Campbell, S.J., and Bert A. Rockman (Chatham, NJ: Chatham House, 1991), pp. 1–35. See also Charles O. Jones, "Meeting Low Expectations: Strategy and Prospects of the Bush Presidency," in *The Bush Presidency, First Appraisals,* pp. 37–67. Lockerbie and Borrelli argue that the way in which skill is measured may influence conclusions about the importance of presidential skill. Brad Lockerbie and Stephen A. Borrelli, "Getting Inside the Beltway: Perceptions of Presidential Skill and Success in Congress," *British Journal of Political Science,* XIX (January 1989), 97–106. Yet presidents can make a difference. After the Bush administration learned that congressman Ralph Regula (R., OH) was not inclined to support the president's budget proposal in 1990, the congressman discovered, despite previously made promises, that he could no longer use the president's box at the Kennedy Center to see a play.

63. Haynes Johnson, *In the Absence of Power* (New York: Viking Press, 1980), p. 216. President Lyndon Johnson described the problem well: "A congressman is like a whiskey drinker. You can put an awful lot of whiskey into a man if you just let him sip it. But if you try to force the whole bottle down his throat at one time, he will throw it up." Quoted in Joseph A. Califano, Jr., *A Presidential Nation* (New York: W. W. Norton, 1975), p. 63.

64. Ibid.

65. Quoted in Paul F. Boller, Jr., *Presidential Anecdotes* (New York: Oxford University Press, 1981), p. 344.

66. Talented liaisons are useful not only for persuading members of Congress but also for bringing information from the Hill that can be turned to strategic and tactical uses. A thorough study of legislative liaison is Abraham Holtzman, *Legislative Liaison* (Chicago: Rand McNally, 1970). For an analysis of legislative liaison in the Eisenhower through Ford administrations, see Stephen J. Wayne, *The Legislative Presidency* (New York: Harper & Row, 1978), pp. 139–77. See also Kenneth E. Collier, *The White House Office of Legislative Affairs* (Pittsburgh: University of Pittsburgh Press, 1997).

67. Davis, "Legislative Liaison in the Carter Administration," pp. 287–301. See also Wayne, *The Legislative Presidency,* pp. 211–17. This argument is supported by the discussion in Matthew Kerbel, "Before the Honeymoon Ends: Presidential Leadership and Congressional Response," *Congress and the Presidency,* XVI (Spring 1989), 11–22. The uses and limits of legislative liaison are examined by Terry Sullivan in "Explaining Why Presidents Count: Signaling and Information," *Journal of Politics,* LII (August 1990), 939–62.

68. Rosenthal, *Governors and Legislatures,* p. 113.

69. Ransone, *The Office of Governor in the United States,* p. 184. Ransone, *The American Governorship,* pp. 142–60, provides a discussion of how formal and informal techniques can be used by governors to influence the making of legislation.

70. Thad A. Beyle, "Governors' Views on Being Governor," *State Government,* LII (Summer 1979), 105.

71. Edwin S. Corwin, *The President, Office and Powers, 1787–1957* (New York: New York University Press, 1957). See also Arthur M. Schlesinger, Jr., *The Imperial Presidency* (Boston: Houghton Mifflin, 1973).

72. A very helpful discussion of problems in determining what presidential success is and how

to measure it is found in Jon Bond and Richard Fleisher, *The President in the Legislative Arena,* Chap. 3. Some problems in using box scores are shown in George Edwards, *At the Margins,* pp. 17–33. Zeidenstein discusses problems of measurement when he looks at the data on presidential popularity as they relate to presidential support in Congress. Harvey G. Zeidenstein, "Presidents' Popularity and Their Wins and Losses on Major Issues in Congress," *Presidential Studies Quarterly,* XV (Spring 1985), 287–300. Providing suitable measures of presidential effectiveness is discussed in Russell D. Renka, "Comparing Presidents Kennedy and Johnson as Legislative Leaders," *Presidential Studies Quarterly,* XV (Fall 1985), 806–20. An excellent discussion of alternative measures of presidential influence on Congress is in George C. Edwards III, "Measuring Presidential Success in Congress: Alternative Approaches," *Journal of Politics,* XLVII (May 1985), 667–85. See also Jon R. Bond, Richard Fleisher, and Glen S. Krutz, "An Overview of the Empirical Findings on Presidential-Congressional Relations," in *Rivals for Power,* ed. James A. Thurber (Washington, DC: Congressional Quarterly Press, 1996), pp. 103–39. A study of similarities and differences in presidential success in dealing with the House and Senate is Brad Lockerbie, Stephen Borrelli, and Scott Hedger, "An Integrative Approach to Modeling Presidential Success in Congress," *Political Research Quarterly,* LI (March 1998), 155–72.

73. Rosenthal, *Governors and Legislatures,* p. 113, provides a series of examples.

74. An insightful discussion of the limits of the box scores compiled by Congressional Quarterly, Inc., is Jeffrey E. Cohen, "The Impact of the Modern Presidency on Presidential Success in the U.S. Congress," *Legislative Studies Quarterly,* VII (November 1982), 516–19. See also Congressional Quarterly, Inc., *Congressional Quarterly Almanac 1997* (Washington, DC: Congressional Quarterly, Inc., 1998), pp. C5–C6. C. Anita Pritchard warns that the CQ support scores merely show executive-legislative agreement and are not necessarily measures of presidential effectiveness. "An Evaluation of CQ's Presidential Support Scores," *American Journal of Political Science,* XXX (May 1986), 480–95. Cary R. Covington reminds us that in some situations presidential influence on Congress can be increased by not taking a public stand on issues but rather by working behind the scenes. "'Staying Private': Gaining Congressional Support for Unpublicized Presidential Preferences on Roll-Call Votes," *Journal of Politics,* XLVIII (August 1987), 737–55. The impact of a president choosing to support or oppose bills is discussed in Cary R. Covington, J. Mark Wrighton, and Rhonda Kinney, "A 'Presidency-Augmented' Model of Presidential Success on House Roll Call Votes," *American Journal of Political Science,* XXXIX (November 1995), 1001–1024.

75. "The Two Presidencies," *Trans-Action,* IV (December 1966), 7–14. This article was reprinted in Aaron Wildavsky, ed., *Perspectives on the Presidency* (Boston: Little, Brown, 1975), pp. 448–61.

76. Among the participants in the argument have been George C. Edwards III, "The Two Presidencies: A Reevaluation," *American Politics Quarterly,* XIV (July 1986), 247–63; Donald Peppers, "The Two Presidencies: Eight Years Later," in *Perspectives on the Presidency,* pp. 462–71; Lance LeLoup and Steven Shull, "Congress versus the Executive: The 'Two Presidencies' Reconsidered," *Social Science Quarterly,* LIX (March 1979), 704–19; Lee Sigelman, "A Reassessment of the Two Presidencies Thesis," *Journal of Politics,* XLI (November 1979), 1195–205; and Harvey G. Zeidenstein, "The Two Presidencies Thesis Is Alive and Well and Has Been Living in the U.S. Senate Since 1973," *Presidential Studies Quarterly,* XI (Fall 1981), 511–25. Some useful analyses on this subject are reprinted in Steven A. Shull, ed., *The Two Presidencies* (Chicago: Nelson-Hall, 1991). James Meernik argues that since the Vietnam War, presidents have had to focus on building specific issue-based coalitions rather than assuming congressional support on foreign policy issues. "Presidential Support in Congress," *Journal of Politics,* LV (August 1993), 562–87. See James M. Lindsay and Wayne R. Steger, "The 'Two Presidencies' in Future Research: Moving Beyond Roll-Call Analysis," *Congress and the Presidency,* XX (Autumn 1993), 103–17.

77. Bond and Fleisher, *The President in the Legislative Arena,* Chap. 6. Randall Ripley asserts that the forces determining congressional behavior in foreign policy are very similar to those in domestic policy. "Congress and Foreign Policy: A Neglected Stage," in *Great Theatre,* ed. Herbert F. Weisberg and Samuel C. Patterson (Cambridge: Cambridge University Press, 1998), pp. 248–68.

78. M. Nelson McGeary, "The Governor's Veto in Pennsylvania," *American Political Science Review,* XLI (October 1947), 944.

79. Joseph F. Zimmerman, *Comparative State Politics Newsletter,* 1 (January 1980), 12.

80. Joel M. Fisher, Charles M. Price, and Charles G. Bell, *The Legislative Process in California* (Washington, DC: American Political Science Association, 1973), p. 109. Larry N. Gerston and Terry Christensen, *California Politics and Government* (Belmont, CA: Wadsworth, 1995).

81. Robert Spitzer, *The Presidential Veto,* pp. 72–73.

82. Richard Neustadt, "Congress and the Fair Deal: A Legislative Balance Sheet," *Public Policy, 1954* (Cambridge, MA: Harvard University Graduate School of Public Administration, 1954), pp. 380–81.

83. This problem of evaluation is discussed in Bert A. Rockman, "An Imprint but Not a Revolution," in *The Reagan Revolution,* ed. B. B. Kymlicka and J. V. Matthews (Chicago: Dorsey Press, 1988). See also Charles O. Jones, ed., *The Reagan Legacy* (Chatham, NJ: Chatham House, 1988).

84. For an elaboration of this theme, see Mark Peterson, *Legislating Together.* An analysis placing the president in the context of U.S. politics and demonstrating that presidents need Congress to govern is Charles O. Jones, *The Presidency in a Separated System* (Washington, DC: Brookings Institution, 1994).

85. In a study of the attitudes of legislators in eleven states, a majority of legislators in eight of these states found the balance between governor and legislature to be "proper." E. Lee Bernick and Charles W. Wiggins, "Executive-Legislative Power Relationships," *American Politics Quarterly,* IX (October 1981), 470–475.

86. Edwards, *At the Margins,* especially pp. 213–24. Mark Peterson concludes after looking at about three decades of executive-legislative relations in the national government that compromise and consensus prevail 43 percent of the time. *Legislating Together,* p. 96.

# 12

# Legislative Oversight of the Bureaucracy

Policies made by government may be imperfect for several reasons: the depth and complexity of problems exceed our knowledge about how to deal with them; conflicts arise between public desires and policy necessities; and disputes are common within our highly diversified society over what should be done. For example, as the 1990s ended, government faced hurdles in regulating the Internet because policy could not keep up with rapid technological change. The challenges posed by problems in foreign relations continue to multiply the difficulty of finding the type of answers that so many people prefer: those that are quick, painless, and effective.

Presidential initiative sometimes helps government function more effectively. But who keeps track of the president and a powerful bureaucracy? Many expect Congress to do so, but that expectation can seldom be met in a systematic manner. The reasons lie in the immensity of the task and the way that Congress normally operates. The need for legislative oversight perpetually outstrips the ability of legislatures, both national and state, to deliver. Legislative performance in oversight often lags behind public expectations.

## POLITICS, POLICY, AND ADMINISTRATION

Complex industrial societies require trained specialists to deal with problems. In government, these people are often found in the bureaucracy, but the importance of bureaucracy does not eliminate politics. Especially at the higher levels of the executive branch, bureaucrats do not replace politicians; they join them. The importance of the bureaucracy means even more participants in policymaking. Administration has become an important part of the political process. The expansion of bureaucratic activity means that more and more people are affected by what bureaucrats do. People who find their lives shaped by bureaucratic behavior become more concerned with it. Those who make important policy decisions do not remain immune to the pressures of politics. Organized interests gravitate to those who exercise real political power. Political attention comes to those who gain policy importance.

If the bureaucrats make important policy, and they do, concern arises about who the bureaucrats are and how they are organized. Policy results relate to those who make decisions and who set the rules of the game. Frustration with administrative inaction or anger at an administrative policy sometimes spills over onto the legislature. As bureaucrats act with policy consequences, the gap between politics and administration blurs.[1]

That bureaucrats allocate values in society explains attempts to influence them through the political process. Key decisions in the bureaucracy involve both political and technical considerations. Technical experts can decide how to design a guided missile with the longest range. Whether the missile should be built involves choices based on both technical considerations and value judgments. Technical specifications are not automatically translated into policy. Legislators soon discover that technical experts may differ among themselves, that top-level bureaucrats make policy judgments. These insights lead some legislators to feel fully capable of effective involvement in decision making. The position of the top-level bureaucrats vis-à-vis their departmental technical experts is similar to the relationship of the legislator to these experts. In each instance, a nonexpert is attempting to weigh the merits of technical proposals, the details of which he or she may not completely comprehend. Understandably, legislators sometimes try to second-guess those who run administrative departments.

If policy and politics provide the motivation for legislative oversight, law provides the opportunity. Constitutions grant legislatures the power to set public policy, create executive departments, provide revenue for their operation, and establish personnel practices. These powers provide legal levers for influence.

When they see a connection between their own political lives and bureaucratic activity, legislators have a compelling reason to oversee the bureaucracy. Reelection or advancement to higher office may depend as much on the announcing of contracts, the building of veterans hospitals, or the successful intervention on behalf of constituents as on their overall voting records. Legislators act accordingly. Even members who favor cutting defense budgets raise a furor at proposals to eliminate military bases in their state or district. Members do try to influence bureaucrats in an effort to promote policy objectives but also so that they can claim credit for promoting goals valued in their own constituency. The political lives of the legislator and the bureaucrat can come together. Yet the legislature finds it difficult to compete with the bureaucracy. Multiple priorities, limited time, lack of expertise, and low political payoffs can stand in the way. Former Representative Dan Glickman (D., KS) related the effort to conduct oversight to the desires of committee chairs: "And few want to because oversight is complex and it isn't sexy."[2]

Legislative oversight of bureaucracy takes many forms. Legislators may investigate to see how a particular program is working; some estimate that Congress has conducted more than 600 such investigations. They may be concerned with the administration of programs in a general area such as energy policy. They may be worried about the qualifications and conduct of the people running a program. They may probe how the structure of a department or agency affects executive behavior. Although the legislature cannot implement the programs that it passes, it finds ways to affect that implementation. Although Congress as a body seems unable to understand the details of missile policy, a few of its members can; and all of them see the impact of awarding contracts to their home districts. Although many legislators do not understand the details of complex scientific research, they can keep bureaucrats on the defensive by publicizing expenditures for research on such superficially trivial subjects as senility in salmon. Although the legislature seems unlikely to solve problems of unemployment, it can pressure the bureaucracy to move in desired directions.

The inadequacies of legislators are often those of top executives as well. Hence both groups stress the high relevance to decision making of intelligence, diligence, and that elusive quality labeled political skill. On these revised grounds, legislators feel, rightly or wrongly, that they possess the necessary credentials for oversight of the bureaucracy.

## WHAT DO LEGISLATORS OVERSEE, AND HOW?

With rare exceptions, legislative oversight of administration, at least in Congress, follows well-established patterns. Myriad potential controls over policy, personnel, structure, and expenditures exist. The same factors that shape executive involvement in the legislative process—that is, societal factors, legal structures and procedures, partisan relationships, and personal aspects—influence the ability and desire of legislators to oversee. These elements emerge in concrete questions. Is the country at war? Does the same political party control both Congress and the presidency? Are the president and the Speaker of the House at personal and political loggerheads? What do the public opinion polls show?

According to law, legislatures should oversee all executive structures, processes, and behavior. In reality, bureaucratic activity is too extensive and complex for systematic legislative control. Choices have to be made concerning which techniques of control will be applied to which executive agencies, how often, with how much perseverance, and by whom.

Congress is not organized to provide a coherent pattern of choice.

Decisions come from committees, their chairpersons, party leaders, and individual members of Congress.[3] Member incentives and skills as well as committee structures and resources are relevant to the process of choice. Oversight inevitably will be partial and selective. How and in what areas is it carried out?

### Oversight: Formal and Informal

The following sections focus mainly on formal techniques of oversight, even though such a discussion does not tell the whole story. This attention is partly because these techniques can be seen and analyzed, but much oversight occurs informally and hence is more difficult to discover and document.

With these cautions in mind, we can now look at oversight in four areas: oversight over policy implementation; oversight over administrative structures; oversight over the persons who implement policy; and oversight over the expenditure of public funds. The techniques used to oversee in these areas are many and varied. They include hearings, investigations, the legislative veto, required reports, casework, confirming the appointment of selected bureaucrats, regulating their conduct, removal of bureaucrats, controlling the expenditure of money, and studies by units such as the General Accounting Office (GAO), the Congressional Research Service, and the Congressional Budget Office.

### Oversight over Policy Implementation

Legislation is frequently drafted in generalized language using such terms as "serving the public interest" and "fair standards." Such imprecise wording suggests that when legislative bodies confront complex and difficult policy conflicts, they shift the burden of more precise definition to bureaucrats who confront concrete problems. Legislators thus create opportunities for the exercise of administrative discretion. In the state of New York, Eric Lane writes,

> Poorly crafted laws translate into vast discretion for agency bureaucrats, who must try to figure out the Legislature's intent without benefit of committee reports, transcripts of floor debates, or other common legislative records.[4]

Since such bureaucratic behavior involves heavy policy overtones, legislative interest in its substance should not be too surprising.

The concern of Congress with policy oversight is intermittent. In 1991, media reports revealed failures in the Reagan and Bush administrations to implement congressional policy in areas such as pollution, tobacco health warnings, patient care in nursing homes, aid to the homeless, and the cleaning up of storage sites for waste materials. Clearly, Congress was not bringing intense, sustained pressure on the executive to act.[5]

The first demand in law for systematic oversight came in the Legislative Reorganization Act of 1946, stipulating that each committee should exercise "continuous watchfulness" over the activities of those administrative units acting within the subject matter jurisdiction of that committee. The Legislative Reorganization Act of 1970 reiterated this concern:

> Each standing committee shall review and study, on a continuing basis, the application, administration, and execution of those laws, or parts of laws, the subject matter of which is within the jurisdiction of that committee.

Congress continues intermittently to add to its oversight authority, for example, in the reforms passed in the House of Representatives in 1974 and in the Budget and Impoundment Control Act of 1974, in the Government Performance and Results Act of 1993, and in the Contract with America Advancement Act of 1996 providing for the possibility of congressional review of agency regulations.

*Legislative veto.* Congress has used several techniques for oversight of policy. One of the most prominent of these was the legislative veto. This oversight technique was employed by Congress for many years. Congress might require that the executive branch notify one or more of its committees before acting in a specified area. On occasion, advance approval for bureaucratic action was even demanded. Thus, Congress projected itself or its committees into the administrative decision-making process. Instead of exercising oversight only by checking on executive implementation of law, Congress assumed a direct role in the process of policy implementation. The necessity for speed, the burdens of complexity, and the barriers of secrecy contributed to Congress's use of the legislative veto.[6] All recent presidents have objected to the legislative veto. Some even vetoed several bills containing provisions for "veto by committee."

The legislative veto was more than a potential threat. Table 12.1 shows that, on presidential plans to reorganize the executive branch, Congress played more than a passive role. The use of the legislative veto increased for some forty years (see Figure 12.1). By the early 1980s, some members of Congress proposed that all administrative regulations be subject to it. Such proposals were receiving serious consideration when, in 1983, the U.S. Supreme Court ruled the legislative veto to be unconstitutional.[7]

This decision upset a common practice. Justice Byron White, in his dissenting decision, assumed that the majority had stricken down some two hundred acts of Congress, more than the Supreme Court had declared unconstitutional in its entire history. Such prominent legislation might be disallowed, it was argued, as the War Powers Resolution of 1973 permitting Congress to order the president to withdraw troops that he had sent overseas; the National Emergencies Act of 1976, which allowed Congress to terminate a presidential declaration of national emergency; and the International Security

TABLE 12.1    Presidential reorganization plans in Congress:
Proposals and rejections, 1949–84

| Years | President | Plans Proposed | Plans Rejected | Percentage Rejected |
|---|---|---|---|---|
| 1949–52 | Truman | 41 | 11 | 27 |
| 1953–60 | Eisenhower | 17 | 3 | 18 |
| 1961–63 | Kennedy | 10 | 4 | 40 |
| 1964–68 | Johnson | 17 | 1 | 1 |
| 1969–April 1973 | Nixon | 8 | 0 | 0 |
| 1977–81 | Carter | 14 | 0 | 0 |
| April–December 1984 | Reagan | 0 | 0 | 0 |

NOTE: Reorganization authority expired in April 1981 and was renewed in April 1984. It expired again in December 1984 and has not been renewed.

SOURCE: Data from *Congressional Quarterly Weekly Report*, October 16, 1976, p. 3012, supplemented by relevant issues of the *Congressional Record* and the 1983 *Congressional Quarterly Almanac*.

Assistance and Arms Control Act of 1976, which permitted Congress to disapprove presidential commitments to sell major defense equipment to other countries.

Congress incorporated the legislative veto in some two hundred statutes. Its utility was not in the frequency of its application; for example, the device has never been applied successfully in the foreign affairs area. But the threat of its use did push Presidents Carter and Reagan to be more accommodating. Presidents have, on controversial issues of foreign policy such as major arms sales, had to assess what would make their contemplated actions more palatable to Congress and by so doing to remove the threat of a possible legislative veto. Despite the Supreme Court's decision in 1983, controversy still continues over the utility and the legality of the legislative veto.[8]

With the legislative veto legally dead, how did Congress replace it? Several options have been tried: detailed statutes limiting executive discretion; more systematic efforts at legislative oversight of bureaucratic activity; a refusal to allow the executive broad grants of power. In reality Congress has always had these options, but for reasons compelling to it, had not regularly used them. Congress preferred the legislative veto partly because it was easy to insert in legislation and gave the appearance of action. It was thus symbolically useful. The threat of its use inspired executive sensitivity to congressional preferences. Now members of Congress have to rely more on joint resolutions, on prescribing waiting periods, and on informal understandings with executive agencies.[9]

In the states, use of the legislative veto has declined partly because some state courts have declared the device to be unconstitutional.[10] As the prominence of the legislative veto faded in the states, legislative review of

**FIGURE 12.1    Growth in the use of the legislative veto, 1932–75**

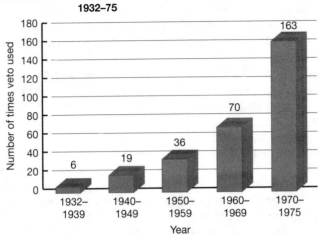

SOURCE: Data from Clark F. Norton, *Congressional Review, Deferral and Disapproval of Executive Actions: A Summary and an Inventory of Statutory Authority* (Washington, DC: Congressional Research Service, 1976), p. 8.

administrative agency regulations gained in use. Here state agencies are required to submit proposed regulations, usually to a legislative committee, often for advisory purposes, before formal implementation. More than 75 percent of the states make use of some version of this procedure.[11]

*Required reports.*   Congress seeks to alert itself to administrative actions and to sensitize bureaucrats to congressional interest in their behavior by requiring departments and agencies to file written reports on specified activities from time to time. Requiring a report is hardly the same as direct legislative intrusion in the decision-making process. Yet, indirectly, this requirement can stimulate legislative oversight.[12] The traditional annual reports from the executive departments are now supplemented by literally hundreds of reports each year.[13] Many of these documents remain undigested and perhaps even unread by members of Congress, but they do provide information for members and thus promote an opportunity for legislative oversight. Members of Congress seem to agree since they continue to provide for these reports—for example, in the Government Performance and Results Act of 1993 where agencies were required to set goals, measure performance, and report their findings. The regular written reports that form the grist of the governmental process are supplemented by scores of executive officials trooping before congressional committees to testify.

*Casework.*   Legislative concern with how administrative policy is applied derives from many sources, including newspaper accounts of alleged wrongdoing, congressional staff reports, and, on occasion, complaints of individuals. The legislature may hear that a law is too harsh, that it is being improperly interpreted, or simply that constituents need relief from the demands of the law. Such complaints arise from organized interests (described in Chapter 10), but also from individuals. In February 1963, an airman wrote to Senator Jacob Javits (R., NY) protesting against an Air Force questionnaire that asked, "Are you a member of an interracial marriage?" The Air Force dropped the question from the form after several protests from Senator Javits.[14]

Legislators, both national and state, receive countless requests from constituents for help. Their constituents may wish benefits to be provided more quickly. Businesspeople may ask for support when they seek contracts from the government. They may be outraged at government actions toward them that they perceive to be abuses of bureaucratic power. Legislators attempt to facilitate these requests whenever possible.

These efforts raise ethical questions, as illustrated by the "Keating Five" inquiry. In 1991, the Senate Ethics Committee heard evidence regarding five senators who had intervened with federal regulators in behalf of Charles H. Keating, Jr., and his failed Lincoln Savings and Loan of Irvine, California. The committee asked, "Was this routine constituent service; were the meetings with and repeated phone calls to regulators merely 'status inquiries' as the senators contend?" Special counsel for the committee, Robert S. Bennett, argued no: "If I'm sitting on a park bench, and an 800-pound gorilla comes along and says, 'Excuse me, I'm just making a status inquiry if there are any seats available,' you say, 'You're damn right, there's a seat available.' And there's a lot of 800-pound gorillas around this place."[15]

A stimulus may yield a response. But it is easy to overestimate the consequences of casework for oversight of the bureaucracy. The legislator's office sees this work primarily as service to constituents. Hardly any offices keep records to identify patterns of complaints. On the executive side, few agencies keep systematic files either. Both legislators and bureaucrats are concerned mainly with responding to the individual request. So, while casework may occasionally stimulate oversight efforts, that is the exception.[16]

Congressional oversight is generally exercised as part of a desire to note and record deficiencies in current policy and to recommend appropriate corrective legislation. Oversight is also used from time to time to propose that the executive branch reconsider and perhaps redraw its policies.

Partly as a result of the perceived disasters arising from United States involvement in Vietnam in the 1960s and early 1970s, congressional committees probed government policies in Southeast Asia and extended their surveillance to defense policy areas seldom investigated with such seriousness. For example, in 1972, Congress stipulated that the texts of all executive agreements made by the president with foreign countries be submitted to Congress within sixty days of signing. Congress was generally worried about the increasing use of executive agreements instead of treaties. Some members of Congress were concerned specifically with agreements to establish military bases in Spain and Portugal. Senators would have preferred that such arrangements be made through treaties requiring approval by the Senate.

The desire for oversight is increased, in foreign policy as elsewhere, as the administration makes decisions unpopular with segments of Congress. Yet even then members of Congress are more likely to speak out against an administration policy than is Congress to act concretely to challenge the chief executive.

## Oversight and the Structure of the Executive Branch

How government is organized may well affect what policies emerge. Numerous examples throughout this book have shown that committee structures, patterns of party organization, and the bicameral legislature can affect policy. Structure, although it usually does not determine policy, surely should be added to the list of things that make a difference. Presidents realize if they wish to achieve new policy objectives or to diminish the importance of programs, organizational change may assist them to do so. To achieve substantial organizational change, the president must ask Congress for help.

Congress has the constitutional authority to determine the basic features of the executive branch. When President Reagan sought to abolish the Department of Education, he needed Congress to do the job. When he wanted a new Department of Trade, he had to ask Congress to provide it. Congress thus plays a significant role in forming and amending the structure of the executive branch. All of this activity takes place in a context of policy preferences and political gains and losses. Congress realizes that structures can hinder or enhance policy proposals, so requests for structural change are examined carefully.

*Presidential reorganization plans.* The growth in size and complexity of the bureaucracy has made it impossible for Congress to monitor all structural change in the executive branch. Therefore, beginning in 1949, Congress authorized the president to make some structural changes on his own, subject to the exercise of the legislative veto.[17] How presidents used this authority, and the congressional response, were shown in Table 12.1. Since all presidents have opposed the legislative veto, it may seem strange that reorganization authority subject to the legislative veto has been sought by these same chief executives.[18] The answer to this riddle is quite simple: Presidents generally applaud those steps that help them achieve their purposes and look askance at those that diminish their ability to do so. In the states, limited executive reorganization power subject to a legislative veto exists in about half of the units.[19]

*Sunset laws.* The most spectacular technique for legislative oversight is the so-called "sunset law." Under this procedure, the legislature authorizes a program for a specified number of years. At the end of that time, the program comes up for review. The legislature must formally extend the life of the program or the program expires. About 60 percent of the states have adopted some form of sunset legislation. The experience with these laws in the states has been mixed. At the national level, Congress has discussed such proposals but has shown no inclination to adopt them into law.

## Oversight of Administrative Personnel

Legislative oversight is also exercised through controls over personnel. From a constitutional standpoint, legislative interest in the personnel of government and their conduct stems from the requirement that certain executive appointees be confirmed by the Senate, that the House shall impeach, and that the Senate shall try civil officers of the United States. More immediately, legislative interest derives from the realization that personnel and policy may be politically inseparable. Who applies a policy may be just as significant as what the policy provides, especially when policy is set down in general terms. Legislative anxiety over the personnel of the executive branch centers on three aspects of personnel policy: the appointment, conduct, and removal of officeholders.

*Personnel selection.* National and state governmental bureaucrats are selected in accordance with statutory provisions that sometimes detail large parts of the selection process. A substantial proportion of national bureaucrats is chosen through the examination and rating practices charted in the rules of merit systems. Each year the U.S. Senate is called upon to give its advice and consent to thousands of executive nominations and candidates for promotion. Almost all such nominees are approved in routine fashion.[20] That so few are considered at length and that even fewer are rejected masks as much as it reveals. Quantitatively, most of these cases involve military and foreign service appointments and promotions. Such proceedings normally personify the perfunctory. Data on civilian nominations are provided in Figure 12.2.

More attention is usually given to the appointment of ambassadors and members of the president's cabinet, but here also confirmation is generally the rule. Throughout U.S. history, only nine presidential nominees for cabinet positions have been rejected outright by the Senate—only three of these in the twentieth century.[21]

The quality of the Senate confirmation process has been the target of considerable criticism. A survey of the confirmation process for fifty top-level nominees in the Carter administration provides useful insights into the process more generally. Most Senate committee hearings on nominees were quite brief, one only 176 words. For many of the nominees, the questioning

**FIGURE 12.2  Presidential civilian nominations and confirmations, 1984–98**

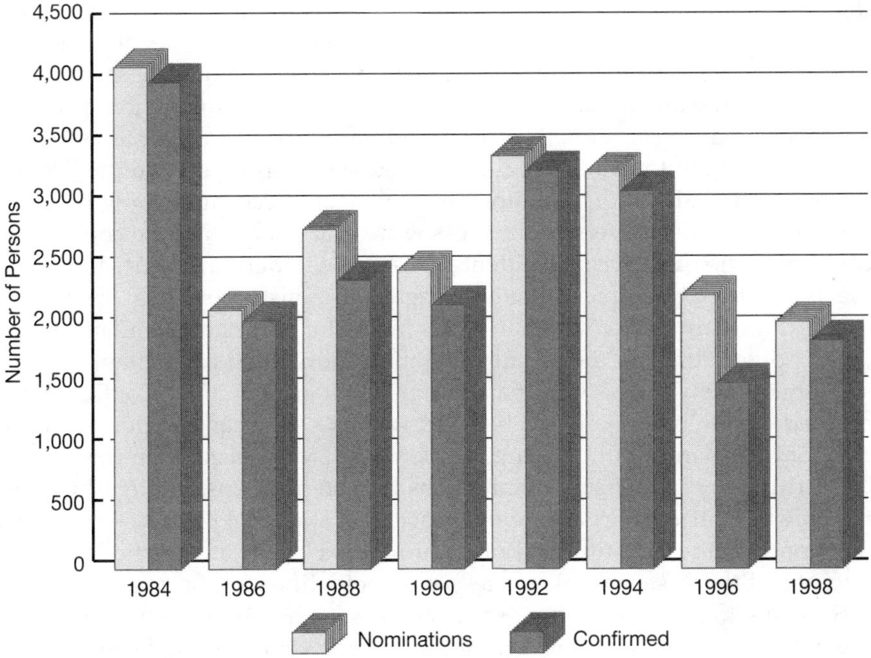

SOURCE: *Congressional Record*, Daily Digest, Resume of Congressional Activity for the relevant years.

by the Senate committees was pro forma. Printed committee hearings or reports were available for the entire Senate before the final confirmation vote in only six of the fifty cases.[22]

The confirmation proceedings for Bert Lance, President Carter's nominee to be director of the Office of Management and Budget, provides a case in point. Lance, a close personal friend of President Carter, was easily confirmed by the Senate after only nominal scrutiny. Not long after he assumed office, evidence surfaced of questionable practices during Lance's previous career in banking. Most observers agreed that a careful Senate inspection of Lance's earlier behavior should have yielded at least some of the evidence that stimulated Lance to resign his position when it was discovered later. Bruce Adams and Kathryn Kavanagh-Baran refer to the superficial confirmation hearings as "not merely unfortunate aberrations."[23]

What can make the seemingly simple task of the confirmation process —to establish the fitness of the nominee for office—exceedingly complex is trying to decipher the record of individuals with extensive involvement in business or the professions. In the words of one congressional observer: "It ain't as easy as looking for the old boy's arrest record."[24] Further complicating the confirmation process is the use of *holds,* more than forty in 1997, whereby individual senators can block or delay nominations by implicitly threatening a filibuster.

Even if the Senate confirms most top-level nominees, Senate reaction may provide a warning to the administration that it should be more concerned with the quality or the policy orientation of subsequent nominees. In the Reagan administration, the nomination of Ernest W. Lefever as assistant secretary of state for human rights aroused such controversy in the Senate that the Foreign Relations Committee voted against recommending his confirmation. Such an adverse vote was so rare that students of the committee could recall no other recent incidents. One of the underlying issues here was the perception by some that the Reagan administration was "watering down" President Carter's human rights policy for international affairs.

If proceedings in the Senate on ambassadorial and cabinet appointees sometimes seem tinged with partisan or ideological conflict, confirmation proceedings involving a job to be filled within a state can provide an occasion for truly fierce political struggles. Senators try to bolster their own political fortunes by influencing nominations to such positions as judgeships for the federal district courts. Here the practice of *senatorial courtesy*—nowhere mentioned in the Constitution but enshrined in U.S. Senate practice—comes into play. Briefly, senatorial courtesy may be defined as the practice of the U.S. Senate to accept the veto of the senators of the same political party as the president for an appointment in the senator's home state. When an appointment is made to such a position and sent to the Senate to be confirmed, if a senator of the president's party rises and objects to the nomination, the Senate, as a whole, will usually vote it down, regardless of the experience and competence of the nominee. Realizing this, an astute president will clear relevant appointments with appropriate senators. The record of few Senate rejections is primarily evidence not of senatorial submission to executive choice but rather of an extensive system of prior clearance.

Senate interrogation of appointees need not be confined to matters of high policy. In 1975, when Roderick M. Hills was appointed to the Securities and Exchange Commission, Senator William Proxmire (D., WI), an inveterate jogger, asked the appointee whether he would need a government-provided limousine to drive to work. Hills replied: "I shall not, nor shall I jog."[25]

Legislative influence over appointments in the states is so varied as almost to defy description. Statutory restrictions, confirmation requirements, and investigations are the relevant techniques. More than half the states have extensive systems of merit appointments, which serve to limit direct legislative influence on appointments. A few states use merit systems only because they take part in federal grant-in-aid programs in which this is required. The particular pattern through which patronage is dispensed in each state will determine the extent to which legislators can influence the job-selection process.

Legislative interest in the appointment process stems from concern with policy, personalities, legislative prerogatives, and building one's electoral fortunes. Under these circumstances it becomes easier to understand why legislators make the choices that they do. Whether such involvement enhances the quality of personnel selected or contributes to political responsibility remains unsettled.

*Control of administrative conduct.* Once administrative officials are appointed, legislative attention turns to their conduct in office. Laws are passed regarding advancement and promotions, creating codes of ethics, formulating rules about disclosure of information, and delegating power to executive agencies to prescribe rules of administrative conduct. Beyond such everyday statutes, legislators have attempted, at times, to regulate subversive activities, to limit partisan political activity of bureaucrats, and to guard against conflicts of interest. If such statutes are the staples of legislative oversight of bureaucratic conduct, investigations can provide the spice of the legislative diet. Legislative forays in quest of peculation and the peculators, inefficiency and the inefficient, subversion and the subversives are characteristic aspects of legislative oversight.

Congress has created in the last several decades two highly visible offices aimed indirectly at improving the performance of the executive departments and agencies: inspectors general (IGs) and independent counsels (ICs).

The Inspector General Act of 1978, enacted following financial and management scandals in the late 1970s, provided authority for the appointment of these officers whose task was to reduce "waste, fraud, and abuse." Now existing in all cabinet departments and in more than forty agencies, these inspectors are to regularly report their findings to Congress and to agency heads. The impact of their work has varied from agency to agency, but it is fair to state that the problems they were designed to deal with are still with us. Paul C. Light suggests:

> The IG's, however, cannot fix all the shortcomings in government without help. They cannot force the president to appoint good people, the Senate to take the confirmation process seriously, and Congress to exercise more systematic oversight.[26]

Inspectors general do their work routinely and quietly. Their efforts rarely reach the media headlines. Independent counsels are creatures of crisis. Created in 1978 following the Watergate scandal in the Nixon administration, an IC is appointed to investigate allegations of misconduct by a particular high-level administrator. In some cases, the ICs have provided material for many media headlines. Of the twenty ICs appointed, perhaps the most visible have been Lawrence Walsh, who investigated the Iran-contra problem in the Reagan administration, and Kenneth Starr, whose investigations of President Clinton led to a referral to the House of Representatives recommending impeachment of the president.

The assumption that no administration could investigate thoroughly and fairly the conduct of its own senior officials struck many as entirely reasonable. Experience with independent counsels has shaken that belief so substantially that Congress in 1999 did not renew their authorization. New structures can assist in ameliorating problems of executive misconduct; they are unlikely by themselves to eliminate or substantially reduce it.

A brief discussion of two subjects—limiting the political activity of bureaucrats and conflict of interest—sheds light on legislative efforts to regulate bureaucratic conduct. How to promote merit in appointments to bureaucratic positions and how to protect bureaucrats from being coerced by politically oriented superiors to contribute money and to work in political campaigns has long concerned members of Congress. The Civil Service Act of 1883 represented an early congressional attempt to promote the competence and efficiency of the federal bureaucracy by requiring appointments based on merit rather than primarily on patronage. The Hatch Act in 1939 limited political activity by bureaucrats and thus insulated them from political pressure.

The debate over whether bureaucrats can be politically active and yet function efficiently and effectively in their jobs continued in the 1990s. A 1993 amendment to the Hatch Act only slightly altered the status quo. At issue are the rights of bureaucrats to participate in politics as do other citizens, their freedom from coercion at work from their politically selected superiors, and issues of partisan advantage.

As is often the case in legislative oversight, sorting out motivations can be difficult. For example, in the debate in Congress in 1990 and 1991 over whether to widen opportunities for political participation by bureaucrats, Democrats, many of whom supported such legislation, tended to argue for the political rights of bureaucrats, whereas Republicans, who tended to oppose lowering the barriers to participation, focused on how the Democrats would gain in campaign contributions of money and activity. Whether a congressperson's position is taken on the basis of general principles or on specific concerns for partisan advantage is seldom fully clear. Both principles and expediency are involved in determining what oversight will be done.

Conflict-of-interest statutes and regulations are designed to separate the private economic gain of the bureaucrat from his or her administrative duties.[27] Concern over the possible confusion of public and private interests is as old as politics itself. For Plato, the solution was to remove the possibility of such conflict by withdrawing wives, children, and property from his philosopher-kings. In U.S. society, less extreme measures have been adopted. At the national level, several statutes on this subject cover such areas of conduct as prohibiting officials to assist outsiders in their dealings with the government, requiring officials not to act in government matters in which they have a personal economic interest, and prohibiting outside pay for governmental work.

Earlier in American history, when government reached fewer sectors of society and spent less money, a public-private distinction might have been realistic. By the year 2000, when the impact of government is so pervasive, the utility of this distinction has diminished. The profundity of this problem, as well as congressional difficulties in dealing with it, is exemplified clearly in the circumstances surrounding the appointment and confirmation of Charles E. Wilson as secretary of defense by President Eisenhower.

In 1953, when Eisenhower assumed the presidency, his intention was to seek the best business talent of the country to advise him. Viewing the Department of Defense as a citadel of complexity, President Eisenhower nominated as secretary Charles E. Wilson, president of General Motors, one of the country's largest corporations. A disturbing fact to many was that General Motors was a very large defense contractor. Would Wilson, then, as secretary of defense, function in the public interest or in the interest of General Motors?

Rejecting Wilson's equation of these two interests—"What was good for our country was good for General Motors, and vice versa"[28]—a majority of the Senate Armed Services Committee, in the course of confirmation hearings, argued that Wilson must divest himself of his General Motors stock before the committee could recommend his confirmation. Somehow, the committee apparently thought, Wilson's life's labor in General Motors would be set aside if he sold his stock. A profound problem was settled by a simple and superficially satisfactory example of congressional diligence. C. Wright Mills calls this performance "a purifying ritual,"[29] implying that the congressional action made people feel good but that not much had really been accomplished. Mills's judgment is one that is widely shared.[30]

The problem of conflict of interest has become pervasive. By and large, top governmental executives are recruited from the business and professional communities. As government becomes more and more involved in defense and research contracts and associated with universities and research associations, the task of attracting suitable top-level administrators not affected by conflict-of-interest problems becomes ever more difficult. President Carter, sensing the depth of these problems, made a strong effort by issuing guidelines concerning financial disclosure, divestiture of holdings, and post-government-service employment to screen his nominees to top positions. His efforts were not completely successful.[31] Every recent administration wrestles with these same issues; Congress, too, has found no effective solutions.

At the national level, problems of conflict of interest are profound and solutions remain scarce. At the state level, comprehensive consideration of the topic of conflict of interest has been largely a phenomenon of the last few decades. About 80 percent of the states have comprehensive conflict-of-interest laws; all have passed some type of legislation.

*Removal of bureaucrats.* Legislative concern with the conduct of executive officials leads in extreme cases to questions of removal. The most potent legal power of removal that Congress possesses is that of impeachment. Article I of the U.S. Constitution gives the House the sole power of impeachment and empowers the Senate to try those who have been impeached. A two-thirds vote of those senators present is required to convict. Subject to impeachment, according to Article II, are the president, vice-president, and all civil officers of the United States. Impeachment proceedings may be brought only on charges of "treason, bribery, or other high crimes and misdemeanors."

The House has voted to impeach some sixteen times in American history and only three times has the process involved the executive branch. President Andrew Johnson was acquitted. President Grant's secretary of war, William Belknap, resigned after formal charges had been brought against him; still, the Senate placed him on trial, but a two-thirds vote could not be mustered for conviction.[32] President William J. Clinton was impeached by the House but was acquitted by the Senate in 1999. The power to impeach is rarely invoked; it is simply too strong to use in the normal conduct of legislative oversight and to resolve disputes between the legislature and the executive.

Impeachment is too powerful a weapon at the state level as well. Governors in all of the states but Oregon are subject to impeachment. Here, too, the power is seldom used. Arizona governor Evan Mecham was impeached, convicted, and removed from office in 1988. His was the first such removal in over fifty years.

The power to impeach provides Congress with a legal justification to seek out wrongdoing. Partisan clashes, policy differences, and personal clashes may also stimulate such congressional activity. To be effective, Congress does not need to impeach and convict. Senate pressure on President Grant led him to ask his attorney general to resign. Congressional committees during the Eisenhower administration had similar success, when their investigations spotlighted evidence that forced the resignation of several high-ranking officials. Almost every administration, including, most recently, the Clinton administration, has its own examples.

### The Power of the Purse: Control over Expenditures

A fourth area in which legislative bodies exercise oversight is through checking on the expenditure of money. Historically, consultative assemblies bargained with kings by refusing to assent to new taxes until grievances were settled. The maturing of legislative control over expenditures provides an incentive, not always used diligently or wisely, to oversee executive activity.

At the state level, review of the budget is a primary instrument for oversight. In the words of a Kentucky legislator, "If you grab them by their budgets, their hearts and minds will follow."[33] Legislative concern with the finances of government manifests itself at two different stages: (1) when a program is formulated and money provided to the executive; (2) when attempting to ascertain whether appropriated funds are disbursed according to legislative intent. Alan Rosenthal indicates:

> As of now, performance auditing appears to be the principal technique by means of which legislatures are attempting to review state policies and programs and thereby to exercise greater control.[34]

Regarding Congress, the constitutional mandate is clearly established in Article I, Section 9: "No money shall be drawn from the Treasury, but in Consequence of Appropriations made by Law." Congress has, throughout American history, attempted to build a structure of power on this foundation. The net result often has been dissatisfaction and anxiety over control of expenditure. Policies difficult to control by law may be equally difficult to control through appropriations.

The statutory basis for monitoring expenditures through legislative oversight begins with the Legislative Reorganization Act of 1946. In brief, programs are formulated with amounts of money specified to carry them out. The authorization stage, dominated by the substantive standing committees, sets a ceiling for expenditure. The actual money is provided through appropriations, at which stage the appropriations committees and subcommittees dominate. Since 1974, the House and Senate budget committees have added several new dimensions to legislative concern with expenditures (see the fuller discussion in Chapter 11). Opportunities exist, then, at many stages for checking on administrative expenditures.

The overall quality of oversight varies from issue to issue and there is strong evidence of striking unevenness. At times, appropriations committee oversight focuses sharply on details while leaving larger problems and priorities blurred.[35] An immediate and overwhelming crisis diminishes the role of Congress even more. According to former Speaker Sam Rayburn, the House of Representatives appropriated $800 million to develop the atom bomb without even being aware of where the money was going.[36]

The record of legislative oversight is somewhat more impressive in matters of domestic policy, partly because issues seem less complex, partly because information is more accessible, and partly because these issues seem more vital to more people. The inherent difficulty of the legislative task is compounded by a fundamental role conflict for some legislators who desire rationality, efficiency, and economy in the abstract, but want expenditures and projects for their state or district.

Any deficiencies in oversight are rarely a result of a lack of help. All congressional committees have a great deal of assistance available to them when they want to use it. For example, the General Accounting Office, created by Congress to monitor executive expenditures, has a vast array of personnel and skills for Congress to rely on. Originally concerned largely with technical financial matters, the GAO has shifted its emphasis toward more general review of executive programs.

Here, again, policy helps shape process. The GAO attempts to be very responsive to congressional requests for help. The unrest in segments of Congress in the 1970s and 1980s over defense spending has led to heavier reliance on the GAO for data and analysis that members of Congress need to be more effective in oversight activity.[37] "In fiscal year 1988, fully 80 to 100 percent . . . of GAO's resources were involved in responding to specific congressional requests."[38]

Even this brief analysis suggests that as problems of policy become more complex, especially in that portion of the budget that goes for defense, the possibility of close, effective legislative oversight decreases. Members of Congress may become irritated at executive reprogramming and shifting of funds from one project to another; they may chafe at the size of emergency and contingent funds over which the executive has sole control. Focusing this frustration in terms of careful, sustained analysis is much more difficult for them.[39]

## LEGISLATIVE OVERSIGHT: GOALS AND EFFECTIVENESS

Legislative oversight, it is argued, promotes rationality, efficiency, and responsibility in the bureaucracy. Legislators do pursue these goals, but they are also concerned with promoting their own careers and causes. Legislative oversight occurs in concrete situations where personal motives and broader goals may become hopelessly intermingled.[40] Speaker of the House Newt Gingrich (1995–98) could urge an aggressive program of oversight targeting the White House, whereas in 1999 his successor, Dennis Hastert, favored a more normal concern focused on what programs work and how departments are being run.[41]

The end product of oversight is usually a mix of asset and liability. Oversight may stimulate desirable change; legislative scrutiny may also serve, at times, mainly to frustrate conscientious officials, to secure special favors, and to disrupt carefully conceived executive programs.

## The Quest for Rationality and Responsibility

Despite the discomforting aspects of legislative oversight, most observers continue, rightly, to stress the importance of this legislative function. Far from self-evident, however, is what legislative behavior can most effectively promote executive responsibility.

Two broad models of executive-legislative relations provide a focus for analysis. The first may be sketched as follows. Legislative bodies should set only broad policy and not interfere with the details of administration. Legislative bodies can represent the interests of society, but neither their structure nor practices seem conducive to effective control over details. The chief executive and the top subordinates are viewed, on the other hand, as possessing more potential for success in supervising the bureaucracy.[42] The implications of these propositions are that legislative bodies should set structure, personnel, and fiscal policies only in the broadest sense. Their objective should be to promote centralization of control through the top echelons of the executive branch. Bureaucratic breaches then become the primary responsibility of the chief executive, who can be controlled through elections, impeachment, statutes, or investigations. Other control is exercised through top subordinates, and for their actions the chief executive assumes responsibility. Proponents allege that such a pattern stimulates efficiency and rationality and pinpoints responsibility.

An alternative model might look like this. A primary task of legislative bodies is to further bureaucratic responsibility. The legislative body must be concerned with all policy, both broad and detailed. Despite the claim of chief executives to superior representative character, the heterogeneity of the nation is best reflected in Congress, that of the state in the state legislature. Accordingly, since the people are best represented by legislative assemblies, the chief executive cannot be as effective as the legislature in controlling the bureaucracy in the public interest. Indeed, legislative bodies must watch chief executives themselves to ensure that responsible government is achieved.

A third model suggests a mixed pattern. Congress, while routinely collecting information about the bureaucracy, merely keeps a watchful eye unless some substantial problem arises or until some external pressure forces action. What is suggested here is that Congress only intermittently engages in significant oversight, but that the potential for legislative involvement is always present.[43]

These models place in sharp focus some critical questions: Should Congress or the president be given the responsibility of creating executive units and altering executive structures? Should legislative grants of authority go to the chief executive to be distributed among many subordinates, or should such grants go directly to subordinate executive departments, agencies, or even bureaus? Should statutes embodying personnel policy be written in minute detail, or should the top executives be allowed to fill in details? Should there be precise, rigidly allocated appropriations for the executive branch, or should the executive be given discretion in spending? Should legislators investigate the smallest details of administrative behavior, or should investigations generally be directed at broader questions of fundamental policy?

Each of these approaches can be supported in theory. Circumstances determine which approach is used. A continuing bargaining and accommodation process is at work. In legislative-executive struggles, Congress as a whole seldom engages the executive branch as a whole. The more common pattern is for congressional committees and executive bureaus to form alliances against other such combinations or against their respective branches of government as a whole.

The forms that executive-legislative conflict can take are illustrated through a discussion of some perennial problems that arise in two areas of legislative oversight: oversight of intelligence agencies and executive privilege.

*Oversight of intelligence agencies.* The problems of performing effective legislative oversight are heightened in regard to intelligence agencies such as the Central Intelligence Agency. As is true with other units of the executive branch, Congress has the responsibility to regularly oversee the CIA. The normal obstacles to effective oversight are highlighted in this case by the need for discretion and secrecy in looking into matters of intelligence collection and especially into examples of covert action.

CIA officials typically view Congress as a leaky sieve and hence are less than enthusiastic about fully sharing sensitive information. Many members of Congress, in turn, are dazzled by the intelligence mystique. The net result is that Congress is often rather casual in performing its oversight function in this area until some disaster strikes. Even then, as is illustrated in the Iran-contra episode, the attention of Congress is fitful and few enduring solutions emerge.

Explanations for these phenomena are clear. The particular context for oversight of intelligence activities and especially of covert action places strong barriers in front of desires to oversee.[44] As the twentieth century ends, congressional committees continue their nearly thirty-year quest for answers to these enduring problems.

*Executive privilege.* Problems over executive secrecy arise when Congress asks the executive branch for data that it deems useful in reaching policy decisions. Although the executive branch sends reams of routine data to members of Congress and to congressional committees, there are times when, for reasons of administrative efficiency, national security, or even political advantage, it declines to comply with congressional requests. The conflicts that arise are usually settled by bargaining and accommodation. In the

George Washington administration, executive papers were turned over to Congress to satisfy its demands for information on General St. Claire's military defeat, but the executive branch declined to provide information to the House of Representatives concerning the Jay Treaty. Thomas Jefferson and John Tyler were among the early presidents who refused to send information to Congress.[45] All of these disputes seem to produce the same charges of legislative meddling or of executive cover-ups. No conclusive determination seems to result. Each case opens up the problem anew.

These problems became acute after World War II when Congress steadily sought sensitive personnel information lodged in executive files. In 1948, President Truman ordered confidential loyalty reports of the Federal Bureau of Investigation and other investigative agencies to be released to Congress only on his authority. Again, in 1954, President Eisenhower ordered certain types of intra-agency documents to be withheld from congressional investigators. Executive explanations for these actions did not diminish the irritation felt by some members of Congress. Accommodations continued to be worked out piecemeal. Compromise seems to be the governing practice. Such disputes are muddled further by the fact that much executive secrecy is authorized by Congress itself in statutes.[46]

The tradition of conflict followed by comity was shattered under President Nixon as administration claims of executive privilege soared beyond precedents.[47] The congressional response was anger, and then an attempt to pass a statute setting firmer limits on executive usage.[48]

In the 1960s and 1970s disputes flared over executive secrecy regarding U.S. foreign aid programs in Vietnam, defense weapons systems, and assorted activities of the CIA. Those in Congress who thought that executive policies were wrong and that fundamental errors were being concealed were the most vocal critics of executive secrecy. Yet because the complexity of the situation was widely understood, pragmatic accommodation rather than absolute showdown normally prevailed. Recent presidents, in an attempt to blunt congressional concern, have stated that executive privilege would be invoked in their administration only with their explicit permission. In reality, executive officials subordinate to the president have implicitly invoked this defense.

Executive-legislative conflicts over secrecy continued into the 1980s and 1990s as congressional committees flayed the Reagan, Bush, and Clinton administrations, charging excessive secrecy in testimony before congressional committees and too much classification of government documents. These issues, however, are not one-sided. The Reagan administration especially challenged the behavior of some members of Congress in publicizing intelligence activities abroad. Public statements from congressional sources about United States covert activity in Nicaragua led to charges and countercharges concerning partisanship and the need for legislative involvement in foreign policy.

During the Clinton presidency, court decisions seemed to sharpen and clarify what had traditionally been opaque and hence negotiable. Rejected were administration claims of executive privilege for some presidential conversations with advisers and for testimony from Secret Service persons protecting the president. In each instance, the courts acknowledged that executive privilege was a valid claim unless overridden by specific circumstances, for example, the need for information by Independent Counsel Kenneth Starr.

The problem of selecting spokespersons from the executive branch to testify before congressional committees also highlights alternative notions of responsibility. Committees themselves have difficulty in deciding what they want. At times, committees are mainly interested in hearing department heads; at other times, they want to hear from lower-level employees, on the grounds that they are the persons who actually know what is going on. In the model that calls for centralizing responsibility in the executive branch, it would be appropriate for Congress to hear only a department's top political officials. If Congress is the primary agent for promoting a responsible bureaucracy, then it is presumably appropriate for it to hear any officials that it thinks can supply the information it wants.

Conflicts over what information is to be released to Congress occur in almost every administration. In the Reagan administration, a flurry of excitement arose as a series of administration officials refused, for various reasons, to provide information requested by congressional committees. Secretary of the Interior James Watt, Environmental Protection Agency administrator Ann Gorsuch Burford, and EPA official Rita Lavelle were all threatened with contempt citations by the Congress. Usually after informal negotiations, some information was provided and any contempt citations were quashed.[49] Similar arguments occurred in the Clinton administration over such issues as alleged political use of FBI files and "Travelgate." Threats of contempt of Congress citations resulted in the release of some previously withheld documents.

Executive-legislative disputes over executive privilege and which executive branch officials shall testify before congressional committees seem to have no ultimate solution. Recurring conflict between the two branches is to be expected; settlements are never more than temporary.

Occasional public conflicts mask much executive-legislative cooperation:

> By all accounts, most congressional demands for information are handled without confrontation, and it is clear that most agencies respond to most requests by providing whatever information Congress is seeking. It follows, in most cases, if Congress is not getting the information it needs, the problem is not agency unresponsiveness to congressional demands, but something else. Indeed, in many contexts, Congress's main problem is as likely to be a surfeit of information, or at least of unfocused information, as it is to be an information deficit.[50]

## The Effectiveness of Oversight

Jack Brooks (D., TX), chairman of the House Government Operations Committee in 1979, summarized widely held feelings:

> The ability of any Member of Congress or any subcommittee or any committee to ferret out fraud or waste or mismanagement is very limited. And, I speak from over a quarter century of experience in overseeing the shenanigans of bureaucrats. Unless you watch them closely all the time, they always go back to the cookie jar. Congress simply does not have enough time or resources to review adequately every aspect of the Federal Government on a continuing basis.[51]

A 1983 interview with a veteran investigator for congressional committees elicited even more pointed remarks. He alleged that congressional oversight was done "very, very poorly." Oversight activity was described as "a scandal." Trying to systematically oversee the vast bureaucracy was said to be "impossible." "It's like trying to sweep back the ocean."[52]

Events over the last forty years sometimes confirm these indictments, but there is some contradictory evidence that should not be ignored. Legislative oversight is not systematic; it is frequently not profound. Yet congressional inquiries sometimes do focus attention on significant problems. They have provoked executive reexamination of some policies and procedures.[53] As one witness from the Office of Management and Budget told a congressional committee: "And I'll tell you, when the Congress is interested, it sends the fear of God into the executive branch."[54] They have broadened the scope of alternatives considered by the executive. In short, legislative oversight has sometimes been an effective agent of innovation and change. One could argue, for example, that reforms of the Internal Revenue Service were stimulated by congressional investigations in 1997–98 and then by legislation.

A former congressional committee staff member suggested some of the problems in accurately assessing legislative oversight:

> The great bulk of congressional oversight, however, is conducted out of the public's eye. Nearly every day that Congress is in session, oversight hearings are held which go unnoticed by the general public. These hearings go a long way to shape public policy as government agencies and the President often take steps to avoid embarrassment by even the least-noticed oversight panel. . . .

> Countless examples can be provided that demonstrate the positive impact congressional oversight has had on the administration of government, but they gain little public recognition because they are largely ignored by the press. These investigative hearings lead to substantial reforms in government regulation or decisions to spend or stop spending federal tax dollars on a particular program. The threat of hearings has forced the White House to take specific actions and often, the president will announce a major initiative on the eve of a congressional hearing so that he can later claim credit for pursuing the cause.[55]

There is now extensive quantitative evidence that Congress has been paying more attention to oversight in recent years[56] (see Figure 12.3). Another measure of the increased attention to oversight is the money authorized to congressional committees for investigations. Budgets for investigations are much larger than they used to be. Joel Aberbach argues that oversight patterns change as context changes. More oversight was conducted during the 1980s than in previous decades because of declining opportunities to create new programs, tighter budgets, and different political parties in control of Congress and the presidency.[57]

Does divided government have an impact on legislative oversight of bureaucracy? Analysts disagree. David Mayhew, for example, sees no substantial difference for legislative oversight under unified or divided government. Others argue otherwise. Ogul found clear differences; Oleszek

**FIGURE 12.3  Days of oversight, committee hearings, and meetings, 1961–83**

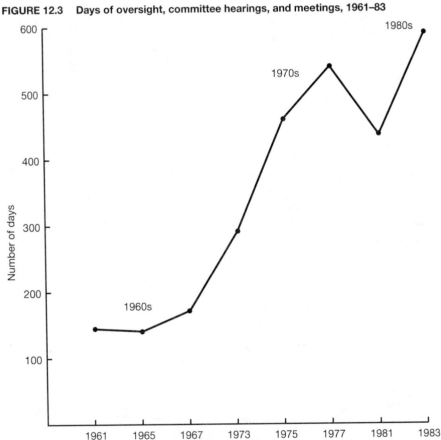

SOURCE: Data from Joel D. Aberbach, *Keeping a Watchful Eye* (Washington, DC: Brookings Institution, 1990), p. 35.

suggests: "In the 104th [Congress], Republicans conducted investigations. . . . to embarrass the Clinton White House." O'Halloran associates divided government with stricter controls over legislative delegations to the executive branch in trade policy; McCarty and Razaghian see divided government as fostering delays in Senate confirmation of presidential appointees; Kiewiet and McCubbins find increased conflict between Congress and the Budget Bureau (now the Office of Management and Budget) under divided government.[58]

One of the great difficulties in assessing legislative oversight is that so much of it is performed through daily, informal interactions that are impossible to document and quantify. If formal oversight attempts seldom match the demands of law, informal efforts can sometimes close the gap. Aberbach shows that there are extensive and continuing interactions between congressional committee staff members and bureaucrats; in addition, oversight occurs during legislative hearings on bills, in the processing of casework, through comments in the committee reports on bills, and in other activities not actually called oversight.[59] What these activities add to oversight cannot be precisely measured, but they probably add quite a bit. If the formal techniques of legislative oversight seem underused and only partially effective, part of the explanation may be that less visible informal actions are promoting some of the same goals.

Fragmentary evidence concerning legislative oversight in the states points in two directions: The job has not been done well, and it is now being done better. Alan Rosenthal, writing in 1972, found that few legislators in six states rated their performance in exercising oversight as "excellent" or "good." He suggests that these perceptions are typical in the states: "the performance of oversight undoubtedly maintains its status as a neglected stepchild."[60] A more complex picture emerges from thirty years of data collected by the American State Administrators' Project. State administrators report that they engage in considerable communication with state legislators and their staffs, as well as with the governor and his or her staff.[61] Moreover, many of them perceived the legislature as exercising significant control over their agency along with the governor. Table 12.2 reports these perceptions during a thirty-year period.[62]

**TABLE 12.2** **Executive and legislative control over state administration: Perceptions of state agency heads, 1964–94 (percentages)**

| Greater Control Over Agency | 1964 | 1974 | 1984 | 1994 |
|---|---|---|---|---|
| Governor | 32 | 47 | 42 | 41 |
| Legislature | 44 | 26 | 35 | 31 |

SOURCE: Data from Cynthia J. Bowling and Deil S. Wright, "Change and Continuity in State Administration: Administrative Leadership Across Four Decades," *Public Administration Review*, LVIII (1998), 436.

The traditional picture of oversight activity in the states needs to be amended. Attention to oversight has been growing rapidly in recent decades in some states. The most visible symptom is the emergence of new structures and procedures for conducting it. The adoption of sunset laws and provisions for legislative review of administrative rules and regulations are among the most visible. About 60 percent of the states have some form of sunset legislation; about 80 percent of states provide for legislative review of administrative rule making.

Barriers to the effectiveness of legislative oversight have typically been traced to structural factors, such as deficiencies in legal authority and staff. Congress has established a substantial structure for conducting oversight. There is a well-established committee system, and staffing is largely adequate. Other support mechanisms, such as the Congressional Research Service, the Congressional Budget Office, and the General Accounting Office, are in place. Additions to legislative oversight authority and to legislative staff may indeed be somewhat useful in improving oversight performance. The experience in Congress since the passage of the Legislative Reorganization Act of 1946 suggests, however, no direct correlation between structural change and the effective performance of oversight.

In many states, however, where the structural preconditions for oversight are frequently fragile, progress in establishing new structures and procedures may indeed predict increased oversight activity. Alan Rosenthal concludes, after examining legislative oversight in fifteen states, that some institutional factors do promote oversight, but that these pressures are seldom substantial enough to stimulate most legislators to get involved in what they perceive to be a long-range activity; the eye of the legislator is normally firmly focused on the short run.[63]

The incentives for legislators to oversee need to be added to the analysis. Legislators, given their many and diverse obligations, must regularly choose where to focus their efforts. Most legislators, most of the time, feel that they will derive greater benefits from activities other than oversight.[64] According to Representative Norman Mineta (D., CA): "It's very tough. . . . It's time consuming, painstaking investigative work. And there's no political appeal in it. There's much more appeal in getting a bill passed."[65]

If legislators do not oversee systematically, do they do enough? This question elicits little consensus among analysts. The traditional answer is to point to deficiencies in performance. Marcus Ethridge, for example, notes that increases in oversight do not necessarily mean that the job is being done well: "the existence of greater oversight activity can be reconciled with the continuing failure of legislators to achieve systematic monitoring and consistent evaluation of administrative activity."[66]

Mathew McCubbins and Thomas Schwartz argue, however, that Congress does not neglect oversight. Congress, they assert, is merely expressing a preference for one type of oversight—that performed in response to complaints from their supporters. These authors view such highly selective oversight as rational and appropriate.[67]

Despite lingering uncertainties about precisely how much oversight is being done and what impact it has, several conclusions are clear: Oversight is "an intensely political activity."[68] Its performance varies with changes in political climate.[69] It remains "more opportunistic than comprehensive."[70]

## NOTES

1. For an argument that organizations are inherently political, see Karen M. Hult and Charles Wolcott, *Governing Public Organizations* (Pacific Grove, CA: Brooks/Cole, 1990). At the state level, see Priscilla Wohlstetter, "The Politics of Legislative Oversight: Monitoring Legislative Reform in Six States," *Policy Studies Review*, IX (Autumn 1989), 50–65. The enduring nature of executive-legislative conflict over control of the bureaucracy is illustrated in James R. Bowers, "Looking at OMB's Shared Regulatory Review Through a Shared Powers Perspective," *Presidential Studies Quarterly*, XXIII (Spring 1993), 331–45. A similar thesis is developed in Cathy Marie Johnson, *The Dynamics of Conflict Between Bureaucrats and Legislators* (Armonk, NY: M. E. Sharpe, 1992). A defense of political decisions being made at times by bureaucrats is in Jerry L. Mashaw, *Greed, Chaos, and Governance* (New Haven, CT: Yale University Press, 1997). For analyses of research on oversight, see Bert A. Rockman, "Legislative-Executive Relations and Legislative Oversight," *Legislative Studies Quarterly*, IX (August 1984), 387–440; and Morris S. Ogul and Bert A. Rockman, "Overseeing Oversight: New Departures and Old Problems," *Legislative Studies Quarterly*, XV (February 1990), 5–24. Kenneth R. Mayer argues that congressional micro management attempts toward the Department of Defense grow from suspicions that the DOD will not necessarily faithfully carry out congressional preferences and from understanding that policy and administration cannot be separated completely. "Policy Disputes as a Source of Administrative Controls: Congressional Micro-Management of the Department of Defense," *Public Administration Review*, LIII (July/August 1993), 293–302.

2. Quoted in David Segal, "A House Divided," *Washington Monthly*, January/February 1994, p. 31.

3. An unusually insightful analysis of legislative oversight is Joel D. Aberbach, *Keeping a Watchful Eye: The Politics of Congressional Oversight* (Washington, DC: Brookings Institution, 1990). An extended analysis can be found in Morris S. Ogul, *Congress Oversees the Bureaucracy* (Pittsburgh: University of Pittsburgh Press, 1976). The problem of jurisdiction is highlighted in the area of foreign policy where almost all Senate committees and more than 80 percent of House committees have some role to play. Dale Vinyard cites some important limits to committee oversight efforts in "Public Policy and Institutional Politics," *Aging and Public Policies*, ed. W. Browne and L. Olson (Westport, CT: Greenwood Press, 1983), pp. 181–99. The continuing problems in studying oversight are illustrated in Michael J. Scicchitano, "Congressional Oversight: The Case of the Clean Air Act," *Legislative Studies Quarterly*, XI (August 1986), 393–407. Oversight hearings sometimes serve a political purpose within Congress as committees strive to expand their jurisdiction into subject areas not explicitly assigned to a particular unit. See Jeffery Talbert, Bryan D. Jones, and Frank R. Baumgartner, "Nonlegislative Hearings and Policy Change in Congress," *American Journal of Political Science*, XXXIX (May 1995), pp. 383–406.

4. Eric Lane, "Albany's Travesty of Democracy," *City Journal*, VII (Spring 1997), 55.

5. For a detailed report, see *New York Times*, March 31, 1991, p. 1. See also Alan Rosenthal, *Governors and Legislatures: Contending Powers* (Washington, DC: Congressional Quarterly Press, 1990), especially pp. 186–93.

6. See Barbara Hinkson Craig, *The Legislative Veto* (Boulder, CO: Westview Press, 1983). For an excellent discussion, see Joseph Cooper and Patricia A. Hurley, "The Legislative Veto: A Policy Analysis," *Congress and the Presidency*, X (Spring 1983), 1–24.

7. *Immigration and Naturalization Service* v. *Chadha*, 103 S. Ct. 2764 (1983).

8. Jessica Korn argues that the demise of the legislative veto does not cripple congressional oversight efforts. See "The Legislative Veto and the Limits of Public Choice Analysis," *Political Science Quarterly*, CIX (Winter 1994–95), 873–94; and *The Power of Separation* (Princeton, NJ: Princeton University Press, 1996). For an argument that the legislative veto has had significant consequences for foreign policy decision making, see Martha L. Gibson, *Weapons of Influence* (Boulder, CO: Westview Press, 1992).

9. "Judicial Misjudgments About the Lawmaking Process: The Legislative Veto Case," *Public Administration Review*, special issue (November 1985), 705–11. See also Frederick M. Kaiser, "Congressional Control of Executive Actions in the Aftermath of the Chada Decision," *Administrative Law Review*, XXXVI (Summer 1984), 239–76.

10. For examples, see Rosenthal, *Governors and Legislatures*, pp. 182–84; and L. Harold Levinson, "The Decline of the Legislative Veto: Federal/State Comparisons and Interactions," *Publius*, XVII (Winter 1987), 115–32.

11. See Rosenthal, *Governors and Legislatures*, p. 182; James Bowers, *Regulating the Regulators* (New York: Praeger, 1990); and Marcus E. Ethridge, *Legislative Participation in Implementation: Policy Through Politics* (New York: Praeger, 1985).

12. John R. Johannes, "Study and Recommend: Statutory Reporting Requirements as a Technique of Legislative Initiative in Congress—A Research Note," *Western Political Quarterly*, XXIX (December 1976), 589–96; and Ogul, *Congress Oversees the Bureaucracy*, pp. 175–80.

13. In 1990, listing the reports required by Congress required a 194-page document; 126 of these pages described reports from the president and the executive branch. Congress seems of two minds in requiring these reports. The numbers required grow regularly, yet on occasion, as in 1995, Congress reduced the number of reports required.

14. This incident is reported in *New York Times*, July 3, 1963, p. 12.

15. *Congressional Quarterly Weekly Report*, January 19, 1991, p. 169. This paragraph dealing with the "Keating Five" was prepared by Lisa Campoli.

16. The fullest discussion of casework and its impact is John R. Johannes, *To Serve the People: Congress and Constituency Service* (Lincoln: University of Nebraska Press, 1984). See also Ogul, *Congress Oversees the Bureaucracy*, pp. 162–75. Richard C. Elling, "The Utility of State Legislative Casework as a Means of Oversight," *Legislative Studies Quarterly*, IV (August 1979), 353–79; and Richard C. Elling, "State Legislative Casework and State Administrative Performance," *Administration and Society*, XII (November 1980), 350. Freeman and Richardson studied legislative oversight in four states. Their conclusions show that the electoral basis for casework is strong in some states as well as in Congress. Patricia K. Freeman and Lilliard E. Richardson, Jr., "Exploring Variation in Casework Among State Legislators," *Legislative Studies Quarterly*, XXI (February 1996), 41–56.

17. This authority has lapsed from time to time, usually to be renewed eventually. In early 1984, Congress extended this authority, but only until December 1984. It has not been renewed since. An excellent study of attempts in the twentieth century to reorganize the executive branch is Peri E. Arnold, *Making the Managerial Presidency* (Lawrence: University Press of Kansas, 1998). Arnold stresses the relations between reorganization and the roles of the president.

18. Louis Fisher and Ronald C. Moe, "Presidential Reorganization Authority: Is It Worth the Cost?" *Political Science Quarterly*, XCVI (Summer 1981), 308.

19. Rosenthal, *Governors and Legislatures*, p. 172.

20. A study of nominations by presidents from 1965 to 1994 revealed that on important nominations the median number of witnesses at confirmation hearings was one, frequently only the nominee. Glen S. Krutz, Richard Fleisher, and Jon S. Bond, "From Abe Fortas to Zoe Baird: Why Some Presidential Nominations Fail in the Senate," *American Political Science Review*, XCII (December 1998), 873. Senator Mike Monroney (D., OK) noted in June 1952 that one hundred appointments to postmasterships had been approved in committee in thirty seconds. Joseph P. Harris, *The Advice and Consent of the Senate* (Berkeley: University of California Press, 1953), p. 355. In a study of nominations by presidents from 1961 to 1993, Nolan McCarty and Rose Razaghian find that presidents employ strategic anticipation in making

nominations subject to Senate confirmation. They see presidents as highly responsive to the possibility of opposition to their appointees. "Hitting the Ground Running: The Timing of Presidential Appointments in Transition," in *Presidential Power: Forging the Presidency for the 21st Century,* ed. Robert Shapiro, Lawrence Jacobs, and Martha Kumar (New York: Columbia University Press, forthcoming).

21. Harris, *The Advice and Consent,* p. 259, notes seven rejections. Subsequent to the publication of the Harris study, the Senate, in 1958, disapproved the nomination of Lewis L. Strauss to be secretary of commerce. In 1989, the Senate rejected the nomination of John Tower to be secretary of defense. A description and analysis of the confirmation process is G. Calvin Mackenzie, *The Politics of Presidential Appointments* (New York: Free Press, 1981). On occasion, protracted confirmation proceeding do occur. In the Clinton administration, the nomination of Alexis Herman to be secretary of labor required some 113 days of confirmation proceedings. Nolan McCarty and Rose Razaghian argue that the time required to confirm nominees varies with such factors as divided government and ideological polarity in the Senate. "Advice and Consent: Senate Responses to Executive Branch Nominations, 1885–1996," *American Journal of Political Science,* XLIII (1999), 1122–143.

22. Bruce Adams and Kathryn Kavanagh-Baran, *Promise and Performance: Carter Builds a New Administration* (Lexington, MA: D. C. Heath, 1979), p. 166.

23. Ibid., p. 169.

24. Quoted in *President Carter, 1978* (Washington, DC: Congressional Quarterly Press, 1979), p. 170. For an argument that "insiders" receive a warmer reception in the Senate and that that status is more easily granted to men than to women, see Mary Anne Borrelli, "Gender, Credibility, and Politics: The Senate Nomination Hearings of Cabinet Secretaries-Designate, 1975–1993," *Political Research Quarterly,* L ( March 1997), 171–97.

25. The story is reported in *New York Times,* October 7, 1975, p. 57.

26. Paul C. Light, *Monitoring Government* (Washington, DC: Brookings Institution, 1993), p. 222.

27. A classic study of the problem of conflict of interest is the Association of the Bar of the City of New York, *Conflict of Interest and Federal Service* (Cambridge, MA: Harvard University Press, 1960). The following section leans heavily on this work. For the story of the Carter administration's efforts to cope with conflicts of interest, see Adams and Kavanagh-Baran, *Promise and Performance,* pp. 87–98. A history of attempts to regulate conflicts of interest is Robert N. Roberts, *White House Ethics: The History of the Politics of Conflict of Interest Legislation* (New York: Greenwood Press, 1988).

28. Hearings Before the Senate Committee on Armed Services on the Nomination of Charles E. Wilson et al., 83rd Cong., 1st Sess., p. 26.

29. C. Wright Mills, *The Power Elite* (New York: Oxford University Press, 1959), p. 285.

30. New York City Bar Association, *Conflict of Interest,* p. 108.

31. Adams and Kavanagh-Baran, *Promise and Performance,* pp. 93–96.

32. For details, see Leonard White, *The Republican Era* (New York: Macmillan, 1958), pp. 368–69.

33. Quoted in Alan Rosenthal, *Legislative Life: People, Process, and Performance in the States* (New York: Harper & Row, 1981), p. 286.

34. Alan Rosenthal, *Legislative Performance in the States* (New York: Free Press, 1974), p. 69. See also Rosenthal, *Governors and Legislators,* pp. 188–93.

35. For some examples, see Ogul, *Congress Oversees the Bureaucracy,* pp. 155–57.

36. W. B. Ragsdale, "An Old Friend Writes of Sam Rayburn," *U.S. News & World Report,* October 23, 1961, pp. 70 and 72.

37. Two descriptions and analyses of the functions of the General Accounting Office are Joseph Pois, *Watchdog on the Potomac* (Washington, DC: University Press of America, 1979); and Frederick C. Mosher, *The GAO: The Quest for Accountability in American Government* (Boulder, CO: Westview Press, 1979).

38. Harry S. Havens, *The Evolution of the General Accounting Office: From Voucher Audits to Program Evaluations* (Washington, DC: U.S. General Accounting Office, 1990), p. 14.

39. See Louis Fisher, *Presidential Spending Power* (Princeton, NJ: Princeton University Press,

1975). An argument that budgetary controls over bureaucracy may be important partly for the signals that changes send to agencies is made by Daniel P. Carpenter, "Adaptive Signal Processing, Hierarchy, and Budgetary Control in Federal Regulation," *American Political Science Review,* XC (June 1996), 283–302.

40. How these factors interact is illustrated in Ogul, *Congress Oversees the Bureaucracy,* Chaps. 2–5. See also Aberbach, *Keeping a Watchful Eye.*

41. *Congressional Quarterly Weekly Report,* February 6, 1999, p. 328.

42. William F. West and Joseph Cooper argue that "the emergent model of political oversight, which advocates centralized presidential control over agency policy making while prescribing a passive role for Congress, ignores key goals of our political system as well as important external influences and internal constraints that shape institutional behavior." West and Cooper, "Legislative Influence v. Presidential Dominance: Competing Models of Bureaucratic Control," *Political Science Quarterly,* CIV (Winter 1989–90), 581–606. Some problems in arguing congressional dominance are discussed in John T. Woolley, "Conflict Among Regulators and the Hypothesis of Congressional Dominance," *Journal of Politics,* LV (February 1993), 92–114.

43. A variant of this model is presented in Mathew D. McCubbins and Thomas Schwartz, "Congressional Oversight Overlooked: Police Patrols versus Fire Alarms," *American Journal of Political Science,* XXVIII (February 1984), 165–79.

44. This overall perspective is shared by L. Britt Snider, *Sharing Secrets with Lawmakers: Congress as a User of Intelligence* (Washington, DC: Center for the Study of Intelligence, 1997). Snider has had extensive experience from several perspectives in the intelligence community. Some excellent studies of congressional attempts to oversee intelligence agencies are found in Loch K. Johnson, *America's Secret Power: The CIA in a Democratic Society* (New York: Oxford University Press, 1990); Loch K. Johnson, *A Season of Inquiry* (Louisville: University Press of Kentucky, 1985); Frank J. Smist, Jr., *Congress Oversees the United States Intelligence Community, 1947–1994* (Knoxville: University of Tennessee Press, 1994); Rhodri Jeffreys-Jones, *The CIA and American Democracy* (New Haven, CT: Yale University Press, 1989); and Frederick Kaiser, "Congress and the Intelligence Community," in *The Post-Reform Congress,* ed. Roger Davidson (New York: St. Martin's Press, 1991), Chap. 14.

45. For more detailed accounts, see Francis E. Rourke, *Secrecy and Publicity* (Baltimore: Johns Hopkins University Press, 1961); for examples of the executive providing information to Congress, see Stephen W. Stathis, "Executive Cooperation: Presidential Recognition of the Investigating Authority of Congress and the Courts," *Journal of Law and Politics,* III (Fall 1986), 183–294. See also Mark J. Rozell, *Executive Privilege: The Dilemma of Secrecy and Democratic Accountability* (Baltimore: Johns Hopkins University Press, 1994).

46. See Peter M. Shane, "Negotiating for Knowledge: Administrative Responses to Congressional Demands for Information," *Administrative Law Review,* XLIV (Spring 1992), 197–244.

47. Role does influence behavior since Nixon, as a member of Congress in 1948, had stated: "The point has been made . . . that . . . the Congress has no right to question the judgment of the President in making that decision [to withhold information from Congress]. I say that the proposition cannot stand from a constitutional standpoint or on the basis of the merits." *Congressional Record,* 80th Cong., 2nd Sess., April 22, 1948, p. 4783.

48. During the Nixon administration, the Supreme Court confronted directly, for the first time, the issue of executive privilege. In *U.S. v Nixon* (1974), the Court argued that a general claim of executive privacy, while valid, fell before the need for specific evidence in a grand jury investigation of a crime. The Senate Watergate Committee, in another case, sought access to some of President Nixon's tape recordings. The Court of Appeals of the District of Columbia ruled that the committee did not demonstrate that these tapes were vital to fulfilling its function. In any case, the House impeachment proceedings were underway. See *Senate Select Committee v. Nixon* (1974). A discussion of the basis for and limits on executive privilege can be found in Rozell, *Executive Privilege.*

49. See Ronald L. Claveloux, "Congressional Oversight: The Gorsuch Controversy," *Duke Law Journal,* 1983 (December 1983), 1333–358.

50. Shane, "Negotiating for Knowledge: Administrative Responses to Congressional Demands for Information," pp. 200–201.

51. Hearings on the Failure of Departments and Agencies to Follow Up on Audit Findings Before the Legislation and National Security Subcommittee of the Government Operations Committee, U.S. House of Representatives, 96th Cong., 1st Sess., 1979, p. 2.

52. Quoted in Donald Lambro, "Congress Bungles Oversight," *Pittsburgh Press*, June 15, 1983, p. B2. Analysts in the "congressional dominance" school see Congress as actually in full control of the bureaucracy. Some limits to this dominance argument are noted in Terry M. Moe, "An Assessment of the Positive Theory of Congressional Dominance," *Legislative Studies Quarterly*, XII (November 1987), 475–520.

53. Robert J. Art formulates an iron law of executive-legislative relations: "because the Congress reacts, the executive anticipates." In "Congress and the Defense Budget: Enhancing Policy Oversight," *Political Science Quarterly*, C (Summer 1985), 248. See also Aberbach, *Keeping a Watchful Eye*.

54. "The Abuse and Mismanagement of HUD," Hearings before the HUD/MOD Rehab/Investigation Subcommittee of the Committee on Banking, Housing, and Urban Affairs, U.S. Senate, 101st Cong., 2nd Sess., 1990, p. 158.

55. Kevin Sabo, "Congressional Investigations of the Presidency," *Extensions*, Fall 1998, pp. 18, 19.

56. Aberbach, *Keeping a Watchful Eye*, Chaps. 2 and 3. Lawrence C. Dodd and Richard L. Schott, *Congress and the Administrative State* (New York: John Wiley, 1979), p. 169. See also Frederick C. Kaiser, "Oversight of Foreign Policy: The U.S. House Committee on International Relations," *Legislative Studies Quarterly*, II (August 1977), 255–79. Kaiser shows that oversight in foreign policy, just as in domestic policy, is based on opportunities and inducements.

57. Aberbach, *Keeping a Watchful Eye*, Chaps. 2 and 3. Hammond and Knott argue that variation is to be normally expected because autonomy varies from agency to agency and with changing circumstances and conditions. Thomas H. Hammond and Jack H. Knott, "Who Controls the Bureaucracy? Presidential Power, Congressional Dominance, Legal Constraints, and Bureaucratic Autonomy in a Model of Multi-Institutional Policy-Making," *Journal of Law, Economics, and Organization*, XII (April 1996), 119–66. Nicholas W. Jenny has compiled data on formal oversight hearings spanning more than a century. These data clearly show sharp variations over time in the days of oversight hearings conducted. "Variations in Congressional Oversight," paper presented at the annual meetings of the Midwest Political Science Association, Chicago, April 15, 1999.

58. David R. Mayhew, *Divided We Govern* (New Haven, CT: Yale University Press, 1991), Chap. 7; Ogul, *Congress Oversees the Bureaucracy*, Chaps. 1–5; Walter J. Oleszek, "The New Era of Congressional Policy Making," in *Rivals for Power*, ed. James A. Thurber (Washington, DC: Congressional Quarterly Press, 1996), p. 60; Sharyn O'Halloran, *Politics, Process and American Trade Policy* (Ann Arbor: University of Michigan Press, 1994), pp. 76, 97; see also David Epstein and Sharyn O'Halloran, "Divided Government and the Design of Administrative Procedures," *Journal of Politics*, LVIII (May 1996), 373, 394; in an elaborate, systematic discussion and analysis, David Epstein and Sharyn O'Halloran show that the impact of divided government on how Congress establishes the institutions of delegation to the executive branch (and hence executive discretion) is substantial. They argue that executive discretion will be higher during periods of unified government. *Delegating Powers: A Transaction Cost Politics Approach to Policy Making Under Separate Powers* (New York: Cambridge University Press, forthcoming). See also Nolan McCarty and Rose Razaghian, "Advice and Consent: Senate Responses to Executive Branch Nominations, 1885–1996," *American Journal of Political Science* XLIII (October 1999), 1122–1143; D. Roderick Kiewiet and Mathew D. McCubbins, *The Logic of Delegation* (Chicago: University of Chicago Press, 1991), pp. 182–84.

59. Aberbach, *Keeping a Watchful Eye*, Chap. 4. The concept of latent oversight (that which occurs during legislative activity not normally labeled as oversight) is developed and illustrated in Ogul, *Congress Oversees the Bureaucracy*, Chap. 6. See also Lawrence C. Dodd and Richard L. Schott, *Congress and the Administrative State*, pp. 164–65. Hamilton and Schroeder point out astutely that informal arrangements between legislators and bureaucrats can work to the advantage of both. James Hamilton and Christopher Schroeder, "Strategic Regulators and the Choice of Rulemaking Procedures: The Selection of Formal versus Informal Rules in Regulating Hazardous Waste," *Law and Contemporary Problems*, LVII (Spring 1994), 11–60.

60. "Legislative Review and Evaluation—The Task Ahead," *State Government*, XLV (Winter 1972), 43. Rosenthal provides some useful insights into oversight at the state level in *Legislative Performance in the States*, Chaps. 4 and 5. See also Rosenthal, *Governors and Legislatures*, pp. 186–93.

61. Cynthia J. Bowling and Deil S. Wright, "Change and Continuity in State Administration: Administrative Leadership Across Four Decades," *Public Administration Review*, LVIII (September/October 1998), 434–36. For a related study, see Cynthia J. Bowling and Deil S. Wright, "Public Administration in the Fifty States: A Half-Century of Administrative Revolution," *State and Local Government Review*, XXX (Winter 1998), 52–64.

62. Glenn Abney and Thomas P. Lauth report related data. "The Governor as Chief Administrator," *Public Administration Review*, XLIII (January/February 1983), 41. William A. Pearson and Van A. Wigginton find that state legislators perceive their oversight efforts as the most effective device to control state bureaucrats. "Effectiveness of Administrative Controls: Some Perceptions of State Legislators," *Public Administration Review*, XLVI (July/August 1986), 328–31.

63. "Legislative Behavior and Legislative Oversight," *Legislative Studies Quarterly*, VI (February 1981), 115–31.

64. This is a major theme in Ogul, *Congress Oversees the Bureaucracy*. See also David R. Mayhew, *Congress, the Electoral Connection* (New Haven, CT: Yale University Press, 1974). Most scholars argue that reelection incentives dominate member motivation. Diana Evans presents a convincing case that member goals are more complex and that reelection goals are not always the most powerful. "Congressional Oversight and the Diversity of Members' Goals," *Political Science Quarterly*, CIX (Fall 1994), 669–87. Huber, Shipan, and Pfahler link incentives, political context, and legislative capacity to oversee to whether state legislatures will delegate powers to executive bureaucracies. They show effectively that decisions concerning oversight are essentially political decisions. John D. Huber, Charles R. Shipan, and Madeleine Pfahler, "The Choice of Instruments for Controlling the Bureaucracy in Alternative Institutional Contexts," paper presented at the annual meeting of the American Political Science Association, Boston, September 1998.

65. *Congress and the Nation, 1977–80* (Washington, DC: Congressional Quarterly Press, 1981), p. 17.

66. Ethridge, *Legislative Participation in Implementation, Policy Through Politics*, p. 10.

67. Mathew D. McCubbins and Thomas Schwartz, "Congressional Oversight Overlooked: Police Patrols versus Fire Alarms." Their argument is expanded in Hugo Hopenhayn and Susanne Lohmann, "Fire-Alarm Signals and the Political Oversight of Regulatory Agencies," *Journal of Law, Economics, and Organization*, XII (April 1996), 196–213.

68. Joel D. Aberbach, "Congress and the Agencies: Four Themes on Congressional Oversight of Policy and Administration," in *The United States Congress*, ed. Dennis Hale (New Brunswick, NJ: Transaction Books, 1983), p. 285.

69. Joel D. Aberbach, "The Congressional Committee Intelligence System: Oversight and Change," *Congress and the Presidency*, XIV (Spring 1987), 69. Aberbach's most comprehensive statement is in *Keeping a Watchful Eye*. Oversight efforts and goals may also vary with the policy area. See Kathleen Bawn, "Political Control versus Expertise: Congressional Choices About Administrative Procedures," *American Political Science Review*, LXXXIX (March 1995), 62–73.

70. Aberbach, "The Congressional Committee Intelligence System," p. 71. Cathy Marie Johnson finds conflict between the executive and legislative branches to be both persistent and sometimes productive; see *The Dynamics of Conflict Between Bureaucrats and Legislators* (Armonk, NY: M. E. Sharpe, 1992). James Meernik suggests that in foreign policy matters involving the commitment of U.S. troops abroad, Congress challenges executive action only if there are substantial political incentives to do so. Even then, members of Congress are more likely to criticize than to take other forms of action. "Congress, the President, and the Commitment of the U.S. Military," *Legislative Studies Quarterly*, XX (August 1995), 377–97.

# 13

# Legislative-Judicial Relations

Because courts are involved in making public policy, they too should be considered part of the legislative process. Courts, like legislatures, create and interpret law. Each makes public policy and, in translating societal preferences into the language of law, serves as a representative. This description of the relationship between legislatures and courts contradicts the usual stereotype: politics is the domain of the legislature; law is the domain of the courts. Such a distinction misses an important point. There are many basic similarities existing alongside some subtle yet significant differences.[1]

## COURTS AND LEGISLATURES: COMPARISON AND CONTRAST

Legislatures differ from courts in their constitutional mandates. Congress and state legislatures, according to their constitutions, create public policy by making law and determining expenditures. The basic constitutional task of courts is to settle particular disputes in cases that properly come before them. But in legislating, representative assemblies inevitably interpret their respective constitutional documents; in deciding cases, courts unavoidably read meaning into both legislative acts and constitutional phrases.

The members of legislative bodies are selected through the political process. Federal judges, appointed rather than elected, may gain office on the basis of political as well as legal considerations. In the states, judges, like legislators, most often run for election on partisan slates; the difference typically lies in the longer terms of judges and in their less overt partisanship. Legislators face the possibility of removal each time they encounter the electorate. Federal judges serve during "good behavior." Judges too work within the boundaries of the political process but are more insulated from some of its operations than are legislators.

Legislators and judges carry on their activities in much different environments. Legislators work out their roles and seek reelection within a highly political environment. The judge, in contrast, has markedly greater freedom, due in some part to continuing public respect for the law. Possibly the difference in context is less today than in the past, since one impact of modern legal theory has been to separate the voice of the judge from that of God. That judges are engaged steadily in making political decisions is recognized by parts of the public, by political action groups, and by scholars.

Recognizing the political dimensions of the judicial process, pressure groups seek access to both legislator and judge. They supply the legislator with campaign funds, but they also provide money for individuals pressing cases before the courts. They offer legal support in court cases, just as they send lobbyists to testify before Congress. They seek support to pressure legislatures, just as they search for cases that may goad the courts into action. Money, energy, and skills are the resources needed to influence both legislatures and courts.

The manner of access rather than the attempt at influence distinguishes pressure-group efforts in the legislative and judicial arenas. Buttonholing the legislator is commonplace; contacting judges for unofficial sessions is commonly seen as irregular. Both legislator and judge receive reams of information from organized interests, but the judge has a greater role in determining the form in which the data are presented. The federal judge is immune from the threat of retaliation in the next election, and the lengthy terms of some state judges may create a similar effect. The legislator is more fearful about interest-group opposition in the next election. Pressure groups, attempting to influence judges, act not only under more formal procedures but under the taboos imposed by a society that views its judges as defenders of the purity of the Constitution.

Legislative and judicial bodies share a dependence on the executive branch to implement their decisions. In turn, each has an identifiable if somewhat different impact on the behavior of the executive. Each institution acts mainly outside the public gaze, but public concern focuses on legislative activity more regularly than on judicial decision making.

The power of a legislature is rooted in its representative character as fortified by its legal authority; the ultimate strength of the courts, especially of the U.S. Supreme Court, rests on its public status as guardian of the Constitution. In the words of Robert McCloskey: "If the public should ever become convinced that the Court is merely another legislature . . . the Court's future as a constitutional tribunal would be cast in grave doubt."[2]

In sum, the similarities between the judicial and the legislative processes are substantial. The differences are often those characteristic in political analysis: more matters of degree than of kind. At times these differences do become crucial. In 1965, the U.S. Supreme Court overturned Connecticut's birth control laws. A participant in the struggle explained: "We went to Hartford a number of times trying to get the laws changed through the legislature, but it never worked. Finally . . . [her husband insisted] the court is the only way."[3]

Functioning in related and overlapping but poorly defined spheres, legislatures and courts inevitably clash at critical intersections in the political process. Whether legislatures and courts will quarrel or cooperate is determined in some degree by constitutional provisions. Constitutions either settle questions about the size of courts, their structure, their procedures, and their powers, or grant legislative bodies the authority to do so. The result is that policy conflict sometimes emerges in the form of disputes over personnel, structures, rules, and procedures.

## THE COURTS: PERSONNEL, STRUCTURE, PROCEDURES

### The Judges

*Selection.* Congress plays a key role in the selection of most federal judges. The constitutional mandate, Article II, Section 2, gives the president the power to appoint judges to the Supreme Court with the advice and consent of the Senate. Congress determines the method of appointment for judges of "inferior courts"; the procedure adopted matches that for the Supreme Court.[4] About 80 percent of the nominees for the Supreme Court sent to the Senate have been confirmed. Most of the rejections came before 1900. Nominees were rejected most frequently because of political controversies, senatorial opposition to the president, or personal vendettas; rejection rarely has been based on a nominee's lack of technical qualifications or integrity.[5] When President Bush nominated Clarence Thomas to the Supreme Court, an intense confirmation controversy involving ideology, policy disputes, and charges of personal misbehavior ensued. The Senate in 1991 approved the Thomas nomination by a margin of 52–48, the smallest margin in over a century.[6] Four nominations have been rejected since 1900: John J. Parker in 1930, Clement F. Haynesworth, Jr., in 1969, G. Harrold Carswell in 1970, and Robert Bork in 1987.

The success of presidents in confirming their appointees to the Supreme Court varies with party control of the Senate and with how early or late in a president's term the appointment is made. If the Senate is controlled by the president's party, then 89 percent of the appointees have been confirmed; if the party in control of the Senate is not the same as the president's, the figure drops to 59 percent. If the appointee is selected during the first three years of a president's term, confirmation occurs in 89 percent of the cases; for fourth-year appointments, the confirmation percentage is lowered to 54 percent.[7]

In seeking persons to appoint to federal judgeships, a president usually ends up naming candidates who belong to his own political party. Thus those appointed by Democratic presidents Roosevelt, Truman, Kennedy, Johnson, Carter, and Clinton were Democrats more than 90 percent of the time. And those appointed by Republican presidents Eisenhower, Nixon, Ford, Reagan, and Bush were Republicans more than 90 percent of the time. Congress places firmer limits on the appointment of judges to district courts. The selection process that is specified in law tends to be reversed in fact. Senatorial courtesy dominates the selection process.[8] The senator of the president's party from the state concerned tends to nominate and the president tends to "confirm" the appointee. Once selection is settled through such informal procedures, the president can submit the name of "his" appointee to the Senate for formal confirmation with confidence. Senate control is so ironclad that conflict is most often resolved through negotiations that rarely reach the pages of daily newspapers. Practice is somewhat different if there is no senator of the president's political party from the state concerned. Then, members of the state's House delegation and other state political leaders are consulted.

If the rules of the political game have been followed, rejections are few. From 1977 to 1996, the average percentage of nominees to lower federal courts confirmed by the Senate was 84.5. Figure 13.1 provides additional data. If nominations are rarely rejected, senators can still delay confirmations to gain bargaining advantages.

In law, the selection of federal judges has remained relatively constant.

**FIGURE 13.1   Percentage of lower court nominees confirmed**

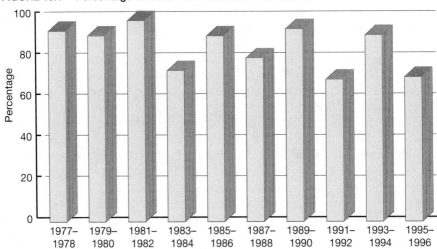

SOURCE: Data from *Congressional Quarterly Weekly Report*, January 10, 1998, p. 83.

The legal pattern in the states has been more variable. In seven of the original states, legislative selection of judges was the pattern; the legislature played a lesser role in the six other states.[9] A marked shift toward the election of judges was characteristic of the Jacksonian revolution. By 1860, about two-thirds of the states were selecting their judges through direct popular election.[10] Each state admitted to the Union since 1846 has provided for popular election of all or most of its judges. Today, most of the states elect a majority of their judges. Judges in other states are appointed by the executive, elected by the legislature, or appointed through some variety of "merit selection." In thirty-one states at least some judges are selected with the help of a "blue ribbon" commission.[11]

Disputes over whether judges should be elected or appointed have raged throughout the legal journals. Evidence of a relationship between selection procedures and judicial behavior is scarce, but Victor Flango and Craig Ducat argue, after examining the relevant literature, that there is no proof that different selection procedures produce differences in judicial opinions.[12]

The term of federal judges is for "good behavior," thus diminishing a potential opportunity for exerting political pressure on them. In the states, the terms of judges vary tremendously. Very few states have terms similar to the federal stipulation. However, the terms of many state judges are long enough to provide some measure of political insulation.

Congress sets the salaries of federal judges, but judicial independence is promoted by the constitutional provision (Article III, Section I), that their salaries "shall not be diminished during their Continuance in Office." Legislatures usually determine judicial salaries in the states, but most states also protect judges against reduction in salary while in office. This safeguard may have been more meaningful years ago. The guarantee has largely symbolic significance today.

*Removal.*   Congress plays a central role in the removal of federal judges since impeachment is the only method available. The House of Representatives has formally impeached twelve judges; five were acquitted and seven were convicted by the Senate.[13] The last federal judge to be impeached and convicted was Walter L. Nixon, Jr., in 1989. Impeachment is such an ultimate weapon that it is rarely used. Congress continues to wrestle with the problem of how to establish disciplinary and removal procedures short of impeachment, but with limited success.[14] Almost all of the states follow the federal pattern for removal of judges through impeachment. Like the national government, most states use the device sparingly. In 1994, the impeachment and conviction of Pennsylvania Supreme Court Justice Rolf Larsen marked the first time in nearly 200 years that this power had been used in the state. Over half of the states use other removal methods involving the legislature. In retention elections, where the voters are asked if they wish to retain the judge named, the voters almost always choose to keep the judge in office. Of 1,499 judges voted on in such elections from 1972 through 1978, only twenty-four, about 2 percent, were *not* retained.[15] Legislatures also use more subtle techniques to ease judges from office. Increasing the value of retirement benefits has provided one attractive lure.

### The Structure of the Courts

The U.S. Constitution directly creates only the Supreme Court. Congress is assigned the task of creating "inferior courts." Congress used this power in 1982 to create a new appellate court by consolidating the U.S. Court of Customs and Patent Appeals with the appellate division of the U.S. Court of Claims. In addition, Congress determines the number of judges for all federal courts. The Judiciary Acts of 1789 generally set the pattern of lower court organization. A study of congressional juggling of the number of federal court judges demonstrates the close relationships between politics and law. The size of the Supreme Court was set at six judges in 1789. The Federalist party lost control of the presidency and Congress in 1800. Before the Jeffersonian majority could take office, Federalists pushed through the Judiciary Act of 1801, which provided that the next Supreme Court vacancy was not to be filled. The new majority in Congress promptly repealed this legislation. The size of the Court was subsequently altered four more times until it was stabilized at nine members in 1869. In 1937, President Roosevelt proposed to increase the size of the Supreme Court by adding a new justice for each one over seventy years of age who refused to retire. President Roosevelt spoke of bringing "young blood" into the Court and of "more rapid justice"; few people failed to recognize the policy implications of this proposal, and Congress refused to accept it.

The growth in size and complexity of the political system provides a basic explanation for the addition of new federal judges. Increases in the number of judgeships are related to partisan politics; ordinarily the number of judges is increased after a political party that has long been out of power regains it.[16] In 1978, Congress created 152 new federal judgeships. This was the largest single group added in U.S. history. Most observers explained this action by noting the increased caseload of the federal courts. Others wondered why previous Congresses controlled by Democrats had not established these positions during the period 1968–76 when Republicans held the presidency. Congressional committees hold hearings annually, if possible, on the geographic organization of the U.S. district courts.

Congress also provides funds to run the federal courts. From 1969 to 1985, Congress granted in appropriations on average more than 95 percent of the budget requests from the judiciary.[17]

It is difficult to generalize about the relationships between court structure and state legislative processes, partly because structures vary greatly in the different states. In almost all states, the court of last appeal is created in the state constitution. Inferior courts are a product either of the constitution itself or of a constitutional grant of authority to the legislature. Constitutions are typically phrased to allow legislative bodies to establish courts other than those named therein. Joel A. Thompson and Robert T. Roper, looking at judicial reorganization in Kentucky, found that legislators' attitudes toward change in the courts depended on how the courts worked *and* on political concerns.[18]

### Procedures and Jurisdictions

Judicial procedures and jurisdictions sometimes are prescribed in constitutions. Legislatures fill in constitutional gaps. Only the jurisdiction of the Supreme Court is spelled out in the U.S. Constitution. The appellate jurisdiction of the Supreme Court is exercised "with such exceptions and under such regulations as the Congress shall make." Few cases come to the Supreme Court under its original jurisdiction; Congress can wield a powerful weapon over the Court through control of appellate jurisdiction. Congress exerts this authority only under exceptional circumstances. Perhaps the most blatant example was in the case of *Ex Parte McCardle*. After the Supreme Court had heard argument on the case but before the decision was announced, Congress acted in 1868. Concerned over the possibility that the Court would declare the Reconstruction Acts unconstitutional, Congress passed a law removing appellate jurisdiction in this case. The Court then dismissed the case, stating that its decisions could only be rendered in instances where the Court had jurisdiction. More commonly, congressional attempts to limit the jurisdiction of the Supreme Court have failed.

Lower federal courts are wholly dependent on Congress for their jurisdiction. Beginning with the Judiciary Act of 1789, Congress has adopted statutes at irregular intervals to modify the jurisdiction of the lower courts. The federal courts of appeals, for example, have been given the duty of reviewing the actions of the many executive agencies that exercise quasi-judicial functions. Among the agencies whose actions come under review are the National Labor Relations Board and the Federal Communications Commission. In 1988, Congress stipulated that cases involving citizens of different states could come before federal courts only if the money involved was more than $50,000. In recent years, Congress has moved to limit access to the federal courts on appeals by "death row" prison inmates and on some class action suits concerning immigration.

Predictably, one can assert that attempts to amend or alter the jurisdiction of the courts are made in reaction to unfriendly court decisions. Clarence Manion, formerly chair of the Commission on Intergovernmental Relations and dean of the Notre Dame Law School, charged: "The record reveals that the chief, if not the only, beneficiaries of the Warren Court's constitutional constructions have been convicted criminals, Communists, atheists, and clients of the NAACP." His remedy was to "strip the Supreme Court of its appellate jurisdiction which it now exercises so prodigally to reverse the sound judgments of all the inferior courts in the country."[19] A majority in Congress did not agree. In 1988, Congress did eliminate most of the Supreme Court's nondiscretionary appellate jurisdiction.

Legislatures can have a sharp impact on the business of the courts through the laws they pass. Many suits were brought, for example, under the provisions of the Civil Rights Act of 1964, the National Environmental Quality Act of 1969, and laws affecting railroad reorganization and endangered species. Congress, it seems, sometimes bucks decision-making authority to the courts.

Congressional prescription of judicial procedure extends beyond the subject of jurisdiction. In the Judiciary Act of 1789, Congress determined the time and place for court sessions and the ability of the courts to issue writs. Congress provided that the courts could "make all the necessary rules for the orderly conduct of their business." Congress was quick to use these powers for political purposes. In its 1802 repeal act, Congress postponed, in effect, the next session of the Supreme Court, thus prohibiting the judges from ruling on other sections of this piece of legislation.

Congress now authorizes the Supreme Court, with few restrictions, to make rules for the federal constitutional courts. The Judicial Conference, created by Congress in 1922, consists of 27 judges who make policy for the administration of the federal courts and adopt rules of procedure for submission to the Supreme Court. These rules, if approved, become effective unless specifically rejected by Congress. Congress itself alters court procedures from time to time, as in 1994 on the matters of arbitration in civil cases and automation in the courts.

A study of judicial rule making in the states finds a "patchwork quilt of pragmatic arrangements and political choices" in which it is difficult to identify patterns.[20]

## LEGISLATURES, COURTS, AND THE SEPARATION OF POWERS

### The Courts and Executive-Legislative Relations

Most questions concerning the relationships between the legislative and executive branches are decided through discussion, bargaining, and compromise. At times, stalemate may result. The courts rarely play a decisive role in such decision making. But, from time to time, issues involving executive-legislative relations are decided in the courts. Those seeking absolute rules from the courts are largely doomed to disappointment. Even when the decision of the

Supreme Court seems clear—the legislative veto is unconstitutional—the underlying argument may be somewhat obscure or questionable. For example, in *Immigration and Naturalization Service* v. *Chadha*, 1983 (the legislative veto case), and in *Bowsher* v. *Synar*, 1986 (the Gramm-Rudman-Hollings case), the Supreme Court seemed to be asserting that any law is unconstitutional if it grants "executive power" to Congress. Yet, in *Morrison* v. *Olson*, 1988 (the independent prosecutor case), the Court seemed to contradict the principle of clear, absolute separation of powers between the branches. The boundaries between the branches are defined mainly through compromise or, less commonly, through court decisions in particular cases. What continues to be missing is a clear, comprehensible rule, judicially or otherwise created, by which one could predict the location of these boundaries.

## Court Impact on Legislative Procedures

The impact of courts on congressional procedure has been visible but surely not decisive. The Constitution authorizes Congress to make its own rules and to judge the election and conduct of its own members. In many states, the identical rule obtains. Where rules of procedure are created by the legislative assembly and no constitutional questions are at issue, courts generally refuse to review these legislative acts. In *United States* v. *Ballin* (1892), the Supreme Court stated:

> The constitution empowers each house to determine its rules of proceedings. It may not by its own rules ignore constitutional restraints or violate fundamental rights, and there should be a reasonable relation between the mode or method of proceeding established by the rule and the result which is sought to be attained. But within these limitations all matters of method are open to the determination of the house.[21]

Court interpretations have been relatively few. In a spectacular exception, the Supreme Court ruled in 1969 that the U.S. House of Representatives had acted unconstitutionally in excluding Congressman Adam Clayton Powell. The Court argued that Powell was duly elected and met the constitutional qualifications for membership: age, citizenship, and residence. The House could not therefore exclude him but could punish or expel him if charges were brought and if he were convicted of them.[22] State courts are much more active in hearing cases concerning legislative procedures since so many state constitutions spell out in minute detail how their legislatures should conduct their business.

Some examples illustrate the impact of the courts. Congress cannot grant the president a line-item veto.[23] The constitutional immunity of members of Congress does not protect them from prosecution for taking a bribe.[24] Congressional immunity extends to congressional staff members if their actions would be protected if performed by a member of Congress.[25]

Congressional employees who feel that their dismissal violates the right to due process can file challenges to that action in court. Thus, a woman fired by a member of Congress because of her sex was entitled to sue.[26] Congressional immunity does not protect members of Congress against libelous remarks that they might make in press releases or newsletters.[27] The way in which the Senate collects evidence for use in impeachment trials, sometimes through a twelve-member committee, is essentially outside of the Court's interest.

In recent years members of Congress have filed many lawsuits in the federal courts. The subjects of these suits included attempts to get information from executive agencies, challenges to executive interpretation or administration of laws, congressional versus presidential authority, and challenges to internal congressional procedures. These suits are usually lost. They are important, however, one analyst claims, for political purposes such as publicizing issues, exposing constitutional problems, and promoting executive-legislative compromise.[28]

On rare occasions the courts do act to umpire executive-legislative conflicts. One example involved a dispute over when the pocket veto could be used. According to the Constitution, if Congress adjourns, thus preventing the president from returning a vetoed bill, the president can pocket veto the bill and thus effectively kill it. But how is an adjournment defined? If Congress takes a recess over a holiday, is that an adjournment? If Congress recesses between sessions, is that an adjournment? The courts over the years have ruled that an adjournment comes only at the end of a Congress as long as during recesses the Congress designates an official to receive presidential vetoes. Presidents Reagan and Bush have argued for a broader definition of the scope of the pocket veto so they could use it more frequently. The courts have mainly sided with those members of Congress who said that the pocket veto should apply only in the narrowest sense, at the end of a Congress when there is a final adjournment.[29]

## LEGISLATURES, COURTS, AND PUBLIC POLICY

Legislative-judicial conflicts are often verbalized in procedural terms. In many cases these procedural disputes simply disguise policy battles. Problems of personnel, jurisdiction, and structure are often problems of power.

> The mechanism of law . . . cannot be dissociated from the ends that law subserves. So-called jurisdictional questions treated in isolation from the purposes of the legal system to which they relate become barren pedantry. After all, procedure is instrumental; it is the means of effectuating policy.[30]

Spectacular battles between the Supreme Court and Congress catch the public eye; less eventful interaction is the more characteristic relationship.

Day after day, the courts decide cases involving the application of public policy reflected in constitutions and legislative acts. The issues involved, while undoubtedly of great consequence to the participants, often have little relevance in the broader forum of the political system. The decision in many cases adds increments of meaning to public law but in such small doses that they escape attention. The great bulk of court decisions passes largely unnoticed into the volumes of court reports.

It is highly unusual for a court decision to make a lasting impact on the political process. Precisely for that reason, legislative bodies rarely concern themselves with the activities of the courts. Record of discussion and debate over the courts and their activities is seldom found in legislative journals; court structure and procedure is the subject of very few bills.

Examples of legislative-judicial conflict should be examined against this background of peaceful cooperation and mutual indifference. Legislative-judicial interaction takes place in the few situations where courts significantly interpret legislative acts or subject them to judgments about constitutionality and where legislators in turn respond to judicial decisions.

**Judicial Interpretation of Public Policy**

Each judicial decision involves some interpretation of law. In fact, more cases involve interpretation of statutes than constitutional questions. Judges are required to match phrases in laws with the facts of concrete cases that come before them. This task is neither simple nor scientific. Precedents may exist for several courses of action, so judges may end up having to choose. It is least difficult in the lower courts, where most cases are decided. Law and fact often match without the judge exerting great discretion. In the appeals courts, and especially in the supreme courts, where the more complex cases inevitably end up, the judge must extend more effort and creativity to reconcile law and fact.

> Ambiguities in statutory language often indicate . . . failure to reach agreement. . . . The legislative history of most important statutes . . . contains conflicting pieces of evidence that can be interpreted in many different ways by agencies and courts.[31]

Some legislators count on the courts to correct their own errors. One senator was quoted as saying:

> I had a senator this afternoon tell me he's going to vote for this [the item veto bill]. He doesn't believe in it. He thinks it's going to be a tragedy if it ever occurred. . . . I'm counting on the Supreme Court to save us from ourselves.[32]

In their decision making, the judges are forced to read precise meaning into legislative acts. This judicial creativity is a necessity for several reasons.

First, the words in statutes are merely "symbols of meaning" phrased with only "approximate precision." Second, the ambiguity in statutes reflects the doubts and compromises of legislative accommodations—the legislature is not always certain of its goals. Third, draftsmanship in statutes is not always characterized by care and creativity. Fourth, the inherent complexity of some subjects defies exhaustive statutory treatment—legislatures cannot anticipate all possible situations. Fifth, "provisions at times embody purposeful ambiguity."[33]

Faced with an obligation to interpret statutes, judges cannot pretend that they are merely supplying the intent of the legislature as they read meaning into statutes.

> The [Supreme] Court no doubt must listen to the voice of Congress. But often Congress cannot be heard clearly because its speech is muffled. Even when it has spoken . . . what is said is what the listener hears. . . . One listens with what is already in one's head.[34]

After analyzing 222 Supreme Court decisions dealing with antitrust policy and labor-management relations, Beth M. Henschen concludes that the way the courts interpret statutes is related to the policy area and to the specificity or vagueness of the wording in the statute. A precise, detailed statute leads judges to look at the words and at legislative history carefully; a more loosely drawn statute leads judges to balance the interests involved. The judges then must fill the gaps.[35] In doing so, judges can often find precedents for many views, so they have some freedom to choose.

Court decisions can push Congress to make changes in legislation. For example, in the early 1980s, when the Social Security Administration began to interpret congressional legislation so as to reduce the number of claimants for benefits under the social security disability insurance program, some of those whose benefits were terminated took their claims to court. The courts responded positively to claimants' pleas and ordered the Social Security Administration to restore claims to thousands of persons. These controversies, in turn, stimulated Congress to enact legislation supporting the court decisions.[36]

### Judicial Review

The most spirited interaction between legislative and judicial bodies occurs when courts exercise the power of judicial review to determine the constitutionality of government actions. Courts make these judgments despite the absence of a specific constitutional mandate to do so. Whatever its origin, judicial review has become so accepted in the American tradition that its existence and its future must be presumed. A brief survey of the practice of judicial review yields insights that are useful to understanding contemporary legislative-judicial relationships.[37]

Judicial review was an accepted practice in the colonies. After the American Revolution, several states adopted the practice. From 1788 to 1802, state courts held state legislation invalid in more than twenty instances in eleven of fifteen states.[38] By 1803, the date of *Marbury* v. *Madison*, judicial review was well established in eight states. In 1789, the Supreme Court had sustained a state legislative act;[39] in 1796, it had upheld an act of Congress.[40] The presumption that the courts could exercise judicial review existed before 1803, but in that year the Supreme Court for the first time declared part of an act of Congress unconstitutional.[41] Seven years later, the Supreme Court for the first time declared a state legislative act unconstitutional.[42]

*Federal courts and acts of Congress.* The significance of John Marshall's decision in *Marbury* v. *Madison* apparently was lost to most observers. Some described the decision as "a perfectly calculated audacity"; others saw it as "a partisan coup." In the heat of the partisan furor over Marshall's oral rebuke to President Jefferson, few people were concerned with the impact of Marshall's pronouncement on judicial review. In particular, congressional reaction was slight. Perhaps part of the sting of *Marbury* v. *Madison* had been removed by the Court's decision six days later upholding an act of Congress.[43]

The Supreme Court did not declare an act of Congress unconstitutional again until the notorious case of *Dred Scott* v. *Sandford*.[44] Justice Taney went out of his way in that case to invalidate a section of the Missouri Compromise of 1820. What was especially perplexing about the Taney decision was that the section declared unconstitutional had been repealed before the Supreme Court had made its decision.[45]

The Supreme Court declared few acts of Congress unconstitutional until after the Civil War. The subsequent increase in judicial activity can be traced in part to disputes arising out of the war. The most intensive exercise of judicial review occurred, however, during the period between 1890 and 1937 when the Court, applying the doctrine of substantive due process, substituted its collective judgment of the reasonableness of legislation for the judgment of Congress. Constitutional guarantees of due process had been regarded previously as ensuring that government would use fair *procedures* in dealing with the citizenry. Now the courts used this constitutional phrase to assess the substantive merits of state and national legislation. Such merits came to be evaluated in terms of the judges' own social and economic philosophies; for most judges this meant laissez-faire and the protection of private property would be given primacy. Under the Court's interpretation, the due process clause came to be associated with "reasonable legislation," and the Court, rather than Congress, became the arbiter of what was "reasonable."

Specifically, the courts found an act of Congress outlawing "yellow-dog" contracts to be unconstitutional.[46] A statute setting minimum wages for the District of Columbia was found to be an unconstitutional deprivation

**TABLE 13.1   Acts of Congress declared unconstitutional in U.S. Supreme Court decisions, 1789–1997**

| Year | Number of Acts of Congress Overturned in Supreme Court |
|------|:---:|
| 1789–1864 | 2 |
| 1865–1936 | 71 |
| 1937–1952 | 3 |
| 1953–October 1999 | 79 |

SOURCE: Data from Henry J. Abraham, *The Judicial Process*, 7th ed. (New York: Oxford University Press, 1998), p. 309. Data for 1998 and 1999 from interview with Henry J. Abraham.

of liberty.[47] The high point in the history of Court reversals of Congress came in 1935 when seven statutes were voided. In 1936, four additional decisions upset acts of Congress. Congress and the president had entered into a new era of policymaking, but the Court was still holding fast to nineteenth-century doctrines. In the 1940s and 1950s, the Supreme Court declared fewer acts of Congress unconstitutional. The broad interpretation rendered to the "commerce clause" has eased the close control by the Court as Congress proceeds to regulate segments of the economic life of the nation. The 1960s through the 1990s saw a flurry of decisions overturning acts of Congress (see Table 13.1).

Judges have to practice creative interpretation. The Constitution provides scant guidance about the constitutionality of anti-abortion legislation, the right to privacy, or regulation of the Internet. Yet the courts regularly must render authoritative judgments. A selection of court decisions will exemplify judicial creativity in deciding the constitutionality of statutes: Congress can provide educational benefits to veterans but can exclude from these benefits conscientious objectors who have completed alternative service;[48] Congress can legislate to protect wild animals on public lands;[49] Congress can create black-lung benefit programs for coal miners.[50] The Supreme Court seldom challenges Congress lightly. In fact, the Supreme Court has reversed more of its own decisions than it has overruled acts of Congress.

> What seems clear—and clearly recognized by both bodies [the Supreme Court and Congress]—is that if the plain legislative intent is plainly distorted by a zealous Court, the reaction of a proud Congress will be plainer still. It is with this understanding that the Court proceeds, where it deems it appropriate, to make, or to shape, or at least to refine, public policy.[51]

***Federal courts and judicial review of state acts.***   Federal courts became concerned with the constitutionality of state legislative acts early in

American history. Before 1800, a circuit court judge had found a state act to be contrary to the Constitution; another state act was declared unconstitutional because of conflict with a treaty. The Supreme Court first voided an act of a state legislature for reasons of unconstitutionality in *Fletcher* v. *Peck* (1810). Until the Civil War, the Supreme Court had declared state legislation void in less than forty cases.[52] With industrialization came an increase in judicial review of the acts of state legislatures. In the last quarter of the nineteenth century, about one hundred state acts were declared unconstitutional.[53] Of the 125 state laws invalidated by federal courts before 1888, fifty concerned commerce, fifty involved the obligation of contracts, and only one was related to due process. In the era when judges most often applied substantive due process, from the 1890s to 1937, some four hundred acts of state legislatures were declared unconstitutional.[54] The explanation for this increased activity is threefold: An increase in the volume of cases, the attitudes of judges applying the "rule of reason," and many legislative experiments aimed at meeting the challenge of industrialization provided a target for judges concerned with maintaining laissez-faire and property rights.[55]

Over the last three decades, the Supreme Court has repeatedly struck down state legislative acts in areas such as racial discrimination and civil rights, reapportionment, and due process for persons accused of crimes. From 1969 to 1991, the Supreme Court declared 238 state acts unconstitutional.[56] In 1995, the Supreme Court declared laws in twenty-three states limiting the term that members of Congress can serve to be unconstitutional. Overall, the Supreme Court has been much more willing to strike down state acts than it has been to declare acts of Congress unconstitutional. Yet the total of state laws and local ordinances overturned from 1790 to 1996 was only 1,233; the overall percentage of state law affected remains very small.[57]

*State courts and state legislation.* In the states, "The active participation of state judges in the policy process is much more taken for granted and much less controversial than the involvement of federal judges in the national government."[58] Judges in the states sometimes seem to feel fewer constraints than do federal judges. In the words of one state judge, "No political thicket [is] too political for us."[59] Judicial review was recognized as early as 1818 as legitimate in all states but Rhode Island. Yet its exercise was infrequent and restricted to relatively few states. In Indiana, few legislative acts were declared unconstitutional between 1816 and 1852; in Pennsylvania, no act of the legislature was held invalid for some fifty years after the adoption of the constitution of 1790; in Massachusetts, one legislative act was voided in 1813, after which none was overruled for thirty-four years; in Ohio, from 1802 to 1851, seven state laws were declared unconstitutional; in Virginia, from 1789 to 1861, two laws were declared invalid on constitutional grounds.[60]

In the post–Civil War era, and especially near the end of the nineteenth century, judicial review in the states was on the upswing. Several factors help explain this trend: (1) Many of the state constitutions drafted in the late nineteenth and early twentieth centuries, reflecting a distrust of legislatures, spelled out the structures and procedures of government in minute detail. (2) Legislative discretion was circumscribed by a detailed listing of powers. (3) The rise of industrialization and urbanization led to an increased volume of governmental activity. According to Arthur Holcombe, nearly four hundred state laws were declared unconstitutional by state courts between 1903 and 1908.[61] Of these four hundred decisions, only thirty-two related to interference with the judiciary, which in earlier years had been a common cause for judicial review. Most related to "defective legislative procedure" or alleged violations of due process of law.[62] Margaret Nelson described a vast increase in the use of judicial review in Virginia, from 1902 to 1928; in New York, from 1906 to 1938, some 136 state statutes were declared unconstitutional; in Ohio, from 1912 to 1936, forty-four state legislative acts were declared void; in Nebraska, from 1920 to 1936, twenty-five statutes were held unconstitutional.[63]

Despite this increase in the use of judicial review, its overall application in the states still remains slight. In a study of judicial review in ten states, Oliver P. Field found that about 1,400 statutes had been declared unconstitutional until 1940.[64] Of the cases involving constitutionality that reached the courts, more than four-fifths of the statutes questioned were upheld. Overall, judicial review at least in many states tends to focus on procedural details and technical formalities rather than on the grand issues of public policy. Martin Hickman concludes that the impact of judicial review on policymaking has been slight in Utah;[65] for Indiana, Field found that most unconstitutional legislation has dealt not with great socioeconomic issues but with "squabbles."[66] After examining the history of judicial review in Virginia, Margaret Nelson concluded:

> The exercise of judicial review in Virginia from 1789 to 1928 was, generally speaking, of little practical significance in that it exerted slight tangible influence upon the course of legislative enactment and played an unimportant role in the shaping of vital public policies.[67]

Despite some studies of judicial review in particular states, the subject generally requires much more attention from scholars before more definitive analysis is possible.[68]

## LEGISLATIVE REACTION TO COURT DECISIONS

Legislative reaction to judicial decisions is not always the same. How and why legislators react can be illustrated through examples involving lobbying and flag burning.

*Lobbying.* In 1946, Congress passed the Federal Regulation of Lobbying Act. The provisions of the statute applied to persons or organizations attempting "to influence, directly or indirectly, the passage or defeat of any legislation by the Congress of the United States." In 1950, a House committee created to investigate "all lobbying activities" subpoenaed the Committee for Constitutional Government, a private group, to provide specified information about some of its contributors. When Edward Rumely, representing this committee, refused to provide the information requested, he was cited and convicted for contempt of Congress.

On appeal, the Supreme Court set aside the conviction on the grounds that the House committee was to investigate "lobbying," a term that the Court defined as excluding indirect efforts at persuasion through such techniques as distributing literature to members of the community. In essence, the Court defined lobbying as only direct activity to influence Congress. The efforts of the Committee for Constitutional Government to "educate the public" could not be regulated as lobbying, and Rumely, therefore, could not be in contempt of Congress for refusing to answer questions about indirect activities.[69]

The Rumely decision seemed to modify substantially the Federal Regulation of Lobbying Act. Yet it made no great impact on Congress. The explanation is perhaps threefold: (1) Congress itself was strongly divided on the definition of lobbying and how to regulate lobbies. (2) No immediate, organized, and substantial interests pressured Congress to act. (3) No self-evident threat to the integrity of the political system was posed by this decision.

*Flag Burning.* In contrast, many members of Congress were greatly agitated when the Supreme Court in 1989 declared that statutes punishing burning of the American flag were unconstitutional because they interfered with freedom of expression granted under the Constitution. The response in Congress was immediate and impassioned. Legislation and proposed amendments to the Constitution were rapidly introduced. Congress passed the Flag Protection Act of 1989, designed to overturn the Court decision.

When the Supreme Court in 1990 declared this latest statute to be unconstitutional, serious debate on a proposed constitutional amendment began. Such a proposal gained a majority vote in each house of Congress but not the two-thirds vote required for passage. Two subsequent attempts, in 1995 and 1998, to pass constitutional amendments also failed. One of the key issues in these defeats was concern with limiting freedom of expression as guaranteed in the First Amendment to the Constitution. No member of Congress defended desecration of the flag, but many wondered whether the proposed remedy was appropriate for relatively rare flag burnings.

Legislative response to court interpretations varies from inattention to flurries of proposals to alter the structure and procedures of the courts or to change their substantive rulings. Legislative reaction to exercises of judicial review of legislation follows similar patterns. The central fact is that few court decisions are reversed in Congress; when they are, action tends to come quickly.[70]

Congressional reaction seldom means a direct and nasty confrontation with the courts. More frequently, the congressional response will be to seek new legislative means to achieve its ends. Legislative reactions concerning the legislative veto (discussed in Chapter 12) and to court action concerning the Gramm-Rudman-Hollings Act (discussed in Chapter 11) provide good illustrations of how Congress copes.

### Reversal Through Constitutional Amendment

The most direct method of response to judicial declarations of unconstitutionality is to alter these decisions through proposing and passing constitutional amendments. Only a few such attempts have been successful; there are only six examples for the U.S. Constitution. In 1793, the Supreme Court ruled that states could be sued by citizens of other states without the consent of the state.[71] This ruling, seemingly in contradiction to widespread understandings of the Constitution, was quickly overruled by the passage of the Eleventh Amendment in 1798. This amendment provides the only instance in U.S. history of the curtailment of the jurisdiction of federal courts through a constitutional amendment.

The Thirteenth, Fourteenth, and Fifteenth Amendments reversed Supreme Court decisions, or parts of them, such as *Dred Scott* v. *Sandford.*[72] The end of slavery and the establishment of specific criteria for citizenship for all persons had the effect of overruling Justice Taney's assertion that Negroes were not eligible for citizenship and that Congress could not prohibit slavery in the territories.

The fifth example of a reversal came after the decision in *Pollock* v. *Farmer's Loan and Trust Company.*[73] The Court had ruled unconstitutional an act of Congress setting a uniform income tax. Constitutional amendments to offset the impact of this decision were introduced in 1895, 1898, 1907, and 1912. From 1897 to 1909, thirty-three amendments were introduced to override the *Pollock* decision.[74] These efforts were finally successful with the passage of the Sixteenth Amendment in 1913.

The sixth example involves lowering the minimum voting age for state and local elections. In 1970, Congress lowered the minimum voting age to 18. The Supreme Court upheld this action for national elections but ruled that the change was unconstitutional when applied to state and local elections.[75] Early in 1971 a constitutional amendment to lower the voting age in national, state, and local elections was considered in Congress. The proposal passed both houses with unusual haste and was ratified by the states in the record time of slightly over three months, as the Twenty-sixth Amendment.

More typical were the unsuccessful attempts in the 1960s into the 1990s to overturn decisions by the Supreme Court dealing with criminal procedures, school prayer, reapportionment, capital punishment, school busing, and abortion. Of the many constitutional amendments proposed in Congress from 1965 through 1990, 183 in 1989–90 alone, only eleven came to a vote in either house of Congress. Only two were passed and then ratified by the states.

## Reversal Through New Legislation

Congress quite regularly counters Court decisions by the adoption of new legislation. More than 150 provisions of federal laws had been declared unconstitutional by 1997. The court's decision in *I.N.S.* v. *Chadha* (1983), discussed earlier, may have added two hundred more examples to this list. Congress has passed legislation reversing these decisions in whole or in part more than one hundred times. Table 13.2 demonstrates the congressional response over some 150 years. During the 1980s, while congressional reversals were more common, some sixty-two in the decade, those passed were only a small fraction of the bills introduced.

Where the courts have restricted law through interpretation, Congress can act to redraw or replace the statute. This has been the experience since 1937, when the federal courts began to restrict their overseer's role. From 1945 to 1957, Supreme Court interpretations of statutes had been reversed, in effect, by subsequent statutes in twenty-one instances. Reversals were most likely when Congress acted to restore a widespread consensus that had been upset by a court decision. Reversal was most predictable when the groups affected by the Court's decision were politically articulate and united in support of action by Congress; Court decisions that met with less opposition were very rarely upset by Congress.[76] William N. Eskridge finds substantial attention in Congress to court decisions, but points out that attention does not necessarily lead to overrides.[77]

TABLE 13.2   Type of congressional action after U.S. Supreme Court decisions holding legislation unconstitutional within four years after enactment, 1803–1955

| Congressional Action | Major Policy | Minor Policy | Total |
|---|---|---|---|
| Reverse Court's policy | 17 | 2 | 19 |
| None | 0 | 12 | 12 |
| Other | 6 | 1 | 7 |
| Total | 23 | 15 | 38 |

SOURCE: Adapted from Robert Dahl, "Decision-Making in a Democracy: The Supreme Court as National Policy-Maker," *Journal of Public Law*, VI (Fall 1957), 290.

FIGURE 13.2    Congressional reactions, 1950–78, to U.S.
Supreme Court statutory interpretations
on issues concerning labor and antitrust

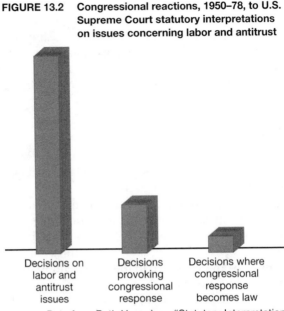

Decisions on labor and antitrust issues

Decisions provoking congressional response

Decisions where congressional response becomes law

SOURCE: Data from Beth Henschen, "Statutory Interpretation of the Supreme Court Congressional Response," *American Politics Quarterly*, XI (October 1983), 443–45.

At least in two policy areas, congressional reaction was found to be rare. In a study of labor and antitrust decisions from 1950 to 1972, Beth M. Henschen found that only 12 percent of the court decisions stimulated a legislative response. Of these, about 90 percent were designed either to modify or reverse the court decisions.[78] Figure 13.2 provides a graphic illustration.

## Attacks on the Courts and Judges

The legislative reaction to judicial decisions may be to lash out at the courts and judges. Many controversial court decisions are followed by legislative attempts to restrict the activities of the courts. A common proposal would require the courts to have more than a simple majority vote before they could declare legislative acts unconstitutional. From 1900 to 1936, thirty-seven proposals were introduced in Congress to limit the power of the courts to declare legislative acts unconstitutional; of these, twenty-five required more than a simple majority to invalidate legislative acts.[79] Proposals to restrict judicial review reached their apogee during the crisis over New Deal legislation. Table 13.3 shows something of the dimensions of congressional antagonism toward the Court in the mid-1930s.

Other, more recent proposals involved alteration of selection and removal procedures and changing the jurisdiction of the courts.

Unable to secure the necessary two-thirds majority to propose a constitutional amendment [dealing with mandatory school busing, prayer in schools, and abortion], various senators and representatives who oppose these Supreme Court decisions have attempted to limit the federal courts' jurisdiction over future prayer, busing, and abortion controversies.[80]

Congress passed few of these proposals. The history of legislative attacks on the courts in the states is about the same. Criticism of the courts is sometimes intense, but direct legislative action seldom results.

Legislatures can also indicate their displeasure indirectly. Thus, in 1964, when Congress voted pay raises for federal judges, Supreme Court judges received a smaller increase ($4,500) than the circuit judges ($7,500). The explanation for this behavior was seemingly simple: A majority in Congress had strong objections to some Supreme Court decisions.

Judges sometimes can defend themselves. In 1980, the Supreme Court found that Congress could not rescind a cost-of-living pay adjustment for judges after the increment has gone into effect. Congress could do so if the scheduled increases had not yet become effective.[81]

The record of legislative response to judicial decision making can be spelled out, but analysis of why these reactions occur and explanations of their success or failure are more difficult. Each major judicial decision is likely to produce new controversy both inside and outside legislative assemblies. Yet the response is seldom translated into effective action. One basic explanation for this is that courts are able to temper their controversial decisions by more restricted action in subsequent cases. In this manner, criticism can be deflected. For example, the Supreme Court's decision in *Stuart* v. *Laird* helped soften the impact of *Marbury* v. *Madison*. In the late 1820s and early 1830s, the Supreme Court rendered decisions modifying earlier and stronger statements on the subjects of impairing obligation of contract and federal

TABLE 13.3   Proposed constitutional amendments designed to limit or deny the U.S. Supreme Court's power to declare acts of Congress unconstitutional, 1935–39

| Year | Number of Amendments Proposed |
|------|-------------------------------|
| 1935 | 3 |
| 1936 | 3 |
| 1937 | 15 |
| 1939 | 1 |

SOURCE: Data from U.S. Congress, Senate, *Proposed Amendments to the Constitution of the United States of America*, 87th Cong., 2nd sess., Doc. 163 (1963).

control of commerce.[82] Much the same thing occurred in the so-called New Deal cases when the famous "switch in time that saved nine" took place. In four months, in 1937, the Supreme Court upheld the validity of several key statutes and thus apparently saved itself from a successful executive and legislative attack.[83] Controversy over the school segregation cases was somewhat diminished by the behavior of the courts in applying these rulings to specific situations.

The failure of most attacks on the courts is explained also by noting that key provisions of the Constitution often have no self-evident meaning. Reasonable persons will differ in their interpretations. Moreover, court decisions rarely antagonize all segments of society. Decisions that offend some groups will please others. Generally, when agreement is lacking in a society, successful opposition to the courts is less likely. The absence of a "unified enemy" is seen most clearly when the courts have declared state legislative acts unconstitutional. Attacks on the Marshall courts were blunted in part for this reason. The same reasoning helps to explain the failures of the Populists and Progressives in the early twentieth century in their efforts to attack the courts.

Finally, legislative bodies are generally organized more to prevent action than to promote it. A successful attack on the courts depends on the ability of legislatures to transcend their typical patterns of behavior. This action is unlikely unless legislative authority is challenged directly or unless powerful organized groups are prodding the legislature to act.[84]

In a sweeping survey of experience in American history, Stuart Nagel finds:

> The factors that have an affirmative correlation with the success of Court-curbing bills . . . [are] as follows: (1) sponsored by the majority party in Congress, (2) party split between the Court and Congress, (3) crisis present and allegedly made more severe by the Court's decisions, (4) public and pressure group support, (5) northern sponsored attack, (6) introduced in the Senate, (7) limited in purpose, and (8) has presidential support and cohesive congressional leadership.[85]

Michael L. Solimine and James L. Walker underscore the difficulty in finding patterns: ". . . the reversal process is still sporadic, not obviously predictable, and relatively rare."[86]

These correlations carry us beyond mere conjecture, but for purposes of causal analysis, Walter Murphy's general conclusion must probably suffice:

> Recognizing the potential threat to their own policy aims which the authority of the High Bench poses, members of Congress and executive officials will continue to view judicial power with a suspicion which will turn to hostility whenever they themselves or articulate segments of their constituencies disapprove

of specific decisions, or when these officials fear that their own policy-making prerogatives are being threatened.[87]

Events in 1990–91 illustrated the accuracy of these conclusions. Members of Congress, moving to alter specific Court decisions concerning civil rights in hiring and in employment, found mustering a sufficient majority to be difficult. In 1989, the Supreme Court rendered a series of decisions dealing with such questions as appropriate testing procedures for employment and racial harassment on the job. The thrust of these decisions was to define the rights of minorities more narrowly. Congressional efforts to reverse these Court decisions required two years of intense bargaining and compromise. These particular efforts were so difficult because both society in general and Congress in particular remained divided, and various factions sought to gain partisan advantage.

## LEGISLATURES, COURTS, AND THE POLITICAL PROCESS

Legislative-judicial relations in the United States are ordinarily marked by harmony and mutual indifference. Such comity is hardly surprising since both legislative and judicial institutions tend to reflect the dominant attitudes and policies in society at a given time. When conflict does occur, the courts tend to be least successful against enduring cohesive political majorities and most successful "against a 'weak' majority; e.g., a dead one, a transient one, a fragile one, or one weakly united upon a policy of subordinate importance."[88] The judiciary is most likely to be successful when it avoids the critical, highly charged political controversies and deals with less substantial issues.[89] Judges demonstrate an awareness of their position in the limitations that they impose upon themselves. These range from a judicial presumption of the constitutionality of statutes to a practice of hearing only cases properly brought before them. Judges avoid "political questions"— that is, questions that they feel are more appropriately resolved by the executive and legislative branches. If possible, they decide cases on other than constitutional grounds. If the courts generally choose to avoid conflict with the legislative branch, it is likely that the judiciary will frequently hold a subordinate position among political institutions.

Ultimately, the political influence of the courts rests heavily on their "unique legitimacy." In public opinion polls, the Supreme Court ranks high in public confidence; Congress ranks lower (see Table 13.4). If popular support of the courts is insufficient to permit them to challenge the legislatures steadily, their standing is nevertheless useful in helping the courts to defend themselves against legislative onslaught. Despite an overwhelming victory

**TABLE 13.4   Public confidence in the U.S. Supreme Court and Congress, 1998**

|  | Great Deal/Quite a Lot | Some | Very Little/None |
|---|---|---|---|
| Supreme Court | 50% | 34% | 13% |
| Congress | 28 | 48 | 22 |

SOURCE: *The Gallup Poll Monthly*, June 1998, p. 22.

in 1936 and the presence of a Democratic majority in Congress, President Roosevelt failed in his attempt to "pack" the Supreme Court in 1937. One explanation for his defeat rests on the "magic of the courts."[90] This unique legitimacy serves other functions besides insulating the courts. In upholding legislative acts, courts can assist legislatures by legitimizing the compromises and practical decisions of the political process.

Judges interpret the generalizations of legislative statutes outside the gaze of the public. Only rarely do the courts challenge legislative bodies and even more rarely do they do so successfully. Unusual instances, as in the school segregation decisions, sometimes place the courts at the center of the lawmaking process. The courts, then, can act as more than a moral stimulus to the legislature in particular and the nation in general. But the role of the courts should be put in perspective. In particular interpretations of law or in specific decisions about what the Constitution means, the courts can be influential in checking legislatures. Yet that is the exception. Much of what Congress and the state legislatures do faces neither scrutiny nor challenge by the courts. The courts are occasional players and not dominating participants in the legislative process.

# NOTES

1. William Mischler and Reginald S. Sheehan see the Supreme Court over the last forty years as "highly responsive to public opinion." "The Supreme Court as a Counter Majoritarian Institution? The Impact of Public Opinion on Supreme Court Decisions," *American Political Science Review*, 87 (March 1993), 93. Wayne McIntosh sees litigation as another form of political activity: "Private Use of a Public Forum: A Long-Range View of the Dispute Processing Role of Courts," *American Political Science Review*, 77 (December 1983), 991–1010. The importance of seeing the Supreme Court as both a legal and political body is stressed by H. W. Perry, Jr., *Deciding to Decide: Agenda Setting in the United States Supreme Court* (Cambridge, MA: Harvard University Press, 1991). Lawrence Baum, *The Puzzle of Judicial Behavior* (Ann Arbor: University of Michigan Press, 1997), applauds progress in research on the courts, but finds that fully adequate explanations for judicial behavior remain a challenge.

2. "Foreword: The Reapportionment Case," *Harvard Law Review*, LXXVI (November 1962), 67. Copyright © 1962 by the Harvard Law Review Association.

3. *New York Times*, June 8, 1965, p. 34.

4. This discussion applies only to the so-called constitutional courts. Legislative courts—those created by Congress on the basis of its authority granted in Article I—tend to be more specialized.

5. Wayne Selfridge, in a study of the Senate confirmation process for Abe Fortas, Clement

Haynsworth, G. Harrold Carswell, and William Rehnquist, concludes that once a nomination becomes controversial, ideology becomes a major predictor of the votes of senators. "Ideology as a Factor in Senate Consideration of Supreme Court Nominations," *Journal of Politics*, 42 (May 1980), 560–67. John Massaro, looking at Supreme Court nominations in the Johnson, Nixon, and Reagan administrations, finds failure due to ideology and timing, the two conventional explanations, but also to presidential mismanagement of the confirmation process. *Supremely Political* (Albany: State University of New York Press, 1990). Confirmation disputes have historically been a political process according to John Anthony Maltese, *The Selling of Supreme Court Nominees* (Baltimore: Johns Hopkins University Press, 1995). A convincing case that constituency pressure must be taken into account in Senate voting on judicial confirmations is L. Marvin Overby, Beth N. Henschen, Michael H. Walsh, and Julie Strauss, "Courting Constituents? An Analysis of the Senate Confirmation Vote on Justice Clarence Thomas," *American Political Science Review*, 86 (December 1992), 997–1003. See also L. Marvin Overby and Beth M. Henschen, "Race Trumps Gender?" *American Politics Quarterly*, 22 (January 1994), 62–73; L. Marvin Overby, Beth M. Henschen, Julie Strauss, and Michael H. Walsh, "African-American Constituents and Supreme Court Nominees," *Political Research Quarterly*, 47 (December 1994), 839–55. The problems and politics of judicial selection are illuminated in National Legal Center for the Public Interest, *Judicial Selection: Merit, Ideology, and Politics* (Washington, DC: National Legal Center for the Public Interest, 1990). The role of interest groups in confirmation proceedings is probed in Christine DeGregorio and Jack E. Rossoti, "Resources, Attitudes and Strategies: Interest Group Participation in the Bork Confirmation Process," *American Review of Politics*, XV (Spring 1994), 1–19. See also Gregory A. Caldeira and John R. Wright, "Lobbying for Justice: Organized Interests, Supreme Court Nominations, and the United States Senate," *American Journal of Political Science*, XLII (April 1998), 499–523. The role of interest groups in confirmations may be different for the lower courts. See Lauren M. Cohen, "Interest Groups and Federal Judicial Appointments," *Judicature*, LXXXII (November–December 1998), 119–23. Stephen L. Carter asserts in *The Confirmation Mess* that the confirmation process has become a political circus (New York: Basic Books, 1994). Mark Silverstein argues that the contemporary confirmation process with its widespread media coverage and public participation does not necessarily lead to the highest quality candidates being nominated and confirmed. *Judicious Choices: The New Politics of Supreme Court Confirmations* (New York: W. W. Norton, 1994). On the politics of the nomination process, see Glen S. Krutz, Richard Fleisher, and Jon R. Bond, "From Abe Fortas to Zoe Baird: Why Some Presidential Nominations Fail in the Senate," *American Political Science Review*, XCII (December 1998), 871–81. See also David Yalof, *Pursuit of Justice: Presidential Politics and the Selection of Supreme Court Nominees* (Chicago: University of Chicago Press, 1999). Robert A. Katzmann argues that interest-group lobbying and the role of the media now must be included in any analysis of judicial nominations. *Courts and Congress* (Washington, DC: Brookings Institution Press/Governance Institute, 1997), p. 18. Bryon J. Moraski and Charles R. Shipan argue that most presidential nominees to the Supreme Court are confirmed by the Senate because presidents, aware of political constraints, act strategically when they make nominations. "The Politics of Supreme Court Nominations: A Theory of Institutional Constraints and Choices," *American Journal of Political Science*, XLIII (1999), 1069–1095.

6. Senator Warren Rudman (R., NH) was quoted in the media as attributing his positive vote in the Thomas confirmation to his desire to continue to influence the appointment of federal judges and to get federal money for New Hampshire. *Pittsburgh Post Gazette*, April 12, 1996, p. A16.

7. Whether a nominee will change the political balance of the Court affects his or her confirmation chances; see P. S. Ruckman, Jr., "The Supreme Court, Critical Nominations, and the Senate Confirmation Process," *Journal of Politics*, 55 (August 1993), 793–805. Lilliard E. Richardson and John M. Scheb II link the appointment of judges who turn out to be moderates in civil rights cases to divided government at the time of appointment. "Divided Government and the Supreme Court: Judicial Behavior in Civil Rights and Liberties Cases, 1954–89," *American Politics Quarterly*, 21 (October 1993), 458–72. Sheldon Goldman shows that divided government can affect how quickly nominees to lower courts are confirmed. "The Judicial Confirmation Crisis and the Clinton Presidency," *Presidential Studies Quarterly*, XXVIII (Fall 1998), 838–84.

8. Hartley and Holmes argue that divided government is of no great consequence for explaining the percentage of lower court judges confirmed by the Senate. Roger E. Hartley and Lisa M. Holmes, "Decreasing Senate Scrutiny of Lower Federal Court Nominees," *Judicature,* LXXX (June 1997), 274–78. Slotnick and Goldman warn that "defeat" should not be measured only by rejection of nominees. Delays in the process and failure to bring nominations to a vote are also useful measures. Elliot Slotnick and Sheldon Goldman, "Congress and the Courts: A Case of Casting," in *Great Theatre,* ed. Herbert F. Weisberg and Samuel C. Patterson (Cambridge: 1998), pp. 197–223. The details of this selection process are described in Daniel J. Meador, "Problems and Uncertainties in the Appointment of Federal Judges," *Miller Center Journal,* V (Spring 1998), 41–50. A thorough study of the selection process for lower court judges is Sheldon Goldman, *Picking Federal Judges: Lower Court Selection from Roosevelt Through Reagan* (New Haven, CT: Yale University Press, 1997).

9. Shelden D. Elliott, *Improving Our Courts* (New York: Oceana, 1959), p. 163.

10. Ibid., p. 164. For a table providing data on constitutional and statutory aspects of judicial selection and tenure in the states from 1776 to the early 1940s, see Evan Haynes, *The Selection and Tenure of Judges* (National Conference of Judicial Councils, 1944, n.p.), pp. 101–35.

11. Larry Berkson, Scott Beller, and Michele Grimaldo, *Judicial Selection in the United States* (Chicago: American Judicature Society, 1981), p. 6.

12. "What Difference Does Method of Judicial Selection Make?" *Justice System Journal,* 5 (1979–80), 25–44. Glick and Emmert find no correlation between the type of selection system and superior judges. Henry F. Glick and Craig F. Emmert, "Selection Systems and Judicial Characteristics: The Recruitment of State Supreme Court Judges," *Judicature,* 70 (December–January 1987), 229–35. C. K. Rowland and Bridget Jeffery Todd argue that policy consequences do accrue from the types of judges appointed by different presidents. "Where You Stand Depends on Who Sits: Platform Promises and Judicial Gatekeeping in the Federal District Courts," *Journal of Politics,* 53 (February 1991), 175–85. One study finds that the method of judge selection does correlate with the perceptions of judges concerning increases in the number of individual rights cases litigated under state constitutions during the early 1980s. Peter L. Collins, Peter J. Galie, and John Kincaid, "State High Courts, State Constitutions, and Individual Rights Litigation Since 1980," *Publius,* 16 (Summer 1986), 151, 158. An article linking judicial activism in the states with the method of selection of judges is James P. Wenzel, Shaun Bowler, and Donald Lanque, "Legislating from the State Bench," *American Politics Quarterly,* XXV (July 1997), 363–79.

13. Russell R. Wheeler and A. Leo Levin, *Judicial Discipline and Removal in the United States* (Washington, DC: Federal Judicial Center, 1979), p. 11. More recently, Judges Harry E. Claiborne, Alcee L. Hastings, and Walter L. Nixon were impeached, convicted, and removed from office. For a complete list of impeached federal judges, see Michael J. Remington, "Impeachment," in *Encyclopedia of the United States Congress,* ed. Donald C. Bacon, Roger H. Davidson, and Morton Keller (New York: Simon & Schuster, 1995), p. 1102. See also Emily Van Tassel and Paul Finkelman, *Impeachable Offenses: A Documentary History from 1787 to the Present* (Washington, DC: Congressional Quarterly Press, 1999). A chronological study of each Senate impeachment trial is Eleanore Bushnell, *Crimes, Follies, and Misfortunes: The Federal Impeachment Trials* (Champaign: University of Illinois Press, 1992).

14. Congress has investigated the conduct of nearly sixty federal judges. In most cases, the judges were absolved of impeachable conduct and formal proceedings were not undertaken. See Carl L. Shipley, "Legislative Control of Judicial Behavior," *Law and Contemporary Problems,* XXXV (Winter 1970), 192. In 1993, the Supreme Court ruled that the Senate had authority to conduct impeachment trials as it saw fit. The courts would not second-guess the Senate on these questions of procedure.

15. Susan B. Carbon and Larry C. Berkson, *Judicial Retention Elections in the United States* (Chicago: American Judicature Society, 1980), p. 24.

16. The impact of politics on administration of the federal courts is explored in Peter Graham Fish, *The Politics of Federal Judicial Administration* (Princeton, NJ: Princeton University Press, 1973). Jon Bond states that the most realistic chance of adding new judges comes if the president and a majority of Congress are of the same political party and if such proposals come early in a president's term. "The Politics of Court Structure," *Law and Politics Quarterly,* 2 (April 1980), 181. One study found that 84 percent of the expansion of the federal appellate

courts occurred when the president and majority of Congress were of the same political party. John M. DeFigueiredo and Emerson H. Tiller, "Congressional Control of the Courts: A Theoretical and Empirical Analysis of Expansion of the Federal Judiciary," *Journal of Law and Economics*, XXXIX (October 1996), 435–62.

17. Thomas E. Walker and Deborah J. Barrow, "Funding the Federal Judiciary: The Congressional Connection," *Judicature*, 69 (June–July 1985), 50.

18. "The Determinants of Legislators' Support for Judicial Reorganization," *American Politics Quarterly*, 8 (April 1980), 221–36.

19. *Manion Forum*, July 14, 1963, p. 3. For a series of articles on issues involved in congressional attempts to regulate Supreme Court jurisdiction, see *Villanova Law Review*, 27 (May 1982), 893–1076.

20. Beth N. Henschen and Edward I. Sidlow, "The Regulation of State Court Systems Through Rulemaking," paper presented at the meeting of the Midwest Political Science Association, 1985, p. 9.

21. 144 U.S. 1. See Frank E. Horack, Jr., *Statutes and Statutory Construction*, 3rd ed. (Chicago: Callaghan, 1943), I, pp. 126–28.

22. *Powell* v. *McCormack*, 395 U.S. 486.

23. *Clinton* v. *City of New York*, 118 S. Ct. 2091 (1998).

24. *U.S.* v. *Brewster*, 408 U.S. 501 (1972).

25. *Gravel* v. *U.S.*, 408 U.S. 606 (1972).

26. *Davis* v. *Passman*, 442 U.S. 238 (1979).

27. *Hutchinson* v. *Proxmire*, 443 U.S. 11 (1979).

28. Eva R. Rubin, "Congress in the Courts: Interinstitutional Lawsuits and the Separation of Powers," paper presented at the meeting of the Southern Political Science Association, 1986.

29. See the Pocket Veto Case of 1929, 279 U.S. 655; *Wright* v. *United States* (1936), 302 U.S. 583; *Kennedy* v. *Sampson* (1974), 511 F. 2nd 430; *Kennedy* v. *Jones* (1976), 412 F. Supp. 353; *Barnes* v. *Kline* (1985), 759 F. 2nd 41 (1985).

30. Felix Frankfurter and James M. Landis, *The Business of the Supreme Court* (New York: Macmillan, 1928), p. 2.

31. R. Shep Melnick, *Regulation and the Courts* (Washington, DC: Brookings Institution, 1983), p. 374. David O'Brien states that in the 1990s about 40 percent of Supreme Court cases dealt with the interpretation of congressional legislation. "Judicial Review" in *The Encyclopedia of the United States Congress*, ed. Donald C. Bacon, Roger H. Davidson, and Morton Keller (New York: Simon & Schuster, 1995), p. 1186.

32. Quoted in *Congressional Quarterly Weekly Report*, March 30, 1996, p. 865.

33. Felix Frankfurter, "Some Reflections on the Reading of Statutes," *The Record*, X (June 1947), 213–15. This analysis was underlined in 1999 as the Supreme Court grappled with the precise meaning of the Americans with Disabilities Act of 1990.

34. Frankfurter, "Some Reflections," p. 224. The complexities involved in interpreting statutes are emphasized in *Judges and Legislators: Toward Institutional Comity*, ed. Robert A. Katzmann (Washington, DC: Brookings Institution, 1988), see especially pp. 170–75. See also Katzmann, *Courts and Judges*, pp. 46–48. Marc N. Garber and Kurt A. Wimmer argue that presidential signing statements designed to interpret legislation should not be used by the courts to establish legislative intent. President Reagan, they suggest, tried to reinterpret the language of legislation to coincide with his own views. "Presidential Signing Statements as Interpretations of Legislative Intent: An Executive Aggrandizement of Power," *Harvard Journal on Legislation*, 24 (Summer 1987), 363–95. His view is shared by William D. Popkin, "Judicial Use of Presidential Legislative History," *Indiana Law Journal*, LXVI (1991), 699–722.

35. "Judicial Use of Legislative History and Intent in Statutory Interpretation," *Legislative Studies Quarterly*, 10 (August 1985), 353–71.

36. This story is told most effectively by Susan Gluck Mezey, *No Longer Disabled: The Federal Courts and the Politics of Social Security Disability* (New York: Greenwood Press, 1988).

37. For two discussions of the evolution and functions of judicial review in the United States, see Jesse H. Choper, *Judicial Review and the National Political Process* (Chicago: University of

Chicago Press, 1980); and Christopher Wolfe, *The Rise of Modern Judicial Review: From Constitutional Interpretation to Judge-Made Law* (New York: Basic Books, 1986).

38. Alfred H. Kelly and Winfred Harbison, *The American Constitution* (New York: W. W. Norton, 1963), p. 229; and Charles Warren, *The Supreme Court in United States History* (Boston: Little, Brown, 1926), I, p. 263.

39. *Calder* v. *Bull*, 3 Dall. 386.

40. *Ware* v. *Hylton*, 3 Dall. 199.

41. *Marbury* v. *Madison*, 1 Cr. 137.

42. *Fletcher* v. *Peck*, 6 Cr. 87.

43. *Stuart* v. *Laird*, 1 Cr. 299.

44. 19 How. 393 (1857).

45. Walter F. Murphy, *Congress and the Court* (Chicago: University of Chicago Press, 1962), pp. 29–31.

46. *Adair* v. *United States*, 208 U.S. 161 (1908).

47. *Adkins* v. *Children's Hospital*, 261 U.S. 161 (1923).

48. *Johnson* v. *Robinson*, 415 U.S. 361 (1974).

49. *Kleppe* v. *New Mexico*, 426 U.S. 529 (1976).

50. *Usery* v. *Turner Elkhorn Mining Company*, 428 U.S. 1 (1976).

51. Stephen P. Strickland, "Congress, the Supreme Court and Public Policy," *American University Law Review*, XVIII (March 1969), 298. Shipan claims that when Congress inserts provisions for judicial review into a statute, it does so for political, not technical legal, considerations. Charles R. Shipan, *Designing Judicial Review: Interest Groups, Congress, and Communications Policy* (Ann Arbor: University of Michigan Press, 1997).

52. Congressional Research Service, *The Constitution of the United States of America: Analysis and Interpretation* (Washington, DC: U.S. Government Printing Office, 1987), p. 1921.

53. Ibid., pp. 1927–940.

54. Kelly and Harbison, *The American Constitution*, p. 541.

55. John B. Gates links U.S. Supreme Court invalidation of state policies to periods of partisan realignment and socioeconomic changes. "Partisan Realignment, Unconstitutional State Policies, and the U.S. Supreme Court, 1837–1964," *American Journal of Political Science*, XXXI (May 1982), 259–80.

56. David M. O'Brien, *Storm Center: The Supreme Court in American Politics*, 3rd ed. (New York: W. W. Norton, 1993), p. 63. See also Gregory A. Caldeira and Donald McCrone, "Of Time and Judicial Activism: A Study of the U.S. Supreme Court, 1800–1973," in *Supreme Court, Activism and Restraint*, ed. Stephen C. Halpern and Charles M. Lamb (Lexington, MA: Lexington Books, 1982), especially pp. 115–23.

57. Lawrence Baum, *The Supreme Court*, 6th ed. (Washington, DC: Congressional Quarterly Press, 1998), p. 203.

58. Hans A. Linde, "Observations of a State Court Judge," in Katzmann, *Judges and Legislators*, p. 117.

59. Quoted in G. Alan Tarr and Mary Cornelia Porter, *State Supreme Courts in State and Nation* (New Haven, CT: Yale University Press, 1988), p. 44.

60. Oliver P. Field, "Unconstitutional Legislation in Indiana," *Indiana Law Journal*, XVII (December 1941), 102; Arthur W. Bromage, *State Government and Administration in the United States* (New York: Harper & Row, 1936), p. 321; and Margaret Virginia Nelson, *A Study of Judicial Review in Virginia* (New York: Columbia University Press, 1947), pp. 204–205.

61. Arthur Holcombe, *State Government in the United States* (New York: Macmillan, 1926), p. 431.

62. Ibid., p. 434.

63. Nelson, *A Study of Judicial Review*, p. 204; Franklin A. Smith, *Judicial Review of Legislation in New York, 1906–1938* (New York: Columbia University Press, 1952), p. 223; and Katherine B. Fite and Louis B. Rubenstein, "Curbing the Supreme Court—State Experiences and Federal Proposals," *Michigan Law Review*, XXXV (March 1937), 774–80.

64. *Judicial Review of Legislation in Ten Selected States* (Bloomington: Indiana University, Bureau of Government Research, 1943). The states are listed on p. 5. A chronological table of statutes declared unconstitutional in each state is provided on p. 14.

65. "Judicial Review of Legislation in Utah," *Utah Law Review*, IV (Spring 1954), 61.

66. Field, *Indiana Law Journal*, XVII, 104.

67. Nelson, *A Study of Judicial Review*, p. 202.

68. Peter J. Galie, "The Other Supreme Courts: Judicial Activism Among State Supreme Courts," *Syracuse Law Review*, XXXIII (1982), 731–93. The impact of state supreme courts on public policymaking is analyzed in *State Supreme Courts, Policymakers in the Federal System*, ed. Mary Cornelia Porter and G. Alan Tarr (Westport, CT: Greenwood Press, 1982).

69. This episode is detailed in Telford Taylor, *Grand Inquest* (New York: Simon & Schuster, 1955), pp. 140–47.

70. See Lori Hausegger and Lawrence Baum, "Behind the Scenes: The Supreme Court and Congress in Statutory Interpretation," in *Great Theatre*, ed. Herbert F. Weisberg and Samuel C. Patterson (Cambridge: Cambridge University Press, 1998), 224–38. Bawn and Shipan argue that failed attempts at overrides can be explained by internal divisions in Congress and by uncertainty about the precise policy preferences of those involved in policymaking. Kathleen Bawn and Charles R. Shipan, "Congressional Responses to Supreme Court decisions: Imperfect Anticipation and Institutional Constraints," manuscript, July 1997.

71. *Chisholm v. Georgia*, 2 Dall. 419.

72. 19 How. 393 (1857).

73. 157 U.S. 429 (1895).

74. M. A. Musmanno, *Proposed Amendments to the Constitution*, 70th Cong., 2nd sess., H. Doc. 551, 1929, p. 212.

75. *Oregon v. Mitchell*, 400 U.S. 112 (1970).

76. James Meernik and Joseph Ignani, "Judicial Review and Coordinate Construction of the Constitution," *American Journal of Political Science*, XLI (April 1997), 447–67.

77. William N. Eskridge, Jr., "Overriding Supreme Court Statutory Interpretation Decisions," *Yale Law Journal*, CI (Spring 1991), 331–445, shows that congressional attempts at overrides are not rare. See especially his data on p. 338. See "Congressional Reversal of Supreme Court Decisions, 1945–1957," *Harvard Law Review*, LXXI (May 1958), 1326–1336. Court-Congress interactions on the issues of school busing, school prayer, and abortion are discussed in Edward Keynes with Randall K. Miller, *The Court* vs. *Congress: Prayer, Busing, and Abortion* (Durham, NC: Duke University Press, 1989). Meernik and Ignani studied 569 cases between 1954 and 1990 where federal or state laws had been declared unconstitutional. In 78 percent of these, there was no congressional attempt to reverse the decisions; in those instances where reversal was attempted, some 33 percent passed. James Meernik and Joseph Ignani, "Judicial Review and Coordinate Construction of the Constitution." See also Joseph Ignani and James Meernik, "Explaining Congressional Attempts to Reverse Supreme Court Decisions," *Political Research Quarterly*, XLVII (June 1994), 353–71; and James Meernik and Joseph Ignani, "Congressional Attacks on Supreme Court Rulings Involving Unconstitutional State Laws," *Political Research Quarterly*, XLVIII (March 1995), 43–59. Ignani, Meernik, and King argue that political imputs are basic to explaining congressional responses. Joseph Ignani, James Meernik, and Kimi Lynn King, "Statutory Construction and Congressional Response," *American Politics Quarterly*, XXVI (October 1998), 459–84. The Supreme Court, at times, actually invites Congress to reverse Court statutory interpretations. See Lori Hausegger and Lawrence Baum, "Inviting Congressional Action: A Study of Supreme Court Motivations in Statutory Interpretation," *American Journal of Political Science*, XLIII (January 1999), 162–85. See also Richard A. Paschal, "The Continuing Colloquy: Congress and the Finality of the Supreme Court," *Journal of Law and Politics*, VIII (Fall 1991), 143–226.

78. Beth Henschen, "Statutory Interpretation of the Supreme Court, Congressional Response," *American Politics Quarterly*, 11 (October 1983), 441–58.

79. Fite and Rubenstein, "Curbing the Supreme Court," pp. 763–64; Musmanno, *Proposed Amendments*, 94.

80. Keynes with Miller, *The Court* vs. *Congress*, p. xv.

81. *United States* v. *Will*, 449 U.S. 200 (1980).

82. Murphy, *Congress and the Court*, p. 27. For a related analysis, see Stuart S. Nagel, *The Legal Process from a Behavioral Perspective* (Homewood, IL: Dorsey Press, 1969), p. 278.

83. Kelly and Harbison, *The American Constitution*, pp. 759–64. Henry J. Abraham points out that the Supreme Court does in fact modify its own decisions on constitutional questions; it did so in 169 instances between 1937 and 1997. *The Judicial Process*, 7th ed. (New York: Oxford University Press, 1998), p. 366.

84. Clark and McGuire argue that congressional responses to Supreme Court decisions are subject to the same pressures and considerations that affect Congress more generally. John A. Clark and Kevin T. McGuire, "Congress, the Supreme Court, and the Flag," *Political Research Quarterly*, XLVIII (December 1996), 771–82. See also Hausegger and Baum, in *Great Theatre*, Chap. 10. Legislators are not frequently successful in challenging court decisions, but court decisions can stimulate legislators to rethink a problem. For evidence, see Beth M. Henschen and Edward I. Sidlow, "The Supreme Court and the Congressional Agenda-Setting Process," *Journal of Law and Politics*, V (Summer 1989), 685–724.

85. Nagel, *The Legal Process*, p. 279. David W. Brady, John Schmidhauser, and Larry L. Berg present evidence suggesting that those members of Congress who are lawyers do not protect the Supreme Court differently from their non-lawyer colleagues. "House Lawyers and Support for the Supreme Court," *Journal of Politics*, XXXV (August 1973), 724–29. Mark C. Miller disagrees, arguing that the legal training of some members of Congress does make some difference in their attitudes toward the courts. "Lawyers in Congress: What Difference Does It Make?" *Congress and the Presidency*, XX (Spring 1993), 1–23.

86. "The Next Word: Congressional Responses to Supreme Court Statutory Decisions," *Temple Law Review*, LXV (Summer 1992), 438.

87. Murphy, *Congress and the Court*, p. 268.

88. Robert Dahl, "Decision-Making in a Democracy," *Journal of Public Law*, VI (Fall 1957), 286. Epstein and Knight suggest that even if the Court seeks to anticipate the reactions of Congress, the judges "do not know with certainty" what Congress will do. Lee Epstein and Jack Knight, *The Choices Justices Make* (Washington, DC: Congressional Quarterly Press, 1998), pp. 140–141. See also Barry Friedman, "Attacks on Judges, Why They Fail," *Judicature*, LXXXI (January–February 1998), 150–155.

89. Robert McCloskey, *The American Supreme Court* (Chicago: University of Chicago Press, 1960), p. 229. Hausseger and Baum, in *Great Theatre*, pp. 233–35, offer three hypotheses to explain why Congress overrides some Supreme Court decisions but largely ignores the rest.

90. John Schmidhauser and Larry L. Berg find that patterns of congressional voting on judiciary issues are not markedly different from "normal" patterns of voting. *The Supreme Court and Congress: Conflict and Interaction, 1945–1968* (New York: Free Press, 1972), Chap. 7. Joseph Tanenhaus and Walter F. Murphy find substantial diffuse support for the Supreme Court, "Patterns of Public Support for the Supreme Court: A Panel Study," *Journal of Politics*, XLIII (February 1981), 24–39. Gregory A. Caldeira argues that popular confidence in the Supreme Court does have some relationship to Court behavior on policy issues. "Neither the Purse nor the Sword: Dynamics of Public Confidence in the Supreme Court," *American Political Science Review*, LXXX (December 1986), 1209–1226. John M. Scheb II and William Lyons provide additional data on public perceptions of Congress and the Supreme Court. "Public Perceptions of the Supreme Court in the 1990's," *Judicature*, LXXXII (September–October 1998), 66–69.

# 14

# The Legislative Process: Problems and Perspectives

The responsibilities of the American legislature are numerous and varied. In broad terms, the legislature lends legitimacy to government by being responsive and accountable to the people. In the process of representing the people, the legislature helps to illuminate and resolve conflict and to build consensus. It listens to grievances, addresses public problems, explores alternatives, protects or alters past decisions and policies, considers future requirements, and does what the people are not organized to do for themselves. And not surprisingly, it also thinks about itself, its public standing, how well it is doing its job, and how it might do things differently.

## EFFORTS TO REFORM THE LEGISLATURE

### Congress

Every now and then Congress turns to reform, seeking ways to improve its organization and better methods for handling persistent problems. Numerous changes have been made since the first Congress assembled in 1789, but only a few have had a major impact on the congressional system.

The principal object of reform has been the committee system. Change has taken two forms. In the first, occurring in the early nineteenth century, Congress abandoned its preoccupation with creating numerous special committees and moved to a more orderly system of standing committees. The second involved a continuing struggle to streamline the structure by eliminating those committees no longer useful. Until recently, battles to cut out committees were more often lost than won. Early in the twentieth century, there were well over one hundred standing committees in the House and Senate. A good many had lost their reason for existence and others plainly were moribund; ambiguous and conflicting jurisdictions compounded the problem. A number of committees were erased in the 1920s, but it was not until 1946 that a significant paring down took place. The Legislative Reorganization Act of that year reduced the number of standing committees in the House from forty-eight to nineteen and in the Senate from thirty-three to fifteen. Currently, following a shake-up in the 104th Congress (1995–96), there are nineteen standing committees in the House and seventeen in the Senate.

Many changes in congressional organization and practices in the nineteenth century had the function of centralizing authority. The Rules Committee of the House, for example, began its rise to power in 1841, when it was given the power to report at any time. Later on, in 1858, its position was enhanced further when the Speaker was installed as its chair. Its sphere of influence was widened again in 1883 when it was given the power to report special orders fixing the terms of floor debate. During the tenure of Speakers Reed and Cannon, the Committee on Rules became the principal agency for controlling the House.

Another change in congressional organization worth noting occurred in 1865, when a separate Appropriations Committee was formed in the House; responsibility for appropriations formerly had been entrusted to the Committee on Ways and Means. Conflict over the authority of the Appropriations Committee soon developed, however, and in 1885 the House chose to vest the power to report appropriations bills in a number of committees, one for each of the executive departments. Not until the passage of the Budget and Accounting Act of 1921 was the appropriations function again consolidated in a single committee.[1]

Although the houses of Congress have frequently made organizational and procedural alterations, the record suggests that in only three cases, all in the twentieth century, has the overhauling been of major proportions. The first occurred in 1910–11, when the autocratic Speaker of the House, Joseph G. Cannon, was stripped of his most important powers. A "reorganization" in the broadest sense, a political revolution in the strictest sense, the changes found the Speaker shorn of his right to appoint standing committee members and of his membership on the Rules Committee; in addition, his power over recognition was curtailed. Perhaps no other action in the history of Congress has altered so fundamentally the internal distribution of power.

The second major attempt to transform Congress took place in 1946 when, following lengthy study and substantial bargaining, the Legislative Reorganization Act was passed.[2] Unlike the 1910–11 episode, this one was "bloodless," and in its final form the act contained little of *political* significance. As we have noted, the historic gambit of eliminating and revamping committees was invoked. A number of housekeeping provisions involving committee organization, records, and meetings were introduced. Staff assistance for legislators and committees was augmented, and the Legislative Reference Service and the Office of Legislative Counsel were strengthened. To enhance congressional control over spending, the act provided for a legislative budget that would set a ceiling on appropriations for each fiscal year; this was tried once in 1948 and promptly abandoned. Another feature of this legislation was Title III, requiring lobbyists to register and file financial reports. Rounding out the modernization effort in pleasant style were provisions that increased legislative salaries and expense accounts and made legislators eligible for a retirement plan.

The third major period of congressional change took place during the 1970s. Although more important changes were to come later, this period began with the passage of the Legislative Reorganization Act of 1970. The leading provisions of the 1970 act concern the committee system. Among other things, the act provides that committees may sit while the House is in session (unless a bill is being read for amendment), requires committees to provide a week's notice of hearings to be held except in unusual circumstances, empowers a committee majority to provide for broadcasting or televising of hearings subject to certain conditions, eliminates proxy voting (unless otherwise provided by a committee), permits minority-party members to have at least one day during the course of any committee hearing to call witnesses of their choosing, requires that a committee report on a bill be filed within seven days after a committee majority makes such a request, and brings the Senate into agreement with the House by permitting a committee majority to call a special meeting if the chair fails to call a meeting on request.

Still other provisions of the 1970 act permit teller votes to be recorded if demanded by twenty members, permit ten minutes of debate on any amendment printed in the *Congressional Record*, provide for ten minutes of debate on any motion to return a bill to committee with instructions, and divide time for debate on a conference report between the majority and minority. These changes, like those involving the committee system, were designed not only to "open up" the legislative process but also to provide safeguards for the individual member. The main thrust of these procedural changes has been to diminish arbitrary rule by the chairs of the standing committees.

The other changes since 1970 have been of much larger significance. One string of changes was induced by decisions of the Democratic caucus. Laying the groundwork for later actions, the caucus in 1971 provided for secret ballots on nominees for committee chairmanships. This was the opening gun fired against the seniority system. Two years later the caucus strengthened this provision by requiring each chair to be considered separately by the caucus and to obtain a majority vote to retain office. At the same time, the caucus formed a Steering and Policy Committee, to be chaired by the Speaker and to include a number of other party officers. Turning to the committee system, the caucus adopted a resolution known as the Subcommittee Bill of Rights, the broad objective of which was to curtail the powers of committee chairs while vesting new authority in subcommittees.

The mood of reform was even more pronounced as the 94th Congress opened in 1975. Bolstered by seventy-five freshmen members, the Democratic caucus rejected three committee chairs, transferred the authority to make committee assignments from the Democratic members of the Ways and Means Committee to the Steering and Policy Committee, significantly increased the size of the Ways and Means Committee (as a means of increasing its liberal contingent) and ordered it to create subcommittees, stipulated that the chairs of the Appropriations subcommittees be ratified by the caucus, and vested in the Speaker the authority to nominate the Democratic members of the Rules Committee (subject to caucus approval).

By any reckoning, these were significant changes in the House. In most respects the powers of the Speaker, wrenched loose in the 1910–11 revolution, were restored (see Chapter 9). Caucus authority over committees, and particularly over their chairs, was reasserted. As the committees lost ground, however, subcommittees gained in independence, and junior members came to play a more important role in their proceedings and decisions. The overall result was that the changes of the 1970s served the interests of a decentralized system about as fully as those of a centralized one, centered in the Speaker and the caucus.

The second line of changes, less important than the first, stemmed from the creation of the House Select Committee on Committees (the Bolling Committee) in the 93rd Congress and the Temporary Select Committee to Study the Senate Committee System (the Stevenson Committee) in the 94th Congress. Each committee was charged with examining the chamber's committee system in order to make recommendations for committee reorganization.

The recommendations of the Bolling Committee covered a wide range of committee matters. Among its numerous proposals were those that would have abolished two standing committees, substantially shifted the jurisdiction of many others, and split the Committee on Education and Labor. In addition, the Bolling Committee's reorganization plan sought to strengthen the oversight activities of the House by directing all standing committees except Appropriations to create oversight committees and by enlarging the powers of the Committee on Government Operations. A third major proposal in the Bolling Committee report provided for early (December) organizational caucuses to be held by the parties for the purpose of selecting leaders, making committee assignments, and tending to other party business. A miscellany of other provisions dealt with increases in staff resources, proxy voting in committee, limitations on major committee assignments, funds for minority staffs, and the Speaker's authority over bill referral.

In the process of satisfying members' demands, most of the major features of the Bolling report were abandoned: The significant shifts in committee jurisdictions were eliminated; committees destined for elimination were retained and, in one case, strengthened; the Committee on Education and Labor was kept intact. A number of oversight proposals were retained (although the mandated creation of oversight subcommittees for each standing committee was eliminated), as were provisions for increases in staff allowances. Provision was made for early organizational caucuses and for increasing the Speaker's authority over bill referral.

In its final form, this reorganization effort achieved much less than was intended. The original jurisdictional package—the main feature of the plan—was lost because it "threatened too many careers and political relationships."[3] Or as the House Majority Leader Thomas P. O'Neill (D., MA) explained, "The name of the game is power, and the boys didn't want to give it up."[4] The committee reorganization proposals of the House Select Committee on Committees in the 96th Congress (1979–80)—the Patterson Committee—met about the same fate and for the same reason. Attempts to realign committee jurisdictions inevitably produce intense conflict as members struggle to defend their "turf." And their efforts are typically successful.

The reorganization of the Senate committee system in 1977 accomplished several things. Three standing committees were abolished and their responsibilities transferred to other committees. Several joint committees and numerous subcommittees were eliminated. A number of changes in committee jurisdictions were made. And "antimonopoly" provisions were adopted that limited the number of committee and subcommittee chairmanships that a member could hold, thus bringing greater equality in members' committee workloads while offering junior members a better opportunity to secure subcommittee chairmanships.[5]

Congress has never had a profound, continuing interest in reform, and for good reasons. Ambitious reform proposals rarely find much acceptance, invariably threaten power arrangements, and lead to intense partisan wrangling. And there is a good chance that nothing will come of them. Nevertheless, in the midst of public opinion surveys showing enormous public disaffection with Congress, the House and Senate agreed in 1992 to create another Joint Committee on the Organization of Congress to study and make recommendations for overhauling the institution.

The two houses eventually made separate reports in late 1993. Among the proposals approved by the Senate members of the Joint Committee were the following: a modest curb that would preclude filibustering on motions to proceed to consider a bill; a limit of three committee assignments per member, only one of which would be on a "Super A" committee, such as Appropriations or Finance; a sharp reduction in subcommittees and also in the number of subcommittee assignments per member; a tightening up of waivers under which members would gain extra assignments; the elimination of joint committees; procedures for the abolition of unpopular committees; limitations on proxy voting in committee; publication of committee attendance and voting records; a sharp cut in committee staffing levels; and provisions for a two-year budget.

The proposals approved by the House members of the Joint Committee were similar in their treatment of committees. They called for a reduction in subcommittees, limits on members' assignments (two committees and four subcommittees), stricter limits on waivers for committee assignments, a method for abolishing unpopular committees, and the publication of committee attendance and voting records. In addition, proposals were adopted to institute a two-year budget cycle, to expand the minority party's prerogatives in floor procedures, to use private citizens for initial investigations in ethics cases, and to make Congress subject to the same labor laws that it imposes on others.

Unlike the reorganizations of 1946 and 1970, none of the proposals in the House and Senate plans was adopted. Even changes of modest significance—a fair depiction of most of the proposals endorsed by Joint Committee members—proved unattainable. The reality is that the ultimate test of institutional reforms is not their fit or wisdom, but rather their impact on careers. It is not so much that members are attached to inherited institutions and practices, but rather that they are unwilling to risk changes that appear to threaten their influence and the interests of their constituencies, parties, and colleagues. Except in unusual circumstances, institutional change that matters is hard to bring about.

The midterm election of 1994 created these unusual circumstances. Republicans captured both houses of Congress—the lower house for the first time since 1952. Changing the power structure of the House, in keeping with campaign promises, became a prime objective of the new Republican majority under the aggressive leadership of Speaker Newt Gingrich (R., GA). Supported by a remarkably cohesive party, one-third of whom were freshmen, Gingrich quickly won support for a series of actions and rules changes (several of which were drawn from the recommendations of the Joint Committee on the Organization of Congress). Arguably the most important of the rules changes were those designed to reduce the independence and influence of subcommittees—which had prospered under Democratic rule—constrain committees in general, and centralize power in the speakership.

Under the House reforms of 1995, three standing committees were abolished, seniority was disregarded in the appointment of three committee chairs, numerous subcommittees were eliminated, staff hiring for subcommittees was transferred from subcommittee chairs to committee chairs, committee staff was pared by one-third, and limits were placed on committee and subcommittee assignments. Other provisions in the rules package abolished proxy voting in committee (thus diminishing the chairs' power), restricted opportunities for committee chairs to claim jurisdiction over politically attractive bills by eliminating joint multiple referrals (see Chapter 6), and limited committee and subcommittee chairs to three consecutive terms. And to top off the leadership's venture in harassing committees and centralizing power, the party's Steering Committee was reconstituted to augment the Speaker's influence over the assignment of members to committee.

Other changes to make the House more open and accountable were adopted. A Congressional Accountability Act was passed to end Congress's exemption from federal workplace laws and to permit congressional employees to sue Congress if their rights under federal labor laws are violated. The requirement for open committee meetings was further strengthened, and committees are now required to publish their votes. In addition, under the new rules, mandatory roll-call votes are required on revenue and appropriations bills and on the annual budget resolution, retroactive tax increases are prohibited, and a three-fifths majority vote is required for any bill that contains an income-tax increase. House Republicans also adopted several procedural changes to enlarge opportunities for the minority party to offer floor amendments and thus to establish a public record on their alternative proposals. Primarily of symbolic importance, a new rule limits the term of the Speaker to a maximum of four consecutive two-year terms.

The House Republican majority could not deliver, however, on one of its key provisions in the "Contract with America": to waylay career politicians by adopting a constitutional amendment that would impose term limits on members of Congress. Several different plans were handily defeated by a coalition of Democrats and senior Republicans. Shortly thereafter, the Supreme Court held unconstitutional term-limits provisions that twenty-three states had adopted for their congressional delegations. All things considered, 1995 was a bad year for term limits.

The essence of legislative reform is not subtlety. Provisions are usually hammered out on the run—to make a break with the past, to respond to immediate and highly visible problems, to signal and consolidate a redistribution of power, to legitimize a new order. Against the backdrop of minimal institutional change since the mid-1970s, the changes ushered in by a Republican House majority in 1995 were clearly substantial—particularly in terms of narrowing committee and subcommittee autonomy and centralizing power in the party leadership. (The institutional upheaval in the House had no counterpart in the Senate.)

Significant reform, ordinarily, is elusive. Reasonable men and women differ not only on the need for reform but also on the objectives and probable consequences of it. Most changes, it turns out, are crammed with unforeseen consequences. How Congress is evaluated, what is more, depends on where the viewer stands. Critics who see Congress through "executive" eyes, classifying the institution as an obstacle to be overcome, are not interested in the same changes as those who want to strengthen legislative independence and autonomy. Advocates of strong legislative parties view Congress in a different light from those persons, including some legislators, who are skeptical of the concentration of legislative power in any quarter. Legislators who hold key positions, moreover, are chary of change that may seem to threaten their power or the power of their party, friends, state delegations, constituencies, or regions. Proposals for legislative change often fail outright or are reshaped to the point of innocuousness because they cannot meet the critical test of political feasibility—a test established by all legislators, not just by legislative leaders.

## State Legislatures

During the last two decades, states have made substantial progress in modernizing their legislative institutions. Their principal efforts to improve capabilities have focused on the committee system, sessions, salaries, staff, information systems, and rules and procedures. The states have made marked advances in streamlining cumbersome committee systems. Emulating Congress, they have cut out a potpourri of bogus and extraneous standing committees. The typical lower house today has fewer than twenty standing committees, less than half the number it had in the 1940s; the typical senate has fewer than fifteen permanent committees. Several New England states have adopted and found effective a system of joint committees; elsewhere this arrangement has been used sparingly. Despite improvements, however, it is not unusual to find legislative houses in which members continue to serve on four or five committees during a session. But the overall record of committee modernization is impressive.

Trends in legislative sessions are also worth recalling at this point. More states now have annual sessions than at any time since the era of disillusionment set in late in the nineteenth century. There were only eight states that held annual sessions in 1950; currently forty-three states meet annually. Thirty states now empower their legislatures to call themselves into special session, as compared with twelve states in 1960. Moreover, legislatures are in session for much longer periods today than they were two or three decades ago. It continues to be true in many states, however, that the legislature is only partly master of its chambers, and whether its work is finished or not, it must end its session by a certain date.

The most significant contribution to legislative renewal in this century is the creation and development of service agencies and professional staff to provide legislators with information and assistance.[6] The principal agencies are legislative reference services and legislative councils, but increased use is also made of various kinds of interim (between-session) legislative commissions. The service agencies engage in a number of related activities, including research and reference assistance, bill drafting, statutory revision, codification, preparation of recommendations for legislation, and review of state revenues and appropriations. A few states empower their legislative councils to screen administrative proposals and even to take the testimony of interested citizens concerning proposals. At one time substantial innovations, reference services and councils have become indispensable units in the legislative process.

More and more states now provide for the appointment of professional staffs for legislators. Individual members are given a year-round personal staff by twenty-three state senates and seventeen state houses; another six state senates and nine state houses provide for personal staff during sessions. Senators in seven states and representatives in six states are also given year-round district staff; other states make no distinction between personal and district staff or else leave it to the legislator to decide where to place his or her staff. Thirteen states make no provision whatsoever for personal staff (Alaska, Arizona, Georgia, Indiana, Maine, Mississippi, Montana, New Hampshire, North Dakota, Rhode Island, South Dakota, Vermont, and Wyoming).[7] States such as California, Michigan, New York, New Jersey, Pennsylvania, Wisconsin, Florida, Texas, and Illinois have led the way in providing staffs for members and standing committees. In most state chambers, members share staffs or rely on a staff pool for assistance. Overall, the number of staff working in state legislatures increased by about 24 percent during the decade of the 1980s.[8] Many legislators and legislative observers believe that the key to increasing the capabilities of the legislature is to be found in the provision of professional staffs for members and standing committees. But the general public may not see it this way. In 1990, California voters approved a voter-initiated law that not only imposed term restrictions on state legislators (three 2-year terms for the lower house and two 4-year terms for the upper house) but also cut the legislature's operating budget by 38 percent. As a result, hundreds of staff positions were abolished and the budgets of standing committees sharply reduced.

A miscellany of other legislative improvements in recent years should be noted. For example, bill drafting has been improved; more states now have provisions for presession filing of bills; presession orientation conferences for freshman legislators are increasingly common; committee research staffs have been developed in some states; local and special legislation have declined markedly; expeditious ways of handling noncontroversial bills have been implemented; new concern over redistributing committee work loads is in evidence; and legislative salaries in many states have been raised to more realistic levels (on an hourly basis it is still more remunerative to collect garbage than to legislate in some states).

The reform of state legislatures has centered on improving their decision-making capabilities. A state legislature ranking high in functional capability, according to Legis 50/The Center for Legislative Improvement, would have unrestricted annual sessions, competent staff support for members, well-developed information systems, individual offices for members, rules of procedure that foster individual and collective accountability, substantial budget and subpoena powers, oversight and audit capabilities, and comprehensive public records. In addition, it would have a membership of modest size, a limited number of committees, and a high salary level for members. By and large, state legislatures that rank high in one respect rank high in all respects, and those at the bottom show a similar consistency. The California and New York legislatures rank near the top in virtually all categories. The Illinois legislature also ranks high in functional capability. Southern legislatures tend to be clustered among those states that rank low in legislative capability. Florida is a conspicuous exception among southern states.[9] Overall, it is plain that a number of state legislatures today are characterized by a growing professionalism, a rising concern for standards of performance, and an increased sensitivity to the need to improve the legislature's standing among the public. Moreover, there is good reason to think that states will continue to be concerned about the vitality of their legislative institutions.

The era of state legislative reform has resulted in significant changes in the way legislatures conduct their business. According to Alan Rosenthal, the reform movement has increased the capacity of legislatures, promoted specialization, contributed to the democratization of the institution, and improved legislative ethics. The greatest change has come in *legislative capacity*, in large part because of the addition of professional staffs. But modernization has not been an unmixed blessing. Although increased staff assistance has enabled legislators to do their jobs better, it has also made them more independent, more inclined to pursue their particularistic goals. Staffs have become an important resource for identifying, promoting, and defending district interests. At the same time, democratization of the legislature has given the individual member a more important role in policymaking. The influence of legislative leaders has declined correspondingly. The net result has been a dispersal of legislative power. State legislatures have become increasingly fragmented—this argument runs—making it difficult for members to reach agreement on matters of communal interest. "Individual legislators are out for their own district, their own client groups, their own programs, their own reelection, their own political advancement. The individual is way out front, but where in all of this is the legislature as an institution?"[10]

For some time, the dominant movement in the states thus has been directed toward reforms that culminate in full-time, professional legislatures.[11] "State legislatures," in Rosenthal's view, "are entering an era of congressionalization. If legislatures do not attend to the drift in where they are going institutionally, legislatures in a majority of states will resemble minicongresses." And some legislators worry about the problems that are likely to accompany the congressional model: the loss of "citizen" legislators in a full-time legislative environment, the rising costs of campaigns and the need for members to focus on fund-raising, members' preoccupation with reelection, and the heightened importance of staffs in policymaking.[12]

The main task that confronts the modern state legislature is to increase legislative *integration*. Legislatures are more than the sum of their parts.[13] To achieve integration, more attention will have to be paid to the welfare of the institution and less to the welfare of the individual member.[14] The heart of the problem is the fragmentation of legislative power—a problem that is becoming more acute according to a recent study.[15] Thus the chief requirement would seem to be a strengthened legislative leadership, one better able to combat the individualistic and centrifugal forces so apparent in many state legislatures.[16]

There is a final matter to be raised concerning the reform of state legislatures. Does a legislature that makes major changes in its structure and processes produce different policy outputs? The question is by no means settled, but a study casts doubt on the proposition that reform has an *independent* impact on state politics. When controls for personal income and political culture are introduced, there is scant association between the presence of a "reformed" legislature and policy outputs as represented by such indicators as education and welfare expenditures or per capita general revenue.[17] This finding is consistent with numerous studies showing that the policies states adopt are more a function of their economic well-being than of anything else.

Yet we are left to wonder about other possible consequences of legislative reform. No one's credulity ought to be sharply strained by the following surmises: Major reforms are likely to improve the quality of legislative life, making it a more desirable institution in which to work; to enhance the members' respect for the institution and to heighten their sense of political efficacy; to raise the attentive public's esteem for the institution; to increase the legislature's effectiveness in overseeing the bureaucracy; to strengthen the legislature's position vis-à-vis the governor; to decrease its reliance on lobbies; and to lead to the adoption of policies that cannot be so easily measured as state expenditures and revenues.

A study of the fifty states by Joel A. Thompson concludes that legislative reform has strengthened legislative autonomy and capability. He finds that reformed legislatures are "more capable of making independent budgetary decisions, more capable of obtaining information about policies and proposing new or alternative policies, and more capable of overseeing the implementation of those policies once they have been made."[18]

Legislative institutionalization, of course, is not a cure-all for political systems. John R. Hibbing writes:

> There is the well-known popular desire in many parts of the world, and especially in the United States, for more citizen-based and less institutionalized legislatures. The popular yearning for term limits, staff reductions, salary cuts, easy methods for demanding recall votes, and more referenda and initiatives all bespeak a public turned off by any sort of developed legislative structure. Many citizens in the United States wonder what they are getting for their investment in an institutionalized legislature. They see only entourages, boondoggles, and unbecoming subservience to special interests and political parties. One serious problem with legislative institutionalization is that ordinary people do not like it one bit.[19]

# THE CONTINUING PROBLEMS

Many of the most aggravating problems of the American legislature cannot be addressed either directly or in a coherent fashion through reform legislation. Rather, they are problems involving political power, representation, the careers of members, and the expectations of constituents.

## Minority Power

Legislatures are frequently criticized because their structures for decision making endanger rule by the majority. In the past, critics have had a substantial argument in the case of Congress. The seniority rule that conferred great advantage on southern Democrats, the power of a House Rules Committee loosely attached to the party leadership, the extraordinary powers of committee chairs to obstruct legislation, the unrepresentativeness of committees, the filibuster—in varying degrees each has had a corrosive effect on majority rule in Congress.

More recently these elements of minority rule have been of less significance. The seniority system is no longer automatic and violations of it are more common, the House Rules Committee has been shorn of much of its independence, standing committee chairs have become increasingly responsive to the leadership and to the conference or caucus, and various institutional changes (particularly in the House) have led to greater centralization of power.

Although the Senate is a more democratic institution now than in the past, it is still far from becoming a majority-rule body. Increasingly, senators pursue their own agendas without much regard for the institution's capacity to solve public problems or its general well-being. Barbara Sinclair defines the problem in this way:

> The growth of obstructionism and the Senate's tolerance of it greatly complicates Senate decision making. Senators regularly hold "must" legislation hostage and extract a ransom in policy concessions. One senator or a small group of senators may be able to block altogether consideration of less-than-top priority legislation. A large minority may be able to stop passage of even major legislation favored by a Senate majority. Thus minorities, even small ones, can wield inordinate influence over legislative decisions.[20]

Commenting on the bitter conflicts in the 103rd Congress (1993–94) over crime and health care legislation, former House member Donald Pease (D., OH) offered these observations:

> Congress has no trouble acting when there is a clear public consensus. In fact, it moves in jig time. Where it goes haywire is when there is no consensus, and the situation only gets worse when a powerful minority with strongly held views weighs in and thwarts a majority. This is a particularly serious problem in the

Senate, where the filibuster plays right into the hands of strongly motivated minorities.[21]

Minority rule thus persists as a problem. Committees and subcommittees will sometimes thwart majority preferences in the chamber. Moreover, collective-choice analysis suggests that because there is an incentive for committee members to conceal private information, in order to manipulate the decision-making process, any committee decision may in fact reflect or overrepresent the interests of a minority.[22] Filibusters and threats of filibusters will continue to frustrate majority plans. (Campaign finance reform, for example, has regularly been filibustered to death in the Senate.) Rules and practices that enhance the power of blocs and individual members will sometimes immobilize majorities. Nevertheless, opportunities for outright minority rule are fewer today than formerly. And the pervasive openness of congressional processes should make such instances more visible to attentive and organized publics.

## Unrepresentativeness

A traditional explanation for the failure of legislatures to come to grips with important problems has centered on their unrepresentativeness, as reflected either in the overrepresentation of certain areas (usually rural) in the membership as a whole or in the overrepresentation of certain elements in the "power structure" of the institution.

Over the years no fact of daily civics has been more familiar to legislative observers than malapportionment. Prior to *Baker* v. *Carr*, equitable apportionment, like the legislature itself, remained largely unexamined and surely unvisited in most states. It scarcely exaggerates the situation to remark that in certain states the equal-population doctrine enunciated by the Supreme Court appeared to many legislators as a totally new concept, so accustomed were they to old apportionments and inherited arrangements. Rural power in virtually all legislatures was inflated. Typically, critics pointed out, major shifts in American social and economic life had not been accompanied by shifts in the locus of legislative power. The world had changed, but many of those who sat in the legislatures and held the key positions saw it as it used to be. The inevitable result, in this interpretation, was that unrepresentative legislatures not only had failed to address themselves to many important questions of public policy but also had neglected or directly damaged the interests of the nation's urban populations. Beyond that, of course, malapportioned legislatures were out of harmony with the idea that one person's vote should be equal to any other person's vote.

Today the problem of malapportionment is of minimal significance, so great has been the impact of the Supreme Court's reapportionment rulings. Particularly interesting is the 1986 decision of the Supreme Court in *Davis* v. *Bandemer*.[23] It ruled that gerrymandering will be found unconstitutional when it consistently degrades the influence of individuals and groups in the political process. The significance of this case can be better judged when subsequent decisions disclose the Court's tolerance for districting plans that appear to reflect partisan considerations.

Unrepresentativeness in the power structure of legislatures is another aspect of the overall problem. At one time or another all legislatures come under criticism for the existence of disparities in the distribution of power among members. Obviously, individual members do not share equally in legislative power. Senior members typically have more influence than junior members.[24] Leadership positions, committee chairmanships, and the allocation of seats on key committees may benefit one element of the party over another or one region over another. Legislators from rural areas, for example, invariably dominate some state legislative houses, whereas big-city (Democratic) members dominate others. At the congressional level, when the Democrats have been in a majority over most of the last half-century, southern Democrats have often held a disproportionate number of chairmanships. Conversely, when Republicans are in control, conservatives dominate the leadership positions.

The representativeness of committees themselves is worth examining.[25] Some committees, such as Armed Services and Agriculture, are significantly more conservative than the House as a whole. Other committees, such as Foreign Affairs and Judiciary, are distinctly more liberal. There are similar examples in the Senate.[26] The stacking of committees with liberals and conservatives may have an impact on policy outcomes. And it is reasonable to suppose that those committees whose ideological composition differs sharply from the membership as a whole encounter more difficulty with their recommendations on the floor.

Instructive research by E. Scott Adler and John S. Lapinski shows convincingly that a number of House committees are decidedly unrepresentative of the chamber as a whole when the committee members' districts are compared with a cross section of all House districts. The politics of the assignment process are unmistakable. Members win assignments to these outlier committees in order to deliver particularized policy benefits to the "high-demand" constituencies they represent, believing that there is an electoral payoff in their good work. Thus members from agriculturally oriented districts gain assignment to the Committee on Agriculture, members from districts with military installations gravitate toward Armed Services, members from rural districts with large sections of land controlled by the Interior Department flock to Resources, members from coastal districts opt for Merchant Marine and Fisheries, members from districts with heavy union concentrations select Education and the Workforce, and so on.[27] The policy needs of constituencies thus shape the formation of a number of congressional committees and, of course, many state legislative committees as well.

The remedy for unrepresentative committees is presumably to be found in the parent chamber. But is it realistic to believe that the chambers can steadily control their committees? Roger Davidson writes:

> [In the short run] the full house is an imperfect counterweight to committee bi-ases. Floor amendments can bring committee bills into line, but it is often futile to challenge committee members' expertise. Indeed, disparities of information are sometimes such that legislators may be quite unaware of the biases hidden in committee bills. It is even harder to cope with the nondecisions of the committees. When a committee chooses not to pursue a given line of inquiry, there is little the parent house can do. Committee special-ization is a cherished norm on the Hill, and an extreme sanction, such as the discharge petition, is invoked only rarely.[28]

Committee power may be especially nettlesome for freshman members of the legislature. "The committee system means that bills come to the House floor with little input except by the committee that drafts them," a freshman member observes. "But the new members' interests are much broader than the committees on which they serve. Part of the frustration of the new mem-bers is—how do they have impact on problems not within their committee jurisdictions?"[29]

It remains to be mentioned that legislatures come under strictures for their failure to accommodate sufficiently all elements of the population. Leg-islatures are never microcosms of the population. The black community is underrepresented in most states as well as in Congress. Women face a simi-lar problem of underrepresentation in all but a few legislatures.

### Inefficiency, Trivialism, and Inside Electioneering

Still another weakness of the American legislature, according to some critics, is that with too few members tending the shop of public priorities, the ma-chinery tends to become clogged by trivia, "politicing," and the politics of self-protection. Much of the legislature's and legislator's time is consumed on questions of slight moment or on routine chores. Whether power shrivels for want of use may or may not be true, but it is clear that the energies of members are often dissipated on minor matters. Several reasons help to ex-plain this problem. One is the two-year term of office for members of the lower house. Affecting Congress and the states alike, the two-year term caus-es many legislators to campaign more or less continuously, with the result that there is less time for the public's business.

A second, related reason is that many legislators feel insecure in their positions. Each election appears threatening. The need to build political sup-port impels legislators to cater to their constituents—to run errands for them, to entertain them when they visit the capital, to intercede with administrative agencies for them, to campaign steadily among them. Any delegation of consequence that visits Washington or the state capital can meet with the local representative or senator, as can the single constituent if he or she is persistent. The legislator's time is seldom his or her own. Gaylord Nelson (D., WI), who ran unsuccessfully for a fourth term in the U.S. Senate in 1980, observed,

> Some days I had somebody from the state in my office every 15 minutes. Seventy-five percent of my time, or maybe 80 percent, was spent on nonlegislative matters. . . . The floor is being used as an instrument of political campaigning far more than it ever has before. People seem to expect that. Constituents judge their senators on how much crap the senator is sending them. The less legislating and the more campaigning you do the better legislator you are perceived to be. There isn't much thinking in the Senate any more.[30]

Few problems nag legislators more than the financing of their campaigns. Fund-raising consumes inordinate amounts of time for members and their staffs, doubtlessly to the detriment of members' performance as legislators:

> The present system does not even allow the incumbents with new ideas to get them into place. We are too busy out engaging in the money chase. We cannot be here in the committees, we cannot be here on the floor doing our work. . . . We are kept so busy out there knocking on doors all over the country, seeking money, asking for money, begging for money, getting on our hands and knees for money, we do not have time to give thought to new ideas and to be putting them into creative legislation. [Senator Robert C. Byrd, D., WV][31]

> The talent of many senators and their staffs for developing and incubating policy innovations is squandered by activities that are, at best, peripheral to their functions as legislators and representatives of their states. In large part, the fault lies with the current system of campaign finance that requires senators and their staffs to spend too much time, throughout their term, raising money for their next campaign. Quite apart from the implications of reform proposals for winning and losing elections, therefore, more serious consideration should be given to the consequences of campaign finance practices for senators' legislative and representative responsibilities. [Steven S. Smith][32]

Veterans' claims, immigration and deportation cases, and a variety of personal and local problems find their way to congressional offices. A good staff can take care of many of these problems, but there is still a heavy drain on the lawmaker's time. Thus a New York member of Congress reports, "In my district, one half of my time is taken up running errands." A southern member complains, "I would say that answering correspondence (we average more than 100 letters a day from our district) and doing favors for constituents, totally unrelated to the business of legislating (arguing veterans' cases, handling Social Security matters and the like), take up the greater part of my time."[33]

A third reason why legislatures may appear to be foundering arises from the weakness of legislative party organizations in most states and typically in Congress. Concerted party action leading to the adoption of party policies is not a common occurrence; in the great majority of legislatures the party neither originates most legislation nor sees it through the legislature. In the void created by party weakness, legislators clutch at all straws. Sensitive to the power of interest groups and apprehensive over their electoral support, legislators are responsive to all manner of narrow demands in order to maintain and attract political support. Members usually find it easy to put party on the back burner.

And fourth, the failure of legislatures to deal promptly and imaginatively with major problems may be the result of their emphasis on the rights of individual members at the expense of institutional cohesion. The power of individual legislators has never been greater. Although the U.S. Senate once followed a rule that debate must be germane to the subject at hand ("No one is to speak impertinently or beside the question, superfluously, or tediously"), it no longer does. Filibustering and other dilatory tactics, such as offering numerous amendments, at times can paralyze the Senate. And it seems likely that there is more individual free wheeling and obstructionism today than in the past. Consider these blunt observations by members and former members of the Senate:

> Senate custom is to go along to get along. But I don't do that. If I'm not the most popular guy in the Senate—well, I can live with that. [former Senator Howard M. Metzenbaum, D., OH]

> If I can slow down a markup or find some tactic to keep a bill off the floor, I'll do it. I don't particularly have loyalty to tradition. [former Senator Jake Garn, R., UT]

> The parties play a limited role now, and that's what they should play. Every individual senator should have an equal chance to express himself. [former Senator William Proxmire, D., WI]

> The obstructionists have always been able to do what they really wanted. But the obstructionists were often the giants of the Senate. It wasn't somebody trying to get 14 seconds on the evening news. [Patrick J. Leahy, D., VT][34]

Members of Congress pay less attention (or deference) to committee decisions than in the past. The proposal of floor amendments by noncommittee members is now a frequent occurrence. For the individual member, making a record and protecting one's constituency shape strategy and behavior. Before he retired, Barber Conable, Jr. (R., NY), reflected on how Congress had changed in this respect:

> Throughout the Congress everybody feels that he has to be part of every decision that's made. We have a tendency to transfer a lot of the decision making to the floor of the House now. . . . And that means we are deciding things less

efficiently and probably with lesser expertise, because everybody wants to be a part of every issue.[35]

State legislatures sometimes come under critical review because of the improbable, bizarre behavior of their members. The following accounts of two sessions of the Texas legislature are far from novel; indeed, such unrehearsed if not entirely spontaneous antics have very likely occurred in most state legislatures:

> One night, in a bitter floor debate in the lower house, one legislator pulled the cord out of the amplifier system, another hit him from the blindside with a tackle; there was mass pushing, hitting, clawing, and exchanges about one another's wives, mistresses, and forebears. Sweethearts and wives, who were allowed on the floor with friends and secretaries cowered near the desks. In the middle of the brawl, a barbershop quartet of legislators quickly formed at the front of the chamber and, like a dance band during a saloon fight, sang "I Had a Dream Dear."[36]

> The 63rd session cleaned up the House rules and passed a campaign-reporting law with teeth in it and some species of ethics legislation, and that exhausted ree-form for the year. Ree-form expired totally about halfway through the session on Apache Belle Day. The Apache Belles are a female drill and baton-twirling team that performs during half time at college football games. They are real famous in their field, so the House set aside a special day to honor them for their contributions to the cultural life of Texas. . . . The Belles, all encased in tight gold lamé pants with matching vests and wearing white cowboy boots and hats, strutted up the center aisle of the House with their tails twitching in close-order drill. They presented the speaker's wife with a bouquet of Tyler roses, and made the speaker an honorary Apache Beau for the day. Then [the legislator serving as master of ceremonies] commenced his address by noting that not all the Apache Belles were on the floor of the House. Upon [his] instruction, everyone craned his neck to look up at the House gallery, where, sure enough, six extra Belles were standing. At a signal . . . the six turned and pertly perched their gold-laméd derrières over the brass rail of the gallery. Upon each posterior was a letter, and they spelled out R*E*F*O*R*M.[37]

It is a nagging fact of life in the state legislature that members occasionally become engrossed in matters only a notch above absurdity. Should the term describing the study of foot disorders be changed from *chiropody* to *podiatry*? Should the citizenry be permitted to drink beer in taverns while standing up? Should the state permit women to serve as bartenders? Should the great dane or cocker spaniel or possibly the beagle be designated as the official state dog? Should the bedbug, "which has left marks of distinction on the people of this great state for generations," be designated the official state bug? Should insectivorous birds be protected by a state law requiring cats to be strolled on a leash? Should individuals be permitted to advertise for matrimonial purposes? Should chili, barbecue, or chicken gumbo be chosen as the official state dish? Should the state's automobile license plates be painted maroon and gold, the colors of one of the state's leading universities, or red and blue, the colors of the other? Should drum majorettes be permitted to parade their talents at the state university? Should shows that feature horses and mules diving off towers into pools of water be outlawed? Should it be legal for citizens to collect and consume road kill? Should the dog-faced butterfly be anointed as the official state insect? Should ministers be allowed to carry concealed weapons? Should Colby be the official state cheese? Would it be sound public policy to make it unlawful to shoot a deer that is "albino or predominantly white"?

MR. McCORMACK: Mr. Speaker, I would like one of the sponsors of the bill to clarify for me . . . the word "predominantly."

MR. BRETH: Mr. Speaker. . . . If you would see enough white or if there were enough white on a deer to be seen clearly, you would know that you were shooting either an albino or a part albino.

MR. FILO: Mr. Speaker. . . . [How] can you see both sides of a deer at the same time?

MR. BRETH: To my mind, Mr. Speaker, that would be decided by the magistrate or by the arresting officer. If the deer had his brown side toward me, the bullet that killed it would enter the brown side; if the white side were toward me, the bullet would enter the white side. . . .

MR. ADAMS: Mr. Speaker. . . . You have enough trouble finding a deer in the woods that has legal horns on it and being able to shoot it without having to go out and measure how much of it is white and how much of it is brown. . . . You kill it thinking it is a brown deer, you go over and pick it up and find that one side of it is white and then the man is nailed. . . .

MR. HARTLEY: Mr. Speaker. . . . When you find an albino, you have certainly found a rare specimen and a freak of nature. Therefore, you would want to have it mounted. . . .

MR. MAXWELL: Mr. Speaker, the gentlemen made a statement that these white deer are freaks.

MR. GRAMLICH: In my opinion, they are. In all the history of it, the albino deer is a freak.

MR. MAXWELL: Mr. Gramlich, what color are you?

MR. GRAMLICH: Well, I do not know. I might be a freak, but I did not know anybody was concerned about it. And, Mr. Speaker, I only have two legs and pink skin.

MR. MAXWELL: Mr. Speaker, I did not hear the gentleman's answer but I suppose he said he was white.

THE SPEAKER PRO TEM: The gentleman says he is pink.

MR. MAXWELL: Well then, the gentleman has called himself what he calls the deer, because there are more brown, yellow, and black people in this world than there are white. . . . Now, ladies and gentlemen, in closing, practically every country in the world respects the color of white. We have the sacred white cow, we have the sacred white elephant, we have the sacred white cat. Even the American Indians have the white buffalo as their most powerful and their most sacred medicine. Now can we do any less in Pennsylvania except to pass the white deer bill?

MR. ADAMS: Mr. Speaker. . . . [The] gentleman who just spoke would lead us to believe that an albino buck would go out and hunt an albino doe in order to propagate the white species. I think it is very unlikely that that thing would happen out in the woods. . . . I have been hunting in the woods for about 24 years and I only saw one partial albino deer and that did not have any horns, so I just had to watch it walk away.[38]

No state legislature spends most of its time weighing the merits of white-deer bills or considering the dangers that bounding majorettes pose for university propriety and public morality. Not every Iowa legislator can expect his birthday to be celebrated by a belly dancer performing in the rotunda of the capitol. There is no chance that silly or minor bills, mixed with "fun and games," will cause the collapse of the fifty republics. The astonishing fact about these sorties into the world of trivia, however, is the public response. We have the word of the late Richard L. Neuberger, a state legislator in Oregon and subsequently a U.S. senator, that "the legislative mail pouch frequently gets its biggest bulge . . . from some bill that may appear irresponsibly frivolous to the detached observer."[39]

It is easier to raise questions concerning the style and habits of legislatures and to identify their arcane arrangements than to prescribe acceptable methods of improving operations. Reform proposals invariably clash with other values. Moreover, it is no more than a guess—perhaps a good one—that a legislature bent on increasing its efficiency will, if successful, provide better representation, write better laws, or otherwise help to restore institutional vitality. Will the time saved legislators by eliminating certain minor but burdensome tasks and anachronistic practices be spent in useful ways? What could result, of course, is simply more and improved errand running.

### Parochialism

Each legislator "belongs" to a number of groups. Members of Congress, for example, belong to a political organization in their home constituency, to one or more interest groups in their constituency (veterans', business, church, and so on), to several different legislative groups (committees or blocs), to the national party, and to the government of the United States. They are formal and participating members of some of these groups; they may simply sympathize with the objectives of other groups. One and all press demands on them.

This introduction leads us to the following problem: Substantial dissatisfaction with the legislature traces to its excessive parochialism—the tendency of legislators to look only to their home districts for guidance, to defer to the claims made by individuals and organizations that help make up their individual constituencies, and to treat indifferently matters of national (or statewide) significance. Thus, among the groups to which the legislators belong or to which they defer, those based at home (interest groups and the constituency political organization, especially the former) have first claim. Theirs may be the only claims that are heard.

Parochialism is a problem because it concentrates the attention of legislators on narrow, often special-interest politics. For reasons we shall enumerate later, lawmakers come to Washington lacking a national viewpoint or to Albany or Austin lacking a state viewpoint. Elected by radically different constituencies, they bring with them a concern for local problems and local advantage. Critics of localism contend that in the process of ministering to localized demands, legislators overlook the most obvious statewide or national needs. When being lobbied to support the energy program proposed by President Carter, a New York member of Congress remarked, "You're asking me to vote for things that will cost my constituents money and make life less convenient, and they won't see any benefit from it for the next five elections. And I'll tell you something else, if I do what you want, the last four of those elections, I'll be out."[40]

The legislator's orientation toward his or her locality—the constituency comes first—is a major fact about Congress and the state legislatures. Localism and logrolling are joined when decisions are made to build highways, hospitals, post offices, flood control projects, airports, and military installations. A former state legislator observes,

> Among the other bills that were before us, pork barrels abounded. Literally millions of dollars were earmarked for a slew of goodies ranging from state funding for a national track and field hall of fame in Kanawha County to subsidizing a chronically flooded historical site. The projects were tied together politically into a coalition vote since none could easily survive on its own merits as a "priority" use of state tax dollars. Thus, as we prepared to vote on a pork barrel for Wood County, a Kanawha County delegate blurted out, "O.K., everybody. Vote yes. Wood County is going for the Hall of Fame."[41]

Few policy questions are more likely to alert the typical legislator than the allocation of funds for public works projects. Consider the observations of a member of the House Public Works Committee:

> If you're going to stay around here, you've got to take care of the folks back home. And, if you're not, you don't belong here. You're supposed to be representing them and if you don't, somebody else will. We are all national legislators in a sense and we have to be but the national issues don't mean a damn thing back home—oh, sure, they read about it in the newspapers but it doesn't mean much to them. They've got to see something; it's the bread and butter issues that count—the dams, the post offices and the other buildings, the highways. They want to know what you've been doing. You can point to all these things you've done and all of them go through my committee.[42]

Protecting local interests through public policy is an overriding concern of legislators everywhere. James L. Sundquist sketches its dimensions in congressional policy:

[Whatever] the merits of the local or regional claim, it must be pressed. Representatives of Texas must see the national interest in terms of oil, those of South Dakota in terms of cattle, and those of Detroit in terms of automobiles. Foreign policy seen through the eyes of a constituency may predispose a representative toward the Greek, the Israeli, or the Irish view of particular problems. The budget appears as a "pork barrel" to be distributed among districts as well as a fiscal program for the country. What weapons the military forces should get are liable to be judged by what factories are located in a state or district. And so it goes across the whole range of policy. Political incentives propel the member—especially the House member who represents more specialized constituencies—from the broad to the narrow perspective.[43]

The force of localism and the members' sensitivity to constituents' concerns shape not only the contents of legislation and voting decisions, but also the members' explanations of their behavior. Explanations can be as important as the vote itself.[44] An increasingly skeptical and cynical public has put legislators on the defensive, and they look for ways to justify their actions. "To the extent that public discourse is all anger and hostility," Senator John C. Danforth (R., MO) observed in 1994, "the need for a politician is to take a position which is very easily explained." Along these lines, Senator Trent Lott (R., MS) once remarked, "You do not ever get into trouble for those budgets which you vote against."[45] Voting *for* taxes, spending, and programs, of course, does require careful and imaginative explanation.

There are not many major pieces of legislation that pass through Congress without being shaped to confer special advantage on certain interests. When trade-agreement legislation is before Congress, pressures are massed to protect the domestic steel industry from foreign imports, to restrict the importation of cheese, to require the labeling of alien trout, to unload farm surpluses through foreign trade policy, to require a certain share of foreign aid cargoes to be shipped in American vessels, ad infinitum. In the consideration of foreign economic policy, Holbert Carroll observes, the House "mirrors the varying approaches . . . of the diverse components of the executive branch. What the House adds to this confusion is the babble of more localized pressures applied to wool, textile, coal, soybean, shipping, and scores of other interests."[46]

Another sign of parochialism appears in the development of a large number of informal policy caucuses in Congress, especially in the House. Organized to advance economic, geographical, race, gender, and other interests, they carry such names as Congresswomen's Caucus, Congressional Black Caucus, Vietnam Veterans' caucus, Steel Caucus, Auto Task Force, Metropolitan Area Caucus, Congressional Sunbelt Caucus, New England Congressional Caucus, Northeast-Midwest Congressional Coalition, Congressional Rural Caucus, Suburban Caucus, Coal Caucus, Alcohol Fuels Caucus, Mushroom Caucus, Textile Caucus, and Ad Hoc Committee for Irish Affairs. Such groups are an important source of information and policy options for their members. They also contribute to agenda setting and coalition formation. The overriding objective of each group, of course, is to promote the welfare of a distinctive interest. The effect of this fragmentation may be to make it difficult for the party and committee systems to integrate policymaking.[47]

Scott Ainsworth and Frances Akins describe the caucuses from a somewhat different perspective. They see them as a rival source of information to that provided by committees. Typically, "the caucus system acts to counterbalance the inherent biases of the committee system by providing the floor with an informational perspective unrepresented within the committee system."[48]

A certain amount of controversy has always surrounded the caucuses, or Legislative Service Organizations (LSOs). They have been criticized for contributing to divisiveness in the House, for their links to outside lobby organizations, for their use of public funds, and for occupying office space on Capitol Hill. When the Republicans took control of the House in the 104th Congress (1995–96), one of their first decisions was to bar the diversion of funds from members' office allowances to support the activities of twenty-eight LSOs, including such well-known ones as the Democratic Study Group, the House Republican Study Committee, the Congressional Black Caucus, and the Congressional Caucus for Women's Issues. Republicans justified their action as consistent with their campaign pledge to cut spending and reduce the size of government, while some Democrats viewed it as a move to undermine opponents, such as the black and women's caucuses.

The unflagging parochialism of legislatures, easily visible on all sides, is not difficult either to account for or to understand. To sum up a long story, it traces to the decentralization of American politics, to the influence of interest groups resulting from the inability of the parties to generate legislation or to hold their lines intact, to the custom that legislators must reside in the districts they represent, to the insecurity of short-term legislators loosely linked to party, to the dispersal of power within the legislature, to the weakness of party organizations at *all* levels of government, and to the heterogeneous quality of American life. In addition, the parochial spirit is at the root of much of the buffeting between the executive and the legislature; their constituencies dissimilar, one sees the need for a broad plan of action, the other the need to keep things at home in repair.

Members of Congress who yield to local pressures and who spend their time satisfying constituents' requests are following the surest route to reelection.[49] If, in the course of supporting local claims, they oppose national party positions, there is not much the party can do about it. They wear the party label whether the party likes them or not, and they can rise to power in Congress without the party's blessing. However, if they support the party and the president at the expense of their district, they have gained virtually nothing and may have lost their bid for reelection. The national party will be of little direct assistance to them in their campaign, and possibly their identification with it may hurt their chances. Hence the cards are stacked in favor of the members who are sensitive to the interests of their district and accord priority to its claims. Under the circumstances, it may be surprising that any members will risk the wrath of their constituents (or organized groups) to support a position unpopular at home. Yet many do. A majority, it would seem, play it safe.

On controversial, district-sensitive issues, even party leaders may stray off the reservation, opposing a majority of their party or their own president. When the Clinton administration's North American Free Trade Agreement (NAFTA) came before Congress in 1993, both the House Democratic majority leader (Richard A. Gephardt, D., MO) and whip (David E. Bonior, D., MI) were active opponents of the legislation, making it necessary for then Speaker Thomas S. Foley (D., WA) to create an ad hoc whip organization to round up votes. "David Bonior wasn't elected by the national party," said the chair of the Macomb County (Michigan) Democratic committee, "and he's sensitive to that."[50]

Though it supplies no broad or national vision, localism in moderation is neither harmful nor undesirable. Local interests require representation in national (or statewide) legislation, and there are obvious values to keeping "distant" government responsive to the people at home. The grounds for criticizing localism are more circumscribed than might appear at first glance. They become relevant as parochialism becomes rampant, as broad purposes become blighted or vitiated through obsessive concern for local advantage.

### Fragmentation of Power and Erosion of Autonomy

Each legislature has a profile of its own. But though no legislature is precisely the same as any other, all have certain features in common. In greater or lesser degree, all are troubled by problems of minority control, unrepresentativeness, inefficiency, obstructionism, excessive electioneering, and localism. Another factor, the fragmentation of party and legislative power, increases the severity of the foregoing problems. Localism, for example, gets out of hand because legislators lack strong attachments to institutions that transcend their constituencies, notably party. Minority power sometimes turns to minority domination because the majority is unable to organize its power by consolidating its forces and by ordering the ground rules of the legislature so that majority control is a distinct and continuing possibility.

All this is familiar ground by now; we need come back to only a few points. The key for understanding American legislatures lies in the absence of party rule and party discipline. Because the party is not equipped to mass persistent majorities, responsible rule goes by default. Effective power may come to rest with transient bipartisan majorities—sometimes brought into being through the pressure of a vigorous executive, sometimes the product of careful engineering by a perennial bipartisan coalition (for example, southern Democrats and Republicans), sometimes no more than the deft concoction of an alliance of logrollers, and sometimes purely accidentally.

Whatever may be the advantages of coalition rule and majority-by-logrolling—and it is difficult to attribute more to them than unadorned expediency—they are not consonant with the idea of responsible party government. At no point in the political process are these combinations accountable for their behavior. Never required to produce a platform or to campaign on a collective program or to submit their record to the voters, coalitions can work their extravagancies without significant restraint. In only the vaguest sense can it be said that the public is able to take account of what they do, approving or rejecting it. With each election campaign, coalition members find their way back to the same old parties for a short stay. Once the election is out of the way, the air cleared of programs and promises, and members returned to the legislature, the process begins anew.

The weakness of the parties is accompanied by a dispersal of power in the legislature. The latter owes its existence to the former. Were the parties strong agencies of majority rule the legislature would function much differently. Committee and subcommittee power would be linked firmly to party power, committee and subcommittee chairs to party leaders, and rules of procedure to party requirements. Such is not the case in most American legislatures.

The inability of the party to integrate the separate elements of the legislature and to control individual members opens up the legislature to manipulation by interest groups. When private organizations have unrestricted access to centers of public decision making and when the response of the legislature is simply to referee group struggles, the autonomy of the government is threatened. Public policy may come to be simply the expression of the preferences of organized interests. In truth, the business of the legislature is more than the total of all private business brought before it. The legislature's role is both creative and regulatory—creative in the sense of enlarging opportunities for popular direction of government and popular review of national goals, and regulatory in the sense that any government worthy of its name is required to prevent interests from trampling one another or any one interest from gaining ascendancy over all others. Neither task can be discharged by a legislature that is the captive of those it seeks to regulate. The legislature "can't be everybody's friend all the time," as Roland Young observed.

> If a legislature is subjected to such rigorous external pressures that it cannot maintain its own identity, if rules having the sanction of government are in effect made by private groups, society may shortly find itself deprived of the benefit of a stable and effective political authority. Government would be up for grabs, with individuals and groups appropriating indiscriminately the symbols of government for their own purposes.[51]

The leading scholar of American state legislatures, Alan Rosenthal, deplores the fragmentation of legislative power and the weakened position of legislative leaders:

> Power within legislatures, which was never highly concentrated, is now [late 1990s] even more dispersed. Just as the legislature's external environment is fragmented, so is its internal environment. Connected as they are to their constituencies, members maintain independence of party and of leadership in the legislature. They have their personal careers and individual agendas to promote. Each has his or her own bottom line, which legislative leaders are obliged to respect. . . . To ensure their positions and their power, leaders have to do more and more service for their members, catering to their individual needs even at substantial cost. There is less threat nowadays, if there ever was, of autocratic legislative leadership; the greater threat is of demanding members and more submissive leadership.[52]

### The Nagging Problem of Clientelism

Nowhere does the fragmentation of legislative power manifest itself more directly than in the phenomenon of clientelism—that form of policymaking in which interested individuals and groups come together to shape the decisions that affect their welfare, with little or no regard for the public interest. In congressional clientelism, the beneficiaries of public policy are the primary designers of it.[53]

Clientele politics is centered in the committees and subcommittees. It is here that the bargains and trade-offs are worked out within the "unholy trinity: the long-standing underground alliance of a committee member with a middle-level bureaucrat and a special interest lobbyist concerned with the same subject matter."[54]

Clientelism helps to shape legislative career patterns. Members seek assignments on committees whose policy jurisdictions coincide with the dominant interests of their constituencies. The result is that legislators from farm-belt areas predominate on the Committee on Agriculture, westerners gain disproportionate representation on Interior, urban liberals win seats on Education and Labor, and members with military bases and arsenals in their districts gravitate toward Armed Services—to mention just a few. As a western congressman explained his preference for Interior and Insular Affairs:

> I was attracted to it, very frankly, because it's a bread and butter committee for my state. I guess about the only thing about it that is not of great interest in my state is insular affairs. I was able to get two or three bills of great importance to my state through last year. I had vested interests I wanted to protect, to be frank.[55]

Although it cannot be said for all committees, it can be said for many that they have become partisans for the interests of particularistic clienteles, including interest groups and segments of the bureaucracy. Advantages accrue for members as well as for their clienteles:

> [The] fact that there is little change among the membership of a committee for years makes members of key committees the focus of special treatment by special interests. If those in the automotive industry or the oil industry or the tobacco industry know that they will be working for years with a particular congressman, it is not surprising that they direct their attention to that congressman and his district. . . . The lack of movement within and among committees promotes a situation in which many committees become lobbying committees, with special interests overwhelmingly represented among the members of the panel.[56]

The deficiencies of clientele-oriented policymaking are made clear by Roger Davidson:

> The corpus of public policy derived from clientele-oriented decision making typically lacks coherence, dissipating resources in contradictory efforts which often cancel out one another. . . . Ultimately, every member of the society pays for benefits distributed to certain segments of the society, no matter how innocuous the distributions may appear when considered separately. If it is true that war is too important to be left to generals, it follows equally that it is unwise to leave agricultural policy to the farmers, banking regulation to the bankers, communications policy to broadcasters, or environmental protection to the environmentalists. Yet this is what frequently passes for representative policy making.[57]

### The Failure to Represent the Unorganized Public

"All power is organization and all organization is power. . . . A man who has no share in any form of organized power is not independent of organized power. He is at the mercy of it. . . ."[58]

The proposition that legislators listen only to those who make the loudest noise is not wholly true. But there is little doubt that it is mainly true. Legislators seldom constitute an audience attentive for sounds coming from the unorganized public. If they listen at all, and some do, they hear very little; and it could hardly be otherwise amid the noisy clamor of organized voices. Congress has often been criticized for its failure to represent adequately the "have nots" in American society. Duane Lockard wrote,

> Whatever else may be said of congressional power, this much is true: it is exercised so as to render difficult or impossible the task of developing policies addressed to the needs of those in the most desperate straits. It is far easier to get a mammoth defense budget through Congress than to keep an antipoverty program alive. Defense budgets have formidable support: they are endorsed by the President; they have the awesome backing of the military-industrial complex; they are difficult to oppose, for to do so may appear to be failing the troops in battle or "endangering" the safety of the society; and they are, after

all, a test of the national power, which arouses nationalistic feelings in the patriot. . . . To get through the needle's eye of Congress, a law to protect farm workers attempting to form unions or to curb the power of the oil industry is another matter. For there are almost limitless ways in which an intensely interested minority can block such laws. In this respect, Congress perverts the priorities of the nation; it responds to money, to organized power, to vested interests of various kinds; but it has little sympathy for migrant farm workers, the poor, or the prisoner.[59]

In the view of many members of Congress, the influence of organized groups on decision making is much greater now than in the past:

Lobbying has reached a new dimension and is more effective than ever in history. It has become a big computerized operation in which the Congress and the public are being bombarded by single-issue groups. [Former Senator Abraham Ribicoff, D., CO][60]

We have the best Congress money can buy. Congress is awash in contributions from special interests that expect something in return. [Senator Edward M. Kennedy, D., MA][61]

I have been around here for 25 years [and] I have never seen such extensive lobbying. [Thomas P. O'Neill, former Speaker of the House][62]

What we are seeing in the Senate [concerning the banking industry's massive 1983 campaign to block a withholding tax on interest and dividend income] . . . and what we will see in the House is [that] when a letter-writing campaign is ginned up, when a newspaper ad campaign is ginned up, members of the Congress of the United States crumble like cookies. [former Senator John C. Danforth, R., MO][63]

If you've got enough money and send in enough mail, you'll probably get results. It doesn't say a whole lot for the Senate. [Senator Robert Dole, R., KS][64]

There's a danger that we're putting ourselves on the auction block every election. It's now tough to hear the voices of the citizens in your district. Sometimes the only things you hear are the loud voices in three-piece suits carrying a PAC check. [former Representative Leon Panetta, D., CA][65]

## CONCLUSION

The belief that Congress and the state legislatures are not functioning properly is widely held. Opinion surveys regularly report that a large majority of the public does not approve of the way Congress is doing its job. Popular support for state legislatures may be even more limited. Generalized discontent over the legislature, in fact, is a key factor in the drive to impose term limits on legislators. The Supreme Court's decision in 1995 holding unconstitutional state limitations on congressional terms is likely to lead to renewed efforts to secure term limits through a constitutional amendment.

Although legislatures are fair game for critics of all kinds, they also have their supporters. The essence of the defender's position is the belief that legislatures perform about as well as could be expected in a pluralistic political system, where the values of accommodation, bargaining, and decentralization are important. Hence, if the legislature is slow to act, which it often is, it cannot easily make abrupt changes in public law. If the legislature lacks hierarchy, it nonetheless offers legislators opportunities to pursue their individual goals and private citizens opportunities to gain access to the legislative process. If the diffusion of legislative power makes it perplexing to fix responsibility, it also makes it difficult to undo or abandon traditional arrangements. If legislative procedure makes it difficult for the majority to work its will, it also assures the minority of its right to be heard and to press its case. If legislators subordinate broad interests to provincial ones, they nevertheless make government responsive to local claims and opinions. If the legislature is slow to respond to pressure for change, it is also less likely to act capriciously.

The numerous criticisms lodged against the legislature are not necessarily well taken. The limitations under which the legislature operates are often ignored. Great size alone makes it difficult to operate with the speed its critics would prefer. Lawmaking is slow because the process of reconciliation is slow, inevitably so in an institution with limited hierarchy and decentralized power. The need to build majorities, piece by piece, concession by concession, usually means that the changes from existing law will be smaller rather than larger, patched together rather than integrated, incremental rather than comprehensive.

Legislative politics and decision making often appear to both outsiders and insiders as awkward, unpredictable, and disorganized. Richard Bolling, a former well-known member of the House of Representatives from Missouri, made this observation:

> I happen to think that the House is messy, the House will continue to be messy. It was messy under Cannon, under Clay, under Rayburn, under Albert, and it will be messy under whomever comes along. I think there is a very good reason. It is that the democratic process is messy. . . .[66]

Second thoughts are also in order concerning the petty quarreling and partisanship that at times make the legislature its own worst enemy. Unlike judges and administrators, who have their quarrels and make their decisions in relative privacy, legislators live in glass houses, where anyone may observe their foibles and disputes.[67] And what appears as ugly partisanship to one individual, moreover, is no more than simple justice to another. Disputes and bickering, in other words, come with the territory.

In the case of Congress, dissatisfaction focuses more on the institution than on the individual member. To quote former Congressman Les AuCoin (D., OR),

> In the district, Congress is held in low esteem, like a used car salesman. As an institution, Congress has never been very popular. Yet people have a high respect for their individual congressman. I didn't fully appreciate that dichotomy till I got here.[68]

This distinction stems from the fact that the public applies different standards in evaluating members and the institution. "For the individual the standard is one of representativeness—of personal style and policy views." For the institution, in contrast, the standard involves its ability to find solutions to complex national problems; when it fails, as it often does, the public is frustrated. The unenviable position of Congress also derives in part from the members' concern over reelection: They worry more about their standing among the public than they do about the legislature's standing. Moreover, many members "run for Congress by running *against* Congress,"[69] and Congress as an institution suffers.

The public is easily aroused over legislative happenings that, by most standards, are not of large significance. In 1991, for example, it was disclosed that dozens of representatives had bounced checks on their House bank accounts, without interest or penalty, and had run up congressional restaurant tabs of several hundred thousand dollars. Shortly after these revelations, a *New York Times*/CBS poll found that only 27 percent of all adults approved of "the way Congress is handling its job." Worse yet, 29 percent thought that most members of Congress were "financially corrupt," and an additional 28 percent thought that "about half" the members were corrupt. Such transgressions obviously do serious damage to the institution. But at the same time that the public was lambasting Congress for its arrogance and privileges, 56 percent said they approved of the way the representative from their district was handling his or her job.[70]

In considering the performance of legislatures, it is important to recognize that the issues thrust before them are extraordinarily complex. Some of the issues originate in the legislature, but many others are handed over to it because they cannot be resolved satisfactorily anywhere else. "The flight to government," E. E. Schattschneider observed, "is perpetual." It occurs because the losing contestants in private conflicts seek relief, new and more favorable settlements, from a public authority.[71] Conflict is not easily managed in the legislature since on every major issue there are clashing opinions of powerful groups. Our expectations are unreasonable if they include the notion that the resolution of issues, or lawmaking, can be handled easily and without intense controversy. And impasse and stalemate should occasion no surprise. Barber Conable, a well-known New York congressman who retired in the mid-1980s, put the matter this way:

[People] who want Congress to move quickly and easily don't really want representative government at all. Congress does what's necessary—frequently at the last possible moment after a crisis has already developed. But representative government is always going to be behind the curve. If you understand that, you won't be disappointed in your expectations of our government.[72]

American legislatures represent all manner of economic interests; social classes; ethnic and religious groups; and assorted values, beliefs, and sentiments. Although groups sometimes agree on certain broad goals, they often go their separate ways when their interests are at stake. Thus there are frequent collisions in the legislature between the parochial interests of one group and those of another. The truth is that American society is simply too heterogeneous to permit the emergence of a single majority, including party, able to speak authoritatively for most citizens. American diversity, Herbert Agar observed in his classic book, requires acceptance of the fact that

> most politics will be parochial, most politicians will have small horizons, seeking the good of the state or the district rather than of the Union, yet by diplomacy and compromise, never by force, the government must water down the selfish demands of regions, races, classes, business associations, into a national policy which will alienate no major group and which will contain at least a small plum for everybody. This is the price of unity in a continentwide federation.[73]

The underlying problem of government is thus to find means by which diverse and antagonistic groups can be held together and conflict over policy kept within tolerable limits. For several reasons, the American polity performs this job better than most, and legislatures play a key role in this achievement. First, by bending extreme positions toward the middle or by isolating them, the system narrows the range of conflict. Second, the system makes it difficult for a majority (some of whose members may feel indifferently about the issue) to force its preferences on a vigorous minority (whose members are likely to feel intensely about the issue). Third, by encouraging compromise and accommodation, the political system diminishes the likelihood of class conflict. Fourth, the flexibility and tolerance found within the system make it easier for minorities to accept majority verdicts because the settlements are rarely as disagreeable as they could have been—the majority seldom wins completely; the minority seldom loses completely. To conclude this argument, in the usual policymaking scenario, a persistent lawmaking majority eventually gets most of what it wants.

Finally, it is useful to remember that legislatures reflect the realities of American society. Legislatures are not isolated institutions but rather are strongly influenced by their environment—the argument that introduced this book. They are primarily *reactive* institutions. More than any other branch of government, in fact, legislatures are sensitive to popular impulses, preferences, and doubts. Legislators hear a great deal from the public, and the moods that dominate it are soon reflected in their attitudes and behavior.[74] When the public is uncertain and divided on important questions, legislators are uncertain and divided. They talk, listen, and buy time. When the public decides what it wants, or will tolerate, legislatures act. Any interpretation of the legislative system that underestimates the legislature's responsiveness to its environment or the members' responsiveness to their constituencies ends up exaggerating the independence and autonomy of the members and the institution.

## NOTES

1. The House decision in 1885 to manipulate the Appropriations Committee's jurisdiction, removing nearly one-half of the total federal budget from its control, occurred because of growing House dissatisfaction over the independence and imperialism of the committee, along with its excessive "economy-mindedness." The move to strip the committee of its jurisdiction was led by members of the most powerful committees of the House, including Ways and Means, Rules, Judiciary, Banking and Currency, and Commerce. Members of those committees that would assume some portion of the Appropriations Committee's jurisdiction heavily supported the change. When this decision was reversed decades later, members from those committees that would lose jurisdiction were the principal opponents of consolidating the appropriations function. See Richard F. Fenno, Jr., *The Power of the Purse: Appropriations Politics in Congress* (Boston: Little, Brown, 1966), pp. 42–46.

2. The modern Congress begins with the passage of the Legislative Reorganization Act of 1946. See Roger H. Davidson, "The Legislative Reorganization Act of 1946," *Legislative Studies Quarterly*, XV (August 1990), 357–73.

3. Roger H. Davidson and Walter J. Oleszek, "Adaptation and Consolidation: Structural Innovation in the U.S. House of Representatives," *Legislative Studies Quarterly*, I (February 1976), 49. Their book-length study of the Bolling Committee should also be consulted: *Congress Against Itself* (Bloomington: Indiana University Press, 1977). Also see David E. Price, "The Ambivalence of Congressional Reform," *Public Administration Review*, XXXIV (November–December 1974), 601–608.

4. Richard L. Strout, "Democrats Ax House Reform," *Christian Science Monitor*, June 28, 1974; as quoted in Davidson and Oleszek, "Adaptation and Consolidation," 49.

5. See an analysis by Judith H. Parris, "The Senate Reorganizes Its Committees," *Political Science Quarterly*, XCIV (Summer 1979), 319–37.

6. See Samuel Rothstein, "The Origins of Legislative Reference Services in the United States," *Legislative Studies Quarterly*, XV (August 1990), 401–11.

7. *Book of the States, 1998–1999* (Lexington, KY: Council of State Governments, 1999), p. 110.

8. Rich Jones, "The State Legislatures," in *Book of the States, 1990–1991* (Lexington, KY: Council of State Governments, 1991), p. 115.

9. *Report on an Evaluation of the 50 State Legislatures* (Kansas City, MO: Citizens Conference on State Legislatures, 1971).

10. See Alan Rosenthal, "Beyond Legislative Reform," *State Legislatures*, VIII (July–August 1982), 17–21 (quotation on p. 19).

11. A study by Morris P. Fiorina finds that legislative professionalization is particularly attractive for Democractic state legislators, inducing them to stay in the legislature, because full-time service carries increased compensation. By contrast, the state legislature is less attractive to Republican members because they have more opportunities in the private sector. Professionalization thus contributes to divided government, as experienced Democrats are able to retain their seats even when a Republican governor is reelected. The decline in unified government is largely a decline in unified Republican government. "Divided

Government in the American States: A Byproduct of Legislative Professionalization," *American Political Science Review*, LXXXVIII (June 1994), 304–16. Peverill Squire finds some support for Fiorina's hypothesis, but contends that the increase in divided government is more likely to have resulted from changes in the behavior of legislators than from changes in the characteristics of the institution. "Another Look at Legislative Professionalization and Divided Government in the States," *Legislative Studies Quarterly*, XXII (August 1997), 417–32.

12. Rich Jones, "The Legislature 2010: Which Direction?" *State Legislatures*, July 1990, 22–25 (quotation on p. 24).

13. Peverill Squire finds a relationship between professionalization and membership diversity. The most professionalized legislatures (e.g., California, Michigan, Massachusetts, and New York) proportionately have more blacks and fewer women as members. Geographic concentration improves the chances for blacks to win, and professionalization makes winning seats worthwhile. Women are more likely to be elected in northern, liberal, and less professionlized states. "Legislative Professionalization and Membership Diversity in State Legislatures," *Legislative Studies Quarterly*, XVII (February 1992), 69–79.

14. See the evidence of Peverill Squire on the enduring quality of institutional arrangements in the state legislatures of California, Connecticut, and New York: "Member Career Opportunities and the Internal Organization of Legislatures," *Journal of Politics*, L (August 1988), 726–44.

15. Gary F. Moncrief, Joel A. Thompson, and Karl T. Kurtz, "The Old Statehouse, It Ain't What It Used to Be," *Legislative Studies Quarterly*, XXI (February 1996), 57–72.

16. Rosenthal, "Beyond Legislative Reform," 17–21. Also see William J. Keefe, "Legislative Leadership: A Time to Rebuild," *State Legislatures*, VII (May 1981), 22–25.

17. Albert K. Karnig and Lee Sigelman, "State Legislative Reform and Public Policy: Another Look," *Western Political Quarterly*, XXVIII (September 1975), 548–52. See also Leonard Ritt, "State Legislative Reform: Does It Matter?" *American Politics Quarterly*, I (October 1973), 499–510.

18. Joel A. Thompson, "State Legislative Reform: Another Look, One More Time, Again," *Polity*, XIX (Fall 1986), 27–41. For a study that finds that the level of professionalism of state legislatures is affected by the socioeconomic characteristics of its population, its governmental structures, and the extent of legislative professionalism found in its sister states, see Christopher Z. Mooney, "Citizens, Structures, and Sister States: Influence on State Legislative Professionalism," *Legislative Studies Quarterly*, XX (February 1995), 47–67.

19. John R. Hibbing, "Legislative Careers: Why and How We Should Study Them," *Legislative Studies Quarterly*, XXIV (May 1999), 149–72. Also see Charles Mahtesian, "The Sick Legislature Syndrome and How to Avoid It," *Governing* (February 1997), 16–20.

20. Barbara Sinclair, *The Transformation of the U.S. Senate* (Baltimore: Johns Hopkins University Press, 1989), p. 140.

21. *Pittsburgh Post-Gazette*, August 28, 1994.

22. David Austen-Smith and William H. Riker, "Asymmetric Information and the Coherence of Legislation," *American Political Science Review*, LXXXI (September 1987), 897–918.

23. *Davis* v. *Bandemer*, 106 S. Ct. 2810 (1986).

24. Although the apprenticeship norm is less important in Congress today, senior members nevertheless have disproportionate influence both in committees and on the floor. See the recent evidence marshalled in studies by John R. Hibbing, "Contours of the Modern Congressional Career," *American Political Science Review*, LXXXV (June 1991), 405–28; and Richard L. Hall, "Participation and Purpose in Committee Decision Making," *American Political Science Review*, LXXXI (March 1987), 105–27.

25. See Kenneth A. Shepsle, *The Giant Jigsaw Puzzle* (Chicago: University of Chicago Press, 1978); and Hall, "Participation and Purpose," 105–27.

26. See Norman J. Ornstein, Thomas E. Mann, and Michael J. Malbin, *Vital Statistics on Congress, 1993–1994* (Washington, DC: Congressional Quarterly Press, 1994), 206–16.

27. E. Scott Adler and John S. Lapinski, "Demand-Side Theory and Congressional Committee Composition: A Constituency Characteristics Approach," *American Journal of Political Science*, XLI (July 1997), 895–918.

28. "Representation and Congressional Committees," *The Annals*, CDXI (January 1974), 58.

29. *Congressional Quarterly Weekly Report*, August 2, 1975, p. 1674.

30. This quotation is from an instructive article by Alan Ehrenhalt, "The Individualistic Senate," *Congressional Quarterly Weekly Report*, September 4, 1982, pp. 2176–177.

31. *Congressional Record*, 101st Cong., 1st sess., May 11, 1990, p. S6038. (Daily edition.)

32. Steven S. Smith, "Informal Leadership in the Senate: Opportunities, Resources, and Motivations," in *Leading Congress: New Styles, New Strategies*, ed. John J. Kornacki (Washington, DC: Congressional Quarterly Press, 1990), p. 82.

33. *U.S. News & World Report*, September 12, 1960, p. 60.

34. Ehrenhalt, "The Individualistic Senate," pp. 2175–182.

35. *Congressional Quarterly Weekly Report*, November 3, 1984, p. 2870.

36. Willie Morris, "Legislating in Texas," *Commentary*, November 1964, p. 43.

37. Molly Ivins, "Inside the Austin Fun House," *Atlantic Monthly*, March 1975, p. 50.

38. *Pennsylvania Legislative Journal*, March 13, 1961, pp. 742–44. The bill failed.

39. *Adventures in Politics* (New York: Oxford University Press, 1954), p. 84.

40. *Washington Post*, April 18, 1977, p. 1.

41. Larry Sonis, "'O.K., Everybody Vote Yes': A Day in the Life of a State Legislator," *Washington Monthly*, June 1979, p. 25.

42. Quoted in James T. Murphy, "Partisanship, Party Conflict and Cooperation in House Public Works Committee Decision-Making," paper presented at the Annual Meeting of the American Political Science Association, Washington, DC, 1968. A revised edition appears in the *American Political Science Review*, LXVIII (March 1974), 169–85.

43. James L. Sundquist, "Congress and the President: Enemies or Partners?" in *Congress Reconsidered*, ed. Lawrence C. Dodd and Bruce I. Oppenheimer (New York: Praeger, 1977), p. 230.

44. For a perceptive treatment of legislators' explanations, see Richard F. Fenno, Jr., *Home Style: House Members in Their Districts* (Boston: Little, Brown, 1978), Chap. 5.

45. *Congressional Quarterly Weekly Report*, April 2, 1994, p. 786.

46. *The House of Representatives and Foreign Affairs* (Pittsburgh: University of Pittsburgh Press, 1966), p. 73.

47. See Arthur G. Stevens, Jr., Daniel P. Mulhollan, and Paul S. Rundquist, "U.S. Congressional Structure and Representation: The Role of Informal Groups," *Legislative Studies Quarterly*, VI (August 1981), 415–37; Burdett A. Loomis, "Congressional Caucuses and the Politics of Representation," in *Congress Reconsidered*, ed. Lawrence C. Dodd and Bruce I. Oppenheimer (Washington, DC: Congressional Quarterly Press, 1981), pp 204–20; Susan Webb Hammond, Daniel P. Mulhollan, and Arthur G. Stevens, Jr., "Informal Congressional Caucuses and Agenda Setting," *Western Political Quarterly*, XXXVIII (December 1985), 583–605; and Susan Webb Hammond, "Committee and Informal Leaders in the U.S. House of Representatives," in *Leading Congress: New Styles, New Strategies*, ed. John J. Kornacki (Washington, DC: Congressional Quarterly Press, 1990), pp. 57–69.

48. Scott H. Ainsworth and Frances Akins, "The Informational Role of Caucuses in the U.S. Congress," *American Politics Quarterly*, XXV (October 1997), 407–30 (quotation on p. 407).

49. See a study of constituency influence on the voting behavior of senators in the confirmation of Justice Clarence Thomas to the U.S. Supreme Court: L. Marvin Overby, Beth M. Henschen, Michael H. Walsh, and Julie Strauss, "Courting Constituents? An Analysis of the Senate Confirmation Vote on Justice Clarence Thomas," *American Political Science Review*, LXXXVI (December 1992), 997–1003.

50. *Congressional Quarterly Weekly Report*, September 11, 1993, p. 2374.

51. Roland Young, *The American Congress* (New York: Harper & Row, 1958), p. 267. See pp. 267–69 for further discussion of the need for legislative autonomy.

52. Alan Rosenthal, *The Decline of Representative Democracy: Process, Participation, and Power in State Legislatures* (Washington, DC: Congressional Quarterly Press, 1998), pp. 330–31.

53. Roger H. Davidson, "Breaking Up Those 'Cozy Triangles': An Impossible Dream?" paper

prepared for the Symposium on Legislative Reform and Public Policy, University of Nebraska, Lincoln, March 11–12, 1976.

54. *Hearings on Committee Organization in the House Before the Select Committee on Committees,* U.S. House of Representatives, 93rd Cong., 1st sess., 1973, III, p. 242. The statement is by John W. Gardner, chair of Common Cause.

55. Richard F. Fenno, Jr., *Congressmen in Committees* (Boston: Little, Brown, 1973), p. 6.

56. *Hearings on Committee Organization in the House,* p. 270. The statement is by Ralph Nader.

57. Davidson, "Breaking Up Those 'Cozy Triangles,'" pp. 1–3. But also see a study that finds that committee clientelism breaks down when members perceive an issue to have high public salience. In such cases, members are more likely to adopt positions that are in conflict with those of organized groups. David E. Price, "Policy Making in Congressional Committees: The Impact of 'Environmental' Factors," *American Political Science Review,* LXXII (June 1978), 569–70. Also see a study of energy policy subgovernments by Charles O. Jones and Randall Strahan, "The Effect of Energy Politics on Congressional and Executive Organization in the 1970s," *Legislative Studies Quarterly,* X (May 1985), 151–79.

58. Harvey Fergusson, *People and Power* (New York: William Morrow, 1947), pp. 101–102.

59. *The Perverted Priorities of American Politics* (New York: Macmillan, 1976), pp. 131–32.

60. *Time,* August 7, 1978, p. 15.

61. *U.S. News & World Report,* January 29, 1979, p. 24.

62. *Congressional Quarterly Weekly Report,* February 11, 1978, p. 323. Speaker O'Neill made this comment following the defeat of a bill to establish a federal Office of Consumer Protection.

63. *Congressional Quarterly Weekly Report,* April 23, 1983, p. 771.

64. Ibid. This remark was prompted by the Senate's 91–5 vote to delay tax withholding on interest and dividend income.

65. *Time,* March 3, 1986, p. 35.

66. *Hearings on Committee Organization in the House Before the Select Committee on Committees,* U.S. House of Representatives, 93rd Cong., 1st sess., 1973, II, p. 58.

67. The image of the legislature is difficult to protect. A single incident is likely to trigger a vast amount of public criticism. Consider these observations by a state legislator in Wisconsin: "We're all tarred with the same brush. What one legislator does affects all 133 of us. I can give you an illustration of that. A few years ago, some of the boys were whooping it up over in the Belmont Hotel and they amused themselves at night by throwing beer cans out of the window where they clattered musically down on the pavement below and the police were called and it was headlines in the paper. When I returned that weekend, as other legislators did, although I personally was not involved in the beer can throwing incident, we became the beer can throwing legislature. My constituents were saying to me: 'Is that all you've got to do down there is throw beer cans around?'" Quoted in Ronald D. Hedlund and Wilder Crane, Jr., *The Job of the Wisconsin Legislator* (Washington, DC: American Political Science Association, 1971), p. 69.

68. *Congressional Quarterly Weekly Report,* August 2, 1975, p. 1677.

69. Richard F. Fenno, Jr., "If, as Ralph Nader Says, Congress Is 'The Broken Branch,' How Come We Love Our Congressman So Much?" in *Congress in Change: Evolution and Reform,* ed. Norman J. Ornstein (New York: Praeger, 1975), pp. 277–87 (quotations on pp. 278 and 280).

70. *New York Times,* October 10, 1991.

71. E. E. Schattschneider, *The Semisovereign People* (New York: Holt, Rinehart & Winston, 1961), p. 40.

72. *U.S. News & World Report,* August 20, 1984, p. 30.

73. Herbert Agar, *The Price of Union* (Boston: Houghton Mifflin, 1950), p. xiv.

74. See the evidence of Suzanna De Boef and James Stimson that the composition of the U.S. House reflects the policy preferences of the electorate. When the preferences of the public change, that change is reflected in the membership of the House. "The Dynamic Structure of Congressional Elections," *Journal of Politics,* LVII (August 1995), 630–48.

# INDEX

Aberbach, Joel D., 417, 448, 449, 451, 455, 456
Abernethy, Byron R., 73
Abney, Glenn, 418, 224, 419, 456
Abraham, Henry J., 470, 486
Abramowitz, Alan I., 107, 130, 147, 148, 150, 151
Adams, Brock, 141
Adams, Bruce, 435, 453
Adler, E. Scott, 195, 223, 500, 519
Agar, Herbert, 517, 521
Ainsworth, Scott, 287, 509, 520
Aistrup, Joseph A., 147
Akins, Frances, 509, 520
Albert, Carl, 336
Albino deer, 505–06
Albritton, Robert B., 74, 383, 418
Alford, John R., 49, 146, 148
Alt, James E., 421
Althoff, Philip, 338
Alvarez, R. Michael, 36, 51
Ambrosius, Margery M., 185
Andrade, Lydia, 419
Ansolabehere, Stephen, 149
Apache Belles, 504
Apportionment (*see also* Representation)
    constitutional and statutory provisions, 86–87
    criteria for, 85
    gerrymandering, 88–89, 97–103
    impact, 103–105
    malapportionment, 88–92, 499–500
    majority-minority districts, 98–103, 109, 323, 340–41
    multimember districts, 96–97
    reapportionment, 89–105
Arnold, Peri, 452
Arnold, R. Douglas, 417
Art, Robert J., 455
Asher, Herbert B., 189, 289, 341
Aspin, Les, 39
AuCoin, Les, 516
Austen-Smith, David, 386, 519
Ayres, Q. Whitfield, 90, 107

Bach, Stanley, 259, 260, 263, 287
Bacheller, John M., 383
Bacon, Donald C., 482, 483
Bacot, A. Hunter, 146
Baer, Michael, 384, 386
Bagehot, Walter, 30
Bailey, Stephen K., 50, 345, 382, 387
Baker, John R., 184

Baker, Ross K., 336, 339
Barber, James David, 112, 145, 171, 173, 174, 188, 421
Barenblatt, Lloyd, 241
Barrett, Andrew, 421
Barrett, Edith J., 185
Barrow, Deborah J., 483
Bartels, Larry M., 341
Barthelmes, Wes, 48
Basehart, Harry, 91, 107, 227
Bauer, Monica, 131, 151
Bauer, Raymond A., 105, 386
Baum, Lawrence, 480, 484, 485, 486
Baumgartner, Frank R., 225, 235, 254, 451
Bawn, Kathleen, 338, 456, 485
Beer, Samuel, 385
Bell, Charles G., 106, 227, 255, 342, 386, 424
Beller, Scott, 482
Benjamin, Gerald, 74, 418
Bennett, Linda L. M., 47
Bennett, Robert S., 432
Bennett, Stephen Earl, 47
Berard, Stanley P., 340
Berg, Larry L., 486
Berkman, Michael B., 158, 184, 186, 188, 226
Berkson, Larry, 482
Bernick, E. Lee, 420, 424
Bernstein, Robert A., 145, 185
Berry, Gregory, 341
Beyle, Thad, 401, 417, 420, 422
Bianco, William T., 151
Bibby, John F., 74, 147
Bicameralism, 72–73, 404
Bicker, William E., 109
Bickers, Kenneth N., 36, 51
Bicknell, Patricia L., 108
Biden, Joseph, Jr., 178
Biersack, Robert, 153
Bimes, Terri L., 342
Binder, Sarah, 48
Binkley, Wilfred, 417
Bledsoe, Timothy, 151
Bloom, Howard S., 148
Blumenthal, Sidney, 233
Boller, Paul F., Jr., 422
Bolling, Richard, 206, 224, 302, 336, 490, 515
Bolling Committee, 490–91
Bond, Jon R., 146, 150, 151, 288, 414, 421, 422, 423, 452, 481, 482
Bone, Hugh A., 287, 334
Bonior, David E., 287, 510

**522**

Bookheimer, Samuel, 339
Borah, William E., 115
Born, Richard, 48, 107, 145, 146, 147, 189
Borrelli, Mary Anne, 453
Borrelli, Stephen A., 338, 339, 422, 423
Borris, Thomas J., 153
Bowers, James R., 451, 452
Bowler, Shaun, 482
Bowling, Cynthia J., 449, 456
Boyd, Steven R., 419
Boyd, Thomas A., 50
Boyd, William J. D., 107
Brace, Paul, 152
Bradley, Robert B., 289
Brady, David W., 154, 226, 304, 335, 337, 338, 339,
    340, 341, 342, 486
Breaux, David, 151, 152
Broach, Glen T., 341
Broder, David S., 48, 153
Brody, Richard, 335
Bromage, Arthur W., 484
Brooks, Jack, 447
Brown, Deborah Dwight, 186
Browne, William P., 49, 255, 385
Brunell, Thomas L., 47
Brunk, Gregory, 386
Bryce, James, 312
Buchanan, Scott, 152
Buchanan, William, 75, 81, 82, 106, 144, 145, 183,
    189, 289, 382
Budgetary and appropriations process, 11–12, 202,
    267, 391–96, 488, 518
Bullock, Charles S., III, 107, 119, 152, 184, 226, 339,
    340
Bumpers, Dale, 11, 270
Bupp, Irvin C., 418
Burford, Ann Gorsuch, 446
Burke, Edmund, 79, 106, 311
Burrell, Barbara C., 185
Bushnell, Eleanore, 482
Butler, David, 98, 108
Button, James, 159, 184
Byrd, Robert C., 295, 309


Cain, Bruce E., 98, 107, 108, 146
Caldeira, Gregory A., 313, 339, 481, 484
Califano, Joseph A., Jr., 422
Calvert, Randall L., 147, 421
Cameron, Charles, 109
Camobreco, John F., 74
Campagna, Janet, 90–91, 107
Campbell, Colin, 417, 420, 422
Campbell, James E., 123, 147, 152, 421
Campoli, Lisa, 452
Cannon, Joseph G., 260, 261, 291, 302, 488
Canon, David T., 109, 150, 187, 299, 335
Carbon, Susan B., 482
Carey, John M., 70, 75
Carlson, Eric H., 341
Carlucci, Carl, 106
Carpenter, Daniel P., 454
Carr, Robert K., 255
Carroll, Holbert N., 192, 223, 508
Carter, Stephen L., 481
Carver, Joan S., 109

Cary, William, 379
Cassie, William, 152, 153, 384
Celler, Emanuel, 226, 385, 387
Chafee, John, 316, 317, 320
Chappell, Henry, 384
Chase, Harold W., 255
Chief executive:
    administrative leader, 400–402
    agenda setting, 340
    appointments, 29–30
    budget making, 391–96
    crisis, 390
    fast tracking, 420
    impact on legislative elections, 122–23, 147
    impeachment of, 14–15
    and impoundment, 392–93
    item veto, 396, 398
    messages, 399–400
    patronage, 29–30, 402
    representative character, 402–03, 416
    special sessions, 400
    term of office, 404–405
    veto, 396–99, 419, 466
Chief executive, bases for influence:
    legal base, 327, 390–405
    partisan-political, 327, 406–08
    personal dimension, 408–12
    societal base, 389–90
Chief executive, effectiveness:
    measurement of, 412–15, 423
    proposal-passage ratio, 413–14
    vetoes overridden, 414–15
Cho, Yong Hyo, 109
Choike, James R., 185
Choper, Jesse H., 484
Christensen, Terry, 424
Cigler, Allan J., 347, 380, 383, 387
Clapp, Charles L., 74, 149, 188, 189, 336
Clark, Janet, 185
Clark, John A., 188, 486
Clausen, Aage R., 289, 421
Claveloux, Ronald L., 454
Clay, Henry, 271, 302, 303
Clem, Alan L., 147, 153, 154, 339
Clubb, Jerome M., 314, 338
Clucas, Richard A., 337, 338
Clynch, Edward J., 418
Coelho, Tony, 14
Cohen, Jeffrey E., 147, 152, 421, 423
Cohen, Julius, 238, 254
Cohen, Lauren M., 481
Coleman, John J., 339
Collender, Stanley E., 417
Collie, Melissa P., 146, 226, 315, 338, 339
Collier, Kenneth, 422
Collins, Peter L., 482
Collins, Susan, 316, 317, 320
Comer, John, 91, 107
Committees in Congress:
    assignment to, 209–11, 304, 500
    chair, 40, 208, 213, 215, 406, 489–90, 491
    committee-floor relations, 194, 250–51, 503–04
    conference, 193–94, 201–04, 352
    efficient element, 192
    executive sessions, 32–33, 245
    hearings, 230–36

Committees in Congress—(*Cont.*)
  House Rules Committee, 258–62, 269, 275, 286, 302, 332, 333, 488, 498
  investigating, 239–44, 244–45
  joint, 200–01
  jurisdiction, 206–08, 491
  power of, 190, 191–95, 211, 246–54, 350, 501
  prestige of, 212–13
  reports, 246–50
  representativeness, 195–97, 500–01
  select, 198–99
  seniority, 39, 213–17, 292, 332, 333
  sessions, 245–46
  staff, 218–21, 222, 230, 250
  standing, 190, 197–98, 199, 493
  subcommittees, 204–06, 214
Committees in state legislatures:
  assignment to, 212
  chair, 307
  hearings, 236–37
  power of, 351
  seniority, 227
Conable, Barber, 503, 516
Congressional Budget and Impoundment Control Act of 1974, 393
Congressional Budget Office, 428
Congressional Research Service, 428
Constitutional amendment process, 25–27
Contract with America, 8, 205, 333, 493
Cook, Timothy E., 48, 148, 151, 223
Cooper, Joseph, 154, 187, 223, 337, 338, 339, 451, 454
Copeland, Gary W., 51, 151
Cornwell, Elmer E., Jr., 227
Cortner, Richard C., 108
Corwin, Edwin S., 422
Cosgrove, Kenneth M., 102, 109
Costain, Anne N., 47, 387
Costain, W. Douglas, 387
Cover, Albert D., 50, 146, 147, 148
Covington, Gary R., 146, 150, 423
Cowden, Jonathan A., 153
Cox, Gary W., 150, 152
Craig, Barbara Hinkson, 451
Crane, Wilder, Jr., 383, 521
Cranor, John D., 107
Cranston, Alan, 299
Crawley, Gary L., 107
Crew, Robert E., Jr., 417
Crisp, Charles, 260
Crook, Sara Brandes, 75, 79, 106

Dabelko, Kirsten la Cour, 185
Dahl, Robert A., 475, 486
Dalton, Robert, 401, 420
D'Amato, Alphonse, 138
Danforth, John C., 11, 508, 514
Daniels, R. Steven, 339
Darcy, Robert, 185
Dauer, Manning J., 109
Davidson, Roger H., 20, 47, 48, 74, 106, 223, 224, 336, 454, 483, 501, 513, 518, 520, 521
Davis, Eric L., 388, 417, 422
Davis, Frank L., 384
Dawes, Roy A., 146
Daynes, Byron W., 420

Deakin, James, 384
Deber, Raisa B., 185
De Boef, Suzanna, 154, 521
Deckard, Barbara, 189
Deering, Christopher J., 225, 253, 256, 336
DeFigueiredo, John M., 483
de Grazia, Albert, 106
DeGregorio, Christine, 221, 228, 235, 254, 371, 386, 481
Demetrius, Nelson C., 420
DeNuccio, William J., 227
Derge, David R., 341
Dexter, Lewis A., 78, 83, 105, 106, 386
Dillon, Sonja G., 337
Dimock, Michael A., 151
Dingell, John D., 357
Dodd, Lawrence C., 49, 146, 148, 187, 338, 455, 520
Dolan, Kathleen, 184–85
Dole, Robert, 514
Donovan, John C., 51
Drew, Elizabeth, 224
Durant, Robert F., 146
Durden, Garey C., 384
Durenberger, David F., 8

Earmarking, 37–38
Edwards, George C., III, 147, 408, 416, 417, 420, 421, 422, 423, 424
Ehrenhalt, Alan, 11, 48, 520
Ehrmann, Henry W., 385
Eismeier, Theodore J., 153
Eldersveld, Samuel J., 385
Ellickson, Mark C., 49
Elling, Richard C., 289, 452
Elliott, Shelden D., 482
Emmert, Craig F., 482
Endersby, James W., 226
Enelow, James M., 288
Engler, Robert, 383
Entman, Robert E., 341
Epstein, David, 109, 226, 335, 455
Epstein, Lee, 486
Erickson, Brenda, 334
Erikson, Robert S., 109, 146
Eskridge, William N., Jr., 475, 485
Ethridge, Marcus, 450, 452, 456
Eulau, Heinz, 75, 81, 82, 106, 144, 145, 183, 184, 189, 289, 382
Evans, C. Lawrence, 205, 224
Evans, Diana M., 51, 146, 255, 351, 383, 384, 386, 456

Feingold, Russell D., 142
Feinstein, Dianne, 138
Feldman, Paul, 51, 149
Fenno, Richard F., Jr., 17, 19, 32, 48, 50, 146, 180, 189, 202, 203, 224, 225, 284, 290, 324, 334, 341, 383, 418, 518, 520, 521
Ferejohn, John A., 146, 147, 421
Ferguson, LeRoy, C., 75, 81, 82, 106, 144, 145, 183, 189, 289, 382
Fergusson, Harvey, 521
Fett, Patrick J., 74
Field, Oliver P., 472, 484, 485

Filibustering, 31–32, 271–74, 498
Finer, Herman, 191
Finkelman, Paul, 482
Fiorina, Morris P., 145, 146, 148, 168, 188, 225, 342, 406, 420, 518
Firestone, Juanita M., 185
Fischer, John, 192
Fishel, Jeff, 154
Fisher, Joel M., 227, 255, 424
Fisher, Louis, 393, 417, 418, 452, 453
Fite, Katherine B., 484–85, 486
Flathman, Marcus, 264, 287, 296, 335
Fleisher, Richard, 146, 150, 151, 288, 414, 421, 422, 423, 452, 481
Flemming, Gregory N., 147, 421
Flinn, Thomas A., 341
Foley, Thomas S., 17, 70, 301, 304, 336, 510
Ford, Lynne E., 185
Fortenberry, C. N., 227
Forth, Rod, 222
Fowler, Linda L., 113, 145
Fox, Harrison W., Jr., 188, 228
Fox, Sharon E., 223
Francis, Wayne L., 74, 226, 227, 255, 293, 334
Frankfurter, Felix, 483
Franking privilege, 169
Franklin, Charles H., 149
Frantzich, Stephen E., 187
Frederickson, H. George, 109
Freeman, J. Leiper, 255
Freeman, Patricia K., 51, 383, 452
Frendreis, John P., 384
Friedman, Barry, 486
Friedman, Sally, 187, 225
Friedrich, Carl J., 76, 77, 105, 342
Friesema, H. Paul, 106
Fritsch, Jane, 383
Froman, Lewis A., Jr., 66, 337, 342
Frost, Richard T., 387
Frye, Alton, 50
Frymer, Paul, 342
Fuller, Hubert Bruce, 287, 288

Gabler, Eugene J., 131
Gaddie, Ronald Keith, 148, 152, 384
Galbraith, J. Kenneth, 342
Galie, Peter J., 482, 485
Gamm, Gerald, 223
Garand, James C., 146, 149, 152, 336
Garber, Marc N., 483
Gardner, John W., 521
Garn, Jake, 503
Gates, John B., 484
Gelman, Andrew, 91, 107, 129, 149, 150
General Accounting Office (GAO), 428, 442, 453
George, Alexander, 421
George, Juliette, 421
Gephardt, Richard, 138, 139, 510
Gerber, Alan, 149, 153, 160, 184
Gerber, Elisabeth R., 60, 74, 383
Gere, Edwin Andrus, 383
Gerston, Larry N., 424
Gertzog, Irwin N., 185, 225
Gibbons, Sam, 357
Gibson, Martha L., 421, 452

Gierzynski, Anthony, 152
Giles, Michael, 153
Gingrich, Newt, 8, 126, 137, 205, 214, 244, 258, 297, 301, 304, 333, 336, 442, 492
Glazer, Amihai, 290
Glick, Henry F., 482
Glickman, Dan, 426
Goidel, Robert K., 149
Goldman, Sheldon, 481, 482
Goodman, Jay S., 227
Goodman, Marshall R., 50
Goodwin, George, Jr., 225
Gormley, Ken, 89, 107
Gosling, James, 398, 419
Gottlieb, Joel, 109
Gove, Samuel K., 89, 107, 227, 255
Graham, Peter, 482
Gramm, Phil, 339
Gramm-Rudman-Hollings Acts, 11–12, 394–95
Grau, Craig H., 151, 152
Gray, Virginia, 74, 383, 418
Green, Donald Phillip, 150, 153, 154
Greenstein, Fred, 408
Greider, William, 417, 418
Grenzke, Janet, 384
Grier, Kevin B., 140, 153, 225
Griffin, Robert, 341
Griffith, Ernest S., 225
Grimaldo, Michele, 482
Grofman, Bernard, 47, 91, 106, 107, 108, 184, 225, 341
Groseclose, Timothy, 151
Gross, Bertram, 288
Gross, Debra S., 50
Gross, Donald A., 146

Hacker, Andrew, 107
Haddon, Michael, 74, 187
Hahn, Harlan, 337
Hale, Dennis, 456
Hall, Richard L., 148, 177, 187, 189, 197, 205, 223, 224, 225, 384, 519
Halpern, Stephen C., 484
Hamilton, James, 455
Hamilton, Lee H., 78
Hamm, Keith E., 74, 217, 227, 255, 289, 337, 341, 342, 386
Hamman, John A., 147, 421
Hammond, Susan Webb, 188, 228, 520
Hammond, Thomas H., 455
Handberg, Roger B., 418
Handley, Lisa, 184
Hansen, Susan B., 73, 418
Harbison, Winfred, 484, 486
Harmel, Robert, 226, 334, 337, 341
Harris, Joseph P., 452, 453
Hartley, Roger E., 482
Hastert, J., Dennis, 8, 205, 301, 304–05, 334, 336
Hatfield, Mark, 176
Hausegger, Lori, 485, 486
Havens, Harry S., 453
Haynes, Evan, 482
Haynes, George H., 215, 226, 288
Hechler, Ken, 289, 336
Hedge, David, 159, 184
Hedger, Scott, 423

Hedlund, Ronald D., 73, 74, 106, 217, 226, 227, 383, 521
Helms, Jesse, 316, 317
Henkin, Louis, 26, 49
Henschen, Beth M., 227, 468, 476, 481, 483, 486, 520
Herrera, Cheryl L., 340
Herrera, Richard, 340
Herrick, Rebekah, 186, 189, 335
Herring, E. Pendleton, 402
Herring, Mary, 159, 184
Herrnson, Paul S., 112, 145, 153, 185
Herzberg, Donald G., 385, 386
Hibbing, John R., 39, 49, 51, 75, 79, 106, 131, 146, 148, 151, 164, 176, 180, 186, 187, 188, 189, 223, 289, 497, 519
Hickman, Martin, 472
Hill, Jeffrey S., 108
Hill, Kevin A., 109, 341
Hill, Kim Quaize, 418
Hill, Marjorie Renee, 417
Hills, Roderick M., 436
Hinckley, Barbara, 149, 335
Hird, John A., 51, 148
Hobbs, Edward H., 227
Hodson, Timothy, 74, 75
Hofeller, Thomas, 106
Hoff, Samuel B., 419
Holbrook, Thomas M., 152
Holcombe, Arthur, 484
Holmes, Lisa M., 482
Holtzman, Abraham, 422
Hopenhayn, Hugo, 456
Horack, Frank E., Jr., 483
Hoyer, Robert, 74, 187
Hrebenar, Ronald, 368, 383, 386
Huber, John D., 456
Huckshorn, Robert J., 154
Huffington, Michael, 138
Huitt, Ralph K., 232, 295, 334
Hult, Karen M., 451
Humphries, Craig, 153
Hunt, Margaret A., 385
Hunter, Kenneth, 386
Huntington, Samuel, 328
Hurley, Patricia A., 154, 335, 338, 339, 342, 451
Hutchings, Vincent L., 184
Hutchison, Tony, 418, 419
Hyde, Henry J., 15, 167, 188
Hyneman, Charles S., 156, 166, 184, 187, 188

Ignani, Joseph, 485
Impeachment process, 43
Initiative and referendum, 59–61, 383, 495
Interest groups:
  access to legislature, 350–52, 368
  alliances between, 362–63, 385
  bribery, 354–60, 514
  campaign contributions, 354–60, 384
  and democratic government, 4–7, 344–47, 377–82
  demonstrative lobbying, 361–62
  effectiveness, 366–70, 386–87
  grass-roots (indirect) lobbying, 363–65
  inspired communications, 352–54
  legislator-lobbyist relations, 370–73, 514
  lobbyists, 347–49

political action committees (PACs), 6–7, 138–43, 211, 225, 354–60, 384
  and political parties, 316, 317, 318–19, 346, 365–66
  regulation of, 373–78
  social lobby, 359–61, 385
  techniques, 352–63
Ivins, Molly, 47, 520

Jackson, John S., III, 187
Jackson, Robert A., 150
Jacob, Herbert, 74, 369, 383, 386, 418, 420
Jacobs, Lawrence, 298, 335, 453
Jacobson, Gary C., 146, 148, 149, 151, 154, 330, 342
James, Kathy, 418
Jameson, Patricia E., 337
Javits, Jacob, 432
Jeffords, James, 316, 317
Jeffreys-Jones, Rhodri, 454
Jenkins, Jeffrey A., 224
Jenny, Nicholas W., 455
Jewell, Malcolm E., 50, 151, 152, 153, 384, 403, 420
Johannes, John R., 50, 146, 150, 452
Johnson, Cathy Marie, 451, 456
Johnson, Haynes, 422
Johnson, Loch K., 454
Johnson, Nancy L., 220
Jondrow, James, 51
Jones, Bryan D., 225, 235, 254, 451
Jones, Charles O., 9, 45, 47, 49, 52, 119, 254, 342, 422, 424, 521
Jones, Rich, 74, 75, 518, 519
Jones, Ruth S., 153
Judicial impact on legislative process:
  flag burning, 473
  interpretation of law, 467–68, 483–84
  judicial review, 468–72
  lobbying, 473
  politics and law, 479–80, 482–83
  procedures, 465–66
  public policy, 466–72
  reapportionment, 92–105

Kahn, Kim Fridkin, 149, 162, 186
Kaiser, Frederick, 452, 454, 455
Kammerer, Gladys, 218
Karlan, Pamela S., 108
Karnig, Albert K., 519
Kasich, John R., 309
Kathlene, Lyn, 186
Katz, Jonathan N., 150
Katzmann, Robert A., 481, 483
Kau, James B., 384
Kavanagh-Baran, Kathryn, 435, 453
Kawato, Sadafumi, 226
Kazee, Thomas A., 113, 145, 151
Keating, Charles H., 360, 432
Keating Five, 14, 360, 432
Keefe, William J., 49, 147, 341
Keith, Gary, 342
Keller, Morton, 482, 483
Kelley, Stanley, 364, 385
Kelly, Alfred H., 484, 486
Kennedy, Edward M., 514

Kenney, Patrick J., 145
Kenny, Christopher, 149
Kephart, Thomas, 224, 336
Kerbel, Matthew, 422
Kessel, John H., 420
Key, V. O. Jr., 114, 342
Keynes, Edward, 485, 486
Kiewiet, D. Roderick, 146, 148, 187, 449, 455
Kim, Jay C., 36
Kim, Thomas P., 342
Kimball, David, 19, 49, 184
Kincaid, Diane D., 185
Kincaid, John, 482
Kinder, Donald R., 148
King, David C., 207, 208, 225
King, Gary, 91, 107, 129, 149, 150
King, Kimi Lynn, 485
Kingdon, John W., 106, 289
Kinney, Rhonda, 423
Kirkpatrick, Evron M., 343
Kite, Darla W., 337
Knight, Jack, 486
Knott, Jack H., 455
Koehler, David H., 288
Koetzle, William, 154
Kofmehl, Kenneth, 188
Korn, Jessica, 452
Kornacki, John J., 334, 336, 338, 520
Kornberg, Allan, 184
Koven, Steven G., 109
Kozak, David C., 52, 106, 227, 283, 289, 421
Krasno, Jonathan S., 150, 153, 154
Krassa, Michael A., 147, 421
Krehbiel, Keith, 151, 223, 225
Krutz, Glen S., 423, 452, 481
Kuklinski, James H., 342
Kumar, Martha, 453
Kunkel, Joseph A., III, 145
Kurtz, Karl T., 74, 75, 222, 228, 383, 519
Kymlicka, B. B., 424

Lacy, Alex B., Jr., 227
La Follette, Robert M., Jr., 198, 273
Lamb, Charles M., 484
Lambro, Donald, 455
Lance, Bert, 435
Landis, James M., 483
Lane, Eric, 10, 47, 267, 288, 337, 428, 451
Langbein, Laura I., 189, 384
Langue, Donald, 482
Lapinski, John S., 195, 223, 500, 519
Latham, Earl, 50, 344
Lauth, Thomas P., 224, 418, 419, 456
Lavelle, Rita, 446
Lawrence, Eric D., 335
Leahy, Patrick J., 503
LeBlanc, Hugh L., 341
Lee, Frances E., 39, 51, 107
Lee, Jeong-Hwa, 223, 225
Lefever, Ernest W., 436
Legislation:
   bill introduction, 49
   complexity, 31
   "fetcher" bills, 15
   initiative and referendum, 59–61
   local and special, 58
   logrolling, 23–24
   "pork," 36–37, 38
Legislative functions:
   checking the administration, 27–30, 425–56
   educating the public, 30–33
   judicial, 42–43
   leadership selection, 43–44
   making law, 8–9, 21–27, 45–47
   representation, 33–42
Legislative oversight of bureaucracy:
   appointments, 434–37, 452–53
   budgetary control, 440–41
   casework, 40, 50, 431–32, 452, 502
   conduct of administrators, 437–40
   conflict of interest, 438–40, 453
   effectiveness, 442–51
   executive privilege, 444–46, 454
   foreign policy, 432–33, 436, 445, 456
   informal techniques, 428, 449, 455
   Inspector General, 437–38
   intelligence, 444
   latent oversight, 455
   legislative veto, 429–31, 452, 475
   personnel, 434–40
   policy implementation, 428–33
   political activity of bureaucrats, 438
   politics and administration, 425–27, 451
   removal of bureaucrats, 440
   reorganization of executive branch, 429–30,
      433–34, 452
   reports required, 431, 452
   structure of executive branch, 433–34
Legislative oversight of judiciary (see also Judicial
      impact on legislative process)
   procedure and jurisdiction, 463–64
   reaction to judicial decisions, 472–79, 485–86
   salary, 461, 477
   selection and removal of judges, 459–62, 480–81
   structure of courts, 462–63
Legislative procedure:
   amendments, 268–71
   bill referrals, 206–07
   calendars, 257–58
   Calendar Wednesday, 258, 262–63
   closed and open rules, 259–60, 269
   debate, 271–82, 503
   discharge rule, 262–63, 265–66
   five-minute rule, 276, 288
   holds, 274, 435–36
   logjams, 266–67
   privileged bills, 258
   riders, 270–71
   rules, 8–9, 65–66, 259, 271–84
   scheduling legislation, 264–68
   suspension of the rules, 263–64, 276
   voting, 283–86, 503
Legislative Reorganization Act of 1946, 218, 219,
      293, 374–76, 429, 441, 487, 488
Legislative Reorganization Act of 1970, 285, 429, 489
Legislative veto (see Legislative oversight of
      bureaucracy)
Legislators:
   African-American, 159–60
   backgrounds, 155–63
   bases for voting, 283–87, 337, 338, 339

Legislators—(*Cont.*)
  and bedbugs, 504
  and beer-can throwing, 521
  and bounced checks, 169
  businessmen, 157, 158
  casework, 40, 50, 431–32, 452, 502
  clientelism, 512–13
  educational achievement, 157
  election of, 117–33, 163–67, 421
  ethics, 12–17, 169, 211
  farmers, 157, 158
  financing elections, 134–43, 338–39
  goals, 501–06
  Hispanic, 159, 161
  honoraria, 12–13
  incumbents, 7, 19, 36, 91, 92, 115–16, 118, 128–32, 165–66, 384
  lawyer members, 157, 158
  midterm elections, 123–27
  nominations, 114–17
  norms, 175–81, 189
  parochialism, 10, 506–10, 517
  pay and perquisites, 167–70
  privileges and immunities, 170
  recruitment, 110–14, 173–74
  religion, 159, 161
  roles, 188
  scandals, 13–16, 57
  senatorial courtesy, 29
  socialization of, 156–57, 170–81, 346
  staff, 169, 442
  tenure and turnover, 163–67
  women, 161–62, 184–85, 186, 225
Legislature:
  approval of public, 184, 497, 514, 521
  confidence in, 17–20
  constitutional status, 54–61
  discontent over, 3–20
  fragmentation of power, 496–97, 510–12
  functions of, 21–44
  and innovation, 7–8
  and majority rule, 498–99
  norms, 24, 278, 335, 519
  organizing the, 59–63
  and political system, 497, 517–18
  presiding officers, 63–65
  professionalization, 518–19
  reform, 487–97
  sessions, 71–72, 494
  size, 66–67, 405, 515
  terms, 67–68, 501
  term limits, 69–70, 514–15
LeLoup, Lance T., 418, 423
Levin, A. Leo, 482
Levinson, L. Harold, 452
Levitt, Steven, 150
Lewinsky, Monica, 43, 233–34
Leyden, Kevin M., 338, 339
Light, Paul C., 437, 453
Linde, Hans A., 484
Lindsay, James M., 50, 423
Lippmann, Walter, 10, 50, 80, 106
Little, Thomas H., 152, 304, 337
Livingston, Robert L., 15, 304
Livingston, Steven G. , 187
Lockard, Duane, 7, 365, 385, 513

Lockerbie, Brad, 422, 423
Logrolling, 267, 511
Lohmann, Susanne, 456
Lonergan, Edward, 152
Long, Huey, 273
Longworth, Nicholas, 303
Loomis, Burdett A., 334, 335, 336, 347, 380, 383, 387, 520
Lott, Trent, 316, 317, 508
Lotwis, Mark A., 384
Lowell, A. Lawrence, 312
Lowery, David, 339
Lowry, Robert C., 421
Lublin, David Ian, 109, 150, 184
Luce, Robert, 198, 224, 230, 237, 254, 261, 283, 287, 289, 290
Luttbeg, Norman R., 187
Lynn, Naomi B., 341, 342
Lyons, William, 486

Macartney, John D., 52
Mackenzie, G. Calvin, 453
Maestas, Cherie, 145
Maggiotto, Michael A., 109
Mahtesian, Charles, 519
Maisel, L. Sandy, 113, 145
Majstorovic, Steven, 47
Malachowski, James, 339
Malbin, Michael J., 22, 51, 74, 124, 147, 188, 219, 223, 225, 227, 228, 254, 519
Maltese, John Anthony, 481
Maltzman, Forrest, 48, 194, 223
Manley, John, 203, 221
Mann, Thomas E., 22, 51, 124, 147, 188, 223, 225, 227, 254, 418, 519
Mansfield, Mike, 295
Margolis, Michael, 343
Marra, Robin F., 148
Marsh, Paul E., 387
Martin, Joe, 336
Marz, Roger H., 152
Mashaw, Jerry L., 451
Massaro, John, 481
Mather, Jeanie, 224
Mathias, Charles, 48
Matland, Richard E., 186
Matthews, Donald R., 144, 156, 175, 180, 183, 188, 189, 278, 288, 371, 386, 421
Matthews, J. V., 424
Maurer, Lynn M., 49
May, Richard, 309
Mayer, Kenneth R., 451
Mayhew, David R., 47, 51, 127, 146, 147, 148, 149, 331, 334, 339, 342, 448, 455, 456
Mazzoli, Romano L., 211
McAdams, John C., 50, 146, 150
McBurnett, Michael, 149
McCain, John, 142
McCartney, John D., 289
McCarty, Nolan, 449, 452, 453, 455
McClain, Paula D., 108
McCloskey, Robert, 458, 486
McClure, Robert D., 113, 145
McCormack, John W., 175
McCormick, James M., 408, 421

McCrone, Donald, 484
McCubbins, Mathew D., 146, 449, 450, 454, 455, 456
McCurdy, Karen M., 226
McCurley, Carl, 147
McGeary, M. Nelson, 254, 255, 424
McGuire, Kevin T., 486
McIntosh, Wayne, 480
McKay, David, 419
McKean, Dayton, 383
McManus, Susan A., 108
Meador, Daniel J., 482
Meernik, James, 423, 456, 485
Meier, Kenneth J., 51
Melnick, R. Shep, 483
Metzenbaum, Howard M., 503
Mezey, Susan Gluck, 483
Michel, Robert H., 297
Milbrath, Lester, 381, 383, 385, 386, 387
Miller, Arthur H., 49
Miller, Edward J., 420
Miller, James N., 48
Miller, Mark C., 486
Miller, Randall K., 485, 486
Miller, Warren, 83
Mills, C. Wright, 10, 439, 453
Mills, Wilbur, 406
Mineta, Norman, 450
Mischler, William, 480
Mitchell, George J., 309
Moe, Ronald C., 452
Moe, Terry M., 455
Moncrief, Gary F., 74, 75, 144, 184, 186, 187, 221, 228, 342, 383, 519
Mondak, Jeffrey J., 74–75, 147
Mondale, Walter F., 229
Monroney, A. S. Mike, 198, 452
Moon, David, 50
Mooney, Christopher Z., 289, 519
Moore, Michael K., 39, 51, 164, 186, 187, 189, 335
Moraski, Byron J., 481
Morehouse, Sara McCally, 341, 342, 421
Morgenstern, Scott, 152
Morin, Richard, 48
Morris, Jack H., 255
Morris, William D., 152
Morris, Willie, 520
Morse, Wayne, 273
Mosca, Angelo A., Jr., 227
Mosely-Braun, Carol, 159
Mosher, Frederick C., 453
Muchmore, Lynn R., 417
Muller, Keith J., 420
Mulhollan, Daniel P., 520
Munger, Michael C., 140, 153, 225
Murphy, James T., 520
Murphy, Walter F., 478, 484, 486
Murtha, John P., 38
Musmanno, M. A., 485

Nader, Ralph, 521
Nagel, Stuart, 478, 486
Nagler, Jonathan, 223
Natchez, Peter B., 418
Nechemias, Carol, 185

Nelson, Candice J., 146
Nelson, Gaylord, 502
Nelson, Margaret Virginia, 472, 484, 485
Neuberger, Richard L., 362, 506
Neustadt, Richard E., 399, 403, 410, 415, 420, 424
Nice, David C., 386, 419
Niemi, Richard G., 70, 75, 106, 108, 187
Norpoth, Helmut, 147, 148
Norris, George W., 261, 302
Norton, Clark F., 431
Nownes, Anthony J., 383
Nye, Mary Alice, 339, 340

Obey, David R., 37, 214
O'Brien, David M., 483, 484
O'Brien, Lawrence F., 411
O'Connor, Robert E., 186
Oden, William E., 227
Ogle, David B., 224
Ogul, Morris S., 50, 448, 451, 452, 453, 454, 455, 456
O'Halloran, Sharyn, 109, 226, 449, 455
Oleszek, Walter J., 224, 336, 448–49, 455, 518
Olson, David M., 337, 338
O'Neill, Thomas P. (Tip), 11, 303, 336, 491, 514, 521
Opheim, Cynthia, 74, 187, 387
Oppenheimer, Bruce I., 49, 84, 106, 107, 146, 148, 187, 338, 520
Ornstein, Norman J., 22, 48, 51, 124, 147, 188, 223, 225, 227, 254, 418, 519
O'Rourke, Timothy G., 108
Ostdiek, Donald, 107
Ostrum, Charles W., Jr., 148
Ottinger, Richard L., 6, 357
Overby, L. Marvin, 102, 109, 187, 481, 520
Owens, John R., 146

Palmer, Harvey, 149
Panetta, Leon E., 24, 514
Parker, Frank R., 108
Parker, Glenn R., 20, 48, 146, 149
Parker, Suzanne L., 146
Parris, Judith H., 518
Paschal, Richard A., 485
Patterson, Samuel C., 19, 49, 184, 226, 288, 298, 304, 313, 334, 335, 337, 339, 423, 482, 485
Payne, James L., 146, 254
Peabody, Robert L., 105, 294, 299, 308, 334, 335, 337
Peake, Jeffrey, 421
Pearson, James B., 299
Pearson, William A., 456
Pease, Donald, 498
Peppers, Donald, 423
Perkins, Lynette Palmer, 50, 225
Perry, H. W., Jr., 480
Peterson, Mark A., 388, 394, 417, 418, 422, 424
Petracca, Mark, 75
Pfahler, Madeleine, 456
Pinderhughes, Dianne M., 108
Pitkin, Hanna F., 105
Pitney, John J., Jr., 287, 337
Plumlee, John Patrick, 418
Pois, Joseph, 453
Political Action Committees (PACs) (*see* Interest Groups)

Political parties:
    caucus or conference, 261, 291–93, 332, 489
    conservative coalition, 4, 321–23, 326, 340
    Democratic Study Group, 11, 326–27, 509
    discipline, 117, 295, 303, 340, 346, 502–03, 511
    and divided government, 47, 330–31, 342–43,
        407–08, 421, 448–49, 455, 482
    floor leaders, 264, 274, 295–300, 332, 336, 337, 340
    and informal caucuses, 508–09
    intra-party divisions, 309–10, 320–23
    leadership selection, 308–09, 335
    and liberalism-conservatism, 316–20, 328–29
    nomination of legislators, 116–17
    party responsibility, 8–9, 41, 293, 325–26, 331–33,
        343, 510
    party voting in Congress, 311–20, 339
    party voting in the states, 305, 324–28
    policy and steering committees, 209, 214, 261,
        293–95
    and policy change, 316–20, 324, 340, 341, 342
    rural-urban conflict, 325, 328
    separation of powers, 329–31
    whips, 300–01
Pollock, Philip H., III, 153
Polsby, Nelson W., 105, 107, 109, 193, 215, 226, 336
Pomper, Gerald M., 343
Ponder, Daniel E., 74
Pool, Ithiel deSola, 105, 386
Poole, Keith T., 289
Popkin, William D., 483
Porter, H. Owen, 288
Porter, Mary Cornelia, 484
Posler, Brian D., 298, 335
Powell, Adam Clayton, 465
Powell, Lynda W., 70, 75, 108
Prewitt, Kenneth, 184
Price, Charles M., 106, 227, 255, 424
Price, David E., 25, 49, 227, 518, 521
Price, H. Douglas, 148
Pritchard, Anita, 151, 153, 423
Proxmire, William, 436, 503
Putnam, Robert D., 417

Quinlan, Stephen V., 49
Quinn, John C., 383
Quirk, Paul J., 7, 47

Radcliff, Benjamin, 387
Rader, Dotson, 47, 336
Ragsdale, Lyn, 146, 148, 149, 151
Ragsdale, W. B., 453
Ranney, Austin, 343
Ransone, Coleman B., Jr., 397, 417, 419, 422
Ray, Bruce A., 196, 223
Ray, David, 255, 305, 337, 387
Rayburn, Sam, 303, 336, 441
Razaghian, Rose, 449, 452–53, 455
Reed, Thomas B., 260, 276, 291, 302, 303
Regens, James L,, 384
Reingold, Beth, 185, 186
Remington, Michael J., 482
Renka, Russell D., 423
Representation:
    representative-constituency relations, 77–84, 176,
        289–90, 499–501, 513–14, 521

Rhee, Jungho, 223, 225
Rhodes, Carl M., 296, 335
Rhodes, John, 297
Ribicoff, Abraham, 514
Rice, Tom W., 145
Richardson, Lilliard E., Jr., 51, 452, 481
Richardson, Sula P., 249
Riddick, Lloyd, 262
Riddlesperger, James W., 255
Riker, William H., 519
Ringelstein, Albert C., 419
Ringquist, Delbert J., 255
Ripley, Randall B., 49, 252, 256, 336, 337
Ritt, Leonard, 519
Robbins, Marc, 290
Roberts, Brian E., 226
Roberts, Chalmers, 107
Roberts, Robert N., 453
Robinson, James A., 334
Rockman, Bert A., 417, 422, 424, 451
Rogers, Lindsay, 277, 288
Rohde, David W., 145, 225, 315, 339, 419
Romer, Thomas, 357, 384
Romero, David W., 130, 150
Roper, Robert T., 463
Rosen, Corey M., 189
Rosenthal, Alan, 152, 187, 222, 227, 228, 388, 406,
        412, 417, 419, 420, 421, 422, 423, 441, 449, 450,
        451, 452, 453, 456, 496, 512, 518, 519, 520
Rossiter, Clinton, 295
Rossoti, Jack E., 481
Rostenkowski, Dan, 246
Rothstein, Samuel, 518
Rourke, Francis E., 50, 454
Rowland, C. K., 482
Rozell, Mark J., 454
Rubenstein, Louis B., 485, 486
Rubin, Eva R., 483
Rubin, Paul H., 384
Ruckman, P. S., Jr., 481
Rudman, Warren, 481
Rudolph, Thomas J., 384
Rule, Wilma, 185
Rundquist, Barry S., 196, 223, 224, 225
Rundquist, Paul S., 520

Sabatier, Paul, 222, 228, 289
Sabato, Larry, 391
Sabo, Kevin, 455
Saiz, Martin, 387
Salisbury, Robert H., 52
Sanders, Francine, 130, 150, 339
Saving, Jason L., 36, 51
Schantz, Harvey L., 119, 145
Schattschneider, E. E., 5, 47, 338, 342, 343, 344, 382,
        387, 516, 521
Scheb, John M., II, 481, 486
Scheele, Raymond H., 107
Schick, Allen, 393, 394, 395, 417, 418
Schier, David, 339
Schiller, Wendy J., 49
Schippers, David P., 233
Schlesinger, Arthur M., Jr., 422
Schlesinger, Joseph, 119, 121, 335, 420
Schlozman, Kay Lehman, 387
Schmidhauser, John, 486

Schneier, Edward V., 338
Schott, Richard L., 455
Schousen, Matthew M., 109
Schroeder, Christopher, 455
Schumer, Charles, 138
Schwartz, Thomas, 450, 454, 456
Scicchitano, Michael J., 451
Sciortino, John, 152
Scott, Andrew M., 385
Scott, Ruth K., 383
Segal, David, 451
Selfridge, Wayne, 480
Seligman, Lester, 111, 144, 145
Sellers, Patrick J., 37, 51, 109
Senatorial courtesy, 436
Seniority (*see* Committees in Congress, Committees
    in state legislatures, Legislators, and Political
    parties)
Serra, George, 50
Shaffer, William R., 339
Shan, Chao-Chi, 152
Shane, Peter M., 454
Shannon, Wayne, 342
Shapiro, Robert, 298, 335, 453
Sheehan, Reginald S., 480
Shelley, Marc C., III, 340
Shepsle, Kenneth A., 52, 74, 183, 193, 206, 215, 223,
    224, 226, 519
Shields, Todd G., 149
Shin, Kwang S., 187
Shipan, Charles R., 456, 481, 484, 485
Shipley, Carl L., 482
Shull, Steven, 423
Sidlow, Edward I., 227, 483, 486
Sigelman, Lee, 48, 189, 519
Silberman, Jonathan, 384
Silverman, Corinne, 342
Simon, Dennis M., 419
Simon, Paul, 48, 268
Sinclair, Barbara, 50, 180, 189, 223, 251, 256, 274, 288,
    303, 310, 334, 336, 338, 339, 340, 341, 417, 418,
    519
Slotnick, Elliot, 482
Smist, Frank J., Jr., 454
Smith, Eric R.A.N., 150, 340
Smith, Frank E., 189
Smith, Franklin A., 484
Smith, Richard A., 386
Smith, Steven S., 194, 223, 224, 225, 253, 256, 259,
    260, 264, 287, 288, 296, 298, 335, 520
Smith, T. V., 283
Snider, L. Britt, 454
Snowe, Olympia, 316, 317, 320
Snyder, James M., Jr., 357, 384
Solimine, Michael L., 478
Songer, Donald R., 289, 337
Sonis, Larry, 287, 290, 337, 520
Sorauf, Frank J., 110, 144
Speaker of the House, 63–64, 251, 258, 259, 260, 261,
    291, 301–05, 336, 442, 488, 490
Speaker, state legislature, 305–08, 337
Spear, Mary, 159, 184
Specter, Arlen, 316, 317, 320
Spencer, Robert C., 154
Spitzer, Robert J., 419, 424
Squire, Peverill, 107, 150, 151, 166, 184, 187, 188, 227,
    305, 337, 519

Starr, Kenneth, 233, 437
Stathis, Stephen W., 454
Steger, Wayne R., 423
Stein, Robert M., 36, 51
Steiner, Gilbert Y., 89, 107, 202, 224, 227, 255
Stevens, Arthur G., Jr., 249, 520
Stevenson, Adlai, 398
Stewart, Joseph, Jr., 108
Stimson, James A., 148, 521
Stockman, David, 391
Stokes, Donald, 83
Stone, Walter J., 113, 145, 341
Stonecash, Jeffrey M., 152, 153, 187–88
Strahan, Randall, 521
Strain, Judith A., 342
Strauss, Julie, 481, 520
Strauss, Lewis L., 453
Strickland, Stephen P., 484
Strom, Gerald S., 224
Strout, Richard L., 518
Studlar, Donley T., 162, 186
Sullivan, Terry, 422
Sullivan, William E., 335
Sulzner, George T., 383
Summers, Joe, 123, 147
Sundquist, James L., 507, 520
Sunset laws, 434
"Sunshine" rules (*see* Committees in Congress:
    executive sessions)
Sussman, Glen, 420
Swanson, Wayne R., 334
Swers, Michele L., 186
Swift, Elaine K., 75, 223

Tacheron, Donald G., 188
Taggart, William A., 146
Talbert, Jeffrey C., 151, 225, 235, 254, 451
Tanenhaus, Joseph, 486
Tarr, G., Alan, 484
Tatalovich, Raymond, 339
Taylor, Andrew J., 421
Taylor, Telford, 485
Theilmann, John, 384
Theriault, Sean M., 187
Thomas, Clive, 368, 383, 386
Thomas, Martin, 289
Thomas, Norman, 184
Thomas, Robert D., 418
Thomas, Scott J., 154
Thomas, Sue, 180, 186, 189
Thompson, Joel A., 74, 152, 153, 184, 186, 187, 221,
    228, 342, 383, 384, 392, 418, 463, 497, 519
Thompson, Pat, 419
Thornberry, Mary C., 113, 145
Tidmarch, Charles M., 152
Tiller, Emerson H., 483
Tobin, Richard J., 145
Todd, Bridget Jeffery, 482
Traficant, James A., 38
Traugott, Santa A., 314, 338
Truman, David B., 188, 230, 231, 252, 254, 297, 334,
    335, 377, 386
Thurber, James A., 423, 455
Thurmond, J., Strom, 273
Tubbesing, Carl D., 188
Tucker, Harvey J., 152, 266, 287

Tufte, Edward R., 126, 148
Turner, Henry A., 385
Turner, Julius, 312, 313, 338

Udall, Morris K., 188, 268
Udall, Stewart L., 288
Unekis, Joseph K., 289
Underwood, James M., 337
Underwood, William D., 337
Unruh, Jesse, 359, 370, 385, 386

Van Dunk, Emily, 150
Van Houweling, Robert P., 187
Van Tassel, Emily, 482
Vardys, V. Stanley, 224
Vega, Arturo, 185
Vincent, Brian, 149
Vines, Kenneth N., 369, 383, 386, 420
Vinyard, Dale, 451
Vogel, Ronald, 149
Vogler, David, 203, 224
von Dalen, Hendrik, 369, 386

Wade, Larry, 146
Wahlke, John C., 75, 81, 82, 106, 144, 145, 183, 189, 289, 382
Walker, James L., 478
Walker, Robert S., 288
Walker, Thomas E., 483
Walsh, Lawrence, 437
Walsh, Michael H., 481, 520
Ward, Daniel S., 314, 339
Waterman, Richard W., 148, 384
Watson, Richard A., 419
Watt, James, 446
Wayman, Frank W., 384
Wayne, Stephen J., 422
Webber, David J., 148
Weber, Robert P., 225
Weber, Ronald E., 152
Weber, Vin, 298
Weicker, Lowell P., 48
Weingast, Berry R., 74, 193, 223
Weisberg, Herbert F., 50, 289, 341, 423, 482, 485
Weissberg, Robert, 84, 106
Weissert, Carol S., 222
Welch, Susan, 162, 185, 186, 341, 385
Welch, W. P., 384
Wenzel, James P., 482
West, William F., 187, 454
Westlye, Mark C., 150
Wheeler, Russell R., 482
Whitby, Kenny J., 151, 184

White, Leonard, 453
White, William S., 296
Whiteman, David, 90, 107, 222, 228, 254, 289
Whitten, Jamie, 39
Wicker, Tom, 287
Wiggins, Charles W., 227, 288, 341, 342, 385, 386, 397, 415, 419, 421, 424
Wigginton, Van A., 456
Wilcox, Clyde, 153, 384
Wildavsky, Aaron, 413, 414, 423
Wilhite, Allen, 384
Wilkerson, John D., 149
Will, George F., 11, 75
Wilson, Charles E., 439
Wilson, Laura, 386
Wilson, Rick W., 335
Wilson, Woodrow, 30, 31, 49, 50, 190, 197, 223, 239, 254, 382
Wimmer, Kurt A., 483
Wink, Kenneth, 149
Winsky, Laura R., 187
Wise, Sidney, 50, 227, 254, 334, 385, 419
Witmer, T. Richard, 163, 186
Wittkopf, Eugene A., 408, 421
Wlezien, Christopher, 418
Wohlstetter, Priscella, 451
Wolcott, Charles, 451
Wolfe, Christopher, 484
Wolfram, Catherine D., 150
Wood, B. Dan, 417
Wood, Robert C., 387
Woolley, John T., 454
Wright, Benjamin Fletcher, 382
Wright, Deil S., 420, 449, 456
Wright, Gerald C., 52, 146
Wright, Jim, 14, 66, 129, 301, 336
Wright, John R., 150, 384, 386, 481
Wrighton, J. Mark, 423
Wyden, Ron, 274

Yalof, David, 481
Yiannakis, Diana (*See* Evans, Diana M.)
Young, Garry, 419
Young, H. P., 106
Young, Roland, 50, 288, 511, 520

Zeidenstein, Harvey G., 423
Zeigler, Harmon, 369, 384, 386
Zeller, Belle, 224, 227, 287, 385
Zeng, Langche, 187
Zimmerman, Joseph F., 419, 424
Zisk, Betty H., 184
Zwier, Robert, 222